Contents

CW00321903

This atlas divides Scotland into eight colour-coded tourist regions. Each region has an introductory page followed by a section of road maps and ends with an alphabetical list of places of interest within that area.

Route planning

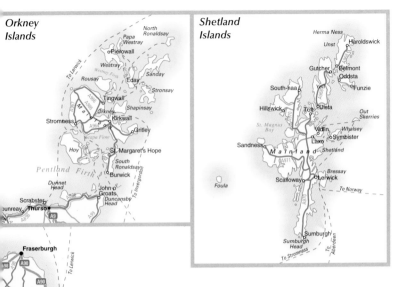

Orkney Islands

Shetland Islands

Planning your journey

Many visitors choose to see Scotland by road. If you want to get to your destination quickly, the motorways and primary roads are generally fast and efficient, with plenty of services en route. If, on the other hand, you are not in a hurry, take time out to follow one of the many designated routes and trails. Scotland has 12 National Tourist Routes that take the visitor off the motorways and primary roads along attractive routes passing a variety of things to see and do. They are all well signposted and easy to follow. There are also varied special interest trails - from the Malt Whisky Trail in Speyside to the Castle Trail in Aberdeen. Contact the Scottish Tourist Board (see inside front cover) for further information.

National Tourist Routes

National Tourist Routes are numbered on the map and their alignments are highlighted in purple.

① **Borders Historic Route (95miles/152km)**
Travelling between the great border city of Carlisle and Scotland's capital, Edinburgh, this tour savours the area which has been at the heart of Scotland's history and culture for centuries.

② **Galloway Tourist Route (96miles/154km)**
This route stretches from Gretna to Ayr, linking Robert Burns' attractions in Dumfries and Ayr. En route, it gives you an introduction to the Galloway Forest Park and the industrial heritage of the Doon Valley.

③ **Clyde Valley Route (42miles/67km)**
This follows the River Clyde through an area of contrasting landscapes, rich in historical interest.

④ **Forth Valley Route (39miles/62km)**
This short route from Edinburgh to Stirling takes in the attractive old burgh of South Queensferry, dominated by the mighty Forth Bridges.

⑤ **Fife Tourist Route (70miles/112km)**
Extending between the Firths of Forth and Tay, this journey travels through the historic Kingdom of Fife. En route is St Andrews, home of golf and seat of Scotland's oldest university.

⑥ **Argyll Tourist Route (149miles/238km)**
Touring from Tarbet on the banks of Loch Lomond along the shores of Loch Fyne to Lochgilphead this excursion then meanders north to Fort William at the foot of Ben Nevis.

⑦ **Perthshire Tourist Route (45miles/72km)**
Beginning just north of Dunblane and ending at Ballinluig near Pitlochry, this route runs through both fertile farmland and the rugged splendour of the Sma' Glen.

⑧ **Deeside Tourist Route (107miles/171km)**
From Perth all the way to Aberdeen, enjoy spectacular views of the Highland landscape as the route climbs to 2182ft (665m) on Britain's highest main road.

⑨ **Angus Coastal Route (58miles/93km)**
This begins in Dundee, with its fascinating industrial heritage and maritime traditions, and takes you north along a spectacular coastline towards Aberdeen.

⑩ **Highland Tourist Route (118miles/189km)**
From Aberdeen through the lovely valley of Upper Donside and on up to Tomintoul in the fringes of the Cairngorms, this tour then journeys through Grantown-on-Spey, a popular salmon fishing centre, to Inverness, capital of the Highlands.

⑪ **Moray Firth Tourist Route (80miles/128km)**
A semi-circular route around three of the most beautiful inlets on the east coast of Britain – the Beauly, Cromarty and Dornoch Firths – north from Inverness into the heart of the northern Highlands.

⑫ **North & West Highlands Route (140miles/225km)**
Starting at the fishing village of Ullapool, the route wends its way north through magnificent mountain country to Durness. Then east along Scotland's north coast through gradually softening scenery to John o'Groats.

Road distances

Distances between two selected towns in this table are shown in miles and will be found at the intersection of the respective vertical and horizontal rows, for example, the distance between Edinburgh and London is 378 miles. In general, distances are based on the shortest routes by classified roads.

Aberdeen	Ayr	Carlisle	Dumfries	Edinburgh	Fort William	Glasgow	Inverness	Kyle of Lochalsh	Perth	Stirling	Stranraer	Thurso	Ullapool	London
175														
221	90													
200	61	37												
125	73	96	80											
165	132	179	200	146										
145	33	96	75	42	104									
105	198	262	235	158	66	166								
188	211	275	256	225	79	183	83							
81	94	136	125	44	105	61	112	184						
116	63	114	93	36	96	30	142	175	34					
239	51	111	68	126	192	84	260	271	155	110				
226	315	371	367	278	183	285	132	209	237	274	369			
165	268	327	307	220	142	232	61	87	176	205	316	141		
503	390	301	338	378	497	397	536	576	415	415	402	651	629	

Key to regions

The eight colour-coded tourist regions used in this atlas are shown on the map below.
   Each region has an introductory page followed by a section of road maps and ends with an alphabetical list of places of tourist interest within that area. All places of interest are also referenced in the main index at the back of the atlas. For further information about each region, contact the relevant Area Tourist Board. There are 14 Area Tourist Boards in Scotland and their addresses, telephone numbers and web-sites are given on the introductory page to each region. Some of the regions in this atlas are covered by more than one Area Tourist Board. For more specific details about smaller areas or towns, contact the local Tourist Information Centre. Addresses and telephone numbers for all of Scotland's Tourist Information Centres are given down the side of the relevant road map page where the information centre is located.

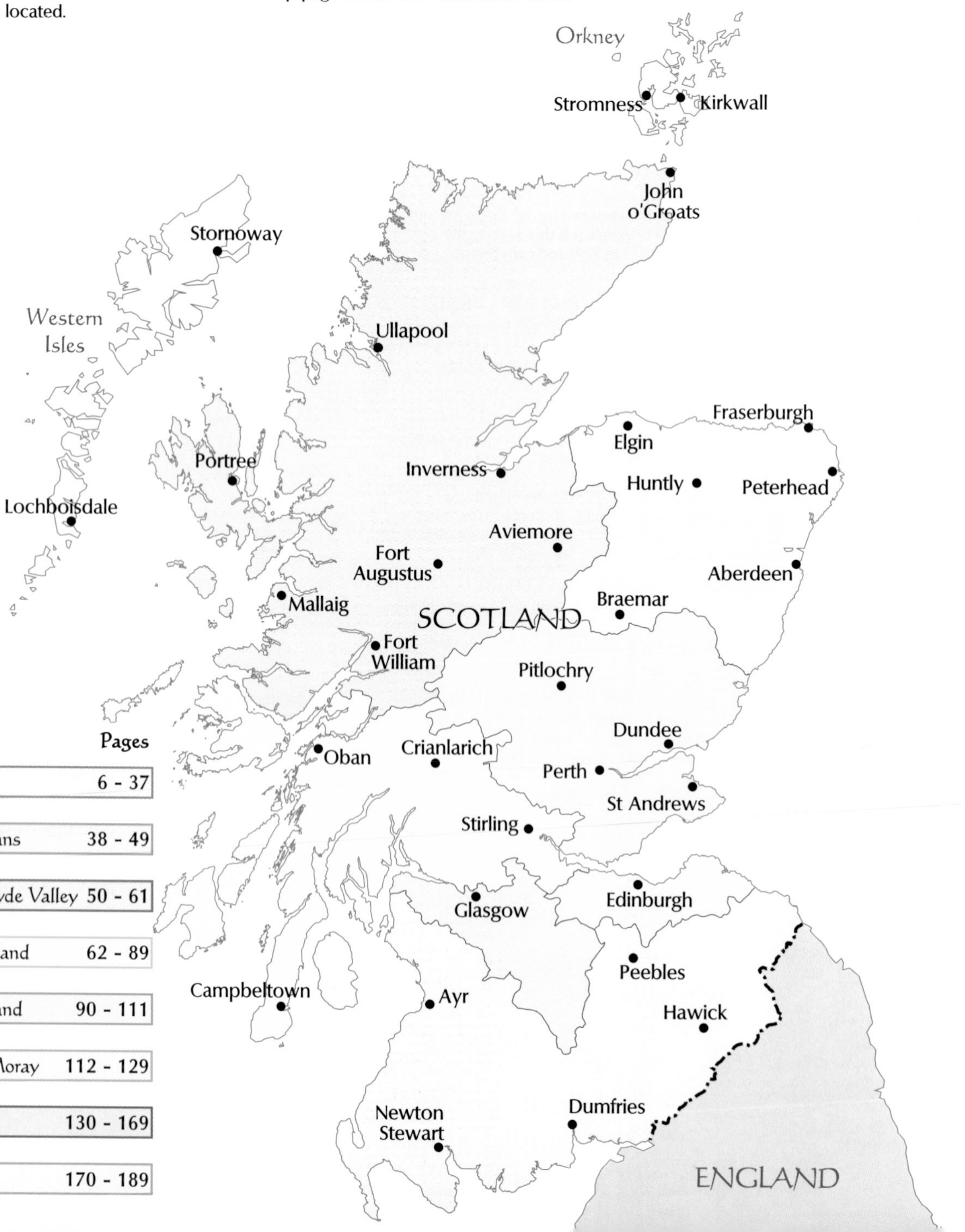

Shetland
Lerwick

Orkney
Stromness   Kirkwall

John o'Groats

Stornoway

Western Isles

Ullapool

Fraserburgh

Elgin

Portree

Inverness

Huntly   Peterhead

Lochboisdale

Aviemore

Aberdeen

Fort Augustus

Mallaig

SCOTLAND

Braemar

Fort William

Pitlochry

Dundee

Crianlarich

Oban

Perth

St Andrews

Stirling

Region	Pages
South of Scotland	6 - 37
Edinburgh & Lothians	38 - 49
Glasgow & the Clyde Valley	50 - 61
Central West Scotland	62 - 89
Central East Scotland	90 - 111
Aberdeenshire & Moray	112 - 129
Highlands & Skye	130 - 169
Outer Islands	170 - 189

Glasgow   Edinburgh

Peebles

Campbeltown

Ayr

Hawick

Newton Stewart   Dumfries

ENGLAND

Key to map symbols

Road maps

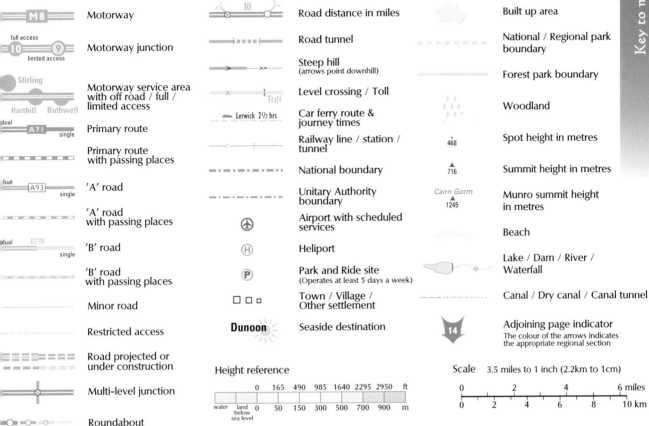

M8	Motorway
full access / limited access	Motorway junction
Stirling / Harthill / Bothwell	Motorway service area with off road / full / limited access
dual A71 single	Primary route
	Primary route with passing places
dual A93 single	'A' road
	'A' road with passing places
dual B778 single	'B' road
	'B' road with passing places
	Minor road
	Restricted access
	Road projected or under construction
	Multi-level junction
	Roundabout

10	Road distance in miles
	Road tunnel
	Steep hill (arrows point downhill)
Toll	Level crossing / Toll
Lerwick 2½ hrs	Car ferry route & journey times
	Railway line / station / tunnel
	National boundary
	Unitary Authority boundary
✈	Airport with scheduled services
Ⓗ	Heliport
Ⓟ	Park and Ride site (Operates at least 5 days a week)
□ □ ▫	Town / Village / Other settlement
Dunoon	Seaside destination

	Built up area
	National / Regional park boundary
	Forest park boundary
	Woodland
468	Spot height in metres
▲ 716	Summit height in metres
Cairn Gorm ▲ 1245	Munro summit height in metres
	Beach
	Lake / Dam / River / Waterfall
	Canal / Dry canal / Canal tunnel
14	Adjoining page indicator The colour of the arrows indicates the appropriate regional section

Height reference

	0	165	490	985	1640	2295	2950	ft
water	land below sea level	0	50	150	300	500	700	900	m

Scale   3.5 miles to 1 inch (2.2km to 1cm)

0	2	4	6 miles
0	2	4	6	8	10 km

Places of interest & tourist features

♱	Ancient monument	🚩 9 18	Golf course 9 hole / 18 hole	🏓	Picnic site
⚔	Battlefield		Guided tour / Nature trail		Pleasure boat trip
⛺	Campsite	🏠	Historic house (with or without garden)		Preserved railway
🚐	Caravan site		Lighthouse		Skiing
♜	Castle	🏆	Major sports venue		Theatre / Arts centre
	Country park	🏛	Museum / Art gallery		Theme park
🚲	Cycle trail	(NTS)	National Trust for Scotland	i i	Tourist Information Centre (all year / seasonal)
	Distillery / Brewery	🦆	Nature reserve		Viewpoint
✝	Ecclesiastical building	🚶	Outdoor activity centre	♥	Wildlife park / Zoo
✿	Garden	£	Outlet / Shopping village	★	Other place of interest
				★	Symbols highlighted in yellow are notable tourist attractions

City centre plans

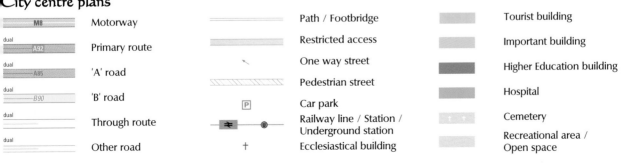

M8	Motorway
dual A92	Primary route
dual A85	'A' road
dual B90	'B' road
dual	Through route
dual	Other road

	Path / Footbridge
	Restricted access
	One way street
	Pedestrian street
Ⓟ	Car park
	Railway line / Station / Underground station
✝	Ecclesiastical building

	Tourist building
	Important building
	Higher Education building
	Hospital
	Cemetery
	Recreational area / Open space

South of Scotland

The Scottish Borders is an area of tranquil villages and textile towns, with a soft rolling landscape and a rugged coastline.

Visitors can enjoy a wide range of attractions, from craft workshops to magnificent historic houses and the great Border abbeys.

Culzean castle

Ayrshire & Arran

This area offers all the contrasts of mainland and island life. The island of Arran has been a playground for generations of outdoor enthusiasts. It is easily reached by ferry from Ardrossan. On the mainland visitors can explore the area's industrial history, numerous golf courses and enjoy the heritage of Robert Burns, Scotland's most famous poet.

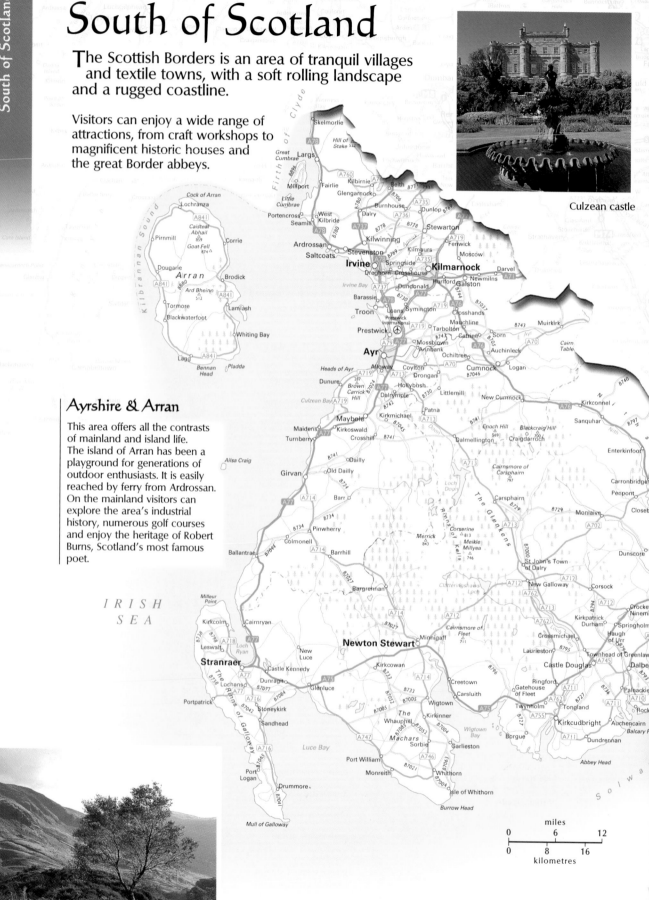

miles
0   6   12
0   8   16
kilometres

Glen Trool, Galloway Forest Park

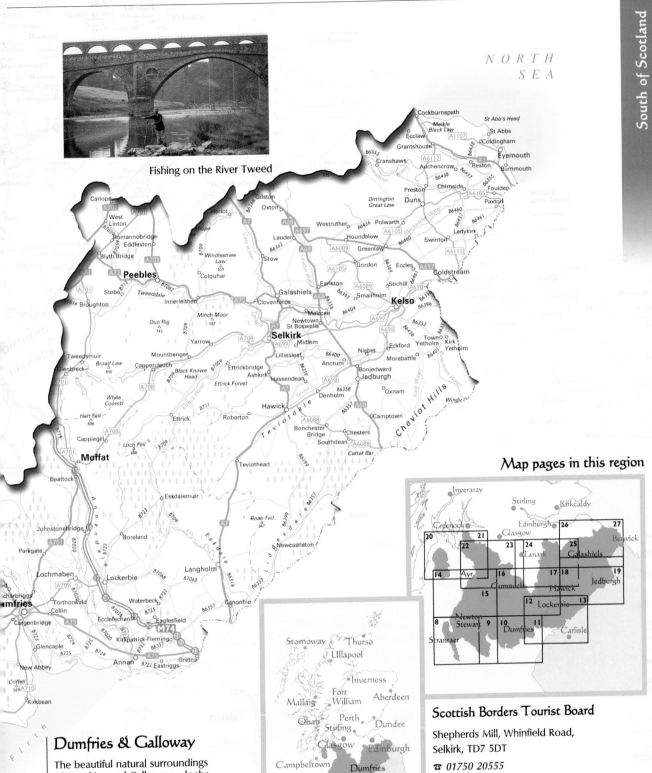

Fishing on the River Tweed

NORTH SEA

Map pages in this region

Dumfries & Galloway

The beautiful natural surroundings of Dumfries and Galloway – lochs and craggy hills, rugged cliffs and long sandy beaches, are ideal for fishing, golfing, walking and cycling. There is plenty to entertain the visitor, including birdwatching and a large number of beautiful gardens.

Ayrshire & Arran Tourist Board

15 Skye Road, Prestwick, KA9 2TE

☎ 01292 262555

www.ayrshire-arran.com

Scottish Borders Tourist Board

Shepherds Mill, Whinfield Road, Selkirk, TD7 5DT

☎ 01750 20555

www.scot-borders.co.uk

Dumfries & Galloway Tourist Board

64 Whitesands, Dumfries, DG1 2RS

☎ 01387 253863

www.dumfriesandgalloway.co.uk

South of Scotland

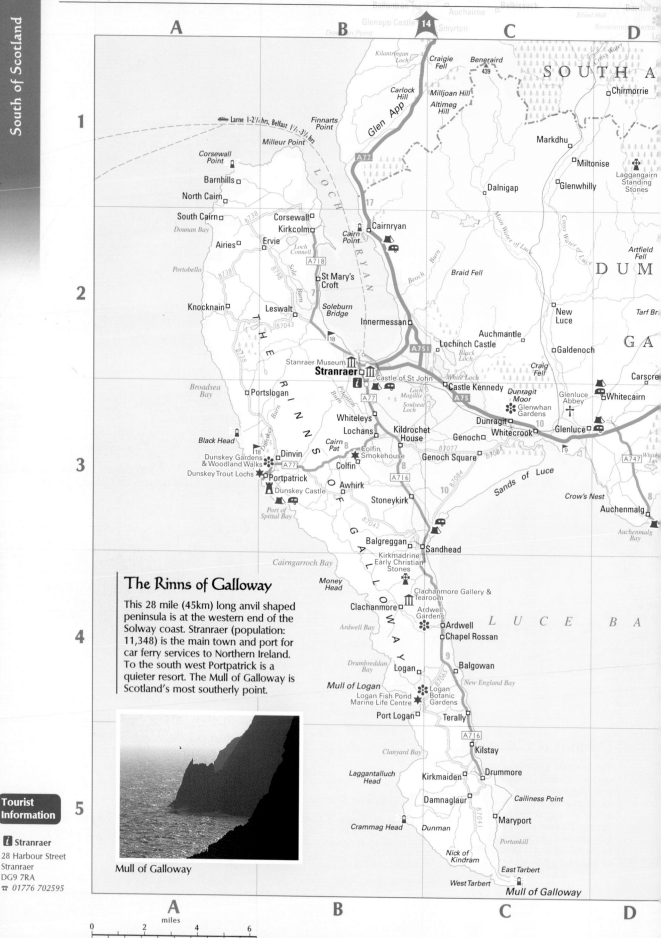

A | B | C | D

Mains of Tig

Ballantrae Auchaire Balkissock Shiel Hill Barwinnock Burn

Glenapp Castle **14** Smyrton

Downan Point

Kilantringan Loch Craigie Fell Benerard 439 S O U T H A

Carlock Hill Milljoan Hill Chirmorrie

Glen App Altimeg Hill

Larne 1-2½ hrs, Belfast 1½-3½ hrs Finnarts Point

Milleur Point A77 Markdhu

Corsewall Point Miltonise D U M

Barnhills Dalnigap Glenwhilly Laggangairn Standing Stones

North Cairn 17

South Cairn Corsewall Artfield Fell

Dounan Bay Kirkcolm Braid Fell New Luce

Airies Ervie Cairnryan Tarf Br

Portobello Loch Connell Cairn Point Auchmantle G A

Knocknain St Mary's Croft Soleburn Bridge Lochinch Castle Galdenoch

Leswalt Innermessan Black Loch Carscre

Main Water of Luce Craig Fell

18 A751 Craig Fell Whitecairn

Stranraer Museum White Loch Castle Kennedy Dunragit Moor Glenluce Abbey

Stranraer Castle of St John A75 Glenwhan Gardens

Broadsea Bay Loch Magillie Dunragit 10 Glenluce

Portslogan Soulseat Loch Whitecrook

Pikenhom Burn Whiteleys Kildrochet House Genoch 9 A747

Black Head Lochans Genoch Square B7084 White Loch

Dunskey Gardens & Woodland Walks Cairn Pat Colfin Smokehouse A716 10 Crow's Nest 8

Dunskey Trout Lochs Dinvin Colfin Awhirk Sands of Luce Auchenmalg

Portpatrick A77 Stoneykirk Auchenmalg Bay

Dunskey Castle B7042 10

Port of Spittal Bay Balgreggan Sandhead

Cairngarroch Bay Kirkmadrine Early Christian Stones

Money Head Clachanmore Gallery & Tearoom L U C E B A

The Rinns of Galloway

This 28 mile (45km) long anvil shaped peninsula is at the western end of the Solway coast. Stranraer (population: 11,348) is the main town and port for car ferry services to Northern Ireland. To the south west Portpatrick is a quieter resort. The Mull of Galloway is Scotland's most southerly point.

Clachanmore Ardwell Gardens Ardwell

Ardwell Bay Chapel Rossan

Drumbreddan Bay 9 Balgowan

Logan New England Bay

Mull of Logan Logan Botanic Gardens

Logan Fish Pond Marine Life Centre Terally

Port Logan A716

Clanyard Bay Kilstay

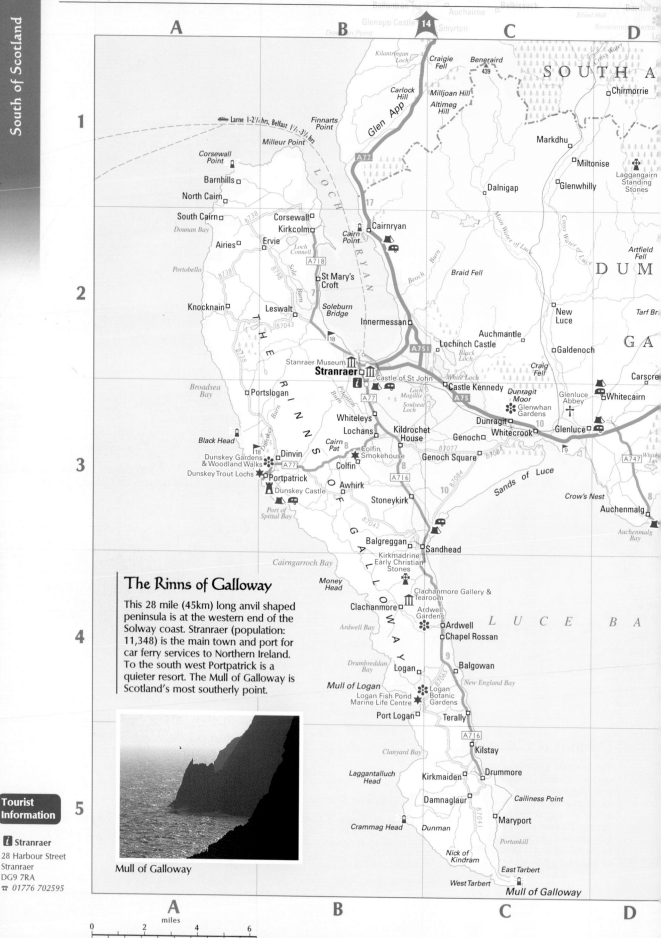

Mull of Galloway

Laggantalluch Head Kirkmaiden Drummore

Damnaglaur Cailiness Point

Crammag Head Dunman Maryport

Portankill

Nick of Kindram East Tarbert

West Tarbert **Mull of Galloway**

Tourist Information

_i_ **Stranraer**
28 Harbour Street
Stranraer
DG9 7RA
☎ 01776 702595

A | B | C | D

miles
0 2 4 6

0 2 4 6 8 10
kilometres

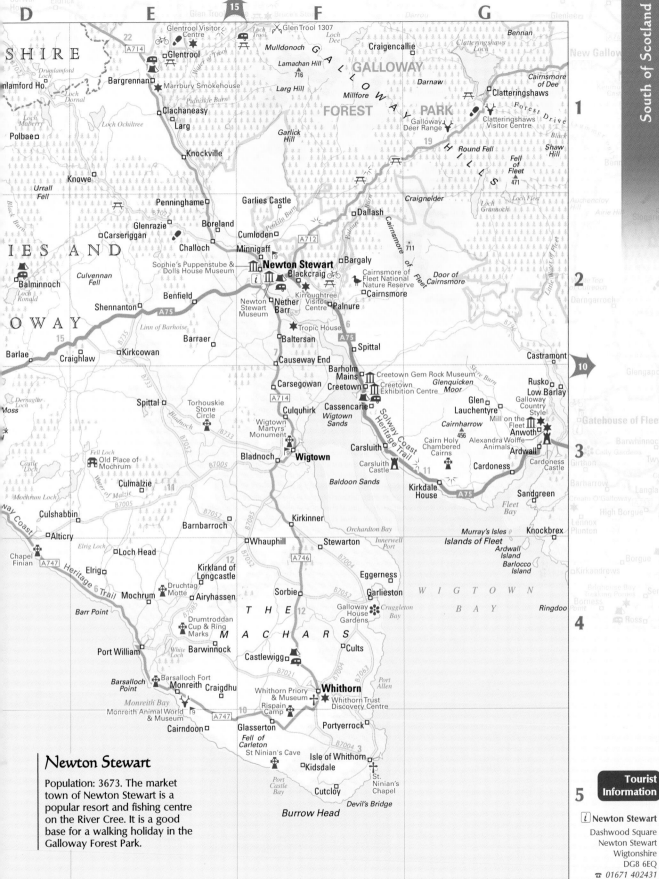

D | E | F | G

Newton Stewart

Population: 3673. The market town of Newton Stewart is a popular resort and fishing centre on the River Cree. It is a good base for a walking holiday in the Galloway Forest Park.

Tourist Information

ⓘ **Newton Stewart**
Dashwood Square
Newton Stewart
Wigtonshire
DG8 6EQ
☎ 01671 402431

D | E | F | G

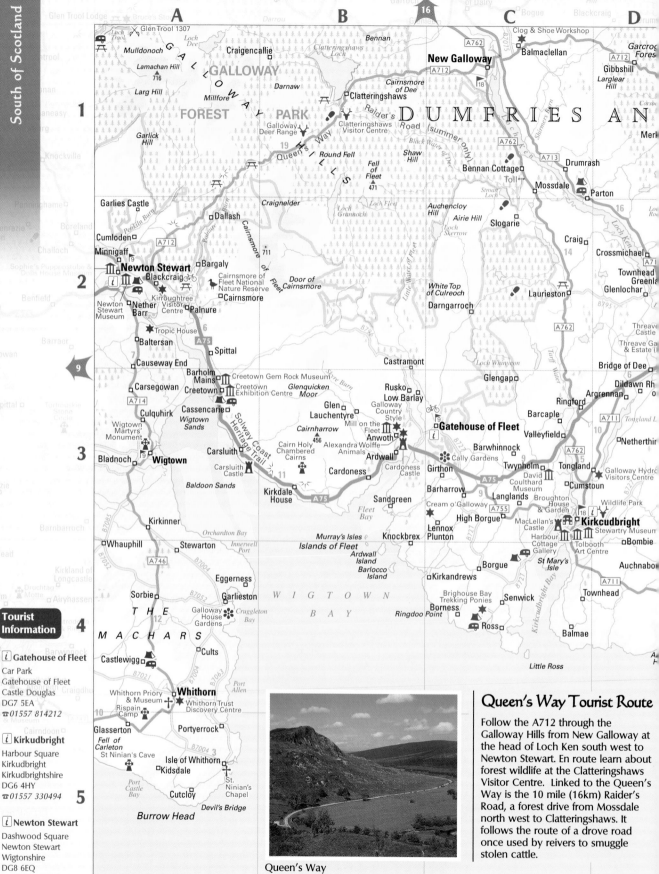

Palgowan • Craignaw • Silver Flowe National Nature Reserve • Meikle Millyea 746 • Corriedoo • Water
Glen Trool Lodge • Glen Trool 1307 • Bruce's Stone • Loch Dee • Craignaw • Garroch • St John's Town of Dairy • Bogue • Blackcraig
Mulldonoch • Loch Trool • Craigencallie • Bennan • New Galloway • Clog & Shoe Workshop • Balmaclellan • A712 • Garcrog Forest
Lamachan Hill 716 • Darnaw • Clatteringshaws Loch • Clatteringshaws • A762 • A2075 • Gibbshill • Larglear Hill
Larg Hill • Millfore • Cairnsmore of Dee • A712 • 18 • Drumrash
FOREST • **PARK** • Raider's Road (summer only) • **DUMFRIES AN** • A762 • A713 • Mossdale • Parton
Galloway Deer Range • 19 • Round Fell • Shaw Hill • Bennan Cottage Toll • Stroan Loch
Garlick Hill • Fell of Fleet 471 • Black Water of Tree • 16
Garlies Castle • Craignelder • Loch Grannoch • Auchencloy Hill • Airie Hill • Slogarie • Loch Skerrow • Craig • 14 • Crossmichael
Dallash • Door of Cairnsmore • 711 • White Top of Culreoch • Darngarroch • Laurieston • Townhead Greenla • Glenlochar
Cumloden • A712 • Cairnsmore of Fleet National Nature Reserve • Little Water of Fleet • Threave Castle • Threave Ga & Estate
Minnigaff • 19 • Bargaly • Cairnsmore • A762
Newton Stewart • Blackcraig • Castramont • Loch Whinyeon • Glengap • Bridge of Dee
Newton Stewart Museum • Kirroughtree Visitor Centre • Palnure • 6 • Rusko • Dildawn Rh • Argrennan
Nether Barr • Tropic House • Low Barlay • Galloway Country Style • Ringford • Barcaple • A711
Baltersan • A75 • Spittal • Silver Burn • Glen • Lauchentyre • Mill on the Fleet • **Gatehouse of Fleet** • Valleyfield • Netherthir
Causeway End • Cairnharrow 456 • Anwoth • Barwhinnock • A762 • Tongland • Galloway Hydro Visitors Centre
Carsegowan • Barholm Mains • Creetown Gem Rock Museum • Glenquicken Moor • Cairn Holy Chambered Cairns • Ardwall • Cally Gardens • Twynholm • David Coulthard Museum • Cumstoun
Culquhirk • Creetown • Creetown Exhibition Centre • Alexandra Wolffe Animals • Cardoness Castle • Girthon • Langlands • Broughton House & Garden • Wildlife Park
Cassencarie • Wigtown Sands • Cardoness • Barharrow • A75 • 9 • 18 • **Kirkcudbright**
Wigtown Martyrs' Monument • Solway Coast Heritage Trail • Carsluith • Kirkdale House • 11 • Sandgreen • Cream o'Galloway • A755 • MacLellan's Castle • Stewartry Museum
Bladnoch • **Wigtown** • Carsluith Castle • Baldoon Sands • Fleet Bay • Lennox Plunton • High Borgue • Harbour Cottage Gallery • Tolbooth Art Centre • Bombie
Kirkinner • Orchardton Bay • Murray's Isles • Knockbrex • Borgue • St Mary's Isle • Auchnabo
Whauphill • Innerwell Port • Islands of Fleet • Ardwall Island • Barlocco Island • Kirkandrews • A711
Stewarton • A746 • B7004 • **WIGTOWN** • **BAY** • Brighouse Bay Trekking Ponies • Senwick • Townhead
Sorbie • Eggerness • Garlieston • Cruggleton Bay • Borness • Ross • Auchnabo
THE • **MACHARS** • 12 • Galloway House Gardens • Ringdoo Point • Balmae
Cults • Little Ross
Castlewigg • B7021 • Port Allen
Whithorn Priory & Museum • **Whithorn** • Whithorn Trust Discovery Centre
Rispain Camp • Portyerrock
Glasserton • Fell of Carleton • St Ninian's Cave
10 • B7004 • Isle of Whithorn • Kidsdale • St Ninian's Chapel
Port Castle Bay • Cutcloy • Devil's Bridge
Burrow Head

Tourist Information

i **Gatehouse of Fleet**

Car Park
Gatehouse of Fleet
Castle Douglas
DG7 5EA
☎ 01557 814212

i **Kirkudbright**

Harbour Square
Kirkudbright
Kirkudbrightshire
DG6 4HY
☎ 01557 330494

i **Newton Stewart**

Dashwood Square
Newton Stewart
Wigtonshire
DG8 6EQ
☎ 01671 402431

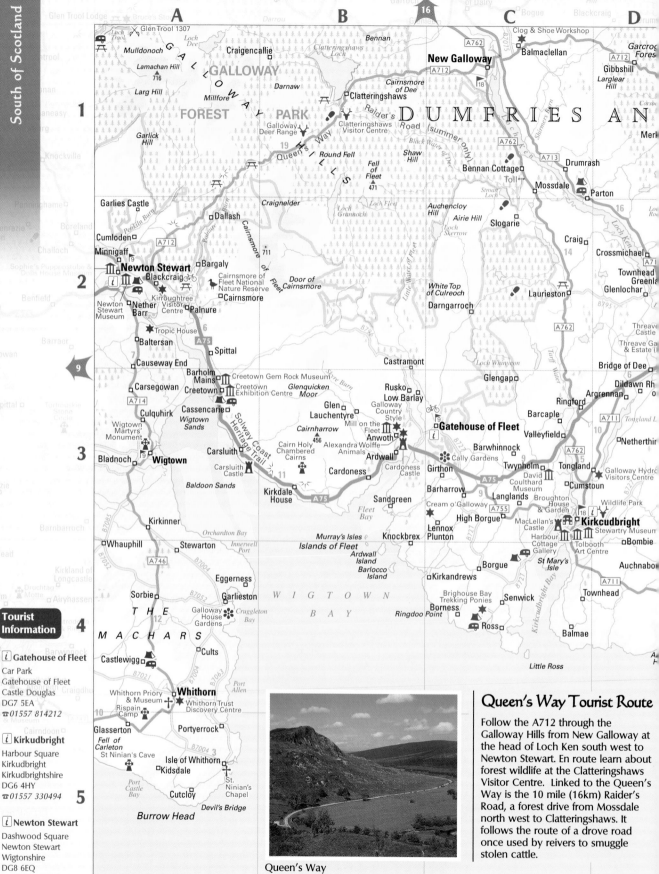

Queen's Way

Queen's Way Tourist Route

Follow the A712 through the Galloway Hills from New Galloway at the head of Loch Ken south west to Newton Stewart. En route learn about forest wildlife at the Clatteringshaws Visitor Centre. Linked to the Queen's Way is the 10 mile (16km) Raider's Road, a forest drive from Mossdale north west to Clatteringshaws. It follows the route of a drove road once used by reivers to smuggle stolen cattle.

miles
0   2   4   6
0   2   4   6   8   10
kilometres

The Solway Coast

The Solway Firth is a shallow arm of the Irish Sea between the coasts of Cumbria in England and Dumfries & Galloway in Scotland. Fringed by tidal marshes, much of the coast is remote and a haven for bird-life. Follow the coast using the Solway Coast Heritage Trail, a 190 mile (306km) sign-posted route from Annan to the Mull of Galloway. Along the way are historic monuments, castles, abbeys and gardens as well as the pretty harbours of coastal towns and villages.

Rough Firth

Tourist Information

ℹ️ **Castle Douglas**
Market Hill Car Park
Castle Douglas
DG7 1AE
☎ 01556 502611

ℹ️ **Dumfries**
64 Whitesands
Dumfries
Dumfries and
Galloway
DG1 2RS
☎ 01387 253862

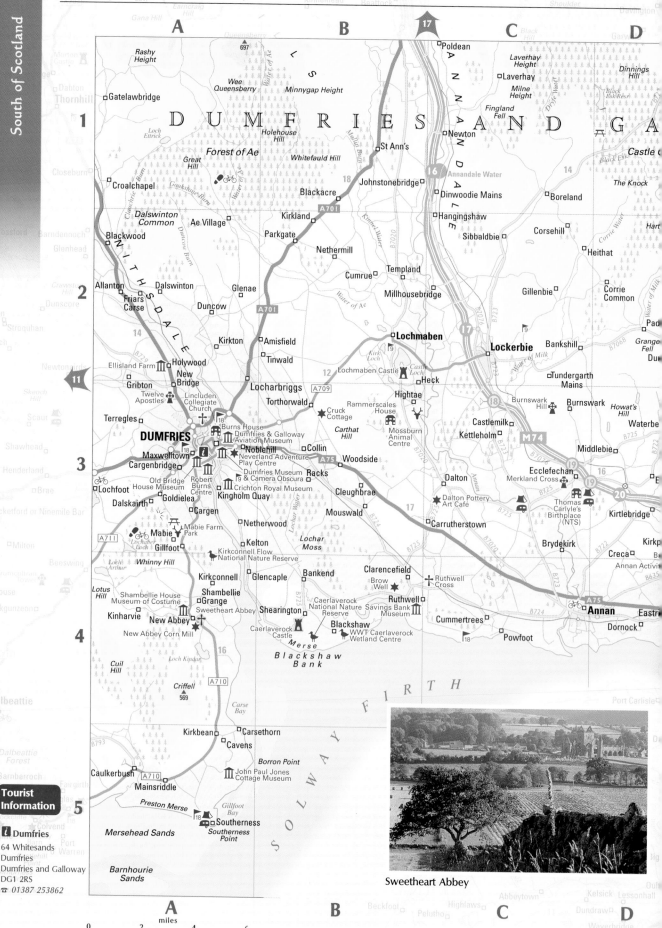

Sweetheart Abbey

Tourist Information

i Dumfries
64 Whitesands
Dumfries
Dumfries and Galloway
DG1 2RS
☎ 01387 253862

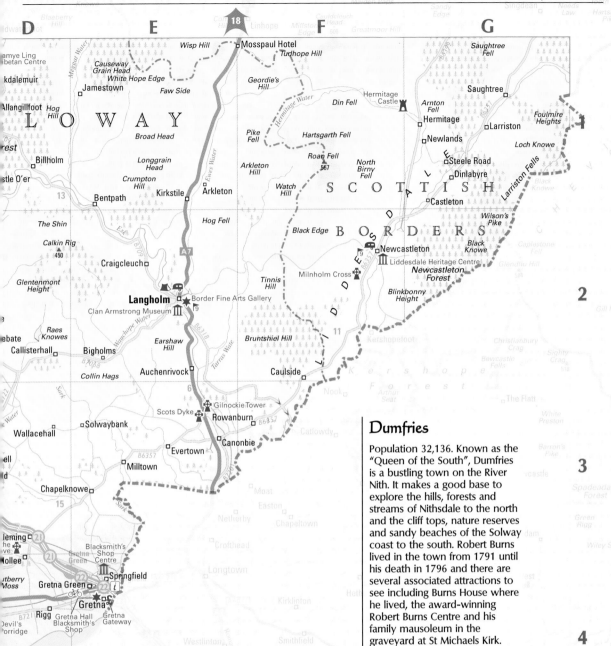

Dumfries

Population 32,136. Known as the "Queen of the South", Dumfries is a bustling town on the River Nith. It makes a good base to explore the hills, forests and streams of Nithsdale to the north and the cliff tops, nature reserves and sandy beaches of the Solway coast to the south. Robert Burns lived in the town from 1791 until his death in 1796 and there are several associated attractions to see including Burns House where he lived, the award-winning Robert Burns Centre and his family mausoleum in the graveyard at St Michaels Kirk.

Gretna Green

Sited just across the border from England, Gretna Green is famed as the location of runaway marriages in former times. The tradition is explained at the Blacksmith's Shop centre, where marriage ceremonies are still performed at the anvil.

Midsteeple and fountain, Dumfries

Tourist Information

ℹ️ **Gretna Green**
Old Headless Cross
Gretna Green
Dumfriesshire
DG16 5EA
☎ 01461 337834

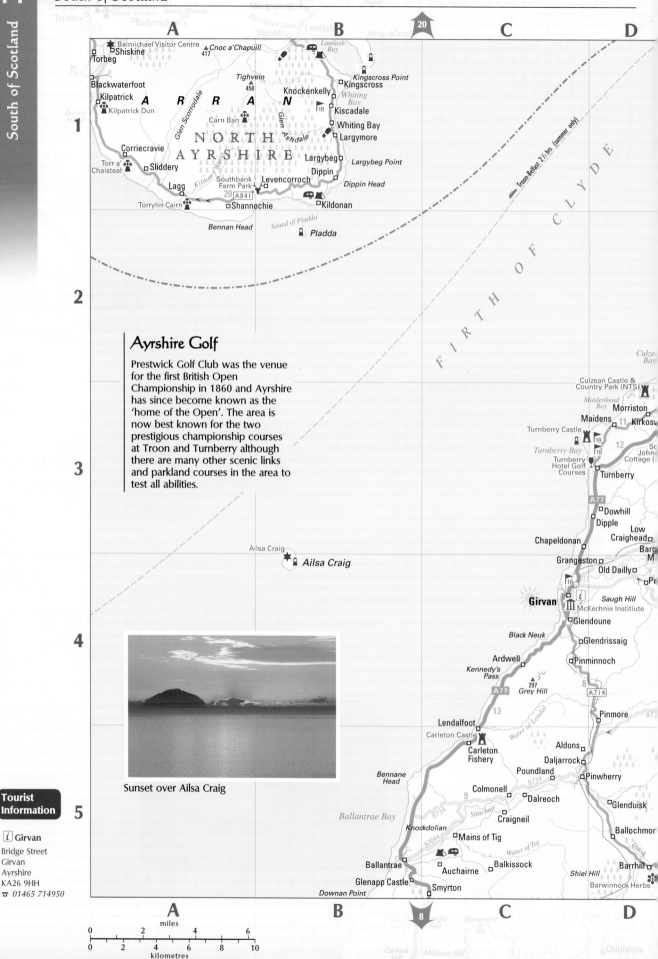

Ayrshire Golf

Prestwick Golf Club was the venue for the first British Open Championship in 1860 and Ayrshire has since become known as the 'home of the Open'. The area is now best known for the two prestigious championship courses at Troon and Turnberry although there are many other scenic links and parkland courses in the area to test all abilities.

Sunset over Ailsa Craig

Tourist Information

ⓘ **Girvan**
Bridge Street
Girvan
Ayrshire
KA26 9HH
☎ 01465 714950

Map labels:

Machrie, A'Chruach, Torr Mor, Stone Circles, Ballymichael, Morganaglach, Glenkiln, Lamlash, Holy Island, Clauchlands Point

Balmichael Visitor Centre, Shiskine, Torbeg, Cnoc a'Chapuill, 417, Lamlash Bay, Blackwaterfoot, Tighvein, 458, Knockenkelly, Kingscross, Kingscross Point, Kilpatrick, Kilpatrick Dun, A R R A N, Carn Ban, Glen Scorrodale, Glen Ashdale, Whiting Bay, Kiscadale, 18, Corriecravie, N O R T H, A Y R S H I R E, Whiting Bay, Largymore, Torr a' Chaisteal, Sliddery, Largybeg, Largybeg Point, Lagg, Southbank Farm Park, Levencorroch, Dippin, Dippin Head, Torrylin Cairn, 20, A841, Shannochie, Kildonan, Bennan Head, Sound of Pladda, Pladda

F I R T H   O F   C L Y D E

Troon-Belfast 2¼ hrs (summer only)

Culzean Bay, Culzean Castle & Country Park (NTS), Maidenhead Bay, Morriston, Maidens, 11, Kirkosw, Turnberry Castle, 18, 12, Sc John Cottage, Turnberry Bay, 18, Turnberry Hotel Golf Courses, Turnberry, A77, Dowhill, Dipple, Low Craighead, Chapeldonan, Barg M, Grangeston, Old Dailly, Pe, 18, Saugh Hill, Girvan, McKechnie Institiute, Glendoune, Black Neuk, Glendrissaig, Ardwell, Pinminnoch, Kennedy's Pass, 297, Grey Hill, 8, A714, Lendalfoot, 13, Pinmore, Carleton Castle, Water of Lendal, B7, Carleton Fishery, Aldons, Bennane Head, Poundland, Daljarrock, Pinwherry, Colmonell, Dalreoch, B734, 9, Glenduisk, Craigneil, Ballantrae Bay, B734, Stinchar, Ballochmor, Knockdolian, B7044, Mains of Tig, Balkissock, Water of Tig, Shiel Hill, Barrhill, Ballantrae, Auchairne, Barwinnock Herbs, Glenapp Castle, Smyrton, Downan Point, Carlock Hill, Miljoan Hill, Chirmorie

Ailsa Craig, Ailsa Craig

Scale:
miles: 0 2 4 6
kilometres: 0 2 4 6 8 10

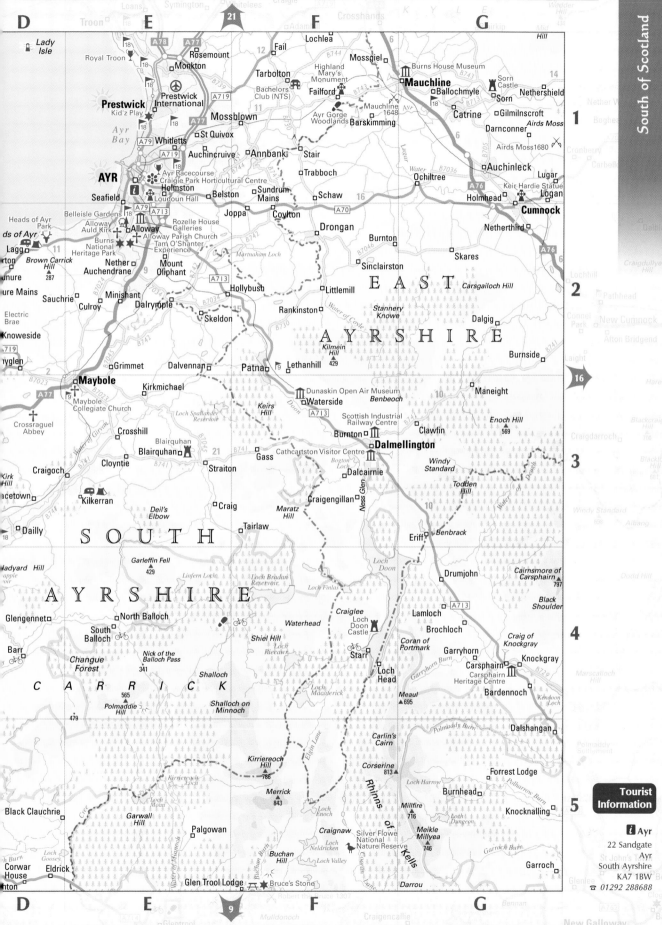

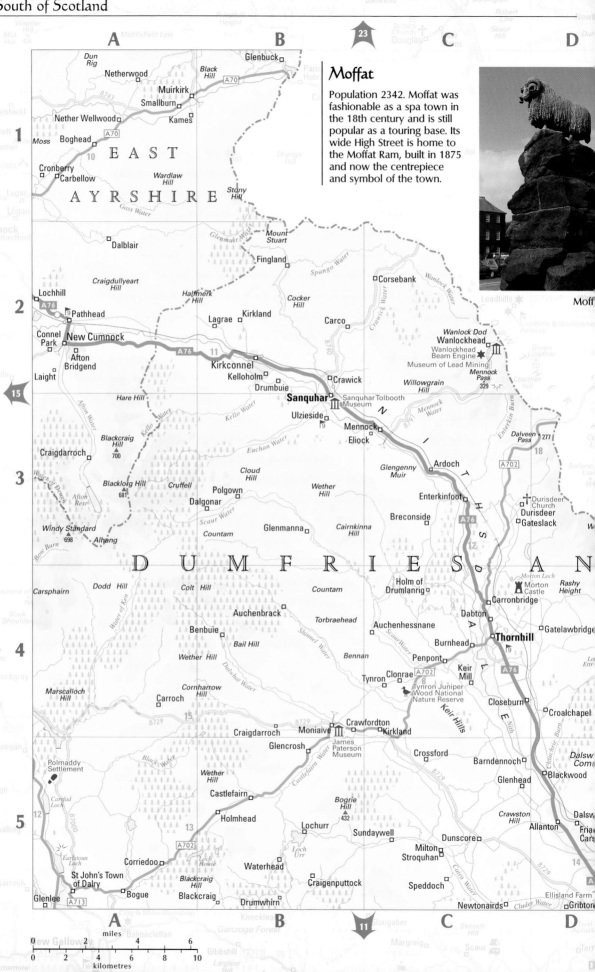

Moffat

Population 2342. Moffat was fashionable as a spa town in the 18th century and is still popular as a touring base. Its wide High Street is home to the Moffat Ram, built in 1875 and now the centrepiece and symbol of the town.

Moff

Map labels:

A B 23 C D

1

Dun Rig
Netherwood
Black Hill
Glenbuck
A70
Muirkirk
Smallburn
Kames
Nether Wellwood
Boghead
Moss
A70
10
Cronberry
Carbellow
Wardlaw Hill

EAST AYRSHIRE

Gass Water
Stony Hill
Drygns Hill

Dalblair
Fingland
Mount Stuart
Spango Water
Corsebank
Wanlock Water

2

Lochhill
A76
Pathhead
Craigdullyeart Hill
Halfmerk Hill
Cocker Hill
Carco
Wanlock Dod
Wanlockhead
Connel Park
New Cumnock
Lagrae
Kirkland
Wanlockhead Beam Engine
Museum of Lead Mining
Afton Bridgend
A76
11
Kirkconnel
Crawick
Willowgrain Hill
Mennock Pass 329
Laight
Kelloholm
Drumbuie
Hare Hill
Sanquhar
Sanquhar Tolbooth Museum
Leadhills & Wanlockhe...
Green Lowther
732

15

Blackcraig Hill 700
Ulzieside
9
Mennock
Eliock
Mennock Water
Dalveen Pass 277
18
Craigdarroch
Afton Water
Kello Water
Euchan Water
Cloud Hill
Wether Hill
Glengenny Muir
Ardoch
A702

3

Blacklorg Hill 681
Cruffell
Polgown
Dalgonar
Scaur Water
Glenmanna
Cairnkinna Hill
Breconside
Enterkinfoot
A76
Durisdeer Church
Durisdeer
Gateslack
Windy Standard 698
Alhang
Bow Burn
Countam
12

DUMFRIES AN

Carsphairn
Dodd Hill
Colt Hill
Countam
Holm of Drumlanrig
Morton Loch
Morton Castle
Rashy Height
Carronbridge
Dabton
Gatelawbridge

4

Marscalloch Hill
Benbuie
Auchenbrack
Bail Hill
Torbraehead
Shinnel Water
Auchenhessnane
Scaur Water
Burnhead
Thornhill
A76
Wether Hill
Bennan
Penpont
Keir Mill
9
Carroch
Cornharrow Hill
Dalwhat Water
Tynron
Clonrae
A702
8
Tynron Juniper Wood National Nature Reserve
Keir Hills
Closeburn
Croalchapel
15
B729
Craigdarroch
Moniaive
Kirkland
Crossford
Barndennoch
Glenhead
Blackwood
Dalsw Com

5

12
Polmaddy Settlement
Carsfad Loch
B7000
Black Water
Glencrosh
James Paterson Museum
Crawfordton
Castlefairn Water
Crossford
E Nith
Crawston Hill
Allanton
Dals
Fria Cars
Earlstoun Loch
Wether Hill
Castlefairn
Bogrie Hill 432
Lochurr
Sundaywell
Dunscore
Milton Stroquhan
Speddoch
14
A
13
A702
Holmhead
Loch Howie
Loch Urr
Waterhead
Craigenputtock
St John's Town of Dalry
Corriedoo
Blackcraig Hill
Blackcraig
Drumwhirn
Ellisland Farm
Glenlee
A713
Bogue
Newtonairds
Gribton

A miles B 11 C D
0   2   4   6
0 2 4 6 8 10
kilometres

New Galloway

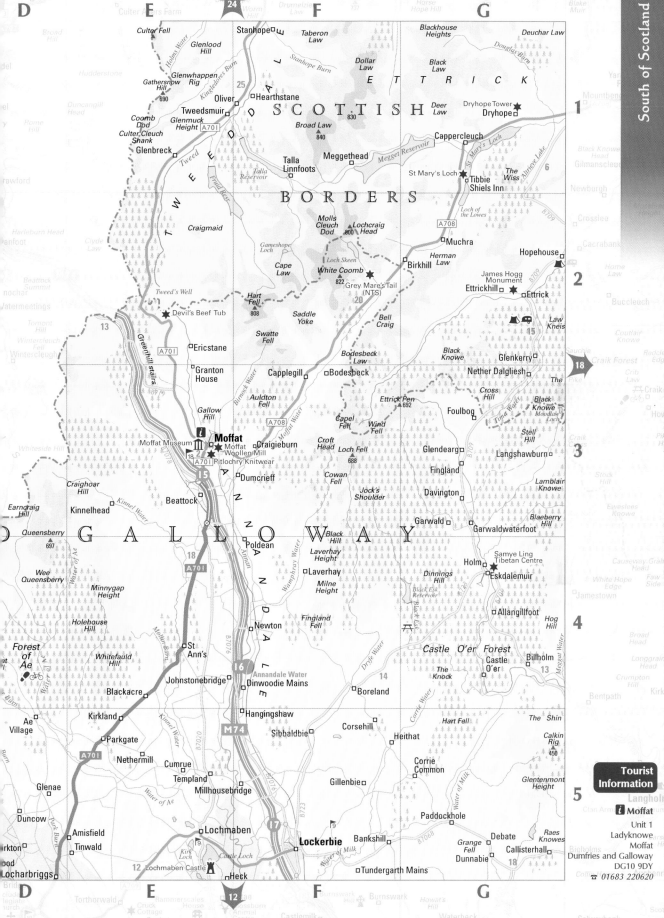

Tourist Information

i Moffat

Unit 1
Ladyknowe
Moffat
Dumfries and Galloway
DG10 9DY
☎ 01683 220620

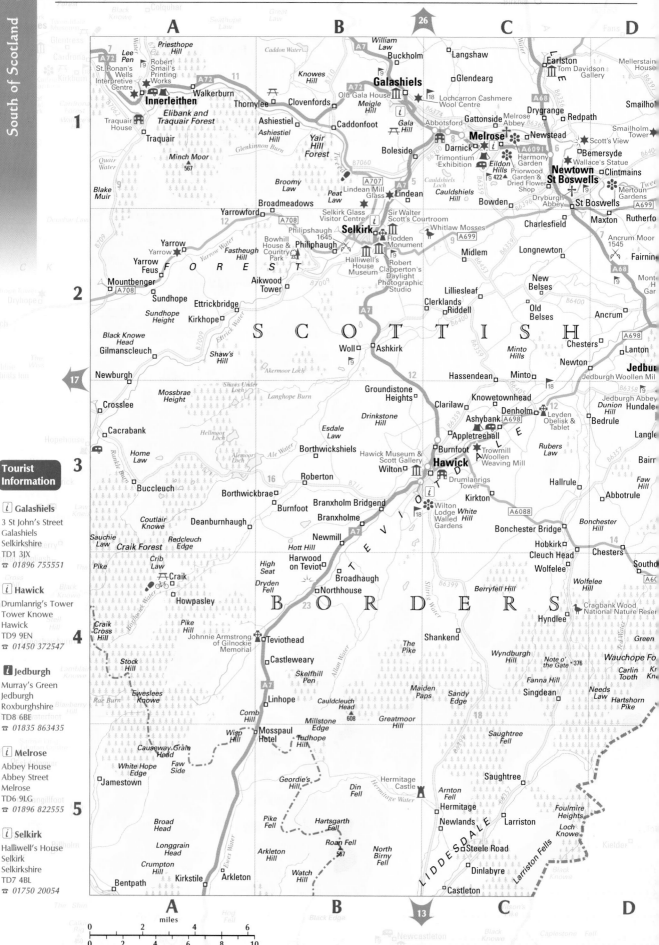

26
17
13

Tourist Information

i Galashiels

3 St John's Street
Galashiels
Selkirkshire
TD1 3JX
☎ 01896 755551

i Hawick

Drumlanrig's Tower
Tower Knowe
Hawick
TD9 9EN
☎ 01450 372547

i Jedburgh

Murray's Green
Jedburgh
Roxburghshire
TD8 6BE
☎ 01835 863435

i Melrose

Abbey House
Abbey Street
Melrose
TD6 9LG
☎ 01896 822555

i Selkirk

Halliwell's House
Selkirk
Selkirkshire
TD7 4BL
☎ 01750 20054

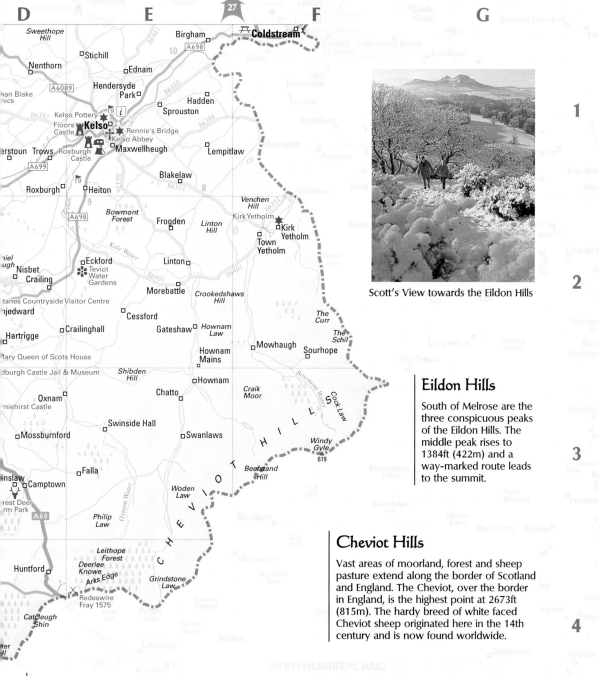

Scott's View towards the Eildon Hills

Eildon Hills

South of Melrose are the three conspicuous peaks of the Eildon Hills. The middle peak rises to 1384ft (422m) and a way-marked route leads to the summit.

Cheviot Hills

Vast areas of moorland, forest and sheep pasture extend along the border of Scotland and England. The Cheviot, over the border in England, is the highest point at 2673ft (815m). The hardy breed of white faced Cheviot sheep originated here in the 14th century and is now found worldwide.

Border Towns

The peace and tranquility of the Borders that visitors find so attractive belies a turbulent past. There were times when Border people lived under constant threat of invasion and this history has left a legacy of castles, abbeys and great country houses to explore. Melrose, Jedburgh and Kelso are all abbey towns that are best explored on foot. Hawick (population 15,812), famous for knitwear and rugby, is the largest of the Border towns and is a frequent winner of national floral awards.

Cheviot Hills

Tourist Information

i **Kelso**

Town House
The Square
Kelso
Roxburghshire
TD5 7HF
☎ 01573 223464

South of Scotland

Glen Sannox, Arran

Isle of Arran

Often called 'Scotland in Miniature', the Isle of Arran offers a diversity of terrain and holiday experiences for the visitor. In the north the island is mountainous and unspoilt, peaking with Goat Fell at 2866ft (873m). The area offers a challenge to hillwalkers, climbers and cyclists. The milder south is more fertile and forested, with seaside resorts and impressive Bronze Age standing stone circles. The island is also known for its locally produced food and drink and the 'taste of Arran' includes cheeses, smoked fish, traditional ice cream and speciality ales from the Arran Brewery as well as whisky from Scotland's newest distillery.

Tourist Information

i **Brodick**

The Pier
Brodick
Isle of Arran
KA27 8AU
☎ 01770 302140

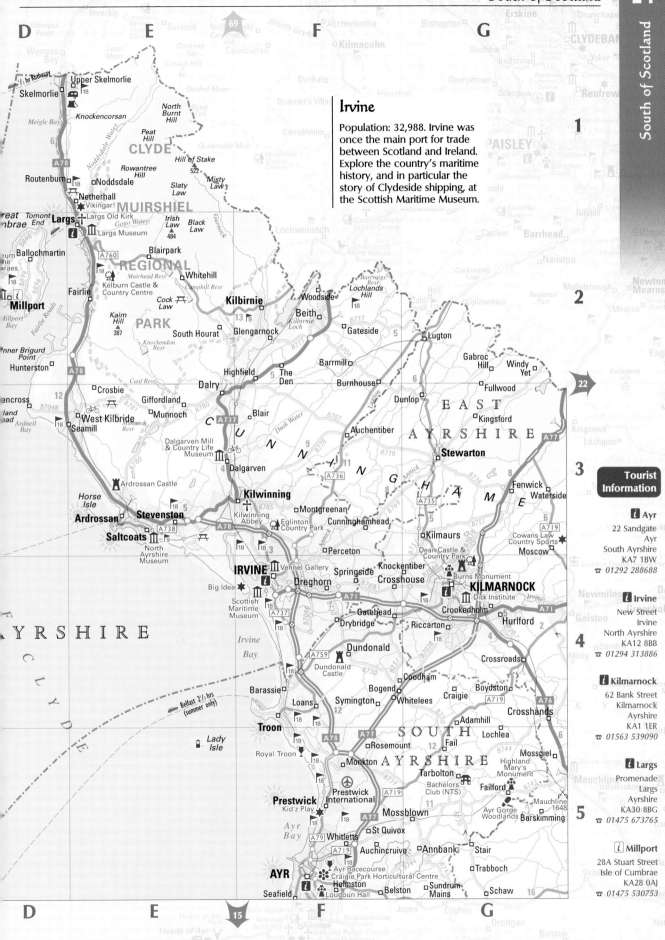

Irvine

Population: 32,988. Irvine was once the main port for trade between Scotland and Ireland. Explore the country's maritime history, and in particular the story of Clydeside shipping, at the Scottish Maritime Museum.

Tourist Information

_i_ Ayr
22 Sandgate
Ayr
South Ayrshire
KA7 1BW
☎ 01292 288688

_i_ Irvine
New Street
Irvine
North Ayrshire
KA12 8BB
☎ 01294 313886

_i_ Kilmarnock
62 Bank Street
Kilmarnock
Ayrshire
KA1 1ER
☎ 01563 539090

_i_ Largs
Promenade
Largs
Ayrshire
KA30 8BG
☎ 01475 673765

_i_ Millport
28A Stuart Street
Isle of Cumbrae
KA28 0AJ
☎ 01475 530753

Tourist Information

ℹ Ayr
22 Sandgate
Ayr
South Ayrshire
KA7 1BW
☎ 01292 288688

ℹ Irvine
New Street
Irvine
North Ayrshire
KA12 8BB
☎ 01294 313886

ℹ Kilmarnock
62 Bank Street
Kilmarnock
Ayrshire
KA1 1ER
☎ 01563 539090

ℹ Largs
Promenade
Largs
Ayrshire
KA30 8BG
☎ 01475 673765

Map labels (grid A–D, rows 1–5):

Largs Old Kirk, Largs, Largs Museum, Irish Law, Black Law 484, Blairpark, Whitehill, REGIONAL, Kelburn Castle & Country Centre, Cock Law, Kaim Hill 387, Fairlie, Crosbie, NORTH PARK, Kilbirnie, Woodside, Beith, Lochlands Hill, Lugton, Gabroc Hill, Windy Yet, Kingswell, Lochgoin, South Hourat, Glengarnock, Gateside, Fullwood, AYRSHIRE, Giffordland, The Den, Highfield, Burnhouse, Dunlop, Kingsford, Munnoch, Dalry, Blair, Auchentiber, Tayburn, West Kilbride, Seamill, Dalgarven Mill & Country Life Museum, Dalgarven, CUNNINGHAME, Stewarton, Fenwick, Waterside, Ardrossan Castle, Kilwinning, Kilwinning Abbey, Montgreenan, Cunninghamhead, Kilmaurs, Cowans Law Country Sports, Moscow, Horse Isle, Ardrossan, Stevenston, Saltcoats, North Ayrshire Museum, Perceton, Dean Castle & Country Park, Loudoun Castle Theme Park, IRVINE, Vennel Gallery, Springside, Knockentiber, Burns Monument, KILMARNOCK, Greenho..., Big Idea, Dreghorn, Crosshouse, Dick Institute, Newm..., Scottish Maritime Museum, Gatehead, Crookedholm, Hurlford, Galston, Drybridge, Riccarton, Sornhill, Irvine Bay, Dundonald, Dundonald Castle, Coodham, Crossroads, Milrig, Barassie, Bogend, Whitelees, Craigie, Boydston, Middlea..., Belfast 2½ hrs (summer only), Loans, Symington, Adamhill, Lochlea, Crosshands, KYL..., Troon, SOUTH AYRSHIRE, Fail, Mossgiel, Blai..., Lady Isle, Rosemount, Tarbolton, Highland Mary's Monument, Mossblown, Burns House Museum, Royal Troon, Monkton, Bachelors' Club (NTS), Failford, Ayr Gorge Woodlands, Mauchline 1648, AYR..., Prestwick, Prestwick International, Mauchline, Balloch..., Kid'z Play, St Quivox, Ayr Bay, Whitletts, Auchincruive, Annbank, Stair, Trabboch, Ochiltree, AYR, Ayr Racecourse, Craigie Park Horticultural Centre, Holmston, Belston, Sundrum Mains, Schaw, Seafield, Loudoun Hall, Joppa, Coylton, Drongan, Belleisle Gardens, Rozelle House Galleries, Burnton, Alloway Auld Kirk, Alloway, Alloway Parish Church, Tam O'Shanter Experience, Martnaham Loch, Heads of Ayr Park, Burns National Heritage Park, Nether Auchendrane, Mount Oliphant, Sinclairston, Lagg, Fisherton, Brown Carrick Hill 287, Dunure, Hollybush, Littlemill, Sk..., Dunure Mains, Sauchrie, Culroy, Minishant, Dalrymple, Rankinston, Stannery Knowe, Electric Brae, Knoweside, Skeldon, Kilmein Hill 429, Culzean Bay, Pennyglen, Grimmet, Dalvennan, Patna, Lethanhill, Maybole, Crosshill

Scale: miles 0 2 4 6 / kilometres 0 2 4 6 8 10

D   E   F   G

Fishing at Irvine Beach

Ayr

Population: 47,962. Ayr is the commercial and administrative centre of the area, as well as being the largest town on the Forth of Clyde coast. It became a resort in the 19th century and continues to attract visitors to its long sandy beach, racecourse and numerous golf courses.

The Ayrshire coast

Sailing is popular in the sheltered waters of the Firth of Clyde. There are marinas and sailing clubs at Troon, Ardrossan and Largs. Sea fishing is also popular with boat trips providing the opportunity to catch haddock, cod, conger and skate.

Robert Burns

Ayrshire is probably best known as the birthplace and early home of the world renowned poet Robert Burns. Scotland's most famous bard is celebrated annually at Burns Night Suppers on 25th January. He was born into a poor background in the village of Alloway in 1759 and much of his life was spent in a struggle against poverty. Many places in 'Tam o'Shanter', such as Alloway Churchyard and the Brig o'Doon can be visited and there is a Burns Heritage Trail linking all sites with a connection to his life and works.

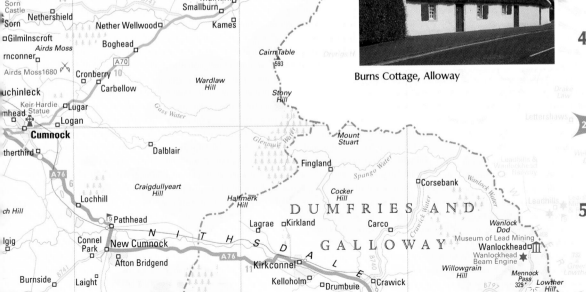

Burns Cottage, Alloway

D   E   F   G

Peebles

Population: 7065. Peebles is a pleasant Borders town in an attractive setting on the banks of the River Tweed. It is surrounded by hills and is a popular area for walking and cycling. The 90 mile (145km) Tweed Cycleway from Biggar to Berwick-upon-Tweed passes nearby.

Selkirk

Population: 5922. The ancient Royal Burgh of Selkirk was once a prosperous textile town. Many of the old stone woollen mills are no longer working, but there are a number of specialist tweed shops in the town. Selkirk also has a strong association with Sir Walter Scott which is explained at the Sir Walter Scott Courtroom in the town centre.

St Mary's Loch

Tweeddale

The Tweeddale valley runs north east, carrying the River Tweed from its source to the confluence with Lyne Water 3 miles (4km) west of Peebles. A roadside sign marks the place at Tweed's Well where the river starts its 97 mile (156km) journey to the sea. The first part of that journey passes through a wide and peaceful glen to the pretty village of Tweedsmuir.

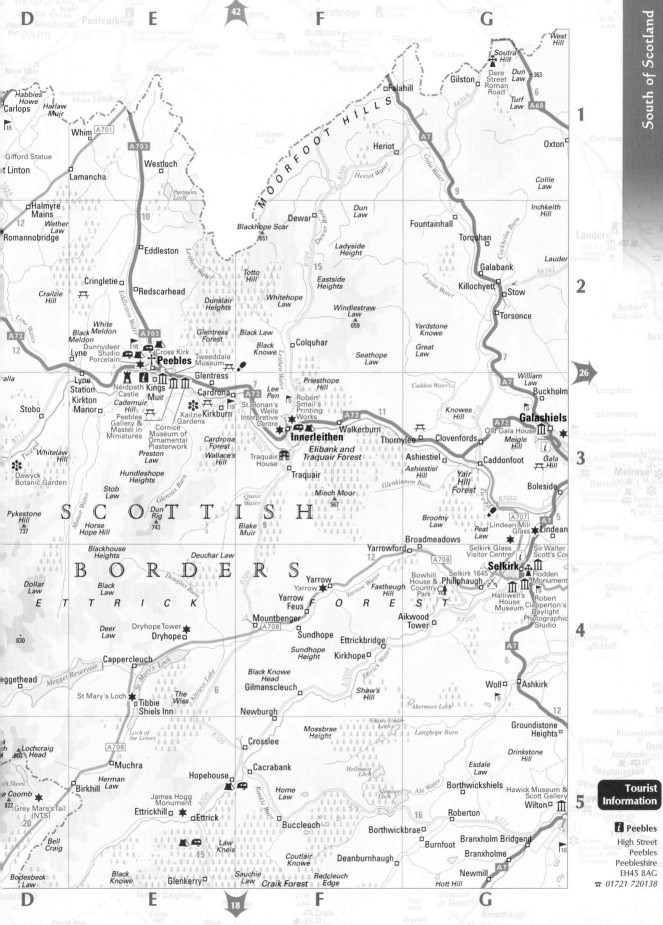

Tourist
Information

i Peebles
High Street
Peebles
Peeblesshire
EH45 8AG
☎ 01721 720138

South of Scotland

Coldingham Beach

Auk, St Abb's Head

Berwickshire Coast

The east coast of the Borders region offers a range of scenery from the historic town and harbour of Eyemouth and the coves and small fishing villages of St Abbs, Burnmouth and Coldingham to the high cliffs and seabird colonies of St Abb's Head. Clear waters also make this a popular area for scuba divers.

42

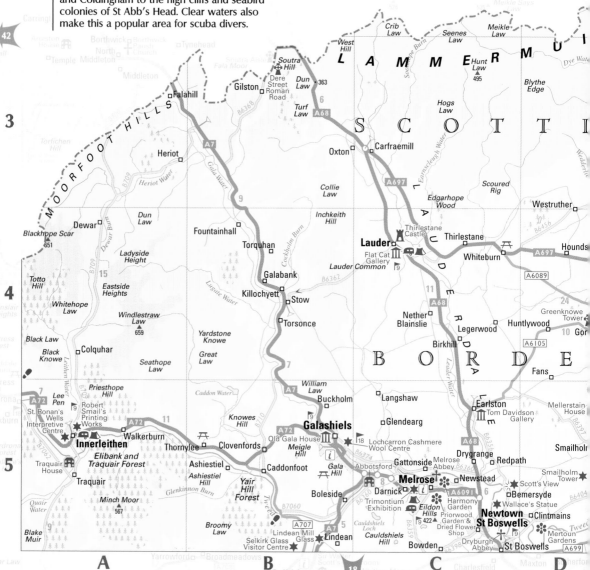

D E 43 F G

N O R T H   S E A

1

Dunbar

Reed Point
Pease Bay
Cove
Cockburnspath

Siccar Point
Fast Castle
Wheat Stack
Telegraph Hill
St Abb's Head
National Nature Reserve
St Abb's Head

Lumsdaine
Cross Law
Coldingham Loch
Northfield
St Abbs

Ecclaw
Meikle Black Law
A1107
Coldingham Moor
Coldingham
Coldingham Bay

Ecclaw Hill
Blackburn Rig
Grantshouse
Eyemouth Museum
Eyemouth

2

Heart Law
Laughing Law
Houndwood
Cairncross
20
A1
Reston
Ayton Castle
Ayton
Burnmouth

HILLS

Abbey St Bathans
Cranshaws
Ellemford
Horseley Hill
Auchencrow
Ayton Hill
Lamberton Beach

Cranshaws Hill
12
Drakemire
B6438
Millerton Hill
Hilton Bay

Wrunk Law
Cockburn Law
Edin's Hall Broch
A6112
Marygold
Lamberton

Longformacus
Preston
Lintlaw
B6355
Chirnside
Foulden Tithe Barn
Mordington Holdings

Dirrington Great Law
Edrom Church
Chirnsidebridge
Whiteadder Water
Foulden
9
A6105

Jim Clark Room
Edrom
Allanton
Clappers
Needles Eye

Dirrington Little Law
Manderston
Hutton
Paxton
Berwick-upon-Tweed

Duns
Cheeklaw
Whitelaw
Blackadder
Sunwick
Paxton House
Fishwick

Gavinton
Choicelee
A6112
6
Whitsome
Union Suspension Bridge
Horncliffe

Polwarth
Sinclair's Hill
B6461
12
Tweedmouth

Hule Moss
A6105
Fogo
Horndean
Spittal

Greenlaw Moor
7
Fogorig
Swinton
Ladykirk Church
Ladykirk

Greenlaw
Blackadder Water
Swintonmill
A6112
Simprim
Upsettlington

4

Purves Hall
Leitholm
B6461
6

Easter Howlaws
Orange Lane
A697

Hume
Humehall
Eccles
The Hirsel
Lennel

Hume Castle
Legars
Coldstream Museum
Coldstream

Sweethope Hill
Birgham
A698
Tweed Bridge

Nenthorn
Stichill
Ednam
10

5

Hendersyde Park
Hadden
Sprouston

Kelso Pottery
Floors Castle
Kelso
Rennie's Bridge
Kelso Abbey
Lempitlaw

Roxburgh Castle
Maxwellheugh
Blakelaw

Roxburgh
Heiton
B6352

D E 19 F G

Tourist Information

Coldstream
Town Hall
76 High Street
Coldstream
Berwickshire
TD12 4DH
☎ 01890 882607

Kelso
Town House
The Square
Kelso
Roxburghshire
TD5 7HF
☎ 01573 223464

Floors Castle

South of Scotland

🏠 Abbotsford   `26 C5`

Abbotsford, on the B6360 between Selkirk and Melrose. The house which Sir Walter Scott, the 19th century novelist, built in 1812 on the site of the Cartley Hole farmhouse, and where he lived until he died in 1832. Features Scott's collection of historical relics, including armour and weapons, Rob Roy's gun and Montrose's sword; his library with over 9000 rare volumes, and other rooms including the chapel.
☎ 01896 752043

✱ Ailsa Craig   `14 B4`

Island in the Firth of Clyde, 10 miles (17km) west of Girvan. A granite island rock, 1114ft (339.5m) high with a circumference of 2 miles (3km). The rock itself was used to make some of the finest curling stones and the island has a gannetry and colonies of guillemots and other sea birds.

✱ Alexandra Wolffe Animals   `9 G3`

The Tollhouse, Gatehouse-of-Fleet. A small working ceramic studio making individual statuettes and portrait models of animals.
☎ 01557 814300

✝ Alloway Auld Kirk   `22 B5`

Alloway, 2.5 miles (4km) south of Ayr on the B7024. Ancient church, a ruin in Burns' day. William Burnes, the poet's father, is buried in the churchyard. In the poem, Tam o' Shanter, Burns described the 'warlocks and witches in a dance, within Alloway's auld haunted kirk'.
☎ 01292 441252

✝ Alloway Parish Church   `22 B5`

Alloway, 2.5 miles (4km) south of Ayr. Built between 1858 and 1890 by architect Campbell Douglas, this church has a fine collection of stained glass including works by Adam Small, W. and J. J. Kier, Whall, Webster, Clayton, Bell and Susan Bradbury (The Seasons and Robert Burns Memorial Window, 1996 and 2001).
☎ 01292 441252

🏃 Annan Activities   `13 D4`

Westlands, on the B6357 between Annan and Kirkpatrick Fleming. The 70 acre (29ha) site has activities for all the family: quad bike tracks and safari, crazy golf, paintball, fishing pond, fly fishing lochans, clay pigeon shooting, go-karts for children and adults. Activities suitable for all ages. All equipment available for hire.
☎ 01461 800274   www.westlands-activities.co.uk

🏰 Ardrossan Castle   `22 A2`

Ardrossan, on a hill overlooking Ardrossan Bay. Mid 12th century castle with fine views of Arran and Ailsa Craig. The castle was destroyed by Cromwell and only part of the north tower and two arched cellars remain.

✱ Ardwell Gardens   `8 B4`

On the A716, 10 miles (16km) south of Stranraer. Gardens surrounding an 18th century country house (not open to the public) with the formal layout around the house blending into the informality of woods and shrubberies. Daffodils, azaleas, camellias, rhododendrons. Walled garden and herbaceous borders. Walks and fine views over Luce Bay.
☎ 01776 860227

✱ Arran Aromatics Visitor Centre   `20 C4`

The Home Farm, 1 mile (1.5km) from Brodick on the road north to Lochranza. Visitors can watch the production of natural soaps and body care products. Set in a courtyard next to a cheese factory and seafood restaurant.
☎ 01770 302595   www.arranaromatics.com

🍶 Arran Brewery   `20 C4`

Cladach, 1 mile north of Brodick. Arran's first and only commercial craft brewery, producing three different real ales using traditional methods. Visitors may see the beer fermenting and watch the bottling and labelling. Displays explain the story of brewing and questions about the process are welcome.
☎ 01770 302353   www.arranbrewery.com

⚱ Auchagallon Stone Circle   `20 B4`

4 miles (6.5km) north of Blackwaterfoot on the Isle of Arran. A Bronze Age burial cairn surrounded by a circle of 15 standing stones.
☎ 0131 668 8800   www.historic-scotland.gov.uk

🌿 Ayr Gorge Woodlands   `22 C4`

At Failford, south of the A758 Ayr – Mauchline road. Gorge woodland, semi-natural, dominated by oak and some coniferous plantation. Situated by the River Ayr. Historic sandstone steps and extensive network of well-maintained footpaths.

🏆 Ayr Racecourse   `22 B4`

Ayr. Scotland's largest racecourse and venue for the Scottish National in April and the Ayr Gold Cup in September. The course was established on its current site in 1907. Corporate hospitality.
☎ 01292 264179   www.ayr-racecourse.co.uk

🏰 Ayton Castle   `27 G3`

Ayton, Eyemouth, 7 miles (11km) north of Berwick. Historic castle, built in 1846 and an important example of the Victorian architectural tradition. Ayton Castle has been restored in recent years and is lived in as a family home.
☎ 01890 781212

🏠 Bachelors' Club   `22 C4`

Sandgate Street, Tarbolton. Robert Burns and his friends founded a debating society here in 1780. Period furnishings.
☎ 01292 541940   www.nts.org.uk

✱ Balmichael Visitor Centre   `20 B4`

Shiskine, Isle of Arran. 7 miles (11km) from Brodick on the B880. Converted farm buildings and courtyard including ice cream parlour and jewellery/craft shop, working pottery, antique and tapestry shops. Adventure playground and indoor play barn. Quad biking for all ages. Heritage area with working mill wheel.
☎ 01770 860430

✱ Barcloy Barn   `11 E3`

Colvend, Dalbeattie. A Portuguese shop selling olive oil produced in the Algarve, together with home-made preserves, almonds, lavender and a large range of Portuguese pottery.
☎ 01556 630341

✝ Barsalloch Fort   `9 E4`

Off the A747, 7.5 miles (12km) west north-west of Whithorn. Remains of an Iron Age hill fort on the edge of a raised beach bluff. Defended by a deep ditch in horseshoe form.
☎ 0131 668 8800   www.historic-scotland.gov.uk

🌿 Barwinnock Herbs   `14 D5`

Barhill, 12 miles (19km) north west of Newton Stewart, off the B7027 near Loch Maberry. A garden and nursery with a fascinating collection of culinary, medicinal and aromatic herbs. Also Rural Life exhibition describing herbs for healing and flavour, and the local countryside, its natural materials and wildlife.
☎ 01465 821338   www.barwinnock.com

🌳 Belleisle Gardens   `22 B5`

Alloway, 1 mile south of Ayr on the A719. Country park and formal gardens with two spectacular golf courses open to the public. Pets' corner and deer park.
☎ 01292 441025

🏛 Big Idea   `22 B3`

The Harbourside, Irvine. The world's first centre devoted to invention and discovery. Take a mind-blowing journey through the history of inventions with over 30,000 square feet (9144 square metres) of attractions to explore. Experience a ride through the history of explosions, interact with exhibits through unique technology and construct inventions in the inventors' workshop.
☎ 01294 461999   www.bigidea.org.uk

✱ Blacksmith's Shop Centre, Gretna Green   `13 E4`

On the Scottish/English border, 15 miles (24km) south of Lockerbie. The Blacksmith's Shop is famous around the world for runaway marriages. The unique Gretna Green Story involves the visitor in the legends of its romantic history and leads into the magnificent anvil and carriage museum. The Tartan Shop presents Scotland's finest independent collection of Scottish and UK merchandise – cashmere, tartans, crystal, luxury foods and gifts. Tartan information centre. Tax-free shopping and worldwide mailing services.
☎ 01461 338441   www.gretnagreen.com/blacksmiths.html

🏰 Blairquhan   `15 E3`

Maybole, 14 miles (22.5km) south east of Ayr. Four families have lived at Blairquhan. The first tower-house was built in 1346. The new house was designed and built by the Scottish architect William Burn between 1821 and 1824. Walled garden with original glasshouse. Pinetum. Sir James Hunter Blair's Collection of Scottish Colourists.
☎ 01655 770239   www.blairquhan.co.uk

🏛 Border Fine Arts Gallery   `13 E2`

Townfoot, Langholm, 20 miles (32km) north of Carlisle. Border Fine Arts have been producing high quality ceramic figurines for over twenty-five years and have many collectors throughout the world. Visitors can see an extensive display of sculptures which collectors find enthralling.
☎ 01387 383033

🏰 Bowhill House & Country Park   `18 B2`

Bowhill, 3 miles (5km) west of Selkirk on the A708. For many generations Bowhill has been the Border home of the Scotts of Buccleuch. Inside the house, begun in 1812, there is an outstanding collection of pictures, including works by Van Dyck, Reynolds, Gainsborough, Canaletto, Guardi, Claude Lorraine, Raeburn. There is also a selection of the world-famous Buccleuch collection of portrait minatures. Also porcelain and furniture, much of which was made in the famous workshop of André Boulle in Paris. Restored Victorian kitchen. In the grounds are an adventure woodland play area, a riding centre, garden nature trails, bicycle hire.
☎ 01750 22204

↻ Brighouse Bay Trekking Ponies   `10 C4`

Borgue, 6 miles (10km) south west of Kirkcudbright. Approved by the British Horse Society, the Trekking Centre offers riding for all abilities. Hard hats are provided. Riding is within the 1200 acre (486ha) holiday/farm complex. Also holiday park.
☎ 01557 870267   www.brighouse-bay.co.uk

🏰 Brodick Castle   `20 C4`

2 miles (3km) north of Brodick on the Isle of Arran. Mainly Victorian castle, built on the site of a Viking fortress. Original parts date from the 13th century, although much of it was destroyed in the 15th and 16th centuries. Fine collections of furniture, paintings, porcelain and silver collected by the Dukes of Hamilton. The castle contains collections of artwork by Gainsborough and Turner. Beautiful walled garden, and woodland garden with famous rhododendron collection. The castle occupies a fine site overlooking Brodick Bay, on the slopes of Goat Fell (2866ft/873m). Nature trail and other walks in country park.
☎ 01770 302202   www.nts.org.uk

🏛 **Broughton Gallery** `24 D3`
On the A701 just north of Broughton village. Sells paintings and crafts by living British artists and makers in Tower House, designed in 1937 by Sir Basil Spence.
☎ 01899 830234

🏠 **Broughton House & Garden** `10 C3`
12 High Street, Kirkcudbright. 18th century town house, home and studio (1901–33) of artist E. A. Hornel, one of the Glasgow Boys. Permanent exhibition of his work. Extensive collection of Scottish books including Burns' works. Attractive Japanese-style garden, added by Hornel, leading down to River Dee estuary.
☎ 01557 330437   www.nts.org.uk

✶ **Brow Well** `11 G2`
On the B725, 1 mile (1.5km) west of Ruthwell. Ancient mineral well visited by Robert Burns in July 1796, when at Brow sea bathing under his doctor's orders.

♰ **Bruce's Stone** `15 F5`
North side of Loch Trool, unclassified road off the A714, 13 miles (21km) north of Newton Stewart. A massive granite memorial to Robert the Bruce's first victory over the English, which led to his subsequent success at Bannockburn. Fine views of Loch Trool and the hills of Galloway. Start of hill climb to the Merrick (2764ft/842.5m), the highest hill in southern Scotland.

🏠 **Burns House** `11 F1`
Burns Street, Dumfries. Five minute walk from Dumfries town centre. It was in this ordinary sandstone house that Robert Burns, Scotland's national poet, spent the last years of his brilliant life. Now a place of pilgrimage for Burns enthusiasts around the world. The house retains much of its 18th century character and contains many relics of the poet. Visitors can see the chair in which he wrote his last poems and many original letters and manuscripts. The famous Kilmarnock and Edinburgh editions of his work are also on display.
☎ 01387 255297

🏛 **Burns House Museum** `22 D4`
Castle Street, Mauchline, 11 miles (18km) from Ayr and Kilmarnock. A museum with a gallery devoted to Burns memorabilia. On the upper floor is the room Burns took for Jean Armour in 1788. It has remained intact and is furnished in the style of the period. Models of Jean and Robert plus a full video presentation. Visitors can also see a large collection of Mauchline boxware and an exhibition devoted to curling and curling stones. Nearby is Mauchline churchyard in which are buried four of Burns' daughters and a number of his friends and contemporaries.
☎ 01290 550045

♰ **Burns Monument** `22 C3`
Kay Park, 0.5 mile (1km) from the centre of Kilmarnock. Victorian red sandstone monument with statue of Burns by W. G. Stevenson. Set in an attractive park with boating, pitch and putt, and children's play area.

✶ **Burns National Heritage Park** `22 B5`
Murdochs Lane, Alloway, 2 miles (3km) south of Ayr on the B7024. The Burns National Heritage Park was established in 1995. It embraces Burns' Cottage, Museum, Monument, Auld Brig o' Doon and Alloway Kirk together with the Tam o' Shanter Experience. The old and new are linked in time by a 5-minute walk which transports the visitor from 1759 (when Burns was born) to the exciting, humorous and action-filled Tam o' Shanter Experience.
☎ 01292 443700

♰ **Burnswark Hill** `12 C3`
By unclassified road, 1.5 miles (2.5km) north of the B725, Ecclefechan to Middlebie road. A native hill fort (circa 6th century BC) with extensive earthworks, flanked by a Roman artillery range. Thought to have been a series of Roman practice seige works, best seen from the hilltop. The excavated ditches and ramparts of Birrens Fort are nearby.

🏰 **Caerlaverock Castle** `11 G2`
Glencople, off the B725, 9 miles (14.5km) south of Dumfries. One of the finest castles in Scotland – its remarkable features are the twin-towered gatehouse and the Nithsdale Lodging, a splendid Renaissance range dating from 1638.
☎ 01387 770244   www.historic-scotland.gov.uk

♰ **Cairn Holy Chambered Cairns** `9 G3`
6.5 miles (10.5km) south east of Creetown. Two remarkably complete Neolithic burial cairns situated on a hill giving good views over Wigtown Bay.
☎ 0131 668 8800   www.historic-scotland.gov.uk

❀ **Cally Gardens** `10 C3`
Gatehouse of Fleet, Castle Douglas. A specialist nursery in an 18th century walled garden. There is a unique collection of over 3500 varieties, mainly perennials, planted out in 32 large borders.
☎ 01557 815029

🏰 **Cardoness Castle** `9 G3`
On the A75, 1 mile (2km) south west of Gatehouse of Fleet. The well-preserved ruin of a 15th century tower house, the ancient home of the McCullochs of Galloway. Four storeys with a vaulted basement. Features include the original stairway, stone benches and elaborate fireplaces.
☎ 01557 814427   www.historic-scotland.gov.uk

🏰 **Carleton Castle** `14 C5`
Off the A77, 6 miles (9.5km) south of Girvan. One in a link of Kennedy watchtowers along the coast. Now a ruin, it was famed in a ballad as the seat of a baron who got rid of seven wives by pushing them over the cliff, but who was himself disposed of by May Culean, his eighth wife.

♱ **Carn Ban** `20 B5`
3.5 miles (5.5km) north east of Lagg on the south coast of the Isle of Arran. One of the most famous Neolithic long cairns of south west Scotland.
☎ 0131 668 8800   www.historic-scotland.gov.uk

🏰 **Carsluith Castle** `9 F3`
On the A75, 7 miles (11km) west of Gatehouse of Fleet. The delightful and well-preserved ruin of a 16th century tower house with 18th century ranges of outhouses still in use by the farmer. One of its owners was the last abbot of Sweetheart Abbey.

🏛 **Carsphairn Heritage Centre** `15 F4`
On the A713, 25 miles (40km) south of Ayr and 25 miles (40km) north of Castle Douglas. Carsphairn Heritage Centre houses a permanent display on the parish together with a temporary annual exhibition, featuring local history. There is also a reference section which pays particular attention to family history records relevant to the area and a small display of locally made articles for sale together with other relevant mementoes of the area.
☎ 01644 460653   www.carsphairnheritage.co.uk

🏛 **Castle Douglas Art Gallery** `11 D2`
Market Street, Castle Douglas. First opened in 1938, having been gifted to the town by Mrs Ethel Bristowe, a talented artist in her own right. The gallery now forms an excellent venue for an annual programme of temporary exhibitions between Easter and Christmas, ranging from fine art and craft to photography.
☎ 01557 331643

🏛 **Castle of St John** `8 B2`
Charlotte Street, Stranraer. Medieval tower house built circa 1500. An exhibition tells the castle's story, highlighting its use by Government troops during the suppression of the Covenanters, and its Victorian use as a prison. Family activities.
☎ 01776 705088

🏛 **Cathcartston Visitor Centre** `15 F3`
Cathcartston, Dalmellington. Local history museum with a fine collection of photographs and maps illustrating the Doon Valley over the centuries. Also local history displays combined with changing art exhibitions and a weaving tableau.
☎ 01292 550633

♱ **Chapel Finian** `9 D4`
5 miles (8km) north west of Port William. The foundation remains of a small chapel or oratory, probably dating from the 10th or 11th century, in an enclosure about 50ft (15m) wide.
☎ 0131 668 8800   www.historic-scotland.gov.uk

🏛 **Clachanmore Gallery & Tearoom** `8 B4`
Clachanmore, Ardwell, 10 miles (16km) south of Stranraer, between Sandhead and Ardwell. Changing exhibitions, many featuring the best of Dumfries and Galloway artists. Outside are sculptures by Jeff White.
☎ 01776 860200

🏛 **Clan Armstrong Museum** `13 E2`
Lodge Walk, Langholm. Off the A7 in Langholm, north of Carlisle. The world's largest Armstrong Museum, containing the most extensive Armstrong archives and displaying the history of this formidable Borders' family from the reiving days of the 15th and 16th centuries to the present.
☎ 01387 381610

✶ **Clatteringshaws Visitor Centre** `9 G1`
New Galloway, Castle Douglas. Situated in Galloway Forest Park. Forest wildlife exhibition. Guided walks. Fishing (by permit). Waymarked walks and cycle trails.
☎ 01644 420285   www.forestry.gov.uk

✶ **Clog & Shoe Workshop** `10 C1`
13 miles (21km) north of Castle Douglas in Balmaclellan. Rural workshop where visitors can watch ongoing work which includes the making of modern and traditional clogs, boots, sandals, baby footwear, bags and purses. Footwear can be made to measure.
☎ 01644 420456

🏛 **Coldstream Museum** `27 F4`
Coldstream. 15 miles (24km) west of Berwick-upon-Tweed. Local history displays and section on the Coldstream Guards. Temporary exhibition gallery.
☎ 01890 882630

✶ **Colfin Smokehouse** `8 B3`
Colfin Creamery, 2 miles (3km) from Portpatrick on the A77 at Colfin. Visitors can observe the salmon smoking process in detail and purchase the product.
☎ 01776 820622

🏛 **Cornice Museum of Ornamental Plasterwork** `25 E3`
Innerleithen Road, Peebles. The museum is a plasterer's casting workshop virtually unchanged since the turn of the century and illustrates the main methods of creating ornamental plasterwork in Scotland at that time. It also displays probably the largest surviving collection of 'masters' in Scotland.
☎ 01721 720212

✶ **Cowans Law Country Sports** `22 C2`
Hemphill Road, Moscow, Galston. From the A77 take the A719 to Moscow. A 4 acre (1.7ha) trout loch set in the heart of Ayrshire's farming country. Also clay shooting, archery and air rifle range. Families and beginners welcome.
☎ 01560 700666   www.countrysports-scotland.com

❀ **Craigie Park Horticultural Centre** `22 B4`
Craigie Estate, Ayr. Beside the River Ayr with pleasant woodland walks. The Horticultural Centre features tropical and temperate houses.
☎ 01292 263275

★ Cream o' Galloway   10 C3

Rainton, 4 miles (6.5km) south of Gatehouse of Fleet off the A75. Cream o' Galloway is a small farm-based ice cream manufacturer specialising in traditional quality ice cream and frozen yoghurt with unusual flavours. There is a farm shop and a viewing gallery where visitors can watch the manufacturing process. Also illustrated nature walks, extensive adventure playground, treasure hunt and nature quizzes.
☎ 01557 814040   www.creamogalloway.co.uk

🏛 Creetown Exhibition Centre   9 F3

Creetown, Newton Stewart. Creetown is portrayed from its origin as an 18th century fishing hamlet, through the growth and decline of its famous granite quarries, to the present day. Displays include a large collection of old photographs, wartime memorabilia, village shop, information on local nature reserve, work of local artists, woodcarver and sculptor.
☎ 01671 820343

🏛 Creetown Gem Rock Museum   9 F3

Chain Road, Creetown, 7 miles (11km) east of Newton Stewart on the A75. The museum houses one of the finest collections of privately owned gemstones, crystals, minerals and fossils in Europe. Visitors can witness the spectacular volcanic eruption display, the Crystal Cave and a 15-minute audio-visual programme.
☎ 01671 820357   www.gemrock.net

🏛 Crichton Royal Museum   11 F1

Easterbrook Hall, Bankend Road, 1.5 miles (2.5km) south of Dumfries centre on Bankend road. Enter site via Crichton Church Gate. The Museum tells the story of mental health care in south west Scotland over a period of more than 200 years, a story featuring the part played by Dumfries Infirmary in the 18th century; the Crichton family and its wealth; stylish architecture; elegant furniture; stained glass; beautiful gardens; operating theatre and medical equipment; exhibits accruing from the various therapies, especially art therapy; and topical health-related exhibitions.
☎ 01387 244228

✝ Cross Kirk   25 E2

In Cross Road, Peebles. The remains of a Trinitarian friary founded in the late 13th century. Consists of nave, west tower and foundations of domestic buildings.
☎ 0131 668 8800   www.historic-scotland.gov.uk

✝ Crossraguel Abbey   15 D3

On the A77, 2 miles (3km) south west of Maybole. A Cluniac monastery built in 1244 by the Earl of Carrick. Inhabited by Benedictine monks until the end of the 16th century. Extensive and remarkably complete remains of high quality, including the church, cloister, chapter house and much of the domestic premises.
☎ 01655 883113   www.historic-scotland.gov.uk

★ Cruck Cottage   11 G1

Torthorwald, off the A709. An example of an early 19th century thatched cottage, restored using traditional skills and local materials.

🏰 Culzean Castle & Country Park   14 D3

Maybole, on the A719, 12 miles (19km) south of Ayr. High on a cliff above the Firth of Clyde, Robert Adam's Culzean Castle is one of the most romantic in Scotland. Designed at the end of the 18th century, the elegant interior includes the spectacular Oval Staircase and the Circular Saloon. Fascinating associated buildings in the 563 acre (227ha) country park include the Fountain Court and the Camellia House. Swan pond, deer park, woodland and beach walks.
☎ 01655 884455   www.nts.org.uk

🏛 Dalgarven Mill & Country Life Museum   22 A2

On the A737 between Dalry and Kilwinning. A 17th century restored water mill, set in a secluded hollow, housing an exhibition of traditional flour production. In the adjoining granary there is a museum of Ayrshire country life, with collections of farming and domestic memorabilia and local costume, including some good examples of Ayrshire whitework. Room reconstructions of 1880's lifestyle.
☎ 01294 552448   www.dalgarvenmill.org.uk

★ Dalton Pottery Art Café   12 C3

Meikle Dyke, Dalton. Signposted on the B725, 1 mile (2km) towards Dalton from Carrutherstown (off the A75 between Dumfries and Annan). A working pottery where visitors can see a range of porcelain giftware being made and hand decorated. Choose from 40 styles of pot, pre-fired and glazed, and paint your own enamel design to take away. Showroom.
☎ 01387 840236

🏛 David Coulthard Museum   10 C3

Twynholm, Kirkcudbright. The museum traces David Coulthard's motor racing career to date. Visitors can see six racing cars, David Coulthard's trophies, race suits and helmets. Also lots of photographs.
☎ 01557 860050

❀ Dawyck Botanic Garden   25 D3

Stobo on the B712, 8 miles (13km) south west of Peebles. A specialist garden of the Royal Botanic Garden, Edinburgh. A historic arboretum with landscaped walks. The mature trees include the unique Dawyck Beech. There are also many varieties of flowering trees, shrubs and herbaceous plants. Visitors can explore Heron Wood and the world's first Cryptogamic Sanctuary and Reserve to see non-flowering plants. Other notable features include the Swiss Bridge, stonework and terracing created by Italian craftsmen in the 1820s.
☎ 01721 760254

🏰 Dean Castle & Country Park   22 C3

On the A77 Dean Road, Kilmarnock. A magnificent collection of buildings dating from the 1350s. For 400 years Dean Castle was the stronghold of the Boyds of Kilmarnock, and today important collections of arms and armour, musical instruments and tapestries are on display in public rooms. The country park comprises 200 acres (81ha) of mixed woodland. Ranger service and programme of events.
☎ 01563 522702

🏛 Designs Gallery & Café   11 D2

179 King Street, Castle Douglas, on the A75, 18 miles (29km) west of Dumfries. A focal point for arts and crafts in south west Scotland. Changing exhibitions of high quality crafts. Adjacent shop sells cards, prints, ceramics, knitwear, studio glass and jewellery.
☎ 01556 504552   www.designsgallery.co.uk

★ Devil's Beef Tub   24 C5

A701, 6 miles (9.5km) north of Moffat. A huge, spectacular hollow among the hills, at the head of Annandale. In the swirling mists of this out-of-the-way retreat, Borders reivers hid cattle lifted in their raids. Can be seen from the road.

🏛 Devil's Porridge   13 D4

St John's Church, Eastriggs, off the A75 between Gretna and Annan. An exhibition on the fascinating story of the 30,000 women and men who worked in HM Factory Gretna in World War I. Women munition workers mixed the Devil's Porridge, the name coined by Sir Arthur Conan Doyle for the highly explosive mixture of gun cotton and nitro-glycerine which was made into cordite for British shells and bullets. Photographs, video, murals, artefacts and supporting exhibitions including Children at War, the story of the World War II evacuation.
☎ 01461 40460

🏛 Dick Institute   22 C3

Kilmarnock. Temporary and permanent exhibitions over two floors of this grand Victorian building. Fine art, social and natural history collections are upstairs, whilst galleries downstairs house the temporary exhibitions of visual art and craft.
☎ 01563 554343

✝ Druchtag Motte   9 E4

At the north end of Mochrum village, 2 miles (3km) north of Port William. A well-preserved Norman motte castle.
☎ 0131 668 8800   www.historic-scotland.gov.uk

✝ Drumcoltran Tower   11 E2

Off A711, 8 miles (13km) south west of Dumfries. The tower can be found among farm buildings. A well-preserved mid 16th century tower house. Simple and severe.
☎ 0131 668 8800   www.historic-scotland.gov.uk

🏛 Drumlanrig's Tower   18 C3

1 Towerknowe, off the High Street in the centre of Hawick. This 15th century fortified tower house, stronghold of the Douglases, tells the story of Hawick and Scotland using period sets, costumed figures and audio-visuals. Themes include Border Reivers and Hawick's renowned knitwear industry.
☎ 01450 377615

✝ Drumtroddan Cup & Ring Marks   9 E4

Off the A714, 2 miles (3km) north east of Port William. A group of Bronze Age cup and ring markings in bedrock. An alignment of three stones stands 400 yards (365m) south.
☎ 0131 668 8800   www.historic-scotland.gov.uk

✝ Dryburgh Abbey   26 C5

Dryburgh, near Newtown St Boswells on the B6404, 5 miles (8km) south east of Melrose. The remarkably complete ruins of a Premonstratensian abbey. One of the four famous Border abbeys founded in the reign of David I by Hugh de Morville, Constable of Scotland. Mainly remains of transepts and cloisters. Sir Walter Scott and Field Marshall Earl Haig are buried here.
☎ 01835 822381   www.historic-scotland.gov.uk

★ Dryhope Tower   25 E4

Off the A708 near St Mary's Loch, 15 miles (24km) west of Selkirk. A stout tower, now ruinous but originally four storeys high, rebuilt circa 1613. Birthplace of Mary Scott, the Flower of Yarrow, who married the freebooter Auld Wat of Harden in 1576 – ancestors Sir Walter Scott was proud to claim.

🏛 Dumfries & Galloway Aviation Museum   11 F1

Heathhall, Dumfries. Opened in 1977 and regarded as one of the foremost volunteer run aviation museums in the UK. Various aircraft are on display and under restoration, including a Spitfire, Hawker Hunter and a Trident airliner. In the former control tower is a varied collection of memorabilia ranging from aero engines to uniforms and documentation.
☎ 01387 251623

🏛 Dumfries Museum & Camera Obscura   11 F1

The Observatory, 0.5 mile (1km) west of Dumfries centre. Situated in the 18th century windmill tower on top of Corbelly Hill, the museum is the largest in south west Scotland, with collections inaugurated over 150 years ago. Exhibitions trace the history of the people and landscape of Dumfries and Galloway. The camera obscura was installed in 1836 and gives a table-top panorama of Dumfries and the surrounding area. Note no wheelchair access to camera obscura.
☎ 01387 253374

🏛 Dunaskin Open Air Museum   15 F3

Dalmellington Road, Waterside, Patna. Adjacent to the A713 Ayr to Castle Douglas/Dumfries road. Journey back in time at this open-air industrial museum. Local coal, ironstone and limestone was smelted here to make pig iron – the museum describes how the rural valley of Doon was transformed into a busy industrial complex during the 19th century. Craighton Pit Experience contains many original artefacts from local pits and mines. Chapel Row Cottage has been restored to recreate an ironworks cottage of around 1914.
☎ 01292 531144   www.dunaskin.org.uk

🏰 Dundonald Castle   22 B3

Dundonald, on the A759, 5 miles (8km) west of Kilmarnock. A large prominent stone castle, built by Robert Stewart in the 1370s, probably to mark his succession to the Scottish throne as Robert II in 1371. Two great feasting halls, one above the other, with great vaults beneath. The third medieval castle to be built on the site, preceded by a hill fort between 500 and 200 BC. Remains of an earlier, but equally grand 13th century castle of the Stewarts are visible.
☎ 01563 851489

† Dundrennan Abbey · 11 D4

Dundrennan, on the A711, 6.5 miles (10.5km) south east of Kirkcudbright. The beautiful ruins, amid a peaceful setting, of a Cistercian abbey founded in 1142 by King David I. Includes much later Norman and transitional work. The east end of the church and the chapter house are of high quality. It is believed that Mary, Queen of Scots spent her last night in Scotland here in May 1568.
☎ 01557 500262   www.historic-scotland.gov.uk

✱ Dunmydeer Studio Porcelain · 25 E2

Peebles Craft Centre, Peebles. Part of a complex of workshops. Visitors can see a ceramic artist (Duncan Hood) at work and purchase finished products including sculptures and jewellery.
☎ 01721 722875

⚑ Dunskey Castle · 8 B3

Located just to the south of Portpatrick. Impressive 16th century castle ruins in a dramatic cliff top setting overlooking the the Irish Sea. Reach the castle from the cliff top footpath which ascends from the old quarry at the south end of Portpatrick waterfront.

❊ Dunskey Gardens & Woodland Walks · 8 B3

Dunskey House, 1 mile from Portpatrick. A charming, recently renovated 18th century walled garden with working greenhouses, interesting woodland walks, plant sales and tea room.
☎ 07769 662194   www.dunskey.com

✱ Dunskey Trout Lochs · 8 B3

Dunskey House, 1 mile from Portpatrick. Two exclusive trout lochs for fly-fishing only. Boat and bank fishing.
☎ 01776 810364   www.dunskey.com

† Durisdeer Church · 16 C3

6 miles (9.5km) north east of Thornhill on the A702. Dating from 1699, the church houses the Queensberry Marbles, which represent the recumbent figures of the second Duke and Duchess of Queensberry. In the vault lie lead coffins, containing ancient remains of the Clan Douglas.

⚐ Edin's Hall Broch · 27 E3

On the north eastern slope of Cockburn Law, off the A6112 about 4.5 miles (7km) from Grantshouse. One of the few Iron Age brochs in the Scottish Lowlands. Unusually large, sitting in a fort defended by ramparts and ditches, partially overlain with a later settlement. Occupied in Roman times.
☎ 0131 668 8800   www.historic-scotland.gov.uk

† Edrom Church · 27 F3

In Edrom churchyard, Berwickshire, off the A6015, 3.5 miles (5.5km) north east of Duns. A fine Norman chancel arch is carved in the church doorway built by Thor Longus circa 1105.
☎ 0131 668 8800   www.historic-scotland.gov.uk

✱ Electric Brae · 22 A5

On the A719, 20 miles (32km) south of Ayr (also known as Croy Brae). An optical illusion is created so that a car appears to be going up the hill when it is in fact going down.

▥ Ellisland Farm · 12 A2

Holywood, off the A76, 6.5 miles (10.5km) north north-west of Dumfries. The farm which Robert Burns took over in 1788, building the farmhouse and trying to introduce new farming methods. Unsuccessful, he became an exciseman in 1789, and when the stock was auctioned in 1791 he moved to Dumfries. Burns wrote some of his most famous works at the farm, including Tam o' Shanter and Auld Lang Syne. The granary houses an audio-visual display and there are facilities for barbecues.
☎ 01387 740426

▥ Eyemouth Museum · 27 G3

Auld Kirk, Manse Road. The museum contains a magnificent tapestry which was sewn by local ladies to commemorate the Great East Coast Fishing Disaster of 1881, when 189 local fishermen were drowned. Also exhibitions on farming, milling, blacksmith and wheelwright, in addition to local fishing heritage.
☎ 01890 750678

⚑ Fast Castle · 27 F1

Off the A1107, 4 miles (6.5km) north west of Coldingham. The scant and remote but impressive remains of a Home stronghold is perched on a cliff above the sea. The castle passed to the last Logan of Restalrig in 1580, who was outlawed for the Gowrie conspiracy (alleged plot to kill James VI).

⚑ Ferniehirst Castle · 19 D3

Lothian Estates Office, on the A68, 2 miles (3km) south of Jedburgh. A 16th century Border castle and Scotland's frontier fortress. The ancestral home of the Kerr family; restored by the clan chief, the Marquis of Lothian. Information centre, chapel, Kerr museum and private apartments.
☎ 01835 862201

▥ Flat Cat Gallery · 26 C4

2 Market Place, Lauder. Changing exhibitions of paintings, sculpture, ceramics, jewellery and furniture by artists from the Borders and further afield. Also a resident restorer of middle-eastern rugs and textiles. A good stock of carpets on display.
☎ 01578 722808   www.flatcatgallery.com

⚐ Flodden Monument · 18 B2

Located in Selkirk town centre, this monument was erected in 1913 on the 400th anniversary of the battle and is inscribed O Flodden Field. The memorial is the work of sculptor Thomas Clapperton, and commemorates the lone survivor of the 80 Selkirk men who marched to Flodden.

▦ Floors Castle · 27 E5

Located in Kelso, Floors Castle is the home of the Roxburghe family. It is the largest inhabited castle in Scotland. The apartments display an outstanding collection of French 17th and 18th century furniture, many fine works of art and tapestries, Chinese and Dresden porcelain and a Victorian collection of birds. The extensive parkland and gardens overlooking the River Tweed provide delightful walks and picnic areas. The walled garden contains splendid herbaceous borders and is best seen in July, August and September.
☎ 01573 223333

▦ Foulden Tithe Barn · 27 G3

On the A6105, 4 miles (6.5km) south east of Chirnside. A two-storey tithe barn with outside stair and crow-stepped gables.
☎ 0131 668 8800   www.historic-scotland.gov.uk

✱ Galloway Country Style · 9 G3

High Street, Gatehouse-of-Fleet. A kilt-making workshop where visitors can see operations and learn about the history of kilts and how they are made.
☎ 01557 814001

✸ Galloway Deer Range · 9 G1

Laggan O'Dee, 10 miles (16km) from Newton Stewart and 9 miles (14.5km) from New Galloway on the A712. Created in 1977 to enable visitors to see red deer in a semi-natural habitat of 500 acres (200ha). Good photo opportunities.
☎ 07771 748400

❊ Galloway House Gardens · 9 F4

On the A713, 10 miles north of Castle Douglas, on the shore of Loch Ken. Woodland garden with a number of walks through the grounds, leading down to the shore and sandy bay.
☎ 01988 600680   www.garlieston.net/gtardens

✱ Galloway Hydros Visitor Centre · 10 D3

Tongland, 2 miles (3km) north east of Kirkcudbright. Hydro-electric station, built in the 1930s, which provides a third of the power of south west Scotland. Visitor centre with exhibition room, 1930s style office and guided tours of the power station and dam.
☎ 01557 330114

✱ Gilnockie Tower · 13 E3

Hollows, on the A7, 2 miles (3km) north of Canonbie. A tower house built in 1525 by the Border freebooter Johnie Armstrong and originally called Holehouse (from the quarry beside which it stands). Managed by the Clan Armstrong Centre.

† Glenluce Abbey · 8 C3

Off the A75, 2 miles (3km) north of Glenluce. The remains of a Cistercian abbey founded circa 1192, including a handsome early 16th century chapter house. Includes an exhibition of objets trouvès. Lovely tranquil setting.
☎ 01581 300541   www.historic-scotland.gov.uk

✱ Glentrool Visitor Centre · 9 E1

Glentrool, 8 miles north of Newton Stewart, 3 miles west of Loch Trool and Stroan Bridge. The gateway to Glen Trool, Scotland's largest forest park, covering 18,780 acres (7606ha) of forest, moorland and loch. Exhibits on Loch Trool.
☎ 01671 840301   www.forestry.gov.uk

❊ Glenwhan Gardens · 8 C3

Dunragit, off the A75, 6 miles (10km) east of Stranraer. A beautiful 12 acre (5ha) garden overlooking Luce Bay and the Mull of Galloway, begun in 1979 and hewn from the hillside creating two small lakes. A rich habitat for many tender species, including alpines, scree plants and conifers. Woodland with bluebells, snowdrops, specie rhododendrons, azaleas and shrub roses. A plantsman's garden. Also rare ducks, guinea fowl and chickens, and a Primula Arena.
☎ 01581 400222

✱ Goat Fell · 20 B3

Isle of Arran. Access from Cladach on the A841 Brodick to Lochranza road. At 2866ft (873m), Goat Fell is the highest peak on Arran, dominating the skyline of the island and affording impressive views from the top. The climb includes fine rock climbing and ridge walking.
☎ 01770 302462   www.nts.org.uk

⚐ Greenknowe Tower · 26 D4

On the A6089, 0.5 mile (1km) west of Gordon on the Earlston road, Berwickshire. A handsome tower house on an L-plan, built in 1581 and still retaining its iron yett (gate).
☎ 0131 668 8800   www.historic-scotland.gov.uk

£ Gretna Gateway Outlet Village · 13 E4

Gretna. Famous name brands in designer fashion at discounted prices. Over 20 outlets covering fashion, sports, gifts and home. Scotland's only outlet store for some brands.
☎ 01461 339100   www.gretnagateway.com

✱ Gretna Hall Blacksmith's Shop · 13 E4

Gretna Green, 1 mile (1.5km) north of the border with England. Built in 1710, the Gretna Hall blacksmiths has an interesting history associated with weddings, which are still performed here.
☎ 01461 337635   www.gretna-green-weddings.com

✹ Grey Mare's Tail   `25 D5`
Adjacent to the A708, 10 miles (16km) north east of Moffat. Spectacular 200ft (61m) waterfall in landscape of geological interest and rich in wild flowers. Herd of wild goats.
☎ 01556 502575   www.nts.org.uk

🏛 Halliwell's House Museum   `18 B2`
Market Place in Selkirk, 35 miles (56km) south of Edinburgh. A local museum in a row of 19th century cottages. One of the best collections of domestic ironmongery in the country. Based on local history, the museum traces the growth of Selkirk, from the Stone Age to its role as an important textile-producing centre.
☎ 01750 20096

🏛 Harbour Cottage Gallery   `10 C3`
Castlebank, beside the harbour in Kirkcudbright. An 18th century cottage restored and opened in 1957 as a gallery exhibiting the work of artists in Galloway.
☎ 01557 330073

✹ Harestanes Countryside Visitor Centre   `18 D2`
Ancrum, off the A68, 3 miles (5km) north of Jedburgh. Housed in converted farm buildings and comprising both indoor and outdoor attractions. Changing exhibitions, walk routes and guided walks, activities and events. Wildlife garden and wooden games room. Waymarked walks include view of Waterloo Monument. This prominent landmark on the summit of Peniel Heugh (741 ft/226m high) was built after the battle of Waterloo by the Marquess of Lothian and his tenants. No access to interior.
☎ 01835 830306

❀ Harmony Garden   `26 C5`
Opposite Melrose Abbey in Melrose. This attractive walled garden was built in the early 19th century, in a fine conservation area. The garden is lovely throughout the seasons, with a rich display of spring bulbs, colourful herbaceous and mixed borders, and fruiting apricots. The garden is set against the beautiful backdrop of Melrose Abbey ruins, with the Eildon Hills in the distance.
☎ 01721 722502   www.nts.org.uk

🏛 Hawick Museum & the Scott Gallery   `18 B3`
Wilton Lodge Park, Hawick. This 200-year-old mansion house, set in over 100 acres (40ha) of award-winning parkland, houses Hawick's long-established museum and art gallery. A programme of museum and art exhibitions complements permanent displays on local industrial history, natural history, ethnography, domestic bygones and militaria.
☎ 01450 373457

Ⅴ Heads of Ayr Park   `22 A5`
Dunure Road, on the A719, 4 miles (6.5km) south of Ayr. Comprising 125 acres (50.5ha) with beautiful views over the Firth of Clyde. Animals include buffalo, wallabies, rhea and rabbits. Reptile house. Pony and buggy rides. Trampolines, toy tractors. Quad biking. Indoor and outdoor play areas.
☎ 01292 441210   www.headsofayrpark.co.uk

⚔ Hermitage Castle   `18 B5`
In Liddesdale, 5.5 miles (9km) north east of Newcastleton. A vast eerie ruin of the 14th and 15th centuries, consisting of four towers and connecting walls, outwardly almost perfect. Much restored in the 19th century. Associated with the de Soulis family, but with the Douglases after 1341.
☎ 01387 376222   www.historic-scotland.gov.uk

♚ Highland Mary's Monument   `22 C3`
At Failford, on the B743, 3 miles (4.5km) west of Mauchline. The monument commemorates the place where, it is said, Robert Burns parted from his Highland Mary, Mary Campbell. They exchanged vows, but she died the following autumn.

✹ Hirsel, The   `27 F4`
North west Coldstream. Estate of the late Prime Minister Sir Alex Douglas Home. A museum in the grounds depicts the workings of the estate. Lake, picnic area and woodland walks.
☎ 01890 882834

⚔ Hume Castle   `27 E4`
Hume, on the B6364, 6 miles (9.5km) north of Kelso. A ruined castle, destroyed by Cromwell and partially rebuilt by the Earl of Marchmont. Good views of the Tweed valley and beyond.

🍾 Isle of Arran Distillery Visitor Centre   `20 B3`
Lochranza, Isle of Arran. 14 miles (22.5km) north of Brodick. This is the newest single malt whisky distillery in Scotland, and has been in production since August 1995. Tours explain how whisky is made. The visitor centre has interactive displays and a short film illustrating whisky production on Arran over the last 150 years. Audio-visual room set in mock 18th century crofter's inn.
☎ 01770 830264   www.arranwhisky.com

🏛 Isle of Arran Heritage Museum   `20 C4`
Rosaburn, 1.5 miles (2.5km) north of Brodick Pier. An original 18th century croft farm with smiddy, cottage, coach house and stables. Extensive garden and special display area which is changed annually. Exhibits on shipping, geology, archaeology and local history.
☎ 01770 302636

♚ James Hogg Monument   `17 G2`
By Ettrick, 1 mile (1.5km) west of the B7009. A monument on the site of the birthplace of James Hogg (1770 – 1835), a friend of Scott known as the Ettrick Shepherd. His grave is in the nearby church.

🏛 James Paterson Museum   `16 B5`
Meadowcroft, North Street, Moniaive. On the A702, 9 miles (14.5km) from Thornhill. An exhibition dedicated to the life and times of the artist. Memorabilia, reference library and works connected to the Glasgow Boys and other well-known artists of the period.
☎ 01848 200583

✝ Jedburgh Abbey   `18 D3`
Jedburgh. One of the Border abbeys founded by David I circa 1138 for Augustinian canons. The remarkable complete church is mostly Romanesque and early Gothic. The west front has a fine rose window and there is a richly carved Norman doorway. The remains of the cloisters have recently been uncovered and finds from the excavations are displayed. An exhibition portrays life in the monastery.
☎ 01835 863925   www.historic-scotland.gov.uk

🏛 Jedburgh Castle Jail & Museum   `18 D3`
Castle Gate, Jedburgh. A refurbished reform prison dating from 1824 standing on the site of Jedburgh Castle which was razed to the ground in the mid 1400s. Designed by Archibald Elliot to principles advocated by John Howard, the prison reformer. New displays in the Jailer's House provide an insight into the development of the Royal Burgh of Jedburgh, while the history of the jail itself is told in the two adjoining cell blocks. One of the few remaining examples of a Howard reform prison in Britain.
☎ 01835 863254

✹ Jedburgh Woollen Mill   `18 D2`
In Jedburgh on the A68, 10 miles (16km) north of the English border. Visitors can trace their clan and tartan at the Clan Tartan Centre – fully authenticated by the Clan Chiefs of Scotland. A world of tartan from small mementoes to full Highland Dress, the choice is immense. Also golf equipment
☎ 01835 863585

Ⅴ Jedforest Deer & Farm Park   `19 D3`
Mervinslaw Estate, Camptown, on the A68, 5 miles (8km) south of Jedburgh. A Borders working farm with sheep, suckler cows, and red deer. Large display of rare breeds, including sheep, cattle, pigs, goats, poultry and waterfowl. Old and new breeds are compared. Emphasis on physical contact with animals and involvement with farm activities. Display with written and pictorial information. Daily bulletin board, coded walks, adventure land, conservation and wet areas. Birds of prey with daily displays, hawk walks and tuition. Seasonal tractor rides and commentary. Educational resources material and guide book. Ranger-led walks and activities. Crazy golf.
☎ 01835 840364

🏛 Jim Clark Room   `27 E3`
44 Newtown Street, Duns, 15 miles (24km) west of Berwick-upon-Tweed. A museum devoted to the twice world motor racing champion, Jim Clark. A collection of trophies, photographs and memorabilia including a video presentation and souvenirs.
☎ 01361 883960

🏛 John Buchan Centre   `24 D3`
Broughton, on the A703, 6 miles (9.5km) east of Biggar and 28 miles (45km) from Edinburgh. The Centre tells the story of John Buchan, 1st Lord Tweedsmuir, author of The Thirty Nine Steps and also lawyer, politician, soldier, historian, and Governor-General of Canada. Broughton village was his mother's birthplace, and a much-loved holiday home.
☎ 01899 221050

🏛 John Paul Jones Cottage Museum   `11 F3`
Arbigland, Kirkbean, off the A710, 14 miles (22.5km) south of Dumfries. Based around the cottage in which John Paul Jones, the Father of the American Navy, spent his first 13 years before becoming an apprentice in the merchant navy. The original building has been restored to the style of a gardener's cottage of the 1740s, with period furnishings, a replica of the cabin of the Bonhomme Richard, and a room containing a model of John Paul Jones and one of the cannons he is known to have used. The cottage gardens have been laid out in period style. Interpretive display and shop in former kennels.
☎ 01387 880613

♰ Johnnie Armstrong of Gilnockie Memorial   `18 B4`
Carlanrig, Teviothead. Take the A7 south from Hawick for 9 miles (14.5km) then turn right on to unclassified road. Memorial is 100 yards (91m) south on left next to churchyard. A stone marker marks the mass grave of the Laird of Gilnockie and his men, hanged without trial by King James V of Scotland in 1530.

❀ Kailzie Gardens   `25 E3`
2.5 miles (4km) east of Peebles on the B7062. Seventeen acres (6.8ha) of gardens in the beautiful Tweed valley. The 1812 walled garden is semi-formal, with fine herbaceous borders and shrub roses. Formal rose garden and greenhouses. Woodland and burnside walks. Rhododendrons in season. Duck pond and stocked trout pond (rod hire available). Art gallery. Interpretive area in Old Bothy with video of the Garden Year.
☎ 01721 720007

♚ Keir Hardie Statue   `22 D4`
Cumnock town centre. Bust outside the Town Hall to commemorate James Keir Hardie (1856 – 1915), an early socialist leader, and founder of the Independent Labour Party in 1893.

Kelburn Castle & Country Centre `22 A1`
On the A78, about 2 miles (3km) south of Largs. Historic home of the Earls of Glasgow, and still lived in today. The original Norman keep is now enclosed in a castle built in 1581. A new mansion (Kelburn House) was added to this in 1700, followed later by a Victorian wing. The buildings are surrounded by spectacular natural scenery including waterfalls. Breathtaking views over the Firth of Clyde. Activities include glen walks, riding, assault and adventure courses, and Scotland's most unusual attraction – the Secret Forest, with fantasy follies and hidden secrets. Exhibitions and ranger centre. Special events most weekends.
☎ 01475 568685

Kelso Abbey `27 E5`
In Bridge Street, Kelso. The west end of the great abbey church of the Tironensians, who were brought to Kelso in 1128 by David I. One of the great Border abbeys – even in its fragmentary state, this is superb architecture.
☎ 0131 668 8800　www.historic-scotland.gov.uk

Kelso Pottery `27 E5`
In the centre of Kelso in the large car park behind the abbey. A workshop creating a range of simple, practical stoneware pottery, augmented by pit-fired ware.
☎ 01573 224027

Kid'z Play `22 B4`
The Esplanade, Prestwick. An indoor adventure play area for children up to 12 years. Soft play adventure area for under 5s.
☎ 01292 475215　www.kidz-play.co.uk

Kilpatrick Dun `20 B4`
1 mile (2km) south of Blackwaterfoot, Isle of Arran. The ruins of a circular drystone homestead of unknown date, with a more recent enclosure wall.
☎ 0131 668 8800　www.historic-scotland.gov.uk

Kilwinning Abbey `22 B2`
The ruins of a Tironensian-Benedictine abbey. Most of the surviving fragments, which consist of parts of the church and chapter house, appear to date from the 13th century.
☎ 0131 668 8800　www.historic-scotland.gov.uk

King's Cave `20 A4`
2 miles (3.2km) north of Blackwaterfoot, Arran. Reputedly the cave where Robert the Bruce was inspired by the determination of a spider in 1306.

Kinsman Blake Ceramics `26 D5`
Barn House, Smailholm. On the A68, 6 miles (9.5km) east of St Boswells. A small family pottery where visitors are welcome in the workshop to view demonstrations. Specialists in decorative techniques. Well-stocked showroom.
☎ 01573 460666

Kirk Yetholm `19 F2`
Off the B6352, 8 miles (12.5km) south east of Kelso. Attractive village, once famous as the home of the Scottish gypsies, now the northern end of the Pennine Way.

Kirkmadrine Early Christian Stones `8 B4`
In the Rhinns of Galloway, 2 miles (3km) south west of Sandhead. Three of the earliest Christian memorial stones in Britain, dating from the 5th or early 6th century, displayed in the porch of a former chapel.
☎ 0131 668 8800　www.historic-scotland.gov.uk

Kirroughtree Visitor Centre `9 F2`
Galloway Forest Park, Stronord, Newton Stewart. The visitor centre runs various activities during the year. Also waymarked cycle trails, walks and a forest drive.
☎ 01671 402165　www.forestry.gov.uk

Lady Gifford Statue `25 D1`
Village clock, in West Linton, 17 miles (27km) south south-west of Edinburgh. Statue on the front of the village clock at West Linton, carved in 1666 by the Laird Gifford, a Covenanter and skilled stonemason. The clock is on the site of a well, disused since Victorian times. Laird Gifford also executed panels (1660 and 1678) on a house opposite, depicting Lady Gifford and the entire family genealogy.

Ladykirk `27 F4`
4 miles (6.5km) east of Swindon and 0.5 miles (0.5km) from Norham off the B6470. Ladykirk was built in 1500 by James IV, in memory of Our Lady who had saved him from drowning. As the border was only 300 yards away and in constant dispute, he ordered it built to withstand fire and flood – hence the all-stone construction of the kirk with no wooden rafters and, until this century, stone pews. The Wardens of East March met regularly in the parish to resolve disputes between Scotland and England. In 1560, a copy of the last peace treaty between them was signed in Ladykirk, marking the end of sporadic warfare.

Laggangairn Standing Stones `8 D1`
At Killgallioch, New Luce on the Southern Upland Way. Two stones carved with early Christian crosses.
☎ 0131 668 8800　www.historic-scotland.gov.uk

Largs Museum `22 A1`
Kirkgate House, Manse Court, Largs. The museum holds a small collection of local bygones and a library of local history books and photographs, put together by the local history society. Holds the key to the Skelmorlie Aisle, adjacent, which belongs to Historic Scotland.
☎ 01475 687081

Largs Old Kirk `22 A1`
In Bellman's Close, off High Street in Largs. A splendid mausoleum with a painted ceiling illustrating the seasons. Added to the parish church in 1636 by Sir Robert Montgomerie of Skelmorlie. Contains an elaborate carved stone tomb in Renaissance style.
☎ 01475 672450　www.historic-scotland.gov.uk

Leyden Obelisk & Tablet `18 C3`
Denholm, on the A698 north east of Hawick. The village was the birthplace of John Leyden (1776–1811), poet, orientalist and friend of Sir Walter Scott. An obelisk was set up in 1861 and a tablet on a thatched cottage records his birth there. Another famous son of Denholm was Sir James Murray, editor of the Oxford English Dictionary, whose birth is commemorated on a tablet on a house in Main Street, Denholm.

Liddesdale Heritage Centre `13 F2`
Townfoot Kirk, South Hermitage Street, Newcastleton. Liddesdale Heritage Association is a voluntary community group who run Liddesdale Heritage Centre and Museum in the former Congregational Church (built in 1804) within the planned village of Newcastleton (built 1793). Displays on the history of Liddesdale and its people, and a unique commemorative bicentenary tapestry. Many books and articles on the Borders region. Facilities available for genealogical research. Waverley Line railway memorabilia. Exhibitions are staged during July and August.
☎ 01387 375259　www.liddesdaleheritagecentre.scotshome.com

Lincluden Collegiate Church `11 F1`
In Abbey Lane, on western outskirts of Dumfries, 1 mile (2km) from the A76. The rich remains of a collegiate church founded in 1389 by Archibald the Grim, 3rd Earl of Douglas. The splendid chancel was probably added by his son, Archibald, the 4th Earl, and houses the exquisite monumental tomb of his wife, Princess Margaret, daughter of King Robert III.
☎ 0131 668 8800　www.historic-scotland.gov.uk

Lindean Mill Glass `26 B5`
Lindean Mill, Galashiels, on the A7, 1 mile (2km) north of Selkirk. Scotland's premier glass studio where visitors can watch glassware being made by hand. Shop.
☎ 01750 20173　www.lindeanmillglass.co.uk

Loch Doon Castle `15 F4`
Off the A713, 10 miles (16km) south of Dalmellington. An early 14th century castle with an eleven-sided curtain wall of fine masonry. Once known as Castle Balliol. Originally it stood on an island in Loch Doon but it was moved to its present site in the 1930s before its original site was flooded during the construction of a hydro-electric scheme.
☎ 0131 668 8800　www.historic-scotland.gov.uk

Lochcarron Cashmere Wool Centre `26 C5`
Waverley Mill, Huddersfield Street, Galashiels. A woollen mill manufacturing cashmere from spun yarn to finished garment. Produces a huge range of pure wool tartans. Tour of mill and museum illustrating the history of Galashiels and its trade.
☎ 01896 751100　www.lochcarron.com

Lochmaben Castle `12 B2`
On the south shore of Castle Loch, by Lochmaben. Off the B7020, 9 miles (14.5km) east north-east of Dumfries. The ruins of a royal castle, originally built by the English in the 14th century but extensively rebuilt during the reign of King James VI. Surrounded by extensive remains of earthworks, including a rectangular peel (timber pallisaded enclosure).
☎ 0131 668 8800　www.historic-scotland.gov.uk

Lochranza Castle `20 B2`
At Lochranza on the north coast of the Isle of Arran. A fine tower house, probably a 16th century reconstruction of an earlier building. Reputed to be where King Robert the Bruce landed on his return in 1307.
☎ 0131 668 8800　www.historic-scotland.gov.uk

Logan Botanic Garden `8 B4`
Port Logan, 14 miles (22.5km) south of Stranraer, off the B7065. Experience the southern hemisphere in Scotland's most exotic garden. Logan's exceptionally mild climate allows a colourful array of tender plants to thrive. Tree ferns, cabbage palms, unusual shrubs, climbers and tender perennials are found within the Walled, Water, Terrace and Woodland Gardens. The Discovery Centre provides activities and information for all ages and the Soundalive self-guided tours enable visitors to make the most of the garden. Logan Botanic Garden is one of the National Botanic Gardens of Scotland.
☎ 01776 860231

Logan Fish Pond Marine Life Centre `8 B4`
Port Logan, off the B7056, 14 miles (22.5km) south of Stranraer. A fully restored Victorian fish larder in a unique setting – a tidal pool created by a blowhole which formed during the last Ice Age. The rock fissure through which the tide flows is now the setting for the unusual cave marine aquarium, containing a large variety of species from the Irish Sea.
☎ 01776 860300

Loudoun Castle Theme Park `22 D3`
Galston, on the A719 between the A77 and the A71. Set in over 500 acres (202ha) of parkland and woods, in the grounds of the imposing ruins of Loudoun Castle. Thrilling rides, including Galaxy Rollercoaster, road trains, woodland walks, games, stalls, go-carts and pony rides.
☎ 01563 822296

Loudoun Hall `22 B4`
Ayr town centre. Loudoun Hall is one of Ayr's oldest and finest buildings, dating back to the late 15th century. Once the site of a brew house and bake house, the hall has been redeveloped. The forecourt is a public space with integrated art works.
☎ 01292 612000

Mabie Farm Park `11 F1`
Burnside Farm, Mabie. Lots of animals including donkeys, horses and ponies, chicks and guinea pigs. Also adventure playground, giant flume slide, zip-wire, go-carts, quad bikes and bouncy castles.
☎ 01387 259666　www.mabiefarm.co.uk

✚ **Machrie Moor Stone Circles** `20 B4`
3 miles (5km) north of Blackwaterfoot on the west coast of the Isle of Arran. The remains of five Bronze Age stone circles. One of the most important sites of its kind in Britain.
☎ 0131 668 8800 www.historic-scotland.gov.uk

🏰 **MacLellan's Castle** `10 C3`
Off the A711 High Street in Kirkcudbright. A handsome castellated mansion overlooking the harbour, dating from 1577, complete except for the roof. Elaborately planned with fine detail. A ruin since 1752.
☎ 01557 331856 www.historic-scotland.gov.uk

🏛 **Manderston** `27 F3`
Off the A6105, 2 miles (3km) east of Duns. An Edwardian stately home set in 56 acres (22.6ha) and surrounded by formal gardens, stables, dairy, lake and woodland garden. Features include the sumptuous staterooms, the only silver staircase in the world, a racing room and the first privately-owned biscuit tin museum. Domestic quarters in period style.
☎ 01361 883450 www.manderston.co.uk

★ **Marrbury Smokehouse** `9 E1`
On the A714, 9 miles north west of Newton Stewart, near Glentrool. Traditional Scottish smokehouse run by the Marr family, net and cobble salmon fishermen on the local River Cree since 1920. Visitors can enjoy a guided tour of the smoking process. A visitor centre sells smoked food and offers recipes and tips.
☎ 01671 840241

🏛 **Mary, Queen of Scots' House** `19 D2`
Queen Street, Jedburgh. A 16th century castle which is now a visitor centre devoted to the memory of Mary, Queen of Scots, who stayed here in 1566 while she was ill.
☎ 01835 863331

✝ **Maybole Collegiate Church** `15 E3`
South of the A77 in Maybole. The roofless ruin of a 15th century church built for a small college established in 1373 by John Kennedy of Dunure.
☎ 0131 668 8800 www.historic-scotland.gov.uk

🏛 **McKechnie Institute** `14 C4`
Girvan. The red standstone building with its octagonal tower has been a local landmark since 1888 – reopening as a local museum in 1982, with changing exhibitions on local history and fine art.
☎ 01465 713643

🏛 **Mellerstain House** `26 D5`
Gordon, off the A6089, 7 miles (11km) north west of Kelso. A superb Georgian mansion designed by William and Robert Adam. Features exquisite plaster ceilings, beautiful interior decoration, fine period furniture, marvellous art collection. Award-winning terraced garden and grounds.
☎ 01573 410225

✝ **Melrose Abbey** `26 C5`
Main Square, Melrose, off the A7 or A68. The ruins of the Cistercian abbey founded by King David I circa 1136. It was largely destroyed by an English army in 1385 but rebuilt in the early 15th century. It is now probably the most famous ruin in Scotland because of the elegant and elaborate stonework which remains. The Commendator's House contains a large collection of objets trouvès.
☎ 01896 822562 www.historic-scotland.gov.uk

✝ **Merkland Cross** `12 C3`
At Merkland Smithy, near Ecclefechan. A fine carved wayside cross, dating from the 15th century.
☎ 0131 668 8800 www.historic-scotland.gov.uk

❖ **Mertoun Gardens** `26 C5`
On the B6404, 2 miles (3km) east of Newtown St Boswells. Twenty-six acres (10.5ha) of beautiful grounds with delightful walks and river views. Fine trees, herbaceous borders and flowering shrubs. Walled garden and well-preserved circular dovecot. Dogs not permitted.
☎ 01835 823236

★ **Mill on the Fleet** `9 G3`
High Street, Gatehouse of Fleet, Castle Douglas. An exhibition housed in a restored 18th century cotton mill, telling the history of the town. Temporary and permanent exhibits.
☎ 01557 814099

✝ **Milnholm Cross** `13 F2`
One mile (1.5km) south of Newcastleton. Erected circa 1320, and owned by the Clan Armstrong Trust, Milnholm Cross is a memorial to Alexander Armstrong who was murdered in Hermitage Castle some 4 miles (6.5km) away. It faces the ruin of Mangerton Castle, seat of the Armstrong chiefs for 300 years.

🏛 **Moffat Museum** `17 E3`
The Old Bakehouse, The Neuk, Church Gate, Moffat. Located in an old bakehouse with a Scotch oven. Tells the story of Moffat and its people, border raids, Covenanters, education, sports and pastimes, famous people. Includes a short video presentation.
☎ 01683 220868

★ **Moffat Woollen Mill** `17 E3`
Ladyknowe, Moffat. Visit the working weaving exhibition. The mill offers a good selection of cashmere, Aran, lambswool and traditional tartans and tweeds. Trace Scottish clan history and heraldry at the Clan History Centre and receive a certificate illustrating your clan ancestry.
☎ 01683 220134

🐾 **Monreith Animal World & Museum** `9 E4`
Low Knowck Farm, on the A747, 0.5 mile (1km) from Monreith. Collection of animals and birds, including otters, pigmy goats, owls, waterfowl and small mammals, in natural spacious surroundings. Reptile collection. Small museum on Gavin Maxwell.
☎ 01988 700217

❖ **Monteviot House Gardens** `18 D2`
Monteviot, off the B6400, 4 miles (6.5km) north of Jedburgh (off the A68). Gardens on the bank of the River Teviot with several feature areas – river garden, rose terraces and a water garden.
☎ 01835 830380

★ **Moonstone Miniatures** `11 D1`
4 Victoria Street, Kirkpatrick Durham. 14 miles (22.5km) west of Dumfries, 4 miles (6.5km) east of Castle Douglas off the A75 at Springholm. Cabinets of miniature marvels at one-twelfth scale, including stately homes, shops and humble cottages.
☎ 01556 650313

🏰 **Morton Castle** `16 C4`
On the A702, 17 miles (27km) north north-west of Dumfries. Beside Morton Loch. The well-preserved ruin of a fine late 13th century hall house, a stronghold of the Douglases.
☎ 0131 668 8800 www.historic-scotland.gov.uk

✚ **Moss Farm Road Stone Circle** `20 B4`
3 miles (5km) north of Blackwaterfoot, Isle of Arran. The remains of a Bronze Age cairn surrounded by a stone circle.
☎ 0131 668 8800 www.historic-scotland.gov.uk

🐾 **Mossburn Animal Centre** `11 G1`
Hightae, Lockerbie. Off the B7020 from Lochmaben. Mossburn is an animal welfare centre where you can see and handle rescued animals, from pigs and horses to Thai water dragons, who now live in a healthy, happy and secure environment.
☎ 01387 811288

✚ **Motte of Urr** `11 E2`
Off the B794, 5 miles (7.5km) north east of Castle Douglas. The most extensive motte and bailey castle in Scotland, dating from the 12th century AD, although the bailey may have been an earlier earthwork of hillfort type.

🏛 **Museum of Lead Mining** `16 C2`
Wanlockhead, Biggar, on the B797 between Abington (A74) and Mennock (A76). A museum tracing 300 years of lead mining in Scotland's highest village set in the dramatic Lowther Hills. Features heritage trail, beam engine, tours of a lead mine, period cottages, miners' library, displays of minerals. Gold panning centre (you can take some gold home).
☎ 01659 74387

🏛 **Museum of the Cumbraes** `21 D2`
Garrison Stables, Millport, Isle of Cumbrae. The museum tells the story of the islands Great and Wee Cumbrae. Displays show how the town of Millport developed and celebrate Millport's heyday as a holiday resort.
☎ 01475 531191 www.northayrshiremuseums.org.uk

🏰 **Neidpath Castle** `25 E3`
One mile (2km) west of Peebles on the A72. A rare example of a 14th century castle converted into a tower house in the 17th century. Displayed in the great hall is an exhibit of beautiful batiks depicting the life of Mary, Queen of Scots. The Laigh Hall contains informative displays. Good views from the parapet walks. Neidpath Castle is often used as a film location. Resident ghost, the Maid of Neidpath.
☎ 01721 720333

★ **Neverland Adventure Play Centre** `11 F1`
Park Lane, Dumfries. Adventure play centre for children aged up to ten. Themed on J.M. Barrie's story of Peter Pan, the boy who would never grow up. There are rope bridges, slides, a ball pool, Indian encampment and Captain Hook's pirate ship. Special area for under fours. Located beside the River Nith, with a pleasant seating area for adults overlooking the river. Parent/guardian supervision is required.
☎ 01387 249100

★ **New Abbey Corn Mill** `11 F2`
On the A710, in New Abbey, 8 miles (13km) south of Dumfries. A carefully renovated water-driven oatmeal mill in working order and demonstrated regularly to visitors in the summer months.
☎ 01387 850620 www.historic-scotland.gov.uk

🏛 **Newton Stewart Museum** `9 F2`
York Road, Newton Stewart. Contains a wealth of historical treasures and exciting and interesting displays of the natural and social history of Galloway.
☎ 01671 402472

🏛 **North Ayrshire Museum** `22 A2`
Manse Street, Saltcoats. Local history museum housed in a mid 18th century parish church. Displays feature cottage life, Ayrshire whitework, fine art, maritime history, archaeology and natural history. Good reference and photographic collection. Children's activity and discovery area.
☎ 01294 464174 www.northayrshiremuseums.org.uk

🏛 **North Glen Gallery & Workshop** `11 E3`
North Glen, Palnackie, off the A711 between Dalbeattie and Auchencairn. Gallery, workshop and home base of international artist Ed Iglehart who works with many collaborators to produce individual works of glass. Glass-blowing demonstrations. Chandeliers, experimental structures, wine goblets and many other objects. Starting point for many walks.
☎ 01556 600200

🏛 **Old Bridge House Museum** `11 F1`
In Dumfries town centre on the west bank of the River Nith at Devorgilla's Bridge. Built in 1660, the house is furnished in period style to illustrate life in Dumfries over the centuries. Rooms include kitchens of 1850 and 1900, a Victorian nursery and a dental surgery dating from 1900. Devorgilla's Bridge was originally built circa 1280 by Lady Devorgilla Balliol, who endowed Balliol College, Oxford.
☎ 01387 256904

🏛 **Old Gala House** `26 B5`
Scott Crescent, 0.25 mile (0.5km) from Galashiels town centre. Dating from 1583 and set in its own grounds, the former home of the Lairds of Gala is now an interpretive centre. Displays tell the story of the house, its inhabitants and the early growth of Galashiels. Features painted ceilings (1635), a painted wall (1988) and the Thomas Clapperton Room. The Christopher Boyd Gallery hosts an exciting programme of visual art exhibitions.
☎ 01896 752611

🏰 **Old Place of Mochrum** `9 E3`
Off the B7005, 11 miles (17.5km) west of Wigtown. Known also as Drumwalt Castle, this is a mainly 15th and 16th century construction with two picturesque towers.

🏯 **Orchardton Tower** `11 E3`
Off the A711, 6 miles (9.5km) south east of Castle Douglas. A charming and unique circular 15th century tower house. Built by John Cairns.
☎ 0131 668 8800   www.historic-scotland.gov.uk

🏰 **Paxton House** `27 G3`
Paxton, on the B6461, 5 miles (8km) west of Berwick-upon-Tweed. Winner of several tourism awards and one of the finest 18th century Palladian houses in Britain. Designed by John and James Adam and built in 1758 by Patrick Home for his intended bride, Sophie de Brandt, an aristocrat from the court of King Frederick the Great of Prussia. Interiors by Robert Adam. The largest collection of Chippendale furniture in Scotland, and fine Regency furniture by Trotter of Edinburgh. The largest art gallery in any Scottish house or castle, an outstation of the National Galleries of Scotland. Over 80 acres (32ha) of grounds and gardens, including a mile of the River Tweed.
☎ 01289 386291   www.paxtonhouse.com

🏛 **Peebles Gallery & Master in Miniatures** `25 E3`
6 Newby Court, in a craft centre off High Street in Peebles. A gallery with an artist in residence (working on the premises), specialising in miniature art work.
☎ 01721 724747

✶ **Pitlochry Knitwear** `17 E3`
4 Bath Place, Moffat. A shop specialising in ready-made tartan garments, a large selection of Aran and other quality knitwear lines. Souvenirs and gifts. Clan research and certificates.
☎ 01683 220354

✎ **Polmaddy Settlement** `16 A5`
6 miles north of New Galloway on the A713. The last settlement in this area before the clearances of the 19th century. A short waymarked trail has interpretation boards explaining the layout of the settlement. There are some remaining features such as foundations.

❀ **Priorwood Garden & Dried Flower Shop** `26 C5`
Off the A6091 in Melrose. A unique garden overlooked by the ruins of Melrose Abbey, specialising in plants suitable for drying. Visitors can watch and learn about the drying process and buy or order dried flower arrangements in the shop. The adjacent orchard includes many varieties of historic apple trees.
☎ 01896 822493   www.nts.org.uk

🏰 **Rammerscales House** `11 G1`
Hightae, on the B7020, 2.5 miles (4km) from Lochmaben. An 18th century Georgian manor house with magnificent views over Annandale. In Adam style and mostly unaltered. Contains rare contemporary art and a library with 600 volumes. Extensive and attractive grounds with walled garden.
☎ 01387 810229

✶ **Rennie's Bridge** `27 E5`
Situated in Kelso, this is a fine five-arched bridge built over the River Tweed in 1803 by Rennie to replace one destroyed by the floods of 1797. On the bridge are two lamp posts from the demolished Old Waterloo Bridge in London, which Rennie built in 1811. There is also a fine view to Floors Castle.

🏯 **Rispain Camp** `9 F5`
Behind Rispain Farm, 1 mile (2km) west of Whithorn on the A746. A rectangular settlement defended by a bank and ditch. 1st or 2nd century AD.
☎ 0131 668 8800   www.historic-scotland.gov.uk

🏛 **Robert Burns Centre** `11 F1`
Mill Road, Dumfries. Situated on the west bank of the River Nith. Award-winning centre illustrates the connection between Robert Burns, Scotland's national poet, and the town of Dumfries. Situated in the town's 18th century watermill, the centre tells of Burns' last years spent in the busy streets and lively atmosphere of Dumfries in the 1790s. Film theatre shows feature films in the evening.
☎ 01387 264808

🏛 **Robert Clapperton's Daylight Photographic Studio** `18 B2`
The Studio, 28 Scotts Place. One of the oldest surviving daylight photographic studios in the UK. The studio is set up as a working museum and photographic archive, in the building originally used by Robert Clapperton in 1867. Photographic equipment, cameras and prints. Demonstrations of black and white print processing in the original dark room can be arranged. Archive photographs and postcards for sale.
☎ 01750 20523

✶ **Robert Smail's Printing Works** `26 A5`
7-9 High Street, Innerleithen, 30 miles (48km) south of Edinburgh. Restored printing works using machinery and methods of the early 20th century. Visitors can watch the printer at work and try setting type by hand. Victorian office with many historic items. Reconstructed waterwheel.
☎ 01896 830206   www.nts.org.uk

🏯 **Robert the Bruce's Cave** `13 D3`
Kirkpatrick Fleming, 3 miles (5km) north of Gretna Green. Situated in an 80 acre (33ha) estate high above the River Kirtle, the cave is reputed to be where Robert the Bruce hid for three months in 1313.
☎ 01461 800285

✶ **Rockcliffe** `11 E3`
7 miles (11km) south of Dalbeattie, off the A710. The NTS owns several sites in and around the picturesque village of Rockcliffe on the Solway Firth. These include the Mote of Mark which is an ancient hill fort, Rough Island which is a bird sanctuary with access on foot at low tide, and Muckle Lands and Jubilee Path which is a beautiful stretch of coastline between Rockcliffe and Kippford.
☎ 01556 502575   www.nts.org.uk

🏯 **Roxburgh Castle** `27 E5`
Off the A699, 1 mile (1.5km) south west of Kelso. The earthworks are all that remain of the once mighty castle, destroyed in the 15th century, and the walled Royal Burgh which gave its name to the county. The present village of Roxburgh dates from a later period.

🏆 **Royal Troon** `22 B4`
Craigend Road, Troon. Links course created in 1878 and host of several dramatic Open Championships since 1923.
☎ 01292 311555

🏛 **Rozelle House Galleries** `22 B5`
Rozelle Park, Monument Road, 2.5 miles (4km) from Ayr town centre. Built in 1760 by Robert Hamilton, in the style of Robert Adam. Rebuilt in 1830 by David Bryce. Now a gallery for art and museum exhibitions.
☎ 01292 445447

🏯 **Ruthwell Cross** `12 C4`
In Ruthwell Church on the B724, 8.5 miles (13.5km) south east of Dumfries. An Anglian Cross, sculptured in high relief and dating from the end of the 7th century. Considered to be one of the major monuments of Dark Age Europe. Carved with Runic characters.
☎ 0131 668 8800   www.historic-scotland.gov.uk

🐾 **St Abb's Head National Nature Reserve** `27 G3`
Off the A1107, 2 miles (3km) north of Coldingham. The most important location for cliff-nesting sea birds in south east Scotland. Remote camera link to the centre provides glimpses of nesting birds. Spectacular walks around the headland, above 300 ft (91m) cliffs. Exhibition on wildlife.
☎ 018907 71443   www.nts.org.uk

✶ **St Mary's Loch** `17 G1`
Off the A708, 14 miles (22.5km) east south-east of Selkirk. Beautifully set among smooth green hills, this 3 mile (4.5km) long loch is used for sailing and fishing. On the neck of land separating it from Loch of the Lowes, at the south end, stands Tibbie Shiel's Inn. The inn was kept by Tibbie Shiel (Elizabeth Richardson, 1783 – 1878) from 1823, and was a meeting place for many 19th-century writers. Beside the road towards the north end of the loch is a seated statue of James Hogg, the Ettrick Shepherd, author of Confessions of a Justified Sinner and a friend of Scott, who farmed in this district. On the route of the Southern Upland Way.

🏯 **St Ninian's Cave** `9 F5`
At Physgill, on the shore 4 miles (6.5km) south west of Whithorn. A cave traditionally associated with the saint. Early crosses found here are housed at Whithorn Museum. The crosses carved on the walls of the cave are now weathered.
☎ 0131 668 8800   www.historic-scotland.gov.uk

✝ **St Ninian's Chapel** `9 F5`
At Isle of Whithorn, 3 miles (5km) south east of Whithorn. The restored ruins of a 13th century chapel, probably used by pilgrims on their way to Whithorn.
☎ 0131 668 8800   www.historic-scotland.gov.uk

✶ **St Ronan's Wells Interpretive Centre** `26 A5`
Wells Brae, Innerleithen, on the A72, 6 miles (9.5km) from Peebles. A site associated with a novel by Sir Walter Scott. Memorabilia of Scott, information and photographs of local festival. The well water can be tasted.
☎ 01721 724820

✶ **Samye Ling Tibetan Centre** `13 D1`
Eskdalemuir, on the B709, 16 miles (25.5km) from Lockerbie. A magnificent Tibetan temple in traditional Buddhist style, in beautiful surroundings. Also guest house for visitors who attend courses on meditation, therapy, and arts and crafts. Gardens and riverside walk.
☎ 01387 373232   www.samyeling.org

🏛 **Sanquhar Tolbooth Museum** `16 B3`
High Street, Sanquhar. Located in a fine 18th century tolbooth. Tells the story of Upper Nithsdale. Features world famous Sanquhar knitting, mines and miners of Sanquhar and Kirkconnel, history and customs of the Royal Burgh of Sanquhar, three centuries of local literature, life in Sanquhar jail, the earliest inhabitants, and the people of Upper Nithsdale, at home and at work.
☎ 01659 50186

🏛 **Savings Banks Museum** `12 C4`

Ruthwell, off the B724, 10 miles (16km) east of Dumfries. Housed in the original 1800 village meeting place, the museum traces the savings bank movement from its founding here in 1810 by the Rev Henry Duncan, to its growth and spread worldwide. Also displays the work of the Ruthwell Friendly Society from 1795, an early insurance scheme providing sick pay, widows' pensions, funeral grants and the chance to buy staple foods at cost price. Features restoration of the 8th century runic Ruthwell Cross.
☎ 01387 870640

✝ **Scots Dyke** `13 E3`

Off the A7, 7 miles (11km) south of Langholm. The remains of a wall made of clods of earth and stones, which marked part of the border between England and Scotland.

✴ **Scott's View** `26 C5`

B6356, 4 miles east of Melrose. A view over the Tweed to the Eildon Hills, beloved by Scott. Here the horses taking his remains to Dryburgh for burial stopped, as they had so often before for Sir Walter to enjoy this panorama.

🏛 **Scottish Industrial Railway Centre** `15 F3`

Minnivey, Burnton, Dalmellington. 12 miles (19km) south east of Ayr, off the A713. The centre is on the site of the former Minnivey Colliery. Steam locomotives and traditional locomotive shed. Brake van trips. Museum with extensive collection of railway relics and documents. Narrow gauge demonstration line.
☎ 01292 531144   www.dunaskin.org.uk

🏛 **Scottish Maritime Museum** `22 B3`

In Irvine, at Harbourside. The museum reflects all aspects of Scottish maritime history. Vessels can be seen afloat in the harbour and under cover. Visitors can experience life in a 1910 shipyard worker's flat and visit the Linthouse Engine Shop, originally built in 1872, under reconstruction.
☎ 01294 278283

✴ **Selkirk Glass Visitor Centre** `26 B5`

Dunsdale Haugh, on the A7 to the north of Selkirk. Visitors can view the complete glassmaking process and can purchase quality seconds and other gifts in the shop.
☎ 01750 20954

🏛 **Shambellie House Museum of Costume** `11 F2`

New Abbey, on the A710, 7 miles (11km) south of Dumfries. A museum housed in a mid-Victorian country house designed by David Bryce. Costume displays in period room settings from the National Museums Collection. An outstation of the National Museums of Scotland.
☎ 01387 850375

🏛 **Sir Walter Scott's Courtroom** `18 B2`

Market Place in Selkirk, 25 miles (40km) south of Edinburgh. The bench and chair from which Sir Walter Scott, as Sheriff of Selkirk, administered justice for 30 years are displayed, as are portraits of Scott, James Hogg, Mungo Park. Watercolours by Tom Scott RSA. Audio-visual display.
☎ 01750 20096

✴ **Smailholm Tower** `26 D5`

Off the B6404, 6 miles (9.5km) north west of Kelso. A small rectangular 16th century Border peel tower sited on a rocky outcrop within a stone barmkin wall. Well-preserved and containing an exhibition of costume figures and tapestries relating to Sir Walter Scott's Minstrelsy of the Scottish Borders. Scott spent some of his childhood at nearby Sandyknowe Farm.
☎ 01573 460365   www.historic-scotland.gov.uk

🏛 **Sophies Puppenstube & Dolls House Museum** `9 F2`

29 Queen Street, Newton Stewart. A high quality collection of over 50 inhabited house displays which show life through the ages, at home and abroad, in one-twelfth scale. The displays are complemented by over 200 dolls, most of which have been specially commissioned for the individual settings.
☎ 01671 403344

🏰 **Sorn Castle** `22 D4`

Sorn, by Mauchline, Ayrshire. A 14th century castle built on a cliff above the River Ayr. The castle was substantially added to in the 17th and 19th centuries. The interior is mainly Victorian, with many fine paintings by Scottish artists. The grounds are laid out along the riverside with handsome trees and shrubs.
☎ 01290 551555

✴ **Souter Johnnie's Cottage** `14 D3`

On the A77 Main Road in Kirkoswald, 4 miles (6.5km) south west of Maybole. Thatched cottage, home of the souter (cobbler) who inspired the character Souter Johnnie in Robert Burns' poem Tam O'Shanter. Burns memorabilia and reconstructed workshop. Restored alehouse with life-size stone figures of Burns' characters.
☎ 01655 760603   www.nts.org.uk

✵ **South Bank Farm Park** `20 C5`

East Bennan, Isle of Arran, 14 miles (22.5km) south of Brodick. A 60 acre (24ha) working farm exhibiting various rare and minority breeds of farm animals – poultry, Highland cattle, red deer. Farm trail and superb views. Sheepdog demonstrations.
☎ 01770 820221

🏛 **Stewartry Museum** `10 C3`

St Mary Street, Kirkcudbright. A wide range of exhibits reflecting the social and natural history of the Stewartry of Kirkcudbright. Features illustrations, pottery and jewellery by Jessie M. King and the work of her husband, E. A. Taylor, Phyllis Bone and other Kirkcudbright artists. Special temporary exhibitions, family and local history information services.
☎ 01557 331643

🏛 **Stranraer Museum** `8 B2`

Old Town Hall, George Street, Stranraer. Permanent display on local history, archaeology, farming and polar exploration. Temporary exhibition programme throughout the year with supporting educational and family activities. Enquiry and identification service available.
☎ 01776 705088

🍾 **Sulwath Brewery** `11 D2`

Castle Douglas. Located in an old steam bakery, this is a family-run brewery producing handcrafted beer – two ales, a lager and a stout. Visitors can see the production process and sample the beer.
☎ 01556 504525   www.sulwathbrewers.co.uk

✝ **Sweetheart Abbey** `11 F2`

New Abbey, 7 miles (11km) south of Dumfries. Splendid ruin of a late 13th century and early 14th century Cistercian abbey founded by Devorgilla, Lady of Galloway, in memory of her husband John Balliol. Apart from the abbey, the principal feature is the well-preserved precinct wall, enclosing 30 acres (12ha).
☎ 01387 850397   www.historic-scotland.gov.uk

✴ **Tam O' Shanter Experience** `22 B5`

Murdochs Lane, Alloway, 2 miles (3km) south of Ayr. Walk your way through history, and experience the Burns mystery and magic with two audio-visual presentations. The first tells the story of Burns and leads you on to the second presentation which is the poem Tam O'Shanter in the words of Burns, using the latest technology. See also Burns National Heritage Park.
☎ 01292 443700

❀ **Teviot Water Gardens** `19 E2`

Kirkbank House, midway between Kelso and Jedburgh on A698. The water gardens are on four levels, set amidst scenic Borders countryside. The lowest garden flows down to the River Teviot.
☎ 01835 850734

🏠 **Thirlestane Castle** `26 C4`

Off the A68 at Lauder. One of the seven great houses of Scotland, Thirlestane Castle was rebuilt in the 16th century as the home of the Maitland family. It became the seat of the Earls of Lauderdale and was enlarged in the 17th century by the Duke of Lauderdale, who commissioned the magnificent plasterwork ceilings in the state rooms. Still a family home, Thirlestane houses a large collection of early toys in the nursery wing, and the Border Country Life Exhibition. The old servants' hall serves as the café, and there are picnic tables alongside the adventure playground and woodland walk.
☎ 01578 722430   www.thirlestanecastle.co.uk

🏠 **Thomas Carlyle's Birthplace** `12 C3`

The Arched House, on the A74 in Ecclefechan, 5.5 miles (9km) south east of Lockerbie. Birthplace of writer Thomas Carlyle (born 1795). Furnished to reflect domestic life in his time, with an important collection of family portraits and belongings.
☎ 01576 300666   www.nts.org.uk

🏰 **Threave Castle** `10 D2`

North of the A75, 3 miles (5km) west of Castle Douglas. A massive tower built in the late 14th century by Archibald the Grim, Lord of Galloway. Round its base is an artillery fortification built before 1455, when the castle was besieged by James II. The castle is on an island, approached by boat.
☎ 07711 223101   www.historic-scotland.gov.uk

❀ **Threave Garden & Estate** `11 D2`

Off A75, 1 mile (2km) west of Castle Douglas. Threave Garden has a spectacular springtime display of daffodils, colourful herbaceous beds in summer, and striking trees and heathers in autumn. The visitor centre has an exhibition and delightful terraced restaurant. Threave Estate is a wildfowl refuge, with bird hides and waymarked trails.
☎ 01556 502575   www.nts.org.uk

🏛 **Tolbooth Art Centre** `10 C3`

High Street, Kirkcudbright. An interpretive centre located in the 17th century tolbooth. Exhibition about the town's history as an artists' colony, including paintings by important Kirkcudbright artists. Audio-visual presentation. Temporary exhibitions programme.
☎ 01557 331556

🏛 **Tom Davidson Gallery** `26 C5`

High Street, Earlston, Berwickshire. On the A68, 14 miles (22km) north of Jedburgh, 38 miles (61km) south of Edinburgh. A gallery featuring mostly landscape paintings, etchings and linocuts. Davidson is known as one of Scotland's leading exponents of the linocut and he can be seen at work either cutting or printing the block.
☎ 01896 848898

✝ **Torhouskie Stone Circle** `9 E3`

Off the B733, 4 miles (6.5km) west of Wigtown. A Bronze Age recumbent circle of 19 boulders on the edge of a low mound.
☎ 0131 668 8800   www.historic-scotland.gov.uk

✝ **Torr a'Chaisteal Fort** `20 B5`

4 miles (6.5km) south of Blackwaterfoot, Isle of Arran. A circular Iron Age fort on a ridge.
☎ 0131 668 8800   www.historic-scotland.gov.uk

✝ **Torrylin Cairn** `20 B5`

0.25 miles (0.5km) south east of Lagg on the south coast of the Isle of Arran. A Neolithic chambered cairn with its compartments visible.
☎ 0131 668 8800   www.historic-scotland.gov.uk

Traquair House 26 A5
Innerleithen, 6 miles (10km) south east of Peebles. Dating back to the 12th century, this is said to be the oldest continuously inhabited house in Scotland. Twenty-seven Scottish and English monarchs have visited the house, including Mary, Queen of Scots, of whom there are relics. William the Lion held court here in 1175. The well-known Bear Gates were closed in 1745, not to be reopened until the Stuarts should ascend the throne. Ale is regularly produced at the 18th century brewhouse. Exhibitions and special events are held during the summer months. Craft workshops, brewery with ale tasting, woodland and River Tweed walks and maze.
☎ 01896 830323

Trimontium Exhibition 26 C5
The Square, Melrose. An exhibition illustrating daily life on the Roman frontier at Trimontium fortress, the remains of which can be seen on the tour. Museum contains objets trouvès.
☎ 01896 822651   www.trimontium.freeserve.co.uk

Tropic House 9 F2
Langford Nurseries, Carty Port, 2 miles (3km) south of Newton Stewart on the A714. An extensive display of carnivorous plants, including the insects which they eat. In Victorian times, explorers feared that such plants would eat humans. Exotic butterflies fly amongst the tropical plants.
☎ 01671 404050

Trowmill, Woollen Weaving Mill 18 C3
Trowmill, on the A698, 2.5 miles (4km) north east of Hawick. Visitors can tour the weaving unit and view the varied processes in cloth manufacture.
☎ 01450 372555

Turnberry Castle 14 C3
Off the A719, 6 miles (9.5km) north of Girvan. The scant remains of the castle where Robert the Bruce was probably born in 1274.

Turnberry Hotel Golf Courses 14 D3
Turnberry. Two famous world class links courses, Ailsa and Kintyre (formerly Arran), overlooking the isles of Arran and Ailsa Craig, which have hosted many amateur and professional championships. Ailsa was the venue for the Open in 1977, 1986 and 1994.
☎ 01655 331000   www.turnberry.co.uk

Tweed Bridge 27 F4
A698 at Coldstream, 9 miles (14.5km) east north-east of Kelso. The 300ft (91m) long bridge was built in 1766 by Smeaton. In the past the bridge was a crossing into Scotland for eloping couples taking advantage of Scotland's easier marriage laws.

Tweeddale Museum & Gallery 25 E3
Chambers Institute, High Street, Peebles. A 19th century building housing a museum and gallery. Temporary exhibitions of art and craftwork. Gallery of local history and ornamental plasterwork.
☎ 01721 724820

Twelve Apostles 11 F1
Off the B729 towards Dunscore, north of Dumfries. The largest stone circle on mainland Scotland.

Union Suspension Bridge 27 G3
Spans the River Tweed, 2 miles (3km) south of Paxton on an unclassified road. This suspension bridge, the first of its type in Britain, was built by Samuel Brown in 1820, and links England and Scotland.

Vennel Gallery 22 B3
10 Glasgow Vennel, Irvine. Gallery with a programme of changing exhibitions of contemporary art and crafts. The gallery includes the Heckling Shop, where Robert Burns worked, and the Lodging House where he lived in 1781.
☎ 01294 275059   www.northayrshiremuseums.org.uk

Vikingar! 21 E1
Greenock Road, Largs, 25 miles (40km) from Glasgow on the A78. The history of the Vikings in Scotland, including the Battle of Largs in 1263, is told here using multimedia. Other facilities include a swimming pool, sauna and health suite, as well as a 500 seat cinema. There is a Winter Garden café, children's play area and an activity room.
☎ 01475 689777   www.vikingar.co.uk

Wallace's Statue 26 C5
5 miles (8km) from Melrose. A 23ft (7m) high sandstone statue commissioned in 1814 by the Earl of Buchan as a monument to Sir William Wallace.

Wanlockhead Beam Engine 16 C2
In Wanlockhead, Dumfries and Galloway, on the A797. An early 19th century wooden water-balance pump for draining a lead mine, with the track of a horse engine beside it. Nearby is the privately-operated Museum of Lead Mining.
☎ 0131 668 8800   www.historic-scotland.gov.uk

Whithorn Priory & Museum 9 F4
6 Bruce Street, Whithorn, Newton Stewart. The cradle of Christianity in Scotland, founded in the 5th century. The priory for Premonstratensian canons was built in the 12th century and became the cathedral church of Galloway. In the museum is a fine collection of early Christian stone, including the Latinus stone, the earliest Christian memorial in Scotland, and the Monreith Cross, the finest of the Whithorn school of crosses.
☎ 01988 500508   www.historic-scotland.gov.uk

Whithorn Trust Discovery Centre 9 F4
45–47 George Street, Whithorn. Since 1986 archaeologists have been investigating the site of an abandoned town. One thousand years ago the Anglo-Saxons called it Hwiterne; earlier it was called Candida Casa, the Shining House. Fifteen hundred years ago St Ninian, Scotland's first saint, built a church here. Guided tour of original dig site, priory, museum and crypts, discovery centre with archaeology puzzle. Audio-visual show, exhibitions.
☎ 01988 500508

Wigtown Martyrs' Monument 9 F3
Wigtown. Hilltop monument to the 17th century Covenanters who died for their beliefs. Their gravestones are in the churchyard and a stone shaft on the shore marks the spot where two women were drowned at the stake in 1685.

Wildlife Park, Kirkcudbright 10 D3
Lochfergus Plantation, 1 mile (2km) east of Kirkcudbright, on the B727. Over 150 animals and 32 species are found in the hillside woodland setting of this zoological park and wild animal conservation centre: from pandas and monkeys to lynx and Scottish wildcats. On offer are guided tours of the zoo, pet-handling sessions, quizzes for children, animal sponsorship, and involvement in threatened species breeding and wildlife conservation both in the zoo and nature reserve. Also crazy golf.
☎ 01557 331645

Wilton Lodge Walled Garden 18 C3
Wilton Park Road, Hawick. 0.5 mile (1km) from the town centre. Comprises 107 acres (43ha) of garden with extensive shrubberies and a large selection of mature trees.
☎ 01450 378023

WWT Caerlaverock Wetlands Centre 11 G2
East Park Farm, Caerlaverock, 9 miles (14.5km) south east of Dumfries. A 1,350 acre (546ha) nature reserve where many birds can be seen from hides and observation towers. Trails in summer.
☎ 01387 770200   www.wwt.org.uk

Yarrow 18 A2
A708, west from Selkirk. A lovely valley praised by many writers including Scott, Wordsworth and Hogg. Little Yarrow Kirk dates from 1640, Scott's great-great-grandfather was minister there. Deuchar Bridge dates from the 17th century. On the surrounding hills are the remains of ancient Border keeps.

Edinburgh & Lothians

Edinburgh is one of the most attractive and historic cities in Europe. The city has preserved its heritage and embraced the new. It is a vibrant cultural, shopping and business centre with a huge amount to offer the visitor.

The castle dominates the city skyline while the tall buildings and narrow closes of the Old Town cluster along the slope stretching to the east of the crag. In striking contrast, and just five minutes walk away, is the Georgian elegance of the 18th century New Town. The broad streets here include Princes Street, the main shopping thoroughfare of the city.

Greyfriars Bobby

National collections

Edinburgh is the home of many of Scotland's national art and museum collections - visit the Scottish National Portrait Gallery, The National Gallery of Scotland and the Museum of Scotland. Then there are many exciting new visitor attractions. Our Dynamic Earth, the new Museum of Scotland and the former Royal Yacht Britannia are all attractions that have opened in the last few years.

Scottish National Portrait Gallery

Edinburgh Castle from Princes Street

City of Edinburgh

Population: 401,910. Scotland's historic capital is built on a range of rocky crags and extinct volcanoes. It is the administrative, financial and legal centre of Scotland. Its medieval castle, perched high on Castle Rock, was one of the main seats of the Royal Court. At the other end of the Royal Mile is the Palace of Holyroodhouse, the chief royal residence of Scotland.

Salisbury Crags

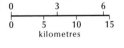

The Lothians

The Lothians surround Edinburgh with country houses and ruined castles and offer space for outdoor activities as well as variety of nature and heritage-based attractions.

Edinburgh Military Tattoo

Map pages in this region

Festivals

Edinburgh's annual festivals are acclaimed worldwide - the Edinburgh International Festival, the Festival Fringe, The Edinburgh Military Tattoo, the Edinburgh Hogmanay and the International Jazz and Blues, Film and Book Festivals present a wide range of events for the visitor.

Edinburgh & Lothians Tourist Board

Edinburgh & Scotland Information Centre
3 Princes Street,
Edinburgh, EH2 2QP

☎ 0131 473 3800

www.edinburgh.org

City of Edinburgh

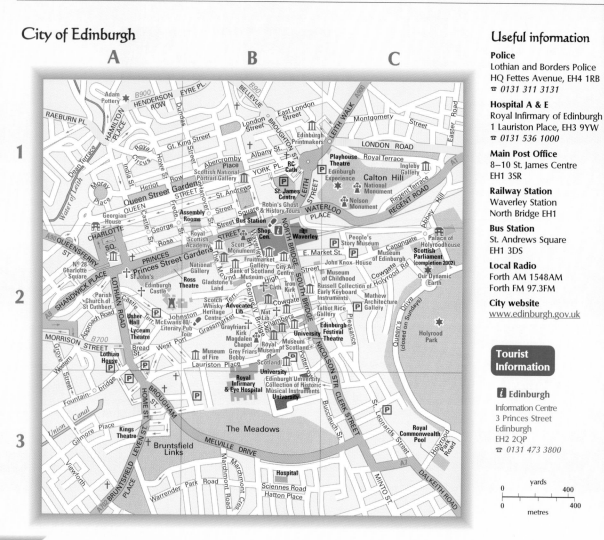

Useful information

Police
Lothian and Borders Police
HQ Fettes Avenue, EH4 1RB
☎ 0131 311 3131

Hospital A & E
Royal Infirmary of Edinburgh
1 Lauriston Place, EH3 9YW
☎ 0131 536 1000

Main Post Office
8–10 St. James Centre
EH1 3SR

Railway Station
Waverley Station
North Bridge EH1

Bus Station
St. Andrews Square
EH1 3DS

Local Radio
Forth AM 1548AM
Forth FM 97.3FM

City website
www.edinburgh.gov.uk

Tourist Information

ℹ️ Edinburgh
Information Centre
3 Princes Street
Edinburgh
EH2 2QP
☎ 0131 473 3800

D4 Royal Mile

Places of interest on the Royal Mile have an index reference of D4

Index to street names

The Royal Mile

Edinburgh's Royal Mile

Sloping gently from the castle to the Palace of Holyroodhouse the Royal Mile is a crowded, historic and romantic jumble of buildings. Today a fashionable area with many fine restored buildings and attractions, the Royal Mile was for a long time home to the poor and many of the old closes in which they lived remain today.

Paragliding in the Pentland Hills

Pentland Hills

This range of grassy hills rises steeply from the southern fringe of Edinburgh and stretches 16 miles (26km) towards Carnwath in South Lanarkshire. The summit is Scald Law at 1898ft (579m). The area provides some delightful hill walking with splendid views towards Edinburgh and beyond to the Pentland Firth.

Tourist Information

i **Edinburgh Airport**

Tourist Information Desk
Edinburgh Airport
Edinburgh
EH12 9DN
☎ 0131 344 3213

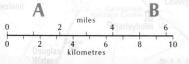

A · B · C · D

Firth of Forth

The estuary of the River Forth widens out into the sea between Fife Ness and North Berwick. At its narrowest point of one mile (2km) it is spanned by the Forth road and railway bridges.

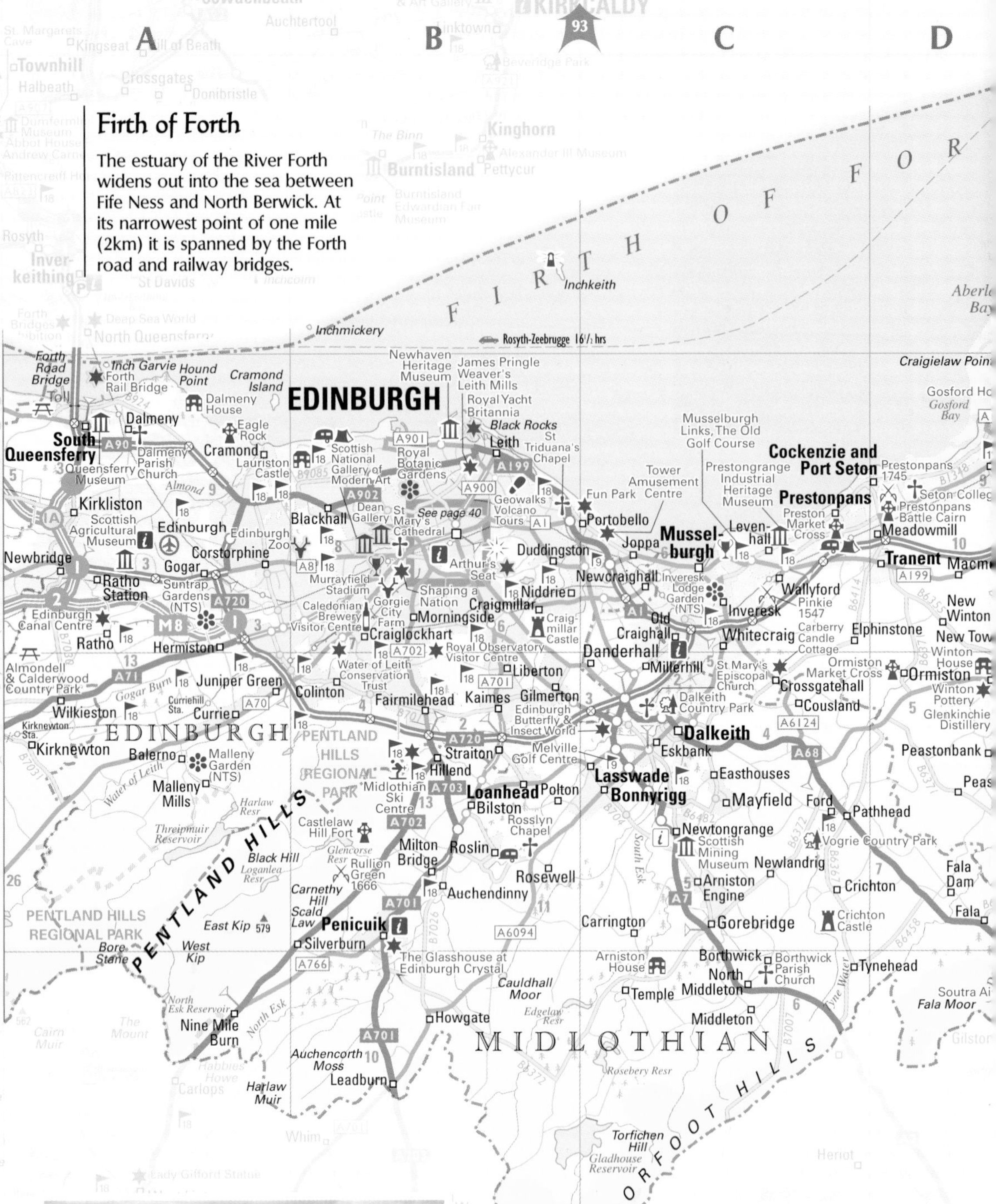

EDINBURGH

Musselburgh

Cockenzie and Port Seton

Prestonpans

Tranent

South Queensferry

i Edinburgh

Edinburgh & Scotland Information
3 Princes Street
Edinburgh
EH2 2QP
☎ 0131 473 3800

i Edinburgh Airport

Tourist Information Desk
Edinburgh Airport
Edinburgh
EH12 9DN
☎ 0131 344 3213

i Newtongrange

Scottish Mining Museum
Lady Victoria Colliery
Newtongrange
Lothian
EH22 4QN
☎ 0131 634262

i Old Craighall

Granada Service Area (A1)
Musselburgh
East Lothian
EH21 8RE
☎ 0131 653 6172

i Penicuik

Edinburgh Crystal Visitor Centre
Eastfield
Penicuik
Midlothian
EH26 8HB
☎ 01968 673846

Calton Hill, Edinburgh

Musselburgh

Population: 20,630. This historic town on the outskirts of Edinburgh at the mouth of the River Esk was once an important trading and fishing port. It also has strong sporting connections with Scotland's oldest racecourse and golf course.

MIDLOTHIAN

PENTLAND HILLS REGIONAL PARK

MOORFOOT HILLS

A · B · C · D

miles
0   2   4   6
0 2 4 6 8 10
kilometres

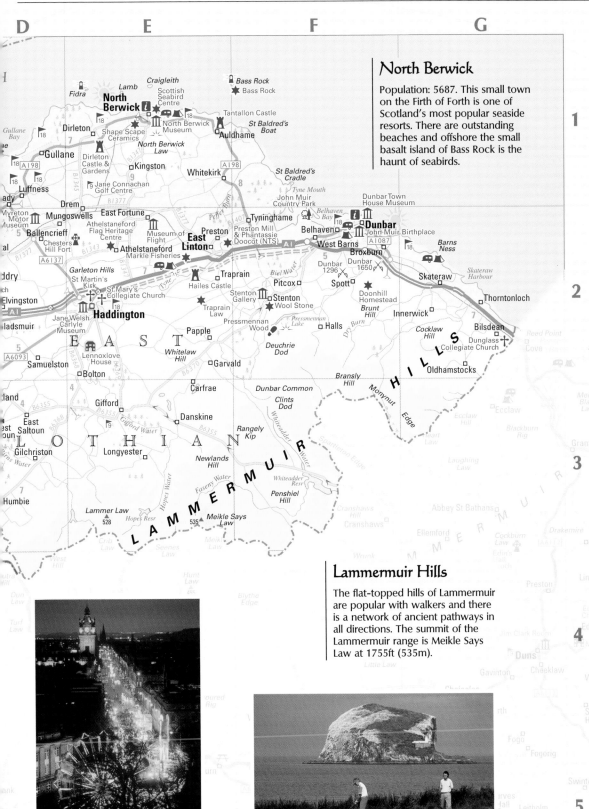

North Berwick

Population: 5687. This small town on the Firth of Forth is one of Scotland's most popular seaside resorts. There are outstanding beaches and offshore the small basalt island of Bass Rock is the haunt of seabirds.

Lammermuir Hills

The flat-topped hills of Lammermuir are popular with walkers and there is a network of ancient pathways in all directions. The summit of the Lammermuir range is Meikle Says Law at 1755ft (535m).

Hogmanay Fair, Edinburgh

Bass Rock

Tourist Information

i **Dunbar**
143 High Street
Dunbar
East Lothian
EH42 1ES
☎ 01368 863353

i **North Berwick**
Quality Street
North Berwick
East Lothian
EH39 4HJ
☎ 01620 892197

† **Abercorn Church & Museum**　　41 C2

Hopetoun Estate, South Queensferry. 6 miles (10km) west of South Queensferry off the A904. There has been a church on this site for 1500 years. Abercorn was the first bishopric in Scotland, dating from 681AD. The present church (dedicated to St Serf) developed from the Reformation to the present day – the present building, on the site of a 7th century monastery, dates from the 12th century. The museum contains Viking burial stones.
☎ 01506 834331

✶ **Adam Pottery, The**　　40 A1

76 Henderson Row, 1 mile (2km) north of Princes Street in Edinburgh. Wheel-thrown stoneware and porcelain with colourful high-fired glaze. Functional and decorative items. Work by other ceramicists also made on the premises. Visitors are welcome to watch any work in progress.
☎ 0131 650 2210

🏛 **Almond Valley Heritage Centre**　　41 C2

Millfield, Livingston Village. Off the A705, 2 miles (3km) from junction 3 on the M8. The history and environment of West Lothian brought to life in an exciting and innovative museum combining a working farm, restored watermill and a history museum. Award-winning interactive displays for children, indoor play areas, nature trail, trailer rides and a narrow-gauge railway.
☎ 01506 414957

🐾 **Almondell & Calderwood Country Park**　　41 C2

On the B7015 at East Calder. Extensive riverside and woodland walks in former estate, with large picnic and grassy areas. The visitor centre, housed in an old stable block, has a large freshwater aquarium, displays on local and natural history, and a short slide show. Ranger service, guided walks programme.
☎ 01506 414957

🏛 **Amiston House**　　42 C3

Gorebridge, on the B6372, 1 mile (2km) from the A7 and 10 miles (16km) from Edinburgh. An outstanding example of the work of William Adam, built in the 1720s. Contains an important collection of furniture and Scottish portraiture.
☎ 01875 830515　　www.arniston-house.co.uk

✶ **Arthur's Seat**　　42 B2

Holyrood Park, Edinburgh. Rising to a height of 822ft (251metres), Arthur's Seat is the igneous core of an extinct volcano, now one of the most prominent landmarks of the city. A path leads from just outside Our Dynamic Earth along the base of the red cliffs and up to the summit. Panoramic views of Edinburgh, the Firth of Forth and the Pentland Hills.

✶ **Athelstaneford Flag Heritage Centre**　　43 E2

Behind Athelstaneford Church. A 16th century dovecot restored to house an audio-visual dramatisation of the battle in 832AD at which an army of Picts/Scots encountered a larger force of Saxons under Athelstan. The appearance of a cloud formation of a white saltire (the diagonal cross on which St Andrew had been martyred) against a blue sky inspired the Scots to victory. Since that time, the St Andrew's Cross has been the national flag of Scotland. There is a viewpoint overlooking the battle site, and visitors can also inspect the Saltire Memorial, the Book of the Saltire, and walk through the historic churchyard.
☎ 01620 880378

🏛 **Bank of Scotland Museum**　　40 B2

Bank of Scotland Head Office, The Mound, Edinburgh. Between the Old and New Towns, just off the Royal Mile. A small but unusual museum telling the 300 year story of Scotland's first bank set against the economic development of the country. Features early adding machines, banknotes and forgeries, bullion chests and gold coins, maps, plans and photographs. Free postcards.
☎ 0131 529 1288　　www.bankofscotland.co.uk

✶ **Bass Rock**　　43 F1

Off North Berwick. A massive 350ft (106.5m) high rock whose many thousands of raucous sea birds include the third largest gannetry in the world.

🐾 **Beecraigs Country Park**　　41 B2

The Park Centre, 2 miles (3km) south of Linlithgow. Nestled high in the Bathgate hills, Beecraigs offers a wide range of leisure and recreational pursuits within its 915 acres (370ha). Archery, orienteering, fly-fishing, walks and trails. Trim course, play area, all-terrain bicycle trail, picnic areas, barbecue sites, fish farm, horse route, deer farm, caravan and camping site. Ranger service.
☎ 01506 844516　　www.beecraigs.com

🏛 **Bennie Museum**　　41 B2

9 – 11 Mansefield Street, Bathgate. Almost 5000 artefacts illustrating the social, industrial, religious and military history of Bathgate, a former burgh town. Displays of postcards and photographs from the 1890s onwards. Fossils, Roman glass and coins, relics from Prince Charles Edward Stuart and the Napoleonic Wars.
☎ 01506 634944　　thornton@benniemuseum.freeserve.co.uk

🏰 **Blackness Castle**　　41 C2

Blackness, on the B903, 4 miles (6.5km) north east of Linlithgow. A 15th century stronghold, once one of the most important fortresses in Scotland and one of the four castles which the Articles of Union left fortified. A state prison in Covenanting times; a powder magazine in the 1870s. More recently, for a period, a youth hostel.
☎ 01506 834807　　www.historic-scotland.gov.uk

† **Borthwick Parish Church**　　42 C3

Borthwick, Gorebridge, 13 miles (21km) south east of Edinburgh. This church, which is largely Victorian, has an aisle and a vault dating from the 15th century, an apse originating in the 12th century, 18th and 19th century memorials (particularly the Dundas family), and two 15th century effigies thought to be the best preserved in Scotland. Associated also with the Borthwick family and clan. Commemorates the birthplace of the great 18th century Scottish Enlightenment figure, Principal William Robertson.

✶ **Brass Rubbing Centre**　　40 D4

Chalmers Close, 81 High Street, Edinburgh. Just off the Royal Mile opposite the Museum of Childhood. Housed in the historic Trinity Apse, thought to have been founded in 1460 by Queen Mary of Gueldres, consort of King James II of Scotland, as a memorial to her husband. Offers a fine collection of replicas moulded from ancient Pictish stones, medieval church brasses and rare Scottish brasses.
☎ 0131 556 4364　　www.cac.org.uk

⚜ **Cairnpapple Hill**　　41 B2

Near Torphichen, off the B792, 3 miles (5km) north of Bathgate. One of the most important prehistoric monuments in Scotland. It was used as a burial and ceremonial site from around 3000 to 1400 BC. Excellent views.
☎ 01506 634622　　www.historic-scotland.gov.uk

🍶 **Caledonian Brewery Visitor Centre**　　42 B2

42 Slateford Road, Edinburgh. On the A7 Lanark road, 2 miles (3km) from Princes Street. A unique reminder of a bygone era when the city boasted over 40 breweries and was one of the great brewing capitals of Europe. Beer is still brewed today using hand selected natural ingredients and the original brewers' equipment – still fired by direct flame and the last of their kind still working in any British brewery.
☎ 0131 623 8066　　www.caledonian-brewery.co.uk

✶ **Camera Obscura**　　40 D4

Adjacent to Edinburgh Castle at the top of the Royal Mile. Edinburgh's oldest attraction. An 1850s camera obscura captures a live panorama of the city below while guides tell Edinburgh's story. Visitors can spy on passers-by or pick vehicles up in the palm of their hand. Three-D hologram display (the largest in Europe) and photographs of old Edinburgh.
☎ 0131 226 3709

† **Canongate Kirk**　　40 D4

The Kirk of Holyroodhouse, Canongate, Edinburgh. Opposite Huntly House Museum in the Royal Mile. Historic 300 year old Church of Scotland, recently renovated and restored. Parish church of the Palace of Holyroodhouse and Edinburgh Castle, with Frobenius organ and Normandy tapestry.
☎ 0131 556 3515

✶ **Carberry Candle Cottage**　　42 C3

Carberry, Musselburgh. Visitors can see live and video demonstrations of candle manufacturing. There is also a factory shop.
☎ 0131 665 5656

🏰 **Castlelaw Hill Fort**　　42 B3

1 mile (2km) north west of Glencorse, off the A702, 7 miles (11km) south of Edinburgh. A small Iron Age hill fort consisting of two concentric banks and ditches. An earth house is preserved in the older rock-cut ditch. Occupied in Roman times.
☎ 0131 668 8800　　www.historic-scotland.gov.uk

🏰 **Chesters Hill Fort**　　43 E2

1 mile (2km) south of Drem on the unclassified road to Haddington, East Lothian. One of the best examples of an Iron Age hill fort with multiple ramparts. A souterrain is built into one of the ditches.
☎ 0131 668 8800　　www.historic-scotland.gov.uk

🏛 **City Art Centre**　　40 B2

2 Market Street, Edinburgh. Houses the City of Edinburgh's permanent fine art collection and stages a programme of temporary exhibitions from all over the world. Six floors of display galleries (with escalators and lifts). Education programme of workshops, lectures, events and educational publications.
☎ 0131 529 3993　　www.cac.org.uk

🏰 **Craigmillar Castle**　　42 B2

Craigmillar Castle Road, off the A68 (Dalkeith road), 2.5 miles (4km) south east of Edinburgh city centre. Imposing ruins of massive 14th century keep enclosed in the early 15th century by an embattled curtain wall. Within are the remains of the stately ranges of apartments dating from the 16th and 17th centuries. The castle was burned by Hertford in 1544. Strong connections with Mary, Queen of Scots.
☎ 0131 661 4445　　www.historic-scotland.gov.uk

🏰 **Crichton Castle**　　42 C3

Crichton, off the A68. A large castle built around a 14th-century keep. The most spectacular part is the arcaded range erected by the Earl of Bothwell between 1581 and 1591. This has a façade of faceted stonework in an Italian style.
☎ 01875 320017　　www.historic-scotland.gov.uk

🐾 **Dalkeith Country Park**　　42 C3

In Dalkeith High Street. The 18th century planned landscape includes farm animals, working Clydesdale horses, adventure woodland play area, nature trails, woodland walks, 18th century bridge, orangery and ice house. Ranger service.
☎ 0131 654 1666

🏛 **Dalmeny House**　　41 D2

South Queensferry. The home of the Earls of Rosebery for over 300 years, but the present Tudor Gothic building, by William Wilkins, dates from 1815. Interior Gothic splendour of hammer-beamed hall, vaulted corridors and classical main rooms. Works of art include a magnificent collection of 18th century British portraits, 18th century furniture, tapestries, porcelain from the Rothschild Mentmore collection and the Napoleon collection. Lovely grounds and a 4.5 mile (7km) shore walk.
☎ 0131 331 1888　　www.dalmeny.co.uk

† **Dalmeny Parish Church**　　41 D2

Main Street, Dalmeny, 10 miles (16km) west of Edinburgh. The best preserved Romanesque (Norman) church in Scotland, dating from the 12th century. Coach tours should book in advance.
☎ 0131 331 1479

Dean Gallery, The
`42 B2`
Belford Road, Edinburgh. Houses the Gallery of Modern Art's extensive collections of Dada and Surrealism. In 1994, Edinburgh-born sculptor Sir Eduardo Paolozzi offered a large body of his work to the National Galleries of Scotland. This collection of prints, drawings, plaster maquettes, moulds and the contents of his studio is now housed in the Dean Gallery. The gallery also accommodates a library and archive of artists' books, catalogues and manuscripts relating in particular to the Dada and Surrealist movement, but also to 20th century art as a whole.
☎ 0131 624 6200   www.natgalscot.ac.uk

Dere Street Roman Road
`42 D4`
On the B6438 (off the A68) beside Soutra Aisle. A good stretch of the Roman road which ran from Corbridge beside Hadrian's Wall to Cramond on the Firth of Forth. Beside the road are scoops, pits from which the gravel for building the road was taken.
☎ 0131 668 8800   www.historic-scotland.gov.uk

Dirleton Castle & Gardens
`43 E1`
Off the A198 in Dirleton. A romantic castle dating from the 13th century with 15th to 17th century additions. First besieged in 1298 by Edward I. Destroyed in 1650. The adjoining gardens include an early 20th century Arts and Crafts garden and a restored Victorian garden. Also a 17th century bowling green.
☎ 01620 850330   www.historic-scotland.gov.uk

DOM Gallery in Edinburgh's Oldest House
`40 D4`
In the centre of Edinburgh. DOM is an international collective of artists, musicians and writers, whose work at Advocate's Close includes an ever-evolving exhibition of works. Number 8 Advocate's Close is Edinburgh's oldest surviving house. Known as Henry Cant's tenement, it was built in the 1480s. This would have been a very prestigious home and the fireplaces bear favourable comparison to those found in Scottish castles of the same period.
☎ 0131 225 9271

Doonhill Homestead
`43 F2`
Off the A1, 2 miles (3km) south of Dunbar. The site of a wooden hall of a 6th century British chief, and of an Anglian chief's hall which superseded it in the 7th century. A rare record of the Anglian occupation of south east Scotland.
☎ 0131 668 8800   www.historic-scotland.gov.uk

Dunbar Town House Museum
`43 F2`
In Dunbar High Street, at the corner of Silver Street. A 16th century town house now containing a museum of local history and archaeology.
☎ 01368 863734

Dunglass Collegiate Church
`43 G2`
Between Bilsdean and Cockburnspath. A handsome cross-shaped church with vaulted nave, choir and transepts, all with stone slab roofs. Founded in 1450 for a college of canons by Sir Alexander Hume.
☎ 0131 668 8800   www.historic-scotland.gov.uk

Eagle Rock
`41 D2`
On the shore of the River Forth about 2.5 miles (0.5km) west of Cramond. A much-defaced carving on natural rock, said to represent an eagle.
☎ 0131 668 8800   www.historic-scotland.gov.uk

Edinburgh Butterfly & Insect World
`42 C3`
Dobbies Garden World, Lasswade. Visitors can walk through an indoor tropical rainforest inhabited by thousands of the world's most beautiful butterflies. Also Bugs and Beasties exhibition, featuring hundreds of live creepy crawlies, snakes, lizards and frogs. Daily 'meet the beasties' handling sessions. Also garden centre, birds of prey centre and children's play parks
☎ 0131 663 4932   www.edinburgh-butterfly-world-co.uk

Edinburgh Canal Centre
`41 D2`
The Bridge Inn, 27 Baird Road, Ratho. Built circa 1750, the inn became a canalside inn with the opening of the Union Canal in 1822. Canal boat restaurants cater for meals, dances, weddings, etc. Sightseeing cruises and Santa cruises in December.
☎ 0131 333 1320   www.bridgeinn.com

Edinburgh Castle
`40 A2`
In the centre of Edinburgh at the top of the Royal Mile. Battlements overlook the Esplanade where the floodlit Military Tattoo is staged each year. The oldest part, St Margaret's Chapel, dates from the Norman period. The Great Hall was built by James IV; the Half Moon Battery by the Regent Morton in the late 16th century. The Scottish National War Memorial was erected after World War I. The castle houses the Crown Jewels (Honours) of Scotland, the Stone of Destiny and the famous 15th century gun Mons Meg.
☎ 0131 225 9846   www.historic-scotland.gov.uk

Edinburgh Dungeon
`40 B2`
Market Street, Edinburgh. The Edinburgh Dungeon transports visitors back to the darkest chapters of Scotland's history. Visitors come face to face with the notorious murderers, Burke and Hare, wander through the plague ravaged streets of old Edinburgh and join James VI on a one-way boat ride to confront the infamous cannibal Sawney Bean in Witchfynder.
☎ 0131 240 1000   www.thedungeons.com

Edinburgh Experience
`40 C1`
City Observatory, Calton Hill. Tells the story of Scotland's capital in a 3-D slide show.
☎ 0131 556 4365

Edinburgh Printmakers
`40 B1`
23 Union Street. Edinburgh's main studio for practising artists who make limited edition prints. Visitors can watch artists at work. Courses in print-making.
☎ 0131 557 2479

Edinburgh Tartan Weaving Mill & Exhibition
`40 D4`
Beside Edinburgh Castle at the top of the Royal Mile. A working mill where visitors can see the production of tartan cloth and try weaving on a 60 year old pedal loom. Visitors can also have their photo taken in ancient Scottish costume. Clans and tartans information bureau.
☎ 0131 226 1555

Edinburgh University Collection of Historic Musical Instruments
`40 B2`
Reid Concert Hall, Bristo Square. Founded circa 1850 and opened to the public in 1982. The galleries, built in 1859 and still with their original showcases, are believed to be the earliest surviving purpose-built musical museum in the world. On display are 1000 items including string, woodwind, brass and percussion instruments from Britain, Europe and from distant lands. The history of the instruments of the orchestra, the wind band, theatre, dance, popular music, domestic music-making and brass bands is shown. Displays include many beautiful examples of the instrument-maker's art over the past 400 years.
☎ 0131 650 2423   www.music.ed.ac.uk/euchmi

Edinburgh Zoo
`42 B2`
134 Corstorphine Road. Established in 1913 by the Royal Zoological Society of Scotland. Over 1000 animals, many threatened in the wild, all set in 80 acres (32ha) of beautiful hillside parkland. Animals range from tiny blue poison arrow frogs to massive white rhinos. The world's largest penguin pool and a magic forest, home to the tiniest primates. A Penguin Parade takes place April – September, daily at 1400.
☎ 0131 334 9171   www.edinburghzoo.org.uk

Forth Rail Bridge
`41 D2`
South Queensferry. Opened on 4 March 1890 by the Prince of Wales. The bridge was designed on the cantilever principle with three towers 340ft (104m) high. The engineers were Sir John Fowler and Benjamin Baker.
☎ 0131 319 1699

Freeport Westwood Outlet Village
`41 B3`
Westwood. Designer fashion brands and home goods at discounted prices.
☎ 01501 763488

Fruitmarket Gallery, The
`40 B2`
45 Market Street, in Edinburgh city centre adjacent to Waverley station. Originally built in 1938 as a fruit and vegetable market, the building now contains an acclaimed art gallery with a national and international reputation for diverse and challenging pro-active exhibitions. Art bookshop and restaurant.
☎ 0131 225 2383   www.fruitmarket.co.uk

Fun Park
`42 B2`
Portobello Promenade, Edinburgh. A family entertainment centre with various amusements – soft play area, dodgems, carousel, juvenile rides (merry-go-round), full-size ten-pin bowling lanes, American pool hall and full-size snooker tables.
☎ 0131 669 1859

Georgian House
`40 A2`
7 Charlotte Square, Edinburgh. A typical house in Edinburgh's New Town, designed by Robert Adam, furnished as it would have been by its first owners in 1796. Video programmes.
☎ 0131 226 3318   www.nts.org.uk

Geowalks Volcano Tours
`42 B2`
Discover extinct volcanoes, hidden views, stunning scenery, the secrets of the local landscape and over 400 million years of history. Explore the beautiful surroundings of Fife and the Lothians, and the dramatic cityscape of Edinburgh. Join Dr Angus Miller for a walk back in time. Walks vary from 2 – 5 hours.
☎ 0131 555 5488   www.geowalks.demon.co.uk

Gladstone's Land
`40 D4`
477b Lawnmarket, Royal Mile, Edinburgh. Typical example of the 17th century tenements of Edinburgh's Old Town, clustered along the ridge between the Castle and the Palace of Holyroodhouse – the Royal Mile. Completed in 1620 and originally home to a prosperous Edinburgh merchant, Thomas Gledstanes, the house contains original painted ceilings and some contemporary furniture.
☎ 0131 226 5856   www.nts.org.uk

Glasshouse at Edinburgh Crystal, The
`42 B3`
In Penicuik, south of Edinburgh. Visitors can watch and talk to the craftsmen, and discover the history of Edinburgh Crystal. Opportunity to try blowing and cutting crystal (must be booked in advance).
☎ 01968 675128   www.edinburgh-crystal.com

Gleneagles Crystal
`41 C2`
37 Simpson Road, East Mains Industrial Estate, in Broxburn. A factory shop with viewing area where visitors can watch crystal cutters at work.
☎ 01506 852566   www.gleneagles-crystal.com

Glenkinchie Distillery
`42 D3`
2 miles (3km) from Pencaitland on the A6093 (signposted). Visitors can see all aspects of the traditional distilling craft, with sample tasting. Exhibition includes a scale model of a malt distillery made for the British Empire Exhibition of 1924.
☎ 01875 342004

Gorgie City Farm
`42 B2`
51 Gorgie Road, Edinburgh. A 2 acre (1ha) farm with various farm animals, commonly kept pets, herbs, vegetables and a wildlife garden. Special events throughout the year, craft classes, educational workshops and tours. Education centre.
☎ 0131 337 4202

Gosford House   `42 D3`

Off the A198, 2 miles (3km) north east of Longniddry. The central part of this mansion is the work of Robert Adam (1800). The north and south wings are by William Young (1890). The south wing contains the celebrated Marble Hall. Extensive grounds, woodland walks, ornamental waters with wildlife.
☎ 01875 870201

Greyfriars Bobby   `40 B2`

By Greyfriars churchyard on the corner of George IV Bridge and Candlemaker Row in Edinburgh. Statue of Greyfriars Bobby, the Skye terrier who, after his master's death in 1858, watched over his grave in the nearby Greyfriars Churchyard for 14 years.

Greyfriars Kirk   `40 B2`

2 Greyfriars Place, in Edinburgh Old Town. Edinburgh's first Reformed Church (1620). On display is the National Covenant (signed at the church in 1638), Scotland's finest collection of 17th and 18th century funeral monuments, fine 19th century windows by Ballantyne, Peter Collins' organ (1990) with carvings of Scottish flora and fauna, memorabilia about Greyfriars Bobby. Millennium window by Douglas Hogg and Millennium kneelers portraying kirk history.
☎ 0131 225 1900

Hailes Castle   `43 E2`

Off the A1, 1.5 miles (2.5km) south west of East Linton. A beautifully-sited ruin incorporating a 13th century fortified manor which was extended in the 14th and 15th centuries. Includes a fine 16th century chapel and two vaulted pit-prisons.
☎ 0131 668 8800   www.historic-scotland.gov.uk

Holyrood Abbey   `40 D4`

At the foot of Canongate (Royal Mile), Edinburgh, in the grounds of the Palace of Holyroodhouse. The ruined nave of the 12th and 13th century Abbey church, built for Augustinian canons. Administered by the Lord Chamberlain.
☎ 0131 668 8800   www.historic-scotland.gov.uk

Holyrood Park   `40 C2`

East of Holyroodhouse Palace, Edinburgh. There has probably been a royal park here since the Augustinian Abbey was founded in the early 12th century, but it was formally enclosed in 1541 during James V's reign. Within the park is a wealth of archaeology, including the remains of four hill forts, other settlements and round them a fascinating landscape of prehistoric and early-medieval farming activity.
☎ 0131 556 1761   www.historic-scotland.gov.uk

Hopetoun House   `41 C2`

South Queensferry. The residence of the Marquis of Linlithgow. Set in 100 acres (40ha) of magnificent parkland on the shore of the Firth of Forth with fine views of the famous bridges. Built 1699 – 1707 by William Bruce and extended by William Adam from 1721. Features original furniture, carriage collection, paintings by famous artists, 17th century tapestries, rococo ceilings and Meissen ceramics.
☎ 0131 331 2451   www.hopetounhouse.com

House of the Binns   `41 C2`

Off the A904, 3 miles (5km) east of Linlithgow. Home of the Dalyell family since 1612. General Tam Dalyell raised the Royal Scots Greys here in 1681. The architecture reflects the early 17th century transition from fortified stronghold to spacious mansion. Elaborate plaster ceilings dating from 1630. Woodland walk to panoramic viewpoint over Firth of Forth. Famous for snowdrops and daffodils in spring.
☎ 01506 834255   www.nts.org.uk

Hub Festival Centre   `40 D4`

348 Castlehill, on the Royal Mile, Edinburgh. The permanent home for the Edinburgh International Festival housed in the former Tolbooth Church. Many of the original, gothic interiors of the church have been maintained and are complemented by new, comtemporary interior design. The centre offers a booking office, exhibition area and café. Special culinary evenings and café concerts.
☎ 0131 473 2000   www.eif.co.uk

Ingleby Gallery   `40 C1`

Carlton Terrace, Edinburgh. Specialises in modern British and contemporary art, with an emphasis on painting, sculpture and photography. Artists include Howard Hodgkin, Andy Goldsworthy, Ian Hamilton Finlay, Sean Scully and Callum Innes.
☎ 0131 556 4441   www.inglebygallery.com

Inveresk Lodge Garden   `42 C2`

Inveresk. Attractive terraced garden in historic village of Inveresk. Excellent range of roses and shrubs and a beautiful display of colour in autumn.
☎ 01721 722502   www.nts.org.uk

James Pringle Weavers Leith Mills   `42 B2`

70 – 74 Bangor Road, Leith. Shops selling woollens, tartans, clothing, gifts, whisky and shoes. Tailor-made outfits. Clan Tartan Centre which will provide visitors with a printed certificate detailing any clan connection, information on the clan chief, origins, heraldic emblems, plant badge and other historic information.
☎ 0131 553 5161

Jane Connachan Golf Centre   `43 E1`

Fenton Barns, on the B1345, between Drem and North Berwick. A floodlit driving range and nine-hole 3-par golf course. Part of a retail and leisure village.
☎ 01620 850475

Jane Welsh Carlyle Museum   `43 E2`

Located at the west end of Haddington High Street. The childhood home of Jane Baillie Welsh has been restored to perpetuate her memory. Jane was the only child of Dr John Welsh, a 19th century Haddington medical practitioner. In 1821, she met and was courted by Thomas Carlyle, writer and philosopher who was to become the 'sage of Chelsea'.
☎ 01620 823738

John Knox House   `40 D4`

43 – 45 High Street, Edinburgh. A picturesque 15th century house associated with John Knox, the religious reformer, and James Mossman, keeper of the Royal Mint to Mary, Queen of Scots. The house contains many original features including the painted ceiling in the Oak Room, and an exhibition on the life and times of John Knox and James Mossman.
☎ 0131 556 9579

John Muir Birthplace   `43 F2`

126 – 128 High Street, Dunbar. The birthplace of John Muir, founding figure of the worldwide conservation movement. He was born in 1838. On the ground floor his father ran a business. His family emigrated in 1849. The flat has been furnished in period style to give an impression of the circumstances in which the family lived, without gas or running water. An audio-visual display tells the story of John Muir, both in Dunbar and the USA.
☎ 01368 860187

John Muir Country Park   `43 F2`

2 miles (3km) west of Dunbar. A coastal conservation area established in 1976 in honour of the conservationist John Muir. The park extends over 8 miles (12km) westward from the ruins of Dunbar Castle, where John Muir played as a boy and includes rugged cliffs, saltmarshes and the sands of Belhaven Bay. Wildlife includes over 220 species of bird and 12 species of butterfly.

Kirk of Calder   `41 C2`

Mid Calder. This 16th century parish church won the West Lothian award for conservation in 1992. Famous visitors include John Knox, David Livingstone, Frederick Chopin and James 'Paraffin' Young. Fine stained glass windows. Visitors can learn about four centuries of Scottish history.

Lauriston Castle   `42 B2`

Cramond Road South, Edinburgh. Set in 30 acres (12ha) this 16th century tower house with extensive 19th-century additions was built about 1590 by Archibald Napier whose son John invented logarithms. In the early 18th century Lauriston was owned by financier John Law who held high office in the court of pre-revolution France. The last private owners were the Reid family, and the castle contains William Reid's extensive collections of furniture and antiques – a snapshot of the interior of a Scottish country house in the Edwardian era.
☎ 0131 336 2060   www.cac.org.uk

Lennoxlove House   `43 E2`

Lennoxlove Estate, on the B6369, 1 mile (2km) from Haddington. The home of the Duke of Hamilton. It features a 14th century keep originally built for Maitland of Lethington, Secretary of State to Mary, Queen of Scots, and houses mementoes belonging to Mary, together with furniture, paintings and porcelain once part of the Hamilton Palace collection.
☎ 01620 823720

Linlithgow Palace   `41 C2`

Kirkgate, Linlithgow. The ruin of a great royal palace beside Linlithgow Loch. The Great Hall and Chapel (late 15th century) are particularly fine. The quadrangle has a richly-carved 16th century fountain. A favoured residence of the Stewart monarchs from James I. Works commissioned by James I, III, IV, V and VI can be seen. Both King James V and Mary, Queen of Scots were born here.
☎ 01506 842896   www.historic-scotland.gov.uk

Linlithgow Story, The   `41 B2`

Annet House, 143 High Street, Linlithgow. A small museum of local history which tells the story, not only of the Stewart kings of Scotland who built and lived in Linlithgow Palace, but also of the ordinary people who lived and worked in the burgh. Housed in a late 18th century merchant house.
☎ 01506 670677   www.linlithgowstory.org.uk

Linlithgow Union Canal Society Museum & Boats   `41 B2`

Canal Basin, Manse Road, Linlithgow. On the Edinburgh and Glasgow Union Canal with small museum in former stable. Boat trips on the Victoria (1/2 hour town trip) and St Magdalene (2 1/2 hour trip to Avon Aqueduct).
☎ 01506 671215   www.lucs.org.uk

Magdalen Chapel (Scottish Reformation Society)   `40 B2`

41 Cowgate, Edinburgh. Built in 1541, the chapel was used by various denominations and also as a guildhall by the Incorporation of Hammermen until 1862, when it was sold to the Protestant Institute of Scotland. Since 1965, it has been in the possession of the Scottish Reformation Society and used as their headquarters with regular services. Features stained glass (the only medieval examples still in the original setting and situation), bell and clock dating from early 17th century.
☎ 0131 220 1450

Malleny Garden   `41 D3`

Balerno. Dominated by four 400 year old clipped yew trees, this peaceful garden features fine herbaceous borders and a large collection of old-fashioned roses. The National Bonsai Collection for Scotland is also housed here.
☎ 0131 449 2283   www.nts.org.uk

Markle Fisheries   `43 E2`

Markle, East Linton. Three spring-fed lakes, totalling 9.5 acres (3.9ha), which are regularly stocked with trout and course fish. Bank fishing. Children's bait pond. Tackle hire and tuition. Also ornamental fish such as koi carp for sale.
☎ 01620 861213   www.marklefisheries.com

Matthew Architecture Gallery   `40 B2`

20 Chambers Street, Edinburgh. Exhibitions of contemporary architecture.
☎ 0131 650 2306

McArthur Glen Designer Outlet   `41 C3`

Livingston. Scotland's largest designer outlet combining shops, multi-screen cinema, food court and bars.
                                     www.mcarthurglen.com

McEwan's 80/- Literary Pub Tour `40 B2`
The Beehive Inn, Grassmarket, Edinburgh. This two hour promenade performance, led by professional actors, begins at the Inn and follows a route through the streets and old taverns. Scotland's great poets, writers and colourful characters from the past 300 years are described, from Robert Burns and Walter Scott to Muriel Spark and Trainspotting.
☎ 0131 226 6665   www.scot-lit-tour.co.uk

Melville Golf Centre `42 C3`
South Melville, Lasswade. Golf centre with a nine hole play-and-pay course, driving range, 22 covered floodlit bays and 12 outdoor bays. Full equipment hire. PGA tuition. Practice area. Putting green.
☎ 0131 663 8038   www.melvillegolf.co.uk

Mercat Walking Tours `40 B2`
These dramatised history and ghost tours of Edinburgh leave from the Mercat Cross beside St Giles Cathedral on the Royal Mile. Visit the wynds and closes of Old Edinburgh, the vaults beneath the South Bridge and the world-famous Mary King's Close.
☎ 0131 557 6464   www.mercattours.com

Midlothian Ski Centre `42 B3`
Hillend, just south of Edinburgh. Europe's longest and most challenging artificial ski slope. Two main slopes, a fun slope and two nursery slopes. Equipment hire, skiing/snowboarding, coaching and instruction for all levels, chair lift and two ski tows. Chairlift open to all visitors, with terrific views.
☎ 0131 445 4433   www.midlothian.gov.uk/contract/skisite/index.htm

Muiravonside Country Park `41 B2`
The Loan, Whitecross, Linlithgow. On the B825. 170 acres (68ha) of woodlands, parkland and gardens of the Muiravonside Estate, home of the Stirling family for 150 years. Exhibition in visitor centre. Auditorium and ranger office. Relics of industrial past. Dovecot, burial ground and summer house. Children's farm.
☎ 01506 845311

Murrayfield Stadium `42 B2`
Murrayfield, Edinburgh. The 67,000 capacity stadium for Scotland's international rugby union team and the venue for home matches during the Six Nations Championship. Built in 1925 by the Scottish Rugby Union and extended and modernised in 1936, 1983 and 1994.

Museum of Childhood `40 D4`
42 High Street, Edinburgh. This unique museum has a fine collection of childhood-related items including toys, dolls, dolls' houses, costumes and nursery equipment.
☎ 0131 529 4142   www.cac.org.uk

Museum of Edinburgh `40 D4`
142 Canongate. A restored 16th century mansion with period rooms and reconstructions relating to the city's traditional industries. There are also collections of Edinburgh silver and glass, Scottish pottery, shop signs and relics relating to Field Marshall Earl Haig, the World War I general.
☎ 0131 529 4143   www.cac.org.uk

Museum of Fire `40 B2`
Lothian and Borders Fire Brigade Headquarters, Lauriston Place, Edinburgh. The history of the oldest municipal fire brigade in the United Kingdom and the development of fire fighting is shown in an exciting and educational way. Displays a range of fire engines from 1806.
☎ 0131 228 2401   www.lothian.fire-uk.org

Museum of Flight `43 E2`
East Fortune Airfield, North Berwick. Scotland's national museum of aviation with a large collection of over 40 aircraft (including Britain's oldest aeroplane, a Spitfire and a Vulcan bomber) in the hangars of a wartime airfield. Special exhibitions on space flight, early aviation, air traffic control and the R34 airship.
☎ 01620 880308   www.nms.ac.uk/flight

Museum of Scotland `40 B2`
Chambers Street, Edinburgh. The Museum of Scotland tells the history of Scotland from its geological beginnings to the present day. Spectacular views of the city from the rooftop. Opened in 1998 as an extension to the Royal Museum of Scotland. A striking piece of architecture to hold the treasured objects of Scotland's past and present.
☎ 0131 225 7534   www.nms.ac.uk

Musselburgh Links, The Old Golf Course `42 C2`
Balcarres Road, at the east end of Musselburgh High Street. Mary, Queen of Scots is said to have played this course in 1567, although the oldest documentary evidence dates from 1672. Between 1874 and 1889 the course hosted six Open Championships. Today golfers can hire hickory clubs and replica balls to emulate the masters of the past.
☎ 0131 665 5438   www.musselburgholdlinks.co.uk

Myreton Motor Museum `43 D2`
Myreton, off the A198 just east of Aberlady. A varied collection of road transport from 1897, including motor cars, cycles, motorcycles, commercials, World War II military vehicles and automobilia. Catalogue and children's quiz book.
☎ 01875 870288

National Gallery of Scotland `40 B2`
The Mound, Edinburgh. It was designed by William Henry Playfair and the foundation stone laid by Prince Albert in 1850. The gallery opened to the public in 1859. Contains outstanding paintings, drawings and prints by the greatest artists from the Renaissance to Post-Impressionism, including Velásquez, El Greco, Titian, Vermeer, Constable, Monet and Van Gogh. It also houses the national collection of Scottish art featuring works by Taggart, Wilkie, Ramsay and Raeburn.
☎ 0131 624 6332   www.natgalscot.ac.uk

National Library of Scotland `40 B2`
George IV Bridge, Edinburgh. Founded in 1682, the library is a treasure house of books and manuscripts, with reading rooms open for research to scholars. For the general public and visitors, it has a programme of exhibitions on Scottish themes.
☎ 0131 226 4531   www.nls.uk

National Monument `40 C1`
Calton Hill, Edinburgh. Unfinished memorial to Scots lost in the Napoleonic Wars.

National War Museum of Scotland `40 D4`
Within Edinburgh Castle. Explores the Scottish experience of war and military service over the last 400 years, housed in mid 18th century buildings.
☎ 0131 225 7534   www.nms.ac.uk

Nelson Monument `40 C1`
On Calton Hill in Edinburgh, above Waterloo Place. One of the first monuments to Admiral Nelson, built between 1807 and 1815. A telescope-shaped tower with a time-ball on the top that is wound up every day (except Sunday) and dropped at 1300. The timeball, like the 1 o'clock gun at Edinburgh Castle, acted as a signal to ships in Leith docks to set their chronometers, enabling them to calculate longitude. Nelson's Trafalgar signal is flown on 21 October. Good views from the top.
☎ 0131 556 2716   www.cac.org.uk

Newhaven Heritage Museum `42 B2`
24 Pier Place, Edinburgh. This museum is situated in the historic fishmarket overlooking the harbour. Find out about fishing and other sea trades, customs and superstitions. Displays tell the stories of the Society of Free Fishermen and the development of this tightly-knit community. Reconstructed sets of fishwives and fishermen, displays of objects and photographs, and first-hand written and spoken accounts of people's lives. Hands-on exhibits, music and video.
☎ 0131 551 4165   www.cac.org.uk

No. 28 Charlotte Square `40 A2`
In Edinburgh city centre. An attractive gallery overlooking Charlotte Square and displaying a collection of 20th century Scottish paintings.
☎ 0131 243 9300   www.nts.org.uk

North Berwick Museum `43 E1`
School Road, North Berwick. The museum, housed in the former Burgh School, offers a wide range of displays. Visitors can see the old town stocks, stroke a gannet in the Bass Rock Room or score an Eagle in the Golf Room.
☎ 01620 895457

Ormiston Market Cross `42 D3`
On the B6371 in Ormiston. A 15th century cross on a modern base in the main street. A symbol of the right of the inhabitants to hold a market.
☎ 0131 668 8800   www.historic-scotland.gov.uk

Our Dynamic Earth `40 C2`
107 Holyrood Road, Edinburgh. Through dramatic special effects, stunning wrap-around images and state-of-the-art interactives, visitors discover the story of the planet, from the start of time to an unknown future. See the Restless Earth volcano erupt, walk through the tropical rainforest thunderstorm and meet an ever-changing menagerie of animals. Take a dramatic helicopter flight over the magnificent Scottish mountains and feel the chill of ice in the polar region.
☎ 0131 550 7800   www.dynamicearth.co.uk

Palace of Holyroodhouse `40 C2`
Canongate in Edinburgh. The official residence of The Queen in Scotland. The oldest part is built against the monastic nave of Holyrood Abbey, little of which remains. The rest of the palace was reconstructed by the architect Sir William Bruce for Charles II. Home of Mary, Queen of Scots for six years and where she met John Knox. Prince Charles Edward Stuart held court here in 1745. The State Apartments house tapestries and paintings. The Picture Gallery has portraits of over 80 Scottish kings painted by De Wet 1684 – 6.
☎ 0131 556 7371

Parish Church of St Cuthbert `40 A2`
Below Edinburgh Castle. This is the seventh church on this site. Tradition has it that St Cuthbert had a small cell church here at the head of the Nor'Loch. Recorded history tells that King David I, gifted lands to 'the Church of St Cuthbert, hard by the Castle of Edinburgh'. The present building was built in 1894 to a design by Hippolyte Blanc, but retained the 1790 tower. Interior was reorganised in 1990 by Stewart Tod. Features Renaissance style stalls, marble communion table, alabaster mural, stained glass by Tiffany. Famous names in graveyard.
☎ 0131 229 1142   www.st-cuthberts.net

Parliament House & Law Courts `40 B2`
11 Parliament Square, Edinburgh. Behind the High Kirk of St Giles, Royal Mile. Built 1632 – 9, this was the seat of Scottish government until 1707, when the governments of Scotland and England were united. Now the Supreme Law Courts of Scotland, Parliament Hall has a fine hammer beam roof and portraits by Raeburn and other major Scottish artists. Access (free) to the splendid Signet Library on an upper floor is by prior written request only, to: The Librarian, Signet Library, Parliament House, Edinburgh. Outside is the medieval Mercat Cross, which was restored in 1885 by W. E. Gladstone. Royal proclamations are still read from its platform.
☎ 0131 225 2595

People's Story Museum `40 D4`
In the picturesque Canongate Tolbooth, built in 1591. Tells the story of the life, work and pastimes of the ordinary working people of Edinburgh from the late 18th century. Sights, sounds and smells. Room reconstructions, rare artefacts and everyday objects.
☎ 0131 529 4057   www.cac.org.uk

Polkemmet Country Park `41 B2`

On the B7066 west of Whitburn. A public park with mature woodland, a 9-hole golf course, golf driving range and bowling green. Also barbecue site (bookable) and large children's play area (the Fantasy Forest). Rhododendrons in summer. Reception and restaurant/bar at the Park Centre.
☎ 01501 743905

Pressmennan Wood `43 F2`

1 mile (2km) south of Stenton. Purchased by the Woodland Trust in 1988, the wood comprises 210 acres (85ha), formerly part of the Biel and Dirleton Estate. Pressmennan Lake was formed artificially in 1819 by constructing a dam at the eastern end of a narrow, marsh glen. Waymarked walks and forest tracks.
☎ 01764 662554　　　　　　www.forestry.gov.uk

Preston Market Cross `42 C2`

0.5 mile (1km) south of Prestonpans. The only surviving example of a market cross of its type on its original site. A fine early 17th century design with a cylindrical base surmounted by a cross-shaft headed by a unicorn.
☎ 0131 668 8800　　　　www.historic-scotland.gov.uk

Preston Mill & Phantassie Doocot `43 E2`

East Linton. Picturesque mill with stone buildings dating from the 18th century. The water wheel and grain milling machinery are still intact and visitors can see them in operation. Attractive surroundings with millponds and a short walk through fields to a 16th century Phantassie Doocot, once home to 500 pigeons.
☎ 01620 860426　　　　　　　　www.nts.org.uk

Prestongrange Industrial Heritage Museum `42 C2`

Morison's Haven, Prestonpans. A museum telling the story of many local industries. Displays include a historic Cornish beam engine. Steam days.
☎ 0131 653 2904

Prestonpans Battle Cairn `42 D2`

East of Prestonpans on the A198. The cairn commemorates the victory of Prince Charles Edward Stuart over General Cope at the Battle of Prestonpans in 1745.

Queensferry Museum `41 D2`

53 High Street, South Queensferry. The town is named in honour of the saintly Queen Margaret (died 1093), who encouraged pilgrims to use the ferry crossing to travel to the shrine of St Andrew in Fife. Describes the development of this Passage, the growth of the former Royal Burgh and the building of the Forth Bridges. Displays on life, work and pastimes, including the annual Ferry Fair and a life-size model of the Burry Man.
☎ 0131 331 5545　　　　　　　　www.cac.org.uk

Rabbie's Trail Burners `40 D4`

207 High Street, Edinburgh. Scottish Highland minicoach tours depart all year to all areas of the Highlands.
☎ 0131 226 3133　　　　　　　　www.rabbies.com

Regimental Museum of The Royal Scots `40 D4`

The museum of the oldest regiment in the British Army, housed in Edinburgh Castle. Contains paintings, artefacts, silver and medals which tell the story of the regiment from its formation in 1633 to the present day.
☎ 0131 220 4387

Robin's Ghost & History Tours `40 B2`

These tours of Edinburgh begin outside the Tourist Information Centre, Princes Mall shopping centre, Princes Street. The tours recreate the dramatic history of Scotland's capital city. The Grand Tour is a journey through the splendours of the Georgian New Town and Edinburgh's medieval heart. At night, the Ghosts and Witches tour is a dark journey through streets haunted by the past.
☎ 0131 557 9933

Rosslyn Chapel `42 B3`

In Roslin, 7 miles (11km) south west of Edinburgh. A 15th century chapel with unique carving throughout, including the legendary Apprentice Pillar, many references to Freemasonry and the Knights Templar. The only medieval church in Scotland used by the Scottish Episcopal Church.
☎ 0131 440 2159　　　　　　www.rosslynchapel.org.uk

Royal Botanic Garden `42 B2`

20a Inverleith Row, Edinburgh. Established in 1670 on an area the size of a tennis court, it now comprises over 70 acres (28ha) of beautifully landscaped grounds. Spectacular features include the world-famous Rock Garden, the Pringle Chinese Collection and a magnificent arboretum. The amazing Glasshouse Experience, featuring Britain's tallest Palm House, leads you on a trail of discovery through Asia, Africa, the Mediterranean and the Southern Hemisphere.
☎ 0131 552 7171　　　　　　　　www.rbge.org.uk

Royal Museum of Scotland `40 B2`

Chambers Street, in the centre of Edinburgh's Old Town. The museum houses international collections in a wonderful Victorian glass-topped building. Collections include applied arts, geology and zoology, natural history, social and technical history, jewellery and costume, Egyptian and African treasures. Lectures, concerts and activities for children.
☎ 0131 225 7534　　　　　　　　www.nms.ac.uk

Royal Observatory Visitor Centre `42 B2`

Blackford Hill, 3 miles (5km) south of Edinburgh city centre. A multi-media gallery with CD-ROMs on space and astronomy. Visitors can experiment with light and see one of the largest telescopes in Scotland. Panoramic views of Edinburgh.
☎ 0131 668 8405　　　　　　　　www.roe.ac.uk

Royal Scottish Academy `40 B2`

Princes Street, Edinburgh. Closed for major refurbishment until July 2003, check website to confirm location of exhibitions until then. The Royal Scottish Academy, established in 1826, is Scotland's oldest art gallery which specialises in showing contemporary art, ranging from works by Academicians and Associates of the Academy to works from students.
☎ 0131 558 7097　　　　www.royalscottishacademy.org

Royal Yacht Britannia, The `42 B2`

Ocean Drive, Leith. Visitors can view the royal family picture gallery, learn about life on board for officers and yachtsmen and see the royal barge. An audio tour takes visitors around the four main decks.
☎ 0131 555 5566　　　　　　　　www.tryb.co.uk

Russell Collection of Early Keyboard Instruments `40 B2`

Niddry Street, Edinburgh Old Town. Scotland's oldest concert hall, built in 1762 for the Edinburgh Musical Society. After many changes of use, it was acquired by the University of Edinburgh and restored to its original use in 1968. It is the home of the Russell Collection of Early Keyboard Instruments, which is of international importance.
☎ 0131 650 2805　　　　　　　　www.music.ed.ac.uk

St Giles' Cathedral `40 D4`

On the Royal Mile in Edinburgh. Founded in the 1100s, a triumph of 14th and 15th century architecture with a crown spire that has dominated the Edinburgh skyline for 500 years. Contains memorials to many great Scots, including the great Covenanting leaders Montrose and Argyll, Robert Louis Stevenson and Robert Burns. Fine Victorian and 20th century stained glass. The Thistle Chapel was designed by Lorimer and is a jewel of Scottish craftsmanship.
☎ 0131 225 9442

St John's `40 A2`

Princes Street, Edinburgh. The Church of St John the Evangelist is one of architect William Burn's early 19th century buildings. Collections of stained glass, modern paintings and sculptures. Outside are the graves of many famous Scots such as Sir Henry Raeburn, Scotland's finest portrait painter, and James Donaldson, the founder of the School for the Deaf.
☎ 0131 229 7565

St Martin's Kirk `43 E2`

On the eastern outskirts of Haddington. The ruined nave of a Romanesque church, altered in the 13th century.
☎ 0131 668 8800　　　　www.historic-scotland.gov.uk

St Mary's Cathedral `42 B2`

Palmerston Place, in the West End of Edinburgh, near Haymarket. An Episcopal cathedral built in 1879, with the western towers added in 1917. The central spire is 276ft (84m) high. Impressive interior. Nearby is the charming Old Coates House, built in the late 17th century and now the Episcopal Church's Theological Institute.
☎ 0131 225 6293

St Mary's Collegiate Church `43 E2`

Sidegate, Haddington. A 14th century cruciform church, East Lothian's Cathedral. Destroyed during the Siege of Haddington in 1548, but completely restored 1971 – 3. Features Burne Jones and Sax Shaw windows; Lammermuir pipe organ. The Lauderdale Chapel is a focus for ecumenical unity.
☎ 01620 823109

St Mary's Episcopal Church `42 C3`

Dalkeith Country Park. Built as a chapel for Dalkeith Palace in 1843 by William Burn and David Bryce. Early English style with many splendid features – double hammerbeam roof, glorious stained glass, heraldic floor tiles by Minton and the only working water-powered Hamilton organ in Scotland (recently restored).
☎ 0131 663 3359

St Michael's Parish Church `41 B2`

Kirkgate, Linlithgow. A medieval parish church consecrated in 1242 on the site of an earlier church. Close association with the royal house of Stewart – Mary, Queen of Scots was baptized here. A contemporary aluminium crown on the tower replaced the medieval stone crown removed in 1820.
☎ 01506 842188

St Triduana's Chapel `42 B2`

At Restalrig Church, off Restalrig Road South, 1.5 miles (2.5km) east of Edinburgh city centre. The lower part of the chapel built by James III, housing the shrine of St Triduana, a Pictish saint. The hexagonal vaulted chamber is unique.
☎ 0131 554 7400　　　　www.historic-scotland.gov.uk

Scotch Whisky Heritage Centre `40 D4`

354 Castlehill, at the top of the Royal Mile. The mystery of Scotch whisky revealed – learn about malt, grain and blended whisky, take a barrel ride through whisky history and meet the resident ghost. Also free taste of whisky for adults. Whisky Bond Bar selling over 250 different whiskies.
☎ 0131 220 0441　　　　　　www.whisky-heritage.co.uk

Scott Monument `40 B2`

East Princes Street Gardens. This imposing Gothic structure is one of Edinburgh's most famous landmarks. It was designed by George Meikle Kemp to commemorate the life and work of the great Scottish writer, Sir Walter Scott (1771 – 1832) and was completed in 1844. It is 200ft (61m) high and inside there are 287 steps to the top rewarding the visitor with superb views of Edinburgh and its surroundings. The monument is decorated with figures from Scott's novels and the statue of Sir Walter Scott at its base was sculpted by Sir John Steell in Carrara marble.
☎ 0131 529 4068

🏛 Scottish Agricultural Museum   `41 D2`
Ingliston, Newbridge, by Edinburgh Airport, off the A8. Scotland's national museum of country life. Interpretive displays feature tools and machinery, including tractors. Audio displays.
☎ 0131 333 2674

🏛 Scottish Mining Museum   `42 C3`
Lady Victoria Colliery, Newtongrange. On the A7, 10 miles (16km) south of Edinburgh. The finest surviving Victorian colliery with Scotland's largest steam engine in the winding house. Visitors can follow a miner's day in the late 19th century and learn about his work. The visitor centre contains interactive displays and exhibits, and a virtual coalface.
☎ 0131 663 7519   www.scottishminingmuseum.com

🏛 Scottish National Gallery of Modern Art   `42 B2`
Belford Road, 20 minute walk from west end of Edinburgh city centre. The building was designed in the 1820s by Sir William Burn and was formerly a school. It has bright spacious rooms and extensive grounds providing the perfect setting for sculptures by Barbara Hepworth, Eduardo Paolozzi, Henry Moore and others. The bulk of the collection, which amounts to almost 4000 works of art, has been amassed since 1960. There are examples of work by Matisse, Kirchner, Picasso, Magritte, Miró, Dali and Ernst. The gallery houses an unrivalled collection of 20th century Scottish art including work by Charles Rennie Mackintosh, Peploe, Fergusson and Cadell. The greatest strengths of the gallery's modern international collection are works by surrealist, German expressionist and French artists.
☎ 0131 624 6332   www.natgalscot.ac.uk

🏛 Scottish National Portrait Gallery   `40 B1`
1 Queen Street, in the city centre, five minute walk from Princes Street in Edinburgh. The gallery, built in the 1880s and designed by Sir Robert Rowland Anderson, provides a unique visual history of Scotland, told through the portraits of the figures who shaped it – royalty, poets, philosophers, heroes and rebels. All the portraits are of Scots but not all are by Scots. The collection holds works by great English, European and American masters such as Van Dyck, Gainsborough, Copley, Rodin, Kokoschka and Thorvaldsen. The gallery also houses the National Photography Collection.
☎ 0131 624 6332   www.natgalscot.ac.uk

✱ Scottish Parliament Visitor Centre   `40 D4`
In the centre of Edinburgh at the junction of George IV Bridge and the Royal Mile. The visitor centre explains the past, present and future of Scotland's Parliaments through colourful displays, exhibitions and state-of-the-art interactive computer systems. Also historical documents from Scotland's earliest days and details of the new Parliament building at Holyrood.
☎ 0131 348 5000   www.scottish.parliament.uk

✱ Scottish Seabird Centre   `43 E1`
The Harbour, North Berwick. Visitors can discover the secret and fascinating world of Scotland's sea birds by studying the birds close up, in their natural environment – without disturbing them. Remote cameras and the latest technology provide amazing live pictures of puffins, gannets and many other sea birds. Breathtaking views across the Firth of Forth to the Bass Rock and Fife.
☎ 01620 890202   www.seabird.org

✝ Seton Collegiate Church   `42 D2`
Longniddry, off the A198, 1 mile (2km) south east of Cockenzie. The chancel and apse of a fine 15th century church. Transept and steeple added in 1513.
☎ 01875 813334   www.historic-scotland.gov.uk

✱ Shape Scape Ceramics   `43 E1`
The Pottery, Station Hill, in North Berwick near the station. A pottery for 40 years, now occupied by a ceramicist. Visitors can buy products designed and made at the pottery.
☎ 01620 893157

✱ Shaping a Nation   `42 B2`
Dundee Street, Edinburgh. Shaping a Nation describes the wonderful achievements and innovative displays made by Scots through informative displays. Interactive exhibits, audio-visual shows and a thrilling motion simulator ride with aerial views of castles, landmarks and Scottish scenery.
☎ 0131 229 0300   www.shapinganation.co.uk

♱ Soutra Aisle   `42 D3`
Soutrahill, 0.5 mile (1km) south of the A68 or 7 miles (11km) north of the A7 on the B6368, near Gilston. From the 12th century to the 17th century, midway between Edinburgh and the magnificent Borders abbeys, stood Soutra medieval hospital – a refuge for wayfarers and the needy, high on the Royal Road, the main Anglo-Scottish highway. Visitors can see the site of the great hospital, the memorial Aisle and the unique archaeo-medical investigations and enjoy the spectacular views.
☎ 01875 833248

🏛 Stenton Gallery   `43 F2`
On the B6370 (Hillfoots Trail), 3 miles (5km) from the A1 at East Linton. Shows the best of contemporary art throughout Scotland. Regularly changing programme of exhibitions.
☎ 01368 850256   www.stentongallery.com

🏛 Stills Gallery   `40 D4`
23 Cockburn Street, in Edinburgh Old Town just off the High Street. A contemporary art gallery, bookshop and café. Open access photography and digital imaging labs open to visitors.
☎ 0131 622 6200

❋ Suntrap Garden   `41 D2`
43 Gogarbank, Edinburgh. Between the A8 and A71, 1 mile (2km) west of the city centre. A 3 acre (1.2ha) site with several gardens in one – Italian, rock, rose, peat and woodland. Started in 1957 by philanthropist and keen amateur gardener George Boyd Anderson, bequeathed to the National Trust for Scotland and Lothian region as a centre for gardening advice and horticultural excellence. Now run by Oatridge Agricultural College, with excellent demonstration facilities.
☎ 01506 854387

🏛 Talbot Rice Gallery   `40 B2`
Old College, South Bridge, in the Old Town, 0.25 mile (0.5km) from the east end of Princes Street and Waverley station. The Red Gallery shows the University of Edinburgh's Torrie Collection. The White Gallery shows seven contemporary exhibitions each year, mainly by mid-career Scottish artists, but also artists from further afield, and occasional historical exhibitions.
☎ 0131 650 2210

♜ Tantallon Castle   `43 E1`
Off the A198, 3 miles (5km) east of North Berwick. Set on the edge of the cliffs looking out to the Bass Rock, this formidable castle was a stronghold of the Douglas family. It features earthwork defences and a massive 50ft (15m) high curtain wall. Display includes replica gun.
☎ 01620 892727   www.historic-scotland.gov.uk

✝ Torphichen Preceptory   `41 B2`
In Torphichen village on the B792, 5 miles (8km) south south-west of Linlithgow. The tower and transepts of a church built by the Knights Hospitaller of the Order of St John of Jerusalem in the 13th century, but much altered.
☎ 01506 654142   www.historic-scotland.gov.uk

✱ Tower Amusement Centre   `42 C2`
49 Figgate Lane, on Portobello Promenade, by the A1, 3 miles (5km) east of the city centre. Edinburgh's largest amusement centre packed with novelty games, prize bingo, children's rides.
☎ 0131 669 8418   www.nobleleisure.com

✱ Traprain Law   `43 E2`
Off the A1, 5 miles (7.5km) west of Dunbar. A whale-backed hill, 734ft (224m) high, with Iron Age fortified site, probably continuing in use as a defended Celtic township until the 11th century. A treasure of 4th century Christian and pagan silver excavated here in 1919 is now in the Museum of Antiquities, Queen Street, Edinburgh.

✱ Tron Kirk   `40 D4`
At the junction of High Street and South Bridge, Edinburgh. A finely proportioned building that takes its name from the tron, or tron, which once stood close by. Built between 1636 and 1647 and in use as a church until 1952. Now serves as the Old Town Information Centre with an exhibition on Old Town history.

🏰 Vogrie Country Park   `42 C3`
2 miles (3km) east of Gorebridge on the B6372. There are over 5 miles (8km) of woodland and riverside walks giving visitors year round interest and variety. Nature trails, interpretation and guided walks. Historic house open to visitors, a Garden centre, model railway, golf course and adventure play area. Events field for hire.
☎ 01875 821990

✱ Water of Leith Conservation Trust   `42 B2`
Water of Leith Centre, 24 Lanark Road, Edinburgh. Based in the Heritage Conservation Centre in Slateford. The trust operates a visitor centre with working models and explanatory displays and provides a central point for information about the river, guided walks and talks. Telephone for details.
☎ 0131 455 7367   www.waterofleith.edin.org

✱ White Horse Close   `40 D4`
Off Canongate, Royal Mile, Edinburgh. A restored group of 17th century buildings off the High Street. The coaches to London left from White Horse Inn (named after Queen Mary's Palfrey), and there are Jacobite links.

⛪ Winton House   `42 D3`
Pencaitland, 14 miles (22.5km) east of Edinburgh off the A1 at Tranent. Lodge gates south of New Winton (B6355) or Pencaitland (A6093). A 15th century tower house restored palatially with famous stone twisted chimneys and magnificent plaster ceilings. Still a family home after 500 years, it houses many treasures which include paintings by many of Scotland's notable artists, fine furniture and an exhibition of family costumes and photographs. The grounds contain specimen trees, woodland walks, terraced gardens and loch.
☎ 01875 341309   www.wintonhouse.co.uk

✱ Winton Pottery   `42 D3`
Winton Estate, Pencaitland, 14 miles (22.5km) south east of Edinburgh on the B6355. The pottery is situated in the grounds of a stately home (see Winton House) in a former stable block. Specialising in thrown and hand-built stoneware for domestic use, as well as plant holders and sundials. Demonstrations are available by arrangement.
☎ 01875 340188

♱ Wool Stone   `43 F2`
In Stenton, B6370, 5 miles (7.5km) south west of Dunbar. The medieval Wool Stone, used formerly for the weighing of wool at Stenton Fair, stands on the green. See also the 14th century Rood Well, topped by a cardinal's hat, and the old doocot.

🏛 Writers' Museum, The   `40 D4`
Lady Stair's Close, Lawnmarket, Edinburgh. Treasure house of portraits, relics and manuscripts relating to Scotland's three great writers – Robert Burns, Sir Walter Scott and Robert Louis Stevenson. Temporary exhibitions on other writers and literary organisations.
☎ 0131 529 4901   www.cac.org.uk

Glasgow & the Clyde Valley

Glasgow is Scotland's largest city and the commercial and industrial capital of the west of Scotland. It is also one of Europe's great cultural destinations, with award-winning museums and galleries and a fine architectural heritage.

It is the UK's biggest retail centre outside London, with the top names in fashion and design as well as all the high street outlets. The Clyde Valley is a complete contrast, with dramatic ruined castles, industrial heritage and country parks.

Princes Square

River Clyde

The winding course of the River Clyde runs from the rolling hills of Lanarkshire through the towns and villages of the 'Garden Valley', through Glasgow and on to the sea via the Firth of Clyde. The Clyde became Glasgow's 'gateway to the Americas' when it was dredged, deepened and widened in the 18th century to make it navigable to the heart of the city. Glasgow consequently prospered and by the 19th century it was the greatest shipbuilding centre in the world.

Armadillo, at the Scottish Exhibition & Conference Centre

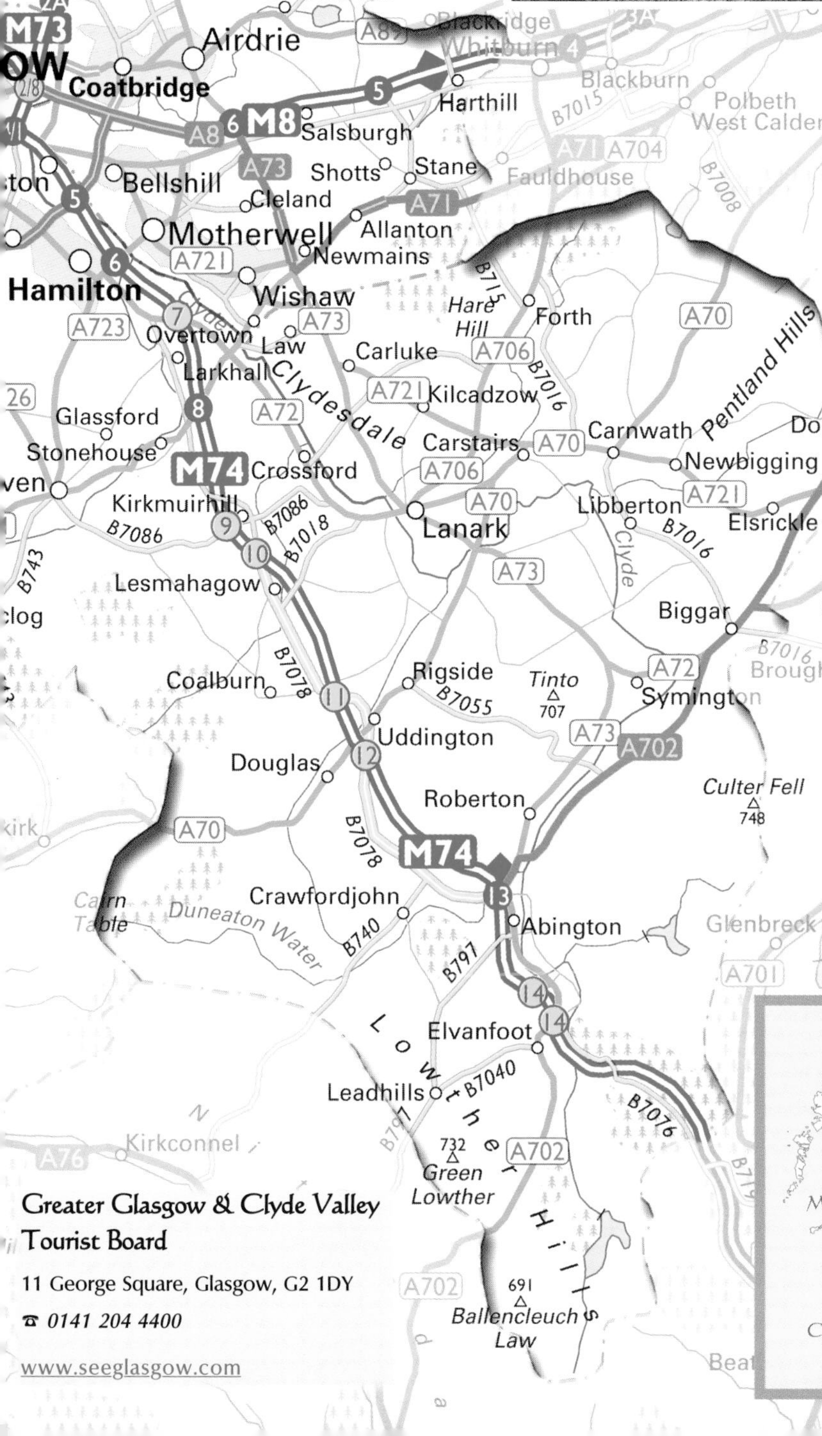
Stirling
Alloa
Clackmannan
Bannockburn
Falkirk
Denny
Kilsyth Hills
Kilsyth
Croy
Cumbernauld
Chryston
Greengairs
Caldercruix
Airdrie
Coatbridge
Armadale
Harthill
Salsburgh
Bellshill
Shotts
Stane
Cleland
Motherwell
Allanton
Newmains
Hamilton
Wishaw
Overtown
Law
Larkhall
Carluke
Forth
Kilcadzow
Clydesdale
Carstairs
Carnwath
Pentland Hills
Dolphinton
Newbigging
Glassford
Stonehouse
Crossford
Kirkmuirhill
Lanark
Libberton
Elsrickle
Lesmahagow
Biggar
Coalburn
Rigside
Tinto 707
Symington
Uddington
Douglas
Roberton
Culter Fell 748
Crawfordjohn
Duneaton Water
Abington
Elvanfoot
Leadhills
Lowther Hills
Green Lowther
Ballencleuch Law
Kirkconnel
M8
M74
M73
M80
M9
M876
M90
A70
A73
A72
A702

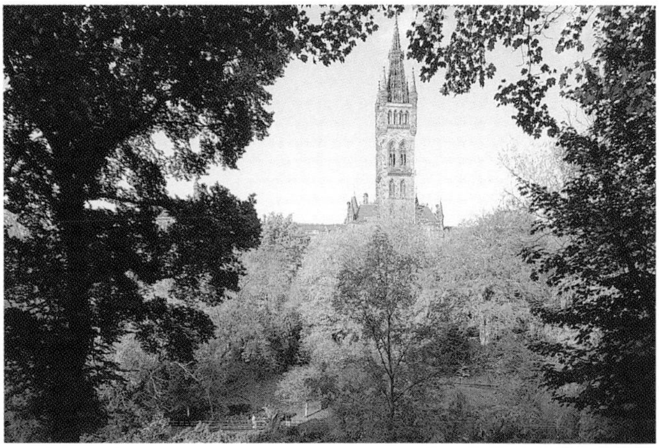

University of Glasgow

Architectural heritage

The architectural heritage of Glasgow is renowned worldwide. The city is home to some of Europe's finest Victorian architecture. Centuries of wealth and achievement have left a legacy of magnificent civic architecture, elegant residential crescents and an industrial heritage to be proud of.

Map pages in this region

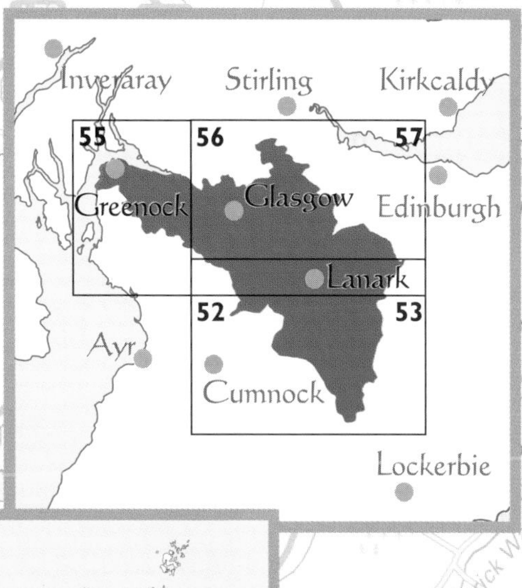
Inveraray
Stirling
Kirkcaldy
55
56
57
Greenock
Glasgow
Edinburgh
Lanark
52
53
Ayr
Cumnock
Lockerbie

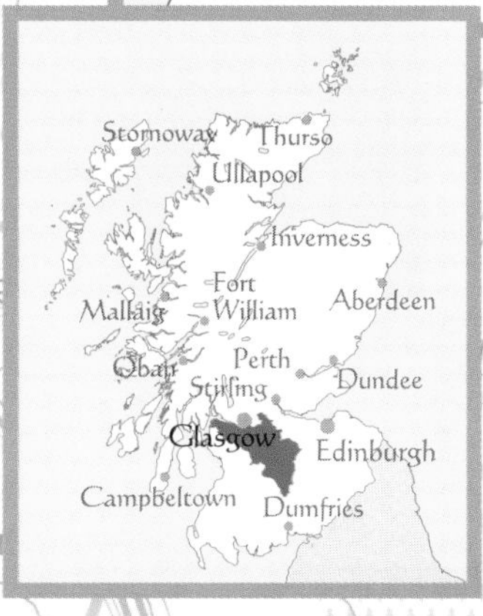
Stornoway
Thurso
Ullapool
Inverness
Fort William
Mallaig
Aberdeen
Oban
Perth
Stirling
Dundee
Glasgow
Edinburgh
Campbeltown
Dumfries

Greater Glasgow & Clyde Valley Tourist Board

11 George Square, Glasgow, G2 1DY

☎ 0141 204 4400

www.seeglasgow.com

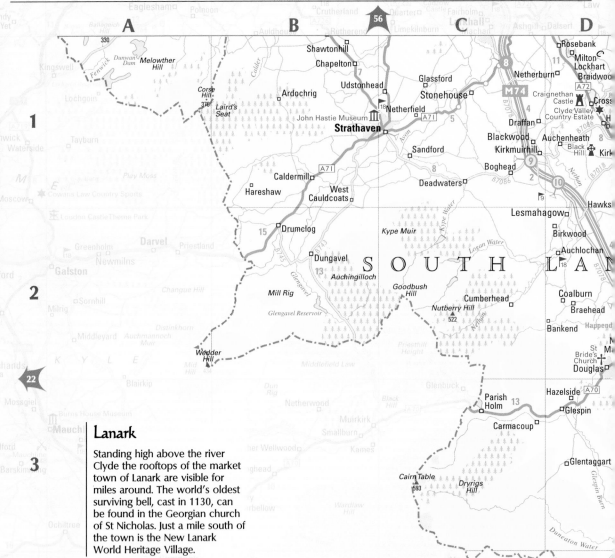

Lanark

Standing high above the river Clyde the rooftops of the market town of Lanark are visible for miles around. The world's oldest surviving bell, cast in 1130, can be found in the Georgian church of St Nicholas. Just a mile south of the town is the New Lanark World Heritage Village.

New Lanark

Lowther Hills

This range of hills between the valleys of the Rivers' Nith and Annan offer a wild landscape of tightly clustered peaks, the highest is Green Lowther at 2403ft (732m). The area once known as 'God's Treasure House' was famed for its silver, gold and lead deposits and many of the stones used in the Scottish crown jewels were mined here.

Tourist Information

i **Lanark**
Horsemarket
Ladyacre Road
Lanark
Lanarkshire
ML11 7LQ
☎ 01555 661661

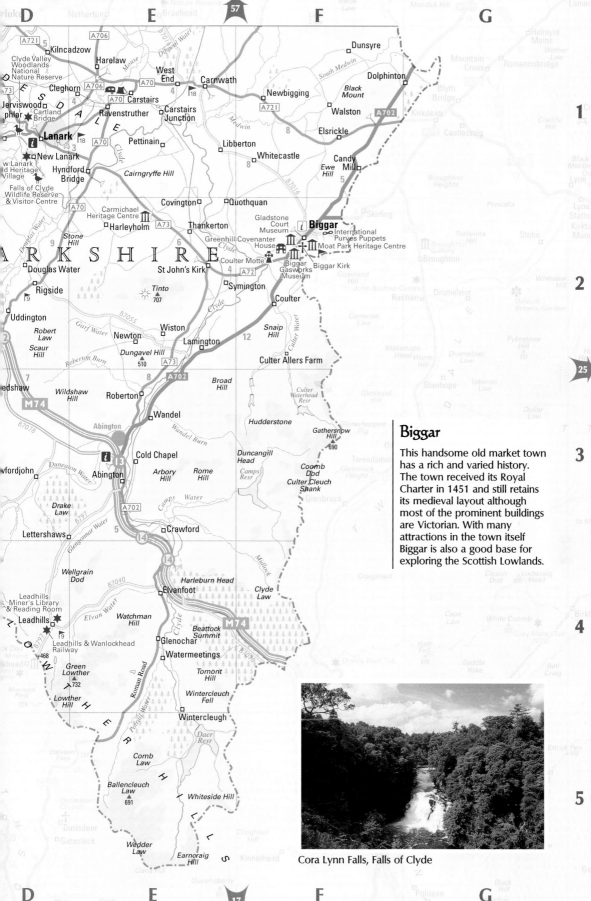

Biggar

This handsome old market town has a rich and varied history. The town received its Royal Charter in 1451 and still retains its medieval layout although most of the prominent buildings are Victorian. With many attractions in the town itself Biggar is also a good base for exploring the Scottish Lowlands.

Cora Lynn Falls, Falls of Clyde

Tourist Information

i Abington
Welcome Break
Service Area
M74 Junction 13
Abington
Lanarkshire
ML12 6RG
☎ 01864 502436

i Biggar
155 High Street
Biggar
Lanarkshire
ML12 6DL
☎ 01899 221066

Glasgow & the Clyde Valley

City of Glasgow

Population: 662,954. On the River Clyde 41 miles (66km) west of Edinburgh, Glasgow is Scotland's largest city. The city grew in importance from the 12th century, becoming a major industrial port during the industrial revolution. Following the decline of the shipbuilding industry in the 1930s Glasgow has restyled itself as a city of culture (European City of Culture 1990 and City of Architecture and Design 1999). Its many museums, galleries and fine buildings are testament to this. Scotland's largest tourist attraction, The Burrell Collection, has more than 8000 objects displayed in an award winning gallery in Pollok Country Park. The 'Oxford Street' of Glasgow is Sauchiehall Street which together with Buchanan Street, the Buchanan Galleries, Argyle Street, Princes Square and the St Enoch centre form the main, mostly pedestrianised shopping area. The city has many theatres and concert halls where productions range from opera, drama, pop, pantomime and musicals.

City Chambers

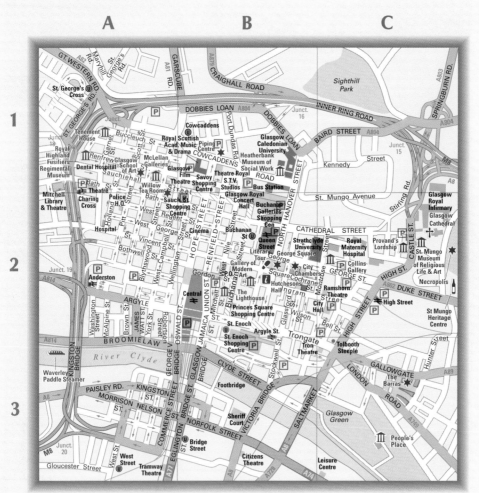

Useful information

Police
Strathclyde Police HQ
173 Pitt Street, G2 4JS
☎ 0141 532 2000

Hospital A & E
Western Infirmary
Dumbarton Road, G11 6NT
☎ 0141 211 2000

Main Post Office
47 St. Vincent Street
G2 5QX

Railway Station
Central Station
Gordon Street

Queen Street Station
Queen Street, G1 2AG

Bus Station
Buchanan Bus Station
Killermont Street, G2 3NP

Local Radio
Clyde 1 102.5FM
Clyde 2 1152 AM

City website
www.glasgow.gov.uk

Tourist Information

i Glasgow
11 George Square
Glasgow
G2 1DY
☎ 0141 204 4400

yards 200
metres 200

Index to street names

Firth of Clyde

The banks of the Clyde are scattered with remnants of the shipbuilding industry which once made this area a great industrial base. The first dock on the Clyde opened in Greenock in 1711. There are spectacular views across the Clyde from many of the small towns along the coast.

Clyde coast

Paisley Abbey

Paisley

This 12th century monastic settlement gave its name to the well known swirling teardrop or pine cone pattern called the Paisley Pattern after the town became the lead manufacturer of the imitation Kashmiri shawls which used the design.

Tourist Information

ℹ️ **Glasgow Airport**
Tourist Information Desk
Glasgow Airport
Paisley
Renfrewshire
PA23 2ST
☎ 0141 848 4440

ℹ️ **Paisley**
9A Gilmore Street
Paisley
Renfrewshire
PA1 1DD
☎ 0141 889 0711

miles
0   2   4   6

kilometres
0   2   4   6   8   10

Glasgow & the Clyde Valley

River Clyde at night

GLASGOW

Tourist Information

i **Glasgow**
11 George Square
Glasgow
G2 1DY
☎ 0141 204 4400

i **Hamilton**
Road Chef Services
M74 Northbound
Hamilton
Lanarkshire
ML3 6JW
☎ 01698 285590

miles
0   2   4   6
0   2   4   6   8   10
kilometres

Charles Rennie Mackintosh

Born in Glasgow in 1868 the quirky, linear, and geometric designs of Mackintosh can be seen all over the city. He studied at the Glasgow School of Art before winning a competition to design their new building which is now considered to be one of his finest works. The Lighthouse, which now houses the Mackintosh Interpretive Centre, the Scotland Street School and House for an Art Lover are all Mackintosh designs to be found around the city, although the House for an Art Lover was only built in 1996. Mackintosh was interested in all aspects of design. When working on the Willow Tea Rooms he designed everything from the building itself to the teaspoons and menu cards.

Glasgow Botanic Gardens

Glasgow parks & gardens

Glasgow has over 70 public parks many of them well worth a visit. Glasgow Green, the oldest public park in Britain, has a special place in the hearts of Glaswegians. In the west end, straddling the banks of the River Kelvin, the trees, slopes and statues of Kelvingrove Park are overlooked by the gothic towers of the University. On the south side of the city there is Pollok Park, home to the Burrell Collection. The Botanic Gardens are to the west of the city and their 42 acres (17ha) are filled with natural attractions, including the celebrated Kibble Palace glasshouse with its fabulous tree ferns, exotic plants and white marble Victorian statues.

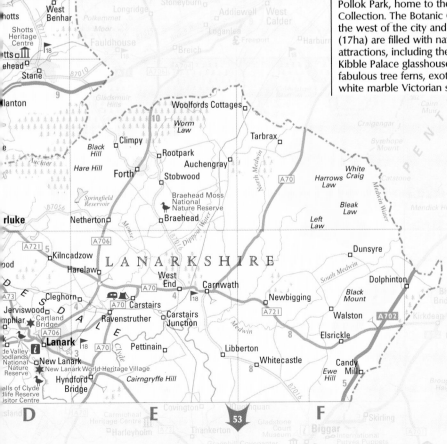

Tourist Information

ℹ️ **Lanark**
Horsemarket
Ladyacre Road
Lanark
Lanarkshire
ML11 7LQ
☎ 01555 661661

Barochan Cross `53 D3`
In Paisley Abbey, in the centre of Paisley. A fine free-standing Celtic cross that formerly stood in Houston parish, west of Paisley.
☎ *0131 668 8800*   www.historic-scotland.gov.uk

Baron's Haugh RSPB Nature Reserve `56 C4`
Motherwell. Baron's Haugh is an urban nature reserve with a variety of habitats: flooded meadow (or haugh), marshland, river, woodland and scrub.
☎ *01505 842663*   www.rspb.org.uk

Barras, The `54 C3`
Gallowgate, 0.25 miles (0.5km) east of Glasgow Cross. Glasgow's world-famous market, with an amazing variety of stalls and shops. Founded one hundred years ago, the Barras is now home to over 800 traders. Look out for the Barras archways, children's crèche and buskers. Numerous licensed premises and cafés.

Biggar Gasworks Museum `53 F2`
On the A702 in Biggar. Typical of a small town coal-gas works, the only surviving example in Scotland (dates from 1839). Managed by the Biggar Museum Trust.
☎ *01899 221050*   www.historic-scotland.gov.uk

Biggar Kirk `53 F2`
The Manse, High Street, Biggar. Cruciform 16th century church with fine examples of modern stained glass.
☎ *01899 221050*

Black Hill `52 D1`
Off the B7018, 3 miles (5km) west of Lanark. This is the site of a Bronze Age burial cairn, Iron Age hill fort, and outlook point over the Clyde Valley.
www.nts.org.uk

Bothwell Castle `56 B3`
At Uddingston off the B7071, 7 miles (11km) south east of Glasgow. In a picturesque setting above the Clyde valley, the largest and finest 13th century stone castle in Scotland. Much fought over during the Wars of Independence. Most of the castle dates from the 14th and 15th centuries.
☎ *01698 816894*   www.historic-scotland.gov.uk

Burrell Collection, The `56 A3`
Pollok Country Park, 2060 Pollokshaws Road, Glasgow. This award-winning building houses a world-famous collection gifted to Glasgow by Sir William Burrell. Visitors can see art objects from Iraq, Egypt, Greece and Italy. Tapestries, furniture, textiles, ceramics, stained glass and sculptures from medieval Europe, and drawings from the 15th to 19th centuries. Regular temporary exhibitions.
☎ *0141 287 2550*

Cadzow Castle `56 C4`
In the grounds of Chatelherault Country Park, Hamilton. Constructed between 1500 and 1550, the castle was known as 'the castle in the woods of Hamilton'.
☎ *0131 668 8800*   www.historic-scotland.gov.uk

Calderglen Country Park `56 B3`
Strathaven Road, 1 mile (1.5km) from East Kilbride. The park consists of over 440 acres (180ha) of attractive wooded gorge and parkland, including several fine waterfalls. Extensive network of paths and nature trails, visitor centre, conservatory, ornamental garden, children's zoo, toddler's play area, adventure and special needs play area centred around the historic Torrance House.
☎ *01355 236644*

Carfin Grotto & Pilgrimage Centre `56 C4`
100 Newarthill Road, Carfin, Motherwell. 12 miles (19km) east of Glasgow. The Pilgrimage Centre is situated adjacent to Carfin Grotto and offers a unique audio-visual and gallery exhibition tracing the history and tradition of pilgrimage worldwide.
☎ *01698 268941*

Carmichael Heritage Centre `53 E2`
Warrenhill Farm by Biggar, 4 miles (6.5km) south of Lanark on the A73. Scotland's only wax model collection tells Scotland's and Carmichael's story using Madame Tussaud quality models. The Clan Centre for southern Scotland concentrates on the Carmichaels but also includes information on many other southern Scottish families, as well as the history of the estate's agriculture and environment. Wind energy exhibit. Deer park. Adventure playground. Animal farm. Horse and pony trekking. Clydesdale horse and cart rides. Heritage walks. Orienteering and way-finding.
☎ *01899 308336*

Cartland Bridge `53 D1`
On the A73 west of Lanark. An impressive bridge built by Telford in 1822 over a gorge, carrying the Mouse Water. It is one of the highest road bridges in Scotland.

Castle Semple Collegiate Church `55 C3`
At Castle Semple, 4 miles (6.5km) west of Howwood. A late gothic church with a three-sided east end with windows of an unusual style.
☎ *0131 668 8800*   www.historic-scotland.gov.uk

Castle Semple Visitor Centre `55 D3`
(Clyde Muirshiel Regional Park)
Castle Semple Outdoor Centre, Lochlip Road, just off the A760 in Lochwinnoch. Located on the edge of Castle Semple Loch. Ranger service, woodland walks and nature trails in the vicinity include Peel Castle, Collegiate Church, grotto, maze and fishponds. Outdoor activities available from the centre (for taught courses, taster sessions and equipment hire) include kayaking, sailing, rowing boats, mountain biking, hill walking, orienteering and archery. Fishing permits are also available.
☎ *01505 842882*   www.clydemuirshiel.co.uk

Chatelherault Country Park `56 C4`
Carlisle Road, Ferniegair, Hamilton. A magnificent hunting lodge and kennels built in 1732 by William Adam. Extensive country walks. Exhibition on the Clyde Valley, geology and natural history of the park, 18th century gardens and parterre.
☎ *01698 426213*

City Chambers `54 B2`
George Square, Glasgow. The City Chambers is the headquarters of Glasgow City Council and arguably Glasgow's finest example of Victorian architecture. The building was opened in 1888 by Queen Victoria and to this day has preserved all its original features.
☎ *0141 287 2000*

Cloch Lighthouse `55 B2`
A770, 3 miles (4.5km) south west of Gourock. This notable landmark stands at Cloch Point with fine views across the upper Firth of Clyde estuary. The white-painted lighthouse was constructed in 1797.

Clyde Marine Cruises `55 E2`
Victoria Harbour, Greenock, 25 miles (40km) west of Glasgow. Cruises, with accommodation for up to 120 persons, to all the scenic lochs and resorts of the Upper Firth of Clyde. Pickups from Greenock, Helensburgh, Kilcreggan, Dunoon, Rothesay, Largs and Millport.
☎ *01475 721281*   www.clyde-marine.co.uk

Clyde Muirshiel Regional Park (Barnbrock Farm) `55 D3`
Kilbarchan, 4 miles (6.5km) north of Lochwinnoch just off the B786. Barnbrock Farm incorporates the headquarters of the Clyde Muirshiel Regional Park. Campsite, picnic area and easy access to nearby Locherwood Community Woodland.
☎ *01505 614791*   www.clydemuirshiel.co.uk

Clyde Valley Country Estate `52 D1`
Crossford, Carluke. Garden centre, narrow gauge railway, bird of prey centre, putting green, woodland walks.
☎ *01555 860691*

Clydebuilt `56 A3`
Scottish Maritime Museum. Clydebuilt tells the history of Glasgow's river, its ships and its people, over the last 300 years. Hands on and interactive computer activities. Also Kyles, the oldest Clyde built ship afloat in the UK.
☎ *0141 886 1013*

Coats Observatory `53 D3`
49 Oakshaw Street West, Paisley. Designed by John Honeyman, Coats Observatory continues a tradition of astronomical, meteorological and seismic observing which started in 1883. Displays relate to the history and architecture of the building, astronomy and astronautics, meteorology and seismicity.
☎ *0141 889 2013*

Collins Gallery `54 C2`
University of Strathclyde, 22 Richmond Street, Glasgow. Temporary exhibition gallery showing annual programme ranging from contemporary, fine and applied art, photography, technology and design, and multi-media installations.
☎ *0141 548 2558*   www.strath.ac.uk/culture/collins

Colzium Estate `56 C2`
Colzium Lennox Estate, Stirling Road, Kilsyth. Outstanding collection of conifers and rare trees in a beautifully designed small walled garden. All trees well labelled. Fabulous display of snowdrops and crocuses in spring. 17th century ice house, glen walk, 15th century tower house, arboretum, curling pond, clock theatre and pitch and putt course.
☎ *0141 304 1800*

Cornalees Bridge Visitor Centre `55 B2`
(Clyde Muirshiel Regional Park)
Loch Thom, Inverkip. Stepped boardwalk trails and woodland walks through Shielhill Glen, access to the Greenock Cut and Kelly Cut for scenic walks and views of the Clyde estuary. Natural and local history exhibitions. Indoor games with environmental themes. Navigation and orienteering courses. Children's activities in the summer, guided walks, ranger service.
☎ *01475 521458*   www.clydemuirshiel.co.uk

Coulter Motte `53 F2`
1.5 miles (2.5km) south west of Biggar. Early medieval castle mound, originally moated and probably surrounded by a palisade enclosing a timber tower.
☎ *01555 860364*   www.historic-scotland.gov.uk

Craignethan Castle `52 D1`
Blackwood, Lesmahagow. An extensive and well-preserved ruin of an unusual and ornate 16th century tower house. It is defended by an outer wall pierced by gun ports, also by a wide and deep ditch with a most unusual caponier (a stone vaulted chamber for artillery). Attacked and dismantled by the Protestant party in 1579. In a very picturesque setting overlooking the River Nethan.
☎ *01555 860364*   www.historic-scotland.gov.uk

Crookston Castle `56 A3`
Off Brockburn Road, Pollok. The altered ruin of an unusual 15th century castle. It consists of a central tower with four square corner towers, set within 12th century earthworks. Affords excellent views of south west Glasgow.
☎ *0131 668 8800*   www.historic-scotland.gov.uk

Cross of Lorraine `55 B2`
Lyle Hill, Greenock (access via Newton Street). Monument to the contribution made by the Free French Navy during World War II. The Cross of Lorraine is situated at a popular viewpoint overlooking the Clyde.

✷ Croy Hill   56 C2
Between Croy and Dullatur. The site of a Roman fort (not visible) on the Antonine Wall. Part of the wall ditch can be seen, beside two beacon platforms on the west side of the hill.
☎ 0131 668 8800   www.historic-scotland.gov.uk

🏛 Cumbernauld Museum   56 C2
Cumbernauld Library. Tells the history of Cumbernauld from the setting of a Roman camp, to the parlour of a 1930s miner. Audio-visual techniques bring the past to life.
☎ 01236 725664

🌿 Dalzell Park   56 C4
Adele Street, Motherwell. Peaceful woodland with spectacular scenery and heritage monuments such as Dalzell House and Lord Gavin's Temple. Wildlife includes woodpeckers, roe deer and squirrels. Ranger service.
☎ 01698 266155

🏛 David Livingstone Centre   56 B3
165 Station Road, Blantyre. In the tenement where Livingstone was born. Displays chart his life, from his childhood in the mills to his exploration of Africa.
☎ 01698 823140   www.nts.org.uk

🐾 Drumpellier Country Park   56 C3
Townhead Road, 2 miles (3km) from Coatbridge. Five hundred acres (202ha) of wood, heath and loch. There is a visitor centre, road train, angling, boating, nature trails, golf course and driving range, butterfly house, pets' corner and play areas.
☎ 01236 422257

⚓ Dullatur   56 C2
0.6 mile (1km) east of Dullatur. A well-preserved section of ditch. Part of the Antonine wall.
www.historic-scotland.gov.uk

🐪 Falls of Clyde Wildlife Reserve & Visitor Centre   53 D1
The Scottish Wildlife Trust Visitor Centre, New Lanark. One of Britain's most spectacular waterfalls set in a mosaic of ancient woodland, meadow and ancient monuments. Over 100 species of birds have been recorded on the reserve, with unsurpassed views of breeding peregrine falcons. The ranger service based at the visitor centre provides a comprehensive events programme, including badger watches, bat walks, insect expeditions and waterfall day walks.
☎ 01555 665262   www.swt.org

✷ Forth & Clyde Canal   56 A2
One of the biggest canal restoration projects in Europe, the Millennuim Link has brought the 69 miles (110km) of canal, from Glasgow to Edinburgh and the Forth to the Clyde, back to life. The towing path provides delightful walks through town and country with plenty of interest for both nature and history enthusiasts. Excursions by canal boat are available.
☎ 01324 671217   www.scottishcanals.co.uk

✷ Fossil Grove   56 A3
Victoria Park, Glasgow. Fossil stumps and roots of trees which grew here 350 million years ago. Discovered by accident and now designated a Site of Special Scientific Interest.
☎ 0141 950 1448

🏛 Gallery of Modern Art   54 B2
Queen Street, Glasgow. The elegant Royal Exchange building displays works by living artists from around the world. A wide range of temporary exhibitions plus a programme of events including music, drama, dance and workshops.
☎ 0141 229 1996

✷ George Square   54 B2
Glasgow city centre. The heart of Glasgow with the City Chambers and statues of Sir Walter Scott, Queen Victoria, Prince Albert, Robert Burns, Sir John Moore, Lord Clyde, Thomas Campbell, Dr Thomas Graham, James Oswald, James Watt, William Gladstone and Sir Robert Peel.

🏛 Gladstone Court Museum   53 F2
North Back Road, Biggar. On the A702, 26 miles (41.5km) south of Edinburgh. An indoor street museum of shops and windows. Grocer, photographer, dress maker, bank, school, library, ironmonger, chemist, china merchant, telephone exchange.
☎ 01899 221573

❀ Glasgow Botanic Garden   56 A3
730 Great Western Road, Glasgow, 1.5 miles (2.5km) west from the city centre. The gardens were formed in 1817 to provide a source of plant material for use in teaching medicine and botany. Today they are valued by tourists and as a centre for education, conservation and research. Specialist plant collections include exotic Australian tree and filmy ferns, orchids and tropical begonias.
☎ 0141 334 2422

✝ Glasgow Cathedral   54 C2
Cathedral Square, Cathedral Street. The only Scottish mainland medieval cathedral to have survived the Reformation complete (apart from its western towers). Built during the 12th and 13th centuries over the supposed tomb of St Kentigern. Notable features are the elaborately vaulted crypt, the stone screen and the unfinished Blackadder Aisle. The parish church of Glasgow.
☎ 0141 552 6891   www.historic-scotland.gov.uk

✷ Glasgow Ducks   56 A3
The Clyde River Boatyard, Kings Inch Road, Renfrew. The only tour company in Scotland offering a city tour and river experience rolled into one. Visitors can enjoy a journey through the city and on the River Clyde on an amphibious craft.
☎ 0870 013 6140   www.glasgowducks.com

✷ Glasgow School of Art   54 A1
167 Renfrew Street, Glasgow. Charles Rennie Mackintosh's architectural masterpiece. The Mackintosh Building has taken its place as one of the most influential and significant structures of the 20th century. Regular guided tours let you experience this famous and fascinating art school.
☎ 0141 353 4526   www.gsa.ac.uk

✷ Glasgow Science Centre   56 A3
On the south bank of the River Clyde. Three attractions on one site. Scotland's first IMAX theatre, a large screen format offering a 2D/3D sound and visual experience. The Science Mall, four floors of dynamic and engaging science exhibits. The Glasgow Tower, which at 328ft (100m) high is the highest free-standing structure in Scotland, and the only 360 degree rotating structure in the world.
☎ 0141 4205000   www.gsc.org.uk

⅄ Glasgow Zoopark   56 B3
Calderpark, Uddingston, 6 miles (9.5km) east of Glasgow city centre. Spacious enclosures set in wooded parkland and featuring a regular programme of animal and parrot displays, bird of prey flying displays, and snake handling. Animals include lions, tigers, monkeys, rhinos and bears.
☎ 0141 771 1185

❀ Greenbank Garden   56 A4
Flenders Road, Clarkston, 6 miles (10km) south of Glasgow city centre. Attractive garden surrounding an elegant Georgian house. Wide range of ornamental plants – especially interesting for owners of small gardens.
☎ 0141 639 3281   www.nts.org.uk

🏠 Greenhill Covenanter House   53 F2
Burnbraes in Biggar. Farmhouse, rescued in a ruinous condition and rebuilt, 10 miles (16km) from its original site. Exhibits include relics of local Covenanters, Donald Cargill's bed (1681), 17th century furnishings and costume dolls.
☎ 01899 221572

🏛 HM Customs & Excise Museum & Exhibition   55 E2
Custom House, Custom House Quay, Greenock, 25 miles (40km) west of Glasgow. A magnificent building which has been used as a customs office since its completion in 1819. The museum shows the diverse and colourful history of the organisation and highlights the great variety of work undertaken by the department.
☎ 01475 726331

⚱ Hamilton Mausoleum   56 C4
In the centre of Hamilton, just off the M74. A grandiose family tomb commissioned by the 10th Duke of Hamilton in the 18th century. An enormous cupola, massive bronze doors, an octagonal chapel guarded by stone lions and an Egyptian sarcophagus crowning a marble pedestal. The chapel was never used for worship – it has a notorious resounding echo which lasts for 15 seconds.
☎ 01698 328232

🏆 Hamilton Park Racecourse   56 C4
Hamilton, 15 miles (24km) south east of Glasgow. Daytime, evening and weekend horse race meetings with annual themed events. Public enclosure with access to grandstand. Corporate hospitality.
☎ 01698 283806   www.hamilton-park.co.uk

🏆 Hampden Park Stadium   56 A3
Hampden Park, Glasgow. Scotland's national football stadium and home of Queen's Park FC. It has retained its oval shape since opening in 1903. Extensive redevelopment in the 1990s brought the capacity to 52,500.
☎ 0141 620 4000   www.hampden.org.uk

🏛 Heatherbank Museum of Social Work   54 B1
Glasgow Caledonian University, City Campus, Cowcaddens Road, Glasgow. Permanent and temporary exhibition to highlight public awareness of the social welfare needs of society through contemporary and historical issues. Book, picture resources and ephemera. Libraries and archives available for research.
☎ 0141 331 8637   www.lib.gcal.ac.uk/heatherbank

🏠 Holmwood House   56 A4
61–63 Netherlee Road, off the B767 in Cathcart, Glasgow. Alexander Greek Thomson, Glasgow's greatest Victorian architect, designed this villa for a local mill owner in 1857. Many rooms are richly ornamented in wood, plaster and marble.
☎ 0141 637 2129   www.nts.org.uk

🏛 House for an Art Lover   56 A3
Bellahouston Park, 10 Dumbreck Road, 3 miles (5km) south of Glasgow city centre. A house designed in 1901 by Charles Rennie Mackintosh but not built until 1989–96. Exhibition and film showing the construction. Permanent exhibition of Mackintosh rooms. Sculpture park. Situated in parkland adjacent to magnificent Victorian walled gardens.
☎ 0141 353 4770   www.houseforanartlover.co.uk

✷ Hunter House   56 B3
Maxwelton Road, Calderwood, 3 miles (4.5km) east of East Kilbride town centre. An exhibition about the lives of John and William Hunter, pioneering 18th century medical surgeons. Audio-visual presentation on East Kilbride new town.
☎ 01355 261261

🏛 Hunterian Art Gallery   56 A3
82 Hillhead Street, in the west end of Glasgow. A prestigious art gallery housing many important works by old masters, impressionists and Scottish paintings from the 18th century to the present day. Includes works by Chardin, Rembrandt and Koninck and Whistler. The print gallery has a changing display from a collection of 15,000 prints. Also houses the Mackintosh House, a reconstructed interior of the architect's own house in Glasgow, using original furniture, prints and designs.
☎ 0141 330 5431

🏛 **Hunterian Museum**   56 A3

University of Glasgow in the west end of Glasgow. Scotland's first public museum was established in 1807 based on the vast collections of Dr William Hunter (1718–83). Many items from his valuable collections are on display.
☎ *0141 330 4221*   www.hunterian.gla.ac.uk

✹ **Hutchesons' Hall**   54 B2

158 Ingram Street, in Glasgow city centre. Built 1802–5, this is one of the most elegant buildings in Glasgow. Incorporates statues from an earlier building (1641) of local philanthropists George and Thomas Hutcheson. Enlarged in 1876.
☎ *0141 552 8391*   www.nts.org.uk

👣 **International Purves Puppets**   53 F2

Biggar Puppet Theatre, Broughton Road, Biggar. A unique Victorian puppet theatre seating 100 and set in beautiful grounds. Mysterious glowing scenery, large-scale puppets, secret passages and magical starry ceiling. Regular performances in many languages for all ages. Backstage and museum tours.
☎ *01899 220631*   www.purvespuppets.com

🏛 **John Hastie Museum**   52 B1

8 Threestanes Road, 6 miles (10km) south of East Kilbride. A local history museum with displays on the town, weaving, commerce, Covenanters, ceramics.
☎ *01357 521257*

🏛 **Kelvingrove Art Gallery & Museum**   56 A3

Kelvingrove in the west end of Glasgow. This fine national art collection contains superb paintings and sculptures, silver and ceramics, European armour, weapons and firearms, clothing, and furniture. The natural history of Scotland is treated in depth and there are displays of relics from Scotland's history and prehistory. Activities for children and temporary exhibitions.
☎ *0141 287 2699*

✞ **Kempock Stone**   55 B2

Castle Mansions of Gourock. Granny Kempock's stone, of grey schist 6ft (2m) high, was probably significant in prehistoric times. In past centuries it was used by fishermen in rites to ensure fair weather. Couples intending to wed used to encircle the stone to get Granny's blessing.

✹ **Leadhills & Wanlockhead Railway**   53 D4

Leadhills, 6 miles (9.5km) from the M74. Britain's highest adhesion railway, reaching 1498ft (456.5m) above sea level. Originally built in 1900 for the transport of refined lead to central Scotland. The diesel hauled journey takes approximately 25 minutes through picturesque countryside.
☎ *01555 820778*   www.leadhillsrailway.co.uk

✹ **Leadhills Miners' Library & Reading Room**   53 D4

15 Main Street, Leadhills. The lead miners' subscription library established in 1741 with rare books, detailed 18th century mining documents and local records.
☎ *01659 74326*

🏛 **Lighthouse, The**   54 B2

11 Mitchell Lane, in Glasgow city centre. The Lighthouse is Scotland's Centre for Architecture, Design and the City and is the long term legacy of Glasgow 1999 UK City of Architecture and Design. It is the imaginative conversion of Charles Rennie Mackintosh's first public commission. Mackintosh Interpretation Centre, interactive play environment for young children, IT hotspot and the Young Designers Gallery.
☎ *0141 225 8414*   www.thelighthouse.co.uk

✐ **Literary Tour**   54 B2

Meet at George Square by the statue of Sir Walter Scott. This two hour promenade performance, led by professional actors moves between George Square and the Merchant City, past Glasgow Cathedral and other historic streets and buildings, exploring Glasgow's influence on writers and poets, ancient and modern.
☎ *0131 226 6665/7*   www.scot-lit-tour.co.uk

🐦 **Lochwinnoch RSPB Nature Reserve**   55 C3

Lochwinnoch, south west of Glasgow. A varied nature reserve encompassing marshland, open water and woodland. A range of wildlife can be seen all year round, including great-crested grebes and the elusive otter. Visitor centre.
☎ *01505 842663*

🏛 **Low Parks Museum**   56 C4

129 Muir Street, Motehill, Hamilton. Combines the former Hamilton District Museum with the Cameronians (Scottish Rifles) Regimental Museum. Displays on the Hamilton Estate, coal mining, textiles, agriculture and Covenantors.
☎ *01698 328232*

✹ **Lunderston Bay (Clyde Muirshiel Regional Park)**   55 B2

Lunderston Bay on the Clyde Coast. Panoramic views to the Cowal peninsula, ranger service, coastal walks, rock pools, children's play area, beach and picnic spots.
☎ *01475 521458*   www.clydemuirshiel.co.uk

✹ **Mackinnon Mills**   56 C3

Kirkshaws Road, Coatbridge, 10 miles (16km) east of Glasgow. Factory shopping with knitwear, designer label garments and everything for the golfer.
☎ *01236 440702*

🏛 **McLean Museum & Art Gallery**   55 B2

15 Kelly Street, Greenock. A museum showing local history, maritime exhibits, ethnography, Egyptology, big game mounts and fine art. Also items relating to James Watt. Programme of temporary exhibitions in the art galleries.
☎ *01475 715624*

🏛 **McLellan Galleries**   54 A1

270 Sauchiehall Street, Glasgow. This purpose-built exhibition gallery which opened in 1854 provides Glasgow with a superb temporary exhibition venue, the largest outside London.
☎ *0141 332 7521*

🏛 **Moat Park Heritage Centre**   53 F2

Kirkstyle, Biggar. A former church adapted to display the geology and history of the Upper Clyde and Tweed Valleys, from the days of the volcano and the glacier to the present. A fine collection of embroidery, including the largest known patchwork cover containing over 80 figures from the 1850s. Archaeology collection.
☎ *01899 221050*

👣 **Motherwell Concert Hall & Theatre**   56 C4

Civic Centre, Motherwell. Venue for performances by some of the foremost stars of theatre, television and stage. Doubles as Motherwell Moviehouse showing a programme of popular films.
☎ *01698 267515*

🏛 **Motherwell Heritage Centre**   56 C4

1 High Road, Motherwell. A superb new attraction, telling the story of the Motherwell area from Roman times to the present day. Visit the Technopolis interactive media display and walk through time to see the industrial heyday of the area, social and political upheavals and the development of the modern town.
☎ *01698 251000*

🦉 **Muirshiel Visitor Centre (Clyde Muirshiel Regional Park)**   55 C3

4 miles (6.5km) north west of Lochwinnoch, off the B786. In Calder Glen, originally a Victorian sporting estate. Woodland, riverside and waterfall walks and coded trails, picnic and barbecue sites and boardwalk access to scenic viewpoint, Windyhill. The area is rich in archaeological sites including a barytes mine.
☎ *01505 842803*   www.clydemuirshiel.co.uk

🏛 **Museum of Scottish Country Life**   56 B3

East Kilbride. This unique museum offers visitors an insight into the working lives of people in rural Scotland and shows how the countryside was once worked by generations of farmers. The museum houses the national collection of country life exhibits, an events area and the original Georgian farmhouse and steading. The farm follows a pattern of seasonal work to show ploughing, seed time, haymaking and harvest. Special events are held throughout the year.
☎ *01355 224181*   www.nms.ac.uk/countrylife

🏛 **Museum of Transport**   56 A3

Kelvin Hall, 1 Bunhouse Road. The history of transport on land and sea with vehicles from horse-drawn carriages to motorcycles, fire engines, railway engines, steam and motor cars. The Clyde Room contains ship models. Also a recreated Glasgow street circa 1938, and a reconstructed underground station.
☎ *0141 287 2720*

✹ **Necropolis**   54 C2

Castle Street, behind Glasgow Cathedral. Remarkable and extensive burial ground laid out in 1833, with numerous elaborate tombs of 19th century illustrious Glaswegians and others; of particular interest is the Menteith Mausoleum of 1842.
☎ *0141 287 3961*

✹ **New Lanark World Heritage Village**   53 D1

1 mile (2km) south of Lanark. New Lanark is the best example in Scotland of an industrial heritage village. Founded in 1785 by Scottish industrialist David Dale, it was the scene of early social experiments by Dale's son-in-law Robert Owen (1771–1858), whose far-reaching ideas on the care of his workers and the formation of man's character made New Lanark famous. The award-winning visitor centre gives visitors a glimpse of life under Owen's paternalistic management, especially through the New Millennium Experience, an innovative dark ride. Passport ticket also includes the Millworkers' House, Village Store, Robert Owen's House and Robert Owen's School. New Lanark is a nominated World Heritage Site.
☎ *01555 661345*   www.newlanark.org

🏰 **Newark Castle**   55 C2

On the A8 in Port Glasgow. A large turreted mansion house in a remarkably good state of preservation, with a 15th century tower, a courtyard and hall.
☎ *01475 741858*   www.historic-scotland.gov.uk

✝ **Old Parish Church, Hamilton**   56 C4

Strathmore Road, Hamilton. The oldest building in Hamilton, a Georgian masterpiece designed by William Adam 1732–34, and the only church designed by him. Embroidery work and exceptionally detailed glass windows depicting the history of the church. Well-preserved 11th century Netherton Cross.
☎ *01698 281905*

✝ **Paisley Abbey**   55 D3

Abbey Close, Paisley. A fine Cluniac abbey church founded in 1163. Some 12th century walls remain, but most of the nave dates from the 14th and 15th centuries. Restored transept and choir. Fine medieval carvings in St Mirin Chapel, stained glass and Cavaille-Coll Organ. The Abbey contains the Barochan Cross, a weathered Celtic cross attributed to the 10th century.
☎ *0141 889 7654*

🏛 **Paisley Museum & Art Galleries**   55 D3

High Street, Paisley. Displays a world-famous collection of Paisley shawls. Also the local, industrial and natural history of Paisley and Renfrewshire. Important ceramic collection and many 19th century Scottish paintings.
☎ *01505 842615*

Palacerigg Country Park   56 C2

Palacerigg Road, 3 miles (5km) east of Cumbernauld. A 700 acre (283ha) country park with a Scottish and north European animal collection. Home to populations of roe deer, owls, bison, wildcat, lynx and moufflon. Nature trails, bridle paths and golf course.
☎ 01236 720047

People's Palace   54 C3

Glasgow Green, Glasgow. Opened in 1898, this collection displays the story of Glasgow and its people, and its impact on the world from 1175 to the present day. Important collections relating to the tobacco and other industries, stained glass, ceramics, political and social movements including temperance, co-operation, woman's suffrage and socialism. Photographs, film sequences and reminiscences bring to life the city's past.
☎ 0141 554 0223

Piping Centre   54 B1

30–34 McPhater Street, Cowcaddens. In Glasgow city centre. A national and international centre of excellence for the bagpipes and their music, incorporating a school with rehearsal rooms and a performance hall, a museum and interpretation centre, a reference library and conference facilities. Housed in a fine listed building.
☎ 0141 353 0220   www.thepipingcentre.co.uk

Pollok House   56 A3

Pollok Country Park, 2060 Pollokshaws Road, 3 miles (5km) south of Glasgow city centre. Built in 1740 and extended in 1890 by Sir John Stirling Maxwell. Set within Pollok Country Park (not NTS), the house contains a renowned collection of paintings and furnishings appropriate for an Edwardian country house.
☎ 0141 616 6410   www.nts.org.uk

Provand's Lordship   54 C2

3 Castle Street, Glasgow. The oldest dwelling in Glasgow, built in 1471 as a manse for the St Nicholas Hospital. Period displays and furniture. Tranquil recreated medieval/renaissance herb garden.
☎ 0141 552 8819

Queen's Cross Church   56 A3

870 Garscube Road, Glasgow. The only church designed by Charles Rennie Mackintosh and now the headquarters of the Charles Rennie Mackintosh Society. Built 1898–9 in a perpendicular Gothic style.
☎ 0141 946 6600   www.crmsociety.com

Renfrew Community Museum   56 A3

41 Canal Street, Renfrew. Located in the former Brown Institute building, the museum illustrates local history.
☎ 0141 886 3149   www.renfrewshire.gov.uk

Rouken Glen   56 A4

Thornliebank, south Glasgow. One of Glasgow's most attractive parks with shaded walks and a waterfall. Children's playground, boating pond and garden centre.
☎ 0141 577 3913

Royal Highland Fusiliers Regimental Museum   54 A1

518 Sauchiehall Street, Glasgow. A museum exhibiting medals, badges, uniforms and records which illustrate the histories of The Royal Scots Fusiliers, The Highland Light Infantry, the Royal Highland Fusiliers and Princess Margaret's Own Glasgow and Ayrshire Regiment.
☎ 0141 332 0961   www.rhf.org.uk

St Bride's Church   52 D2

In Douglas, 12 miles (19km) south-west of Lanark. The restored choir and south side of the nave of a late 14th century parish church. The choir contains three canopied monuments to the Douglas family.
☎ 01555 851657   www.historic-scotland.gov.uk

St Mungo Heritage Centre   54 C2

Sited in the Wellpark Brewery in Glasgow's East End. This is the only surviving brewery in Glasgow and it uses traditional materials and methods. The Heritage Centre contains an extensive array of brewing equipment, much of which has been restored to its former glory.
☎ 0141 552 6552

St Mungo Museum of Religious Life & Art   54 C2

2 Castle Street, next to Glasgow Cathedral. A unique museum exploring the universal themes of life, death and the hereafter through beautiful and evocative art objects associated with different religious faiths. Includes Britain's only authentic Japanese Zen garden.
☎ 0141 553 2557

Scotkart Indoor Kart Racing Centre, Cambuslang   56 B3

Westburn Road, Cambuslang, 4 miles (6.5km) from Glasgow city centre. A large indoor motorsport centre featuring 200cc pro-karts capable of over 40mph. The track can be booked for practice lapping or visitors can compete in a professionally organised race meeting. All equipment and instruction provided.
☎ 0141 641 0222   www.scotkart.co.uk

Scotland Street School Museum of Education   56 A3

225 Scotland Street, 1 mile (2km) south of Glasgow city centre. A magnificent building with twin leaded towers and Glasgow style stone carving designed by Charles Rennie Mackintosh in 1904. Now housing a permanent exhibition on the history of education. There are Victorian, World War II, 1950s and 1960s classrooms, a drill hall and an Edwardian cookery room.
☎ 0141 287 0500

Scottish Exhibition & Conference Centre (SECC)   56 A3

Glasgow. Scotland's national venue for public events and the UK's largest integrated exhibition and conference centre. The Clyde Auditorium or 'Armadillo' forms part of the complex and is an architectural landmark on the riverside.
☎ 0141 248 3000   www.secc.co.uk

Scottish Football Museum   56 A3

Hampden Park, in the Mount Pleasant area in the south of Glasgow. Glasgow was the site of the world's first football international in 1872, when Scotland and England drew 0–0. The museum features the origins and history of the game, women's football, junior football and football fans. Visitors can see the reconstructed changing rooms and press box. Also memorabilia of Scottish football players.
☎ 0141 620 4000   www.scottishfootballmuseum.org.uk

Shotts Heritage Centre   57 D3

Shotts Library, Benhar Road, Shotts. Displays three life-size exhibits – Covenanters, a coal mine and 1940s shop front scene. Photographs and illustrations of local history and heritage.
☎ 01501 821556

Sma' Shot Cottages   53 D3

11–17 George Place, Paisley. A former 18th century weaver's cottage, with domestic accommodation and loom shop, linked by a garden to a 19th century artisan's house, both fully furnished. Exhibition of historic photographs and a fine collection of china and linen. Run by the Old Paisley Society.
☎ 0141 889 1708

Strathclyde Country Park   56 C4

366 Hamilton Road, Motherwell. 10 miles (16km) south of Glasgow. A 1000 acre (404ha) countryside park set in the Clyde valley. Artificial lake, mixed parkland and woodlands, and a variety of recreational facilities, including watersports. Woodland trails, countryside walks, sports pitches, sandy beaches, a caravan site, a hotel, an inn and Scotland's first theme park. The visitor centre depicts the history and wildlife of the park. Also remains of a Roman bathhouse.
☎ 01698 266155

Summerlee Heritage Park   56 C3

Heritage Way, Coatbridge. Summerlee Heritage Park is described as Scotland's noisiest museum, interpreting the history of the local steel and engineering industries and of the communities that depended upon them. It contains reconstructed miners' rows, a mine and a tramway. Guided tours include the coal mine where visitors go underground and see the workings of a mine. The Ironworks Gallery houses a programme of temporary exhibitions.
☎ 01236 431261

Tall Ship at Glasgow Harbour, The   56 A3

100 Stobcross Road, Glasgow. West off Clydeside Expressway. Glasgow's maritime heritage is brought to life at the Tall Ship at Glasgow Harbour, home to the Glenlee (1896). Exhibitions and children's activities.
☎ 0141 339 0631   www.thetallship.com

Tenement House   54 A1

145 Buccleuch Street, Glasgow. A typical late Victorian Glasgow tenement flat, retaining many original features. The furniture and possessions of the woman who lived here for 50 years give a fascinating glimpse of life in the early 20th century.
☎ 0141 333 0183   www.nts.org.uk

Time Capsule   56 C3

100 Buchanan Street, Coatbridge. Swim through primeval swamps, ride the rapids, skate with a 14ft (4m) woolly mammoth and slide down the time tunnel. Also Nardini's Water Babies park, ideal for toddlers.
☎ 01236 449572   www.timecapsule.co.uk

Tollpark & Garnhall   56 C2

West of Castlecary, this is a well-preserved section of the ditch of the Antonine Wall.
☎ 0131 668 8800   www.historic-scotland.gov.uk

Viewpark Gardens   56 C3

New Edinburgh Road, Viewpark, Uddingston. Off the M74 at Bellshill exit. With its ornamental gardens and colourful displays, Viewpark Gardens comprises glasshouse displays, plant collections, horticultural demonstrations, and various themed gardens including Highland, Japanese and Demonstration.
☎ 01698 818269

Waverley Paddle Steamer   54 A3

Anderston Quay, Glasgow. Historically one of the most interesting vessels still in operation in the country, the Waverley is the last paddle steamer to be built for service on the Clyde, and is now the last sea-going paddle steamer in the world. A variety of cruises from Glasgow and Ayr along the Clyde coast.
☎ 0141 221 8152

Weavers Cottage   55 D3

Shuttle Street, Kilbarchan, 5 miles (8km) west of Paisley. This typical cottage of an 18th century handloom weaver contains looms, weaving equipment and domestic utensils. Displays of local, historical and weaving items.
☎ 01505 705588   www.nts.org.uk

Willow Tea Rooms   54 A1

217 Sauchiehall Street, Glasgow. The Willow Tea Rooms are housed in an original Charles Rennie Mackintosh building, designed for Miss Cranston 1904–28. Re-opened in 1983, the tearoom still has the original glass and mirror work and doors, and functions as a restaurant serving light meals, teas and coffees.
☎ 0141 332 0521   www.willowtearooms.co.uk

Central West Scotland

From the islands of Coll and Tiree, lying in the Hebridean Sea to the west, to the green slopes of the Ochil Hills east of Stirling, this area of Scotland straddles Highland and Lowland.

Peaceful glens, shapely peaks and clear blue lochs contrast vividly with the gentle hills and historic towns of the lowlands. Visit Stirling, which played a leading role in Scotland's past, or travel by ferry from Oban to the Isle of Mull, and on to Iona, cradle of Scottish Christianity.

West coast islands

The western coast is indented with inlets and lochs formed by glaciers thousands of years ago. The larger islands of Coll, Tiree, Mull, Colonsay, Jura and Islay each have their own character though all are part of the Inner Hebrides. Oban is the 'Gateway to the Isles' with ferries to many of the islands. Wildlife tours and cruises are on offer to experience the diverse natural wonders of the area.

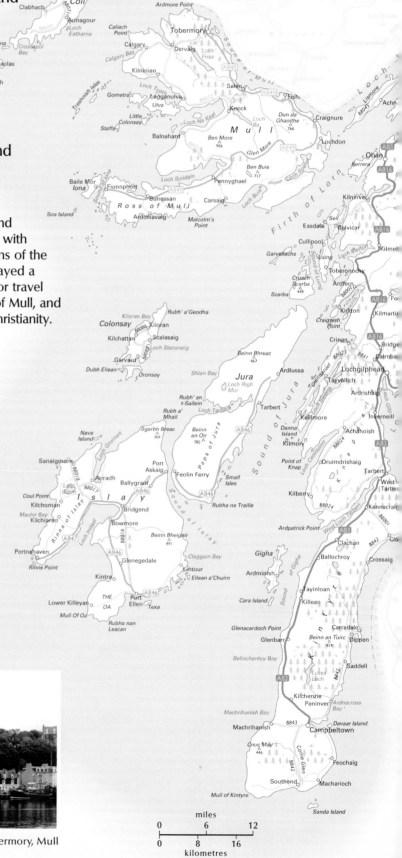

Tobermory, Mull

miles
0   6   12
0   8   16
kilometres

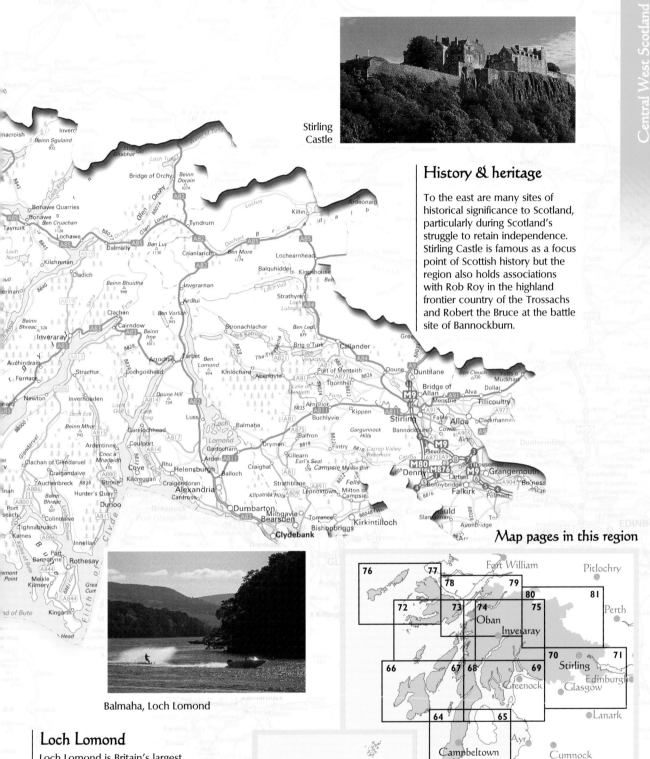

Stirling
Castle

History & heritage

To the east are many sites of historical significance to Scotland, particularly during Scotland's struggle to retain independence. Stirling Castle is famous as a focus point of Scottish history but the region also holds associations with Rob Roy in the highland frontier country of the Trossachs and Robert the Bruce at the battle site of Bannockburn.

Balmaha, Loch Lomond

Map pages in this region

Loch Lomond

Loch Lomond is Britain's largest stretch of inland water. It extends 24 miles (39 km) from Ardlui in the north, to Balloch in the south. Although generally narrow, the loch widens towards the south, where there are a number of wooded islands.

Argyll, the Isles, Loch Lomond, Stirling & Trossachs Tourist Board

Old Town Jail, St. John Street, Stirling, FK8 1EA

☎ 01786 445222

www.visitscottishheartlands.com

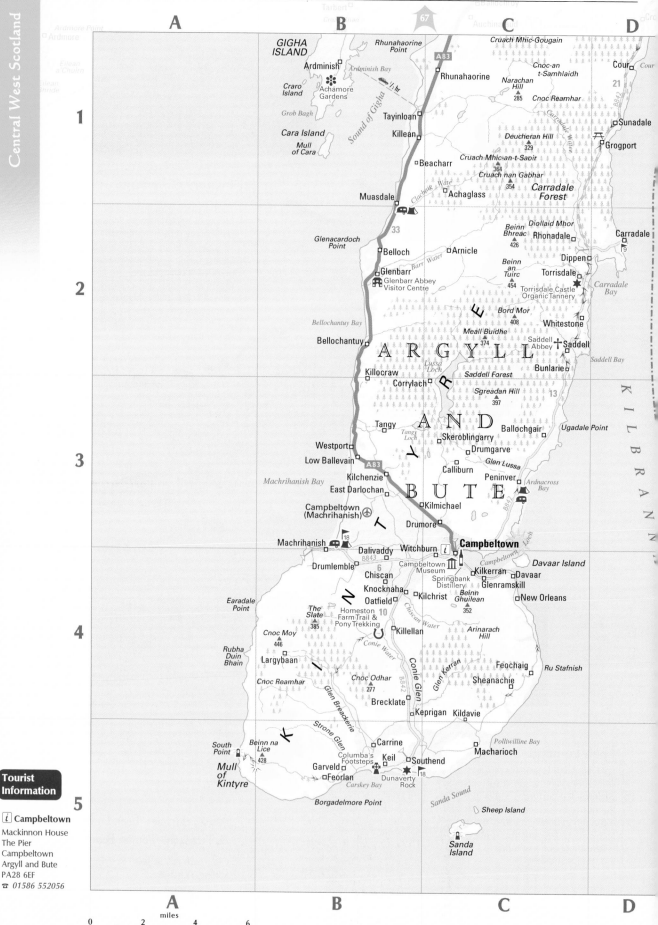

A   B   67   C   D

GIGHA ISLAND

Rhunahaorine Point

Ardminish
Ardminish Bay
1½ hr
Craro Island
Achamore Gardens
Grob Bagh
Tayinloan
Cara Island
Mull of Cara
Killean

A83
Rhunahaorine
Cruach Mhic-Gougain
Cnoc-an t-Samhlaidh
Narachan Hill 285
Cnoc Reamhar
Cour   Cour
21
Sunadale
Grogport
Deucheran Hill 329

Beacharr
Cruach Mhic-an-t-Saoir 364
Cruach nan Gabhar 354
Carradale Forest

Muasdale
Clachaig Wate
Achaglass

Barr Water
Glenacardoch Point
Belloch
Arnicle
Beinn Bhreac 426
Diollaid Mhor
Rhonadale
Carradale 9
Dippen

Glenbarr
Glenbarr Abbey Visitor Centre
Beinn an Tuirc 454
Torrisdale
Torrisdale Castle Organic Tannery
Carradale Bay

Bellochantuy Bay
Bellochantuy
Bord Mor 408
Meall Buidhe 374
Whitestone

Lussa Loch
Killocraw
Saddell Forest
Saddell Abbey
Saddell
Saddell Bay

Corrylach
Sgreadan Hill 397
13
Bunlarie

Tangy
Tangy Loch
Skeroblingarry
Ballochgair
Ugadale Point

KILBRANN

Westport
Drumgarve
Glen Lussa
Low Ballevain
A83
Calliburn
Peninver
Ardnacross Bay
Machrihanish Bay
Kilchenzie
East Darlochan
Kilmichael

Campbeltown (Machrihanish)
Drumore

Machrihanish 18
Dalivaddy
B843
Witchburn
Campbeltown
Campbeltown Museum
Davaar Island
Davaar
Davaar
Glenramskill
Drumlemble
6
Chiscan
Springbank Distillery
Kilkerran

Knocknaha
Kilchrist
Beinn Ghuilean 352
New Orleans
Oatfield
10
Homeston Farm Trail & Pony Trekking

The Slate 385
Killellan
Arinarach Hill
Cnoc Moy 446
Conie Water
Chiscan Water

Rubha Duin Bhain
Largybaan
Feochaig
Ru Stafnish
Sheanachie

Cnoc Reamhar
Choc Odhar 277
Glen Breackerie
Conie Glen
Glen Kerran
B842
Brecklate
Keprigan
Kildavie

South Point
Beinn na Lice 428
K
Strone Glen
Carrine
Polliwilline Bay
Machrioch

Mull of Kintyre
Columba's Footsteps
Garveld
Keil
Southend 18
Feorlan
Carskey Bay
Dunaverty Rock

Borgadelmore Point
Sanda Sound
Sheep Island

Sanda Island

miles
0   2   4   6
0   2   4   6   8   10
kilometres

Tourist Information

[i] **Campbeltown**

Mackinnon House
The Pier
Campbeltown
Argyll and Bute
PA28 6EF
☎ 01586 552056

D   E   68   F   G

Campbeltown

Population: 5722. Set in a sheltered bay, Campbeltown is the chief town and port of Kintyre. The town was a prosperous fishing port in the 1800s. It was also once a major centre for whisky distilling although today Springbank is the only producing distillery remaining from a former total of 34 in the area.

Common seal pups

Kintyre

Separated by only a very narrow isthmus of land at Tarbert, the 40 mile (64km) long peninsula of Kintyre is almost an island. The often windswept west coast has many beautiful beaches such as Machrihanish and there are fine views across to the islands of Jura, Islay and Gigha. The narrow east coast road crosses river gorges through moorland and forest with views across Kilbrannan Sound to the mountains of Arran.

Thistle, the national emblem of Scotland

Port Righ, Mull of Kintyre

Mull of Kintyre

Follow the spectacular road down to the headland at the south west end of Kintyre. The Mull of Kintyre was popularised by the Paul McCartney song in 1977. From the lighthouse it is only 12 miles (19km) across the water to Ireland.

1

2

14

3

4

5

Central West Scotland

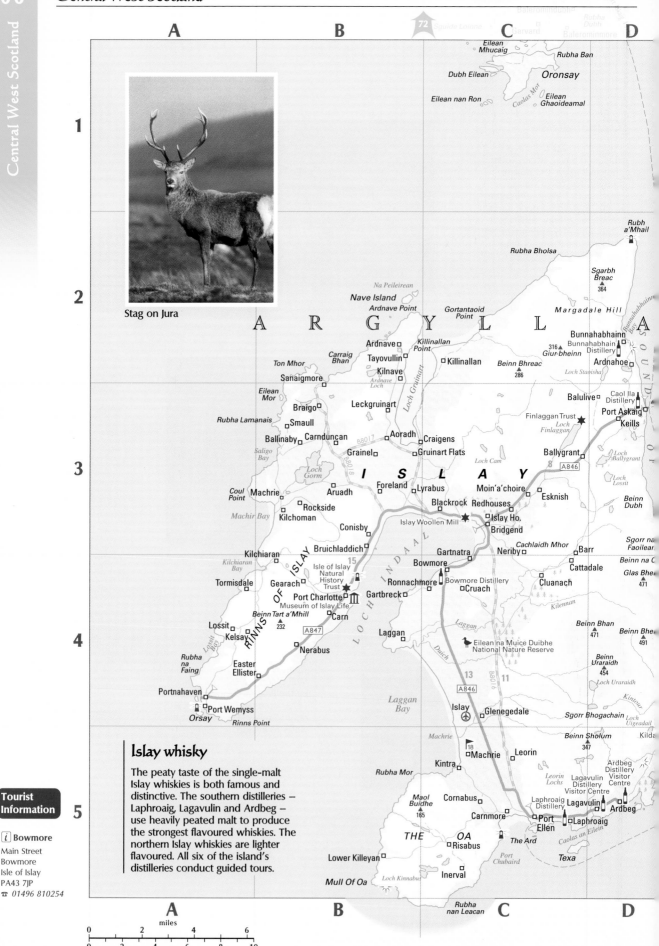

Stag on Jura

Islay whisky

The peaty taste of the single-malt Islay whiskies is both famous and distinctive. The southern distilleries – Laphroaig, Lagavulin and Ardbeg – use heavily peated malt to produce the strongest flavoured whiskies. The northern Islay whiskies are lighter flavoured. All six of the island's distilleries conduct guided tours.

Tourist Information

i **Bowmore**
Main Street
Bowmore
Isle of Islay
PA43 7JP
☎ 01496 810254

Oronsay

Eilean Mhucaig
Rubha Ban
Dubh Eilean
Eilean nan Ron
Caolas Mor
Eilean Ghaoideamal

Rubh a'Mhail
Rubha Bholsa
Sgarbh Breac 364
Margadale Hill

Na Peileirean

Nave Island
Ardnave Point
Gortantaoid Point
Beinn Bhreac 286
Bunnahabhainn
Bunnahabhain Distillery
316 *Giur-bheinn*
Ardnahoe

A R G Y L L A

Ardnave
Tayovullin
Killinallan Point
Killinallan
Caol Ila Distillery
Balulive
Port Askaig
Keills

Ton Mhor
Carraig Bhan
Kilnave
Sanaigmore
Ardnave Loch
Loch Gruinart
Leckgruinart

Eilean Mor
Braigo
Rubha Lamanais
Smaull
Ballinaby
Carnduncan
Aoradh
Craigens
Grainel
Gruinart Flats
Loch Cam
Finlaggan Trust
Loch Finlaggan
Ballygrant
Loch Ballygrant

Saligo Bay
Loch Gorm

I S L A Y

Loch Lossit

Coul Point
Machrie
Aruadh
Foreland
Lyrabus
Moin'a'choire
Esknish
Beinn Dubh

Rockside
Kilchoman
Blackrock
Redhouses
Islay Ho.
Bridgend
Cachlaidh Mhor
Barr
Sgorr na Faoilean

Machir Bay
Conisby
Islay Woollen Mill
Neriby
Beinn na C
Glas Bhei 471

Bruichladdich
Gartnatra
Cattadale
Cluanach
Beinn na

R I N N S   O F   I S L A Y
Kilchiaran
Isle of Islay Natural History Trust
15
Bowmore
Beinn Bhan 471
Beinn Bhe 491

Kilchiaran Bay
Gearach
Ronnachmore
Bowmore Distillery
Cruach
Kilennan

Tormisdale
Port Charlotte
Museum of Islay Life
Gartbreck

Lossit
Beinn Tart a'Mhill 232
Carn
A847
Laggan
Eilean na Muice Duibhe National Nature Reserve
Beinn Uraraidh 454
Loch Uraraidh

Kelsay
Nerabus

L O C H   I N D A A L
Laggan
Dutch
13
B8016
11
A846
Kintour

Rubha na Faing
Easter Ellister
Lossit Bay

Portnahaven
Port Wemyss
Orsay
Rinns Point

Laggan Bay
Islay ✈
Glenegedale
Sgorr Bhogachain
Loch Uigeadail

Beinn Sholum 347
Kilda

Machrie
18
Machrie
Leorin
Leorin Lochs
Lagavulin Distillery Visitor Centre
Ardbeg Distillery Visitor Centre

Rubha Mor
Kintra
Laphroaig Distillery Visitor Centre
Lagavulin
Ardbeg

Maol Buidhe 165
Cornabus
Carnmore
Port Ellen
Laphroaig

T H E   O A
Risabus
The Ard
Caolas an Eilein

Lower Killeyan
Texa
Port Chubaird

Inerval
Mull Of Oa
Loch Kinnabus
Rubha nan Leacan

Scale

miles
0   2   4   6

kilometres
0   2   4   6   8   10

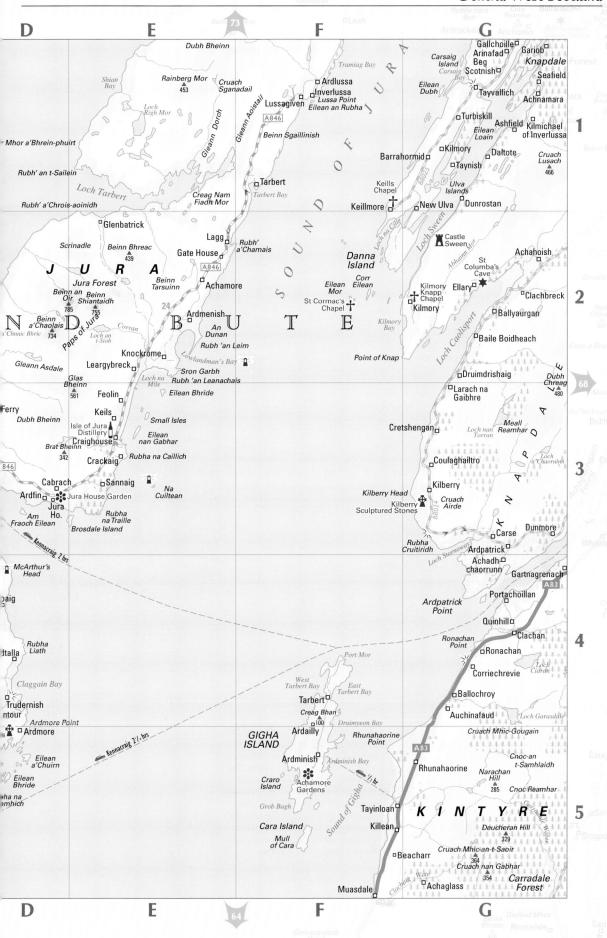

D E F G

73

Knapdale

Dubh Bheinn

Tramiag Bay

Shian Bay
Rainberg Mor
453
Cruach Sganadail

Gallchoille
Arinafad Beg
Gariob
Scotnish
Seafield

Carsaig Island
Carsaig Bay

Eilean Dubh
Tayvallich
Achnamara

Ardlussa
Inverlussa
Lussa Point
Eilean an Rubha

Lussagiven

A846

Mhor a'Bhrein-phuirt

Loch Righ Mor

Gleann Dorch

Gleann Aoistail

Beinn Sgaillinish

Turbiskill
Eilean Loain
Ashfield
Kilmichael of Inverlussa

1

Rubh' an t-Sailein

Barrahormid
Kilmory
Daltote
Cruach Lusach
466

Taynish

Rubh' a'Chrois-aoinidh

Loch Tarbert

Creag Nam Fiadh Mor

Tarbert

Tarbert Bay

Keills Chapel
Keillmore
New Ulva
Ulva Islands
Dunrostan

Glenbatrick

Lagg

Rubh' a'Chamais

Castle Sween
Abhainn Mor
Achahoish

Scrinadle
Beinn Bhreac
439

Gate House

A846

Danna Island

Loch na Cille
Loch Sween

St Columba's Cave
Ellary
Clachbreck

J U R A

Jura Forest

Beinn Tarsuinn

Achamore

Eilean Mor

St Cormac's Chapel

Corr Eilean

Kilmory Knapp Chapel
Kilmory

Achahoish

2

Beinn an Oir
785
Beinn Shiantaidh
755

Ardmenish

An Dunan

Rubh 'an Leim

Loch Caolisport

Ballyaurgan

N D

Beinn a'Chaolais
734

Corran

B U T E

Baile Boidheach

a'Chnuic Bhric

Paps of Jura

Loch an t-Siob

24

Kilmory Bay

Cnoc a'Bharaile

Point of Knap

Druimdrishaig

Dubh Chreag
480

68

Gleann Asdale

Knockrome

Lowlandman's Bay

Larach na Gaibhre

Meall Reamhar

Glas Bheinn
561

Leargybreck
Feolin

Loch na Mile

Sron Garbh
Rubh' an Leanachais

Eilean Bhride

Cretshengan

Loch nan Torran

Meall Reamhar

Dubh Bheinn

Keils

Small Isles

Eilean nan Gabhar

Coulaghailtro

Loch a'Chaorunn

Ferry

846

Isle of Jura Distillery
Craighouse

Brat Bheinn
342

Crackaig

Rubha na Caillich

Kilberry

K N A P D A L E

3

Cabrach

Sannaig

Na Cuiltean

Kilberry Head
Kilberry Sculptured Stones

Cruach Airde

B8024

Carse

Dunmore

Ardfin
Jura Ho.
Jura House Garden

Rubha na Traille

Am Fraoch Eilean

Brosdale Island

Rubha Cruitiridh

Ardpatrick

Achadh chaorunn

McArthur's Head

Kennacraig 2 hrs

Gartnagrenach

A83

Portachoillan

craig

Ardpatrick Point

Quinhill
Clachan

4

Rubha Liath

Ronachan Point

Ronachan

ttalla

Port Mor

Corriechrevie

Loch Ciaran

Claggain Bay

West Tarbert Bay
East Tarbert Bay

Ballochroy

Trudernish
ntour

Kennacraig 2¼ hrs

Tarbert
Creag Bhan
100

Auchinafaud

Loch Garasdale

Ardmore Point

Ardailly

Druimyeon Bay

Cruach Mhic-Gougain

Ardmore

GIGHA ISLAND

Rhunahaorine Point

A83

Crossaig

Eilean a'Chuirn

Ardminish

Ardminish Bay

Rhunahaorine

Cnoc-an t-Samhlaidh

Eilean Bhride

Craro Island

Achamore Gardens

½ hr

Narachan Hill
285

Cnoc Reamhar

ha na
amhich

Grob Bagh

Sound of Gigha

Tayinloan

K I N T Y R E

5

Cara Island
Mull of Cara

Killean

Deucheran Hill
329

Sunadale

Cruach Mhic-an-t-Saoir
364

Grogport

Beacharr

Cruach nan Gabhar
354

Carradale Forest

Muasdale

Achaglass

D E F G

64

Bute

An island of heather hills and flat farmland, Bute is separated from mainland Argyll by the narrow channel of the Kyles of Bute. The northern hills of Bute are most popular with walkers as they offer panoramic views. The Victorian resort of Rothesay is the island's capital. It is known for its winter gardens and colourful promenade flower displays in summer.

Tourist Information

Lochgilphead
Lochnell Street
Lochgilphead
Argyll and Bute
PA31 8JL
☎ 01546 602344

Rothesay
15 Victoria Street
Rothesay
Isle of Bute
PA20 0AJ
☎ 01700 502151

Tarbert
Harbour Street
Tarbert
Argyll and Bute
PA29 6UD
☎ 01880 820429

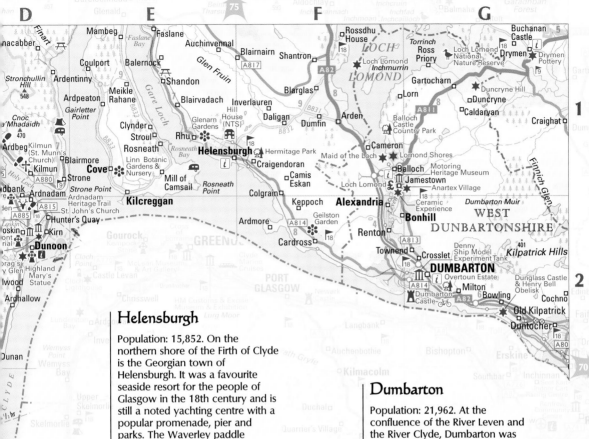

Helensburgh

Population: 15,852. On the northern shore of the Firth of Clyde is the Georgian town of Helensburgh. It was a favourite seaside resort for the people of Glasgow in the 18th century and is still a noted yachting centre with a popular promenade, pier and parks. The Waverley paddle steamer stops at Helensburgh on its route along the Firth of Clyde. The town is also the birthplace of J.L. Baird (1888 – 1946), the inventor of television.

Dumbarton

Population: 21,962. At the confluence of the River Leven and the River Clyde, Dumbarton was once important as a centre for engineering and shipbuilding. The Cutty Sark was built here in 1869. An ancient castle overlooks the town.

Dunoon

Population: 9038. Sited on the Firth of Clyde, Dunoon is the main resort on the Cowal peninsula. There are ferry services to Gourock and pleasure cruises to enjoy the coastal scenery. Dunoon is also an ideal base for exploring the network of walking trails in the nearby Argyll Forest Park.

Kyles of Bute

Tourist Information

i **Balloch**

The Old Station
Building
Balloch Road
Balloch
West Dunbartonshire
G83 8LQ
☎ 01389 753533

i **Drymen**

Drymen Library
The Square
Drymen
G63 0BL
☎ 01360 660068

i **Dumbarton**

Milton
A82 Northbound
Dumbarton
G82 2TZ
☎ 01389 742306

i **Dunoon**

7 Alexandra Parade
Dunoon
Argyll and Bute
PA23 8AB
☎ 01369 703785

i **Helensburgh**

The Clock Tower
Helensburgh
Dunbartonshire
G84 7PA
☎ 01436 672642

80
12
69
52

Tourist Information

i Stirling

41 Dumbarton Road
Stirling
Stirlingshire
FK8 2LQ
☎ 01786 475019

i Stirling Pirnhall

Pirnhall Motorway
Service Area
M9 Junction 9
Stirlingshire
FK7 8ET
☎ 01786 814111

i Stirling Royal Burgh

Royal Burgh of Stirling
Visitor Centre
Stirling
Stirlingshire
FK8 1EH
☎ 01786 479901

Falkirk

Population: 35,610. Falkirk once marked the northernmost frontier of the Roman Empire. Several sections of the Antonine Wall fortification are still visible in the town and the best of these is the ditch of Watling Lodge.

Campsie Fells

Campsie Fells

The rolling hills of the Campsie Fells reach a height of 1896ft (578m) at Earl's Seat. The source of the River Carron is on the slopes of the fells 3 miles (4km) north of Lennoxtown. Walkers can follow the Campsie Fells Trail which links pretty villages such as Balfron, Kippen and Fintry.

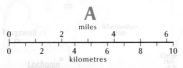

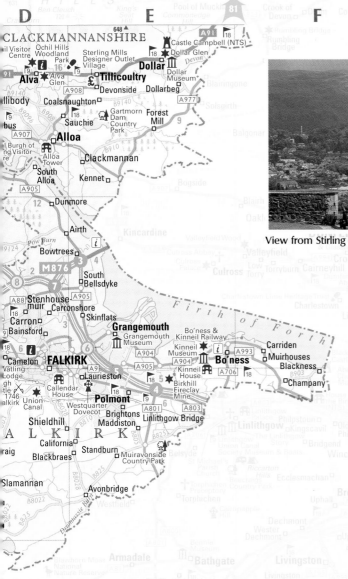

View from Stirling Castle

Stirling

Population: 30,515. This historic town sits on a volcanic rocky outcrop above the banks of the River Forth. The town grew up around the castle, and the original 16th century town walls are still visible today. There are many sites of interest within the town – the medieval castle, Cambuskenneth Abbey, Argyll's Lodging, Mar's Wark and Stirling Old Bridge. Stirling means 'Place of Strife' and it has been the site of many battles over the centuries. Two miles (3.2km) south of the town one of the most famous battles in Scottish history is explained at the Bannockburn Heritage Centre.

Blair Drummond Safari & Adventure Park

Glass blowing at Village Glass

A   B   C   D

1

Bac Mor or
Dutchman's Cap

Bac Beag

Maol na Mine
Maisgeir

Beinn
Eolasary

ULVA

Boathouse
Visitor
Centre

Acharonich

Killiemor

A'Chrannag

Eorsa

Loch Na Keal

Staffa
Eilean Dubh

Little
Colonsay

Samalan
Island

18

Fingal's
Cave

Staffa
(NTS)

Inchkenneth Chapel

Inch
Kenneth

Clachandhu

Dhiseig

Beinn
a'Ghra...

Balnahard

Beinn
Fhada

Erisgeir

Balmeanach

Coirc
Bheinn
561

Ben More
966

Guibe
Uluv...

2

Reidh
Eilean

Eilean Chalbha

Maclean's
Cross

Dun I

Iona Gallery & Pottery
Port an
Duine Mhairbh
Iona Abbey

Baile Mòr

Iona Heritage Centre

Iona (NTS)

Ruanaich

Iona

Fionnphort

Stac
an
Aoineidh

St. Columba
Centre

Fidden

Rubha
na
Carraig-geire

Sound of Iona

Rubha
nan
Cearc

Kintra

Beinn Chladan

Aridhglas

A849

Loch
na
Lathaich

Aird na h-
Iolaire

Creach
Bheinn
491

Ardmeanach

Bearraich

Burg
(NTS)

Carraig Mhic
Thomais

Ardchrishnish

Eorabus

Ardtun

Bunessan

Isle of Mull
Angora
Rabbit Farm

Lee

Gib Bheinn

Port na
Croise

Kilfinichen Bay

LOCH

SCRIDAIN

Port an
Aird Fhada

A849

Cruachan Min
376

Beinn
na
Sreine
519

Balevulin

Loch Beg

Aird of
Kinloch

Maol na
Coille
Moire

Dererach

Maol nan
Uan

Pennygha...

Killunaig

Brolass

Beinn
Chreagach
376

Cars...

Creachan
Mor

Nun's Pass

Carsais
Bay

Soa Island

Erraid

Eilean
Dubh

Eilean
a'Chalmain

Torr Fada

Aird Mor

Eilean
Mor

Knockvologan

Ardalanish

Rubh' Ardalanish

Uisken

Ardchiavaig

Port Mor

Scoor

Rubha
nam
Braithrean

Malcolm's Point

Carsaig Arches

Ross of Mull

Loch
Assapol

3

Dearg
Sgeir

Torran Rocks

Na Torrain

Ruadh Sgeir

West
Reef

McPhail's Anvil

Torran
Sgoilte

Sgeir
Ghobhlach

Otter Rock

A R G Y L L

A N D

B U T E

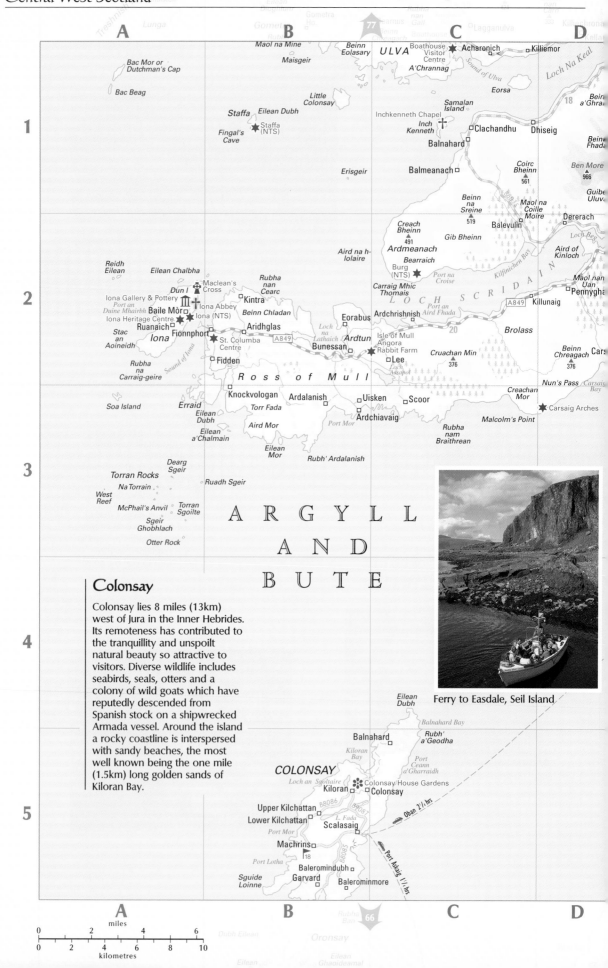

Ferry to Easdale, Seil Island

Colonsay

Colonsay lies 8 miles (13km)
west of Jura in the Inner Hebrides.
Its remoteness has contributed to
the tranquillity and unspoilt
natural beauty so attractive to
visitors. Diverse wildlife includes
seabirds, seals, otters and a
colony of wild goats which have
reputedly descended from
Spanish stock on a shipwrecked
Armada vessel. Around the island
a rocky coastline is interspersed
with sandy beaches, the most
well known being the one mile
(1.5km) long golden sands of
Kiloran Bay.

4

Eilean
Dubh

Balnahard Bay

Balnahard

Rubh'
a'Geodha

Port
Ceann
a'Gharraidh

Kiloran
Bay

COLONSAY

Loch an Sgoltaire

Kiloran

Colonsay House Gardens

Colonsay

Oban 2 1/4 hrs

5

Upper Kilchattan

Lower Kilchattan

B8086

Scalasaig

B8087

L. Fada

Port Askaig 1 1/4 hrs

Port Mor

Machrins

18

B8085

Port Lotha

Baleromindubh

Sguide
Loinne

Garvard

Balerominmore

A   B   C   D

miles

0   2   4   6

0 2 4 6 8 10

kilometres

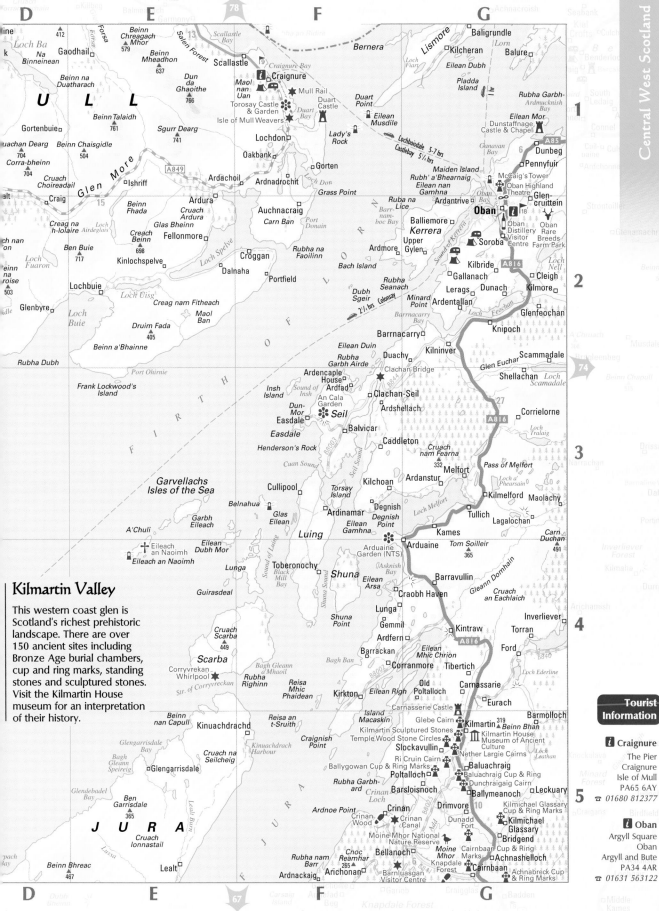

Kilmartin Valley

This western coast glen is Scotland's richest prehistoric landscape. There are over 150 ancient sites including Bronze Age burial chambers, cup and ring marks, standing stones and sculptured stones. Visit the Kilmartin House museum for an interpretation of their history.

Tourist Information

ℹ️ **Craignure**

The Pier
Craignure
Isle of Mull
PA65 6AY
☎ 01680 812377

ℹ️ **Oban**

Argyll Square
Oban
Argyll and Bute
PA34 4AR
☎ 01631 563122

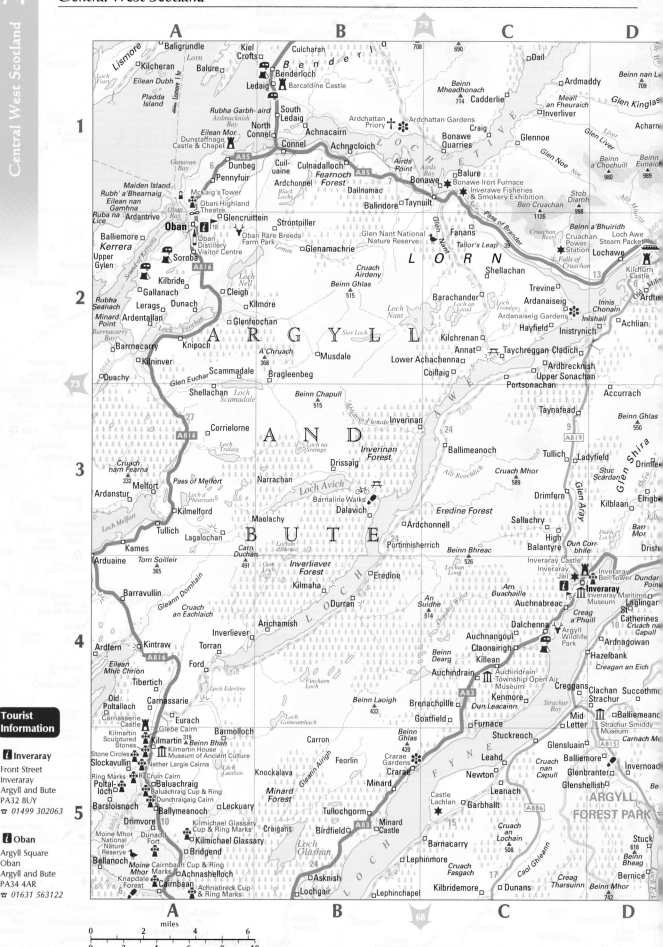

Tourist Information

i Inveraray
Front Street
Inveraray
Argyll and Bute
PA32 8UY
☎ 01499 302063

i Oban
Argyll Square
Oban
Argyll and Bute
PA34 4AR
☎ 01631 563122

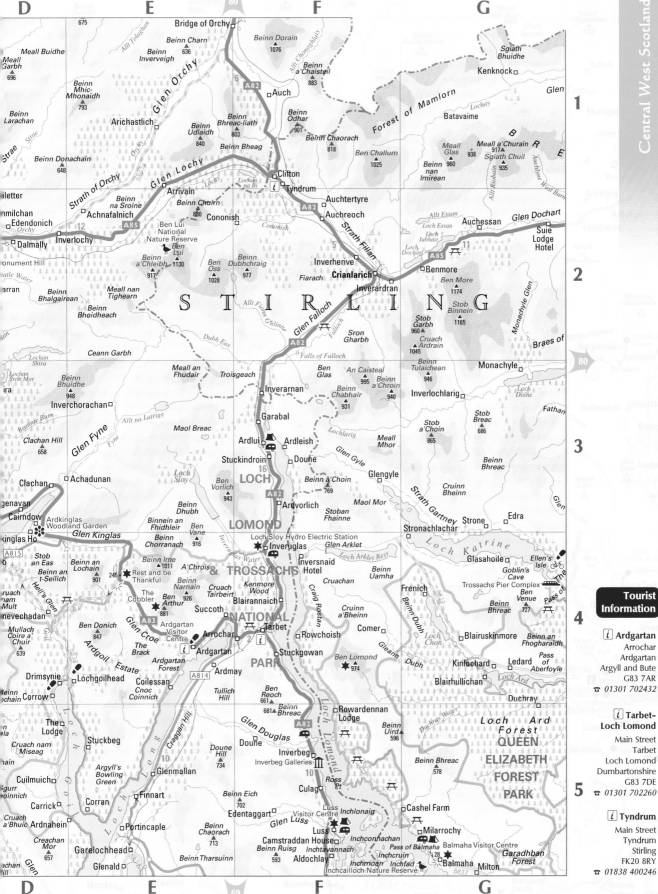

Central West Scotland

Map labels

D E F G

675
Meall Buidhe
Garbh 696
Beinn Larachan
Beinn Mhic-Mhonaidh 793
Arichastlich
Meall Garbh
Beinn Donachain 648
Strath of Orchy
Achnafalnich
Edendonich
Dalmally
Inverlochy
Monument Hill
attle Water
Beinn Bhalgairean
Beinn Bhoideach
Ceann Garbh
Loch Shira
Lochan Sron Mor
Beinn Bhuidhe 948
Inverchorachan
Clachan Hill 658
Glen Fyne
Allt na Lairige
Achadunan
Clachan
Cairndow
Ardkinglas Woodland Garden
Glen Kinglas
A815
Stob an Eas
Beinn an t-Seilich
Cruach nam Miseag
nevechadan
Mullach Coire a' Chuir 639
Ardgoil Estate
Drimsynie
Corrow
The Lodge
Stuckbeg
Cruach nam Miseag
Cuilmuich
Carrick
Cruach a' Bhuic
Ardnahein
Creachan Mor 657
Garelochhead
Glenald

Bridge of Orchy
Beinn Charn 636
Beinn Inverveigh
Glen Orchy
Beinn Udlaidh 840
Beinn Breac-liath 803
Beinn Bheag
Glen Lochy
Beinn Chuirn 880
Beinn na Sroine
Arrivain
Clifton
Tyndrum
Cononish
Ben Lui National Nature Reserve
Ben Lui
Beinn a'Chleibh 917
1130
Ben Oss 1028
Ben Dubhchraig 977
Fiarach
Beinn Dubhcraig
S T I R L I N G
Meall nan Tighearn
Allt Fionn Ghlinne
Glen Falloch
Dubh Eas
Falls of Falloch
Meall an Fhudair
Troisgeach
Inverarnan
Garabal
Maol Breac
Ardlui
Ardleish
Stuckindroin
Doune
LOCH
Ben Vorlich 943
Ardvorlich
Beinn Dhubh
Beinn Ime 1011
A'Chrois
Binnein an Fhidhleir
Beinn Chorranach 916
Rest and be Thankful
The Cobbler
245
Ben Arthur 881
Beinn Narnain 926
Cruach Tairbeirt
Kenmore Wood
Blairannaich
Succoth
& TROSSACHS
NATIONAL
Ardgartan Visitor Centre
The Brack
Arrochar
Ardgartan
Tarbet
Rowchoish
Stuckgowan
Glen Croe
A83
Ardgartan Forest
Ardmay
A814
Tullich Hill
PARK
Coilessan
Cnoc Coinnich
Ben Reoch 661
Ben Bheag
Lochgoilhead
Craggan Hill
Glen Douglas
Doune Hill 734
Inverbeg
Inverbeg Galleries
Argyll's Bowling Green
Glenmallan
Finnart
Corran
Portincaple
Beinn Eich 702
Edentaggart
Glen Luss
Beinn Chaorach 713
Camstraddan House
Beinn Ruisg
Doune
Culag
Ross Pt
Visitor Centre
Luss
Inchlonaig
Inchconnachan
Inchtavannach
Pass of Balmaha
Aldochlay
Inchcruin
Inchmoan
Inchfad
Inchcailloch Nature Reserve

Beinn Dorain 1076
Beinn a'Chaisteil 883
Auch
Beinn Odhar 901
Beinn Chaorach 818
Clifton
Auchertyre
Auchreoch
Strath Fillan
Inverherive
Crianlarich
Inverardran
Cononish
Sron Gharbh
Ben Glas
An Caisteal 995
Beinn Chabhair 931
Beinn a'Chroin 940
Lochlarig
Meall Mhor
Ben a'Choin 769
Glen Gyle
Glengyle
Stoban Fhainne
Maol Mor
LOMOND
Loch Sloy
Loch Sloy Hydro Electric Station
Inveruglas
Inversnaid Hotel
Glen Arklet
Loch Arklet Resr
Beinn Uamha
Cruachan
Craig Rostan
Cruinn a'Bheinn
Comer
Gleann Dubh
Ben Lomond 974
Rowardennan Lodge
Beinn Uird 596
Loch Lomond
Glen Douglas
Loch Chon
Beinn Bhreac 578
Beinn Bhreac
Cashel Farm
Milarrochy
Balmaha Visitor Centre
Garadhban Forest
28
Balmaha
Milton

Forest of Mamlorn
Kenknock
Glen
Sgiath Bhuidhe
B R E
Batavaime
Lochay
Meall Glas 960
Meall a'Churain 917
Sgiath Chuil 935
938
Ben Challum 1025
Beinn nan Imirean
Loch Essan
Allt Essan
Auchessan
Glen Dochart
Loch Iubhair
Suie Lodge Hotel
A85
Loch Dochart
Benmore
Ben More 1174
Stob Binnein 1165
Stob Garbh 960
Cruach Ardrain 1045
Beinn Tulaichean
Inverlochlarig
Monachyle
Loch Doine
Fathan
Braes of
Stob a'Choin 865
Stob Breac 686
Beinn Bhreac
Cruinn Bheinn
Strath Gartney
Cruach Bheinn
Strone
Edra
Loch Katrine
Stronachlachar
Glasahoile
Goblin's Cave
Trossachs Pier Complex
Ellen's Isle
The
Pass of
Ben Venue 727
Frenich
Beinn Bhreac
Blairuskinmore
Kinlochard
Blairhullichan
Loch Ard
Beinn an Fhoghairaidh
Ledard
Pass of Aberfoyle
Duchray
Loch Ard Forest
QUEEN
ELIZABETH
FOREST
PARK
Duchray Water

80
69

Tourist Information

Tourist Information

i **Ardgartan**
Arrochar
Ardgartan
Argyll and Bute
G83 7AR
☎ 01301 702432

i **Tarbet-Loch Lomond**
Main Street
Tarbet
Loch Lomond
Dumbartonshire
G83 7DE
☎ 01301 702260

i **Tyndrum**
Main Street
Tyndrum
Stirling
FK20 8RY
☎ 01838 400246

Central West Scotland

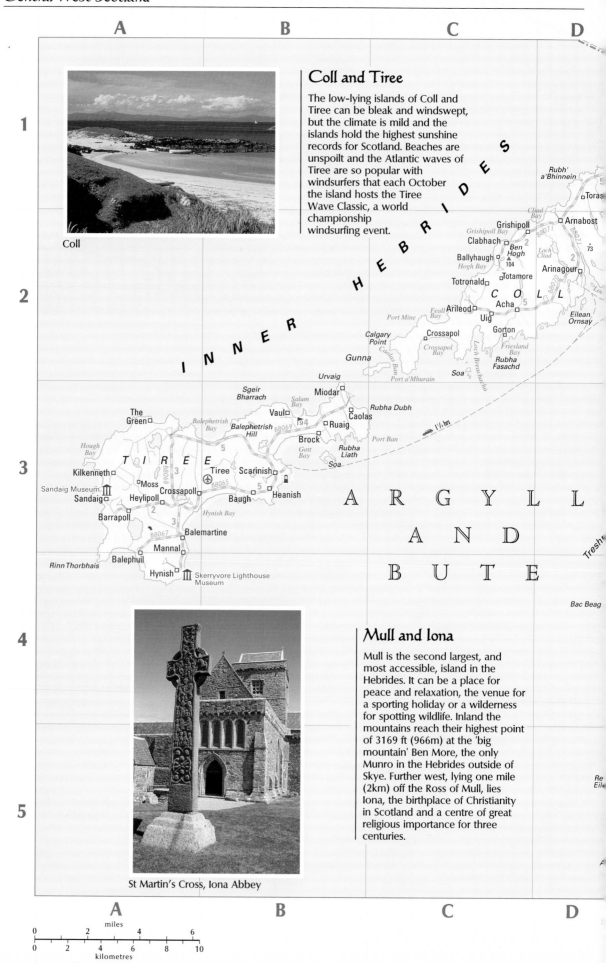

Coll and Tiree

The low-lying islands of Coll and Tiree can be bleak and windswept, but the climate is mild and the islands hold the highest sunshine records for Scotland. Beaches are unspoilt and the Atlantic waves of Tiree are so popular with windsurfers that each October the island hosts the Tiree Wave Classic, a world championship windsurfing event.

Coll

INNER HEBRIDES

ARGYLL AND BUTE

COLL

Rubh' a'Bhinnein
Toras
Arnabost
Cliad Bay
Grishipoll
Grishipoll Bay
Clabhach
Ben Hogh 104
Loch Cliad
73
Ballyhaugh
Hogh Bay
Arinagour
Totamore
Totronald
Acha 5
Arileod
Uig
Gorton
Eilean Ornsay
Calgary Point
Port Mine
Feall Bay
Crossapol
Crossapol Bay
Friesland Bay
Loch Breachachd
Gunna
Rubha Fasachd
Caolas Ban
Soa
Port a'Mhurain

TIREE

Urvaig
Sgeir Bharrach
Miodar
Salum Bay
Vaul
Rubha Dubh
The Green
Balephetrish Bay
Balephetrish Hill
B8069
94
Caolas
Ruaig
Brock
Port Ban
Hough Bay
Kilkenneth
Tiree
Scarinish
Gott Bay
Rubha Liath
Soa
1½ hrs
Moss
B8068
3
Crossapoll
B8065
5
Heanish
Sandaig Museum
Heylipoll
Baugh
Sandaig
2
Hynish Bay
Barrapoll
3
B8067
Balemartine
Rinn Thorbhais
Mannal
Balephuil
Hynish
Skerryvore Lighthouse Museum

Tresh
Bac Beag
Re Eil

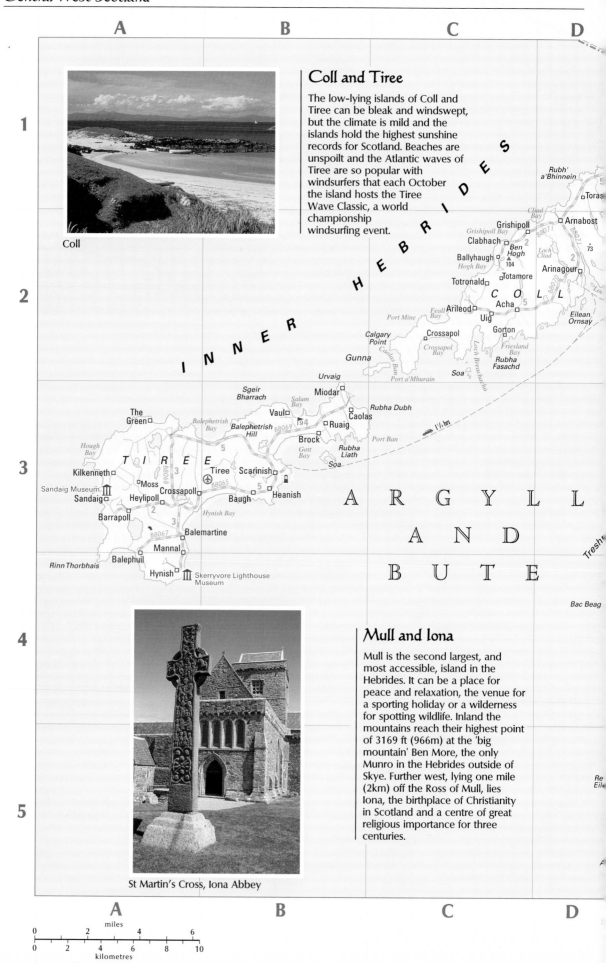

Mull and Iona

Mull is the second largest, and most accessible, island in the Hebrides. It can be a place for peace and relaxation, the venue for a sporting holiday or a wilderness for spotting wildlife. Inland the mountains reach their highest point of 3169 ft (966m) at the 'big mountain' Ben More, the only Munro in the Hebrides outside of Skye. Further west, lying one mile (2km) off the Ross of Mull, lies Iona, the birthplace of Christianity in Scotland and a centre of great religious importance for three centuries.

St Martin's Cross, Iona Abbey

miles
0   2   4   6
0 2 4 6 8 10
kilometres

D   E   132   F   G

Tobermory

Population: 700. Built as a fishing village in the late 18th century, Tobermory is now the main town of Mull. Surrounded by wooded hills and with its brightly coloured buildings along the pier, it is an attractive place to visit or stay.

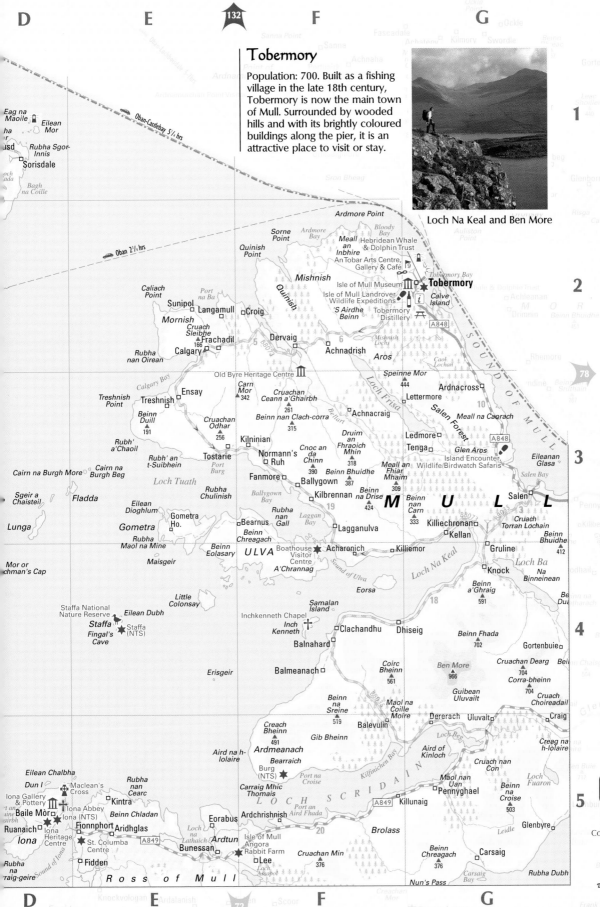

Loch Na Keal and Ben More

Oban-Castlebay 5¼ hrs

Oban 2¼ hrs

Eag na Maoile
Eilean Mor
Rubha Sgor-Innis
Sorisdale
Bagh na Coille

Ardmore Point

Sorne Point
Ardmore Bay
Bloody Bay

Quinish Point
Meall an Inbhire
Hebridean Whale & Dolphin Trust
An Tobar Arts Centre, Gallery & Cafe
Isle of Mull Museum
Tobermory
Tobermory Bay
Isle of Mull Landrover Wildlife Expeditions
'S Airdhe Beinn
Tobermory Distillery
Calve Island
A848

Caliach Point
Mishnish
Quinish
Port na Ba

Sunipol
Langamull
Croig
Dervaig
Achnadrish
Aros
Mishnish Lochs
Caol Lochan

Mornish
Cruach Sleibhe
Frachadil
166
Calgary
Rubha nan Oirean
Old Byre Heritage Centre
Speinne Mor 444
Ardnacross
SOUND OF MULL

Calgary Bay
Ensay
Carn Mor 342
Cruachan Ceann a'Ghairbh 261
Lettermore
Meall na Caorach
Salen Forest

Treshnish Point
Treshnish
Beinn Duill 191
Cruachan Odhar 256
Beinn nan Clach-corra 315
Achnacraig
Loch Frisa
Ledmore
Tenga
Glen Aros
Island Encounter Wildlife/Birdwatch Safaris
A848
Eileanan Glasa

Rubh' a'Chaoil
Kilninian
Normann's Ruh
Cnoc an da Chinn
Druim an Fhraoich Mhin 318
Meall an Fhiar Mhaim 309

Cairn na Burgh More
Cairn na Burgh Beg
Rubh' an t-Suibhein
Tostarie
Fanmore
Ballygown
Kilbrennan
Beinn Bhuidhe 387
Beinn na Drise 424
Salen

Sgeir a Chaisteil
Fladda
Loch Tuath
Rubha Chulinish
Ballygown Bay
Rubha nan Gall
Laggan Bay
M U L L
Beinn nan Carn 333
Killiechronan
Cruach Torran Lochain
Beinn Bhuidhe 412

Lunga
Eilean Dioghlum
Gometra Ho.
Bearnus
Beinn Chreagach
Laggan Bay
Lagganulva
Kellan
Cruach Torran Lochain

Mor or chman's Cap
Gometra
Rubha Maol na Mine
Beinn Eolasary
Boathouse Visitor Centre
A'Chrannag
Acharonich
Killiemor
Loch Na Keal
Gruline
Knock
Beinn a'Ghraig 591
Loch Ba
Na Binneinean

Maisgeir
ULVA
Eorsa
Sound of Ulva
18

Little Colonsay
Samalan Island
Staffa National Nature Reserve
Eilean Dubh
Inchkenneth Chapel
Inch Kenneth
Clachandhu
Dhiseig
Beinn Fhada 702
Gortenbuie

Staffa
Staffa (NTS)
Fingal's Cave
Balnahard
Coirc Bheinn 561
Ben More 966
Cruachan Dearg 704
Corra-bheinn 704
Cruach Choireadail

Erisgeir
Balmeanach
Beinn na Sreine 519
Maol na Coille Moire
Balevulin
Dererach
Uluvalt
Craig
Creag na h-Iolaire

Eilean Chalbha
Dun I
Maclean's Cross
Iona Gallery & Pottery
Kintra
Iona Abbey (Iona NTS)
Rubha na Cearc
Beinn Chladan
Aird na h-Iolaire
Bearraich
Burg (NTS)
Creach Bheinn 491
Gib Bheinn
Ardmeanach
Port na Croise
Aird of Kinloch
Cruach nan Con
Maol nan Uan Pennyghael
Beinn na Croise 503
Loch Fuaron

Baile Mòr
Ruanaich
Iona
Iona Heritage Centre
St. Columba Centre
Fionnphort
Aridhglas
A849
Eorabus
Ardchrishnish
Isle of Mull Angora Rabbit Farm
Ardtun
Lee
Bunessan
Fidden
20
Brolass
Carraig Mhic Thomais
Port an Aird Fhada
A849
Killunaig
L O C H   S C R I D A I N
Cruachan Min 376
Beinn Chreagach 376
Carsaig

Rubha na raig-geire
Ross of Mull
Nun's Pass
Carsaig Bay
Rubha Dubh

D   E   72   F   G

1
2
78
3
4
5

Tourist Information

ℹ **Tobermory**

Columba Buildings
Main Street
Tobermory
Isle Of Mull
PA75 6NU
☎ 01688 302182

Central West Scotland

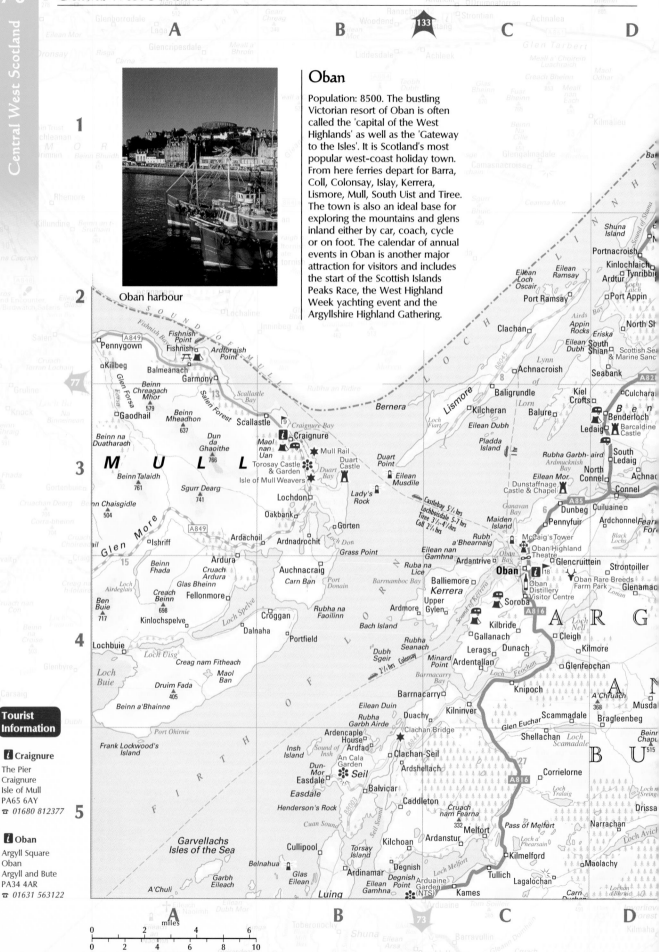

Oban harbour

Oban

Population: 8500. The bustling Victorian resort of Oban is often called the 'capital of the West Highlands' as well as the 'Gateway to the Isles'. It is Scotland's most popular west-coast holiday town. From here ferries depart for Barra, Coll, Colonsay, Islay, Kerrera, Lismore, Mull, South Uist and Tiree. The town is also an ideal base for exploring the mountains and glens inland either by car, coach, cycle or on foot. The calendar of annual events in Oban is another major attraction for visitors and includes the start of the Scottish Islands Peaks Race, the West Highland Week yachting event and the Argyllshire Highland Gathering.

Tourist Information

Craignure

The Pier
Craignure
Isle of Mull
PA65 6AY
☎ 01680 812377

Oban

Argyll Square
Oban
Argyll and Bute
PA34 4AR
☎ 01631 563122

miles
0   2   4   6

kilometres
0   2   4   6   8   10

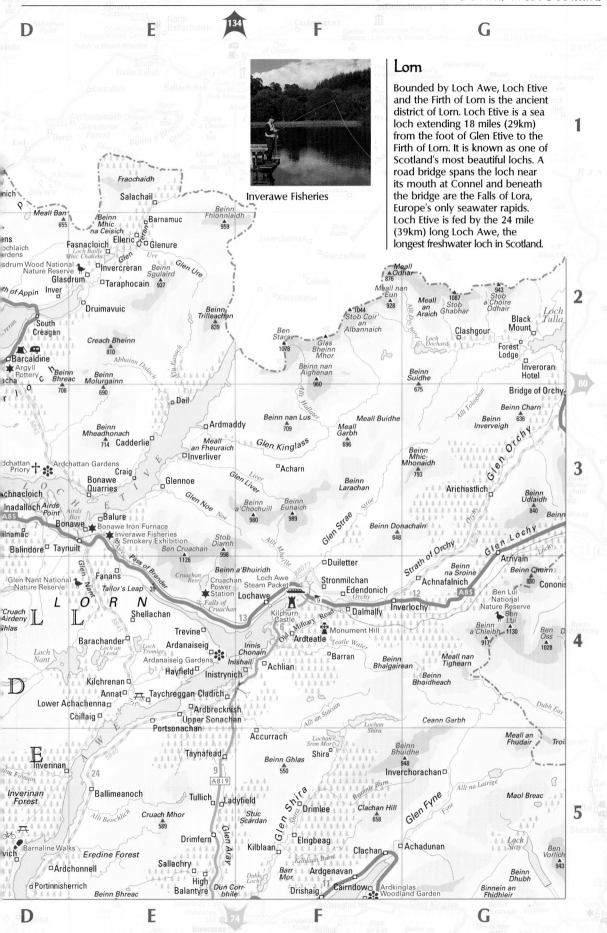

Inverawe Fisheries

Lorn

Bounded by Loch Awe, Loch Etive and the Firth of Lorn is the ancient district of Lorn. Loch Etive is a sea loch extending 18 miles (29km) from the foot of Glen Etive to the Firth of Lorn. It is known as one of Scotland's most beautiful lochs. A road bridge spans the loch near its mouth at Connel and beneath the bridge are the Falls of Lora, Europe's only seawater rapids. Loch Etive is fed by the 24 mile (39km) long Loch Awe, the longest freshwater loch in Scotland.

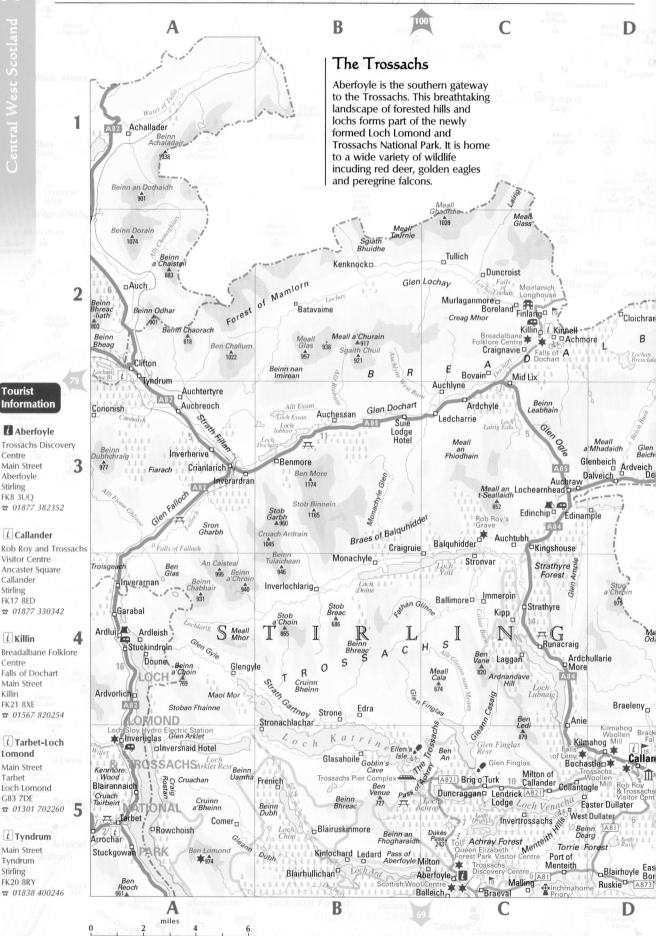

The Trossachs

Aberfoyle is the southern gateway to the Trossachs. This breathtaking landscape of forested hills and lochs forms part of the newly formed Loch Lomond and Trossachs National Park. It is home to a wide variety of wildlife incuding red deer, golden eagles and peregrine falcons.

Tourist Information

ℹ️ **Aberfoyle**
Trossachs Discovery Centre
Main Street
Aberfoyle
Stirling
FK8 3UQ
☎ 01877 382352

ℹ️ **Callander**
Rob Roy and Trossachs Visitor Centre
Ancaster Square
Callander
Stirling
FK17 8ED
☎ 01877 330342

ℹ️ **Killin**
Breadalbane Folklore Centre
Falls of Dochart
Main Street
Killin
FK21 8XE
☎ 01567 820254

ℹ️ **Tarbet-Loch Lomond**
Main Street
Tarbet
Loch Lomond
G83 7DE
☎ 01301 702260

ℹ️ **Tyndrum**
Main Street
Tyndrum
Stirling
FK20 8RY
☎ 01838 400246

Loch Katrine

Loch Katrine

This 8 mile (13km) long loch stretches from Glen Goyle to the Trossachs. It was the setting for Sir Walter Scott's poem Lady of the Lake in 1810. Visitors can cruise the loch on the Victorian steamer SS Sir Walter Scott.

1

Breadalbane

The area of the Grampian Mountains between Glen Lyon and Strathearn is known as Breadalbane, meaning the 'high country of Scotland' in Gaelic. The powerful Falls of Dochart rush through the village of Killin, making it a popular centre for exploring the area.

2

Callander

Population: 2622. Callander is the main tourist base for the Trossachs. The Rob Roy & Trossachs Visitor Centre explains the life of the notorious outlaw and folk hero, Robert MacGregor (1671–1734) who is famed for raiding rich Lowland properties to feed the Clan Gregor.

Cycling in the Ochil Hills

3

Ochil Hills

The rugged Ochil Hills range extends from Bridge of Allan eastwards to the flood plain of the Firth of Tay at Newburgh. The summit is Ben Cleuch at 2363ft (720m).

Paragliding in the Ochil Hills

4

5

Tourist Information

i **Dunblane**
Stirling Road
Dunblane
Stirling
FK51 9EP
☎ 01786 824428

❈ Achamore Gardens · 64 B1
Isle of Gigha, Argyll. 1.5 miles (2.5km) from ferry. Rhododendrons, camellias, azaleas and many semi-tropical shrubs and plants may be seen at these gardens which have been developed over the past 40 years. There is also a spring bank and a viewpoint with fine views of Islay and Jura.
☎ 01583 505254 · www.isle-of-gigha.co.uk

✿ Achnabreck Cup & Ring Marks · 73 G5
Kilmartin Glen. 1.5 miles (2.5 km) north west of Lochgilphead. The exposed crest of a rocky ridge with well-preserved cup and ring marks. Bronze Age.
☎ 0131 668 8800 · www.historic-scotland.gov.uk

❈ Achnacloich Gardens · 79 D3
Connel, off the A85, 8 miles (13km) east of Oban. A woodland garden of around 35 acres (14ha) developed over a period of 130 years. Small walled garden. Planted ponds. Wide variety of shrubs, many from the southern hemisphere.
☎ 01631 710221

✿ Adam's Grave · 69 D2
Near Ardnadam Farm, 3 miles (3km) north of Dunoon. Local name for a Neolithic cairn. Two portals and one cap stone still remain and are believed to date from 3500 BC.

⌂ Alloa Tower · 71 D1
Alloa Park on the A907 in Alloa. Formerly the ancestral home of the Earls of Mar and Kellie for four centuries. The present building dates from 1497 and was built by the 3rd Lord Erskine. In the early 18th century, the 6th Earl remodelled the tower to tie in with the adjoining mansion house, which was destroyed by fire in 1800. Impressive parapet walk around the tower's battlements offering spectacular views of the Forth. Fine family portraits, including works by Jamesone and Raeburn.
☎ 01259 211701 · www.nts.org.uk

❈ Alva Glen · 71 D1
Situated above the village of Alva, at the foot of the Ochil Hills. Formal gardens and a more rugged area, offering views down into a steep gorge. Also the remnants of an old dam that supplied the mills with fast flowing water to drive their machines. A kestrel is often spotted in the upper part of the glen around the rocky cliffs. A long tailed grey wagtail can also be seen in the lower part of the glen all year round.
☎ 01259 450000

❈ An Cala Garden · 73 F3
Isle of Seil, Argyll. A garden laid out in the 1930s with many features redolent of that era, including streams, waterfall, ponds, herbaceous borders, rockeries and Japanese cherry trees.
☎ 01852 300237

✹ An Tairbeart Heritage Centre · 68 A3
0.5 mile (0.8km) south of Tarbert. An Tairbeart explores the rich heritage of this unique coastline. Native woodland with hill and pasture and wonderful views, plus a wealth of wildlife. There is a varied programme of events, such as children's activities, local food tastings, rural skills demonstrations, storytelling, art exhibitions and ceilidhs. An Tairbeart is also a shop window for local produce, stocking a wide range of fresh and smoked produce and local delicacies.
☎ 01880 820190

⌐ An Tobar Arts Centre, Gallery & Café · 77 F2
Argyll Terrace, Tobermory, Isle of Mull. Based in a renovated Victorian primary school, the building has retained its historic detail and atmosphere and commands breathtaking views over Tobermory Bay. Monthly touring local art and craft exhibitions. The best of traditional and contemporary music. Concerts and informal ceilidhs, usually on Tuesday and Friday evenings. Art, craft and music workshops with local and visiting artists.
☎ 01688 302211 · www.antobar.co.uk

✹ Antartex Village · 69 F1
Alexandria, 1 mile (2km) from the A82, 15 miles (24km) north of Glasgow. Watch the famous Antartex sheepskins being made and choose from a vast selection of sheepskin and leather goods. Also golfing equipment and whisky tasting. Restaurant offers traditional Scottish dishes.
☎ 01389 752393

⚑ Antonine Wall · 70 D3
From Bo'ness to Old Kilpatrick, best seen off the A803 east of Bonnybridge, 12 miles (19km) south of Stirling. This Roman fortification stretched from Bo'ness on the Forth to Old Kilpatrick on the Clyde. Built circa 142–3AD, it consisted of a turf rampart behind a ditch, with forts approximately every two miles. It was probably abandoned around 163AD. Remains are best preserved in the Falkirk/Bonnybridge area.
☎ 0131 668 8800 · www.historic-scotland.gov.uk

❈ Ardanaiseig Gardens · 79 E4
Ardanaiseig Hotel, Kilchrenan, on the B845, 10 miles (11.5km) east of Taynuilt. Ardanaiseig Gardens comprises over 100 acres (40.5ha) of Victorian woodlands on the shores of Loch Awe, under the shadow of Ben Cruachan. Many exotic shrubs and trees.
☎ 01866 833333 · www.ardanaiseig-hotel.com

♙ Ardbeg Distillery Visitor Centre · 66 D5
3 miles (5km) east of Port Ellen on the southern tip of Islay. Take a step back in time and experience the history and mystique of the Ardbeg Distillery. Visitors enjoy a personal guided tour and a dram of Ardbeg's extraordinary malt whisky.
☎ 01496 302244 · www.ardbeg.com

❈ Ardchattan Gardens · 79 D3
Ardchattan Priory, on the north shore of Loch Etive, 5 miles (8km) east of Connel. Four acres (1.6ha) of garden surrounding Ardchattan Priory, a private home, with a ruined chapel and interesting stones. Herbaceous borders and extensive lawn facing the loch. Rose, sorbus and many varieties of hebe.
☎ 01796 481355

✝ Ardchattan Priory · 79 D3
On the north side of Loch Etive, 6.5 miles (10.5km) north east of Oban. The ruins of a Valliscaulian priory founded in 1230 and later converted to secular use. The meeting place in 1308 of one of Robert the Bruce's parliaments. Burned by Cromwell's soldiers in 1654. The remains include some carved stones.
☎ 0131 668 8800 · www.historic-scotland.gov.uk

❈ Ardencraig Gardens · 68 D3
Ardencraig Lane, 2 miles (3km) from Rothesay, Isle of Bute. A working greenhouse and garden which produces plants for floral displays on Bute, built between 1919 and 1923. Plus rare plants, an aviary and fish ponds.
☎ 01700 504644

✎ Ardgartan Visitor Centre · 75 E4
Glen Croe, on the A83 west of Arrochar on the Cowal Peninsula. Situated in Argyll Forest Park. Many special events are held throughout the year (nominal charge) and include Deer Watch, guided walks on the hills to see local wildlife and archaeology, and barbecues.
☎ 01301 702432 · www.forestry.gov.uk

❈ Ardkinglas Woodland Garden · 75 D3
Ardkinglas Estate in Cairndow, on the A83, 8 miles (13km) north of Inveraray. One of the finest collections of conifers in Britain, including Europe's mightiest conifer and the tallest tree in Britain. Also a spectacular display of rhododendrons and a gazebo.
☎ 01499 600261

✎ Ardnadam Heritage Trail · 69 D2
Near the village of Sandbank, 3 miles (5km) north of Dunoon. This is an excellent walk including a climb to the Dunan viewpoint, approximately 2 miles (3.2km) long.

❈ Arduaine Garden · 73 F4
Arduaine, on the A816, 20 miles (32km) south of Oban. A 20 acre (8ha) garden on promontory with fine views overlooking Loch Melfort. Noted for rhododendrons, azaleas, magnolias and other interesting trees and shrubs.
☎ 01852 200366 · www.nts.org.uk

ᛜ Argyll & Sutherland Highlanders Regimental Museum · 70 C1
Stirling Castle, Stirling. A fine museum which brings alive the history of the Regiment from 1794 to the present day. Features weapons, silver, colours, uniforms, medals, pictures, music, World War I trench.
☎ 01786 475165 · www.argylls.co.uk

✹ Argyll Pottery · 79 D2
Barcaldine, on the A828, on the south shore of Loch Creran. A pottery producing mostly domestic ware on the wheel, with some individual pieces.
☎ 01631 720503

⚘ Argyll Wildlife Park · 74 C4
Dalchenna, on the A83, 1.25 miles (2km) from Inveraray. A 55 acre (22ha) park with many animals wandering freely. Ponds with water birds. Natural surroundings to view red, silver and arctic foxes, red and fallow deer, wallabies, racoons, monkeys, scottish wild cats, badgers, buzzards, owls and others.
☎ 01499 302264

⌂ Argyll's Lodging · 70 C1
Castle Wynd, Stirling. A superb mansion built around an earlier core in about 1630 and further extended by the Earl of Argyll in the 1670s. It is the most impressive town house of its period in Scotland.
☎ 01786 461146 · www.historic-scotland.gov.uk

❈ Ascog Hall, Fernery & Gardens · 68 D3
Ascog, 3 miles (5km) south of Rothesay on the A886. Built circa 1870, this magnificent Victorian fernery, with beautiful rock work and water pools, has been restored and restocked with an impressive collection of sub-tropical ferns. The only surviving fern from the original collection is said to be around 1000 years old. The large garden is partly restored.
☎ 01700 504555 · www.york.ac.uk/depts/biol/units/ground/ascog/welco

ᛜ Auchindrain Township Open Air Museum · 74 C4
6 miles (10km) south west of Inveraray on the A83. Auchindrain is an original West Highland township of great antiquity and the only communal tenancy township in Scotland to have survived on its centuries-old site, much of it in its original form. The township buildings look as they would have done at the end of the 19th century and give visitors a fascinating glimpse of Highland life.
☎ 01499 500235

ᛜ Auld Kirk Museum · 70 B3
The Cross, Kirkintilloch. The Auld Kirk Museum dates back to 1644 when it was the parish church of Kirkintilloch. Recently refurbished, it is now a museum describing the domestic and working life of people in the area. Temporary exhibition programme of crafts, photography and local history throughout the year.
☎ 0141 578 0144

⛲ Balloch Castle Country Park · 69 F1
Balloch, north of Dumbarton off the A811. Within the boundaries of Loch Lomond and The Trossachs National Park, the country park comprises 200 acres (81ha) at the southern end of Loch Lomond. Mature woodland, gardens, shore walks and wonderful views. The castle, one of the first modern Gothic style castles to be built in Scotland, houses a visitor centre.
☎ 01389 722600

✠ Ballygowan Cup & Ring Marks — 73 G5
Kilmartin Glen. 1 mile (2km) south west of Kilmartin, near Poltalloch. Bronze Age cup and ring marks on natural rock faces.
☎ 0131 668 8800 — www.historic-scotland.gov.uk

✹ Balmaha Visitor Centre — 75 G5
Balmaha, on the A811 north west of Drymen. Visitor centre offering information on Loch Lomond and Trossachs National Park. Audio-visual show and exhibition.
☎ 01360 870470

✠ Baluachraig Cup & Ring — 73 G5
Kilmartin Glen. 1 mile (2km) south south-east of Kilmartin, Argyll. Several groups of Bronze Age cup and ring marks on natural rock faces.
☎ 0131 668 8800 — www.historic-scotland.gov.uk

✹ Bannockburn Heritage Centre — 70 C1
Glasgow Road, 2 miles (3.2km) south of Stirling. Site of the famous battle in 1314 when Robert the Bruce, King of Scots, defeated the English army of Edward II. Colourful exhibition with life-size figures of Bruce and William Wallace plus heraldic flags. Equestrian statue of Bruce outside.
☎ 01786 812664 — www.nts.org.uk

✠ Bar Hill Fort — 70 C3
0.5 mile (1km) east of Twechar (signposted from the village). The highest fort on the line of the Antonine Wall, containing the foundations of the headquarters building and bathhouse. A small Iron Age fort lies to the east.
www.historic-scotland.gov.uk

✹ Barbara Davidson Pottery — 71 D2
Muirhall Farm on the A88 on the north side of Larbert. A working pottery in a picturesque converted 17th century farm steading. Products are hand-thrown stoneware, mostly functional.
☎ 01324 554430 — www.barbara-davidson.com

✠ Barcaldine Castle — 78 B3
Ledaig, 9 miles (14.5km) north of Oban off the A85. The oldest intact castle on the Argyll mainland open to the public. Family home of the Campbells of Barcaldine and last of Black Duncan's seven castles remaining in Campbell hands. Historically associated with the massacre of Glencoe and the Appin Murder. Haunted.
☎ 01631 720598 — www.oban.org.uk/attractions/barcaldine.html

✹ Barnaline Walks — 74 B3
Dalavich, on an unclassified road along the west shore of Loch Awe. Walks start from Barnaline car park and picnic site, taking in Dalavich Oakwood Forest Nature Reserve (an interpretive trail with information point), Avich Falls and Loch Avich.

✹ Barnluasgan Visitor Centre — 73 F5
Near Lochgilphead. Follow the B8025 from Bellanoch towards Tayvallich. This unstaffed centre provides information on Knapdale Forest.
www.forestry.gov.uk

✠ Bearsden Bathhouse — 70 A3
On Roman Road, Bearsden, near Glasgow. The well-preserved remains of a bathhouse and latrine built in the 2nd century to serve a fort.
☎ 0131 668 8800 — www.historic-scotland.gov.uk

✹ Ben Lomond — 80 A5
Ardess Lodge, Rowardennan. Rising from the east shore of Loch Lomond to 3194ft (973.5m), the mountain offers exhilarating walking and spectacular views. It is part of the Ben Lomond National Memorial Park commemorating the war dead.
☎ 01360 870224 — www.nts.org.uk

✹ Benmore Botanic Garden — 68 D1
Benmore, 7 miles (11km) north of Dunoon, on the A815. Some of Britain's tallest trees can be found here, as can over 250 species of rhododendrons and an extensive magnolia collection. Other features include an avenue of giant redwoods planted in 1863, a formal garden, and a variety of waymarked trails.
☎ 01369 706261

✹ Birkhill Fireclay Mine — 71 E3
3 miles (5km) west of Bo'ness. The caverns of Birkhill Fireclay Mine are set in the picturesque Avon Gorge. A mine guide takes visitors on a tour of the mine workings where you can discover how fireclay was mined. There are also fossils which are over 300 million years old. The mine can only be reached by descending 130 steps into the Avon Gorge so access for the disabled and elderly is difficult.
☎ 01506 825855 — www.srps.org.uk

✹ Bishop's Glen — 69 D2
Dunoon. Once the source of Dunoon's water supply, now a favoured beauty spot and delightful walk leading to the Bishop's Seat, 1655ft (504m).

✹ Blair Drummond Safari & Adventure Park — 70 C1
Blair Drummond, 4 miles (6.5km) towards Doune on the A84. Drive through wild animal reserves, boat safari around chimpanzee island, pets' farm, adventure playground. Giant astra-glide and flying-fox cable slide across lake. Five-seater pedal boats. Amusement arcade, bouncy castle, dodgem cars.
☎ 01786 841456 — www.safari-park.co.uk

✹ Bo'ness & Kinneil Railway — 71 E2
Bo'ness Station on the A904 and A706. Savour the nostalgia of the railway age and travel by steam train from Bo'ness to visit Birkhill Fireclay Mine. At Bo'ness the Scottish Railway exhibition tells the story of the movement of goods and people before motorway travel with a display of carriages, wagons and locomotives.
☎ 01506 822298

✹ Boathouse Visitor Centre — 77 F4
Ardalum House, Isle of Ulva. Off the west side of Mull. Provides information on the history of Ulva and also the local natural history. There is a restored thatched croft house and five waymarked walking trails.
☎ 01688 500264 — www.ulva.mull.com

✹ Bonawe Iron Furnace — 79 E3
At Bonawe, close to Taynuilt on the A85, 12 miles (19km) east of Oban. The restored remains of a charcoal furnace for iron smelting. Established in 1753, it functioned until 1876. The most complete example of its type.
☎ 01866 822432 — www.historic-scotland.gov.uk

🍾 Bowmore Distillery Visitor Centre — 66 C4
School Street, Bowmore, Isle of Islay. Malt whisky distillery, licensed since 1779 with guided tours. Traditional floor maltings are a major feature. Across the entrance yard, a former warehouse, gifted to the local community, is now a swimming pool heated by waste energy from the distillery.
☎ 01496 810441 — www.morrisonbowmore.co.uk

✹ Bracklinn Falls — 80 D5
1 mile east of Callander. A series of dramatic waterfalls on the Keltie Water. The falls are approached along a woodland walk from a car park by the Callander Crags at Callander.

✹ Breadalbane Folklore Centre — 80 C2
Falls of Dochart, Killin. Includes a Tourist Information Centre, water wheel and healing stones. History of local clans (MacLaren, MacNab, Campbell and MacGregor). Artefacts on Killin heritage. Display boards and visual display units tell the story of Breadalbane. Visitors can also learn about St Fillan, the local patron saint and healer, a 6th century Celtic monk who preached from the original mill building.
☎ 01567 820254

🍾 Bunnahabhain Distillery — 66 D2
Port Askaig, Isle of Islay. Visitors can see the malt whisky distillation process and sample the results. Individuals and groups welcome.
☎ 01496 840646

✹ Burg — 72 C2
Isle of Mull, 7 miles (11km) west of Tiroran off the B8035, then rough path. Car parking at Tiroran. Covering an area of 1405 acres (568.5ha), this is a spectacular and remote part of Mull. The high cliffs here are known as the Wilderness. MacCulloch's Fossil Tree is 50 million years old, and can be reached by a steep iron ladder down to the beach at low tide.
☎ 01631 570000 — www.nts.org.uk

🏛 Bute Museum — 68 C3
Stuart Street, Rothesay, Isle of Bute. Custom-made museum, gifted by the 4th Marquis of Bute in 1926. A recognised source of information on the Island of Bute.
☎ 01700 505067

✠ Cairnbaan Cup & Ring Marks — 73 G5
Kilmartin Glen. Near to the Cairnbaan Hotel on the A841, 2.5 miles (4km) north west of Lochgilphead. Cup and ring marks on a natural rock surface.
☎ 0131 668 8800 — www.historic-scotland.gov.uk

🏠 Callendar House — 71 D3
Callendar Park, 1 mile (2km) east of Falkirk town centre. Encapsulates 600 years of Scotland's history from medieval times to the 20th century and was visited by great historical figures like Mary, Queen of Scots, Cromwell and Bonnie Prince Charlie. Permanent attractions include displays on the Story of Callendar House, and on the Falkirk area during the great social revolution of 1750 – 1850. The house's research centre contains an extensive archive.
☎ 01324 503770

✝ Cambuskenneth Abbey — 70 D1
1 mile (2km) east of Stirling. Ruins of an abbey founded in 1147 as a house of Augustinian canons. Scene of Robert the Bruce's parliament in 1326 and the burial place of James III and his queen. The fine detached tower is the only substantial survivor, but extensive foundations of the rest remain.
☎ 0131 668 8800 — www.historic-scotland.gov.uk

🏛 Campbeltown Museum — 64 C4
Hall Street, Campbeltown, 38 miles (61km) south of Tarbet, Loch Fyne on the A83. A listed building, designed by the renowned Scottish architect J. J. Burnet. The collections are mainly archaeology and natural history with some local history and maritime material.
☎ 01586 552366 — www.abc-museums.demon.co.uk

🍾 Caol Ila Distillery — 66 D3
Port Askaig, on the A846, on the east side of the Islay. A distillery built in 1846 by Hector Henderson. It stands in a picturesque setting at the foot of a steep hill with its own small pier overlooking the Sound of Islay and Paps of Jura.
☎ 01496 840207

✠ Carnasserie Castle — 73 G4
Off the A816, 9 miles (14.5km) north of Lochgilphead, 2 miles (3km) north of Kilmartin, Argyll. A handsome combined tower house and hall, home of John Carswell, first Protestant Bishop of the Isles and translator of the first book printed in Gaelic. Fine architectural details of the late 16th century. The castle was captured and partly blown up during Argyll's rebellion in 1685.
☎ 0131 668 8800 — www.historic-scotland.gov.uk

✱ **Carsaig Arches** `72 D3`
A 3 mile (5km) walk from Carsaig leads to these remarkable tunnels formed by the sea in the basaltic rock. Reached only at low tide. On the way is the Nun's Cave; it is said that nuns driven out of Iona at the time of the Reformation sheltered here. The west wall bears numerous incised carvings, including crosses of various shapes, some of which could be as old as the late 6th century.

🏰 **Castle Campbell** `71 E1`
In Dollar Glen, 1 mile (2km) north of Dollar. Once known as Castle Gloom, the castle was built towards the end of the 15th century by the 1st Earl of Argyll. Burned by Cromwell in the 1650s. The original tower is well preserved. The 60 acres (24ha) of woodland in the glen make an attractive walk to the castle.
☎ 01259 742408 www.historic-scotland.gov.uk

🏛 **Castle House Museum** `68 C2`
Castle Gardens, Dunoon. The museum illustrates the history of Dunoon and district from pre-history to the recent past. Four rooms have been set aside to give the visitor a reflection of life in Victorian times. Set in pleasant gardens, opposite Dunoon's beautiful Victorian Pier with excellent views of the surrounding area.
☎ 01369 701422 www.castlehousemuseum.org.uk

🏰 **Castle Lachlan** `74 C5`
4 miles south west of Strachur on the A886/B8000, Argyll. Ruins standing on the banks of Loch Fyne dating from the 12th century. The MacLachlans are believed to have had lands in Strathlachlan for over 900 years.

🏰 **Castle Sween** `67 G2`
On the east shore of Loch Sween, 15 miles (24km) south west of Lochgilphead. Probably the oldest stone castle on the Scottish mainland. Built in the mid 12th century with later towers in addition to now vanished wooden structures. Destroyed by Sir Alexander Macdonald in 1647.
☎ 0131 668 8800 www.historic-scotland.gov.uk

⛪ **Castlecary** `70 C3`
On the B816, east of Castlecary village. The reduced earthworks of a fort on the Antonine Wall.
☎ 0131 668 8800 www.historic-scotland.gov.uk

✱ **Ceramic Experience** `69 F1`
Alexandria. Visitors can paint their own designs onto a plate or mug. 2 – 3 day holiday classes run for children. Also adult evening classes and children's parties. Soft play area. Ceramics for sale.
☎ 01389 720888

✝ **Church of the Holy Rude** `70 C1`
St John Street, Stirling. Believed to be the only church in the United Kingdom apart from Westminster Abbey which has held a coronation, that of James VI, son of Mary, Queen of Scots. John Knox preached the coronation sermon. Scottish monarchs of the 15th and 16th centuries worshipped here, and developed the church. Extensively renovated during the 1990s. Magnificent romantic organ.
☎ 01786 471848

✱ **Clachan Bridge** `73 F3`
B844 off the A816, 12 miles (19k) south west of Oban. This picturesque single-arched bridge, built in 1792 and linking the mainland with the island of Seil, is often claimed to be the only bridge to span the Atlantic (although there are others similar). The waters are actually those of the narrow Seil Sound, which joins the Firth of Lorne to Outer Loch Melfort, but they can, with some justification, claim to be an arm of the Atlantic.

🏛 **Clydebank Museum** `70 A3`
Town Hall, Dumbarton Road, Clydebank. 2 miles (3km) north west of Glasgow on the A814. Community museum describing local social and industrial history. Displays on ship building, engineering and sewing machines including the Singer Sewing Machine Collection. Technical archive on Singer machines. Display on the Clydebank blitz.
☎ 01389 738702

✱ **Cobbler, The** `75 E4`
Part of the Arrochar Alps, overlooking Arrochar and Loch Long. So-called because of its curious rock formation summit, The Cobbler – or Ben Arthur – is one of Scotland's most distinctive peaks.

❁ **Colonsay House Gardens** `72 B5`
Kiloran, Isle of Colonsay. 2 miles (3km) from pier. Famous rhododendron garden of 20 acres (8ha), adjacent to Colonsay House, home of Lord Strathcona. In the woodland garden, native trees and rare rhododendrons, bluebells and mecanopsis flourish together. Due to the mildness of the climate and the shelter of the woods, many tender and rare shrubs from all parts of the world grow happily including mimosa, eucalyptus and palm trees.
☎ 01951 200211 www.colonsay.org.uk

⛪ **Columba's Footsteps** `64 B5`
West of Southend at Keil, Mull of Kintyre. Traditionally it is believed that St Columba first set foot on Scottish soil near Southend. The footsteps are imprinted in a flat topped rock near the ruin of an old chapel.

✱ **Corryvreckan Whirlpool** `73 E4`
Between the islands of Jura and Scarba. This treacherous tide race, dangerous for small craft, covers an extensive area and may be seen from the north end of Jura or from Craignish Point. The noise can sometimes be heard from a considerable distance.

🦜 **Cowal Bird Garden** `69 D2`
Lochan Wood, 1 mile (2km) north of Dunoon on the A855. Attraction with a wide range of animals such as donkeys, macaws, parrots, rabbits, guinea pigs, pot-bellied pigs, aviary birds, all set in mature woodland. Nature trail through native woodland. Dry sledge slope, slides and children's play area.
☎ 01369 707999

✱ **Cowane's Hospital** `70 D1`
Near Holyrood Church, Stirling. A former almshouse founded by John Cowane between 1637 and 1649, for the guildry members who fell on hard times.
☎ 01786 472247

❁ **Crarae Gardens** `74 B5`
Crarae, 10 miles (16km) south of Inveraray on the A83. A superb natural gorge with a series of waterfalls and extensive walks through a unique collection of rhododendrons, azaleas, conifers and eucalyptus.
☎ 01546 886388 www.crarae-gardens.org

✱ **Crinan Canal** `73 F5`
Crinan to Ardrishaig, by Lochgilphead. Constructed between 1793 and 1801 to carry ships from Loch Fyne to the Atlantic without rounding Kintyre. The 9 mile (14.5km) stretch of water with 15 locks is now almost entirely used by pleasure craft. There are magnificent views to the Western Isles from Crinan. The Crinan basin, coffee shop, boatyard and hotel make a visit well worthwhile.
☎ 01546 603210 www.scottishcanals.co.uk

🌿 **Crinan Wood** `73 F5`
Crinan, 6 miles (9.5km) north west of Lochgilphead on the B841. Crinan Wood is categorised as a temperate rainforest, benefitting from sea mists and plentiful rain. Over 13 types of fern grow here, together with many varieties of mosses and lichens. Waymarked trails and good views of Jura and Corryvreckan to the west, Ben More to the north.
☎ 01764 662554 www.woodland-trust.org.uk

✱ **Cruachan Power Station** `79 E4`
Dalmally, 18 miles (29km) east of Oban on the A85. A guided tour takes visitors 0.5 mile (1km) inside Ben Cruachan to see a reversible pumped storage scheme. An exhibition houses touch screen and computer video technology.
☎ 01866 822618

🏰 **Culcreuch Castle & Country Park** `70 B2`
Fintry, Stirling. A 14th century castle, ancestral home of the Clan Galbraith, set in a 1600 acre estate. Woodland, river and moorland walks. Pinetum. Walled garden and children's play area. The castle also houses a hotel and conference centre.
☎ 01360 860555 www.culcreuch.com

⛪ **Cunninghame Graham Memorial** `70 A1`
Gartmore, 2 miles (3km) south west of Aberfoyle. A cairn commemorates the life of R. B. Cunninghame Graham (1852 – 1936). An interpretive panel shows he was a radical politician, writer, traveller and renowned horseman.
www.nts.org.uk

🏛 **Denny Ship Model Experiment Tank** `69 G2`
Castle Street, Dumbarton. A ship model experiment tank constructed in 1882 and retaining many of its original features. Fully restored to working order by the Scottish Maritime Museum so that the original process can be demonstrated.
☎ 01389 763444

✱ **Dollar Glen** `71 E1`
0.3 miles north of Dollar. At the foot of the Ochil Hills, Dollar Glen is unmistakable with its imposing castle, Castle Campbell, at its head. A path crosses Dollar Burn and follows the west side of the glen to emerge at the rear of the castle.

🏛 **Dollar Museum** `71 E1`
Dollar. A small award-winning museum with frequently changing, temporary exhibitions. Also permanent exhibitions on the history of Dollar, Castle Campbell, Dollar Academy, the Devon Valley Railway and the prehistory of Dollar. Reading room with local history material, including many photographs.
☎ 01259 742895

🏰 **Doune Castle** `81 E5`
Off the A84 at Castle Road, Doune, 8 miles (13km) north west of Stirling. A magnificent late 14th century courtyard castle built for the Regent Albany. Its most striking feature is the combination of tower, gatehouse and hall with its kitchen in a massive frontal block. Later possessed by the Stuarts of Doune, Earls of Moray.
☎ 01786 841742 www.historic-scotland.gov.uk

✱ **Drymen Pottery** `69 G1`
The Square, Drymen. 20 miles (32km) north of Glasgow. Pottery studio with a large coffee and gift shop. Licenced pub upstairs.
☎ 01360 660458

🏰 **Duart Castle** `73 F1`
Off the A849 on the east of Mull. Built on a cliff overlooking the Sound of Mull this is one of the oldest inhabited castles in Scotland and the home of the 28th Chief of Clan Maclean. The keep was built in 1360 adjoining the original courtyard. Because the clan supported the Stewarts, the castle was taken by the Duke of Argyll in 1691. After the 1745 Rising, it was used as a garrison for Government troops and then fell into ruin. It was restored by Sir Fitzroy Maclean in 1911. The keep contains dungeons with figures of prisoners from the Spanish Armada and exhibitions of clan history. Also an exhibition of The Swan, one of Cromwell's ships that sank directly below the castle in 1653.
☎ 01680 812309 www.duartcastle.com

🏰 **Dumbarton Castle** `69 G2`
Castle Road, off the A814 in Dumbarton on Dumbarton Rock. Spectacularly sited on a volcanic rock, the site of the ancient capital of Strathclyde. The most interesting features are the 18th century artillery fortifications, with the 19th century guns. Also mostly modern barrack, a dungeon, a 12th century gateway and a sundial gifted by Mary, Queen of Scots.
☎ 01389 732167 www.historic-scotland.gov.uk

Dunadd Fort — 73 G5
Kilmartin Glen, 1 mile (2km) west of Kilmichael Glassary. A spectacular site occupied since the Iron Age. The well-preserved hill fort is part-Roman, when it was a stronghold of Dalriada, the kingdom of the Scots.
☎ 0131 668 8800   www.historic-scotland.gov.uk

Dunagoil Vitrified Fort — 68 C4
Isle of Bute. On a commanding site at the south of the island, this ancient fort is clear evidence of Iron Age habitation.

Dunaverty Rock — 64 B5
At Southend, Mull of Kintyre, dominating beach and golf course. Formerly the site of Dunaverty Castle, a Macdonald stronghold. In 1647, about 300 people were put to death here by Covenanters under General Leslie. The rock is known locally as Blood Rock.

Dunblane Museum — 81 E5
The Cross, Dunblane, 6 miles (9.5km) north of Stirling. A museum located in barrel-vaulted rooms built in 1624. Contents include paintings, books, and artefacts which illustrate the life of the cathedral and its congregation from St Blane to the restoration in 1893. Large collection of communion tokens.
☎ 01765 823440

Dunchraigaig Cairn — 73 G5
1.25 miles (2km) south of Kilmartin. A Bronze Age cairn excavated in the last century.
☎ 0131 668 8800   www.historic-scotland.gov.uk

Duncryne Hill — 69 G1
Between Balloch and Drymen, just off the A811 east of Gartocharn. Known locally as The Dumpling, due to its shape, this small hill can be climbed using a short steep path. The reward at the top is one of the best views of Loch Lomond.

Dunglass Castle & Henry Bell Obelisk — 69 G2
Ruined castle on the shore of the River Clyde near the village of Bowling. Former seat of the Colquoun family which dates back to the 14th century. Obelisk erected within the grounds to the memory of Henry Bell, first provost of Helensburgh and pioneer of the steam boat.

Dunstaffnage Castle & Chapel — 78 C3
Off the A85 by Loch Etive, 3.5 miles (5km) north of Oban. A fine, well-preserved 13th century castle built on rock. Nearby, ruins of what was an exceptionally beautiful chapel.
☎ 01631 562465   www.historic-scotland.gov.uk

Eileach An Naoimh — 73 E4
On an island of that name in the Garvellach group, north of Jura. The ruins of beehive cells, a chapel and a graveyard. Associated by local tradition with St Columba.
☎ 0131 668 8800   www.historic-scotland.gov.uk

Ettrick Bay — 68 C3
West side of the Isle of Bute. This is a popular and safe beach.

Falkirk Wheel — 71 D2
At the interchange between the Union and the Forth and Clyde canals, close to Tomfourhill, south Falkirk. Opening early 2002, a spectacular wheel will reconnect the Union Canal up 82ft (25m) to the Forth and Clyde Canal. The wheel will weigh 1300 tonnes and be equivalent in height to a nine-storey block of flats. Free visitor centre and park.
☎ 01324 619888   www.scottishcanals.co.uk

Falls of Dochart — 80 C2
Dramatic waterfalls rushing through the centre of the picturesque Highland village of Killin. On the island of Inchbuie in the river is the burial ground of Clan McNab.

Falls of Leny — 80 C5
Falls on the River Leny west of Callander with surrounding woodland walks. The descent is popular with canoeists.

Finlaggan Trust — 66 C3
The Cottage, Ballygrant, Isle of Islay. 2 miles (3km) off the A846 from Port Askaig. Islay, known as the Cradle of Clan Donald and Finlaggan, is the main headquarters of the Lords of the Isles and a place of pilgrimage for clan members today. The interpretive centre describes local history and details the archaeological finds.
☎ 01496 840644

Gartmorn Dam Country Park — 71 E1
Sauchie, near Alloa. The country park is a peaceful retreat for visitors to walk, cycle or to enjoy horse riding or fishing, with an extensive network of paths. Gartmorn Dam itself is a 170 acre (69ha) reservoir engineered by Sir John Erskine to power pumps which drained mines.
☎ 01259 214319

Geilston Garden — 69 F2
On the A814 at the west end of Cardross, 18 miles (29km) north of Glasgow. Small estate typical of those owned on the banks of the Clyde by tobacco barons and factory owners who made their money in 19th century Glasgow. Charming garden with walled area and wooded glen.
☎ 01389 841867   www.nts.org.uk

Glebe Cairn — 73 G5
In Kilmartin Glen. An early Bronze Age burial cairn with two burial chambers (cists).
☎ 0131 668 8800   www.historic-scotland.gov.uk

Glen Finglas — 80 C5
Off the A821, 5 miles (8km) west of Callander. The glen carries the Finglas water south east to the Black Water between Loch Achray and Loch Venacher. Acquired by the Woodland Trust in 1996, there is an ongoing programme of restoration to native woodland. Waymarked walking trails of various grades.
☎ 01764 662554

Glenam Gardens — 69 E1
Rhu, by Helensburgh, Argyll and Bute. A west coast garden in a sheltered glen overlooking the Gareloch, famous for the collection of rare and tender rhododendrons. Also fine magnolias and many other interesting ericaceous plants. Colour all year round. A network of paths with small bridges connect the different parts of the garden – the pond, walled garden, woodland, greenhouse and the productive vegetable patch.
☎ 01436 820493

Glenbarr Abbey Visitor Centre — 64 B2
Glenbarr, Tarbert, on the A83, 12 miles (19km) north of Campbeltown. A house in the 18th century Gothic Revival style, the seat of the lairds of Glenbarr since 1796, designed by James Gillespie Graham. Tours are conducted by the 5th laird, Angus Macalister, whose home this is. Among items displayed are 19th century fashions, Spode, Sèvres and Derby china, gloves worn by Mary, Queen of Scots, thimble collection.
☎ 01583 421247

Glengoyne Distillery — 70 A2
Dumgoyne, Killearn, on the A81, 3 miles (5km) north of Strathblane. First licensed in 1833, this is Scotland's most southerly Highland distillery and the closest to Glasgow. Nestling in the Campsie Hills, it draws water from a waterfall. The distillery produces Scotland's only unpeated whisky. Conducted tours show the main process of distilling. Heritage Room houses cooperage display, old artefacts and shop. Visitors taste a dram in reception room, overlooking dam, glen and waterfall.
☎ 01360 550254   www.glengoyne.com

Grangemouth Museum — 71 E2
Victoria Library, Bo'ness Road, Grangemouth. Display relating to the growth of Grangemouth. Exhibits on local industries, canals, shipping and ship building, and the world's first practical steamship, the Charlotte Dundas.
☎ 01324 504699

Hamilton Toy Collection — 80 D5
On the High Street in Callander, 16 miles (25km) north west of Stirling on the A84. A family-run toy museum comprising five rooms of toys dating from between 1880 and 1980. Teddy bears, trains (running layout), dolls houses and accessories, cars, bygones, planes, ships, children's books, science fiction toys and associated memorabilia.
☎ 01877 330004

Hebridean Whale & Dolphin Trust — 77 G2
Tobermory, Isle of Mull. Visitor centre offering information on marine issues and local species. The trust carries out research projects (such as eco-tourism, minke whale photo ID) and education (school visits).
☎ 01688 302620   www.hwdt.org

Hermitage Park — 69 F1
Helensburgh. Formal gardens, play area, putting green, bowling green. Features a memorial bust to John Logie Baird, the inventor of the television, who was born in Helensburgh.

Highland Mary's Statue — 68 D2
Castle gardens, near Dunoon pier. The statue of Burns' Highland Mary at the foot of the Castle Hill. Mary Campbell was born on a farm in Dunoon and exchanged vows with Burns. However, she died the following autumn and Burns went on to marry Jean Armour.

Hill House — 69 E1
Upper Colquhoun Street, Helensburgh, off the B832, 23 miles (37km) north west of Glasgow. Charles Rennie Mackintosh designed this house for the publisher Walter Blackie in 1904. A masterpiece of domestic architecture synthesizing traditional Scottish style with avant-garde innovation, this extraordinary building still looks modern today. Mackintosh, with his wife Margaret, also designed the interiors and most of the furniture.
☎ 01436 673900   www.nts.org.uk

Holy Trinity Church — 70 C1
12 Keir Street, Bridge of Allan, 2 miles (3km) south of exit 11 on the M9. An attractive 19th century building with fine timbered roof and excellent stained glass windows. The chancel furnishings, consisting of pulpit, communion table, chair, organ screen and choir rail, were designed in 1904 by Charles Rennie Mackintosh in light oak and represent a unique aspect of Mackintosh's style. Four complementing chairs, gifted in 1999, add modern interest.
☎ 01786 834155

Homeston Farm Trail & Pony Trekking — 64 B4
1 mile (2km) off the B842, 5 miles (8km) from Campbeltown. Farm trail to see all sorts of farm animals. Children can feed animals. Pony trekking. Also B&B and residential riding holidays.
☎ 01586 552437   www.ridescotland.com

Inchcailloch Nature Reserve — 75 G5
On Inchcailloch island, Loch Lomond, opposite Balmaha. Protected oak woodland of European importance. The island lies on the highland boundary fault providing a great opportunity to see the distinction between the lowland and highland areas of Loch Lomond. Woodland birds, deer, bluebell wood. Two miles of waymarked paths, taking visitors to a beach with picnic and barbecue facilities.
☎ 01786 450362

✝ **Inchkenneth Chapel** `77 F4`
On the island of Inch Kenneth off the west coast of the Isle of Mull. A simple building of a distinctive west Highland type, with good medieval monuments in the graveyard.
☎ *0131 668 8800*   www.historic-scotland.gov.uk

⚜ **Inchmahome Priory** `80 C5`
On an island in the Lake of Mentieth. The beautifully situated ruins of an Augustinian monastery founded in 1238, with much 13th century building surviving. Briefly housed Mary, Queen of Scots as an infant in 1547.
☎ *01877 385294*   www.historic-scotland.gov.uk

⚜ **Inveraray Bell Tower** `74 D4`
The Avenue, Inveraray. This 126ft (38.5m) high granite tower houses Scotland's finest ring of bells and the world's second-heaviest ring of ten bells. Excellent views, pleasant grounds. Opportunities to see bells and ringers in action. Recordings always available when tower open. Easy staircase to top viewing gallery in bell chamber.

⚔ **Inveraray Castle** `74 C4`
On the A83, 0.5 mile (1km) north of Inveraray. The Duke of Argyll's family, the senior branch of the Campbell Clan, moved from Loch Awe to Inveraray in the first half of the 15th century. The present building, in the style of a castle, was erected between 1745 and 1790 to replace an earlier traditional fortified keep, and marks the start of more settled times. It was designed by Roger Morris and Robert Mylne. On display are the famous collections of armour, French tapestries, fine examples of Scottish and European furniture, and a wealth of other works of art together with a genealogical display in the Clan Room. Gardens open by appointment only.
☎ *01499 302203*   www.inveraray-castle.com

🏛 **Inveraray Jail** `74 C4`
Church Square, Inveraray. Award-winning attraction. Visitors can see a medieval punishment exhibition, listen to trials in the superb 1820 courtroom, visit the airing yards, talk with guides dressed as warders, prisoners and matron, experience life inside prison and try the crank machine, whipping table and hammocks, before comparing all this with a new exhibition In Prison Today.
☎ *01499 302381*

🏛 **Inveraray Maritime Museum** `74 C4`
Arctic Penguin, The Pier, Inveraray. A fascinating collection of maritime displays, memorabilia, archive film and entertaining hands-on activities on board one of the last iron ships built (1911). Graphic tableaux in the hold depict the hardships suffered on emigrant ships during the Highland clearances. Inveraray was the birthplace of Neil Munro, author of the Para Handy stories. Scotland's last working Clyde Puffer (a small cargo vessel) takes visitors on a short cruise of Loch Fyne.
☎ *01499 302213*

✹ **Inverawe Fisheries & Smokery Exhibition** `79 E3`
Inverawe House, Taynuilt. Turning off the A85, 14 miles (22.5km) east of Oban. Visitors can fish on one of the four stocked lochs, take a look at how the smokery works, and wander around the 50 acre (20ha) estate.
☎ *01866 822446*

🏛 **Inverbeg Galleries** `75 G5`
Inverbeg, Loch Lomond. On the A82, 3 miles (5km) north of Luss. An internationally renowned art gallery with one of the largest selections of oil and watercolour paintings and prints in the UK.
☎ *01436 860277*

✹ **Iona** `77 D5`
An island off the south west tip of the Isle of Mull. Car and coach parking at Fionnphort. The island where Columba began to spread the gospel in 563AD. Superb long sandy beaches and turquoise seas. Unrivalled views.
☎ *01631 570000 (National Trust Office)*   www.nts.org.uk

✝ **Iona Abbey** `77 D5`
On the Isle of Iona, off the south west tip of the Isle of Mull. Car and coach parking at Fionnphort. The site of St Columba's landing in 563AD and his original monastery. From here Christianity spread throughout Scotland and beyond. A Benedictine monastery was founded in 1203, but it fell into ruin at the Reformation in the 16th century. The cathedral was restored in 1910 and has a beautiful interior and carvings. The monastic buildings were later restored by the Iona Community who provide week-long programmes for guests. The abbey precincts contain the graves of many kings and chiefs, the restored St Oran's Chapel, and the 10th century St Martin's Cross.
☎ *01681 700512*   www.historic-scotland.gov.uk

🏛 **Iona Gallery & Pottery** `77 D5`
Beside Iona Abbey. A working pottery where visitors can see work in progress. Displays both thrown and hand-built decorative stoneware. Late 19th century and early 20th century paintings and etchings, and contemporary landscapes. Also limited edition prints.
☎ *01681 700439*   www.ionagallery.com

✹ **Iona Heritage Centre** `77 D5`
On the Isle of Iona, off the south west tip of the Isle of Mull, 0.3 mile (0.5km) from the ferry. Located in the old Telford Manse. Displays illustrate the lives of the islanders over the past 200 years.
☎ *01681 700576*

✎ **Island Encounter, Wildlife/Birdwatch Safaris** `77 G3`
Located on the Isle of Mull, the Island Encounter wildlife/birdwatch safaris offer whole day trips for visitors wishing to see and experience wildlife and birds in areas of the island not usually visited. Binoculars, telescopes and lunch provided.
☎ *01680 300441*

✹ **Islay Woollen Mill** `66 C3`
On the Askaig Road, 1 mile (2km) from Bridgend. An early Victorian mill containing a tweed and woollen factory which produces tartan including all the tartans used in the films Braveheart and Rob Roy.
☎ *01496 810563*

✹ **Isle of Islay Natural History Trust** `66 B4`
Islay Wildlife Information Centre, Port Charlotte, Isle of Islay. The Wildlife Information Centre has displays on all aspects of Islay's wildlife and landscape, as well as an extensive reference library, a children's room and a laboratory where children and adults can try a number of hands-on activities such as dissecting owl pellets and making seaweed pictures. Family activity sessions during July and August.
☎ *01496 850288*

🍾 **Isle of Jura Distillery** `67 E4`
Craighouse, Isle of Jura. A distillery built in 1810 on a site where illegal distillation occurred for almost 300 years.
☎ *01496 820240*

✹ **Isle of Mull Angora Rabbit Farm** `72 C2`
Rehmor Croft, on the A849, 1 mile (2km) east of Bunessan. A farm with about 30 Angora rabbits bred for their hair (which is used for knitting yarns on sale). Visitors can hold and stroke the rabbits and learn all about them. Clipping and spinning demonstrations daily.
☎ *01681 700507*

✎ **Isle of Mull Landrover Wildlife Expeditions** `77 F2`
Ulva House Hotel, Tobermory. Explore Mull's wildlife and the island's immensely varied habitats, guided by a Hebridean wildlife expert. Visitors usually see otters, sea eagles, golden eagles, seals, deer, porpoises etc.
☎ *01688 302044*

🏛 **Isle of Mull Museum** `77 G2`
Main Street, Tobermory, Isle of Mull. An exhibition of items, facts and photos of Mull's history.

✹ **Isle of Mull Weavers** `73 F1`
The Steading, Torosay Castle, Craignure. On the A849, 1.5 miles (2.5km) south of Craignure ferry. Weaving demonstrations all day.
☎ *01680 812381*

❈ **Jura House Garden** `67 D3`
Ardfin, Craighouse, Isle of Jura. On the A846, 5 miles (8km) from Feolin Ferry (to Islay). Interesting woodland and cliff walks with points of local historical interest and, for keen natural historians, abundant wildlife and flowers. The organic garden offers a wide variety of unusual plants and shrubs suited to the protected west coast climate, including a large Australasian collection. The house is not open to visitors.
☎ *01496 820315*

✝ **Keills Chapel** `67 F1`
6 miles (9.5km) south west of Tayvallich. A small west Highland chapel housing a collection of grave slabs and Keills Cross.
☎ *0131 668 8800*   www.historic-scotland.gov.uk

✝ **Kilberry Sculptured Stones** `67 G3`
At Kilberry Castle off the B8024, 17 miles (27km) south south-west of Lochgilphead, on the west coast of Knapdale. A fine collection of late medieval sculptured stones gathered from the Kilberry estate.
☎ *0131 668 8800*   www.historic-scotland.gov.uk

⚔ **Kilchurn Castle** `79 F4`
At the north east end of Loch Awe, 2.5 miles (4km) west of Dalmally. A substantial ruin based on a square tower built by Colin Campbell of Glenorchy circa 1550, but much enlarged in 1693 by Ian, Earl of Breadalbane, whose arms are over the gateway with those of his wife. It incorporates the first purpose built barracks in Scotland. Spectacular views down Loch Awe
☎ *0131 668 8800*   www.historic-scotland.gov.uk

✝ **Kildalton Cross** `67 D5`
On the island of Islay, 2 miles (3km) east north-east of Port Ellen. The finest intact High Cross in Scotland, carved in the late 8th century.
☎ *0131 668 8800*   www.historic-scotland.gov.uk

✹ **Kilmahog Woollen Mill** `80 D5`
1 mile (2km) north of Callander. A 250-year-old mill with the original waterwheel. Visitors can trace the history of Scottish clans and tartans. Knitwear, clothing and gifts for sale.
☎ *01877 330268*

🏛 **Kilmartin House Museum of Ancient Culture** `73 G5`
Kilmartin, on the A816, 9 miles (14.5km) north of Lochgilphead. Award-winning archaeological museum which examines the relationship between Scotland's richest prehistoric landscape and its people. Ancient monuments, local artefacts and bookshop.
☎ *01546 510278*   www.kilmartin.org

✝ **Kilmartin Sculptured Stones** `73 G5`
In Kilmartin Churchyard, Kilmartin, on the A816, 9 miles (14.5km) north of Lochgilphead. Carved west Highland grave slabs housed in a former mausoleum and in the church. One cross dates from the 16th century.
☎ *0131 668 8800*   www.historic-scotland.gov.uk

✝ **Kilmichael Glassary Cup & Ring Marks**   `73 G5`
Kilmartin Glen. Near the schoolhouse in the village of Kilmichael Glassary, 5 miles (8km) north of Lochgilphead. Bronze Age cup and ring carvings on a natural rock outcrop.
☎ *0131 668 8800*   www.historic-scotland.gov.uk

✝ **Kilmodan Sculptured Stones**   `68 B1`
At Clachan of Glendaruel, on the A886, 8 miles (13km) north of Colintraive. A group of west Highland carved grave slabs in a churchyard.
☎ *0131 668 8800*   www.historic-scotland.gov.uk

❊ **Kilmory Castle Gardens**   `68 A1`
On the A83, 2 miles (3.2km) from the centre of Kilmory. The garden was started in the 1770s and included around 100 varieties of rhododendron – it supplied plants for Kew Gardens. Now attached to the local council buildings, the gardens have been restored, with woodland walks, nature trails, herbaceous borders and a sensory trail.
☎ *01546 602127*

✝ **Kilmory Knap Chapel**   `67 G2`
On the shore between Loch Sween and Loch Caolisport in South Knapdale. A small medieval west Highland church with a collection of typical grave slabs. In the church is Macmillan's Cross, a splendid piece of medieval carving.
☎ *0131 668 8800*   www.historic-scotland.gov.uk

✝ **Kilmun (St Munn's) Church**   `69 D1`
Kilmun, 6 miles (10km) from Dunoon on the A880. On the site of a 7th century Celtic monastery. The tower of a 15th century collegiate church still stands. The present building by Thomas Burns dates from 1841, with the interior re-modelled in 1899. Important stained glass. Water-powered organ. Ancient graveyard including fine 18th century carved stones. Mausoleum of Dukes of Argyll. Douglas vault. Grave of Elizabeth Blackwell, the first lady doctor.
☎ *01369 840342*

♛ **King's Knot**   `70 C1`
Below the Castle Rock in Stirling. The earthworks of a splendid formal garden, probably made in 1628 for Charles I.
☎ *0131 668 8800*   www.historic-scotland.gov.uk

❊ **Kinlochlaich Gardens**   `78 D2`
Kinlochlaich House, on the A828, entrance beside the police station at Appin. A walled garden behind Kinlochlaich House surrounded by mature trees in outstanding Highland scenery. Built with the house at the end of the 18th century by John Campbell. Garden plant centre offering an extensive range of plants. Dogs not permitted.
☎ *01631 730342*   www.kinlochlaich-house.co.uk

🏠 **Kinneil House**   `71 E3`
On the western outskirts of Bo'ness. A 15th century tower set in a public park. Remodelled by the Earl of Arran between 1546 and 1550 and transformed into a stately home for the Dukes of Hamilton in the 1660s.
☎ *0131 668 8800*   www.historic-scotland.gov.uk

🏛 **Kinneil Museum**   `71 E2`
2 miles (3km) west of Bo'ness town centre. Displays on the history of Kinneil Estate and the social history of Bo'ness.
☎ *01506 778530*

✝ **Kippen Parish Church**   `70 B1`
Fore Road, Kippen, off the A811, 9 miles (14.5km) west of Stirling. A church built in 1824, but modernised in 1924 under the guidance of Sir D. Y. Cameron RA. He and others donated works of art which, with distinguished Webster Windows, make it one of the most beautiful churches in Scotland.

🌿 **Knapdale Forest**   `73 G5`
Near Lochgilphead, Argyll. The name Knapdale is derived from Cnap (hill) and Dall (field). The forest is flanked to the north by the Crinan Canal and to the west by the Sound of Jura and Loch Sween. Historical and archaeological sites include ancient Castle Dounie. Waymarked walks and cycle rides, from where seals, otters and porpoises can be seen.
www.forestry.gov.uk

★ **Kyles of Bute**   `68 B2`
Narrow arm of the Firth of Clyde, between Isle of Bute and Argyll. A 16 mile (25.5km) stretch of water which presents a constantly changing view of great beauty. It can perhaps be best appreciated from the A8003, Tighnabruaich to Glendaruel road, where there are two view indicators. The western indicator (Scottish Civic Trust) looks over the West Kyle and identifies many features. The east one (NTS) looks over Loch Ridden and the East Kyle.

🍾 **Lagavulin Distillery Visitor Centre**   `66 C5`
Port Ellen on the Isle of Islay. 3 miles (5km) from the ferry on the A846. Home of the famous Lagavulin single malt, established in 1816. The distillery is set beside the ruins of Dun Naomhaig Castle, ancient stronghold of the Lords of the Isles. Tours and tastings.
☎ *01496 302730*

✝ **Lamont Memorial**   `69 D2`
Dunoon. Stone Celtic Cross erected in 1906 to mark the massacre of the Lamonts by the Campbells in 1646.

🍾 **Laphroaig Distillery**   `66 C5`
Port Ellen on the Isle of Islay. A working distillery illustrating the whisky making process in depth.
☎ *01496 302418*   www.laphroaig.com

★ **Leighton Library**   `81 E5`
In the centre of Dunblane, 0.25 mile (0.5km) from the station. One of the oldest libraries in Scotland, dating from 1684. Robert Leighton (1611 – 1684) Bishop of Dunblane and later Archbishop of Glasgow left his collection of 1400 books with instructions that they were to be available for the use of the clergy and provided money for a chamber to be built to house the collection. The library later became a subscription lending library from 1734 to circa 1840, with the collection increasing to 4500 books, mainly first editions.
☎ *01786 822296*

🏞 **Levegrove Park**   `69 F2`
Dumbarton. Beautiful open park stretching to the shores of the River Clyde. Formal flower gardens and magnificent trees. Contains the ruins of an old parish church and the burial place of the Dixon family. Putting green, crazy golf.

❊ **Linn Botanic Gardens & Nursery**   `69 E1`
Cove, Helensburgh, on the B833, 10 miles (16km) from Garelochhead. A garden developed since 1971 around a listed Clyde coast villa in the style of Greek Thompson. Thousands of unusual, exotic and rare plants, extensive water garden, formal ponds and fountains, herbaceous borders, glen with waterfall, cliff garden and rockery. Signed route of just over half a mile (1km) through garden.
☎ *01436 842242*

🚢 **Loch Awe Steam Packet**   `79 F4`
25 miles (40km) east of Oban and 2 miles (3km) west of Dalmally on the A85. Steamboat rides to Kilchurn Castle and cruises around Loch Awe on the steamers Lady Rowena and the Flower of Scotland.
☎ *01866 833333*

★ **Loch Fad Fishery**   `68 C3`
Loch Fad, Isle of Bute. On the B878, 0.75 mile (1km) from Rothesay pier. Fishing for rainbow or brown trout from banks or boats.
☎ *01700 504871*   www.lochfad.com

★ **Loch Fyne Miniature Railway**   `68 A1`
The Green, Ardrishaig, 3 miles (5km) from Lochgilphead on the A83. Overlooking Loch Fyne, the railway has two engines: the Flying Scotsman, a steam replica of the original, a real enthusiast's engine; and a diesel-type shunter, yet to be named.
☎ *01546 603250*

★ **Loch Lomond**   `69 F1`
Loch Lomond, the largest stretch of inland water in Britain, and framed by lovely mountain scenery, is a popular centre for all watersports. Cruises are available around the banks and attractive small islands.

★ **Loch Sloy Hydro-Electric Station**   `80 A5`
By Inveruglas on the A82, Loch Lomondside. Opened in 1950, Loch Sloy was the first of the Hydro-Electric Board's major generating plants to come into service. The station is open to organised parties on application (there is a charge). Interesting walk to Loch Sloy dam across the road.
☎ *01796 484000*

★ **Lomond Shores**   `69 F1`
Balloch, at the southern tip of Loch Lomond. Opening in 2002, Lomond Shores will feature a visitor centre introducing visitors to Scotland's first national park, and a large format film theatre screening a specially commissioned film about Loch Lomond. Also indoor and outdoor children's play areas. Stunning views of Ben Lomond.
☎ *01389 721500*   www.lomondshores.com

★ **Luss Visitor Centre**   `75 F5`
Luss, off the A82, 8 miles from Balloch. Visitor centre offering information on Loch Lomond and the Trossachs National Park. Audio-visual show and exhibition. There is also an information point at Inveruglas.
☎ *01301 702785*

✝ **Maclean's Cross**   `77 D5`
On the island of Iona, off the west coast of Mull. A fine 15th century free-standing cross.
☎ *0131 668 8800*   www.historic-scotland.gov.uk

★ **Maid of the Loch**   `69 F1`
Balloch Pier. Maid of the Loch is the largest UK inland waterways vessel ever built, a paddle steamer originally launched in 1953 and laid up in 1981. Now under restoration, visitors can see an exhibition and watch the restoration underway.
☎ *01389 711865*   www.maidoftheloch.co.uk

🏠 **Mar's Wark**   `70 C1`
At the top of Castle Wynd, Stirling. A remarkable Renaissance mansion built by the Regent Mar in 1570, of which the façade is the main surviving part.
☎ *0131 668 8800*   www.historic-scotland.gov.uk

♛ **McCaig's Tower**   `78 C3`
On a hill overlooking Oban. McCaig was a local banker who tried to curb unemployment by using local craftsmen to build this tower (1897 – 1900) as a memorial to his family. Its walls are 2ft (0.5m) thick and from 30 – 47ft (9 – 14m) high. The courtyard within is landscaped and the tower is floodlit at night in summer. An observation platform on the seaward side was added in 1983.

★ **Mill Trail Visitor Centre**   `71 D1`
West Stirling Street, Alva, on the A91, 8 miles (13km) east of Stirling. An exhibition telling the story of spinning and weaving in Clackmannan (the Wee County). Features the experience of a 13-year-old working in the mills. Original weaving and knitting looms. Shop sells wide variety of local craft goods, books and knitwear.
☎ *01259 769696*

Central West Scotland

Moirlanich Longhouse — 80 C2
Off the A827, 1 mile (1.5km) north west of Killin. An outstanding example of a traditional cruck-frame cottage and byre dating from the mid 19th century. Inhabited until 1968, the house retains many original features and is furnished according to archaeological evidence.
☎ 01567 820988
www.nts.org.uk

Monument Hill — 79 F4
Off the old road to Inveraray, 2 miles (3km) south west of Dalmally. Monument to Duncan Ban Macintyre (1724 – 1812), the Burns of the Highlands, who was born near Inveroran.

Morag's Fairy Glen — 69 D2
Dunoon. This delightful glen was gifted to the town by Bailie George Jones.

Motoring Heritage Centre — 69 F1
Main Street, Alexandria. A motor heritage centre situated in what was once the world's largest motor car works, now Loch Lomond Factory Outlets. Display traces the history of the once-famous Argyll marque and the story of Scottish motoring. Visitors can sit in a Model T Ford, see unique archive film and fascinating carts.
☎ 01389 607862

Mount Stuart — 68 D4
Mount Stuart, Isle of Bute. 5 miles (8km) south of Rothesay. Spectacular Victorian Gothic house, the ancestral home of the Marquess of Bute. Splendid interiors, art collection and architectural detail. Mature Victorian pinetum, arboretum and exotic gardens, waymarked walks. Three hundred acres (121ha) of ground and gardens. Audio-visual presentation.
☎ 01700 503877
www.mountstuart.com

Mugdock Country Park — 70 A3
Craigallian Road, Milngavie, 10 miles (16km) north of Glasgow. Eight hundred acres (323ha) of beautiful countryside – lakes, woodland and moorland. Mugdock and Craigend Castles. Countryside events – orienteering, archery. Craigend stables and bridle routes. Also garden centre, craft shops, play areas, walks and Victorian walled garden
☎ 0141 956 6100
www.mugdock-country-park.org.uk

Mull Rail — 73 F1
In Craignure, 0.25 mile (0.5km) south east of the ferry terminal. Scotland's only (narrow gauge) island passenger railway, running between Craignure and Torosay Castle. Scenic journey lasts 20 minutes. Steam and diesel locomotives.
☎ 01680 812494

Museum of Islay Life — 66 B4
Off the A847 in Port Charlotte. The museum illustrates life on Islay from prehistoric times to the early 20th century. Also the Gordon Booth Library, where archives, photographs and books relating to island life may be consulted. In the Wee Museum of Childhood there are hands-on activities and quizzes for all ages.
☎ 01496 850358

National Wallace Monument — 70 D1
Abbey Craig, Hillfoot Road, 1.5 miles (2.5km) north north-east of Stirling. The National Wallace Monument takes visitors back 700 years in time to the days of Scotland's first struggle for independence. The story of William Wallace, freedom fighter and national hero, is told along with background and events that shaped this period of history. Climb the 246 steps of the 220ft (67m) high tower for superb views.
☎ 01786 472140

Nether Largie Cairns — 73 G5
Kilmartin Glen, between Kilmartin and Nether Largie. One Neolithic and two Bronze Age cairns. There is access to the chamber in the north cairn.
☎ 0131 668 8800
www.historic-scotland.gov.uk

North Third Trout Fisheries — 70 C2
Greathill, 5 miles (8km) south west of Stirling. A rainbow trout fly-only fishery with over 120 acres (48ha) of water set in magnificent surroundings and offering both boat and bank angling. Famed for producing large numbers of fish weighing over 10lb (4.5kg) each. Expert advice is available.
☎ 01786 471967

Oban Distillery Visitor Centre — 78 C4
Stafford Street, Oban. Take a guided tour and learn about the ancient craft of distilling. Visitor centre with exhibition tells the history of Oban.
☎ 01631 572004

Oban Highland Theatre — 78 C4
George Street, Oban. A complex of two cinemas, theatre and exhibition area. Occasional videos focussing on Oban, Lorn and the Isles.
☎ 01631 562444

Oban Rare Breeds Farm Park — 78 C4
2 miles (3km) from Oban along the Glencruitten Road. Displays rare breeds of farm animals – cattle, sheep, pigs, poultry, goats. Pets' corner. Woodland walk and beautiful views.
☎ 01631 770608

Ochil Hills Woodland Park — 71 E1
0.5 miles north of the A91 between Alva and Tillicoultry. The remains of the grounds of Alva House (now demolished). Woodland walks and children's play area.

Old Byre Heritage Centre — 77 F3
1.5 miles (2.5km) south west of Dervaig on the Isle of Mull (0.6 mile/1km private road off Torloisk road at Dervaig end). A genuine stone byre which has been converted into a museum, tearoom and gift shop. The social history of Mull has been created in miniature.
☎ 01688 400229

Overtoun Estate — 69 G2
Dumbarton. Historic gardens, picnic areas, spectacular views, Victorian architecture, wildlife. Guided walks through the summer.
☎ 01389 742544

Puck's Glen — 69 D1
6 miles north of Dunoon on the A815, near Benmore Botanic Gardens. A delightful natural walk with a viewpoint and picnic area.

Queen Elizabeth Forest Park Visitor Centre — 80 C5
Located in Aberfoyle, the Queen Elizabeth Forest Park was first designated a Forest Park by the Forestry Commission in 1953, to mark the coronation of Queen Elizabeth II. It encompasses mountain and moorland, forest and woodland, rivers and lochs, and is home to a rich variety of animal and plant life. The visitor centre is situated on a hillside above Aberfoyle, with spectacular views in all directions, and provides information on all aspects of the forest and activities throughout the year. Resident woodcarver. Orienteering routes.
☎ 01877 382258
www.forestry.gov.uk

Queen's View, Loch Lomond — 70 A2
Off the A809, 12 miles (19km) north north-west of Glasgow. From the west side of the road a path leads to a viewpoint where, in 1879, Queen Victoria had her first view of Loch Lomond.

Rest & Be Thankful — 75 E4
At the head of Glen Croe, 4 miles (6km) north west of Ardgartan. Aptly named steep road pass, linking Glen Kinglas and Glen Croe. The original General Wade road, completed in 1750, can still be seen. This was where cattle drovers enjoyed a well deserved break after a tough climb. Also a viewpoint.

Ri Cruin Cairn — 73 G5
Kilmartin Glen, 1 mile (2km) south west of Kilmartin. A Bronze Age burial cairn with the covering removed to reveal three massive cists. Axe heads are carved on one of the cist slabs.
☎ 0131 668 8800
www.historic-scotland.gov.uk

Rob Roy & Trossachs Visitor Centre — 80 D5
Ancaster Square in Callander, 16 miles (25.5km) north west of Stirling on the A84. Discover the truth behind the remarkable life of notorious outlaw Rob Roy MacGregor in an exciting exhibition, which includes a replica black house and the opportunity to dress as a highlander. Audio-visual presentation.
☎ 01877 330342

Rob Roy's Grave — 80 C3
West end of Balquhidder Churchyard, off the A84, 14 miles (22.5km) north north-west of Callander. Three flat gravestones enclosed by railings are the graves of Rob Roy, his wife and two of his sons. The church itself contains St Angus' Stone (8th century), a 17th century bell from the old church, and old Gaelic Bibles.

Rothesay Castle — 68 C3
Castlehill Street, Rothesay, Isle of Bute. By ferry from Wemyss Bay on the A78. A remarkable 13th century castle of enclosure, circular in plan, with 16th century forework. Breaches made by Norsemen in 1240 are evident. A favourite residence of the Stewart kings.
☎ 01700 502691
www.historic-scotland.gov.uk

Rough Castle — 70 D3
Off the B816, 6 miles (9.5km) west of Falkirk. The best preserved length of the Antonine Wall. Consists of a rampart and ditch, together with the earthworks of a fort. Also a short length of military way with quarry pits.
☎ 0131 668 8800
www.historic-scotland.gov.uk

Royal Burgh of Stirling Visitor Centre — 70 C1
Located at Stirling Castle esplanade. The story of Royal Stirling, from the wars of independence and life in the medieval burgh, to the present day. Sound and light exhibition, multi-lingual audio-visual show.
☎ 01786 462517
www.visitscottishheartlands.org

Saddell Abbey — 64 C2
On the B842, 9 miles (14.5km) north north-west of Campbeltown. The abbey was built in the 12th century by Somerled, Lord of the Isles, or his son Reginald. Only the walls of the original building are left, with sculptured carved tombstones.

St Blane's Church — 68 C4
At the south end of the Isle of Bute, 8.5 miles (13.5km) south of Rothesay. By ferry from Wemyss Bay on the A78. The ruins of a 12th century Romanesque chapel set within the foundations of a Celtic Monastery.
☎ 0131 668 8800
www.historic-scotland.gov.uk

St Columba Centre — 72 B2
Isle of Mull, 38 miles (61km) from Craignure and situated behind Fionnphort village, near ferry terminal for Iona. Exhibition on St Columba, Iona and Celtic heritage of interest to all visitors. Opportunities to practice script writing.
☎ 01681 700640
www.historic-scotland.gov.uk

St Columba's Cave — 67 G2
On the west shore of Loch Killisport (Caolisport), 1 mile (1.5km) north of Ellary, 10 miles (16km) south west of Ardrishaig. Traditionally associated with St Columba's arrival in Scotland, the cave contains a rock-shelf with an altar, above which are carved crosses. A large basin, perhaps a Stone Age mortar, may have been used as a font. The cave was occupied from the Middle Stone Age. In front are traces of houses and the ruins of a chapel (possibly 13th century). Another cave is nearby.

St Cormac's Chapel — 67 F2
On Eilean Mor, a small island off the coast of Knapdale in the Sound of Jura. A chapel with a vaulted chancel containing the effigy of an ecclesiastical figure. Probably 12th century.
☎ 0131 668 8800
www.historic-scotland.gov.uk

† St John's Church · 69 D2
Argyll Street, Dunoon. A magnificent nave and aisles church by R. A. Bryden (1877) with Gothic spired tower. Galleried concert hall interior, raised choir behind central pulpit, organ 1895. Interesting stained glass windows, including Lauder Memorial.

† St Mary's Chapel · 68 C3
On the A845, 0.5 mile (1km) south of Rothesay on the Isle of Bute. The late-medieval remains of the chancel of the parish church of St Mary, with fine tombs.
☎ 0131 668 8800   www.historic-scotland.gov.uk

† St Ninian's · 68 C3
South west of Rothesay along the B878 for 2.5 miles, joining the A844 at Milton, then unclassified road to Straad. The foundations of St Ninian's chapel, dating back to the 6th century, together with its surrounding garth wall are still clearly visible on this remote peninsula.

🏛 Sandaig Museum · 76 A3
The Thatched Cottage Museum, Sandaig, western Tiree. Located in a terrace of traditional thatched buildings, the museum houses a unique collection of items illustrating life in a late 19th century cottar's home. The adjoining byre and barn display elements of agricultural work at the croft, a testimony to the Hebridean islanders' self-sufficiency.
☎ 01865 311468   www.hebrideantrust.org

✹ Scotkart Indoor Kart Racing Centre · 70 A4
Clydebank, 5 miles (8km) from Glasgow City Centre. A large indoor motorsport centre featuring 200cc pro-karts capable of over 40mph. The track can be booked for practice lapping or visitors can compete in a professionally organised race meeting. All equipment and instruction provided

✹ Scottish Sealife & Marine Sanctuary · 78 D2
Barcaldine, Connel, on the A828, 10 miles (16km) north of Oban. Visitors can explore over 30 fascinating natural marine habitats, including a unique Herring Ring, and have close encounters with many sea creatures, including seals. In a picturesque setting among pine trees on the shore of Loch Creran.
☎ 01631 720386   www.sealsanctuary.co.uk

✹ Scottish Wool Centre · 80 C5
Off Main Street in Aberfoyle. Visitor centre and theatre telling the story of Scottish Wool, with a live show with live sheep. Children's farm. Traditional spinners in action. Wide range of woollens, knitwear, gifts and souvenirs.
☎ 01877 382850

⚓ Seabegs Wood · 70 D3
1 mile (2km) west of Bonnybridge. A stretch of rampart and ditch of the Antonine Wall with military way behind.
☎ 0131 668 8800   www.historic-scotland.gov.uk

🏛 Skerryvore Lighthouse Museum · 76 A4
At Hynish village, western Tiree. Located in the old signal tower, the museum tells the story of the construction of the lighthouse, visible for over 10 miles (16km) off shore. Skerryvore lighthouse was constructed on the infamous reef of the same name, by a team led by Alan Stevenson (uncle of Robert Louis Stevenson).
☎ 01865 311468

🏰 Skipness Castle & Chapel · 68 B4
On the coast at Skipness on the B8001, 10 miles (16km) south of Tarbert, Argyll. Bus from Tarbert to Skipness, then 0.5 mile (1km) walk. A fine 13th century castle with a 16th century tower house in one corner. Nearby is an early 14th century chapel with fine grave slabs.
☎ 0131 668 8800   www.historic-scotland.gov.uk

🏛 Smith Art Gallery & Museum · 70 C1
Dumbarton Road, Stirling, a short walk from the bus and rail stations. Displays and exhibitions on the history of Stirling. Fine art, natural history. Educational programme (telephone for details).
☎ 01786 471917   www.smithartgallery.demon.co.uk

🍾 Springbank Distillery · 64 C4
In the centre of Campbeltown. Founded in 1828, the distillery remains under the control of the great-great grandson of the original founder. Springbank Distillery is the only distillery in Scotland to carry out the entire distilling process, from traditional malting through to bottling.
☎ 01586 552085

✹ Staffa · 77 E4
Island 6 miles (10km) north east of Iona and 7 miles (11km) west of Mull. Romantic uninhabited island famed for its extraordinary basaltic column formations. The best known of these is Fingal's Cave, inspiration for Mendelssohn's Hebrides overture. Visitors can view the cave from a boat, or land on the island if weather conditions permit. A colony of puffins nests on the island.
☎ 01631 570000   www.nts.org.uk

£ Sterling Mills Designer Outlet Village · 71 E1
Tillicoultry. 7 miles (11km) east of Stirling. Fashion, designer and branded merchandise direct from manufacturers or brand owners. Guaranteed discount off high street prices.
☎ 01259 752100

🏰 Stirling Castle · 70 C1
Castle Wynd, at the head of Stirling old town, off the M9. Considered by many as Scotland's grandest castle, it is certainly one of the most important. The castle architecture is outstanding and the Great Hall and Chapel Royal are amongst the highlights. Mary, Queen of Scots was crowned here and narrowly escaped death by fire in 1561. Medieval kitchen display and exhibition on life in the royal palace.
☎ 01786 450000   www.historic-scotland.gov.uk

✹ Stirling Old Bridge · 70 C1
In Stirling just beside the Customs Roundabout off the A9. A handsome bridge built in the 15th or early 16th century. The southern arch was rebuilt in 1749 after it had been blown up during the '45 rebellion to prevent the Stuart army entering the town.
☎ 0131 668 8800   www.historic-scotland.gov.uk

🏛 Stirling Old Town Jail · 70 C1
St John Street, at the top of the Old Town in Stirling, five minute walk from rail and bus stations. A 150-year-old Victorian Gothic jail, once a military and a civil establishment. Living history performances detail crime and punishment through the ages (Sat – Sun during summer, by arrangement for groups during winter). Audio tour in winter.
☎ 01786 450050

🏛 Strachur Smiddy Museum · 74 D4
The Clachan, Strachur, on the A815 beside Loch Fyne, 20 miles (32km) north of Dunoon and 20 miles (32km) east of Inveraray. Dating from before 1790, now restored to working order. On display are bellows, anvil, boring beam, hammers, tongs and other tools of the blacksmith and the farrier. Occasional demonstrations. Also a craft shop with a selection of modern craftwork.
☎ 01369 860565   www.opraappers.nl/strachursmiddy/museum.htm

✝ Temple Wood Stone Circles · 73 G5
0.25 mile (0.5km) south west of Nether Largie, Argyll. A circle of upright stones about 3000 years old, and the remains of an earlier circle.
☎ 0131 668 8800   www.historic-scotland.gov.uk

✹ Tighnabruaich Viewpoint · 68 B2
North east of Tighnabruaich on the A8003. A high vantage point, with explanatory indicators identifying surrounding sites. Spectacular views over the Kyles of Bute and the islands of the Firth of Clyde.
www.nts.org.uk

🍾 Tobermory Distillery · 77 G2
Tobermory, Isle of Mull. Malt whisky is distilled using traditional methods. Guided tours and a video presentation reveal the ingredients and distilling process.
☎ 01688 302647

❊ Torosay Castle & Gardens · 73 F1
1 mile (2km) south east of Craignure, Isle of Mull. This Victorian family home contains furniture, pictures and scrapbooks dating from Edwardian times. Torosay is surrounded by 12 acres (5ha) of gardens, including formal terraces and a statue walk, set amidst fuchsia hedges. Woodland and water gardens, eucalyptus walk and rockery all contain many and varied plants. The gardens offer extensive views past Duart Castle and the Sound of Mull to the mountains of Arran and Lorne.
☎ 01680 812421   www.holidaymull.org/members/torosay

✹ Torrisdale Castle Organic Tannery · 64 C2
Torrisdale Castle on the B842, 1 mile (1.5km) south of Carradale on the east coast of Kintyre. A small rural tannery using an ancient method of tanning skins to make leather. The only organic tannery in the country. Visitors can see skins being processed by hand. Finished sheepskins for sale, as well as cushions, slippers, and gloves.
☎ 01583 431233   www.torrisdalecastle.com

🏰 Toward Castle · 68 D3
2 miles south of Innellan on the A815. Ruins of the seat of the Clan Lamont, destroyed by the Campbells in 1646.

✹ Trossachs Discovery Centre · 80 C5
Aberfoyle, Stirling. The Discovery Centre contains interactive touch screens and interpretive displays describing local geography, geology and famous local characters. Also shop selling local maps, guides and gifts.
☎ 01877 382352

🚂 Trossachs Pier Complex · 80 B5
Loch Katrine, 8 miles (13km) west of Callander on the A821. Set in the heart of the Trossachs, the complex has extensive lochside walks and cycle routes, and cruises on Loch Katrine on a steam ship first launched in 1899.
☎ 01877 376316

✹ Trossachs Woollen Mill · 80 C5
Kilmahog, 1 mile (2km) north of Callander. Resident weaver demonstrates skilled weaving techniques to produce the unique Trossachs Woollen Rug, available in the mill shop. Also quality knitwear, outerwear and gifts.
☎ 01877 330178

✹ Union Canal · 71 D3
From the south of Falkirk to the centre of Edinburgh via Linlithgow, Broxburn and Ratho. The Forth and Clyde and the Union Canals formed an important commercial transport corridor across central Scotland for nearly two centuries. They fell victim to the roads culture of the 1960s when they were blocked at more than 30 sites and broken up into short sections. One of the biggest canal restoration projects in Europe, the Millennuim Link has brought the 69 miles (110km) of canal, from Glasgow to Edinburgh and the Forth to the Clyde, back to life.
☎ 01324 671217   www.scottishcanals.co.uk

✹ Village Glass · 70 C1
14 Henderson Street, Bridge of Allan, 4 miles (6.5km) north of Stirling on the A9. Unique glass studio. Visitors can witness the beautiful glassware being created.
☎ 01786 832137   www.villageglass.co.uk

✝ Watling Lodge · 71 D2
In Falkirk, signposted from the A9. The best section of the ditch of the Antonine Wall.
☎ 0131 668 8800   www.historic-scotland.gov.uk

✝ Westquarter Dovecot · 71 E3
At Westquarter, near Lauriston, 2 miles (3km) east of Falkirk. A handsome rectangular dovecot with a heraldic panel dated 1647 over the entrance doorway.
☎ 0131 668 8800   www.historic-scotland.gov.uk

Central East Scotland

Located just 80 miles (129 km) north of Edinburgh and Glasgow, this part of Scotland makes an ideal holiday destination.

Perthshire has mountains, lochs and castles, and opportunities for walking, golfing and fishing, as well as fine theatres, museums and restaurants. Angus and Dundee make a good touring base, with mountainous glens, rugged coastline, pleasant beaches and lots of things to see and do. The ancient Kingdom of Fife has plenty of character. The attractive East Neuk fishing villages nestle amongst the natural harbours of the coastline, and St Andrews is the location of the oldest university in Scotland, and, of course the home of golf.

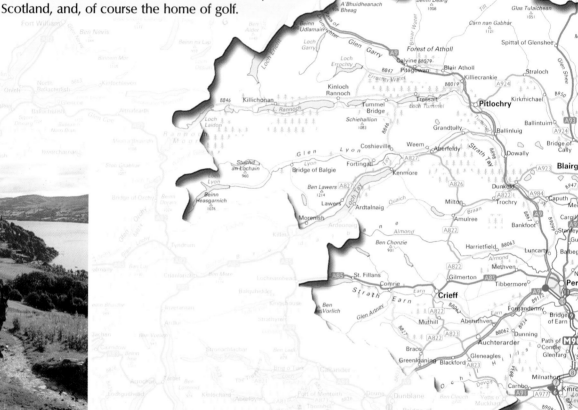

Horse riding, Loch Tay

Fife

The ancient Kingdom of Fife is bounded on three sides by the sea – the Firth of Tay to the north, the North Sea to the east and the Firth of Forth to the south. Although St Andrews is often the focus of attention for visitors there are other areas worth exploring. Rural north Fife is popular for walking, cycling and horse riding. Central Fife is dominated by the port and resort of Kirkcaldy and in the west is Culross, one the best preserved examples of a Scottish burgh in the country.

St Andrews Castle

The Pictish legacy

This area was part of the 8th century Pictish kingdom and many beautifully carved stones still stand as reminders of the past. See the sculptured stones at Aberlemno, St Vigeans, Meigle or the stones in Montrose Museum or Brechin Cathedral.

R.R.S. Discovery

Places to visit in Angus & Dundee

Angus and Dundee boast a variety of innovative and award-winning tourist attractions. See Verdant Works which illustrates Dundee's once thriving jute industry, Pictavia which explores the legacy of the Picts, Discovery Point, home to Captain Scott's polar exploration ship the R.R.S. Discovery, and the Sensation science centre.

Map pages in this region

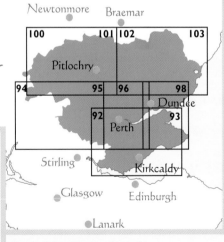

Rafting, Perthshire

Angus & Dundee Tourist Board

21 Castle Street, Dundee, DD1 3AA

☎ 01382 527527

www.angusanddundee.co.uk

Perthshire Tourist Board

Lower City Mills, West Mill Street, Perth, PH1 5QP

☎ 01738 627958

www.perthshire.co.uk

Kingdom of Fife Tourist Board

70 Market Street, St Andrews, Fife, KY16 9NU

☎ 01334 472021

www.standrews.co.uk

Central East Scotland

96
95
41

Tourist Information

Auchterader
90 High Street
Auchterader
Perth and Kinross
PH3 1BJ
☎ 01764 663450

Dunfermline
13/15 Maygate
Dumfermline
Fife
KY12 7NE
☎ 01383 720999

Kinross
Heart of Scotland
Visitor Centre
Junction 6, M90
Kinross
Kinross-shire
KY13 7NQ
☎ 01577 863680

Forth Bridges
Queensferry Lodge Hotel
by North Queensferry
Fife
KY11 1HP
☎ 01383 417759

Perth
Lower City Mills
West Mill Street
Perth
PH1 5QP
☎ 01738 450600

**Perth Caithness Glass
(Inveralmond)**
Caithness Glass Car Park
A9 Western City Bypass
Inveralmond
Perth and Kinross
PH1 3TZ
☎ 01738 638481

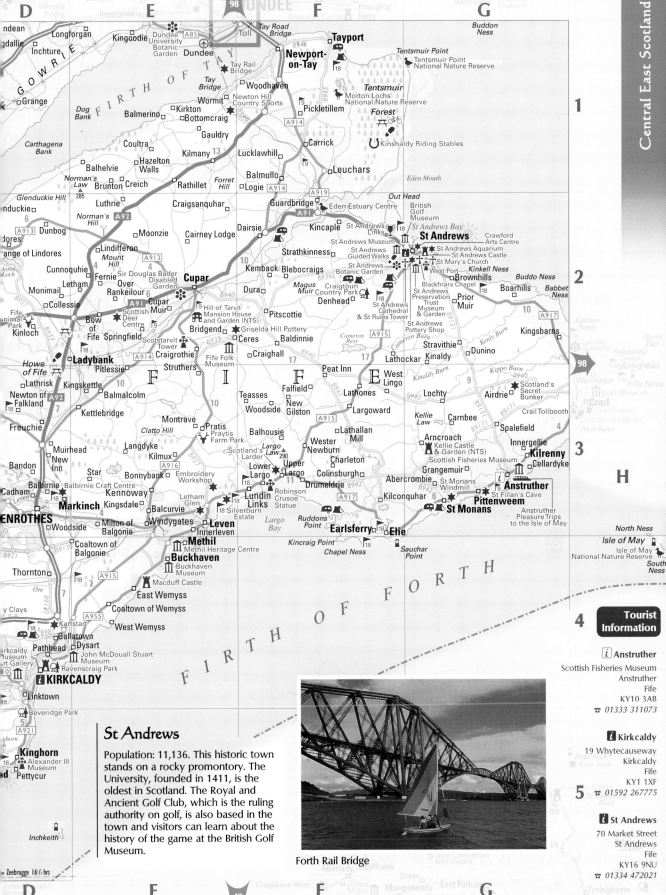

Forth Rail Bridge

St Andrews

Population: 11,136. This historic town stands on a rocky promontory. The University, founded in 1411, is the oldest in Scotland. The Royal and Ancient Golf Club, which is the ruling authority on golf, is also based in the town and visitors can learn about the history of the game at the British Golf Museum.

Tourist Information

ℹ **Anstruther**
Scottish Fisheries Museum
Anstruther
Fife
KY10 3AB
☎ 01333 311073

ℹ **Kirkcaldy**
19 Whytecauseway
Kirkcaldy
Fife
KY1 1XF
☎ 01592 267775

ℹ **St Andrews**
70 Market Street
St Andrews
Fife
KY16 9NU
☎ 01334 472021

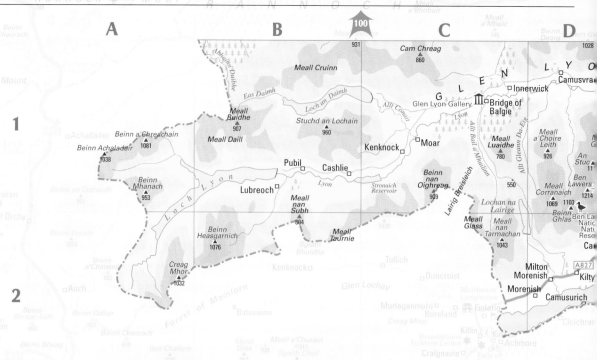

Loch Tay

Loch Tay

This 15 mile (24km) long loch runs north east from Killin to Kenmore. In places it is over 500ft (150m) deep. The loch is noted for its salmon. Just to the north is Ben Lawers, Perthshire's highest mountain.

Gleneagles golf course

Crieff

Population: 6023. This former spa town in the foothills of the Grampians above the River Earn became a popular resort in Victorian times with the arrival of the railway in 1856. It has retained much of its charm and character and is noted for its local crafts, many of which are available at the Crieff Visitors Centre. To the south east is the small town of Auchterader and the championship golf courses of Gleneagles.

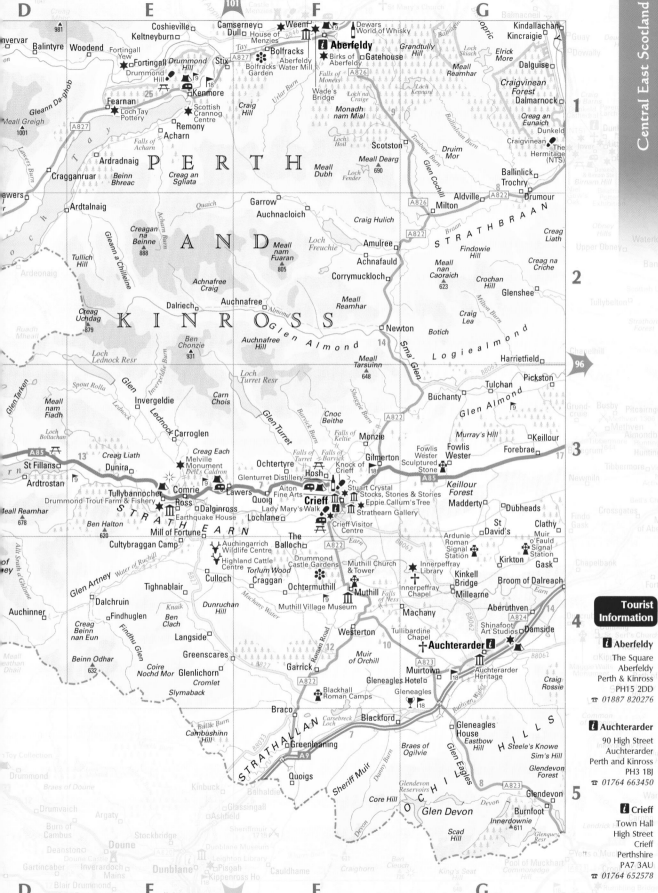

Tourist Information

i Aberfeldy
The Square
Aberfeldy
Perth & Kinross
PH15 2DD
☎ 01887 820276

i Auchterarder
90 High Street
Auchterarder
Perth and Kinross
PH3 1BJ
☎ 01764 663450

i Crieff
Town Hall
High Street
Crieff
Perthshire
PA7 3AU
☎ 01764 652578

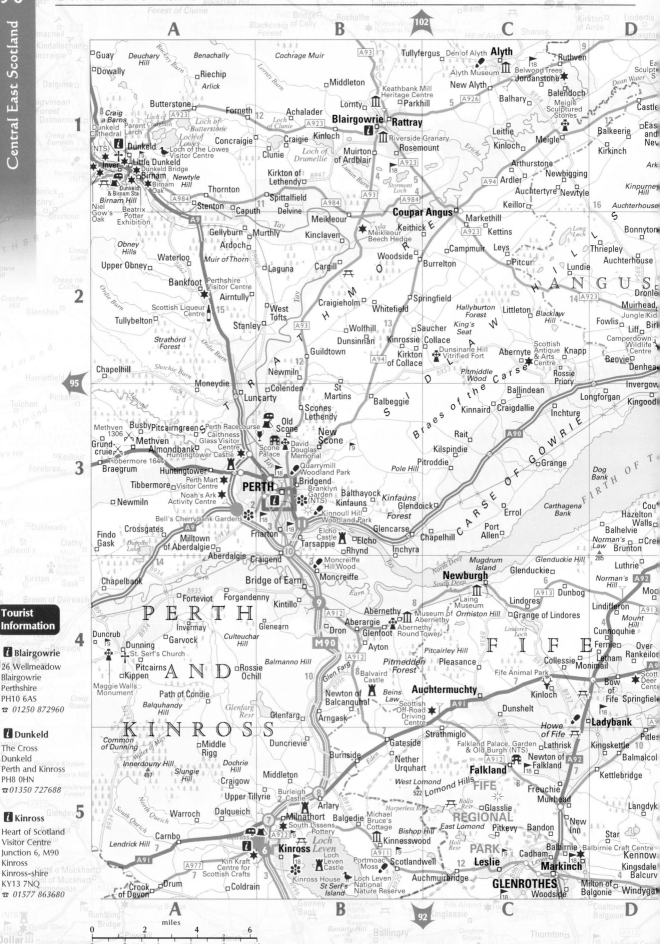

City of Perth

Population: 41,453. Sited on the River Tay 31 miles (50km) to the north of Edinburgh, this ancient cathedral city was Scotland's capital until the 15th century. Perth is a busy market town and a centre for livestock trade. The compact city centre is easily walkable on foot and is home to many interesting attractions. To the north and south of the centre are the Inches, public parks with bloody histories that today offer more sedate activities. The gothic mansion of Scone Palace saw the crowning of 42 Kings of Scotland and is situated just two miles (3km) north of the city.

Useful information

Police
Tayside Police
Barrack Street, PH1 5SF
☎ 01738 621141

Hospital A & E
Perth Royal Infirmary
Taymount Terrace, PH1 1NX
☎ 01738 623311

Main Post Office
109 South Street, PH2 8AF

Railway Station
Leonard Street

Bus Station
Leonard Street, PH2 8ET

Local Radio
Radio Tay 1548 AM
Tay FM 96.4 FM

City website
www.pkc.gov.uk

Tourist Information

i Perth

Lower City Mills
West Mill Street
Perth
PH1 5QP
☎ 01738 450600

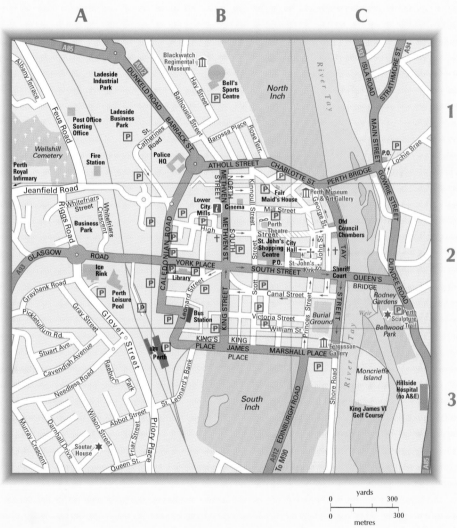

Index to street names

Central East Scotland

City of Dundee

Population: 158,981. Scotland's fourth largest city has a beautiful setting on the north bank of the Firth of Tay, 18 miles (29km) east of Perth. The approach from the south via the Tay Road Bridge gives panoramic views of the city and the good road network north means there is also easy access to the surrounding countryside of the Grampian Highlands. Dundee is a city of considerable historical importance. Robert the Bruce was declared King of the Scots here in 1309, the city suffered severe damage in the civil war and again prior to the Jacobite uprising, before recovering in the 19th century to become one of Scotland's most important trade centres. The Overgate and Wellgate Centres at either end of the High Street provide a good range of shops. Dundee Contemporary Arts Centre which opened in 1997 has boosted the city's cultural standing and the Dundee Repertory Theatre shows contemporary plays. There are many museums and art galleries: three of the best are Discovery Point, Verdant Works and the McManus Galleries.

Useful information

Police
Tayside Police
4 West Bell Street, DD1 9JU
☎ 01382 223200

Hospital A & E
Ninewells Hospital
Ninewells Road, DD1 9SY
☎ 01382 660111

Main Post Office
86 Victoria Road, DD1 2NY

Railway Station
South Union Street

Bus Station
Seagate, DD1 2HR

Local Radio
Radio Tay 1161AM
Wave 102FM
Tay FM 96.4 & 102.8FM

City website
www.dundeecity.gov.uk

Tourist Information

ℹ️ **Dundee**
21 Castle Street
Dundee
DD1 3BA
☎ 01382 527527

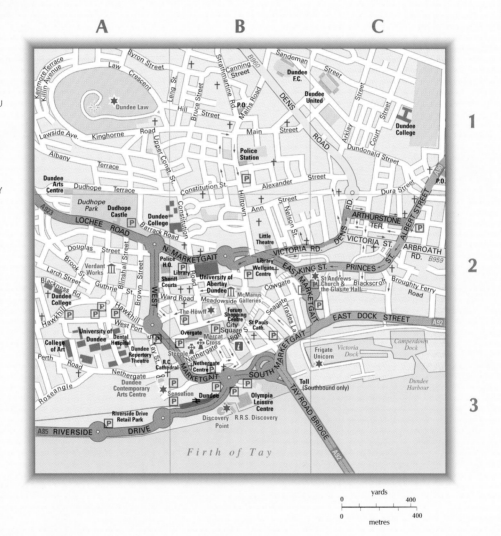

Index to street names

Central East Scotland

Tay Forest Park

10 mile (16km) long Loch Rannoch is dammed at its eastern end. Issuing from the loch is the River Tummel which runs on through Loch Tummel. Bordering both lochs is the Tay Forest Park which includes several forests. The Queen's View Visitor Centre on the northern shore of Loch Tummel is the main interpretive centre for the park and there is a fine view from there across the loch to the peak of Schiehallion.

Loch Tummel from Schiehallion

Pitlochry

Population : 2541. Sited on the banks of the River Tummel and surrounded by mountain scenery, the Victorian resort of Pitlochry makes a good base to stay. There is a visitor centre at the hydro-electric station on the edge of the town, and visitors can watch salmon leaping the fish ladder on their annual migration upstream.

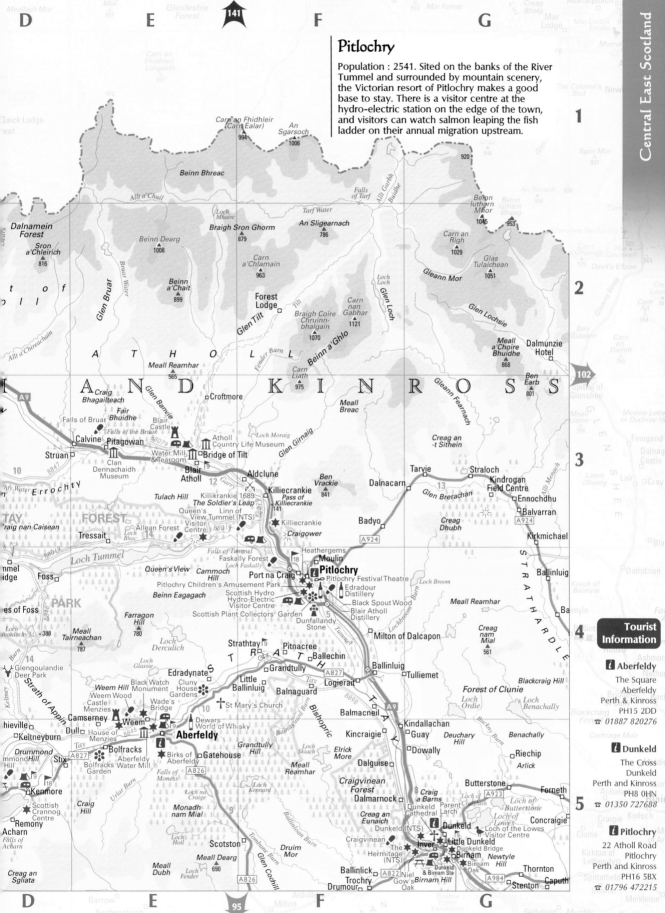

Tourist Information

ℹ️ Aberfeldy

The Square
Aberfeldy
Perth & Kinross
PH15 2DD
☎ 01887 820276

ℹ️ Dunkeld

The Cross
Dunkeld
Perth and Kinross
PH8 0HN
☎ 01350 727688

ℹ️ Pitlochry

22 Atholl Road
Pitlochry
Perth and Kinross
PH16 5BX
☎ 01796 472215

Central East Scotland

Angus glens

The peaceful, heather-clad glens of Angus cut into the Grampian Highlands. Glen Shee and the steep sided glacial valley of Glen Clova are the most popular, but Glen Esk, Glen Prosen and Glen Isla are all also worth exploring.

Tourist Information

ℹ Blairgowrie
26 Wellmeadow
Blairgowrie
Perthshire
PH10 6AS
☎ 01250 872960

ℹ Kirriemuir
St Malcolm's Wynd
Kirriemuir
Angus
DD8 4EF
☎ 01575 574097

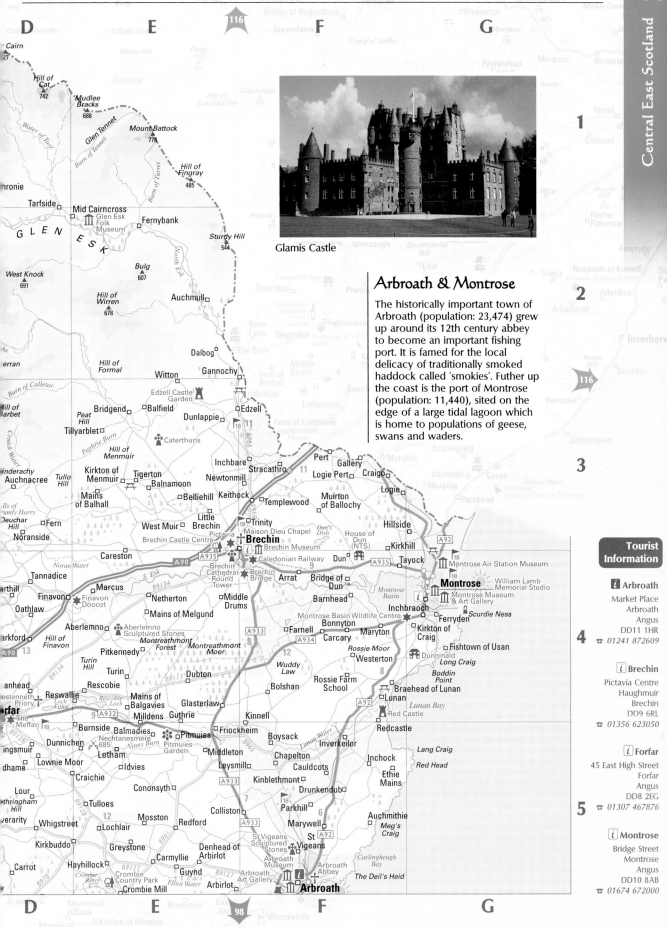

Glamis Castle

Arbroath & Montrose

The historically important town of Arbroath (population: 23,474) grew up around its 12th century abbey to become an important fishing port. It is famed for the local delicacy of traditionally smoked haddock called 'smokies'. Futher up the coast is the port of Montrose (population: 11,440), sited on the edge of a large tidal lagoon which is home to populations of geese, swans and waders.

Tourist Information

Arbroath
Market Place
Arbroath
Angus
DD11 1HR
☎ 01241 872609

Brechin
Pictavia Centre
Haughmuir
Brechin
DD9 6RL
☎ 01356 623050

Forfar
45 East High Street
Forfar
Angus
DD8 2EG
☎ 01307 467876

Montrose
Bridge Street
Montrose
Angus
DD10 8AB
☎ 01674 672000

✸ Abbot House Heritage Centre `92 B5`

Maygate, Dunfermline. In the restored 15th century residence of the Abbot of Dunfermline. Learn Scotland's story from Pictish to modern times and find out about King Robert the Bruce, St Margaret and other figures who played a role in the history of Scotland's ancient capital.
☎ 01383 733266   www.abbothouse.co.uk

🏯 Aberdour Castle `92 C5`

Aberdour, 5 miles (8km) east of the Forth Bridges on the A921. A 13th-century fortified residence overlooking the harbour. Splendid residential accommodation, terraced garden and fine circular dovecot.
☎ 01383 860519   www.historic-scotland.gov.uk

🏛 Aberfeldy Water Mill `95 F1`

Mill Street, Aberfeldy. A mill built in 1825 on a site where there has been a mill for 400 years. The present mill was restored in 1983 and opened to the public in 1988.
☎ 01887 820803   www.aberfeldy-watermill.co.uk

✝ Aberlemno Sculptured Stones `103 E4`

At Aberlemno on the B9134, 6 miles (9.5km) north east of Forfar. A magnificent upright cross-slab sculptured with Pictish symbols stands in the churchyard.
☎ 0131 668 8800   www.historic-scotland.gov.uk

✝ Abernethy Round Tower `96 B4`

In Abernethy on the A913. One of two round towers of the Irish style surviving in Scotland and dating from the end of the 11th century.
☎ 0131 668 8800   www.historic-scotland.gov.uk

🏛 Aiton Fine Arts `95 F3`

63 King Street, Crieff. Family-run art gallery showing contemporary Scottish artists' painting, prints and sculpture.
☎ 01764 655423

✝ Alexander III Monument `93 D5`

By the A921, south of Kinghorn. On the King's Crag, a monument marks the place where Alexander III was killed in a fall from his horse in 1286.

✎ Allean Forest `101 E3`

7 miles west of Pitlochry on the B8019. Magnificent views of Loch Tummel and surrounding mountains from waymarked walks through this working forest.
☎ 01350 727284   www.forestry.gov.uk

🏛 Alyth Museum `96 C1`

Commercial Street, Alyth. Displays of local history.
☎ 01738 632488

🏛 Andrew Carnegie Birthplace Museum `92 B5`

Moodie Street, Dunfermline. Weaver's cottage and the 1835 birthplace of Andrew Carnegie. Tells the rags to riches story of Andrew Carnegie, the weaver's son who emigrated to America and forged a fortune from the furnaces of the American steel industry.
☎ 01383 724302   www.carnegiemuseum.co.uk

🏛 Angus Folk Museum `98 A1`

Kirkwynd, Glamis. The museum is within Kirkwynd Cottages, a row of six reconstructed early 18th century cottages with stone-slabbed roofs. The interiors display one of the finest folk collections of domestic relics in Scotland.
☎ 01307 840288   www.nts.org.uk

🚤 Anstruther Pleasure Trips to the Isle of May `98 C5`

The Harbour, Anstruther. Daily boat trips to the Isle of May nature reserve to view large numbers of sea birds, including puffins. Also colony of grey seals, remains of a 12th century monastery and lighthouses.
☎ 01333 310103

✝ Arbroath Abbey `98 D1`

Abbey Street, Arbroath. The substantial ruins of a Tironesian monastery founded by William the Lion in 1178. This was the scene of the signing of the Declaration of Arbroath in 1320, which asserted Scotland's independence from England.
☎ 01241 878756   www.historic-scotland.gov.uk

🏛 Arbroath Art Gallery `98 D1`

Arbroath. Two galleries feature changing displays from Angus Council's art collections. Also exhibitions from elsewhere and locally generated shows.
☎ 01241 872248

🏛 Arbroath Museum `98 D1`

Signal Tower, Ladyloan, Arbroath. Housed in the shore station for the Bell Rock lighthouse, the museum features displays devoted to this renowned lighthouse as well as exhibits exploring the fishing community. Recreated 1950s schoolroom, Victorian parlour and wash house complete with noises and smells.
☎ 01241 875598

✝ Ardestie and Carlungie Earth Houses `98 B2`

Ardestie. Two examples of large Iron Age earth houses attached to surface dwellings (both now uncovered). At Ardestie the gallery is curved and 80ft (24m) in length. The Carlungie earth house is 150ft (45.5m) long and more complex.
☎ 0131 668 8800   www.historic-scotland.gov.uk

✝ Ardunie Roman Signal Station `95 G4`

At Trinity Gask, 4 miles (6.5km) north of Auchterarder. The site of a Roman watchtower, one of a series running between Ardoch and the River Tay.
☎ 0131 668 8800   www.historic-scotland.gov.uk

🏛 Atholl Country Life Museum `101 E3`

In Blair Atholl on the A924. Folk museum with lively displays showing past life in the village and glen, including blacksmith's smiddy, crofter's stable, byre and living room.
☎ 01796 481232   www.blairatholl.org.uk

🦌 Auchingarrich Wildlife Centre `95 E4`

2 miles (3km) south of Comrie on the B827. Wildlife centre set in 100 acres (40ha) of scenic Perthshire countryside. Abundance of animals and birds including foxes, otters, meerkats, deer, Highland cattle, birds of prey and wildcats.
☎ 01764 679469

🏛 Auchterarder Heritage `95 G4`

Auchterarder Tourist Office, 90 High Street, Auchterarder. History of the town and area told in descriptive panels using old photographs.
☎ 01764 663450

🏛 Aviation Museum `102 C4`

Bellies Brae, Kirriemuir. The museum displays a large collection of ephemera associated with flight.
☎ 01575 573233

✸ Balbirnie Craft Centre `96 C5`

Balbirnie Park, Glenrothes. Independently owned craft workshops producing leather goods, wrought ironwork, paintings and prints, gold and silver jewellery and glass blowing.
☎ 01592 753743

🏯 Balvaird Castle `96 B4`

About 6 miles (9.5km) south east of Bridge of Earn. A late 15th century tower on an L-plan, extended in 1581 by the addition of a walled courtyard and gatehouse.
☎ 01786 431324   www.historic-scotland.gov.uk

✸ Barry Mill `98 C2`

North of Barry village between the A92 and A930, 2 miles (3km) west of Carnoustie. A working 19th century meal mill. Full demonstrations on weekend afternoons.
☎ 01241 856761   www.nts.org.uk

✸ Beatrix Potter Exhibition `96 A1`

Birnam Institute, Station Road, Birnam. A Victorian building erected in 1883. Visitors can enjoy the garden and woodlands where the famous author walked.
☎ 01350 727674

✿ Bell's Cherrybank Gardens `96 A3`

Cherrybank on the western outskirts of Perth. The gardens contain the Bell's National Heather Collection. This is the largest collection in the UK and has over 900 varieties from all over the world, with plants flowering every month of the year.

✸ Belwood Trees `96 C1`

Brigton of Ruthven, Meigle, on the A926 between Blairgowrie and Kirriemuir. Britain's leading large tree specialist with over 250 varieties of semi-mature trees, conifers and specimen shrubs.
☎ 01828 640219

🦌 Ben Lawers National Nature Reserve `94 D1`

Off the A827, 6 miles (9.5km) north east of Killin. Perthshire's highest mountain (3984ft/1214m) noted for the rich variety of mountain plants and the bird population – birds include raven, ring-ouzel, red grouse, ptarmigan, dipper and curlew.
☎ 01567 820397   www.nts.org.uk

🏞 Beveridge Park `93 D4`

Kirkcaldy, Fife. Public park with woodland, formal gardens and extensive leisure facilities.
    www.thebeveridgepark.com

✸ Birks of Aberfeldy `95 F1`

Short walk from the centre of Aberfeldy. Robert Burns wrote The Birks of Aberfeldy here in 1878. A narrow path climbs to a bridge directly above the Falls of Moness, providing spectacular views.
    www.pkc.gov.uk/sport_culture/walks.htm

✸ Birnam Oak `96 A1`

Birnam. An ancient tree believed to be the last surviving remnant of Birnam Wood, the great oak forest made famous in Shakespeare's Macbeth.

✎ Black Spout Wood `101 F4`

South of Pitlochry town centre off the A924. Attractive oak woodland deriving its name from the spectacular waterfall, the Black Spout.
    www.pkc.gov.uk/sport_culture/walks.htm

✝ Black Watch Monument `101 E4`

Taybridge Drive in Aberfeldy. A cairn surmounted by a statue of Private Farquhar Shaw dressed in the uniform of the Black Watch Regiment. To commemorate the first muster of the regiment in May 1740.

🏛 Black Watch Regimental Museum `97 B1`

Balhousie Castle, Hay Street, Perth. The museum describes the regiments' history from 1740 to the present day.
☎ 0131 310 8530

✝ Blackfriars Chapel `98 C4`

South Street, St Andrews. The vaulted side apse of a church of Dominican friars.
☎ 0131 668 8800   www.historic-scotland.gov.uk

✝ Blackhall Roman Camps `95 F4`

Ardoch, 0.5 mile (1km) north of Braco, Perthshire. Parts of the defences of two Roman marching camps, probably dating from the early 3rd century AD.
☎ 0131 668 8800   www.historic-scotland.gov.uk

Blair Atholl Distillery `101 F4`

1 mile (1.5km) south of Pitlochry town centre on the A924. Established in 1798 in the popular Highland resort of Pitlochry, Blair Atholl distillery is the home of Bell's 8 Year Old Extra Special, the biggest selling blended whisky in the UK.
☎ 01796 482003

Blair Castle `101 E3`

Blair Atholl, 7 miles (11km) north of Pitlochry off the A9. A white turreted baronial castle, the traditional seat of the Dukes and Earls of Atholl. The oldest part, Cumming's Tower, dates back to 1269. Fine collections of furniture, portraits, lace, china, arms, armour, Jacobite relics and Masonic regalia. Deer park, woodland, riverside and mountain walks.
☎ 01796 481207   www.blair-castle.co.uk

Bolfracks Garden `95 F1`

2 miles (3km) west of Aberfeldy on the A827. A garden overlooking the Tay Valley. Specialities are rhododendrons, mecanopsis, old and rambling roses, all contained within a walled garden and a less formal wooded garden with stream.
☎ 01887 820207

Branklyn Garden `96 B3`

On the A85 Dundee Road near Perth city centre. Started in 1922 on the site of a former orchard, Branklyn is an outstanding 2 acre (0.8ha) garden with rhododendrons, alpines, herbaceous and peat garden plants.
☎ 01738 625535   www.nts.org.uk

Brechin Bridge `103 F4`

Known locally as the Auld Brig, this is one of the oldest stone bridges in Scotland.

Brechin Castle Centre `103 E3`

Haughmuir, at the southern Brechin junction off the A90. Scottish breeds of domestic animals, pets' corner and pheasantry, farm buildings and display of traditional agricultural machinery and implements.
☎ 01356 626813   www.brechincastlecentre.co.uk

Brechin Cathedral Round Tower `103 E4`

One of the two remaining round towers of the Irish type in Scotland. Built in the late 11th century with a remarkable carved doorway. Capped by a stone roof added in the 15th century.
☎ 0131 668 8800   www.historic-scotland.gov.uk

Brechin Museum `103 F3`

St Ninians Square, Brechin. Local collections tell the story of the development of Brechin from the Celtic church of the 10th century to the last days of the burgh in 1975.
☎ 01356 622687

British Golf Museum `98 C5`

Bruce Embankment, St Andrews. Visitors encounter many famous professionals and amateurs of status. Touch screen videos allow visitors to look deeper into the lives of champions and to test their skills and knowledge of the game.
☎ 01334 478880   www.britishgolfmuseum.co.uk

Broughty Castle `98 B2`

Broughty Ferry. A 16th century tower adapted for changing defence needs during the 19th century. Now houses a branch of Dundee Arts and Heritage Department.
☎ 01382 436916   www.historic-scotland.gov.uk

Buckhaven Museum `93 E4`

College Street, Buckhaven. Museum displays Buckhaven's history with a focus on the fishing industry. Stained glass windows made by local people.
☎ 01592 412860

Burleigh Castle `96 B5`

Off the A911, 2 miles (3km) north east of Kinross. The roofless but otherwise complete ruin of a tower house of about 1500 with a section of defensive barmkin wall and a remarkable corner tower with a square cap-house corbelled out.
☎ 0131 668 8800   www.historic-scotland.gov.uk

Burntisland Edwardian Fair Museum `92 D5`

102 High Street, Burntisland. Permanent display about the Edwardian Fair that visited Burntisland every year, plus displays on the local history of Burntisland.
☎ 01592 412860

Caithness Glass Visitor Centre `96 A3`

Inveralmond Industrial Estate, on the A9 Perth western bypass at the Inveralmond roundabout. See the fascinating process of glass-making. Also paperweight collectors gallery, audio-visual theatre and children's play area. Factory shop.
☎ 01738 492320   www.caithnessglass.co.uk

Caledonian Railway `103 F4`

The Station, 2 Park Road, Brechin. From the unique Victorian terminus at Brechin, board a steam train and journey back in time as you travel the falling grade to the Bridge of Dun. Static display of model trains.
☎ 01356 622992   www.caledonianrailway.co.uk

Cambo Gardens `98 D4`

Cambo Estate on the A917, 2.5 miles (4km) north of Crail. Walled garden full of romantic charm designed around the Cambo burn, which is spanned by ornamental bridges and a greenhouse.
☎ 01333 450313   www.camboestate.com

Camperdown Wildlife Centre `98 A2`

Camperdown Country Park, Coupar Angus Road, 3 miles (4km) north of Dundee on the A923. Over 80 species of native wildlife; brown bears, lynx, arctic foxes and other more unusual species, such as Britain's rarest mammal, the pine marten.
☎ 01382 432689

Captain Scott and Dr Wilson Cairn `102 C3`

In Glen Prosen on unclassified road north west of Dykehead. The cairn replaces the original fountain which was erected in memory of the Antarctic explorers, Captain Scott and Dr Wilson.

Carnoustie Golf Links `98 C2`

Links Parade, Carnoustie. A three course golf links with Burnside, Buddon Links and the Championship course. The latter has a reputation as a demanding test of golfing ability and has hosted the Open many times.
☎ 01241 853789   www.carnoustiegolflinks.co.uk

Castle Menzies `101 E4`

Weem, 1.5 miles (2.5km) west of Aberfeldy. Imposing 16th century castle, a fine example of the transition between a Z-plan clan stronghold and a later mansion house. Seat of the clan chiefs for over 400 years, Castle Menzies was involved in a number of historic occurrences.
☎ 01887 820982

Caterthuns `103 E3`

Near the village of Menmuir about 5 miles (8km) north west of Brechin. Two spectacular large Iron Age hill forts. The Brown Caterthun has four concentric ramparts and ditches; the White Caterthun is a well-preserved fort with a massive stone rampart, defensive ditch and outer earthworks.
☎ 0131 668 8800   www.historic-scotland.gov.uk

Charlestown Lime Heritage Trust `92 B5`

Granary Building, Rocks Road, Charlestown. Charlestown is a very early example of a planned village. Established in 1756 by Charles Bruce, 5th Earl of Elgin and 9th of Kincardine, the village was a self-sufficient complete industrial complex based on the large deposits of limestone in the surrounding area.
☎ 01383 872006

Clan Donnachaidh Museum `101 E3`

Bruar, by Pitlochry. Clan Donnachaidh history and artefacts from the 14th century to the present day.
☎ 01796 483264

Claypotts Castle `98 B2`

South of the A92, near Broughty Ferry. An unusually complete 16th century tower house with circular towers at diagonally opposite corners corbelled out to form overhanging cap houses.
☎ 01786 431324   www.historic-scotland.gov.uk

Cluny Clays `92 D4`

Cluny Mains, Cluny, 2 miles (3km) north of Kirkcaldy on the B922. Outdoor entertainment centre. Golf driving range and 9 hole golf course. Scotland's national clay pigeon shooting and archery centre. Children's playpark and electric trikes, off-road driving, falconry and highland games. Set in beautifully landscaped surroundings in open rolling countryside.
☎ 01592 720374   www.clunyclays.co.uk

Cluny House Gardens `101 E4`

3.5 miles (5.5km) north east of Aberfeldy on the minor road between Weem and Strathtay. Cluny is a Himalayan style woodland garden. Situated on a slope in the Strathtay valley where the climate and soil provide perfect conditions for growing a profusion of primulas, meconopsis, rhododendrons, lilies, trilliums and spring bulbs.
☎ 01887 820795

Craigtoun Country Park `98 B4`

2.5 miles (4km) south west of St Andrews on the B939. Craigtoun Country Park was formerly the grounds of Mount Melville House. The park consists of 50 acres (20ha) including formal gardens, two ponds, landscaped areas, Dutch village and cypress walk.
☎ 01334 473666

Craigvinean `95 G1`

1 mile west of Dunkeld, on the A9. Craigvinean (Gaelic for crag of the goats) is one of Scotland's oldest managed forests. A waymarked walk provides superb views over the Hermitage and Dunkeld to Craig a Barns.
www.forestry.gov.uk

Crail Guided Walks `98 D5`

Crail Museum & Heritage Centre, Marketgate, Crail. Walking tours of the oldest parts of Crail, taking in buildings of architectural and historic interest.
☎ 01333 450869

Crail Museum `98 D4`

62-64 Marketgate, Crail. The museum provides an insight into the past life of this ancient Royal Burgh. Visitors can learn about the seafaring tradition, 200-year-old golf club and HMS Jackdaw, a World War II Fleet Air Arm Station.
☎ 01333 450869

Crail Pottery `98 D5`

75 Nethergate, Crail. Three generations of potters produce a huge variety of hand-thrown pottery from porcelain to gardenware, sculpture, teapots and jardinières.
☎ 01333 451212   www.crailpottery.com

Crail Tolbooth `98 D5`

Marketgate, Crail. The Tolbooth dates from the early 16th century. In the striking Dutch Tower is a bell dated 1520, cast in Holland.

Crawford Arts Centre `98 C5`

93 North Street, St Andrews. The centre provides exciting exhibitions of all kinds of visual art from sculpture and painting to photography, craft and design, and architecture.
☎ 01334 474610   www.crawfordarts.free-online.co.uk

✱ Crieff Visitor Centre `95 F3`

On the A85 Crieff to Comrie road. Traditional whisky flagons, tableware and glass paperweights. Visitors can view the production process and see craftsmen at work.
☎ 01764 654014   www.crieff.co.uk

🦢 Crombie Country Park `98 C1`

Monikie, Broughty Ferry. A Victorian reservoir with the appearance of a natural loch. Set in 250 acres (101ha). Wildlife hide, trails, displays and interpretation centre, ranger service, guided walks and child play park. Barbecue area.
☎ 01241 860360

✝ Culross Abbey `92 A5`

Culross, off the A985, 12 miles (19km) west of Forth Road Bridge. The remains of a Cistercian monastery founded in 1217. The eastern parts of the Abbey Church form the present parish church.
☎ 0131 668 8800   www.historic-scotland.gov.uk

✱ Culross Palace `92 A5`

Culross, off the A985, 12 miles (19km) west of Forth Road Bridge. Built 1597 – 1611 for local entrepreneur Sir George Bruce.
☎ 01383 880359   www.nts.org.uk

🕆 David Douglas Memorial `96 B3`

Located in the grounds of the old church at Scone. David Douglas was one of the greatest plant hunters and explorers of America's north west. He introduced over 200 new plants to Britain.

✱ Deep Sea World `92 C5`

North Queensferry. Visitors can enjoy a spectacular diver's eye view of our marine environment on an underwater safari; come face to face with sand tiger sharks and watch divers hand feed a spectacular array of sea life; touch the live exhibits in the large rockpools; and visit the stunning Amazonian Experience which features ferocious piranhas and electrifying eels.
☎ 0906 941 0077   www.deepseaworld.co.uk

🌿 Den of Alyth `96 C1`

Alyth. The Den of Alyth is a broadleaved woodland through which the Alyth Burn flows. Walks of varying length through shady woods in a steep sided valley.
                                          www.pkc.gov.uk/sport_culture/walks.htm

🍾 Dewars World of Whisky `95 F1`

Aberfeldy Distillery, Aberfeldy. Celebrating the lives of the entrepreneurial Dewer family and the art of blending whisky, visitors will enjoy this interactive, contemporary attraction with a traditional working distillery tour.
☎ 01887 822010   www.dewars.com

✱ Discovery Point `99 B3`

Discovery Quay, Dundee. Centred around Royal Research Ship Discovery, Captain Scott's famous polar exploration ship. Spectacular exhibits and special effects recreate her historic voyages. Visitors can step on board Discovery herself and experience life below decks.
☎ 01382 201245   www.rrsdiscovery.com

🕆 Dogton Stone `92 D4`

Off the B922, at Dogton farmhouse, near Cardenden. 5 miles (8km) north west of Kirkcaldy. An ancient Celtic cross with traces of animal and figure sculpture.
                                                 www.historic-scotland.gov.uk

❊ Drummond Castle Gardens `95 F4`

Drummond Castle, Muthill, 2 miles (3km) south of Crieff. One of Scotland's largest formal gardens with magnificent early Victorian parterre, fountains, terracing and topiary. It is laid out in the form of a St Andrews cross.
☎ 01764 681257

🌿 Drummond Hill `95 E1`

Kenmore, 4.5 miles west of Aberfeldy, off the A827. Drummond Hill has forest walks with stunning views of Loch Tay.
                                                       www.forestry.gov.uk

✱ Drummond Trout Farm and Fishery `95 E3`

1 mile (2km) west of Comrie. Trout farm – feed the fish and see the salmon ladder. You can also fish for trout (two ponds for beginners, three for intermediate fishers and one for fly fishing).
☎ 01764 670500   www.drummondtroutfarm.co.uk

🖐 Dundee Contemporary Arts `99 A3`

152 Nethergate, Dundee. Centre for contemporary art and film with two galleries, cinema, print studio, craft shop, visual research centre and activity room.
☎ 01382 606220   www.dca.org.uk

✱ Dundee Law `99 A1`

The Law is the highest point in the city, and takes its name from the old Scots word for a hill. It is the remains of a volcanic plug and was later the site of an ancient hill fort. Atop the Law is a beacon which is lit four times a year.

❊ Dundee University Botanic Garden `98 A3`

Riverside Drive, Dundee. Botanic and teaching garden with a fine collection of trees and shrubs. Two large tropical and temperate plant houses.
☎ 01382 566939

🕆 Dunfallandy Stone `101 F4`

1 mile (2km) south of Pitlochry. A fine Pictish sculptured stone with a cross on one face and figures on both faces.
☎ 0131 668 8800   www.historic-scotland.gov.uk

✝ Dunfermline Abbey & Palace `92 B5`

St Margaret Street, Dunfermline. The remains of the great Benedictine abbey founded by Queen Margaret in the 11th century. The foundations of her church are under the present nave, built in the 12th century in the Romanesque style. Robert the Bruce is buried in the choir, now the site of the present parish church. Of the monastic buildings, the ruins of the refectory, pend and guest house remain.
☎ 01383 739026   www.historic-scotland.gov.uk

🏛 Dunfermline Museum `92 C4`

Viewfield Terrace, Dunfermline. A 'memory' museum of Dunfermline's social, natural and industrial history, particularly that of damask linen, the industry that made Dunfermline famous in the last century
☎ 01383 313838

✱ Dunkeld `96 A1`

The Ell Shop, Dunkeld. Attractive village with mostly ruined Gothic cathedral on banks of River Tay. The National Trust for Scotland owns many houses dating from the rebuilding of the town in 1689 after the Battle of Dunkeld.
☎ 01350 727460   www.nts.org.uk

✱ Dunkeld Bridge `96 A1`

Over the River Tay at Dunkeld. One of Thomas Telford's finest bridges, a seven-arched bridge and tollhouse built in 1809. An attractive riverside path leads from here downstream to the famous Birnam Oak, last relic of Macbeth's Birnam Wood.

✝ Dunkeld Cathedral `96 A1`

High Street, Dunkeld. Beautifully situated on the banks of the River Tay. Originally 12th century, but nave and great north west tower from 15th century.
☎ 0131 668 8800   www.historic-scotland.gov.uk

🕆 Dunninald `103 G4`

2 miles south of Montrose. Set in a planned landscape dating from 1740, there is an attractive walled garden.
☎ 01674 674842

🕆 Dunsinane Hill Vitrified Fort `96 C2`

South east of Collace, off the A94. Magnificent views from the summit, reached by a steep footpath beginning on the north side of the hill.

🏛 Earthquake House `95 E3`

The Ross, Comrie. Situated on the highland boundary fault line, Earthquake House contains replica and modern seismic measuring instruments. Explanatory boards are on the exterior of the building (no access to the interior).
☎ 01764 652578

🕆 Eassie Sculptured Stone `98 A1`

In Eassie churchyard, near Glamis. A fine elaborately carved monument with Celtic cross on one side and Pictish symbols and processional scenes on the reverse.
☎ 0131 668 8800   www.historic-scotland.gov.uk

🕊 Eden Estuary Centre `98 B4`

Main Street, Guardbridge. By main entrance for paper mill. A small hide overlooking Eden Estuary local nature reserve.
☎ 01333 429785

🍾 Edradour Distillery `101 F4`

Edradour, on the A294, 2.5 miles (4km) east of Pitlochry. The smallest distillery in Scotland, established in 1825. Visitors can taste a hand-crafted single malt whisky.
☎ 01796 472095   www.edradour.co.uk

🏰 Edzell Castle & Garden `103 E3`

At Edzell, off the B966, 6 miles (9.5km) north of Brechin. Late medieval tower house incorporated into a 16th century courtyard mansion. Walled garden with a bathhouse and summerhouse laid out by Sir David Lindsay in 1604.
☎ 01356 648631   www.historic-scotland.gov.uk

🏰 Elcho Castle `96 B3`

Rhynd, 3 miles (5km) south east of Perth. A handsome and complete fortified 16th century mansion. Notable for its tower-like jambs or wings and for the wrought-iron grills protecting its windows.
☎ 01738 639998   www.historic-scotland.gov.uk

✱ Embroidery Workshop `98 A5`

Blacketyside Farm, on the A915 coast road to St Andrews, 0.5 mile (1km) north of Leven. A tiny craft workshop and gift shop, housing an extensive range of original handmade designs. Visitors can watch craftspeople at work.
☎ 01333 423985   www.embroideredoriginals.co.uk

✱ Eppie Callum's Tree `95 F3`

Crieff. A 600 year old oak tree standing 70ft (21m) high. The tree is said to have once sheltered notorious outlaw Rob Roy Macgregor from his enemies.

🏯 Falkland Palace, Garden & Old Burgh `96 C5`

Falkland, Cupar. Country residence of the Stewart kings and queens. The gardens contain the original royal tennis court, built in 1539 and the oldest in Britain.
☎ 01337 857397   www.nts.org.uk

🌿 Falls of Bruar `101 E3`

At Bruar, 10 miles north of Pitlochry. Robert Burns visited the Bruar gorge in 1787 and wrote The Humble Petition of Bruar Water. When Burns died in 1796, the duke created a wild garden in his memory.

🌿 Faskally Forest `101 F4`

1 mile north of Pitlochry on the B8019. Compact, wonderfully mixed woodland beside Loch Faskally.
                                                       www.forestry.gov.uk

Fergusson Gallery — 97 C3
Marshall Place, Perth. An art gallery devoted to the work of the Scottish colourist painter, John Duncan Fergusson (1874 – 1961) and housing the largest collection of his work.
☎ 01738 621152

Fife Airport — 92 D4
Goatmilk, off the B921, 2 miles (3km) west of Glenrothes. A regional airport which is also the home of Fife Flying Club, providing all forms of flying training.
☎ 01592 753792
www.tayviation.co.uk

Fife Animal Park — 96 C4
Collessie, 10 miles from the M90 on the B937. More than 150 species of friendly animals. Children can handle the smaller animals.
☎ 01337 831830

Fife Folk Museum — 98 A4
The Weigh House, High Street, Ceres. A local museum housed in a 17th century tollbooth and 18th century cottages overlooking the Ceres Burn. The collection illustrates the social, economic and cultural history of rural Fife.
☎ 01334 828180

Finavon Doocot — 103 E4
6 miles (10km) north of Forfar, off the A90. A 16th century dovecot, the largest in Scotland, Finavon Doocot had 2400 nesting boxes.
☎ 01738 631296
www.nts.org.uk

Forth Bridges Exhibition — 92 C5
Queensferry Lodge Hotel, St Margaret's Head, North Queensferry. An exhibition telling the fascinating story of the rail and road bridges. The bridges can be viewed from a gallery.
☎ 01383 410000

Fortingall Yew — 95 E1
Fortingall, 9 miles (14.5km) west of Aberfeldy. The surviving part of the great yew in an enclosure in the churchyard is reputedly over 3000 years old, perhaps the oldest tree in Europe. The attractive village is claimed to be the birthplace of Pontius Pilate and has been a religious centre since St Columban times.

Fowlis Wester Sculptured Stone — 95 G3
In the church at Fowlis Wester, 6 miles (9.5km) north east of Crieff. A tall cross-slab carved with Pictish symbols, figure sculpture and Celtic enrichment.
☎ 0131 668 8800
www.historic-scotland.gov.uk

Glamis Castle — 98 A1
Glamis, on the A94, 6 miles (9.5km) west of Forfar. One of the oldest parts is Duncan's Hall, legendary setting for Shakespeare's Macbeth. The present castle was modified in the 17th century. Famous for being the childhood home of Queen Elizabeth, The Queen Mother, and birthplace of Princess Margaret. Fine collections of china, painting, tapestries and furniture. Two exhibitions, Coach House and Elizabeth of Glamis.
☎ 01307 840393
www.great-houses-scotland.co.uk/glamis/index.htm

Glen Esk Folk Museum — 103 E2
The Retreat, Glenesk, Brechin. A museum housing antiques, documents and artefacts reflecting the history of Glen Esk and surrounding area. The interpretive centre houses a large relief model of Glen Esk, a stable in original form and displays on past and present local life.
☎ 01356 670254

Glen Lyon Gallery — 94 C1
Bridge of Balgie, off the B846 at Coshieville, 20 miles (32km) from Aberfeldy. All works are by Alan B. Hayman who specialises in wildlife art and sculpture.
☎ 01887 866260

Gleneagles — 95 G4
The Gleneagles Hotel, Auchterarder. Three prestigious championship golf courses in a splendid moorland setting. The Queens course was founded in 1917, the Kings in 1919 and the PGA Centenary Course, designed by Jack Nicklaus, in 1993.
☎ 01764 662231
www.gleneagles.com

Glengoulandie Deer Park — 101 D4
Glengoulandie, Foss, on the B846, 8 miles (13km) north west of Aberfeldy. Native animals housed in a natural environment. Many endangered species are kept, and there are fine herds of red deer and Highland cattle.
☎ 01887 830261

Glenturret Distillery — 95 F3
The Hosh, on the A85 towards Comrie, 1.25 miles (2km) from Crieff. The oldest Highland malt distillery in Scotland (established in 1775) where whisky is still produced in the traditional manner. Free tasting. Picturesque setting.
☎ 01764 656565
www.glenturret.com

Griselda Hill Pottery — 98 A4
Kirkbrae, Ceres, 3 miles (5km) south east of Cupar. Since 1985, the Griselda Hill pottery has revived the production of Wemyss Ware, beautifully hand-painted cats, pigs and other pottery in bright cheerful colours.
☎ 01334 828273
www.wemyss-ware.co.uk

HM Frigate Unicorn — 99 C3
Victoria Dock, Dundee. Unicorn was launched at Chatham in 1824 and is the third oldest ship, and one of the best preserved, in the world.
☎ 01382 200893

Heathergems — 101 F4
22 Atholl Road, Pitlochry. A Scottish jewellery factory and visitor centre. Visitors can see products being made. Seated video area and a large shop.
☎ 01796 474391

Hermitage, The — 96 A1
Off the A9, 2 miles (3km) west of Dunkeld. Interesting walks in mixed woodland. The focus is a delightful folly, Ossian's Hall, in a gorge of the River Braan.
☎ 01796 473233
www.nts.org.uk

Highland Cattle Centre — 95 E4
Glascorrie Road, Auchingarrich, 2 miles (3km) south of Comrie on the B827. The centre tells the story of the highland cows' evolution and also shows the 6000 year old head of one of their ancestors. See all the different types of highland cattle from the young calves to huge bullocks with 6ft (1.8m) long horns.
☎ 01764 679469

Hill Of Tarvit Mansion House & Garden — 98 A4
Off the A916, 2.5 miles (4km) south of Cupar. Fine Edwardian house designed by Sir Robert Lorimer provides a setting for his important collection of French, Chippendale-style and vernacular furniture. Superb paintings, including works by Raeburn and Ramsay. Formal gardens also designed by Lorimer.
☎ 01334 653127
www.nts.org.uk

House of Dun — 103 F4
On the A935, 3 miles (5km) west of Montrose. Beautiful Georgian house overlooking Montrose Basin, designed in 1730 by William Adam and with superb contemporary plasterwork. Home in 19th century to Lady Augusta Kennedy-Erskine. Many of her belongings remain, as well as her wool work and embroidery. Restored Victorian walled garden and attractive woodland walks.
☎ 01674 810264
www.nts.org.uk

House of Menzies — 95 F1
Castle Menzies Farm, 2 miles out of Aberfeldy on the B846. Situated within an original doocot and cattle court, the House of Menzies features work by contemporary Scottish artists, potters and silversmiths.
☎ 01887 829666
www.houseofmenzies.com

Howff, The — 99 B2
Meadowside, Dundee. An historic graveyard which was formerly the garden of Greyfriars Monastery, gifted to the people of Dundee by Mary, Queen of Scots.

Huntingtower Castle — 96 A3
Huntingtower, off the A85, 3 miles (5km) north west of Perth. A 15th century castellated mansion, known as Ruthven Castle until 1600. Two fine and complete towers, now linked by a 17th century range. There are fine painted ceilings.
☎ 01738 627231
www.historic-scotland.gov.uk

Inchcolm Abbey — 92 C5
On Inchcolm Island in the Firth of Forth. The ruins of an Augustinian house founded circa 1123 and including a 13th century octagonal chapter house.
☎ 0131 331 4857
www.historic-scotland.gov.uk

Innerpeffray Chapel — 95 G4
Innerpeffray, 4 miles (6.5km) south east of Crieff. A rectangular collegiate church founded in 1508. Still retains its altar and evidence of its furnishings.
☎ 0131 668 8800
www.historic-scotland.gov.uk

Innerpeffray Library — 95 G4
Innerpeffray, on the B8062, 4 miles (6.5km) south east of Crieff. The first lending library in Scotland, founded in 1680. A collection of 3000 titles printed between 1500 and 1800 now housed in a purpose-built library completed in 1762. Many rare and interesting volumes.
☎ 01764 652819

Inverkeithing Museum — 92 C5
The Friary, Queen Street, Inverkeithing. Local history of Inverkeithing and Rosyth. Small display on Admiral Greig, founder of the Russian navy.
☎ 01383 313838

J. M. Barrie's Birthplace & Camera Obscura — 102 C4
On A90/A926 in Kirriemuir. Birthplace of J. M. Barrie, creator of Peter Pan. Exhibition about his work, with his first theatre also on display. Camera Obscura, within the cricket pavilion on Kirrie Hill, presented to Kirriemuir by the author.
☎ 01575 572646
www.nts.org.uk

John McDouall Stuart Museum — 93 D4
Rectory Lane, Dysart. An exhibition about the great 19th-century explorer of Australia, located in the house where he was born.
☎ 01592 412860

Jungle Kids — 98 A2
Dronley Road, Birkhill. A large indoor play centre for children up to 12 years, including a selection of slides, ball pools, large climbing frames; soft play area for children under three.
☎ 01382 580540
www.junglekids.co.uk

Jus-Tina Knitwear — 102 C4
Kingoldrum, 3 miles west of Kirriemuir on the B951. A true cottage industry, garments are designed and knitted locally from Shetland lambswool.
☎ 01575 574725
www.justina.co.uk

Kartstart — 93 D4
Just off the A92, Dunfermline to Kirkcaldy link road. 350 metre indoor kart circuit. Offers the opportunity to experience the thrill of real motor sport. All weather facility. Mini-quads, cadet karts, senior karts, pro-karts.
☎ 01592 650200

Central East Scotland

🏛 **Keathbank Mill Heritage Centre**   `96 B1`
Balmoral Road, on the A93, 1 mile (2km) north of Blairgowrie. A mill built in 1864 on the banks of the River Ericht and boasting the largest working water wheel in Scotland. Contains a heraldic museum and workshop displaying clan crests, coats of arms and shields, and an O-gauge model railway.
☎ 01250 872025

🏰 **Kellie Castle & Garden**   `98 C5`
On the B9171, 3 miles (5km) north of Pittemweem. The oldest part of Kellie Castle dates from 1360, and most of the present building was completed around 1606. It was sympathetically restored by the Lorimer family, who lived here in the 1870s.
☎ 01333 720271   www.nts.org.uk

✖ **Killiecrankie**   `101 F3`
On the B8079, 3 miles (5km) north of Pitlochry. Site of the 1689 battle of Killiecrankie, won by the Highland Jacobites under Bonnie Dundee. Visitors can see Soldiers Leap, where a fleeing government soldier made a spectacular jump over the River Garry during the battle.
☎ 01796 473233   www.nts.org.uk

✖ **Kin Kraft Centre for Scottish Crafts**   `96 A5`
Kinross Services Area, Turfhills, off junction 6 on the M90. Visitors can see craftwork demonstrations.
☎ 01577 861300

✎ **Kinnoull Hill Woodland Park**   `96 B3`
1 mile (1.5km) east of Perth. Comprising five hills (Corsiehill, Deuchny Hill, Barnhill, Binn Hill and Kinnoull Hill). Kinnoull Hill, the highest and most impressive, offers spectacular views over the Ochil and Lomond hills.
☎ 01350 727284   www.forestry.gov.uk

❖ **Kinross House**   `96 B5`
Kinross. Kinross House was built by the Surveyor General and Architect to Charles II, Sir William Bruce, as his own home and is one of the finest examples of late 17th century architecture in Scotland. It is set in formal walled gardens with rose gardens, yew hedges, topiary and herbaceous borders.
☎ 01577 862900   www.kinrosshouse.com

♲ **Kinshaldy Riding Stables**   `98 B3`
Kinshaldy Farm, 3 miles (5km) east of Leuchars on unclassified road (signposted to Kinshaldy Beach). Horse treks through 4500 acres (1821ha) of scenic woodland, and along 4 miles (6.5km) of sandy beaches. Suitable for children and adults.
☎ 01334 838527

🏛 **Kirkcaldy Museum & Art Gallery**   `93 D4`
War Memorial Gardens, Kirkcaldy. A collection of fine and decorative arts of local and national importance. There is an outstanding collection of 18th-20th century Scottish paintings and probably the largest public collection of works (outside the National Galleries of Scotland) by William McTaggart and the Scottish colourist S. J. Peploe. There is also an award-winning museum display, Changing Places, which tells the story of the social, industrial and natural heritage of the area.
☎ 01592 412860

🏛 **Kirriemuir Gateway to the Glens Museum**   `102 C4`
Kirriemuir. Housed in Kirriemuir's oldest building (1604). Exhibitions on Kirriemuir, with a stunning model of the town circa 1604. Also features on the western Angus Glens including a Highland wildlife display full of birds and animals.
☎ 01575 575479

✎ **Knock of Crieff**   `95 F3`
Within a short walk from the centre of Crieff. A mixed woodland site located in beautiful Strathearn.
www.pkc.gov.uk/sport_culture/walks.htm

🏆 **Knockhill Racing Circuit**   `92 B4`
On the A823, 6 miles (9.5km) north of Dunfermline. Scotland's National Motor Sports Centre with racing events for motor cars and motor cycles most weekends between April and October. Visitors can watch or participate.
☎ 01383 723337   www.knockhill.co.uk

✎ **Lady Mary's Walk**   `95 F3`
Walk from the centre of Crieff. A favourite walk of Lady Mary Murray, whose family owned the surrounding land in the early 19th century. It provides a peaceful stroll beside the picturesque River Earn, along an avenue of mature trees.
www.pkc.gov.uk/sport_culture/walks.htm

🏛 **Laing Museum**   `96 C4`
Newburgh, Fife. The museum was gifted to the town by Alexander Laing, and first opened in 1896. One gallery is devoted to Laing and his collections while the other holds temporary exhibitions with a local flavour.
☎ 01337 883017

✖ **Letham Glen**   `98 A5`
On the A915, Sillerhole Road on the outskirts of Leven. The nature centre displays information and pictures about wildlife. Nature trail through the glen.
☎ 01333 429231

✎ **Linn of Tummel**   `101 F3`
Walk from Garry Bridge, 2.5 miles (4km) north of Pitlochry on the B8019. Follow a riverside nature trail through mixed woodland to the meeting place of the Rivers Garry and Tummel. The Linn of Tummel (pool of the tumbling stream) comprises a series of rocky rapids in a beautiful setting.
www.nts.org.uk

🏰 **Loch Leven Castle**   `96 B5`
On an island in Loch Leven, by Kinross. A late 14th or early 15th century tower on one side of an irregular courtyard. The prison of Mary, Queen of Scots in 1567.
☎ 07778 040483   www.historic-scotland.gov.uk

🦅 **Loch of Kinnordy RSPB Nature Reserve**   `102 C4`
Loch of Kinnordy, 0.5 miles (0.8km) west of Kirriemuir. Visitors can view wildlife at close quarters from three comfortable hides. There are short trails between the hides and interpretation materials within the hides and at the car park.
☎ 01738 630783   www.rspb.org.uk

🦅 **Loch of the Lowes Visitor Centre**   `96 A1`
2 miles (3km) north east of Dunkeld. A visitor centre with wildlife displays and small aquaria. Observation hide at lakeside with fitted binoculars and telescopes. Birds include breeding ospreys, great crested grebe, tufted duck, coot, mallard, and occasionally cormorants, heron and goldeneye duck.
☎ 01350 727337

✖ **Loch Tay Pottery**   `95 F1`
Fearnan, Aberfeldy. A showroom and workshop in a former croft. Andrew Burt produces a wide variety of stoneware pots.
☎ 01887 830251

🏕 **Lochore Meadows Country Park**   `92 C4`
Crosshill, Lochgelly. Green and pleasant countryside around a large lake reclaimed from coal mining waste in the 1960s. A slide show, displays and ranger-guided walks tell the story of the reclamation. Ancient historical remains.
☎ 01592 414300

🏰 **MacDuff Castle**   `93 E4`
East Wemyss, beside the cemetery overlooking the sea. Reputed to be home of MacDuff of Shakespeare's Macbeth, now in ruins.

♱ **Maggie Walls Monument**   `96 A4`
1 mile (1.5km) west of Dunning, on the B8062. The monument marks the spot where Maggie Wall was allegedly burned as a witch in 1657. It is constructed from rough field boulders and a plinth stone topped with a cross.
☎ 01764 684448

✝ **Maison Dieu Chapel**   `103 F3`
Maison Dieu Lane, Brechin. Part of the south wall of a chapel belonging to a medieval hospital founded in the 1260s, with finely-detailed doors and windows.
☎ 0131 668 8800   www.historic-scotland.gov.uk

🏛 **McManus Galleries**   `99 B2`
Albert Square, Dundee. Victorian Gothic building designed by Sir George Gilbert Scott containing collections of national importance. Features local history, costume, natural history, archaeology, decorative arts and a superb Scottish Victorian art collection. Also the magnificent Albert Hall with its fine stained glass window and vaulted roof.
☎ 01382 432084   www.dundeecity.gov.uk

🏛 **Meffan, The**   `103 D4`
20 West High Street, Forfar. Two art galleries featuring art from contemporary Scottish artists and the Angus collections. The Forfar Story features original Pictish stones from Angus, an interactive guide to the stones, a walk through an old Forfar vennel with its shops and a witch burning scene.
☎ 01307 464123

♱ **Meigle Sculptured Stones**   `96 C1`
On the A94 in Meigle, 12 miles (19km) west south-west of Forfar. One of the most notable collections of Dark Age sculpture in Western Europe.
☎ 01828 640612   www.historic-scotland.gov.uk

✖ **Meikleour Beech Hedge**   `96 B2`
10 miles (16km) east of Dunkeld on the A93. An incredible living wall of beech trees, 100ft (30m) high and one third of a mile (530m) long. Now officially recognised in the Guinness Book of Records as the highest hedge in the world.

♱ **Melville Monument**   `95 E3`
6 miles (9.5km) west of Crieff. The obelisk in memory of Lord Melville stands on Dunmore, a hill of 840ft (256m), with delightful views of the surrounding countryside.

♱ **Mercat Cross**   `99 B3`
Nethergate, Dundee. Standing on the south side of St Mary's Tower, this is a replica of Dundee's old mercat cross which formerly stood in the Seagate. On top of the shaft is a unicorn sculpted by Scott Sutherland, RSA.

🏛 **Methil Heritage Centre**   `93 E4`
272 High Street, Methil, 8 miles (13km) east of Kirkcaldy. A lively community museum, interpreting the social and individual history of the area.
☎ 01333 422100

🏛 **Michael Bruce's Cottage**   `96 B5`
The Cobbles, Kinnesswood, Kinross. An 18th century pantiled weaver's cottage and a museum since 1906. Houses collection relating to the life of the poet, and local history including the manufacture of vellum and parchment.
☎ 01592 840255

✖ **Mills Observatory**   `98 A2`
Balgay Park, Dundee. Constructed in 1935 for the people of Dundee, the Mills Observatory is today Britain's only full-time public observatory. Located in picturesque wooded surroundings, it houses a 10 inch (25cm) refracting telescope.
☎ 01382 435846   www.mills-observatory.co.uk

✖ **Miniature Railway**   `98 D1`
West Links Park, Arbroath. Open since 1935, the small trains run alongside the British Rail Aberdeen to Edinburgh main line from West Links Station, which is complete with platforms, booking office, footbridge, signal box, turntable and locomotive shed. The 0.5 mile (1km) round trip includes a tunnel.
☎ 01241 879249   www.geocities.com/kmr_scotland

Moncreiffe Hill Wood
96 B3

South of Perth, off the M90 at junction 9, take the minor road to Rhynd following tourist signposting. A visit to this spectacular 333 acre (134ha) wood will allow visitors to enjoy outstanding views along the River Tay and Strathearn and you may also catch a glimpse of some of the wildlife which inhabits the wood.
☎ 01764 662554 www.woodland-trust.org.uk

Monikie Country Park
96 B2

Main Lodge, Monikie, off the B962 between Dundee and Arbroath. The country park comprises 185 acres (75ha), with reservoirs, woodland and grassland. Instruction and hire for windsurfing, sailing, canoeing (May – September).
☎ 01382 370202

Montrose Air Station Museum
103 G4

Waldron Road, Montrose. RFC/RAF and wartime artefacts and memorabilia housed in the wartime RAF Montrose HQ. Various aircraft on display outside, also pillbox and Anderson shelter.
☎ 01674 673107

Montrose Basin Wildlife Centre
103 F4

Rossie Braes, 1 mile (1.5km) south of Montrose on the A92. Unique displays show how a tidal basin works and the routes of migrating birds. Magnificent views of wildlife on the basin through telescopes and binoculars. Interactive displays.
☎ 01674 676336 www.montrosebasin.org.uk

Montrose Museum & Art Gallery
103 G4

Panmure Place, Montrose. Tells the story of Montrose from prehistoric times, including local geology and wildlife. On show are various Pictish stones, pottery, whaling and Napoleonic artefacts.
☎ 01674 673232

Muir O' Fauld Signal Station
95 G4

East of Ardunie. The site of a Roman watch tower.
☎ 0131 668 8800 www.historic-scotland.gov.uk

Museum of Abernethy
96 B4

Abernethy. An independent museum housed in a restored 18th century cattle byre and stable in the centre of the historic village of Abernethy. The museum depicts life in the parish of Abernethy from Pictish times to the present day.
☎ 01738 850889

Muthill Church & Tower
95 F4

On the A822 in Muthill. 5 miles (8km) south of Crieff on the A822. The ruins of a 15th century parish church with a tall Romanesque tower at its west end.
☎ 0131 668 8800 www.historic-scotland.gov.uk

Muthill Village Museum
95 F4

Station Road, Muthill, 5 miles (8km) south of Crieff on the A822. Collection of local objects from yesteryear. Model castle and steam railway display.

Newton Hill Country Sports
98 A3

Newton Farm, Wormit, on the B946, 4 miles (6.5km) south of the Tay Road Bridge. Clay shooting, quad bikes, off-road driving and fly fishing.
☎ 01382 542513 www.newtonhillatv.co.uk

Niel Gow's Oak
96 A1

Walk from the Hermitage, near Dunkeld. Famous fiddle player Niel Gow (1727–1807) lived nearby and, according to local folklore, liked to sit here and play.
www.forestry.gov.uk

Noah's Ark Activity Centre
96 A3

Glendevon Farm, Western Edge, off the Perth Western Bypass (A9). A specially equipped and supervised children's softplay barn. Also indoor kart tracks.
☎ 01738 445568 www.noahs-ark.co.uk

Old Steeple
99 B3

Nethergate, Dundee. Scotland's highest surviving medieval tower (154ft/47m), originally part of the great medieval church, is Dundee's oldest building dating from 1485. The tower consists of the ground floor with a vaulted ceiling 50ft (15m) high, four internal levels, bell ringing chamber, belfry and clock room.
☎ 01382 206790 www.oldsteeple.co.uk

Panbride Church
98 C2

Panbride, Carnoustie. The first mention of Panbride was in 1178 when William I gave the church and parish to Arbroath Abbey. At the church gates is a loupin stane used to assist church-goers mounting horses. By the loupin stane there is a footpath which heads north to Muirdrum. Follow this footpath for a few hundred yards and you are at the top of the fairy steps. You are supposed to make a wish on the third step.

Parent Larch
96 A1

Close to Dunkeld Cathedral. The sole survivor from a group of larches planted here as seedlings over 250 years ago. The young trees had been collected from the Tyrol mountains in central Europe in 1738.

Peel Farm Coffee & Crafts
102 B4

Off the B954, 20 miles (32km) north of Dundee. A working farm in an unspoilt area of rural Angus close to the majestic Reekie Linn waterfall. Craft demonstrations.
☎ 01575 560205

Perth Mart Visitor Centre
96 A3

East Huntingtower, on the A85, 2 miles (3km) west of Perth. Visitors are guided through the history of agricultural life in Scotland.
☎ 01738 474170

Perth Museum & Art Gallery
97 C2

George Street, Perth. Collections of local history, fine and applied art, natural history and archaeology. Changing programme of temporary exhibitions.
☎ 01738 632488

Perth Racecourse
96 B3

Scone Palace Park, Perth. Race meetings within the grounds of Scone Palace.
☎ 01738 551597 www.perth-races.co.uk

Perth Sculpture Trail
97 C2

Perth. Perth Sculpture Trail extends through 1 mile (1.5km) of riverside parkland. Permanent public artworks have been specially created by national and international artists.
☎ 01738 475000

Perth Theatre
97 B2

Perth. Perth Theatre is open all year and offers a wide variety of events produced by the Perth Theatre Company and visiting companies, including comedies, musicals, dramatic theatre, children's and family shows.
☎ 01738 621031 www.perth.org.uk/theatre

Perthshire Visitor Centre
96 A2

In Bankfoot, off the A9, 6 miles (9.5km) north of Perth. The Macbeth Experience is a multi-media audio-visual presentation showing the comparison between Shakespeare's play and the real Scottish king.
☎ 01738 787696

Pictavia
103 E3

By Brechin Castle Centre, Haughmuir. Discover Scotland's ancient past through the legacy of the ancient Picts. Pictavia offers an insight into the culture and heritage of these enigmatic people who were central to the foundation of what is now known as Scotland. Interactive exhibits, replicas and artefacts.
☎ 01356 626241 www.pictavia.org.uk

Pitlochry Children's Amusement Park
101 F4

Armoury Road, Pitlochry. Remote controlled cars, trucks, bumper cars, boats, orbiter shuttles, water blasters and rides.
☎ 01796 472876 www.childrensamusementpark.co.uk

Pitlochry Festival Theatre
101 F4

Port-na-Craig, Pitlochry. One of Scotland's most admired repertory theatres with a resident company. Beautifully situated overlooking the river. Art gallery.
☎ 01796 484626 www.pitlochry.org.uk

Pitmuies Gardens
98 C1

House of Pitmuies, Guthrie, 7 miles (11km) east of Forfar. Two walled gardens lead down to a small river with an informal riverside walk with fine trees and two unusual buildings – a turreted dovecote and a Gothic washhouse.
☎ 01241 818245

Pittencrieff House Museum
92 B5

Pittencrieff Park, Dunfermline. A 17th century mansion, converted by Sir Robert Lorimer into three galleries. Displays on the history of the house and park.
☎ 01383 722935

Pittencrieff Park Animal Centre & Glasshouses
92 B5

Dunfermline High Street. Visitors can see a wide range of animals, ranging from rare and endangered species of primates and birds to domestic animals. The glasshouses are planted with a mixture of perennial and seasonal plants. Beautifully landscaped and maintained park.
☎ 01383 313700

Portmoak Moss
96 B5

Between Kinnesswood and Scotlandwell, off the A911. Once a peat bog, today it is under restoration to encourage regeneration of native trees such as birch, rowan, willow and Scots pine. Circular walk within the wood.
www.woodland-trust.org.uk

Praytis Farm Park
98 A5

Leven, Fife. Lots of animals on display, which can be seen close up and touched. There is also a golf driving range, a grass tee area and a 9 hole pitch and putt. An indoor play barn, bouncy castle, wild west adventure fort and go-karting will entertain the family.
☎ 01333 350209

Quarrymill Woodland Park
96 B3

On the outskirts of Perth along the A93 Blairgowrie road. Twenty seven acres of woodland around the Annety Burn. Paths specially designed for disabled visitors.
☎ 01738 633890

Queen's View Visitor Centre
101 E3

Strathtummel, 7 miles (11km) west of Pitlochry on the B8019. The centre, close to the viewpoint, is the focal point of the Tay Forest Park and provides an ideal introduction, describing the history of the people and forests in Perthshire. The view across Loch Tummel to the mountain of Schiehallion and beyond is stunning.
☎ 01350 727284 www.forestry.gov.uk

Rannoch Forest
100 C4

On the south shore of Loch Rannoch, 3 miles (4.8km) west of Kinloch Rannoch. There are fine forest walks offering panoramic views of the loch and distant hills.
www.forestry.gov.uk

Ravenscraig Park
93 D4

Kirkcaldy, Fife. Woodland park, beach and coastal walks. Also putting course, trampolines and access to the ruins of 15th century Ravenscraig Castle.

Red Castle `103 F4`
Off the A92, 7 miles (11km) south of Montrose. This red stone tower on a steep mound beside the sandhills of Lunan Bay probably dates from the 15th century.

Reekie Linn Falls `102 B4`
South west of Kirriemuir on the B954. Spectacular waterfall in the natural gorged woodland, its spume effect accounts for its smoky description.

Restenneth Priory `103 D4`
Off the B9113, 1.5 miles (2.5km) east north-east of Forfar. The ruins of an Augustinian priory church. The lower part of the tower is early Romanesque.
☎ 0131 668 8800 www.historic-scotland.gov.uk

Riverside Granary `96 B1`
Lower Mill Street, Blairgowrie. An art and craft gallery in a converted grain mill.
☎ 01250 873032 www.paintingsandprints.co.uk

Robinson Crusoe Statue `98 B5`
Lower Largo. Bronze statue of Alexander Selkirk, the real life mariner on whom Daniel Defoe based his famous character.

Rumbling Bridge `92 B4`
The River Devon is spanned here by two bridges. A footpath from the north side gives good access to spectacular and picturesque gorges and falls, one of which is known as the Devil's Mill. Another, Cauldron Linn, is a mile downstream, whilst Vicar's Bridge is a beauty spot a mile beyond this.

St Andrew's Church & the Glasite Hall `99 C2`
King Street, Dundee. St Andrew's Church was designed by Samuel Bell and completed in 1772. It was built and paid for entirely by the Nine Trades' Guild of Dundee and there are fine stained glass windows depicting the trades emblems.

St Andrew's Preservation Trust Museum & Garden `98 C4`
12 North Street, St Andrews. A charming 16th century building with a beautiful sheltered garden. Displays include old shops and businesses in the town and some of Scotland's earliest photographs. Changing exhibitions.
☎ 01334 477629

St Andrews Aquarium `98 C4`
The Scores, St Andrews. Over 30 dramatic displays of native sea creatures. Everything from shrimps and starfish to sharks and conger eels. Graceful rays nose the surface of their display to watch you watching them. Visitors can see the resident seals and diving ducks.
☎ 01334 474786

St Andrews Botanic Garden `98 B4`
The Canongate, St Andrews. Eighteen acres (7ha) of impressively landscaped gardens and glasshouses. Peat, rock, heath and water gardens bounded by the Kinness Burn.
☎ 01334 476452 www.st-and.ac.uk/standrews/botanic

St Andrews Castle `98 C4`
The Scores, St Andrews. The ruins of the castle of the Archbishops of St Andrews, dating in part from the 13th century. Notable features include a bottle dungeon and mine, and counter-mine tunnelling made during the siege that followed the murder of Cardinal Beaton in 1546. An exhibition shows the history of the castle and the cathedral.
☎ 01334 477196 www.historic-scotland.gov.uk

St Andrews Cathedral & St Rule's Tower `98 B4`
The Scores, St Andrews. The remains of one of the largest cathedrals in Scotland and the associated domestic ranges of the priory. A museum houses an outstanding collection of early Christian and medieval monuments and other objets trouvés. St Rule's Tower in the precinct is part of the first church of the Augustinian canons at St Andrews, built early in the 12th century.
☎ 01334 472563 www.historic-scotland.gov.uk

St Andrews Guided Walks `98 B4`
Walks depart from St Andrews Pottery Shop, St Andrews. Guided walks of St Andrews cover the area around the cathedral, castle, university and golf course.
☎ 01334 850638

St Andrews Links `98 B4`
St Andrews. There is a 600 year history of golf at St Andrews and the five 18 hole courses now comprise the largest golf complex in Europe. The Old Course, renowned as the 'home of golf' is of great symbolic importance. It attracts thousands of golfers from around the world every year, and has also shaped many of the principles of traditional golf course design.
☎ 01334 466666

www.standrews.org.uk

St Andrews Museum `98 B4`
Kinburn Park, Doubledykes Road, St Andrews. Opened in 1991 in Kinburn House, a Victorian mansion set in pleasant parkland. The museum traces the development of the city as a pilgrimage shrine to St Andrew and a power centre for medieval kings and bishops, with Scotland's largest cathedral and first university.
☎ 01334 412690

St Andrews Pottery Shop `98 C4`
4 Church Square, St Andrews. Shop selling full range of pots made locally by well-known potter, George Young. Video of pottery processes.
☎ 01334 477744

St Bridget's Kirk, Dalgety `92 C5`
Off the A92 at Dalgety Bay. The shell of a medieval church much altered in the 17th century for Protestant worship. At the west end of the building is a burial vault, with a laird's loft above, built for the Earl of Dunfermline.
☎ 0131 668 8800 www.historic-scotland.gov.uk

St Fillan's Cave `98 C5`
Cove Wynd, Pittenweem. A cave associated with St Fillan, a 7th century missionary to the Picts, who lived in the area.
☎ 01333 311495

St John's Kirk `97 C2`
St John's Place, Perth. Consecrated in 1242, this fine cruciform church largely dates from the 15th century and was restored 1923–26. Here in 1559 John Knox preached his momentous sermon urging the 'purging of the churches from idolatry'.
☎ 01738 638482

St Margaret's Cave `92 B5`
Bruce Street, Dunfermline. A site of Catholic pilgrimage where Margaret, 11th century queen and saint, sought refuge for meditation and prayer.
☎ 01383 314228

St Mary's Church, Grand Tully `101 E4`
Off the A827 at Pitcairn Farm, 3 miles (5km) east north-east of Aberfeldy. A simple 16th century parish church with a finely painted wooden ceiling illustrating heraldic and symbolic subjects.
☎ 0131 668 8800 www.historic-scotland.gov.uk

St Mary's Church, St Andrews `98 C4`
Kirkheugh, St Andrews. The foundations of a cruciform church on the edge of a cliff. Destoyed in the Reformation this was the earliest collegiate church in Scotland.
☎ 0131 668 8800 www.historic-scotland.gov.uk

St Monans Windmill `98 C5`
1 mile (2km) west of Pittenweem. A late 18th century windmill.

St Orland's Stone `98 A1`
Near Cossans Farm, 4.5 miles (7km) west of Forfar. An early Christian sculptured slab with a cross on one side and Pictish symbols and figures on the other.
www.historic-scotland.gov.uk

St Serf's Church `96 A4`
The parish church of Dunning, with a square Romanesque tower and tower arch. The rest of the church was rebuilt in 1810 but contains some of the original fabric.
☎ 0131 668 8800 www.historic-scotland.gov.uk

St Vigeans Sculptured Stones `98 D1`
0.5 mile (1km) north of Arbroath. A fine collection of 32 early Christian and Pictish stones set into cottages in the village of St Vigeans.
☎ 0131 668 8800 www.historic-scotland.gov.uk

Scone Palace `96 B3`
On the A93, 2 miles (3km) north east of Perth. A castellated palace, enlarged and embellished in 1803, incorporating the 16th century and earlier palaces. Notable grounds and a pinetum. Magnificent collection of porcelain, furniture, ivories, 18th century clocks and 16th century needlework. The Moot Hill at Scone, known in the 8th century and earlier, was the site of the famous Coronation Stone of Scone (the Stone of Destiny), brought there in the 9th century by Kenneth MacAlpine, King of Scots. In 1296 the Stone was seized by the English and taken to Westminster Abbey. In 1997 the Stone was returned to Scotland and is now in Edinburgh Castle.
☎ 01738 552300 www.scone-palace.co.uk

Scotland's Larder `98 B5`
Upper Largo, (9.5km) east of Leven. Scotland's only visitor attraction offering information on the tradition, variety and quality of Scottish foods.
☎ 01333 360414 www.scotland-larder.co.uk

Scotland's Secret Bunker `98 C5`
Crown Buildings, Troywood, on the B9131, 5 miles (8km) from St Andrews. The amazing labyrinth built 100ft (30.5m) underground where central government and the military commanders would have run the country in the event of nuclear war. Visitors can see the nuclear command centre with its original equipment. Three cinemas show authentic cold war films. There is a display of vehicles in the grounds.
☎ 01333 310301 www.secretbunker.co.uk

Scotstarvit Tower `98 A4`
Off the A916, 3 miles (5km) south of Cupar. A handsome and well-built 15th century tower house remodelled in the mid 16th century. Renowned as the home of Sir John Scot.
☎ 0131 668 8800 www.historic-scotland.gov.uk

Scottish Antique & Arts Centre `96 C2`
Abernyte, 1.5 miles (2.5km) from the A90. A large antique and arts centre.
☎ 01828 686401

Scottish Crannog Centre `95 F1`
Kenmore, 6 miles (10km) west of Aberfeldy on the A827. A unique recreation of an Iron Age loch dwelling, authentically built from evidence obtained from underwater archaeological excavations of crannogs in the loch. Visitors can walk back in time and experience the life of crannog-dwellers.
☎ 01887 830583 www.crannog.co.uk

Scottish Deer Centre `98 A4`
Bow of Fife, on the A91, 3 miles (5km) west of Cupar. Fifty-five acres (22ha) of parkland with more than 160 deer. Falconry displays three times daily.
☎ 01337 810391

Scottish Fisheries Museum `98 C5`
Anstruther. Housed in 16th to 19th century buildings, the museum displays fishing and ships' gear, model and actual fishing boats. Interior of a fisherman's cottage and extended reference library.
☎ 01333 310628 www.scottish-fisheries-museum.org

Scottish Hydro-Electric Visitor Centre `101 F4`
Pitlochry Power Station. An exhibition shows how Scottish Hydro-Electric power stations are controlled and operated. Visitors can also observe salmon coming upstream in the fish ladder and see into the station's turbine hall.
☎ 01796 473152 www.scottish-southern.co.uk

Scottish Liqueur Centre `96 A2`
Hilton, 7 miles (11km) north of Perth at the Bankfoot exit of the A9. The family-run company produces original Scottish liqueurs.
☎ 01738 787044 www.scottish-liqueur-centre.co.uk

Scottish Off-Road Driving Centre `96 C4`
Strathmiglo, Fife. An off-road driving range covering a 100 acre (40ha) site.
☎ 01337 860528 www.scotoffroad.co.uk

Scottish Plant Collectors' Garden `101 F4`
Pitlochry Festival Theatre, Port-na-Craig, Pitlochry. Scotland's newest garden celebrates 300 years of plant collecting by Scotsmen. Art and sculpture are combined with landscape features to provide a unique experience.
☎ 01796 484600 www.scottishplantcollectorsgarden.com

Scottish Vintage Bus Museum `92 B4`
M90 Commerce Park, Lathalmond, 2 miles (3km) north of Dunfermline. A collection of over 150 historic buses from the 1920s, mostly of Scottish origin, which can be seen in all stages of restoration. Also many artefacts depicting Scottish bus history. Visitors can observe restoration work or travel in a vintage bus around the site.
☎ 01383 623380

Sensation `99 A3`
Greenmarket, Dundee. An innovative science centre, housed in a striking building on part of a former rail yard site. Sensation brings science to life with over 65 fun, interactive exhibits, based around the senses and designed for people of all ages.
☎ 01382 228800 www.sensation.org.uk

Shinafoot Art Studios `95 G4`
Shinafoot, Dunning Road, 1 mile (1.5km) north east of Auchterarder on the B8062. Year-round art courses and painting holidays for all ages and abilities.
☎ 01764 663639 www.shinafoot.co.uk

Silverburn Estate `98 A5`
On the A915 Largo Road to the east of Leven. Beautiful gardens and mature woodland, with a variety of wildlife. Includes several paddocks used for summer grazing for domestic animals, including Shetland ponies. The mini farm has a collection of farm animals and farm implements.
☎ 01333 427568

Sir Douglas Bader Disabled Garden `98 A4`
Duffus Park, Carslogie Road, Cupar. The Sir Douglas Bader Garden was opened in 1982 and was designed specifically for disabled visitors. There is a small public garden with raised flower borders, raised ponds and an aviary.
☎ 01334 412831

Soutar House `97 A3`
27 Wilson Street, Perth. This is the former home of the Perth poet William Soutar. The room where he lay bedridden for 14 years, his father's wood panelling of most of the ground floor of the house and the stained glass have been meticulously preserved.
☎ 01738 643687

South Lissens Pottery `96 B5`
22 Church Street, Milnathort. A pottery workshop located in an old Presbyterian church built in 1769. Traditional country pottery and contemporary pots decorated with unusual lustre effects.
☎ 01577 865642

Stocks, Stones & Stories `95 F3`
Crieff. A fascinating exhibition in the basement of Crieff Town Hall, housing three of the town's conserved historical monuments: the Crieff Burgh cross; the Drummond or Mercat cross; and the town stocks – unique in design.
☎ 01764 652578

Strathearn Gallery `95 F3`
Crieff. Regular exhibitions of paintings and applied art by Scottish based artists and craftspeople are held throughout the year.
☎ 01764 656100 www.strathearn-gallery.com

Stuart Crystal `95 F3`
Muthill Road, Crieff. Retail factory shop selling quality Stuart and Waterford crystal and Wedgwood china as well as seconds. Children's play area.
☎ 01764 654004

Tay Rail Bridge `98 A3`
Dundee. The present bridge, carrying the main railway line from London to Aberdeen, was completed in 1887. It replaced the first Tay Rail Bridge which was blown down by a storm in 1879 with the loss of 75 lives.

Tealing Dovecot & Earth House `98 B2`
0.5 mile (1km) down an unclassified road to Tealing, off the A929 5 miles (8km) north of Dundee. The dovecot dates from the late 16th century and is an elegant little building. The earth house, of Iron Age date, comprises an underground passage now uncovered.
☎ 0131 668 8800 www.historic-scotland.gov.uk

Townhill Country Park `92 B5`
Town Loch, Townhill, by Dunfermline. A country park with informal recreation in lochside and woodland setting.
☎ 01383 725596

Tullibardine Chapel `95 G4`
Off the A823, 6 miles (9.5km) south east of Crieff. One of the most complete and unaltered small medieval churches in Scotland. Founded in 1446 and largely rebuilt circa 1500. Good architectural detail.
☎ 0131 668 8800 www.historic-scotland.gov.uk

Valleyfield Wood `92 B5`
On the north side of the A985, High Valleyfield, near Culross. Beautiful woodland walks landscaped by Sir Humphrey Repton.

Vane Farm RSPB Nature Reserve `92 C4`
Kinross, 1 mile (2km) along the B9097 east of junction 5 off the M90. Vane Farm Visitor Centre overlooks Loch Leven where thousands of geese and ducks spend the winter. Two trails take visitors to hides overlooking the wetlands and loch and through woodlands to Vane Hill.
☎ 01577 862355 www.rspb.org.uk

Verdant Works `99 A2`
West Hendersons Wynd, Dundee. A restored 19th century jute works surrounding a cobbled courtyard. Visitors can view the period office (unchanged since the last century), discover why Dundee became the jute capital of the world and see working machinery processing jute to woven cloth.
☎ 01382 225282

Wade's Bridge `95 F1`
On the B846, north of Aberfeldy. The bridge across the River Tay was begun in 1733 by General Wade. It is considered to be the finest of all Wade's bridges.

Water Mill & Tearoom `101 E3`
Ford Road, Blair Atholl. Dating from 1613, this working museum produces oatmeal and flour which is on sale in the tearoom.
☎ 07754 128065

Weem Wood `101 E4`
1.5 miles west of Aberfeldy, on the B846. A circular path takes walkers across ancient woodland-covered crags to St David's Well, a natural spring named after a 15th century local laird who lived as a hermit in one of the caves on the hillside.
www.forestry.gov.uk

West Port `98 C4`
In South Street, St Andrews. One of the few surviving city gates in Scotland, built in 1589 and renovated in 1843.
www.historic-scotland.gov.uk

William Lamb Memorial Studio `103 G4`
Trades Close, High Street, Montrose. The working studio of the famous Montrose sculptor includes displays of his sculptures, etchings, paintings and drawings. Also featured are his workroom and living room with self-styled furniture.
☎ 01674 673232

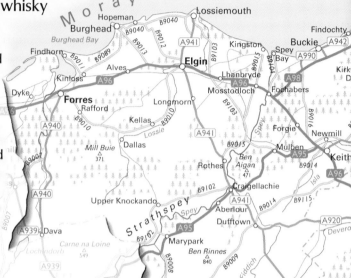

Aberdeenshire & Moray

This quiet corner of Scotland is rich in historic castles, royal connections and whisky distilleries.

There are miles of unspoilt coastline and the Grampian Mountains contain more peaks over 4000ft (1219m) than anywhere else in Scotland. As a gateway to Royal Deeside, the city of Aberdeen has much to offer the visitor. Follow the Castle Trail or the Royal Road along the beautiful Dee valley and visit Balmoral Castle.

Scotland's castle country

Grampian has more castles than any other area of the UK. There are fairy-tale castles with spires and towers, dramatic ruins and stately mansions. Follow the Castle Trail linking some of the region's finest examples - the castles of Huntly, Kildrummy, Corgarff, Craigievar, Fraser, Tolquhon, Fyvie, and Delgattie, and the mansions of Duff House, Haddo House and Leith Hall.

Huntly castle

Grampian gardens

The area's relatively mild climate has helped Aberdeen flourish as the 'Flower of Scotland'. It is renowned for its parks, gardens and floral displays. Away from the city are the gardens of Pitmedden, Crathes Castle and Leith Hall Rock Garden. To the north, Forres is also known as a 'floral town' because of its award-winning parks and gardens.

Pitmedden Garden

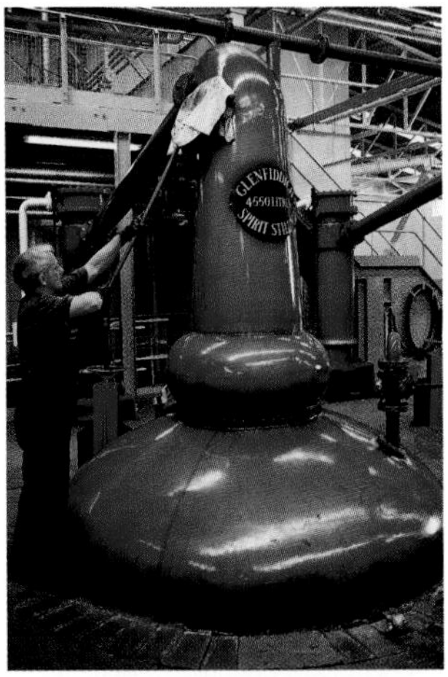

Glenfiddich distillery

The Malt Whisky Trail

Over half of Scotland's distilleries are in Speyside. Scotland's Malt Whisky Trail follows a 70 mile (112km) signposted route linking seven of the world's most famous distilleries. - Glenfiddich, Glenlivet, Strathisla, Glen Grant, Dallas Dhu, Cardhu and Glenfarclas as well as the Speyside Cooperage where barrels are made. All distilleries on the trail have visitor centres and offer guided tours.

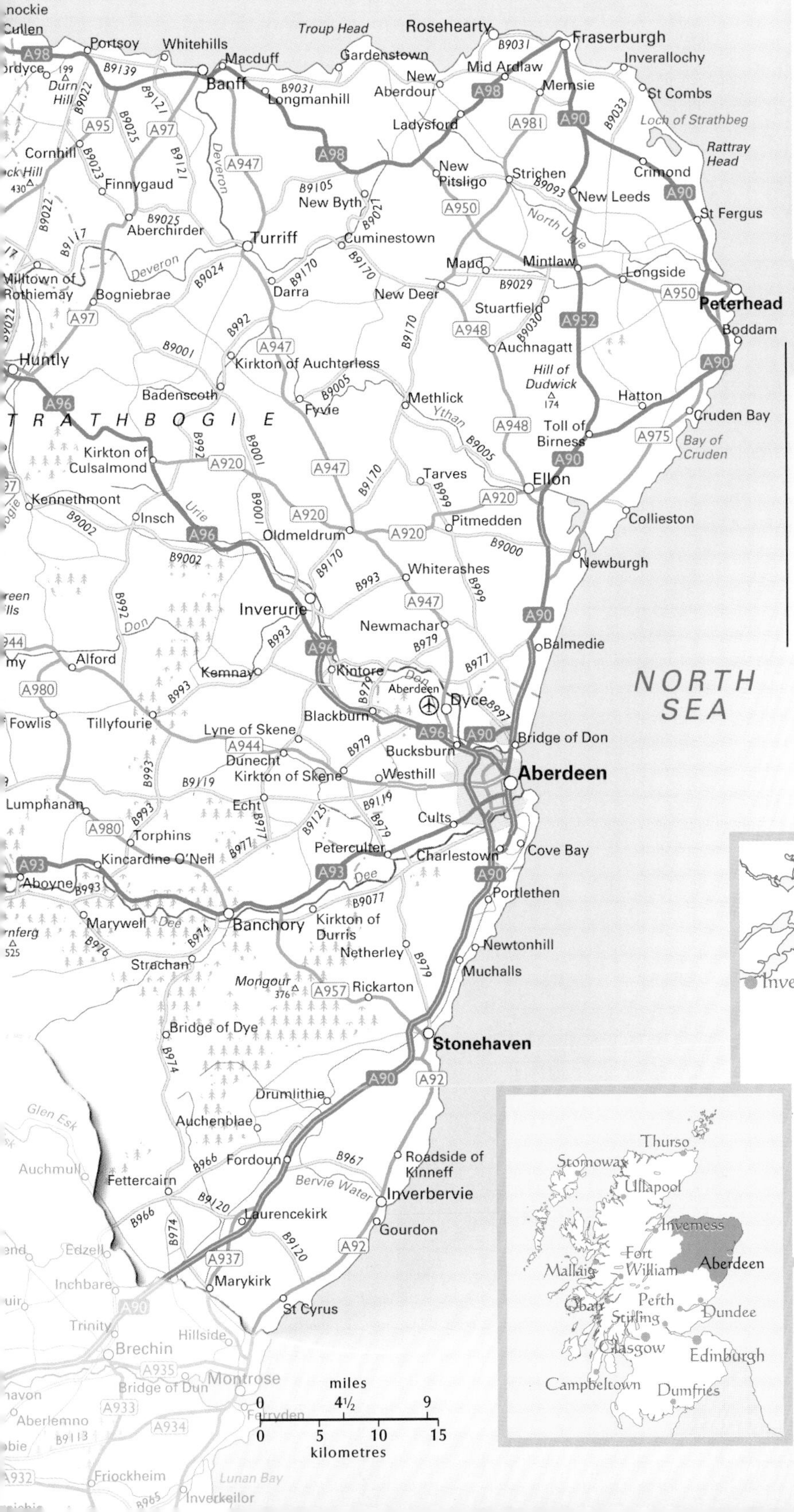
Troup Head
Rosehearty
Fraserburgh
Inverallochy
St Combs
Loch of Strathbeg
Rattray Head
Portsoy
Whitehills
Macduff
Gardenstown
New Aberdour
Mid Ardlaw
Memsie
Banff
Longmanhill
Cullen
Durn Hill
Cornhill
Finnygaud
Ladysford
New Pitsligo
Strichen
New Leeds
Crimond
St Fergus
New Byth
Aberchirder
Turriff
Cuminestown
Maud
Mintlaw
Longside
Milltown of Rothiemay
Bogniebrae
Darra
New Deer
Stuartfield
Peterhead
Boddam
Huntly
Kirkton of Auchterless
Auchnagatt
Hill of Dudwick
Badenscoth
Fyvie
Methlick
Hatton
Cruden Bay
Bay of Cruden
STRATHBOGIE
Toll of Birness
Kirkton of Culsalmond
Tarves
Ellon
Kennethmont
Insch
Pitmedden
Collieston
Oldmeldrum
Newburgh
Whiterashes
Inverurie
Newmachar
Balmedie
Alford
Kemnay
Kintore
Aberdeen
Dyce
NORTH SEA
Fowlis
Tillyfourie
Blackburn
Lyne of Skene
Bridge of Don
Dunecht
Bucksburn
Kirkton of Skene
Westhill
Aberdeen
Lumphanan
Echt
Cults
Torphins
Kincardine O'Neil
Peterculter
Charlestown
Cove Bay
Aboyne
Portlethen
Marywell
Banchory
Kirkton of Durris
Strachan
Netherley
Newtonhill
Muchalls
Mongour
Rickarton
Bridge of Dye
Stonehaven
Drumlithie
Glen Esk
Auchenblae
Auchmull
Fordoun
Roadside of Kinneff
Fettercairn
Bervie Water
Inverbervie
Laurencekirk
Gourdon
Edzell
Inchbare
Marykirk
St Cyrus
Trinity
Brechin
Hillside
Montrose
Bridge of Dun
Ferryden
Aberlemno
Friockheim
Lunan Bay
Inverkeilor
Deveron
Ythan
Urie
Don
Dee
North Ugie
A98
A95
A97
A947
A981
A90
A950
A952
A948
A96
A920
A975
A944
A980
A93
A957
A92
A937
A935
A933
A934
B9031
B9139
B9022
B9025
B9121
B9023
B9105
B9021
B9093
B9033
B9117
B9024
B9170
B9029
B9030
B992
B9001
B9005
B9002
B993
B999
B9000
B979
B977
B997
B9119
B9125
B9077
B974
B976
B966
B967
B9120
B9113
B965
miles
0
4½
9
0
5
10
15
kilometres

Map pages in this region

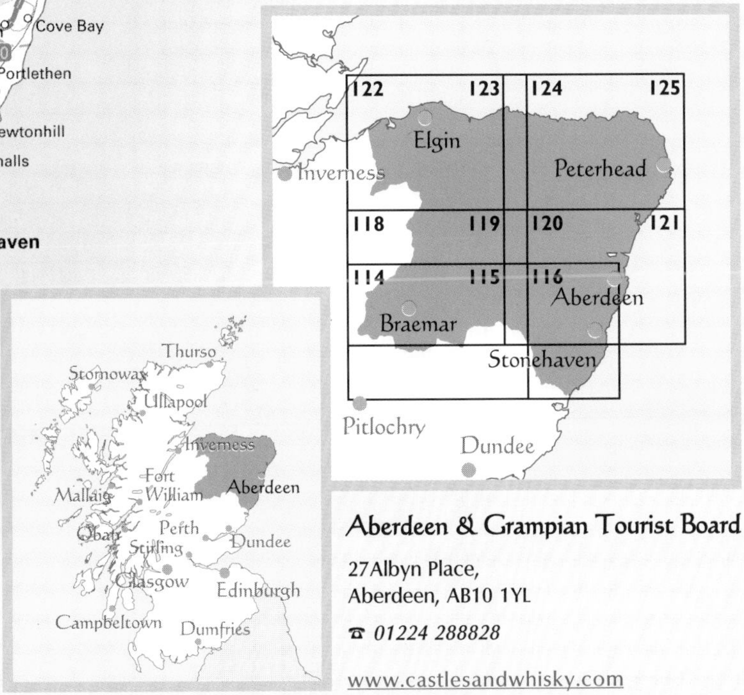
122
123
124
125
Elgin
Inverness
Peterhead
118
119
120
121
114
115
116
Aberdeen
Braemar
Stonehaven
Pitlochry
Dundee
Thurso
Stornoway
Ullapool
Inverness
Fort William
Aberdeen
Mallaig
Perth
Oban
Stirling
Dundee
Glasgow
Edinburgh
Campbeltown
Dumfries

Aberdeen & Grampian Tourist Board

27Albyn Place,
Aberdeen, AB10 1YL

☎ *01224 288828*

www.castlesandwhisky.com

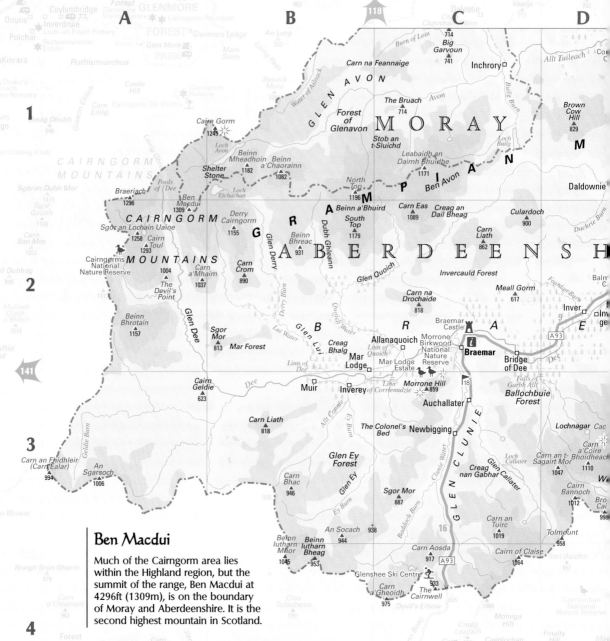

Ben Macdui

Much of the Cairngorm area lies within the Highland region, but the summit of the range, Ben Macdui at 4296ft (1309m), is on the boundary of Moray and Aberdeenshire. It is the second highest mountain in Scotland.

Highland Games

Games are held throughout the region from June to early September. The events are a celebration of all things Scottish including massed pipe bands, highland dancing and international 'heavy' and 'track' events. The Braemar Gathering is held on the first Saturday in September and is always a highlight of the calendar.

Braemar Gathering

Tourist Information

i **Braemar**

The Mews
Mar Road
Braemar
Aberdeenshire
AB35 5YP
☎ 013397 41668

Lochnagar

The Lochnagar mountain ridge is popular with climbers. The steep north east facing cliffs comprise four distinct peaks, the highest of which is Cac Carn Beag at 3788 ft (1155m). Below the ridge is the small loch of Lochnagar.

Ballater

Population: 1362. The former railway town of Ballater lies within magnificent scenery on the River Dee. It is only 8 miles (13km) east of Balmoral and there are many royal warrants displayed on the shop fronts in the town. It is a good touring centre and base for walking on Lochnagar, in Glen Muick to the south west and the woodlands of the Muir of Dinnet Nature Reserve to the east.

Balmoral Castle

Tourist Information

ⓘ **Ballater**
Albert Hall
Station Square
Feus of Ballater
Aberdeenshire
AB35 5QB
☎ 013397 55306

ⓘ **Crathie**
Car Park
Balmoral Castle
Crathie
Aberdeenshire
AB35 5TB
☎ 013397 42414

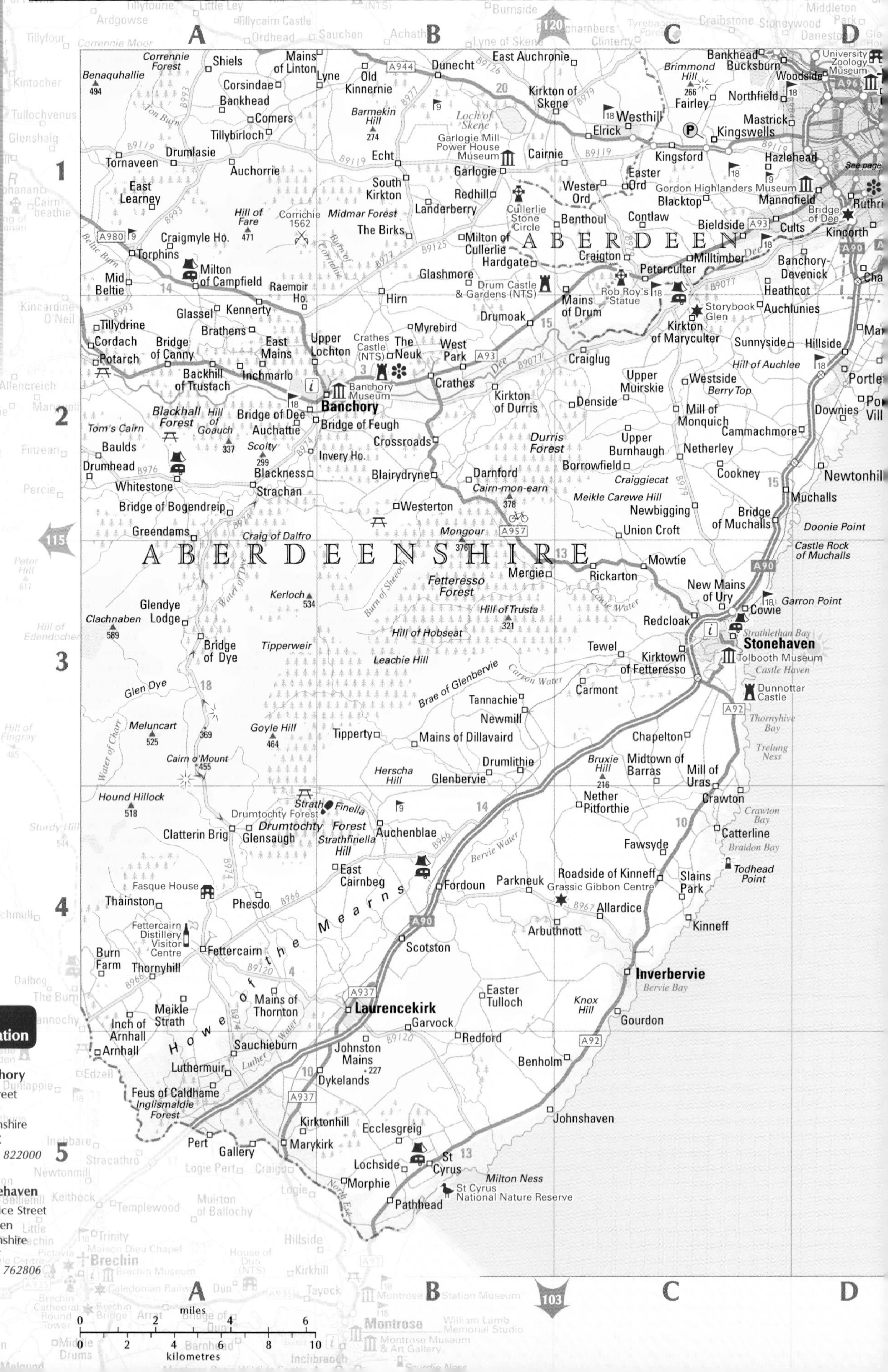

Aberdeenshire & Moray

ABERDEEN

ABERDEENSHIRE

Howe of the Mearns

Tourist Information

ℹ **Banchory**
Bridge Street
Banchory
Aberdeenshire
AB31 3SX
☎ 01330 822000

ℹ **Stonehaven**
66 Allardice Street
Stonehaven
Aberdeenshire
AB39 9ET
☎ 01569 762806

Benaquhallie 494 · Corrennie Forest · Shiels · Mains of Linton · Lyne · Old Kinnernie · Dunecht · East Auchronie · Kirkton of Skene · Brimmond Hill 266 · Fairley · Bankhead · Bucksburn · University Zoology Museum · Woodside · Northfield

Kirkton · Todlachie · Tillyfourie · Little Ley · Tillycairn Castle · Barmekin Hill 274 · Loch of Skene · Westhill · Elrick · Kingswells · Mastrick · Hazlehead · Kingsford

Tornaveen · Drumlasie · Auchorrie · South Kirkton · Echt · Garlogie Mill Power House Museum · Garlogie · Cairnie · Redhill · Landerberry · Wester Ord · Easter Ord · Blacktop · Contlaw · Bieldside · Cults · Bridge of Dee · Kincorth

East Learney · Hill of Fare 1562 · Corrichie 471 · Midmar Forest · The Birks · Glashmore · Milton of Cullerlie · Hardgate · Craigton · Peterculter · Milltimber · Banchory-Devenick · Heathcot

Craigmyle Ho. · Torphins · Mid Beltie · Milton of Campfield · Raemoir Ho. · Hirn · Drumoak · Mains of Drum · Rob Roy's Statue · Storybook Glen · Auchlunies · Sunnyside · Hillside

Tillydrine · Cordach · Potarch · Bridge of Canny · Glassel · Brathens · Kennerty · East Mains · Upper Lochton · Crathes Castle (NTS) · The Neuk · West Park · Craiglug · Kirkton of Maryculter · Hill of Auchlee · Westside · Berry Top · Downies · Portle

Tom's Cairn · Baulds · Drumhead · Whitestone · Blackhall Forest · Hill of Goauch 337 · Bridge of Dee · Auchattie · Banchory · Banchory Museum · Bridge of Feugh · Crathes · Kirkton of Durris · Denside · Upper Muirskie · Mill of Monquich · Cammachmore · Netherley · Newtonhill

Bridge of Bogendreip · Greendams · Craig of Dalfro · Scolty 299 · Blackness · Strachan · Invery Ho. · Crossroads · Blairdryne · Westerton · Darnford · Cairn-mon-earn 378 · Durris Forest · Upper Burnhaugh · Borrowfield · Craiggiecat · Meikle Carewe Hill · Newbigging · Muchalls · Bridge of Muchalls · Doonie Point

Glendye Lodge · Clachnaben 589 · Kerloch 534 · Mongour 376 · Fetteresso Forest · Hill of Trusta 321 · Mergie · Rickarton · Mowtie · Redcloak · New Mains of Ury · Cowie · Garron Point · Castle Rock of Muchalls

Bridge of Dye · Tipperweir · Hill of Hobseat · Leachie Hill · Brae of Glenbervie · Carron Water · Tewel · Kirktown of Fetteresso · Stonehaven · Tolbooth Museum · Castle Haven · Dunnottar Castle

Glen Dye · Meluncart 525 · Goyle Hill 464 · Tipperty · Mains of Dillavaird · Newmill · Drumlithie · Herscha Hill · Glenbervie · Carmont · Chapelton · Bruxie Hill 216 · Midtown of Barras · Mill of Uras · Crawton · Crawton Bay · Thornyhive Bay · Trelung Ness

Hound Hillock 518 · Cairn o' Mount 455 · Drumtochty Forest · Strath Finella · Drumtochty Forest · Strathfinella Hill · Clatterin Brig · Glensaugh · Auchenblae · Nether Pitforthie · Fawsyde · Catterline · Braidon Bay · Todhead Point

Fasque House · Thainston · Phesdo · East Cairnbeg · Fordoun · Parkneuk · Roadside of Kinneff · Grassic Gibbon Centre · Slains Park · Allardice · Kinneff

Burn Farm · Thornyhill · Fettercairn · Fettercairn Distillery Visitor Centre · Scotston · Arbuthnott · Inverbervie · Bervie Bay

Inch of Arnhall · Arnhall · Meikle Strath · Mains of Thornton · Laurencekirk · Easter Tulloch · Knox Hill · Gourdon

Sauchieburn · Luthermuir · Garvock · Johnston Mains 227 · Redford · Benholm

Feus of Caldhame · Inglismaldie Forest · Dykelands · Johnshaven

Pert · Gallery · Kirktonhill · Marykirk · Ecclesgreig · Lochside · St Cyrus · Milton Ness · St Cyrus National Nature Reserve · Morphie · Pathhead

miles 0 1 2 3 4 5 6
kilometres 0 2 4 6 8 10

120 · 115 · 103

City of Aberdeen

Population: 189,707. Situated on the east coast of Scotland 57 miles (92km) north east of Dundee, Aberdeen is the Capital of the Grampians. Since the 13th century the city has been an important centre for trade with the oil industry being the principal employer today. Widely known as 'The Granite City', as local stone was used in constructing many of the city's buildings, the sometimes austere look of the architecture is softened by the many flower gardens, of which Duthie Park Winter Gardens is the most impressive. By far the largest population centre in north east Scotland, Aberdeen has shopping for every taste, from busy shopping malls of designer boutiques and major chain-stores to speciality shops. The large transient population of students and oil workers means that Aberdeen has a bustling nightlife as well. A two mile (3km) long sweeping beach less than a mile (1.6km) from the centre is perfect for a bracing walk.

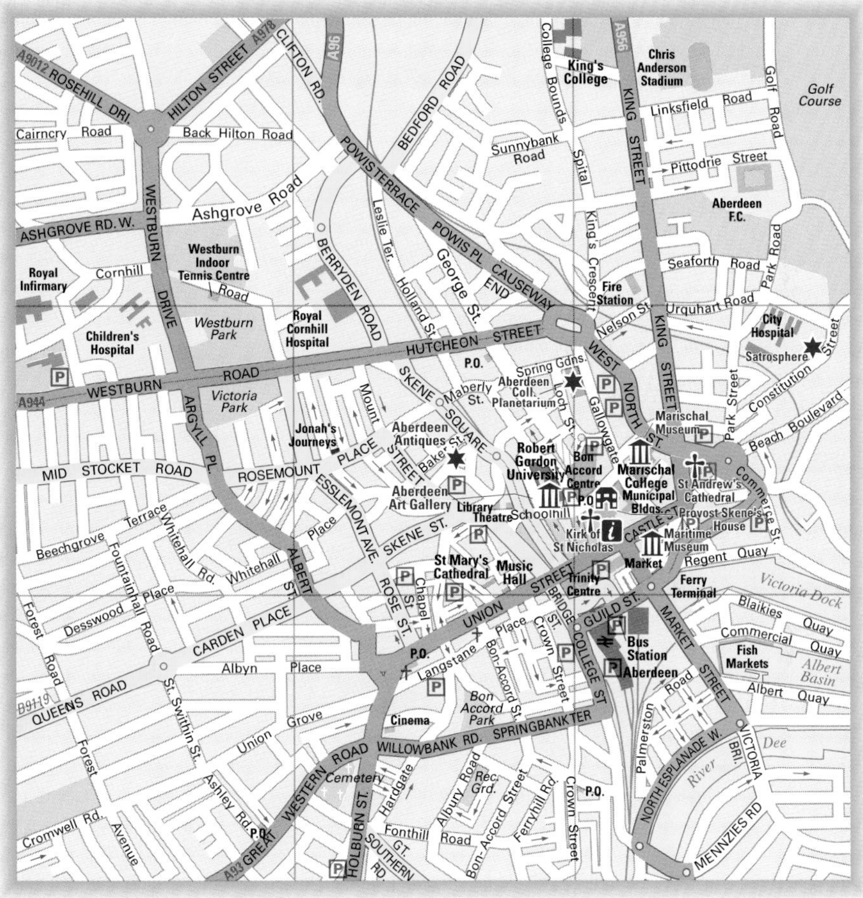

Useful information

Grampian Police Headquarters
Queen Street, AB10 1ZA
☎ 01224 386000

Hospital A & E
Aberdeen Royal Infirmary,
Foresterhill, AB25 2ZN
☎ 01224 681818

Main Post Office
St. Nicholas Shopping Centre
St. Nicholas Street, AB10 1HW

Railway Station
Guild Street
For national enquiries
☎ 08457 484950

Bus Station
Guild Street AB11 6GR

Local Radio
BBC Radio Aberdeen 990 AM
Northsound One 96.9 FM
Northsound Two 1035 AM

City Web-site
www.aberdeencity.gov.uk

Tourist Information

ℹ **Aberdeen**
St. Nicholas House
Broad Street
Aberdeen
AB10 1DE
☎ 01224 632727

Index to street names

yards 0 — 500
metres 0 — 500

Deeside

Royal Deeside

Queen Victoria and Prince Albert began the Royal connection with Deeside when it became their favourite holiday retreat 150 years ago. The tradition continues today. The Victorian Heritage Trail links places of historical interest – including Balmoral, Ballater, Aboyne and Banchory – along a route through spectacular scenery.

Tourist Information

i Braemar
The Mews
Mar Road
Braemar
Aberdeenshire
AB35 5YP
☎ 013397 41668

i Tomintoul
The Square
Tomintoul
Banffshire
AB37 9ET
☎ 01807 580285

miles
0   2   4   6
0   2   4   6   8   10
kilometres

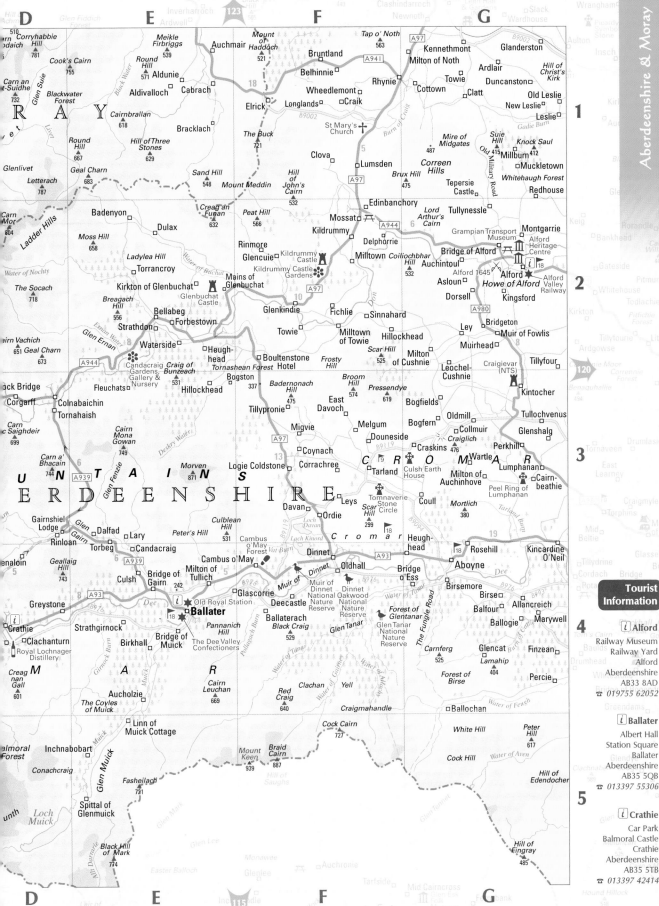

Aberdeenshire & Moray

Tourist Information

ℹ **Alford**
Railway Museum
Railway Yard
Alford
Aberdeenshire
AB33 8AD
☎ 019755 62052

ℹ **Ballater**
Albert Hall
Station Square
Ballater
Aberdeenshire
AB35 5QB
☎ 013397 55306

ℹ **Crathie**
Car Park
Balmoral Castle
Crathie
Aberdeenshire
AB35 5TB
☎ 013397 42414

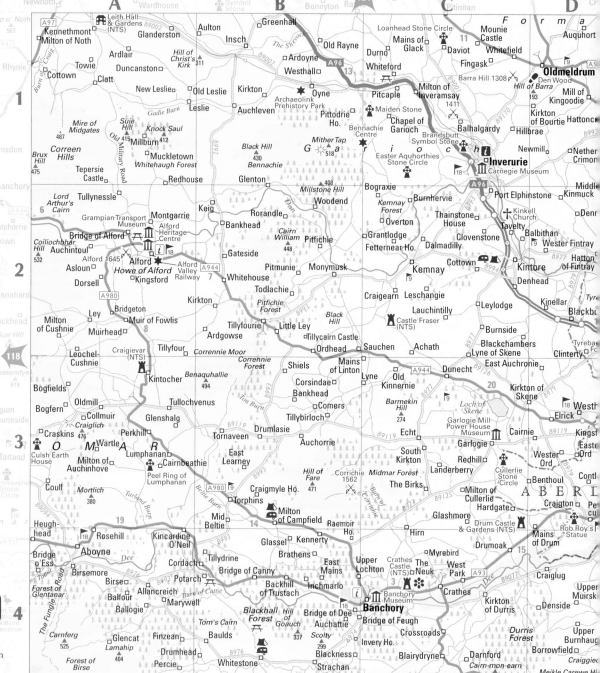

124
118
116

Tourist Information

Alford
Railway Museum
Railway Yard
Alford
Aberdeenshire
AB33 8AD
☎ 019755 62052

Banchory
Bridge Street
Banchory
Aberdeenshire
AB31 3SX
☎ 01330 822000

Inverurie
18 High Street
Inverurie
Aberdeenshire
AB51 3XQ
☎ 01467 625800

0   2   4   6
miles
0   2   4   6   8   10
kilometres

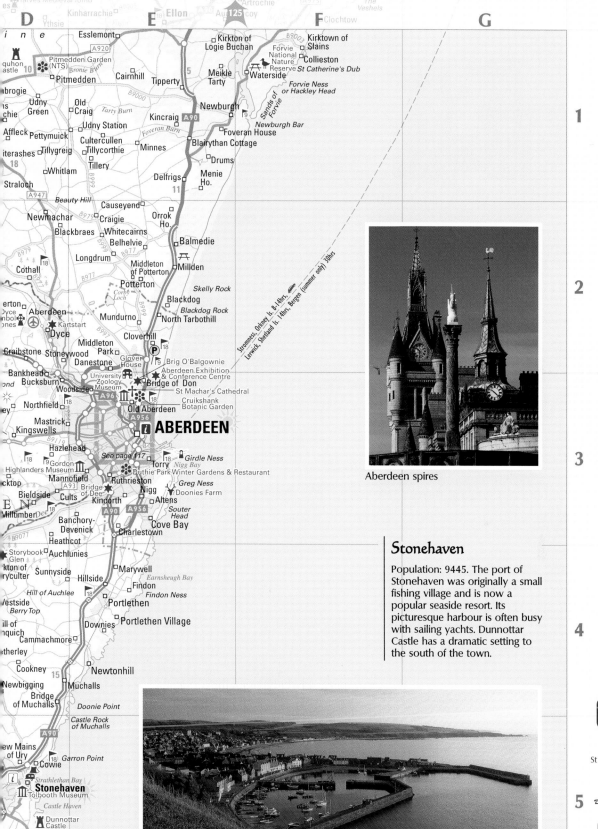

Aberdeen spires

Stonehaven

Population: 9445. The port of Stonehaven was originally a small fishing village and is now a popular seaside resort. Its picturesque harbour is often busy with sailing yachts. Dunnottar Castle has a dramatic setting to the south of the town.

Stonehaven Harbour

Tourist Information

ℹ **Aberdeen**
St Nicholas House
Broad Street
Aberdeen
AB10 1DE
☎ 01224 632727

ℹ **Stonehaven**
66 Allardice Street
Stonehaven
Aberdeenshire
AB39 9ET
☎ 01569 762806

Aberdeenshire & Moray

Elgin Cathedral

Elgin

Population: 19,027. The elegant market town of Elgin was one of the first Scots burghs created in the 12th century. Much of the medieval street layout remains intact. The ruined 13th century cathedral, known as the 'lantern of the north' was once a masterpiece of Scottish architecture.

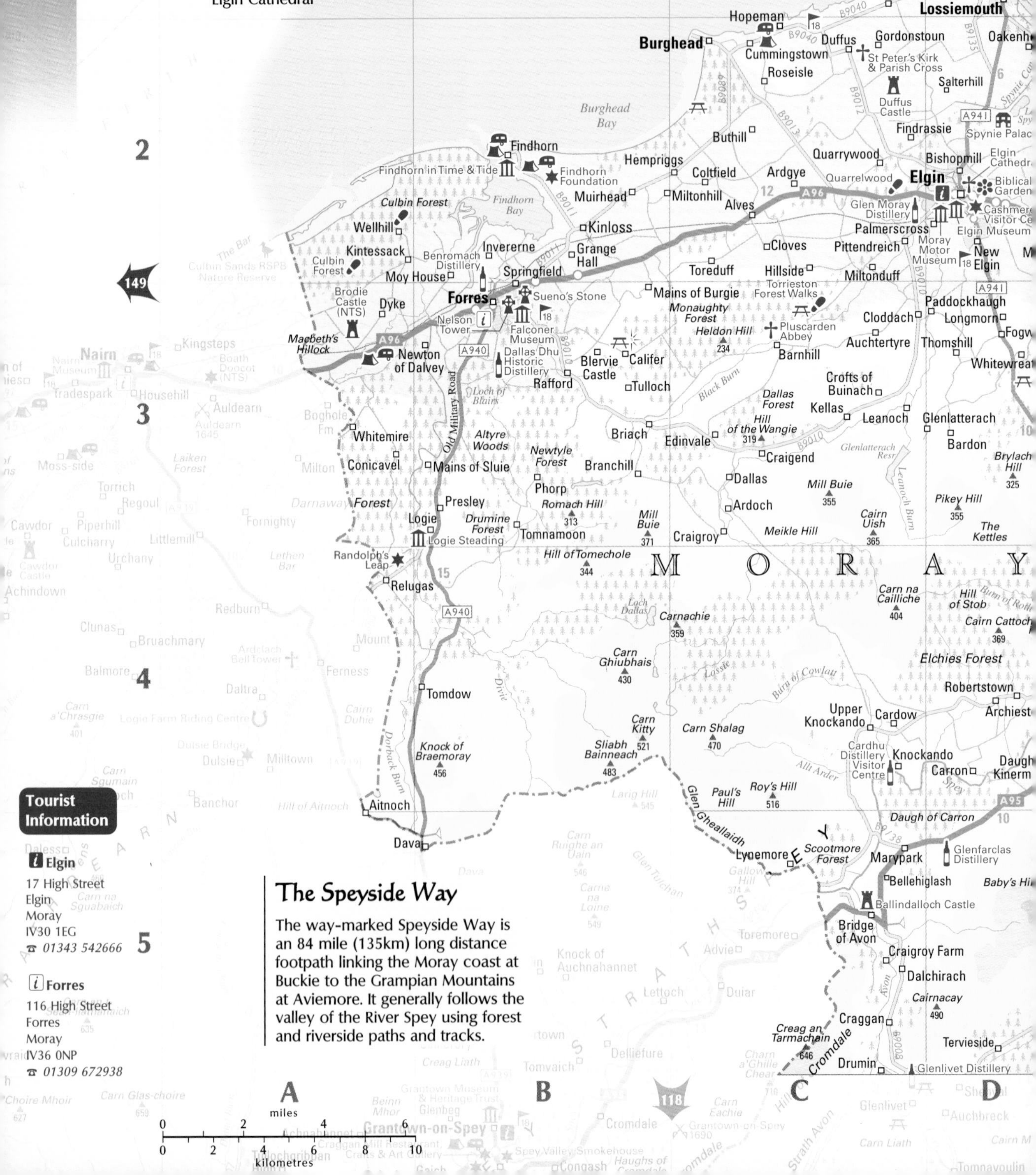

The Speyside Way

The way-marked Speyside Way is an 84 mile (135km) long distance footpath linking the Moray coast at Buckie to the Grampian Mountains at Aviemore. It generally follows the valley of the River Spey using forest and riverside paths and tracks.

Tourist Information

i **Elgin**
17 High Street
Elgin
Moray
IV30 1EG
☎ 01343 542666

i **Forres**
116 High Street
Forres
Moray
IV36 0NP
☎ 01309 672938

MORAY FIRTH

Lossiemouth Fisheries & Community Museum
Halliman Skerries
Covesea Skerries
Clashach Point
Covesea
Stotfield
Brae
Lossiemouth
Hopeman
Duffus
Gordonstoun
Oakenh
Burghead
Cummingstown
St Peter's Kirk & Parish Cross
Roseisle
Duffus Castle
Salterhill
Findrassie
Spynie Palac
Burghead Bay
Buthill
Quarrywood
Elgin Cathedr
Findhorn
Findhorn in Time & Tide
Hempriggs
Coltfield
Ardgye
Quarrelwood
Elgin
Biblical Garden
Findhorn Foundation
Muirhead
Miltonhill
Alves
Glen Moray Distillery
Cashmere Visitor Ce
Culbin Forest
Findhorn Bay
Kinloss
Grange Hall
Cloves
Pittendreich
Palmerscross
Elgin Museum
Wellhill
Invererne
Toreduff
Hillside
Miltonduff
Moray Motor Museum
New Elgin
Kintessack
Benromach Distillery
Springfield
Mains of Burgie
Torrieston Forest Walks
M
Culbin Forest
Moy House
Forres
Sueno's Stone
Monaughty Forest
Heldon Hill 234
Pluscarden Abbey
Cloddach
Paddockhaugh
Longmorn
Brodie Castle (NTS)
Dyke
Nelson Tower
Falconer Museum
Dallas Dhu Historic Distillery
Blervie Castle
Califer
Barnhill
Auchtertyre
Thomshill
Fogw
Macbeth's Hillock
Newton of Dalvey
Rafford
Tulloch
Dallas Forest
Kellas
Crofts of Buinach
Leanoch
Glenlatterach
Whitewrea
Nairn
Kingsteps
Boath (NTS)
Whitemire
Conicaval
Altyre Woods
Newtyle Forest
Branchill
Briach
Edinvale
Hill of the Wangie 319
Craigend
Bardon
Brylach Hill 325
Household
Auldearn
Auldearn 1645
Mains of Sluie
Phorp
Romach Hill 313
Dallas
Mill Buie 355
Ardoch
Mill Buie 371
Pikey Hill 355
The Kettles
Tradespark
Moss-side
Torrich
Regoul
Presley
Drumine Forest
Logie
Logie Steading
Tomnamoon
Craigroy
Meikle Hill
Cairn Uish 365
Laiken Forest
Darnaway Forest
Randolph's Leap
Relugas
Hill of Tomechole 344
MORAY
Carn na Cailliche 404
Hill of Stob
Cairn Cattoch 369
Littlemill
Fornighty
Lethen Bar
Loch Dallas
Carnachie 359
Elchies Forest
Robertstown
Archiest
Cawdor
Piperhill
Culchary
Urchany
Bruachmary
Archtach Bell Tower
Ferness
Mount
Carn Ghiubhais 430
Lossie
Burn of Cowlay
Upper Knockando
Cardow
Daugh Kinerm
Cawdor Castle
Clunas
Balmore
Daltra
Logie Farm Riding Centre
Tomdow
Carn Kitty
Sliabh Bainneach 483
Carn Shalag 470
Cardhu Distillery Visitor Centre
Knockando
Carron
A95
Dulsie Bridge
Dulsie
Milltown
Knock of Braemoray 456
Allt Ander
Roy's Hill 516
Bridge of Avon
Banchor
Hill of Aitnoch
Aitnoch
Dava
Paul's Hill
Lynemore
Scootmore Forest
Marypark
Glenfarclas Distillery
Baby's Hi
Bellehiglash
Ballindalloch Castle
Craigroy Farm
Dalchirach
Knock of Auchnahannet
Lettoch
Cairnacay 490
Creag an Tarmachain 646
Craggan
Cromdale
Tervieside
Drumin
Glenlivet Distillery
Grantown-on-Spey

miles
0   2   4   6
0   2   4   6   8   10
kilometres

Dolphins in the Moray Firth

Tourist Information

ℹ **Dufftown**
Clock Tower
The Square
Dufftown
Banffshire
AB55 4AD
☎ 01340 820501

ℹ **Huntly**
9a The Square
Huntly
Aberdeenshire
AB54 5AE
☎ 01466 792255

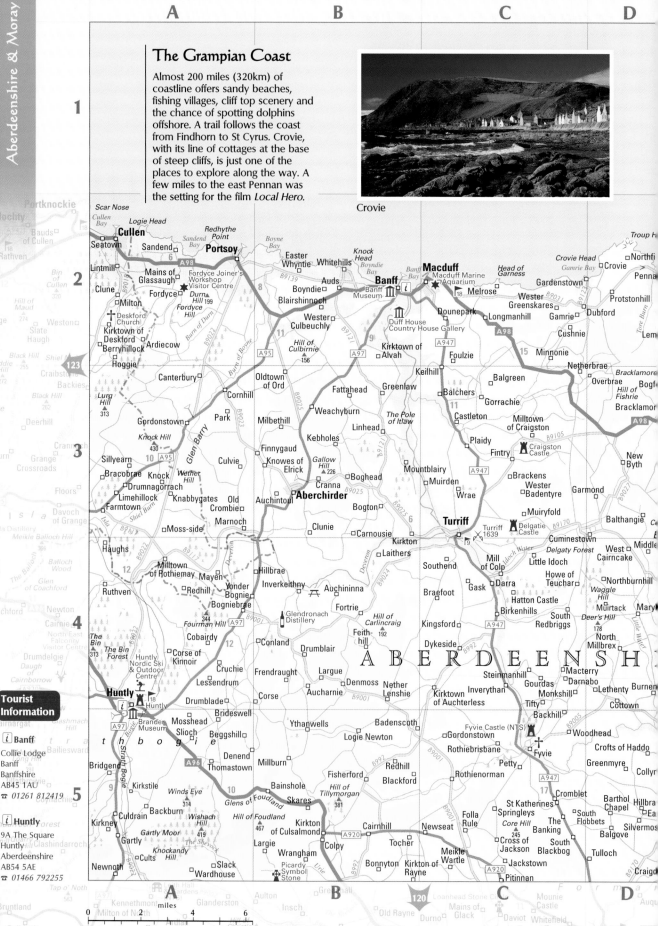

The Grampian Coast

Almost 200 miles (320km) of coastline offers sandy beaches, fishing villages, cliff top scenery and the chance of spotting dolphins offshore. A trail follows the coast from Findhorn to St Cyrus. Crovie, with its line of cottages at the base of steep cliffs, is just one of the places to explore along the way. A few miles to the east Pennan was the setting for the film *Local Hero*.

Crovie

Tourist Information

i Banff
Collie Lodge
Banff
Banffshire
AB45 1AU
☎ 01261 812419

i Huntly
9A The Square
Huntly
Aberdeenshire
AB54 5AE
☎ 01466 792255

miles
0   6
kilometres
0   10

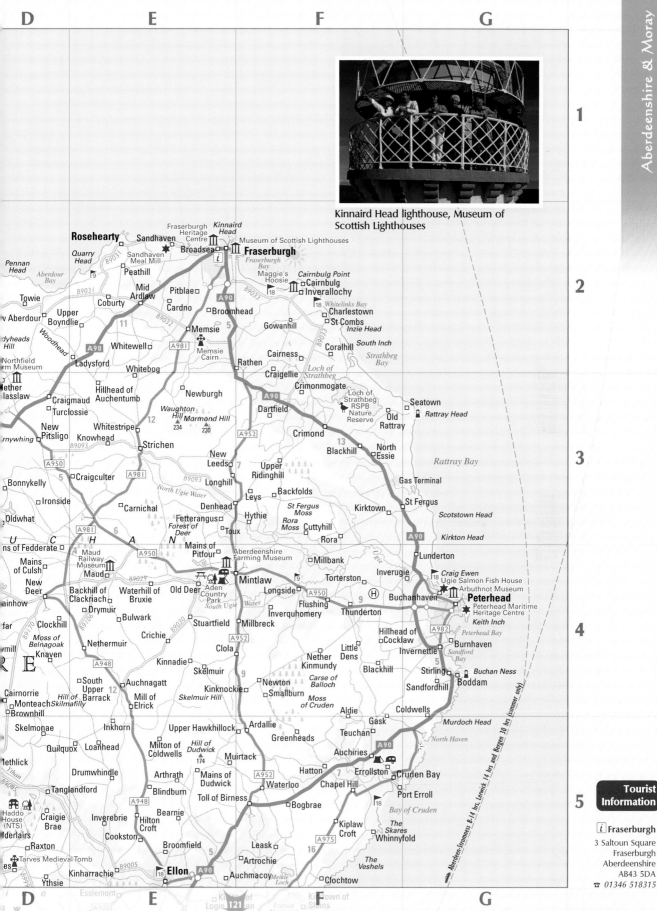

Kinnaird Head lighthouse, Museum of Scottish Lighthouses

D E F G

1

2

3

4

5

Rosehearty
Sandhaven
Fraserburgh Heritage Centre
Kinnaird Head
Museum of Scottish Lighthouses
Broadsea
Fraserburgh
Fraserburgh Bay
Quarry Head
Pennan Head
Aberdour Bay
Peathill
Maggie's Hoosie
Cairnbulg Point
Cairnbulg
Inverallochy
Towie
Upper Boyndlie
Mid Ardlaw
Coburty
Pitblae
Cardno
Broomhead
Gowanhill
Charlestown
St Combs
Whitelinks Bay
Inzie Head
dyheads Hill
Woodhead
Ladysford
Whitewell
Whitebog
Memsie
Memsie Cairn
Rathen
Cairness
Coralhill
South Inch
Strathbeg Bay
Northfield rm Museum
Hillhead of Auchentumb
Newburgh
Craigellie
Crimonmogate
Loch of Strathbeg RSPB Nature Reserve
Seatown
Rattray Head
nether lasslaw
Craigmaud
Turclossie
Waughton Hill 234
Mormond Hill 230
Dartfield
Old Rattray
New Pitsligo
Whitestripe
Knowhead
Strichen
Crimond
Blackhill
North Essie
Rattray Bay
Bonnykelly
Craigculter
New Leeds
Longhill
Upper Ridinghill
Gas Terminal
St Fergus
Scotstown Head
Ironside
Carnichal
Denhead
Leys
Backfolds
Kirkton
Kirkton Head
Oldwhat
Fetterangus
Forest of Deer
Toux
Hythie
St Fergus Moss
Rora Moss
Cuttyhill
Rora
Mains of Culsh
Maud Railway Museum
Maud
Mains of Pitfour
Aberdeenshire Farming Museum
Millbank
Torterston
Inverugie
Lunderton
Craig Ewen
Ugie Salmon Fish House
Arbuthnot Museum
New Deer
Backhill of Clackriach
Waterhill of Bruxie
Old Deer
Aden Country Park
Mintlaw
Longside
Flushing
Thunderton
Buchanhaven
Peterhead
Peterhead Maritime Heritage Centre
Keith Inch
Drymuir
Bulwark
Crichie
Stuartfield
Millbreck
Inverquhomery
Hillhead of Cocklaw
Invernettie
Peterhead Bay
Sandford Bay
Nethermuir
Kinnadie
Clola
Nether Kinmundy
Little Dens
Blackhill
Stirling
Burnhaven
Buchan Ness
Boddam
Knaven
South Upper Barrack
Auchnagatt
Mill of Elrick
Skelmuir
Kinknockie
Skelmuir Hill
Newton
Smallburn
Carse of Balloch
Moss of Cruden
Sandfordhill
Coldwells
Cairnorrie
Monteach
Brownhill
Hill of Skilmafilly
Inkhorn
Loanhead
Milton of Coldwells
Hill of Dudwick 174
Muirtack
Ardallie
Greenheads
Aldie
Gask
Teuchan
Murdoch Head
North Haven
Skelmonae
Quilquox
Drumwhindle
Arthrath
Blindburn
Mains of Dudwick
Waterloo
Hatton
Auchiries
Errollston
Cruden Bay
ethlick
Tanglandford
Bearnie
Toll of Birness
Chapel Hill
Bogbrae
Port Erroll
Bay of Cruden
Haddo House (NTS)
Craigie Brae
Inverebrie
Hilton Croft
Cookston
Broomfield
Leask
Kiplaw Croft
Whinnyfold
The Skares
Raxton
Tarves Medieval Tomb
Kinharrachie
Ellon
Artrochie
Auchmacoy
Meikle Loch
Clochtow
The Veshels
Ythsie
Esslemont

Pitmedden Garden (NTS)
Cairnhill
Tipperty
Meikle Tarty
Waterside
Kirk of Logie
Town of Stains
Collieston
St Catherine's Dub
Forvie National Nature Reserve
Forvie Ness or Hackley Head
Pitmedden

Tourist Information

i Fraserburgh
3 Saltoun Square
Fraserburgh
Aberdeenshire
AB43 5DA
☎ 01346 518315

Aberdeen-Stromness 8-14 hrs, Lerwick 14 hrs and Bergen 30 hrs (summer only)

🏛 **Aberdeen Art Gallery** `117 B2`
School Hill, Aberdeen. Houses one of the finest art collections in the UK dating from the 18th – 20th centuries including British works by Spencer, Nash and Bacon.
☎ 01224 523700 www.aagm.co.uk

✪ **Aberdeen College Planetarium** `117 C2`
Gallowgate, Aberdeen. Built in 1977 for teaching navigation. It is now open to the public and is one the best in Scotland – a unique plaster dome and 2500 stars.
☎ 01224 612130 www.abcol.ac.uk/planetarium

✪ **Aberdeen Exhibition & Conference Centre** `117 D1`
Bridge of Don, Aberdeen. The foremost purpose-built exhibition and events complex in the north of Scotland. Venue for festivals, concerts and shows.
☎ 01224 824824 www.aecc.co.uk

🏛 **Aberdeen University Zoology Museum** `116 D1`
Zoology Building, Tillydrone Avenue, Old Aberdeen. A collection of zoological specimens ranging from flies to whales.
☎ 01224 272850

🏛 **Aberdeenshire Farming Museum** `125 E4`
Aden Country Park, Mintlaw. Unique semi-circular home farm steading where visitors can explore the Aden Estate Story and the Weel Vrocht Grun exhibitions, and visit Hareshowe, a working farm set in the 1950s.
☎ 01771 622906 www.aberdeenshire.gov.uk/heritage

🐾 **Aden Country Park** `125 E4`
Mintlaw, 10 miles (16km) east of Peterhead on the A92. A 230 acre (93ha) country park containing Wildlife Discovery Centre, woodland walks, nature trails, orienteering course, sensory garden, adventure play area, lake and caravan park.
☎ 01771 622857

🏛 **Alford Heritage Centre** `120 A2`
Mart Road, Alford. Features the greatest collection of rural bygones in north east Scotland. The exhibition is designed to give the visitor an insight into the rural life of the ordinary working people of Donside.
☎ 019755 62906

✪ **Alford Valley Railway** `120 A2`
Alford Station, Alford. Narrow gauge railway running a 30 minute trip from the restored Alford Station to Haughton Caravan Park. Train collection includes a former Aberdeen suburban tram, a steam locomotive from Durban in South Africa and three diesel Simplex locomotives.
☎ 019755 62811

🏛 **Arbuthnot Museum** `125 G4`
St Peter Street, Peterhead. One of Aberdeenshire's oldest museums. Features Peterhead's maritime history, Inuit art, Arctic whaling and animals, and one of the largest coin collections in northern Scotland.
☎ 01771 477778 www.aberdeenshire.gov.uk/heritage

✪ **Archaeolink Prehistory Park** `120 B1`
Oyne. Discover Scotland's prehistoric past – from Stone Age to Iron Age. Indoor and outdoor displays make it a unique living history experience.
☎ 01464 851500 www.archaeolink.co.uk

🏰 **Ballindalloch Castle** `122 C5`
Near Aberlour, 13 miles (20km) north east of Grantown-on-Spey. Exemplifies the transition from the stark tower house of 16th century Scotland to the elegant and comfortable country house so beloved of Victorians in the Highlands.
☎ 01807 500206

🏰 **Balmoral Castle** `114 D2`
Balmoral, 8 miles (13km) west of Ballater. The Highland holiday home of the Royal Family since 1852. Exhibition of paintings, works of art and royal tartans in the Castle Ballroom. Wildlife, travel and carriage exhibition in the carriage hall.
☎ 013397 42334 www.balmoralcastle.com

🏰 **Balvenie Castle** `123 E4`
Dufftown. Picturesque ruins of a 13th century moated stronghold with 15th and 16th century additions. Originally owned by the Comyns.
☎ 01340 820121 www.historic-scotland.gov.uk

🏛 **Banchory Museum** `116 B2`
Bridge Street, Banchory. Features the life of Banchory-born musician and composer J. Scott Skinner, the 'Strathspey King', commemorative china, tartans.
☎ 01771 622906 www.aberdeenshire.gov.uk/heritage

🏛 **Banff Museum** `124 B2`
High Street, Banff. One of Scotland's oldest museums, founded in 1828. Features an electrotype copy of the Deskford Carnyx, an Iron Age war trumpet, natural history display, local geology, important collections of Banff silver, arms and armour.
☎ 01771 622906 www.aberdeenshire.gov.uk/heritage

✪ **Baxters Highland Village** `123 E2`
1 mile (1.5km) west of Fochabers. The story of the Baxter family began in 1868 when George Baxter opened a small grocery shop in Fochabers. See the Baxters Story and watch cookery demonstrations.
☎ 01343 820393 www.baxters.com/village

🚲 **Ben Aigan Cycle Trails** `123 E4`
Off the A95, 1.5 miles (2km) south of Mulben. Two forest mountain bike trails giving excellent views over the winding River Spey.
☎ 01343 820223 www.forestry.gov.uk

✪ **Bennachie Centre** `120 C1`
2 miles (3km) south of Chapel of Garioch. The centre describes the local social and natural history. Visitors can participate in guided walks, bat and bird box building, fungal forays and classes for beginners on countryside skills.
☎ 01467 681470 www.forestry.gov.uk

🍶 **Benromach Distillery** `122 B2`
Invererne Road, off the A96. Moray's smallest distillery. The attractive malt whisky centre describes 100 years of history and tradition in whisky making.
☎ 01309 675968 www.benromach.com

❊ **Biblical Garden** `122 D2`
King Street, Elgin. A 3 acre (1.2ha) garden created using the Bible as a reference. A desert area depicts Mount Sinai and the cave of resurrection. Planted with every species of plant mentioned in the Bible.

🏰 **Braemar Castle** `114 C2`
Braemar. A turreted stronghold built in 1628. L-plan with a central round tower and spiral stair. Barrel vaulted ceilings, massive iron gate (yett), underground prison. Star-shaped defensive curtain wall. Fully furnished residence.
☎ 013397 41219 www.braemarcastle.co.uk

🏛 **Brander Museum** `124 A5`
The Square, Huntly. A display about author George Macdonald. Also extensive collection of communion tokens plus arms and armour from 19th century Sudan.
☎ 01771 622906 www.aberdeenshire.gov.uk/heritage

✝ **Brandsbutt Symbol Stone** `120 C1`
Inverurie. An early Pictish symbol stone with an ogham inscription.
☎ 01466 793191 www.historic-scotland.gov.uk

✪ **Bridge of Dee** `116 D1`
On the A90 south west of Aberdeen. Built in the 1520s. Seven arches span 400ft (122m). The medieval solidity of the structure is enlivened by heraldic carvings.

✪ **Brig o' Balgownie** `116 D1`
Bridge of Don. Also known as the Auld Brig o'Don, this massive arch, 62ft (19m) wide, spans the deep pool of the river and is backed by fine woods.

🏰 **Brodie Castle** `122 A3`
Brodie, Forres. The oldest parts of the castle are 16th century. Fine collections of furniture and porcelain and a major art collection. Woodland walk, 4 acre (1.6ha) pond with wildlife observation hides. Famous daffodil collection in spring.
☎ 01309 641371 www.nts.org.uk

🏛 **Buckie Drifter** `123 F2`
Freuchny Road, Buckie. Discover why thousands of north east Scotland's fisherfolk spent their lives following the herring. Clamber on board a Buckie drifter and catch a glimpse of life on a recreated 1920s quayside.
☎ 01542 834646 www.moray.org/area/bdrifter/mbdrifter

🍃 **Cambus o'May Forest** `115 F2`
2.5 miles (4km) east of Ballater on the A93. A wonderful forest with four waymarked walks and a permanent orienteering course.
www.forestry.gov.uk

❊ **Candacraig Gardens, Gallery & Nursery** `119 E2`
Strathdon. An 1830s walled garden and a Gothic summerhouse. There is a display garden featuring specialist plants, some from the Himalayas and the Far East.
☎ 019756 51226

🍶 **Cardhu Distillery Visitor Centre** `122 C4`
Knockando, Aberlour. The origins of Cardhu go back to the heyday of illicit distilling, when farmers made use of their own barley and local water. Licensed since 1824, the Cumming family expanded and improved the distillery.
☎ 01340 872555

🏛 **Carnegie Museum** `120 C1`
Town Hall, The Square, Inverurie. Local archaeology including Beaker folk and Pictish carved stones and transportation.
☎ 01771 622906 www.aberdeenshire.gov.uk/heritage

✪ **Cashmere Visitor Centre** `122 D2`
Elgin. The only British mill to transform cashmere from fibre to garment. The story of luxury fine fibres interwoven with the 200-year history of the Johnstons is told through an audio-visual presentation, hands-on displays and information boards.
☎ 01343 554099 www.johnstonscashmere.com

🏰 **Castle Fraser** `120 C2`
Sauchen, Inverurie. Magnificent castle completed in 1636 and one of the most sophisticated Scottish buildings of the period. Notable paintings and furnishings.
☎ 01330 833463 www.nts.org.uk

✝ **Cathedral Church of St Machar** `116 D1`
The Chanonry, Aberdeen. A twin-towered granite building dating from 1350 – 1520 with stone pillars and impressive stained glass windows on three sides. Outside is the tomb of Bishop Gavin Dunbar.
☎ 01224 485988 www.stmachar.com

🏰 **Corgarff Castle** `114 D1`
Corgarff, Strathdon. A 16th century tower house converted into a barracks for government troops in 1748 by being enclosed within a star-shaped loopholed wall.
☎ 01975 651460 www.historic-scotland.gov.uk

✱ **Craigellachie Bridge** `123 D4`
North of Craigellachie. One of Thomas Telford's most beautiful bridges. It has a 152ft (46m) main span of iron and two ornamental stone towers at each end.

🏰 **Craigievar Castle** `115 G1`
5 miles (8km) south of Alford. A 'fairytale' castle, which seems to grow out of the hillside. Fine collection of family portraits and 17th and 18th century furniture.
☎ 013398 83635 www.nts.org.uk

🏰 **Craigston Castle** `124 C3`
5 miles (8km) from Turriff. Completed in 1607 and still owned by the original family. The main exterior feature is a sculpted balcony unique in Scottish architecture. Interior decoration dates mainly from the early 19th century.
☎ 01888 551228

🏰 **Crathes Castle** `116 B2`
3 miles (5km) east of Banchory. 16th century castle with remarkable original painted ceilings and a collection of Scottish furniture. Famous walled garden contains eight separate gardens designed for colour combinations.
☎ 01330 844525 www.nts.org.uk

❋ **Cruickshank Botanic Garden** `116 D1`
Aberdeen University, Aberdeen. Originally founded in 1898 as a teaching and research garden. The 11 acres (4.5ha) are laid out in an ornamental style. Rock garden and ponds, herbaceous border, rose garden, terrace and arboretum.
☎ 01224 272704

🌲 **Culbin Forest** `122 A2`
Signposted from the A96 between Nairn and Findhorn Bay. Planted from the 1920s to stabilise the drifting sands. Botanical trail. Five waymarked low level walks.
☎ 01343 820223 www.forestry.gov.uk

✝ **Cullerlie Stone Circle** `116 B1`
Near Echt, off the A944. A stone circle enclosing an area on which eight small cairns were later constructed. About 4000 years old.
☎ 01466 793191 www.historic-scotland.gov.uk

✝ **Culsh Earth House** `115 G1`
On the B919 at Culsh. A well-preserved underground passage with roofing slabs intact over the large chamber and entrance. About 2000 years old.
☎ 0131 668 8800 www.historic-scotland.gov.uk

🍾 **Dallas Dhu Historic Distillery** `122 B3`
2 miles (3km) south of Forres. A picturesque small distillery built in 1898.
☎ 01309 676548 www.historic-scotland.gov.uk

✱ **Dee Valley Confectioners** `115 E2`
Station Square, Ballater. Watch the process of colours and flavours being added to the candy, followed by the stretch and pull methods for stripes and lettering.
☎ 01339 755499

🏰 **Delgatie Castle** `124 C3`
3 miles (5km) north east of Turriff. An 11th century tower house. The castle contains late 16th century painted ceilings and has the widest turnpike stair in Scotland.
☎ 01888 563479 www.delgatiecastle.com

🌲 **Den Wood** `120 D1`
4 miles (6km) north of Inverurie. There are a range of woodland habitats and four circular trails offering panoramic views.
☎ 01764 662554 www.woodland-trust.org.uk

✝ **Deskford Church** `124 A2`
Off the B9018, 4 miles south of Cullen, Banffshire. Ruin of a small, late medieval church with a richly carved sacrament house characteristic of north east Scotland.
☎ 01466 793191 www.historic-scotland.gov.uk

🐑 **Doonies Farm** `117 D1`
Nigg, Aberdeen. A 182 acre (74ha) working farm populated with rare breeds.
☎ 01224 875879 www.aberdeencity.gov.uk

🏰 **Drum Castle & Gardens** `116 B1`
Drumoak, Banchory. The 13th century tower of Drum is one of the three oldest tower houses in Scotland. Jacobean and Victorian extensions make this a fine mansion house with notable portraits and furniture, much from the 18th century.
☎ 01330 811204 www.nts.org.uk

🌲 **Drumtochty Forest** `116 B4`
Between Auchenblae and the Cairn o'Mount on the B974. Two waymarked walks along an old mill lade leading through a beautiful small gorge.
www.forestry.gov.uk

🏛 **Duff House Country House Gallery** `124 B2`
Between Banff and Macduff. One of the best examples of Georgian baroque architecture in Britain with a fine collection of paintings, furniture and artefacts.
☎ 01261 818181 www.duffhouse.org.uk

🏰 **Duffus Castle** `122 C2`
5 miles (8km) north west of Elgin. Massive ruins of a fine motte and bailey castle with 14th century tower surrounded by a moat.
☎ 01667 460232 www.historic-scotland.gov.uk

🏰 **Dunnottar Castle** `116 C3`
On the A92, 2.5 miles (4km) south of Stonehaven. A spectacular ruin 160ft (48.5m) above the sea. The site for the successful protection of the Scottish crown jewels against the might of Oliver Cromwell's army.
☎ 01569 762173

❋ **Duthie Park Winter Gardens & Restaurant** `116 D1`
Polmuir Road, Aberdeen. 2 acres (1ha) of covered gardens displaying plants from around the world. Features Bromeliad house, cacti and succulent hall, Victorian corridor and outside gardens, floral hall, corridor of perfumes and fern house.
☎ 01224 585310 www.aberdeencity.gov.uk

✝ **Dyce Symbol Stones** `121 D2`
Dyce Old Church, Dyce. Two fine examples of Pictish symbol stones in the ruined parish church, one with the older type of incised symbols, and the other with symbols accompanied by a Celtic cross and decoration.
☎ 01466 793191 www.historic-scotland.gov.uk

✝ **Easter Aquhorthies Stone Circle** `120 C1`
1 mile (2km) west of Inverurie. A recumbent stone circle about 4000 years old.
☎ 01466 793191 www.historic-scotland.gov.uk

✝ **Elgin Cathedral** `122 D2`
In Elgin on the A96. The superb ruin of what was perhaps the most beautiful cathedral in Scotland. The octagonal chapter house is the finest in Scotland.
☎ 01343 547171 www.historic-scotland.gov.uk

🏛 **Elgin Museum** `122 D2`
High Street, Elgin. Museum interpreting the natural and human heritage of Moray. Internationally known for its fossils and Pictish stones.
☎ 01343 543675 www.elginmuseum.org.uk

🏛 **Falconer Museum** `122 B3`
Tolbooth Street, Forres. Founded in 1871 and now containing a wealth of Moray heritage.
☎ 01309 673701

🏠 **Fasque House** `116 A4`
On the B974, 0.5 mile (1km) north of Fettercairn village. A spectacular example of a Victorian 'upstairs-downstairs' stately home bought by Sir John Gladstone in 1829. Home to Prime Minister William Ewart Gladstone for much of his life.
☎ 01561 340569

🍾 **Fettercairn Distillery Visitor Centre** `116 A4`
Distillery Road, 0.5 mile (1km) west of Fettercairn. Visitor centre with tours which describe the processes of whisky making. Includes a free dram of Old Fettercairn.
☎ 01561 340205

✱ **Findhorn Foundation** `122 B2`
Findhorn, off the A96. The Findhorn Foundation Community was established in 1962. Visitors can see ecological barrel houses, turf roofs, innovative architecture, renewable energy sources such as a wind turbine and solar panels, and a Living Machine natural sewage treatment system.
☎ 01309 690880 www.findhorn.org

🏛 **Findhorn in Time & Tide** `122 B2`
Northshore, Findhorn. Based in two salmon fishers' huts and an ice house. One hut is laid out as a salmon fishers' bothy of days gone by, the other is filled with exhibits which trace the development of Findhorn from pre-historic times.
☎ 01309 690659

🏛 **Fochabers Folk Museum** `123 E3`
High Street, Fochabers. Shows the history of Fochabers over the past 200 years. Includes a large collection of horse-drawn carts and carriages.
☎ 01343 821204

✱ **Fordyce Joiner's Workshop Visitor Centre** `124 A2`
Church Street, Fordyce. Learn about the importance of the rural carpenter to the local community over the last 150 years. Displays of early tools and machinery.
☎ 01771 622906 www.aberdeenshire.gov.uk/heritage

✱ **Fraserburgh Heritage Centre** `125 E2`
Quarry Road, Fraserburgh. The Centre describes the history of Fraserburgh from the bustling quayside to the haute couture of dress designer Bill Gibb.
☎ 01346 512888

🏰 **Fyvie Castle** `124 C5`
Fyvie. Probably the grandest example of Scottish baronial architecture. The five towers enshrine five centuries of history. The oldest part dates from the 13th century. Collection of portraits, arms and armour, and 17th century tapestries.
☎ 01651 891266 www.nts.org.uk

🏛 **Garlogie Mill Power House Museum** `116 B1`
Garlogie, Skene. Visitors can relive the early days of the industrial revolution and see the rare beam engine which powered the woollen mill.
☎ 01771 622906 www.aberdeenshire.gov.uk/heritage

🍾 **Glen Grant Distillery & Garden** `123 D4`
Rothes. Fine single malt whisky has been produced here since 1840. Visitors can tour the distillery, sample a dram in the study or pavillion and explore the garden.
☎ 01542 783318

🍾 **Glen Moray Distillery** `122 C2`
Bruceland Road, Elgin. Constructed in the classic square layout of a Scottish farm, featuring a courtyard surrounded by the buildings where the whisky is produced.
☎ 01343 542577 www.glenmoray.com

✱ **Glen of Rothes Trout Fishery** `122 D3`
8 miles (13km) south of Elgin on the A941. A fishery with 6 acres (2.4ha) of lochs. Visitors can fish for rainbow and brown trout from the banks.
☎ 01340 831888

Glenbuchat Castle `119 E2`
Bridge of Buchat. 14 miles (22.5km) west of Alford. A fine example of a Z-plan tower house, built in 1590.
☎ 01466 793191   www.historic-scotland.gov.uk

Glendronach Distillery `124 B4`
Forgue, between Huntly and Inverurie. A traditional malt whisky distillery established in 1825 with its own floor maltings, peat fire and kiln.
☎ 01466 730202

Glenfarclas Distillery `122 D5`
Glenfarclas, Ballindalloch, on the A95. Established in 1836. Glenfarclas means 'valley of green grass land'. Distillery tours and free tasting.
☎ 01807 500257   www.glenfarclas.co.uk

Glenfiddich Distillery `123 E4`
On the A941, 0.3 mile (0.5km) north of Dufftown. A distillery, opened in 1887, producing the only Highland single malt whisky that is distilled, matured and bottled at its own distillery. Visitors can tour the distillery. Free sample.
☎ 01340 820373

Glenlivet Distillery `122 C5`
Ballindalloch, about 10 miles (16km) north of Tomintoul. Situated in one of the most scenic and romantic glens in the Scottish Highlands. The guided tour also includes the chance to see inside a vast bonded warehouse and to sample a dram.
☎ 01542 783220   www.glenlivet.com

Glenlivet Estate `118 C2`
Tomintoul, Ballindalloch. A large Highland estate encompassing some of the finest landscapes of the Grampian Highlands. A network of over 60 miles of waymarked trails. Learn about the history, countryside, wildlife and management of the area.
☎ 01807 580283   www.crownestate.co.uk

Glenshee Ski Centre `114 C4`
Cairnwell, Braemar. 2000-3504ft (610-1068m) altitude ski area. 38 runs extending over three valleys and four mountains with a diversity of terrain for all standards of skiers and snowboarders. Britain's largest ski lift system.
☎ 01339 741320   www.ski-glenshee.co.uk

Glover House `116 D1`
79 Balgownie Road, Aberdeen. Home of Thomas Blake Glover, the industrial pioneer who introduced modern coal mining and shipbuilding methods to 19th century Japan. The house has been restored to its original Victorian splendour.
☎ 01224 709303

Gordon Highlanders Museum `116 D1`
St Luke's, Viewfield Road, Aberdeen. Striking displays of the regiment's unique collection recalling 200 years of service and gallantry. Housed in the former home and studio of the famous Victorian artist Sir George Reid PRSA.
☎ 01224 311200   www.gordonhighlanders.com

Grampian Transport Museum `120 A2`
Alford, 25 miles (40km) west of Aberdeen. An extensive collection of historic road vehicles housed in a purpose-built hall. Climb-aboard exhibits for children. Driving simulator, video bus featuring motor sport and road transport history.
☎ 019755 62292   www.gtm.org.uk

Grassic Gibbon Centre `116 C4`
Arbuthnott, Laurencekirk. Visitor centre dedicated to the life and times of the novelist Lewis Grassic Gibbon (James Leslie Mitchell).
☎ 01561 361668   www.grassicgibbon.com

Haddo House `125 D5`
Ellon, off the B999. Elegant house designed by William Adam in 1731. Much of the interior is Adam Revival, dating from the 1880s. Beautiful library.
☎ 01651 851440   www.nts.org.uk

Huntly Castle `124 A4`
Castle Street, Huntly. A magnificent ruin of a castle from the 12th century motte to the palace erected in the 16th and 17th centuries by the Gordon family. The architectural details and heraldic enrichments are particularly impressive.
☎ 01466 793191

Huntly Nordic Ski & Outdoor Centre `124 A4`
Hill of Haugh, Huntly. Cross-country ski centre with year-round artificial ski track suitable for all the family. Fifteen miles (25km) of machine-prepared ski trails.
☎ 01466 794428   www.huntly.net/hnoc

Kartstart `121 D2`
Stoneywood Business Centre, Dyce, Aberdeen. The opportunity to experience the thrill of real motor sport. Karting for all ages. All equipment provided.
☎ 01224 772727

Keith & Dufftown Railway `123 E4`
Dufftown Station, Dufftown. This picturesque 11mile (18km) branch line has been fully restored and trains can be boarded from either Keithtown Station or Dufftown.
☎ 01340 821181   www.edge-of-nowhere.demon.co.uk/kdra

Kildrummy Castle `119 F2`
Kildrummy. Called the Queen of Highland castles, this was the headquarters for organising the 1715 Jacobite rising. Scotland's most complete 13th century castle.
☎ 01975 571331   www.historic-scotland.gov.uk

Kildrummy Castle Gardens `119 F2`
Off the A97, 10 miles (16km) west of Alford. The shrub and alpine garden in an ancient quarry are of interest to botanists for their great variety.
☎ 019755 71277

Kings College Centre `117 C1`
College Bounds, Old Aberdeen. In the University of Aberdeen campus, 2 miles (3km) from the city centre. A multi-media centre giving the history of the university.
☎ 01224 273702

Kinkell Church `120 C2`
2 miles (3km) south of Inverurie. The ruins of a 16th century parish church with a fine sacrament house dated 1524 and the grave slab of Gilbert of Greenlaw.
☎ 01466 793191   www.historic-scotland.gov.uk

Kirk of St Nicholas `117 C2`
Aberdeen. 15th century vaulted lower church, 18th century West Kirk, retaining its characteristic reformed layout, 19th century East Kirk, medieval effigies, medieval and 17th century carved woodwork, 17th century needlework, 48-bell carillon.
☎ 01224 643494

Lecht, The `118 D2`
Lecht 2090, Strathdon. 2090-2500ft (640-823m) altitude ski area. 20 runs. Snowboarding funpark. Dedicated snowtubing area. Summer activities include dry ski/snowboard slope, Deval karting track, quad bike circuit and chairlift ride.
☎ 01975 651440   www.lecht.co.uk

Leith Hall & Garden `120 A1`
Huntly, on the B9002. Mansion house in a 286 acre (116ha) estate which was home to the Leith family for 300 years. Exhibition on family's military history.
☎ 01464 831216   www.nts.org.uk

Loanhead Stone Circle `120 C1`
Near Daviot, 5 miles (8km) north west of Inverurie. The best known of a group of recumbent stone circles about 4000 to 4500 year old. Encloses a ring cairn.
☎ 01466 793191   www.historic-scotland.gov.uk

Loch of Strathbeg RSPB Nature Reserve `125 F3`
1 mile (1.5km) from Crimond. The 544 acre (220ha) loch is the largest dune loch in Britain, surrounded by marshes, reedbeds, grassland and dunes.
☎ 01346 532017   www.rspb.org.uk

Loch Park Adventure Centre `123 E4`
Drummuir Castle Estate, on the B9014, 5 miles (7.5km) from Keith. Offers a wide variety of activities, including canoeing, kayaking, gorge walking and archery.
☎ 01542 810334   www.adventure-at-lochpark.co.uk

Logie Steading `122 B3`
6 miles (10km) south of Forres. Originally built as a model farm in the 1920s, now converted to house an unusual visitor centre. Potter, textiles and glass engraving.
☎ 01309 611378   www.logie.co.uk

Lossiemouth Fisheries & Community Museum `122 D1`
2 Pitgaveny Quay, Lossiemouth. Exhibits on the history of fishing and the local community. Features a study of Ramsay McDonald, the first Labour Prime Minister, born in Lossiemouth.
☎ 01343 813772

Macduff Marine Aquarium `124 C2`
High Shore, Macduff. A series of displays covering the marine habitats of the Moray Firth, including rock pools, touch pools and splash tank. Featuring a wave machine and living kelp reef, the main display is the deepest open-topped tank in Scotland.
☎ 01261 833369

Maggie's Hoosie `125 F2`
26 Shore Street, Inverallochy, Fraserburgh. A preserved but and ben fisher cottage with earth floor, box beds and original furnishings.

Maiden Stone `120 C1`
Near Chapel of Garioch, north west of Inverurie. A 9th century Pictish cross-slab bearing a Celtic cross on one side and a variety of Pictish symbols on the other.
☎ 01466 793191   www.historic-scotland.gov.uk

Mar Lodge Estate `114 C2`
5 miles (8km) west of Braemar. Part of the core area of the Cairngorms, internationally recognised as the most important nature conservation landscape in Britain. The estate contains four of the five highest mountains in the UK.
☎ 013397 41433   www.nts.org.uk

Marischal Museum `117 C2`
Marischal College, Broad Street, Aberdeen. Displays the collections of graduates and friends of Aberdeen University over 500 years. Exhibitions include Collecting the World and the Encyclopedia of the North-East.
☎ 01224 274301   www.abdn.ac.uk/diss/historic/museum

Maritime Museum `117 C2`
Shiprow, off Union Street, Aberdeen. Tells the story of the city's long and fascinating relationship with the sea through a collection of ship models, artefacts, computer interaction and set-piece exhibitions. A major display about the offshore oil industry features a 28ft (8.5m) high model of the Murchison oil platform.
☎ 01224 337700

Maud Railway Museum `125 E4`
Maud, 15 miles (24km) west of Peterhead. Sound effects add to the nostalgia of the displays of Great North of Scotland Railway memorabilia and old photographs.
☎ 01771 622906   www.aberdeenshire.gov.uk/heritage

Memsie Cairn `125 E2`
Near Rathen, 3.5 miles (5.5km) south of Fraserburgh. A large stone-built cairn, possibly Bronze Age, but enlarged during field clearance in the last two centuries.
☎ 01466 793191   www.historic-scotland.gov.uk

⚘ Moray Firth Wildlife Centre `123 E2`
At the end of the B9104, 5 miles (8km) north of Fochabers on the A96. Housed in a former salmon fishing station built in 1768 and providing an ideal place to watch ospreys hunting, seals, dolphins, otters and many birds. An exhibition describes the Moray Firth dolphins and the marine environment. Hands-on activities for children.
☎ 01343 820339 www.mfwc.co.uk

⛫ Moray Motor Museum `122 D2`
Bridge Street, Elgin, 30 miles (48km) west of Inverness. Unique collection of high quality cars and motorbikes housed in an old mill building.
☎ 01343 544933

⛫ Museum of Scottish Lighthouses `125 E2`
Kinnaird Head, Fraserburgh. A museum housed in a former castle which became the first lighthouse built by the Northern Lighthouse Board in 1787, now a monument to Scotland's lighthouse service. Tour to the top of the lighthouse.
☎ 01346 511022 www.lighthousemuseum.demon.co.uk

⛢ Nelson Tower `122 B3`
Grant Park, Forres, 11 miles (17.5km) west of Elgin. Nelson Tower was built to commemorate Nelson's victory at Trafalgar. Displays on Lord Nelson and views of old Forres. There are also spectacular views of the Moray Firth from the tower.
☎ 01309 673701

⚘ North East Falconry Visitor Centre `123 F4`
3 miles (5km) north west of Huntly. The centre has almost 65 birds of prey, both indigenous and from overseas, ranging from owls to eagles. None of the birds are caged and they are all clearly visible. Regular flying displays.
☎ 01466 760328

⛫ Northfield Farm Museum `125 D3`
New Pitsligo, 10 miles (16km) south west of Fraserburgh. Vintage tractors and motorcycles, stationary engines, household and horse-drawn farm implements.
☎ 01771 653504

⛢ Old Royal Station `115 E2`
Ballater. Restored Victorian railway station containing displays on the 100 year history of royal use. Unique royal waiting room built for Queen Victoria.
☎ 013397 55306 www.castlesandwhisky.com

⛢ Peel Ring of Lumphanan `115 G1`
0.5 mile (1km) south west of Lumphanan. A major early medieval earthwork 120ft (36.5m) in diameter and 18ft (5.5m) high. The site of a fortified residence.
☎ 01466 793191 www.historic-scotland.gov.uk

⛫ Peterhead Maritime Heritage `125 E4`
The Lido, South Road, Peterhead. Tells the story of Peterhead maritime life in sound and vision. Observation box with telescope views across Peterhead Bay.
☎ 01779 473000 www.aberdeenshire.gov.uk/heritage

⛢ Picardy Symbol Stone `124 B4`
Near Mireton, Insch. One of the oldest Pictish symbol stones, possibly 7th century.
☎ 01466 793191 www.historic-scotland.gov.uk

✱ Pitmedden Garden `121 D1`
Pitmedden, 14 miles (22km) north of Aberdeen near Ellon. Pitmedden's centrepiece is the Great Garden, originally laid out in 1675 by Sir Alexander Seton.
☎ 01651 842352 www.nts.org.uk

✝ Pluscarden Abbey `122 C3`
By the B9010, 6 miles (9.5km) south west of Elgin. Originally a Valliscaulian house, the monastery was founded in 1230. Monastic church services open to the public.
☎ 01343 890257 www.pluscardenabbey.org

⛫ Provost Skene's House `117 C2`
Guestrow, off Broad Street. Splendid room settings including a suite of Georgian rooms, an Edwardian nursery, 17th century ceilings and wood panelling. The painted gallery houses the most important cycle of religious painting in north east Scotland.
☎ 01224 641086 www.aagm.co.uk/psh

⚘ Quarrelwood `122 C2`
0.5 mile (1km) from the A96, west of Elgin. Oakwood and pine forest. Two waymarked trails lead to monuments and to Cutties Hillock, the site of dinosaur finds.
www.forestry.gov.uk

✱ Randolph's Leap `122 B4`
7 miles (11km) south west of Forres. Impressive views of the River Findhorn winding through a deep sandstone gorge.

⛢ Rob Roy's Statue `116 C1`
Peterculter by the A93. Statue of Rob Roy standing above the Leuchar Burn.

🍶 Royal Lochnagar Distillery `115 D2`
Crathie, Ballater. Guided tours of a traditional working distillery, with sample dram.
☎ 012297 42700

✝ St Andrew's Cathedral `117 C2`
28 King Street, Aberdeen. Birthplace of the Anglican Communion overseas. The first Anglican Bishop outside of the UK was consecrated here in 1784.
☎ 01224 640290

✝ St Mary's Church `119 F1`
Near Lumsden, 3 miles (5km) north of Kildrummy. One of the finest medieval parish churches in Scotland, roofless, but otherwise complete. There is a rich early Romanesque doorway and a beautiful early 14th century sacrament house.
☎ 01466 793191 www.historic-scotland.gov.uk

✝ St Ninian's Chapel `123 E2`
3 miles (5km) east of Fochabers. Built in 1755 ostensibly as a sheepcote, but secretly as a Catholic chapel. The oldest post-Reformation Catholic church still in use.
☎ 01542 832196

✝ St Peter's Kirk & Parish Cross `122 C2`
Duffus. The roofless remains of the church include the base of a 14th century western tower, a 16th century vaulted porch and some interesting tombstones.
☎ 01667 460232 www.historic-scotland.gov.uk

✱ Sandhaven Meal Mill `125 E2`
Sandhaven, on the B9031, 2.5 miles (4km) west of Fraserburgh. Visitors can see how oatmeal used to be ground in this typical 19th century Scottish meal mill.
☎ 01771 622906 www.aberdeenshire.gov.uk/heritage

✱ Satrosphere `117 C2`
Located on Constitution Street, this interactive science centre with more than 70 exciting exhibits covers all aspects of science and technology.
☎ 01224 640340 www.satrosphere.net

⛫ Scottish Tartans Museum `123 F2`
The Institute, Mid Street, Keith. The museum contains accounts of famous Scotsmen and explains the developments of tartans and the kilt.
☎ 01542 888419

✱ Speyside Cooperage Visitor Centre `123 D4`
Craigellachie. Visitors can watch coopers and apprentices repairing oak casks for the whisky industry. An exhibition traces cooperage history and development.
☎ 01340 871108

⛨ Spynie Palace `122 D2`
Off the A941, 2 miles (3km) north of Elgin. The residence of the bishops of Moray from the 14th century to 1686. Dominated by the massive 15th century tower.
☎ 01343 546358 www.historic-scotland.gov.uk

✱ Storybook Glen `116 C2`
Maryculter, 6 miles (9.5km) west of Aberdeen. A 28 acre (11.5ha) spectacular theme park with over 100 models of nursery rhymes set in beautiful scenic gardens.
☎ 01224 732941 www.storybookglenaberdeen.com

🍾 Strathisla Distillery `123 F2`
Seafield Avenue, Keith. The oldest working distillery in the Highlands, established in 1786, and home to Chivas Regal blended Scotch whisky. Self-guided tour of the distillery and guided tour of the fitting store and warehouses. Whisky tasting.
☎ 01542 783044

⛢ Sueno's Stone `122 B3`
At the east end of Forres. The most remarkable Pictish sculptured monument in Britain, standing over 20ft (6m) high (now enclosed in glass).
☎ 01667 460232 www.historic-scotland.gov.uk

⛢ Tarves Medieval Tomb `125 D5`
In Tarves churchyard, 15 miles (24km) north west of Aberdeen. The fine altar tomb of William Forbes, the laird who enlarged Tolquhon Castle. Remarkable carving.
☎ 01466 793191 www.historic-scotland.gov.uk

⛫ Tolbooth Museum `116 C3`
The Harbour, Stonehaven. Stonehaven's oldest building, the Earl Marischal's 16th century storehouse which served as Kincardineshire's Tolbooth from 1600 – 1767.
☎ 01771 622906 www.aberdeenshire.gov.uk/heritage

⛨ Tolquhon Castle `121 D1`
Tarves. Built for the Forbes family, the castle has an early 15th century tower with a large mansion around a courtyard. Noted for its highly ornamented gatehouse.
☎ 01651 851286 www.historic-scotland.gov.uk

⛫ Tomintoul Museum `118 C2`
Features a reconstructed crofter's kitchen, smiddy and displays on local wildlife.
☎ 01309 673701

⛢ Tomnaverie Stone Circle `115 F1`
3 miles (5km) north west of Aboyne. A 4000 year old recumbent stone circle.
☎ 01466 793191 www.historic-scotland.gov.uk

⚘ Torrieston Forest Walks `122 C3`
2 miles (3.5km) beyond Pluscarden. Three varied walks on the forested hillside.
☎ 01343 820223 www.forestry.gov.uk

⚘ Tyrebagger Forest `121 D2`
On the A96 west of Aberdeen. Waymarked walks and sculpture trail.
www.forestry.gov.uk

✱ Ugie Salmon Fish House `125 G4`
Golf Road, Peterhead. The Fish House has been used by salmon fishermen for over 100 years. Visitors can see the ancient art of smoking salmon and buy the products.
☎ 01779 476209 www.ugie-salmon.co.uk

⛫ Village Store `123 D4`
98 High Street, Aberlour. A unique time capsule of social history. The shop was bought in 1922 by Mr Affie Macintyre who ran it as a general store until 1978. He never discarded anything and the shelves are still laden with his out-dated stock.
☎ 01340 871243

🚲 Whiteash & Ordiequish Cycle Trails `123 E3`
Fochabers. Three medium grade mountain bike trails through mixed forest.
☎ 01343 820223 www.forestry.gov.uk

Highlands & Skye

No single image can capture the scale and diversity of this region. From the soaring crags of Glen Coe to the wide rolling moors of Caithness, from the old pinewoods of upper Speyside to the spectacular Cuillin mountains of Skye, the north and west offer unmatched scenic splendour.

The Highlands of Scotland are rich in places to visit, with castles, battlefields and forts to remind you of a turbulent past, while distilleries, woollen mills and other crafts contribute to today's diverse Highland economy. Inverness, often called the capital of the Highlands, is a natural gateway to the north. At the other end of the Great Glen, Fort William stands in the shadow of Ben Nevis.

Highland pipers

Skiing, Aonach Mor

Outdoor activities

The Highlands provide year round opportunities for outdoor activities. Many hillwalkers return again and again to the region. Popular areas include the major peaks of Ben Nevis, Cairn Gorm, Glen Coe and Cuillin as well as the hills of Torridon, Wester Ross and Assynt. The three main centres for winter sports are the Nevis Range, Cairngorms and Glencoe. All three offer facilities for all grades of skiers and snowboarders. In summer there are also facilities across the region for white water canoeing, paragliding, golf, birdwatching, pony trekking and water sports. Outdoor activity centres offer packages of specialised activities or multi-activity holidays to suit all ages, abilities and interests.

Pony trekking

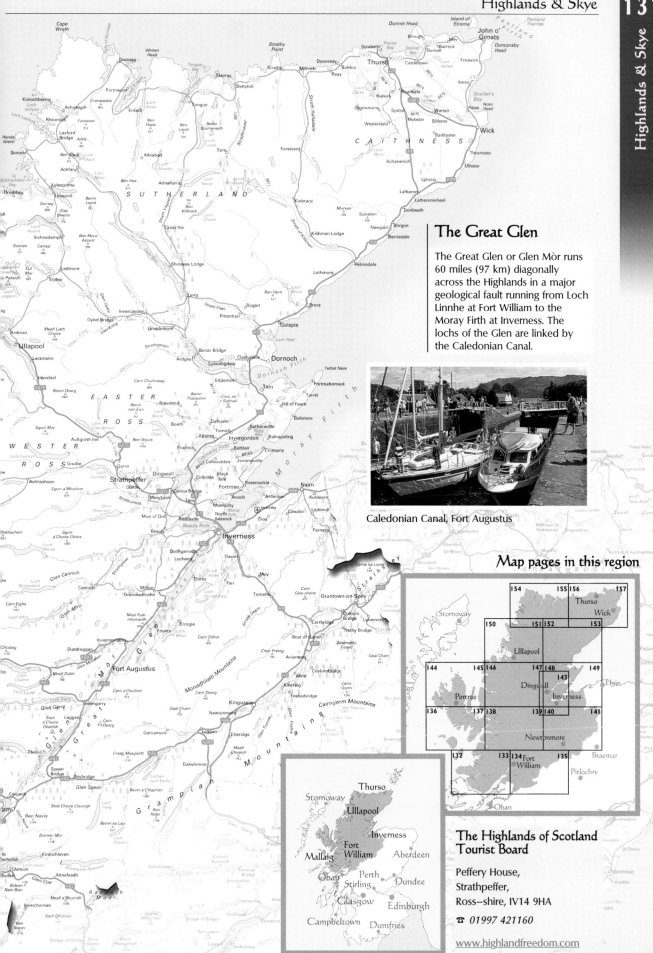

The Great Glen

The Great Glen or Glen Mòr runs 60 miles (97 km) diagonally across the Highlands in a major geological fault running from Loch Linnhe at Fort William to the Moray Firth at Inverness. The lochs of the Glen are linked by the Caledonian Canal.

Caledonian Canal, Fort Augustus

Map pages in this region

The Highlands of Scotland Tourist Board

Peffery House,
Strathpeffer,
Ross-shire, IV14 9HA

☎ 01997 421160

www.highlandfreedom.com

Ardnamurchan

A lighthouse on the Ardnamurchan peninsula marks the most westerly point on the British mainland. This peninsula and the neighbouring regions of Moidart and Morvern are excellent areas for walking, with coastal paths, woodland trails and mountain hikes.

Glenfinnan Monument

Tourist Information

ⓘ **Kilchoan**

Kilchoan
Argyll and Bute
PH36 4LH
☎ 01972 510222

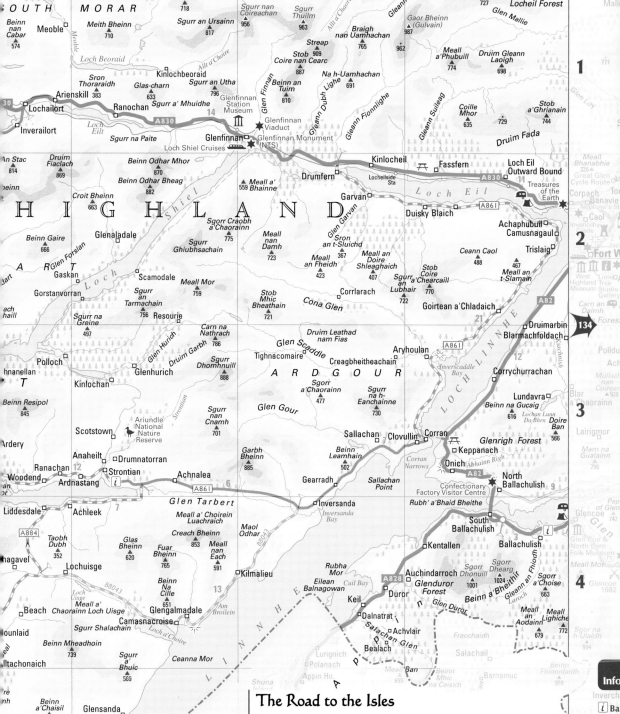

The Road to the Isles

The 46 mile (74km) route along the A830 between Fort William and Mallaig is a journey through dramatic loch and mountain scenery. It is also a journey steeped in history, with several places linked to the failed rebellion of Bonnie Prince Charlie. It was at Borrodale, near Arisaig that he first landed on the Scottish mainland in 1745 and a cairn less than a mile (1.5km) to the east marks the spot from which he escaped as a fugitive in 1746. The Glenfinnan Monument in its spectacular setting at the head of the Loch Shiel valley is a poignant memorial to the Highlanders who fought and died for his cause.

Tourist Information

Ballachulish
Ballachulish Post Office
Loan Fern
Argyll and Bute
PA39 4JB
☎ 01855 811296

Strontian
Strontian
Argyll and Bute
PH36 4HZ
☎ 01967 402131

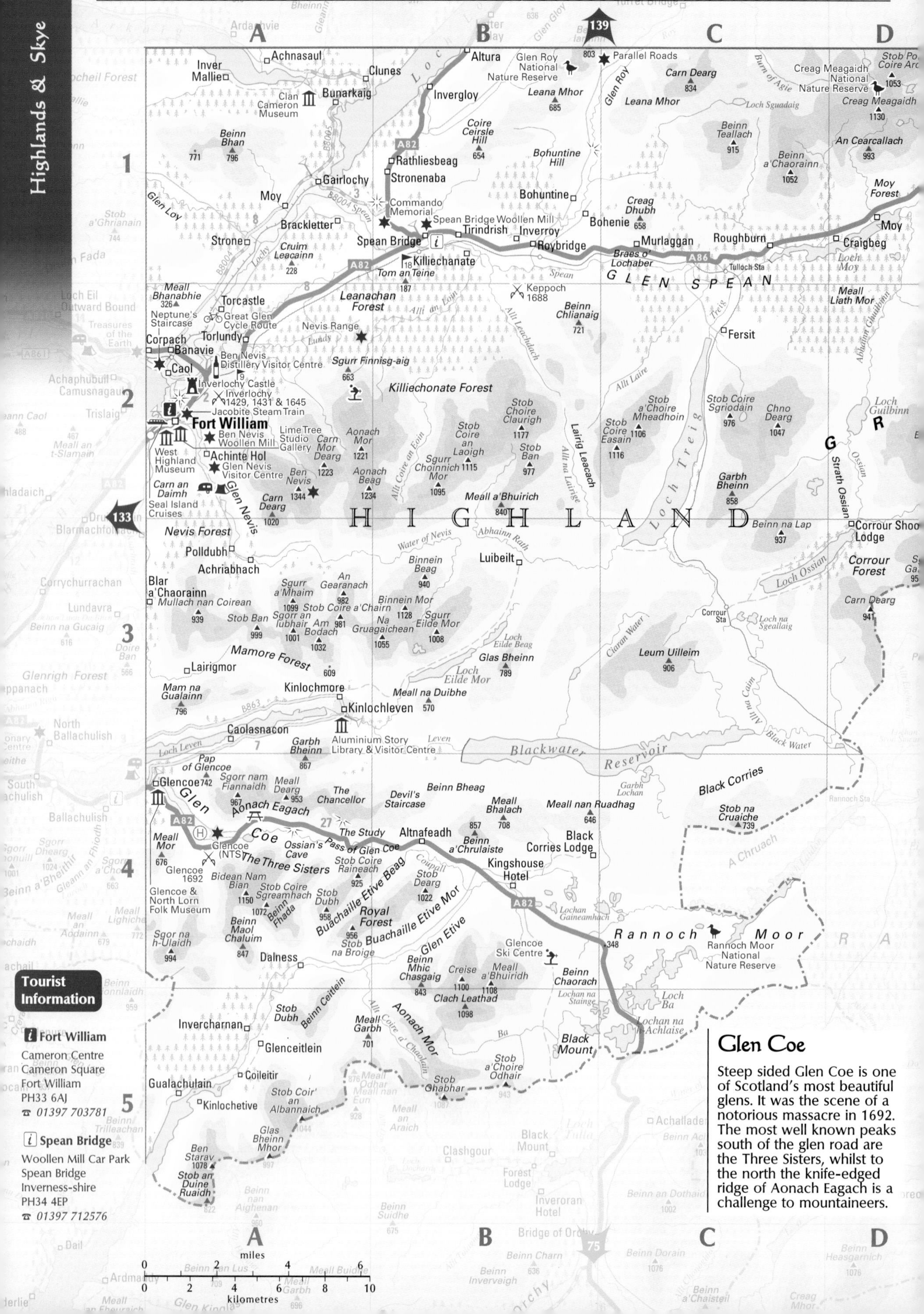

Highlands & Skye

Glen Coe

Steep sided Glen Coe is one of Scotland's most beautiful glens. It was the scene of a notorious massacre in 1692. The most well known peaks south of the glen road are the Three Sisters, whilst to the north the knife-edged ridge of Aonach Eagach is a challenge to mountaineers.

Tourist Information

i **Fort William**
Cameron Centre
Cameron Square
Fort William
PH33 6AJ
☎ 01397 703781

i **Spean Bridge**
Woollen Mill Car Park
Spean Bridge
Inverness-shire
PH34 4EP
☎ 01397 712576

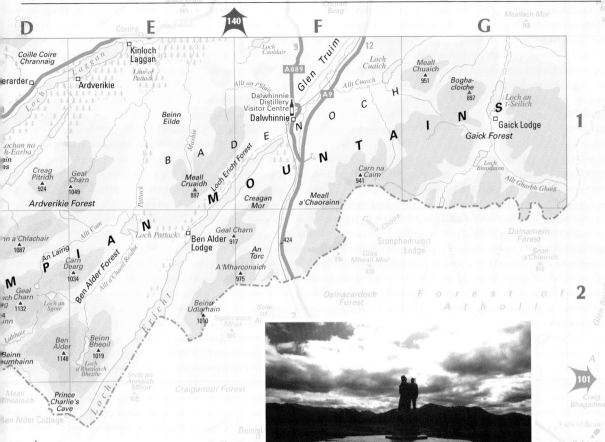

Fort William

Population: 10,391. Set at the foot of Ben Nevis, Fort William is the main tourist and mountaineering centre in the Highlands. The main attraction in winter is the Nevis Range ski centre on Aonach Mor. The attractions of the town itself include the Ben Nevis Distillery, the West Highland Museum and in the summer, a day trip on the Jacobite Steam Train across the Glenfinnan Viaduct and on to Mallaig.

Commando Memorial

Spean Bridge

The bridge was built by Thomas Telford in 1819 but nearby are the remains of an older bridge built by General Wade in 1736 to span the 100ft (30m) gorge. The area was used as a training ground by commandos during World War II and the Commando Memorial is set amongst stunning scenery to the north west of the village as a tribute to them.

Glen Coe

Jacobite Steam Train

Cuillin Hills

In the southern part of Skye the serrated peaks of the Cuillin Hills dominate the landscape. There are 11 Munros in the range, the highest being Sgurr Alasdair at 3258ft (993m). This is some of Britain's most spectacular walking and climbing country, although many of the routes are only for experienced climbers.

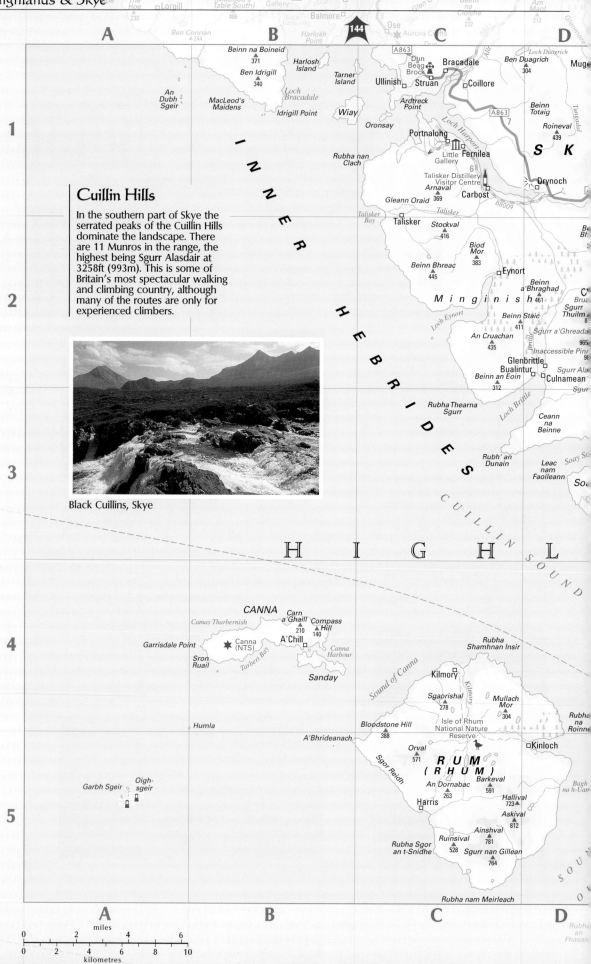

Black Cuillins, Skye

Ramasaig
Ramasaig Bay
Orbost
Roag
Vatten
Healabhal Bheag (Macleod's Table South)
Orbost Gallery
Harlosh
Ben Connan 244
The Hoe
Hoe Rape 233
Lorgill
The Hoe
Glen Ose
Beinn na Cloiche 232
Am Maol 212

Beinn na Boineid 371
Harlosh Island
Balmore
A863
Dun Beag Broch
Bracadale
Ben Duagrich 304
Loch Duagrich
Mug

Ben Idrigill 340
Harlosh Point
Tarner Island
Ullinish
Struan
Coillore
S K

An Dubh Sgeir
MacLeod's Maidens
Loch Bracadale
Idrigill Point
Wiay
Oronsay
Ardtreck Point
Portnalong
A863
Beinn Totaig
Roineval 439
Tungadal

Rubha nan Clach
Little Gallery
Fernilea
Talisker Distillery Visitor Centre
Arnaval 369
Carbost
Drynoch
B8009

I N N E R   H E B R I D E S

Talisker Bay
Talisker
Stockval 416
Gleann Oraid
Biod Mor 383
Eynort
Be Bh

Beinn Bhreac 445
Beinn a'Bhraghad
Bru
Sgurr Thuilm 8

M i n g i n i s h
Loch Eynort
Beinn Staic 411
Sgurr a'Ghreada 965

An Cruachan 435
Inaccessible Pinr 98
Glenbrittle
Bualintur
Sgurr Ala
Beinn an Eoin 312
Culnamean
Sgurr

Rubha Thearna Sgurr
Loch Brittle
Ceann na Beinne

Rubha Dunain
Rubh' an Dunain
Leac nam Faoileann
Soay S

C U I L L I N   S O U N D

H I G H   L

CANNA
Camas Tharbernish
Carn a'Ghaill 210
Compass Hill 140
Rubha Shamhnan Insir

Garrisdale Point
Canna (NTS)
A'Chill
Canna Harbour

Sron Ruail
Tarbert Bay
Sanday

Sound of Canna
Kilmory
Kilmory
Rubha na Roinne

Humla
Sgaorishal 278
Mullach Mor 304

A'Bhrideanach
Bloodstone Hill 388
Isle of Rhum National Nature Reserve
Kinloch

Orval 571
R U M (R H U M)
Bagh na h-Uam

Garbh Sgeir
Oigh-sgeir
Sgor Reidh
An Dornabac 263
Barkeval 591
Hallival 723
Harris
Askival 812

Rubha Sgor an t-Snidhe
Ruinsival 528
Ainshval 781
Sgurr nan Gillean 764

Rubha nam Meirleach

SOUN

144
A863
7
6

miles
0   2   4   6
0   2   4   6   8   10
kilometres

Highlands & Skye

Portree
Castle Keep
Aros Experience
Penifiler
Ben Tianavaig
413
Camastianavaig

D E 145 F G

RAASAY
SOUND OF
Glame
385
Dun Caan
443
Rubha na' Leac
Holoman Bay
Oskaig Point
Oskaig
Raasay Outdoor Centre
Clachan
Beinn na'Leac
319
Inverarish

Applecross
Milton
Camusteel
Camusterrach
Sron na h-Airde Baine
Culduie
Meall Gorm 710
Meall na Ba
Russel
A87

Lower Ollach
Upper Ollach
The Braes
Ben Lee 445
Peinchorran
Suisnish Point
East Suisnish
Meall a' Mhaoil 284
Crowlin Islands
Eilean Meadhonach
Eilean Mor
Toscaig
Meall Loch Airigh Alasdair 352
Uags
Airigh-drishaig
Duirinish
Drumbuie
Erbusaig

Glen Varragill
Glen Sligachan
Sconser
Glamaig 775
Sligachan
Rubh' an Lochain
Scalpay
Mullach na Carn 396
Longay
Camas na Fisteodh
Pabay
Badicaul
Kyle of Lochalsh
Toll
Seafood Cruise

Beinn Dearg
Luib Croft Museum
Luib
Dunan
Caolas Scalpay
Broadford Bay
International Otter Survival Fund
Skye Serpentarium
Kyle Akin
Bright Water Visitor Centre
Kyleakin
L na Beiste
Beinn na Caillich

Am Bastier 958 935 965
Sgurr nan Gillean
Harta Corrie
Marsco 736
Belig
Glas Bheinn Mhor 570
A87
Corry
Broadford
Lower Breakish
Upper Breakish
Skulamus
Sgurr na Coinnich 739

Druim Hain
Garbh-bheinn 806
Beinn Dearg Mhor 732
Beinn na Caillich 732
Broadford
World of Wood
Harrapool
A851
Cnoc Glac na Luachrach
Glen Arroch
Kylerhea
Kylerhea Otter Haven

Sgurr Dubh Mor 324
Garsbheinn 895
Bla Bheinn (Blaven) 928
Torrin
Kilbride
Ben Suardal 283
Strath Suardal
Loch Cill Chriosd
B8083
Kinloch Forest & Letir Fura Walk
Ben Aslak 610
Beinn na Seamraig 561
Beinn Bhreac 436
Ardnameacan

Strathaird
Camasunary
Kirkibost
Kilmarie
Beinn nan Carn 301
Heast
Drumfearn
Sandaig Islands
Sandaig

Loch Scavaig
Beinn Breac 141
Ben Meabost 346
Beinn Bhuidhe 277
Eilean Heast
Duisdealmor
Laurence Broderick Sculpture Exhibition
Isle Ornsay

Bella Jane Boat Trips
Elgol
Drinan
Rubha Suisnish
Loch Eishort
Sgorach Breac 299
Ord
Eilean Iarmain (Isleornsay)
Gaelic Whiskies – Whisky Exhibition
Camus Croise

Prince Charles's Cave
Spar Cave
Glasnakille
Rubha na h-Easgainne
A851
Camascross
Rubh Ard Slisneach

Tarskavaig
Tokavaig
Sgurr na h-Iolaire 292
Loch nam Uamh
Teangue
Knock Bay
Inverguseran
Na Cruachan 583
Beinn na Caillich 785

Tarskavaig Bay
Achnacloich
Sgurr Breac 249
Kilmore
Kilbeg
SLEAT
Airor
Meall Gaothar 422
Druim na Cluain-airighe
Roinn na Beinne 518

Inver Dalavil
Gleann Meadhonach
Sgurr nan Caorach 280
West Highland Heavy Horses
Armadale
Ardvasar
Calligarry
Armadale Bay
Armadale Castle Gardens & Museum of the Isles
Sandaig 441
KNOY
Sgurr Coire na Coinnich 796
Aultvoulin
Inverie

Geur Rubha
Aird of Sleat
Ard Thurinish
Point of Sleat
Rubha Raonuill
Inverie Bay
A'Chruach 395

Lochboisdale 3½ hrs (summer only)
Mallaigvaig
Mallaigmore
Sron Raineach
Gleann

Mallaig
Mallaig Marine World
Mallaig Heritage Centre
Glasnacardoch
Carn a'Ghobhair 522
Sgurr an Eilein Ghiubhais 547
Sgurr Bhuidhe 440

Castlebay 3½ hrs (summer only)
A830
Morar
Loch an Nostarie
Loch an Ghille Ghobaich
Bracora
Bracorina
Stoul
Tarbet

D E 132 F G

Portnaluchaig
Back of Keppoch
Arisaig
Eilean a'Phidhir
NORTH MORAR
Swordland
Loch Morar
Lettermorar

1

2

3

4

5

138

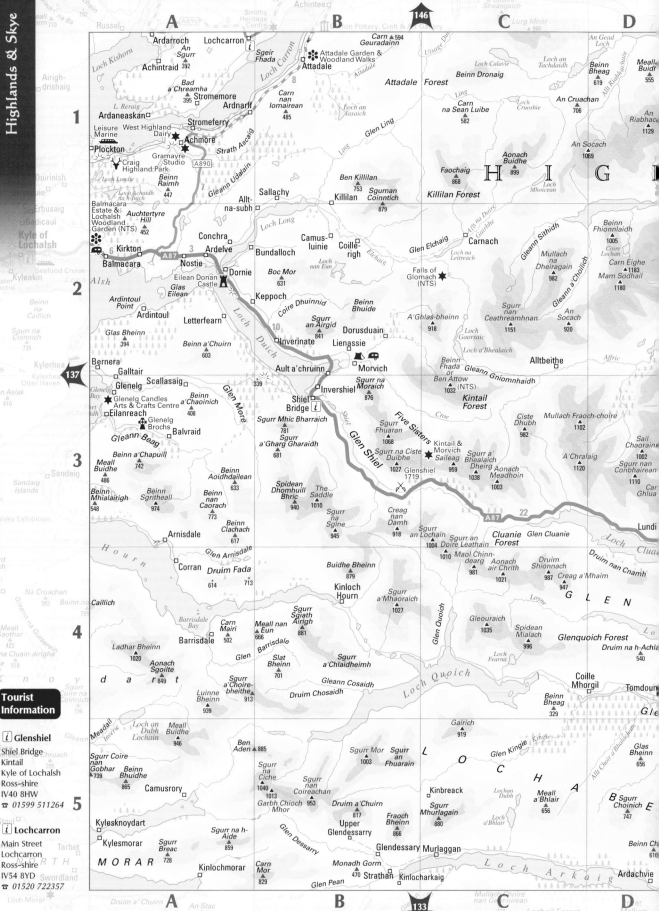

Highlands & Skye

146

137

133

Tourist Information

i Glenshiel

Shiel Bridge
Kintail
Kyle of Lochalsh
Ross-shire
IV40 8HW
☎ 01599 511264

i Lochcarron

Main Street
Lochcarron
Ross-shire
IV54 8YD
☎ 01520 722357

miles
0   2   4   6
kilometres
0   2   4   6   8   10

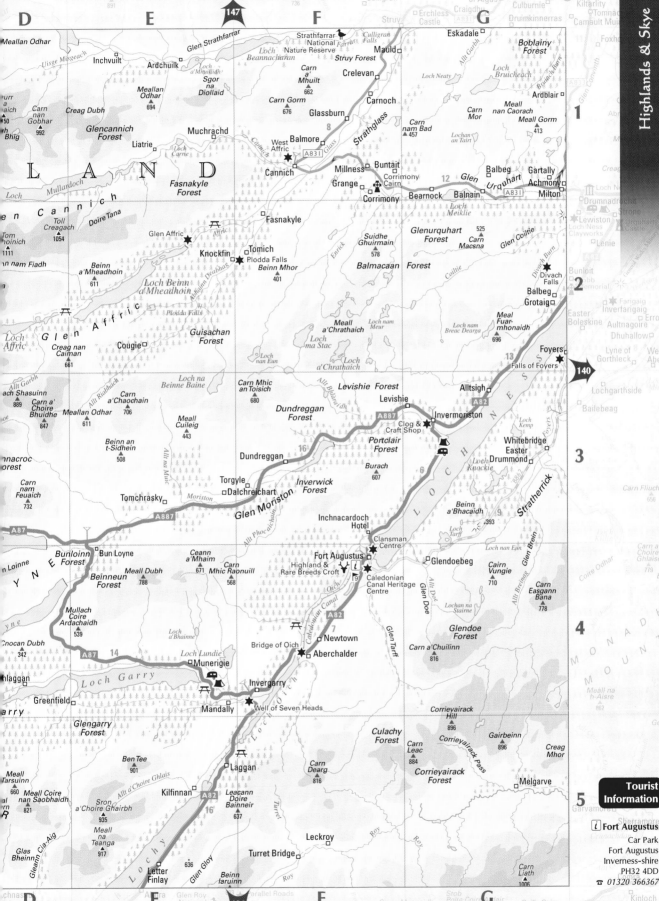

Tourist Information

ℹ Fort Augustus
Car Park
Fort Augustus
Inverness-shire
PH32 4DD
☎ 01320 366367

Cairngorms

This granite mountain mass of rounded summits includes some of Scotland's highest peaks. It is a popular area for hillwalkers, climbers and skiers. The Cairngorms are Britains only example of Arctic tundra vegetation and the area provides a habitat for populations of snow buntings and ptarmigans. Aviemore (population: 2214) is the commercial centre for the area. In winter the village is a mecca for skiers and in summer there are facilities for pony trekking, mountain biking, fishing, sailing, windsurfing and canoeing.

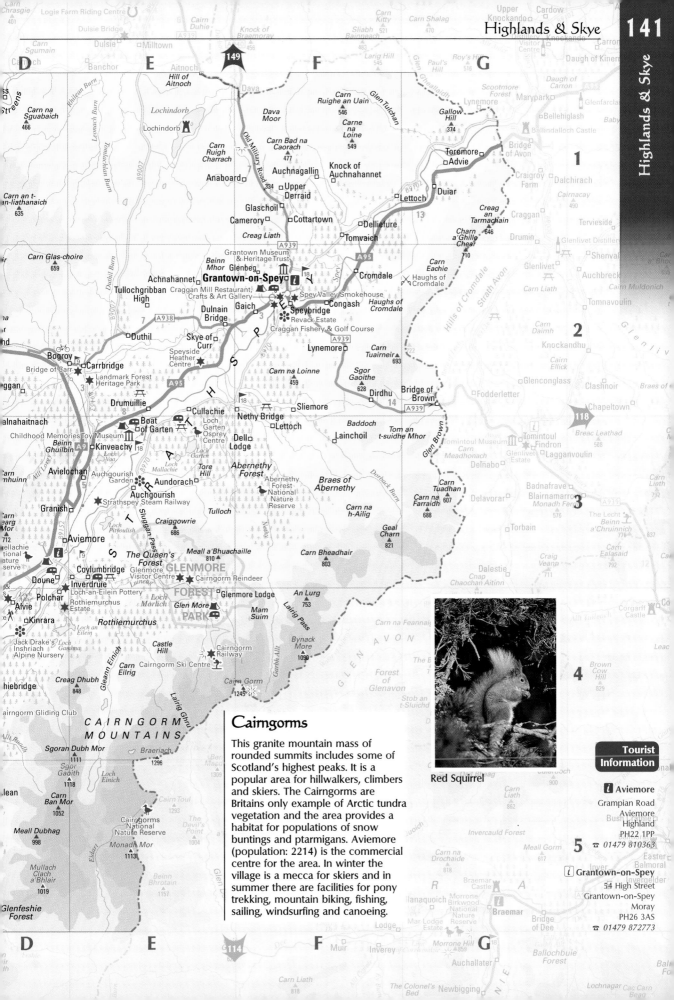

Red Squirrel

Tourist Information

i Aviemore
Grampian Road
Aviemore
Highland
PH22 1PP
☎ 01479 810363

i Grantown-on-Spey
54 High Street
Grantown-on-Spey
Moray
PH26 3AS
☎ 01479 872773

City of Inverness

Population: 41,234. Sited at the mouth of the River Ness 113 miles (169km) north west of Edinburgh and surrounded by spectacular scenery, Inverness is the Capital of the Highlands and the Gateway to the North. Several major rail and road routes radiate from the city, making it an ideal base for exploring northern Scotland in all directions. It is an attractive cosmopolitan city with a compact centre. The imposing red sandstone Victorian castle is not open to the public but there are fine views over Inverness from the castle grounds. For evening entertainment the Eden Court Theatre is popular. For shopping try the modern Eastgate centre, the Victorian style Market Arcade or the pedestrianised High Street. Beyond the city there is a diversity of attractions including dolphin watching in the Moray Firth, Cawdor Castle, Fort George and the battle site at Culloden.

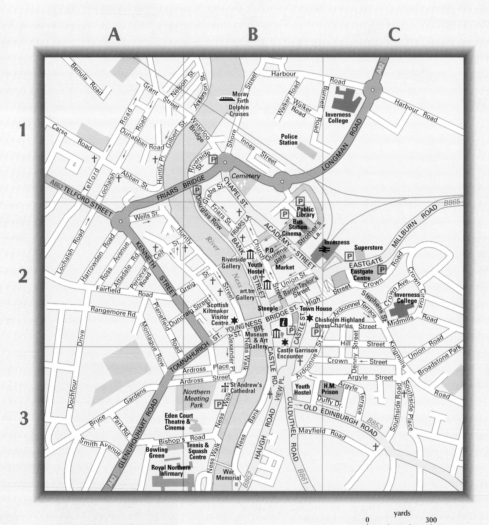

Useful information

Police
Northern Police HQ
Perth Road, IV2 3SY
☎ 01463 715555

Hospital A & E
Raigmore Hospital
Old Perth Road, IV2 3UJ
☎ 01463 704000

Main Post Office
14/16 Queensgate, IV1 1AX

Railway Station
Station Square
Academy Street

Bus Station
Margaret Street, IV1 1LT

Local Radio
Moray Firth Radio
1107AM & 97.4FM

City website
www.highland.gov.uk

Tourist Information

i Inverness
(& Highland
Discovery Centre)
Castle Wynd
Inverness
Inverness-shire
IV2 3BJ
☎ 01463 234353

Index to street names

148

148

148

140

Tourist Information

i **Daviot Wood**
A9 by Inverness
Inverness-shire
IV1 2ER
☎ 01463 772203

i **Inverness**
Castle Wynd
Inverness
Inverness-shire
IV2 3BJ
☎ 01463 234353

i **North Kessock**
North Kessock
Ross-shire
IV1 1XB
☎ 01463 731505

i **Strathpeffer**
The Square
Strathpeffer
Ross-shire
N14 9DW
☎ 01997 421415

Highlands & Skye

Portree

Population: 2126. The port and chief town of Skye lies on Loch Portree on the east coast. It is the island's cultural centre, and has an attractive, colourful harbour. The Aros Experience exhibition south of Portree gives a good introduction to the history of life on the island.

Tourist Information

i **Dunvegan**
2 Lochside
Dunvegan
Isle of Skye
IV55 8WB
☎ 01470 521581

i **Uig**
Ferry Terminal
Uig
Isle of Skye
IV51 9XX
☎ 01470 542404

Trotternish Peninsula

North East Skye

North from Portree the 20 mile (32 km) long Trotternish peninsula has some of the finest coastal scenery on Skye. Ancient landslides have created sheer cliffs and further inland the central spine of the peninsula is also studded with dramatic basalt outcrops. The most spectacular geological features are the Old Man of Storr, Kilt Rock and the pinnacles of the Quirang.

Tourist Information

i Portree
Bayfield House
Bayfield Road
Portree
Isle of Skye
IV51 9EL
☎ 01478 612137

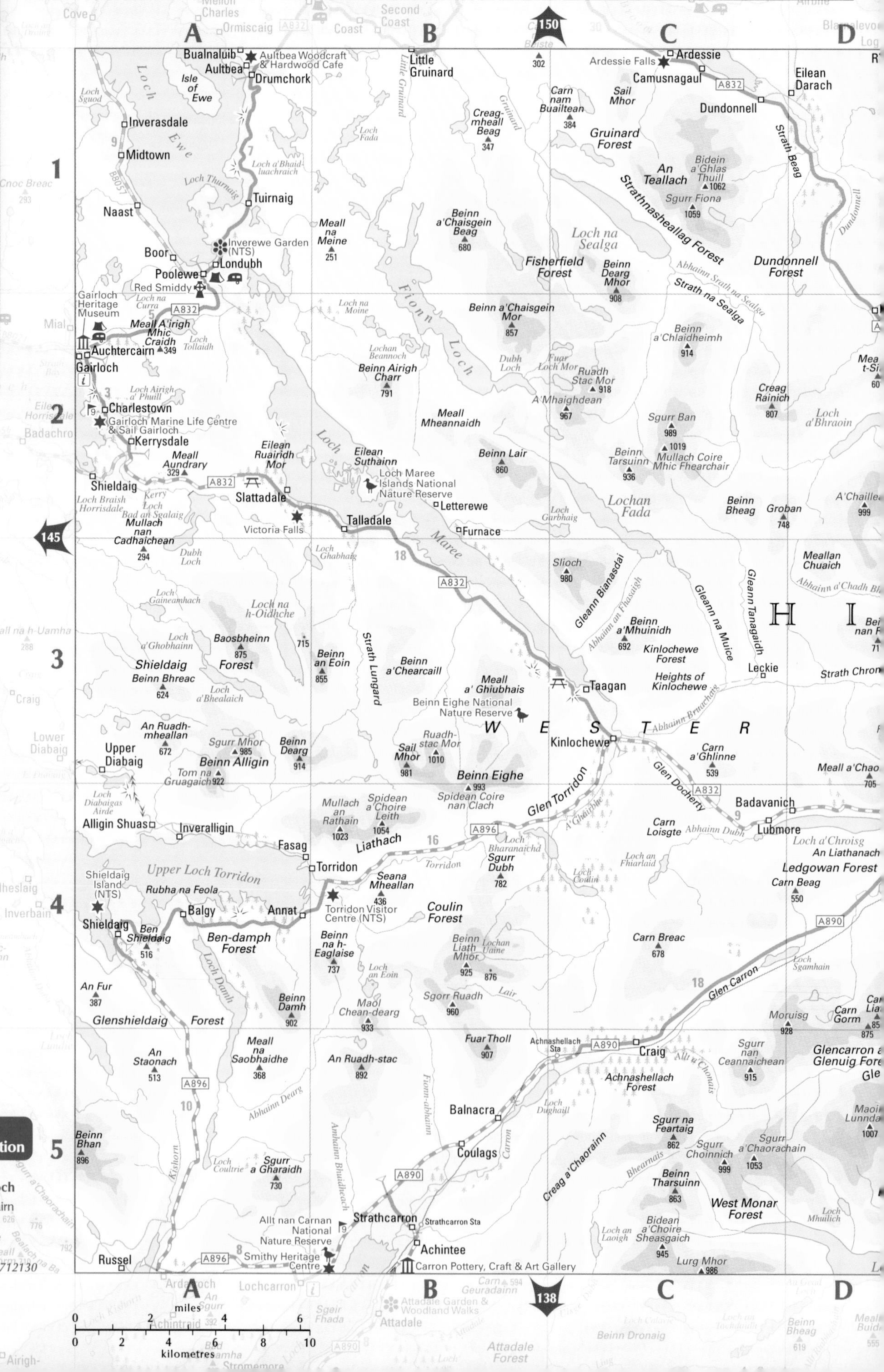

Highlands & Skye

A   B   150   C   D

1

Bualnaluib
Aultbea
Aultbea Woodcraft & Hardwood Cafe
Drumchork
Isle of Ewe
Loch Ewe
Loch Sguod
Inverasdale
Midtown
Loch Thurnaig
Loch a'Bhaid-luachraich
Tuirnaig
Naast
Boor
Inverewe Garden (NTS)
Londubh
Poolewe
Red Smiddy
Loch na Curra
Gairloch Heritage Museum
Meall A'irigh Mhic Craidh 349
Loch Tollaidh
Auchtercairn
Gairloch

Little Gruinard
Little Gruinard
302
Creag mheall Beag 347
Meall na Meine 251
Loch Fada

Carn nam Buailtean 384
Sail Mhor
Ardessie Falls
Camusnagaul
Ardessie
A832
Dundonnell
Eilean Darach
Gruinard Forest
An Teallach
Bidein a'Ghlas Thuill 1062
Sgurr Fiona 1059
Strath Beag
Dundonnell Forest
Strathnasheallag Forest
Loch na Sealga
Abhainn Strath na Sealga
Strath na Sealga
Beinn Dearg Mhor 908
Fisherfield Forest
Beinn a'Chaisgein Beag 680

2

Charlestown
Gairloch Marine Life Centre & Sail Gairloch
Kerrysdale
Meall Aundrary 329
Shieldaig
Loch Braigh Horrisdale
Loch Bad an Sgalaig
Mullach nan Cadhaichean 294
A832
Slattadale
Eilean Ruairidh Mor
Victoria Falls
Talladale

Beinn Airigh Charr 791
Loch a'Phuill
Loch Airigh a'Phuill
Loch na Moine
Lochan Beannoch
Meall Mheannaidh
Eilean Suthainn
Loch Maree Islands National Nature Reserve
Letterewe
Loch Maree
Furnace

Beinn a'Chaisgein Mor 857
Dubh Loch
Fuar Loch Mor
Ruadh Stac Mor 918
A'Mhaighdean 967
Sgurr Ban 989
1019
Mullach Coire Mhic Fhearchair
Beinn a'Chlaidheimh 914
Beinn Lair 860
Beinn Tarsuinn 936
Lochan Fada
Beinn Bheag 748
Groban 748
Creag Rainich 807
Loch a'Bhraoin
Mea t-Si 60
A'Chaille
999

3

145
Dubh Loch
Loch Gaineamhach
Loch Ghabhraig
Strath Lungard
18
A832
Loch Garbhaig
Slioch 980
Gleann Bianasdai
Gleann na Muice
Gleann Tanagaidh
Meallan Chuaich
Abhainn a'Chadh Bh
Loch Ghabhaig
Baosbheinn 875
Shieldaig Forest
Loch a'Ghobhainn
Loch a'Bhealaich
Beinn Bhreac 624
Beinn an Eoin 855
Beinn a'Chearcaill
Beinn Eighe National Nature Reserve
Meall a'Ghiubhais
Taagan
Abhainn an Fhasaigh
Beinn a'Mhuinidh 692
Kinlochewe Forest
Heights of Kinlochewe
Leckie
Strath Chron
HI
Bei nan F 71

4

An Ruadh-mheallan 672
Sgurr Mhor 985
Beinn Deargr 914
Beinn Alligin
Tom na Gruagaich 922
Upper Diabaig
Loch Diabaigas Airde
Alligin Shuas
Inveralligin
Fasag
Torridon
Upper Loch Torridon
Rubha na Feola
Shieldaig Island (NTS)
Balgy
Annat
Shieldaig
Ben Shieldaig 516
Ben-damph Forest
Loch Damh
An Fur 387
Glenshieldaig Forest
Sail Mhor 981
Ruadh-stac Mor 1010
Beinn Eighe 993
Mullach an Rathain 1023
Liathach
Spidean a'Choire Leith 1054
Spidean Coire nan Clach
Glen Torridon
A896
Loch Bharanaichd
Sgurr Dubh 782
Seana Mheallan
436
Torridon Visitor Centre (NTS)
Coulin Forest
Beinn na h-Eaglaise 737
Loch an Eoin
Beinn Liath Mhor 925 876
Sgorr Ruadh 960
Lair
Glen Docherty
A832
Carn a'Ghlinne 539
Carn Loisgte
Abhainn Dubh
Badavanich
Lubmore
Loch a'Chroisg
An Liathanach
Ledgowan Forest
Carn Beag 550
Meall a'Chao 705
Loch Coulin
Loch an Fhiarlaid
Carn Breac 678

5

An Staonach 513
A896
Meall na Saobhaidhe 368
Beinn Damh 902
Maol Chean-dearg 933
An Ruadh-stac 892
Abhainn Dearg
Fuar Tholl 907
Achnashellach Sta
A890
Craig
Achnashellach Forest
Balnacra
Coulags
Loch Dughaill
Glen Carron
18
Moruisg 928
Sgurr nan Ceannaichean 915
Sgurr na Feartaig 862
Sgurr Choinnich 999
Sgurr a'Chaorachain 1053
Beinn Tharsuinn 863
Bidean a'Choire Sheasgaich 945
Lurg Mhor 986
West Monar Forest
Glencarron Glenuig Fore Gle
Carn Gorm
Carn Lia 875
Maoi Lunnda 1007
Loch Sgamhain
Beinn Bhan 896
Sgurr a'Gharaidh 730
Loch Coultrie
Kishorn
Allt nan Carnan National Nature Reserve
Strathcarron
Strathcarron Sta
Achintee
Carron Pottery, Craft & Art Gallery
Russel
A896
Smithy Heritage Centre
Loch Carron

A   B   C   D

Tourist Information

i Gairloch
Auchtercairn
Gairloch
Ross-shire
IV21 2DN
☎ 01445 712130

miles
0   2   4   6
kilometres
0   2   4   6   8   10

D   **E** 151   **F**   **G**

Beinn
Illdeach
550

Ardcharnich
642

Ardindrean
12
Letters

Meall
Dubh
Loch a'Choire
Mhoir

Carn
a'Choin
Deirg
701

Amat Forest

Strathcarron
Wester
Gruinards

The
Craigs

Carn Bhrai
635

1

Loch a'Choire Mhoir

Carn
Mor
649

Bodach Mor
822

Seana
Bhraigh
927

Freevater
Forest

Sron Gun
Aran

Gleann Mor

Glencalvie Forest

Glen Calvie

Carn Ca
nan
Gabha

Inverlael Forest

Lael
est Garden

Inverlael
rbroom
hlunachan
Glackour

Auchindrean
Fasagrianach

Braemore

Corrieshalloch
Gorge (NTS)

Corrieshalloch
Gorge National
Nature Reserve

Creag
Dhubh
522

Lochdrum

Meall
Leacachain
618

Eididh nan
Clach
Geala
928

Meall nan
Ceapraichean
977

Cona'
Mheall
980

Beinn
Dearg
1084

Beinn
Enaiglair
889

Gleann Beag

Abhainn a'Ghlinne Bhig

Glenbeg

Meall
a' Chuaille
628

Carn
Ban

Tollomuick
Forest

Dunan
Liath
691

Beinn
Tharsuinn
714

Diebidale
Forest

Creag
Ruadh
671

Glen Diebidale

Carn
Chuinneag
838

Diebidale

E A S T E

Loch a'Chaorainn

Kildermorie Lodge

eall Mor
738

Meall
a Tuirc
625

Meall
More

Am Faochagach
954

Loch
Coire Lair

Strathvaich
Forest

Tom Ban
Mor
742

Inchbae Forest

Loch
Vaich

Loch
Magharaidh

Beinn
nan Eun
742

Kildermorie
Forest

2

Abhainn

Meall
a'Chrasgaidh
934

Loch
a'Mhadaidh

Beinn Liath
Mhor Fannaich
954

Beinn Liath Bheag
665

Sgurr Mor
1110

Beinn
Liath
Mhor
a'Ghiubhais Li
766

Kinlochluichart
Forest

A835

Strath Vaich

Strath Rannoch

Strathrannoch

Carn
Mor

Loch Bealach
Culaidh

Queen's Cairn

Wyvis
Lodge

Wyvis Forest

Sgurr nan
Clach Geala
1093

Sgurr
nan Each
923

Meall
Gorm
949

Loch
Gorm

Beinn
Dearg
687

Beinn
a'Bhric
442

Aultguish
Inn

Lubfearn

Garbat
Forest

Ben Wyvis
National
Nature
Reserve

Ben Wyvis
1046

Glas
Leathad
Mor

148

all na
rochaide

Glen Glass

Fannich
Forest

Loch Fannich

An Coileachan
923

Carn
na
Beiste
518

An Cabar
558

Meall Mhic
Iomhair
607

Corriemoillie
Forest

Carn na Dubh
Choille
479

Black Water

Achnaclerach

Garbat

An Cabar

Little Wyvis
764

Carn
Gorm
556

Rogie Burn

Meall
na
Speireig

Mill Dearg

Cioch Mhor
482

Heights
of
Brae

Neil M. Gunn
Memorial
Viewpoint

Mountge

H L A N D

R O S S

Lochrosque Forest

Carn Daraich
465

Carn
Chaiseachain
312

Carn Mhartuin
538

Knockban

A832

Studio
Jewellery Workshop
& Gallery

hnasheen

S T R A T H

Sgurr
a'Ghlas
Leathaid
844

Carn an
Leanaidh
574

Scardroy

Lochluichart

Bran

Lochluichart Sta

Loch a'Chuilinn

Loch Achanalt

A832
16

Sgurr
a'Mhuilinn
879

Meallan nan Uan
840

Meall
na Faochaig
680

Glenmeanie

Carnoch

Loch
Beannachan

Inverchoran

B R A N

Carn
na Cre
461

Loch Bhad
Ghaineamhaich

Gruide

Loch nam
Fiadh

A832

Gorstan

Loch
Luichart

Garve

Sgurr
Marcasaidh

Creag
Loch nan
Dearcag
536

Loch
Meig

Falls of Conon

Little Scatwell

Milltown
Porin

Carn na
Coinnich

Meall
nan
Damh
671

Carn na
Cloiche
Moire
591

Sron nan Saobhaidh
408

Glen Orrin

Strathgarve
Forest

A835

Loch
Garve

Tarvie

Rogie Falls

Loch
Achilty

Glensgaich

Bottacks

Water Sampling
Pavilion

Auchterneed

Touchstone Maze

Highland
Museum of Childhood

Strathpeffer 1411

7

James-
town

Torrachilty Wood

Contin

Loch
Achonachie

Strathconon

Marybank

Loch
Achilty

Falls
of Orrin

Faebait

118

Strathpeffer

Lochussie

Strath
Peffer

Dingwall

Maryburgh

A862

Conon
Bridge

Urray

Balvaird

Ale

Sir M
Monu

3

4

Carn
Mhartuin
538

Sgurr Coire nan Eun
789

Bac an Eich
849

Strathconon Forest

Loch na
Caoidhe

An Gorm
Loch

Sgurr
Fhuarthuill
1049

Sgurr
a'Choire
Ghlais
1083

Sgurr
na Ruaidhe
993

Carn
nan
Gobhar
992

Sgurr na
Cairbe

Meallan
Buidhe
766

Orrin
Reservoir

Sgurr a'Phollain
854

Beinn
a'Bha'ach Ard
862

Corriehallie Forest

Alt Goibhre

Gleann Goibhre

Erchless
Forest

Beinn nam
Fitheach
494

Cnoc
Eille
Mor

Loch
nan Eun

Urchany
and
Farley Forest

Kilmorack Gallery

Crask
of
Aigas

Aigas dam

Kilmorack

Oldtown
of Aigas

9

Loch nam
Bonnach

Rheindown

Beauly

Ward
Maus

Tourist
Information

Strathpeffer

Highland Wineries

Kiltarlity

5

Carn
Eiteige
882

Sgurr
na Muice
891

Sgurr
a'Choire
Ghlais
1083

Carn
Ban
736

Neaty Burn

Culligran

Struy

Erchless
Castle

A831

Lochan
Fada

Craigdhu

Culburnie

Druimkinnerras

Made in
Scotland

i Strathpeffer

The Square
Strathpeffer
Ross-shire
N14 9DW
☎ 01997 421415

D   **E** 139   **F**   **G**

Glen Strathfarrar
Ardchuill
Inchvuilt

Struy Forest
Carn
a' Mhuilt

Meallan
Sgor na

National
Nature Reserve

Mauld

Eskadale

Boblainy Forest

Foxhole

Crelevan

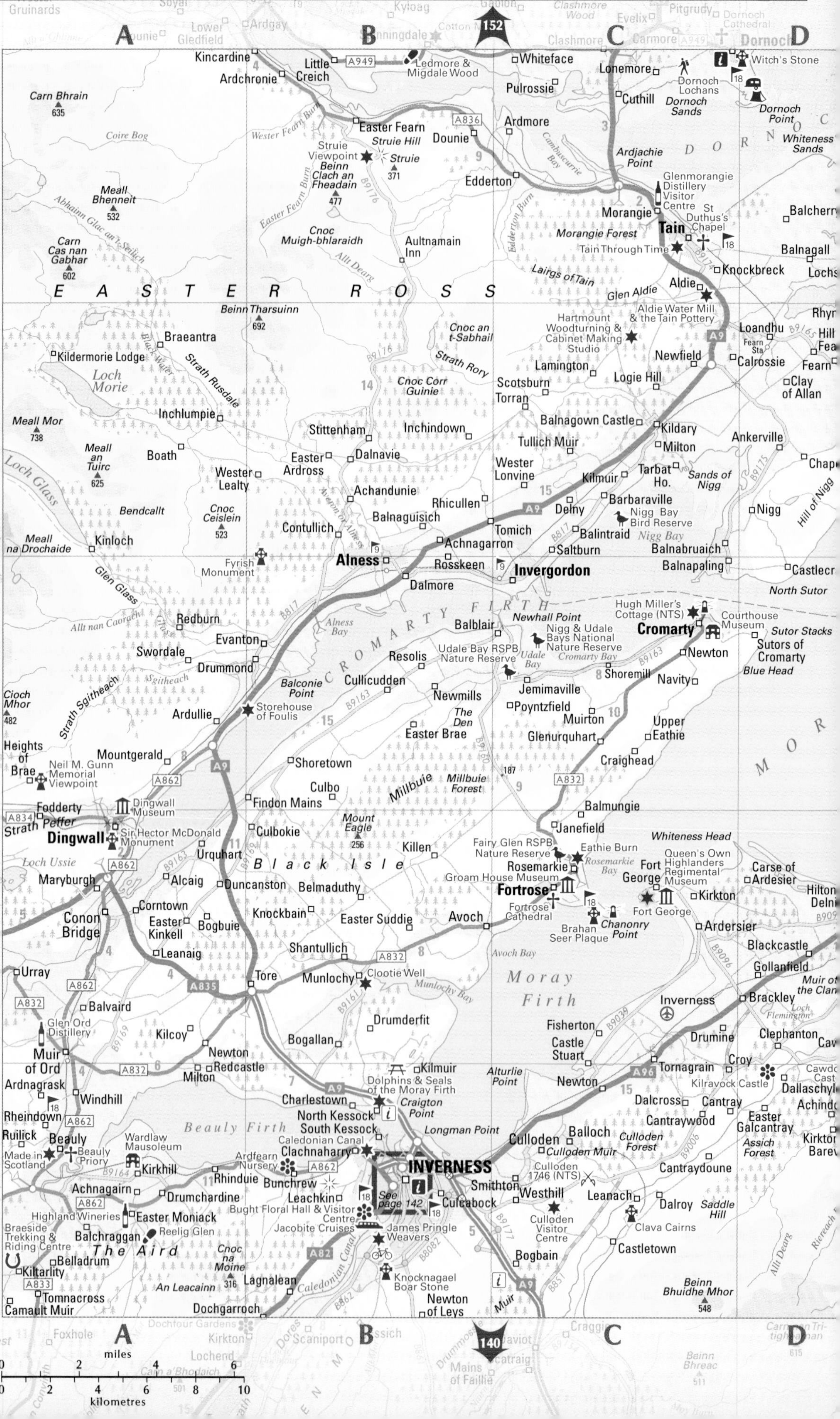

152

147

140

See page 142

Tourist Information

Daviot Wood
A9 by Inverness
Inverness-shire
IV1 2ER
☎ 01463 772203

Dornoch
The Square
Dornoch
Sutherland
IV25 3SD
☎ 01862 810400

Inverness
Castle Wynd
Inverness
Inverness-shire
IV2 3BJ
☎ 01463 234353

North Kessock
North Kessock
Ross-shire
IV1 1XB
☎ 01463 731505

EASTER ROSS

CROMARTY FIRTH

Black Isle

Moray Firth

miles
0   2   4   6

kilometres
0   2   4   6   8   10

Black Isle

Black Isle

The peninsula between Cromarty Firth and the Moray Firth is largely an area of farmland, crossed by many waymarked walks and cycle routes. There are several historic villages such as Avoch and Rosemarkie whilst the main centres are the small towns of Fortrose and Cromarty.

The Pictish Trail

The Pictish trail is a signposted trail for motorists linking important sites of the 8th century Pictish period, including the collection of stones at Groam House Museum in Fortrose, the stone slab at Hilton of Cadboll and an exhibition of local finds at the Tarbat Discovery Centre.

Nairn

Population: 7892. The royal burgh and Victorian seaside resort of Nairn was once a busy fishing port. The harbour was built by Thomas Telford. It has since become known for its fine golf courses, beaches and impressive hotels along a seafront with many family leisure attractions.

Inverness Castle

Tourist Information

i **Nairn**
62 King Street
Nairn
Nairnshire
IV21 4DN
☎ 01667 452753

Highlands & Skye

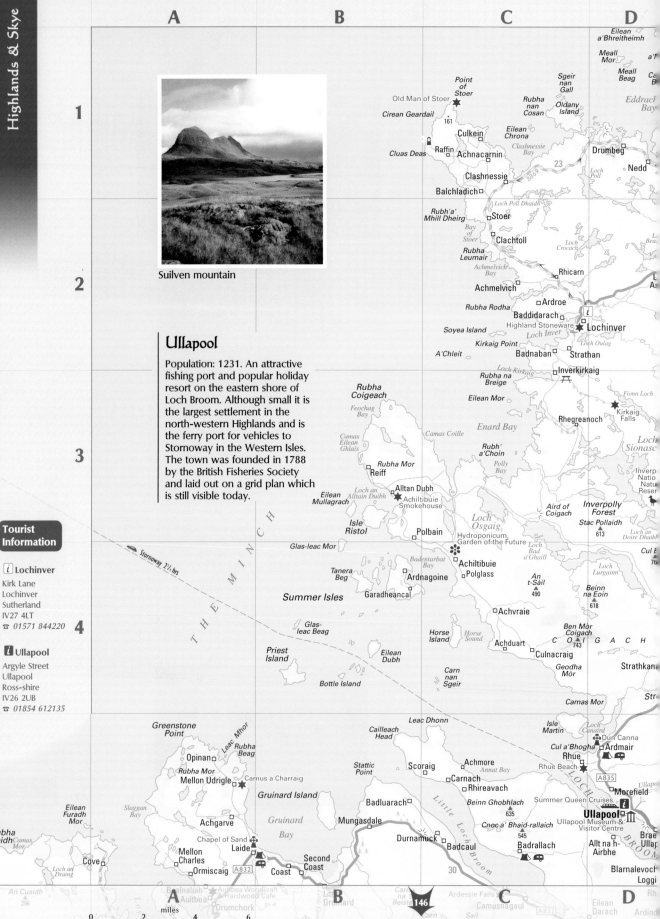

Suilven mountain

Ullapool

Population: 1231. An attractive fishing port and popular holiday resort on the eastern shore of Loch Broom. Although small it is the largest settlement in the north-western Highlands and is the ferry port for vehicles to Stornoway in the Western Isles. The town was founded in 1788 by the British Fisheries Society and laid out on a grid plan which is still visible today.

Tourist Information

ℹ️ **Lochinver**

Kirk Lane
Lochinver
Sutherland
IV27 4LT
☎ 01571 844220

ℹ️ **Ullapool**

Argyle Street
Ullapool
Ross-shire
IV26 2UB
☎ 01854 612135

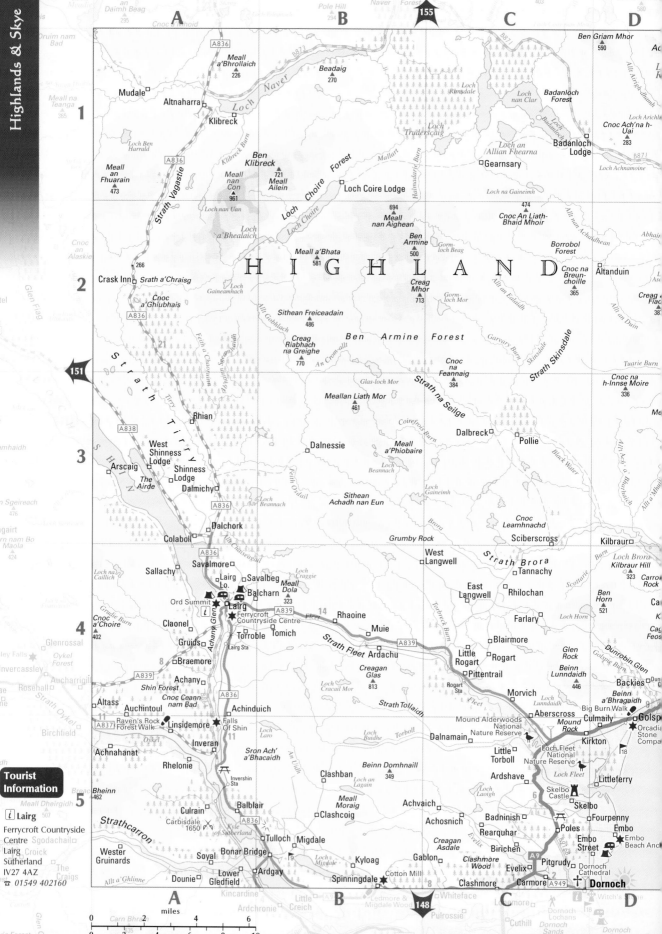

Highlands & Skye

Ben Griam Mhor
590

Cnoc an Daimh Mor
Cnoc an Daimh Beag 295
Pole Hill 294
Naver Forest
Ben Griam Beag

Meall a'Bhrollaich 226
Beadaig 270
Loch Rimsdale
Loch nan Clar
Badanloch Forest
Cnoc Ach'na h-Uai 283

Mudale
Altnaharra
Klibreck
Loch Naver
Loch Truderscaig
Loch Badanloch
Badanloch Lodge

1

Loch Ben Harrald
Meall an Fhuarain 473
Klibreck Burn
Ben Klibreck 721
Meall Ailein
Loch Choire Forest
Mallart
Loch an Allian Fhearna
Gearnsary
Loch Achnamoine

Strath Vagastie
Meall nan Con 961
Loch nan Uan
Loch a'Bhealaich
Loch Choire
Loch Coire Lodge
Loch na Gaineimh
Cnoc An Liath-Bhaid Mhoir 474
Altanduin

Creag Flac 38

H I G H L A N D

Meall nan Aighean 694
Meall a'Bhata 581
Ben Armine 500
Gorm-loch Beag
Borrobol Forest
Cnoc na Breun-choille 365

Crask Inn
Srath a'Chraisg 266
Cnoc a'Ghiubhais
Loch Gaineamhach
Creag Mhor 713
Gorm-loch Mor
Strath Skinsdale

2

Cnoc an Alaskie
Sithean Freiceadain 486
Ben Armine Forest
Cnoc na Feannaig 384
Strath na Seilge
Cnoc na h-Innse Moire 336

Creag Riabhach na Greighe 770
An Crom-allt
Glas-loch Mor
Garvary Burn
Skinsdale
Tuarie Burn

Glen Fiag
Strath Tirry
Rhian
Meallan Liath Mor 461
Coirefrog Burn

Hotel
West Shinness Lodge
Dalnessie
Meall a'Phiobaire
Dalbreck
Pollie
Black Water
Allt Ach' a'Bhraighaidh

3

Arscaig
The Airde
Shinness Lodge
Dalmichy
Loch Beannach
Sithean Achadh nan Eun
Loch Gaineimh
Cnoc Leamhnachd
Sciberscross
Kilbraur

Dalchork
Colaboll
Allt Charsegoal
Grumby Rock
Brora
Strath Brora
Kilbraur Hill 323
Carrol Rock

Loch na Caillich
Sallachy
Savalmore
Savalbeg
Loch Craggie
Meall Dola 323
West Langwell
Tannachy
Ben Horn 521

Cnoc a'Choire 402
Ord Summit
Lairg Lo.
Balcharn
Rhaoine
Muie
East Langwell
Rhilochan
Farlary
Loch Horn
Ca

4

Claonel
Lairg
Ferrycroft Countryside Centre
Torroble
Tomich
Lairg Sta
Strath Fleet
14
Ardachu
Blairmore
Rogart
Glen Rock
Dunrobin Glen
Cag Feos

Gruids
Braemore
8
Achany
Shin Forest
Cnoc Ceann nam Bad
Achinduich
Creagan Glas 813
Little Rogart
Pittentrail
Rogart Sta
Beinn Lunndaidh 446
Golspie Burn
Backies

Glenrossal
Cassley Falls
Oykel Forest
Aucharrigill
Rosehall
Altass
Auchintoul
Achany
Strath Tollaidh
Morvich
Loch Lunndaidh
Mound Rock
Beinn a'Bhragaidh
Big Burn Walk
Golsp

Strath Oykel
Raven's Rock Forest Walk
Linsidemore
Falls Of Shin
11
Inveran
Sron Ach' a'Bhacaidh
Mound Alderwoods National Nature Reserve
Aberscross
Mound Rock
Kirkton
Culmaily
Orcadia Stone Compa

Brae
Dune
Birchfield
Achnahanat
Rhelonie
Invershin Sta
Beinn Domhnaill 349
Clashban
Loch an Lagain
Dalnamain
Loch Fleet
Little Torboll
Loch Fleet National Nature Reserve
18

5

Meall Dheirgidh 507
Bheinn 462
Balblair
Meall Moraig
Achvaich
Ardshave
Skelbo Castle
Skelbo
Littleferry
Fourpenny

Strathcarron
Sgodachail
Culrain
Carbisdale 1650
Kyle of Sutherland
Clashcoig
Achosnich
Badninish
Rearquhar
Poles
Embo Street
Embo
Embo Beach Anch

The Craigs
Carn am Bo Maola 424
Wester Gruinards
Soyal
Tulloch
Migdale
Kyloag
Gablon
Creagan Asdale
Birichen
Pitgrudy
A9
Evelix
Carmore
Dornoch Cathedral
Dornoch

Dounie
Lower Gledfield
Ardgay
Bonar Bridge
9
Loch Migdale
Spinningdale
Cotton Mill
Clashmore Wood
Evelix
Clashmore
Carmore
A949
Dornoch

0   miles   2   4   6
0   2   4   6   8   10
kilometres

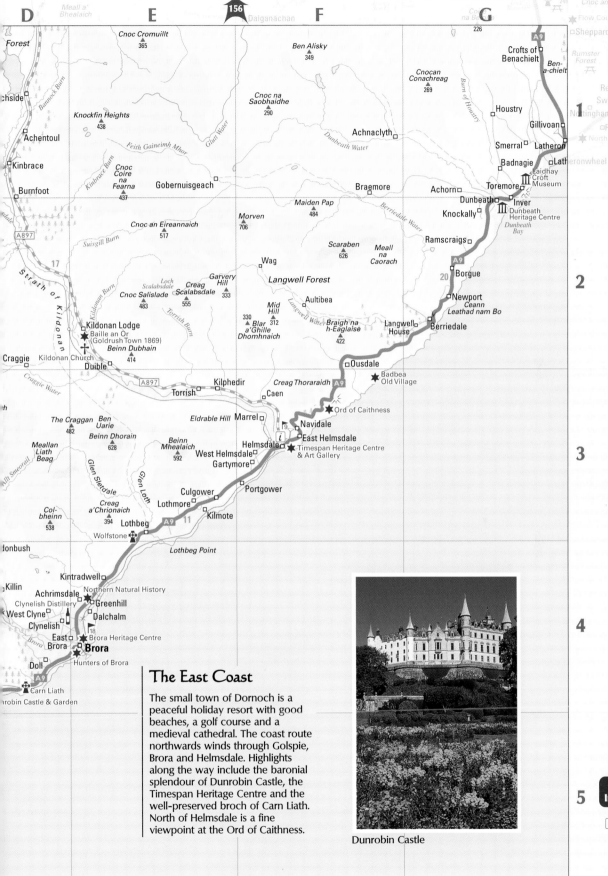

D E F G

156

Dalganachan

Forsinard RSPB
Nature Reserve

Forsinard
Meall a'
Bhealaich

Cnoc nan Gall
275

Achavanich Standing Stones

Flow Country

Cnoc an Ear...
248

Sheppardsto...

Rumster
Forest

chside

Forest

Cnoc Cromuillt
365

Ben Alisky
349

Cnocan
Conachreag
269

226

Crofts of
Benachielt

Ben-
a-chielt

North Sh...

Fors...

Reisg...
Swiney

Nottingham

1

Achentoul

Knockfin Heights
438

Cnoc
Coire
na
Fearna

Cnoc na
Saobhaidhe
290

Achnaclyth

Houstry

Gillivoan

Smerral

Latheron

A9

Kinbrace

Burnfoot

Gobernuisgeach

Braemore

Achorn

Badnagie

Latheronwheel

437

A897

Feith Gaineimh Mhor

Glut Water

Dunbeath Water

Berriedale Water

Toremore

Laidhay
Croft
Museum

Suisgill Burn

Cnoc an Eireannaich
517

Maiden Pap
484

Morven
706

Knockally

Dunbeath

Inver

Dunbeath
Heritage Centre

Dunbeath
Bay

17

Strath of Kildonan

Loch
Scalasdale

Creag
Scalasdale
333

Garvery
Hill

Cnoc Salislade
483

555

Wag

Scaraben
626

Meall
na
Caorach

Ramscraigs

Aultibea

A9

20

Borgue

2

Kildonan Burn

Torrish Burn

Mid
Hill
312

330

Blar
a'Ghille
Dhomhnaich

Braigh na
h-Eaglaise
422

Langwell
House

Newport

Ceann
Leathad nam Bo

Berriedale

Kildonan Lodge
Baille an Òr
(Goldrush Town 1869)

Beinn Dubhain
414

Langwell Forest

Langwell Water

Craggie

Kildonan Church

Duible

A897

Kilphedir

Torrish

Caen

Creag Thoraraidh

A9

Ousdale

Badbea
Old Village

Craggie Water

Eldrable Hill

Marrel

Ord of Caithness

The Craggan
482

Ben
Uarie

Beinn Dhorain
628

Beinn
Mhealaich
592

Navidale

East Helmsdale

Meallan
Liath
Beag

Glen Sletdale

Glen Loth

West Helmsdale

Gartymore

Helmsdale

Timespan Heritage Centre
& Art Gallery

3

Culgower

Lothmore

Portgower

Colbheinn
538

Creag
a'Chrionaich
394

Lothbeg

Kilmote

A9

11

Wolfstone

Lothbeg Point

Kintradwell

Killin

Achrimsdale

Northern Natural History

Greenhill

Clynelish Distillery

West Clyne

Clynelish

Dalchalm

18

Brora Heritage Centre

4

Brora

East
Brora

Brora

Doll

Hunters of Brora

A9

Carn Liath

robin Castle & Garden

The East Coast

The small town of Dornoch is a
peaceful holiday resort with good
beaches, a golf course and a
medieval cathedral. The coast route
northwards winds through Golspie,
Brora and Helmsdale. Highlights
along the way include the baronial
splendour of Dunrobin Castle, the
Timespan Heritage Centre and the
well-preserved broch of Carn Liath.
North of Helmsdale is a fine
viewpoint at the Ord of Caithness.

Dunrobin Castle

**Tourist
Information**

5

i **Helmsdale**

Coupar Park
Helmsdale
Sutherland
KW8 6JX
☎ 01431 821640

D E F G

149

Tarbat
Ness

Port Mor

Wilkhaven

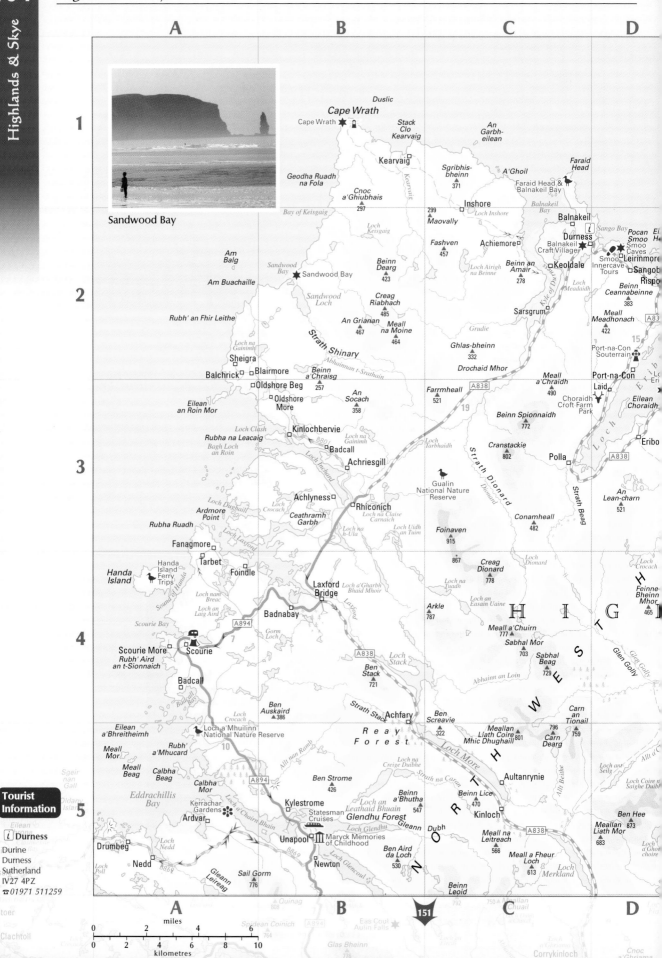

Sandwood Bay

Tourist
Information

i **Durness**
Durine
Durness
Sutherland
IV27 4PZ
☎ 01971 511259

miles
0   2   4   6
0   2   4   6   8   10
kilometres

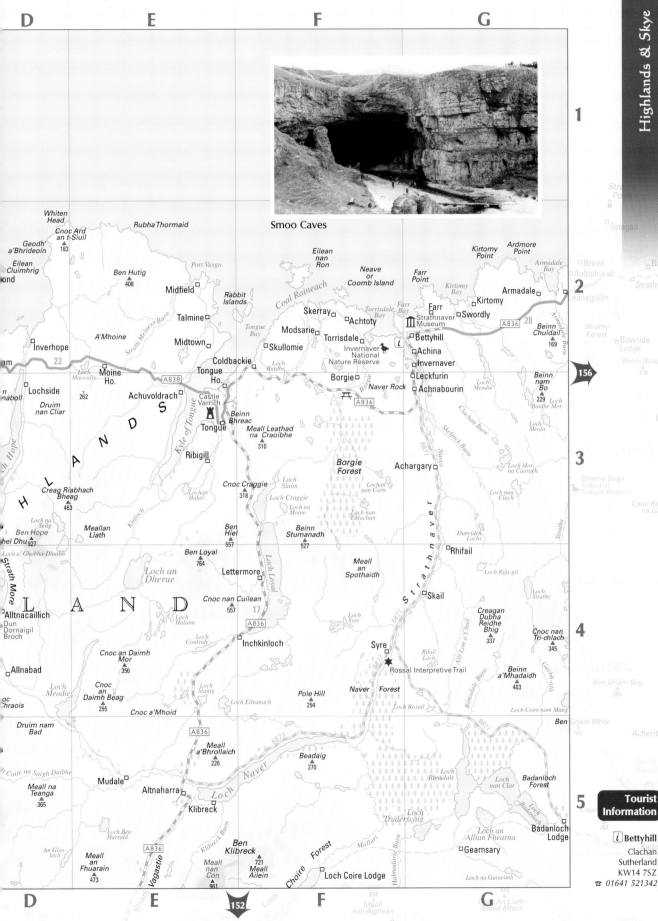

Smoo Caves

Tourist
Information

i **Bettyhill**
Clachan
Sutherland
KW14 7SZ
☎ 01641 521342

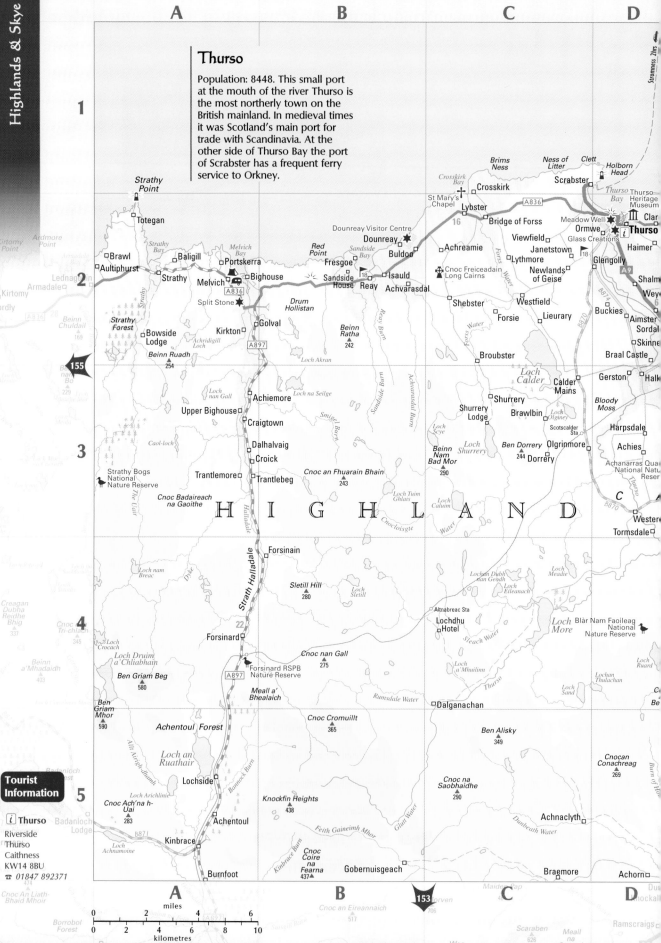

Thurso

Population: 8448. This small port at the mouth of the river Thurso is the most northerly town on the British mainland. In medieval times it was Scotland's main port for trade with Scandinavia. At the other side of Thurso Bay the port of Scrabster has a frequent ferry service to Orkney.

Stromness 2hrs

A B C D

1

Strathy Point

Totegan

Brims Ness
Ness of Litter
Clett
Holborn Head
Scrabster
Thurso Bay
Thurso Heritage Museum
Crosskirk Bay
St Mary's Chapel
Crosskirk
Lybster
Bridge of Forss
A836
16
Meadow Well
Clar
Ormwe
Thurso
Glass Creations
i

Brawl
Aultiphurst
Armadale
Lednagullin
Kirtomy
wordly
A814
Kirtomy Point
Ardmore Point
Strathy Bay
Baligill
Portskerra
Strathy
Melvich
Bighouse
A836
Split Stone
Dounreay Visitor Centre
Red Point
Fresgoe
Sandside House
Reay
18
Isauld
Achvarasdal
Dounreay
Buldoo
Sandside Bay
Cnoc Freiceadain Long Cairns
Achreamie
Viewfield
Janetstown
Lythmore
Newlands of Geise
18
Haimer
Glengolly
A9
Shalm
Wey
B87

2

Beinn Chuldail
169
Strathy Forest
Bowside Lodge
Beinn Ruadh 254
Kirkton
A897
Golval
Drum Hollistan
Achridigill Loch
Loch Akran
Beinn Ratha 242
Reay Burn
Achvarasdal Burn
Forsy Water
Shebster
Forsie
Westfield
Lieurary
Broubster
B870
Buckies
Aimster
Sordal
Skinne
Braal Castle
Gerston
Halk
155
Bc na Bo
229
Achiemore
Loch nan Gall
Loch na Seilge
Smigel Burn
Sandside Burn
Upper Bighouse
Craigtown
Dalhalvaig
Croick
Trantlemore
Trantlebeg
Cnoc an Fhuarain Bhain 243
Caol-loch
Cnoc Badaireach na Gaoithe
Strathy Bogs National Nature Reserve
Loch Scye
Beinn Nam Bad Mor 290
Loch Shurrery
Ben Dorrery 244
Olgrinmore
Dorrery
Shurrery
Shurrery Lodge
Brawlbin
Loch Olguney
Scotscalder Sta
Loch Calder
Calder Mains
Bloody Moss
Harpsdale
Achies
Achanarras Qua National Natu Reser
Thurso
C

3

The Uair
H I G H L A N D
Halladale
Strath Halladale
Loch Tuim Ghlais
Loch Caluim
Water
Chocloisgte
Wester
Tormsdale
B870

4

Creagan Dubha Reidhe Bhig 331
Cnoc Tri-chlach 345
Loch Crocach
Loch Druim a' Chliabhain
Ben Griam Beg 580
Beinn a'Mhadaidh 403
Forsinard
22
A897
Forsinain
Sletill Hill 280
Loch Sletill
Forsinard RSPB Nature Reserve
Meall a' Bhealaich
Cnoc nan Gall 275
Lochan Dubh an Gendh
Loch Eileanach
Loch Meadie
Altnabreac Sta
Lochdhu Hotel
Sleach Water
Loch a'Mhuilinn
Loch More
Blàr Nam Faoileag National Nature Reserve
Loch Ruard
Lochan Thulachan
Loch Sand
C
Be

5

Badanloch Forest
Ben Griam Mhor 590
Achentoul Forest
Loch an Ruathair
Allt Airigh-dhamh
Lochside
Cnoc Ach'na h-Uai 283
Loch Arichlinie
Badanloch Lodge
Achentoul
Kinbrace
B87
Loch Achnamoine
Burnfoot
Cnoc An Liath-Bhaid Mhoir
Borroboll Forest
Knockfin Heights 438
Cnoc Cromuillt 365
Ben Alisky 349
Dalganachan
Gilbit Water
Rumsdale Water
Kinbrace Burn
Feith Gaineimh Mhor
Cnoc Coire na Fearna 437
Gobernuisgeach
Cnoc an Eireannaich 517
Cnoc na Saobhaidhe 290
Dunbeath Water
Achnaclyth
Cnocan Conachreag 269
Burn of Ho
Braemore
Achorn
Du hockall

153

Tourist Information

i Thurso
Riverside
Thurso
Caithness
KW14 8BU
☎ 01847 892371

A   B   C   D

miles
0   2   4   6
0 2 4 6 8 10
kilometres

Stacks of Duncansby

Tourist Information

ℹ **John o'Groats**
County Road
John o'Groats
Caithness
KW1 4YR
☎ 01955 611373

ℹ **Wick**
Whitechapel Road
Wick
Caithness
KW1 4EA
☎ 01955 602596

❊ Abriachan Garden Nursery `143 B5`
North shore of Loch Ness, 9 miles (14.5 km) south west of Inverness on the A82. Exciting garden on Loch Ness side. A combination of native and exotic plants in a beautiful woodland setting. Hardy perennial plantings are a speciality. The adjacent nursery sells many unusual plants. Catalogue available.
☎ 01463 861232

❧ Abriachan Wood `143 B5`
On the shores of Loch Ness, 9 miles (15km) south of Inverness. Abriachan means 'mouth of the steep burn'. These are ancient woods, once coppiced for hazel. The woods were used for commercial forestry but are now under regeneration to return them to native woodland. Waymarked trail and viewpoints.
☎ 01764 662554   www.woodland-trust.org.uk

✝ Achavanich Standing Stones `157 D4`
Situated approximately 5 miles (8km) from Latheron on the A9 to Thurso. The stones are set in an unusual U shape and are thought to date from the Bronze Age. Today 36 stones survive out of a possible 54.

✱ Achiltibuie Smokehouse `150 B3`
The Smokehouse is situated at Altandhu, 5 miles (8km) north west of Achiltibuie village, 25 miles (40km) north west of Ullapool. A smokehouse where visitors can view the work areas and see fish being prepared for smoking and other processes.
☎ 01854 622353

✱ Aigas Dam `143 A4`
By the A831, between Beauly and Struy. This dam, part of the River Beauly Hydro scheme, is by-passed by a fish lift which allows the salmon to migrate upstream to spawn.

✱ Aldie Water Mill & the Tain Pottery `143 D1`
Off the A9, 0.5 mile (1km) south of Tain, 30 miles (48km) north of Inverness. There has been a water mill on the Aldie Estate since 1552. The present mill dates from 1860 and has been restored to working order. There is a selection of Tain pottery for sale, together with other products produced locally, including baskets, weaving and carving.
☎ 01862 893786

🏛 Aluminium Story Library & Visitor Centre, The `134 A3`
Linnhe Road, Kinlochleven. 7 miles (11km) from Glencoe and 21 miles (34km) from Fort William at the head of Loch Leven. The Aluminium Story uses audio-visual displays and a video presentation system to tell the story of the British Aluminium Company which opened a smelter here in 1908. Visitors can learn how the industry and the company's hydro scheme altered the life of the area.
☎ 01855 831663

🏃 Alvie Estate `141 D4`
Kincraig, Kingussie. On the B9152, 4 miles (6.5km) south of Aviemore. A traditional Highland sporting estate which has been in the same family since 1927. Now diversified into tourism – clay pigeon shooting, fishing, horse riding, 4x4 off-road driving, estate tours and corporate entertainment. Spectacular views across the Spey Valley to the Cairngorms.
☎ 01540 651255

🏛 An Tuireann Arts Centre `145 D5`
On the B885, 0.5 mile (1km) from Portree centre. An exhibition gallery for the visual arts and crafts and related educational events.
☎ 01478 613306   www.antuireann.org.uk

✝ Ardclach Bell Tower `149 E5`
Off the A939, 8.5 miles (13.5km) south east of Nairn. A remarkable little two-storey fortified bell tower built in 1655 on the hill above the parish church of Ardclach. The ringing of the bell summoned worshippers to the church and warned in case of alarm.
☎ 01667 460232   www.historic-scotland.gov.uk

✱ Ardessie Falls `146 C1`
Beside the A832 at Dundonnel. Waterfalls and impressive views of Little Loch Broom.

❊ Ardfearn Nursery `143 C4`
Bunchrew, 4 miles (6.5km) west of Inverness on the A862. Horticultural adviser and broadcaster Jim Sutherland and his son Alasdair have created a large family nursery on the shores of the Beauly Firth. Huge variety of plants of extreme hardiness, attractive display beds containing over 1000 species and cultivars, with easy access for all including wheelchair users. Sales area with a wide selection of plants. Panoramic views.
☎ 01463 243250

✱ Ardnamurchan Point Visitor Centre `132 A3`
On the B8007, 6 miles (10km) west of Kilchoan. Ardnamurchan lighthouse is set amongst spectacular scenery on mainland Britain's most westerly point, embracing world-class views of the Hebrides and the Small Isles. Listen to the keepers' radio conversations, learn how the light tower was built, join in the centre's Whale Watch, visit the beautifully restored original room and trace the history of Ardnamurchan through anecdotes of people past and present.
☎ 01972 510210   www.ardnamurchan.u-net.com

🏠 Ardtornish Estate `132 D5`
Morvern, 40 miles (64km) south west of Fort William via the Corran Ferry. Ardtornish estate is a 35,000 acre (14,164ha) Highland estate with 24 acres (10ha) of established gardens around the Grade A listed Ardtornish House. Fly-fishing for brown trout, sea trout and salmon on three rivers and 16 hill lochs. Free loch fishing to residents of estate's self catering properties.
☎ 01967 421288   www.ardtornish.co.uk

♜ Ardvreck Castle `151 E2`
On the A837, 11 miles (18km) east of Lochinver, on Loch Assynt. Built by the MacLeods, who in the mid-13th century obtained Assynt through marriage, the three-storeyed ruins stand on the shores of Loch Assynt. After his defeat at Culrain, near Bonar Bridge, in 1650, the Marquess of Montrose fled to Assynt but was soon captured and confined here before being sent to Edinburgh where he was then executed.

❊ Armadale Castle Gardens & Museum of the Isles `137 F4`
Sleat, Isle of Skye. 0.5 mile (1km) north of Armadale ferry terminal, 21 miles (34km) south of the Skye Bridge at Kyle of Lochalsh on the A851. A 40 acre (16ha) garden set within the 20,000 acre (8094ha) Armadale Estate where some of the flora otherwise associated with warmer climes can be grown because of the gulf stream passing close to these shores. Woodland walks and meadows ablaze with wild flowers, seascapes around every corner. Museum explaining the sometimes complex story of Highland history.
☎ 01471 844305   www.cland.demon.co.uk

✱ Aros Experience `145 D5`
On the A87 Viewfield Road south of Portree. The exhibition tells the story of Skye from 1700 to the present day. An audio-visual presentation introduces the scenery of Skye and a purpose-built auditorium is the location for regular shows on the Gaelic arts, including step dancing, singing and theatre. Walks through Portree Forest.
☎ 01478 613649

🏛 art.tm gallery `142 B2`
20 Bank Street, Inverness. Award winning art gallery exhibiting contemporary painting, prints, new media and applied arts. Also high quality local, national and international jewellery, ceramics and textiles.
☎ 01463 712240   www.arttm.org.uk

❊ Attadale Garden & Woodland Walks `138 B1`
On south shore of Loch Carron, 2 miles (3km) south of Strathcarron on the A890. Attadale House was built in 1755 by Donald Matheson. The gardens and woodlands were started in 1890 by Baron Schroder and planted with rhododendrons, azaleas and specimen trees. Since the storms of the 1980s, more old paths have been revealed, bridges have been built and water gardens have been planted with candelabra primulas, gunnera, iris and bamboo. Restored sunken garden, vegetable and herb gardens. Visitors are advised to wear waterproof shoes.
☎ 01520 722217   www.attadale.com

❊ Auchgourish Gardens `141 E3`
On the B970 between Boat of Garten and Aviemore. A new botanic garden laid out in bio-geographic regions. The first phase of construction includes a large Japanese garden (the largest open to the public in the north of Scotland). Other gardens include plants from Korea, the Himalayas, China, Asia and Europe. Native varieties of plant can be seen in the rockeries which contain Scottish alpine plants. Further areas are being developed.
☎ 01479 831464   www.auchgourishgardens.com

✱ Aultbea Woodcraft & Hardwood Café `146 A1`
Drumchork, off the A832, 6 miles (9.5km) north of Inverewe Garden. A wood-turning workshop, craft shop and tearoom with superb views over loch and mountains. Large display of wood-turning in native and exotic woods. Wood-turning tuition available.
☎ 01445 731394

✱ Aurora Crafts `144 C5`
In Ose, 0.25 mile (0.5km) off the A863, 6 miles (9.5km) south of Dunvegan. A craft shop where visitors can see demonstrations of lace-making on most days. Lace, embroidery, knitwear, spinning, wood-turned articles and other items made on the premises.
☎ 01470 572208

✱ Badbea Old Village `153 F3`
North of Ousdale on the A9. Footpath leads from the lay-by to groups of ruined crofthouses perched above cliffs. Tenants evicted from inland straths during the infamous Clearances founded this lonely settlement. The site is very exposed – tradition has it that children and livestock had to be tethered to prevent them being blown over the cliffs. Many of the inhabitants emigrated to America or New Zealand, as the monument, erected in 1911, testifies.

✱ Baille an Òr (Goldrush Town 1869) `153 E2`
9 miles (14km) north west of Helmsdale, on the A897 Strath of Kildonan road. Gold panning still takes place and you can get all the necessary equipment from the craft shop in Helmsdale.

❊ Balmacara Estate & Lochalsh Woodland Garden `138 A2`
Lochalsh House, Balmacara, on the A87, 3 miles (4.8km) east of Kyle of Lochalsh. A beautiful Highland estate where traditional crofting is still carried out. Includes the village of Plockton, an outstanding conservation area and location for the television series Hamish Macbeth. The garden provides sheltered lochside walks among pine, ferns, fuchsias, hydrangeas and rhododendrons.
☎ 01599 566325   www.nts.org.uk

✱ Balnakeil Craft Village `154 C2`
Balnakeil, 1 mile (1.5km) west of Durness, off the single track road to Balnakeil Bay. Craft village including print and painting galleries, pottery and ceramic sculpture, weaving, spinning and feltwork, clothes, enamelwork, basketry, woodwork and bookshop. Stone polishing and geology display. The well stocked bookshop has a wide range of general titles and features a restaurant serving everything from a pot of tea to a three-course dinner. Theme nights, occasional live music and other events.
☎ 01971 511277

✹ **Beauly Firth & Glens Trust** `143 B4`
Beauly. Local exhibition on Beauly Firth and the glens (Glen Affric, Glen Cannich, and Strathfarrer) and information on local attractions, walks etc for visitors. Products available to purchase. Attractive gardens.
☎ *01463 783444*

✝ **Beauly Priory** `143 B4`
On the A9 in Beauly, 12 miles (19km) west of Inverness. Ruins of a Valliscaulian priory founded in about 1230, although much of the building was later reconstructed. Notable windows and window-arcading.
☎ *01667 460232* *www.historic-scotland.gov.uk*

🐾 **Beinn Eighe National Nature Reserve** `146 C3`
South of Loch Maree near Kinlochewe. The first National Nature Reserve in Britain, acquired primarily to protect an important remnant of Scotland's ancient pinewood. Red deer, roe deer, pine marten and wildcat all inhabit this area. Golden eagle, buzzard and other birds of prey may occasionally be seen. The mountain slopes of Beinn Eighe are also of great geological and botanical interest. Woodland and mountain trail.

🚤 **Bella Jane Boat Trips** `137 E3`
Elgol, Isle of Skye. 15 miles (24km) from Broadford on the B8083. Bella Jane run a three-hour trip from Elgol which sails to Loch Coruisk in the Cuillin Mountains, pausing to see a seal colony then landing ashore. Hot drinks and shortbread are available on the return journey. Knowledgeable skipper and crew. Award-winning. Also day excursions aboard Celtic Explorer to the magical Isles of Rum and Canna.
☎ *0800 7313089* *www.bellajane.co.uk*

✹ **Ben Nevis** `134 A2`
2 miles (3km) from Fort William. Britain's highest (4406ft/1344m) and most popular mountain for both rock climber and hill walker. The Ben Nevis race every September sees runners tackling a course to the summit and back with a record time of 1 hour and 25 minutes. Ben Nevis is best seen from the north approach to Fort William, or from the Gairlochy Road, across the Caledonian Canal.

🍾 **Ben Nevis Distillery Visitor Centre** `134 A2`
Lochy Bridge, on the A82, 2 miles (3km) north of Fort William. Visitors can tour the distillery and taste the famous whisky, the Dew of Ben Nevis. Exhibition and video programme. Award-winning whiskies available.
☎ *01397 702476* *www.bennevis.co.uk*

✹ **Ben Nevis Woollen Mill** `134 A2`
Belford Road, 0.5 mile (1km) outside Fort William town centre at entrance to Glen Nevis. At the end of the West Highland Way, Ben Nevis Woollen Mill stocks fleeces, waterproofs and accessories. Also knitwear, tweeds and Scottish gifts. Whisky shop and daily tastings.
☎ *01397 704244*

🏞 **Big Burn Walk** `152 D4`
Start point of walk in Golspie. One of the finest woodland walks in Sutherland. The extensive and well-maintained paths cross the burn by a series of bridges and allow access up to a waterfall.

🕊 **Boath Doocot** `149 E4`
Auldearn, 2 miles (3km) east of Nairn, off the A96. A 17th century doocot on the site of an ancient motte. Montrose defeated the Covenanters nearby in 1645; battle-plan on display.
www.nts.org.uk

🕊 **Brahan Seer Plaque** `143 D3`
On the shore near Chanonry Lighthouse, Fortrose, Black Isle. Commemorating the burning at the stake of Kenneth MacKenzie (Coinneach Odhar) – the Brahan Seer. This cruel act was instigated by the Countess of Seaforth when the Brahan Seer, on the insistence of the Countess, told of the 'goings on' of her husband who was on state business in Paris and was away longer than his wife thought necessary. The famous Brahan Seer, who lived in the first half of the 17th century, made many prophecies about the Highlands, some of which are still coming true.

✹ **Bridge of Carr** `141 E2`
Carrbridge. High and narrow single-arch bridge. Built by John Niccelsone, mason, in the summer of 1717, for Sir James Grant.

✹ **Bridge of Oich** `139 F4`
On the A82, 4 miles (6.5km) south of Fort Augustus. A splendid suspension bridge designed by James Dredge in 1854. It employs a patented design of double cantilevered chains with massive granite pylon arches at each end.
☎ *01667 460232* *www.historic-scotland.gov.uk*

✹ **Bright Water Visitor Centre** `137 G2`
Kyleakin, approximately 1 mile (1.5km) west of Skye Bridge on the Isle of Skye. Set in idyllic surroundings on the pier in Kyleakin, the Bright Water Visitor Centre makes the ideal, all weather activity. This unique experience unfolds the secrets of the dramatic history of the area and celebrates the wealth of wildlife in the local environment. Also exclusive trips to the nature reserve on the lighthouse island.
☎ *01599 530040* *www.eileanban.com*

❋ **Brin Herb Nursery** `143 C5`
Flichity, Farr, 7 miles (11km) from the A9 on Daviot – Fort Augustus road. Over 300 varieties of herb and wild flower plants are grown in the nursery at 700ft (213m) above sea level. Display gardens give planting ideas. Shop sells herb related products, books, cards and gifts.
☎ *01808 521288*

✹ **Brora Heritage Centre** `153 E4`
Fascally, Brora. Hands-on exhibition illustrating the history of Brora with historical photographs and local artefacts. The story of the area is told from stone age times to the present day, including exhibits on the local whisky, coal and woollen industry, and genealogy. Dinosaur area. Fantastic views.
☎ *01408 622024*
www.highland.gov.uk/cl/publicservices/visitorcentres/broraheritage.htm

🏰 **Bucholie Castle** `157 F2`
South of Freswick on the A9 John o'Groats to Wick road. The 12th century stronghold of Sweyn Asliefson, the Norse pirate. Originally named Lambaborg, the Mowats brought the present name of Bucholie with them from their estates in Aberdeenshire.

❋ **Bught Floral Hall & Visitor Centre** `143 C4`
Bught Lane, Inverness. In Bught Park, off the A82, 1.5 miles (2.5km) from city centre. The Floral Hall, Cacti House and gardens are part of a working horticultural nursery with professional staff. Visitors can stroll along winding paths through a sub-tropical landscape enhanced with a grotto, waterfall, fountain and tropical fish. Ferns and orchids flourish. Rare and fascinating tropical plants. Outside demonstration gardens consist of a number of landscaped areas.
☎ *01463 222755*

✝ **Cairn o' Get** `157 F4`
5 miles (8km) north east of Lybster. A horned and chambered burial cairn.
☎ *01667 460232* *www.historic-scotland.gov.uk*

✹ **Cairngorm Gliding Club** `141 D4`
Feshie Airstrip, Feshiebridge, 2 miles (3km) east of Kincraig. Founded in 1966 by a group of ten pilots and would-be pilots, this members club offers trial lessons and week (5 day) courses.
☎ *01540 651317* *www.gliding.org*

✹ **Cairngorm Railway** `141 E4`
Cairngorm Mountain, 9 miles (15km) east of Aviemore. Scotland's only mountain railway, taking visitors on a spectacular journey to Cairngorm Mountain – the UK's fifth highest mountain. A safe and comfortable adventure for all ages and abilities. Exhibition on the natural history of the area.
☎ *01479 861261* *www.cairngormmountain.com*

✹ **Cairngorm Reindeer Centre** `141 E3`
Reindeer House, Glenmore, 6 miles (10km) east of Aviemore on the A951. Britain's only free-ranging herd of reindeer. Visitors join the guide for a walk to the reindeer's hillside grazing. For visitors unable to make the walk, reindeer can also be seen at the centre. Exhibition and gift shop. Opportunity to adopt your own reindeer.
☎ *01479 861228* *www.reindeer-company.demon.co.uk*

⛷ **Cairngorm Ski Centre** `141 E4`
9 miles (15 km) south east of Aviemore. Scotland's first commercial ski centre and host to Scottish championships for snowboard and freestyle. Skiing at 1800 – 3600ft (600 – 1267m) with one black, nine red, six blue and ten green runs. Sheltered area for beginners.
☎ *01479 861261* *www.skicairngorm.com*

✹ **Caithness & Sutherland Natural History Display** `157 E1`
Dunnet Pavilion, Dunnet, Castletown. On the A836, 7 miles (11km) east of Thurso, next to caravan site. A display illustrating the natural history of Caithness and Sutherland.
☎ *01847 821531*

✹ **Caithness Glass Visitor Centre** `157 F3`
Airport Industrial Estate, on outskirts of Wick beside the airport. Visitors can see glass-making and watch glass cutting, engraving and jewellery making. Factory shop. Exhibition telling the history of the company.
☎ *01955 602286* *www.caithnessglass.co.uk*

✹ **Caledonian Canal** `143 C4`
Canal Office, Seaport Marina, Muirtown Wharf, Inverness. Designed by Thomas Telford and completed in 1822, the Caledonian Canal links the lochs of the Great Glen (Loch Lochy, Loch Oich and Loch Ness). It provides a coast to coast shortcut between Corpach near Fort William and Clachnaharry at Inverness and is the only Scottish canal capable of carrying ships up to 500 tons. The canal has been described as the most beautiful in Europe – the spectacular Highland scenery of lochs, mountains and glens is unusual for a canal. A wide variety of craft use the canal throughout the year and can usually be seen at close quarters as they pass through locks and bridges. There are a number of pleasure cruises available on the canal and small boats are available for hire.
☎ *01463 233140* *www.scottishcanals.co.uk*

✹ **Caledonian Canal Heritage Centre** `139 F4`
Canalside, Fort Augustus. The centre describes the fascinating history of the Caledonian Canal, from its conception to its present day refurbishment. Visitors can see the dramatic lock flight in operation.
☎ *01320 366493* *www.scottishcanals.co.uk*

✹ **Camus a Charraig** `150 A5`
On the main road to Mellon Udrigle, north of Gairloch on the A832. A beautiful white sand beach which borders a broad sandy bay of sparkling blue-green waters surrounded by mountains.

Canna
136 B4

This beautiful Hebridean island offers spectacular views, interesting archaeological remains and fascinating birdlife. The small farming population still uses traditional crofting systems. There is a post office, but no shops, pubs or roads. For details of work camps and holiday accommodation, contact the NTS Head Office in Edinburgh on 0131 243 9300.
☎ 01687 462466
www.nts.org.uk

Cape Wrath
154 B1

12 miles (19.5km) north west of Durness. The most northerly point of Scotland's north west seaboard. A passenger ferry (summer only) connects with a minibus service to the cape. Also mainland Britain's highest sea cliffs at Clo Mor which stand 920ft (280.5m) high.

Carn Liath, Skye
144 D4

Kensalayre. One of the best preserved Neolithic small chambered cairns on Skye.

Carn Liath, Sutherland
153 D4

By the A9, 3 miles (5km) east north east of Golspie. A typical broch, surviving to first-floor level, with associated settlement.
☎ 01667 460232
www.historic-scotland.gov.uk

Carron Pottery, Craft & Art Gallery
146 B4

Cam-Allt, 1 mile (1.5km) south of Strathcarron railway station on the A890. Well-established craft shop selling a wide range of Scottish and local crafts. Visitors can view the pottery attached to the shop. Art Gallery with work by local and professional artists. Occasional solo exhibitions. Sculptures and ceramics.
☎ 01520 722321

Cassley Falls
151 G4

At Invercassley on the A837. An attractive series of cascading falls, particularly impressive after heavy rainfall, and walkway by Rosehall. Salmon can be seen leaping during the summer months.

Castle Garrison Encounter
142 B2

Based at the imposing Inverness Castle, Castle Garrison Encounter portrays life as it was during the Jacobite rebellion period of 1745. Actors depict life as soldiers and tell of conditions while garrisoned at the castle. Visitors sign on as new recruits to the Hanoverian regiment and are taken through the castle basements and into the round tower.
☎ 01463 243363

Castle Keep
145 D5

Unit 7B1, Portree Industrial Estate, on the outskirts of Portree on the Dunvegan Road. 1 mile (1.5km) from the town centre. Bladesmith making hand-forged swords, knives, dirks and traditional Scottish weaponry.
☎ 01478 612114
www.castlekeep.co.uk

Castle of Old Wick
157 F4

1 mile (2km) south of Wick. Also known as the Old Man of Wick, this is one of the oldest surviving stone castles in Scotland. The castle is the ruin of an early Norse tower house on a spectacular site on a spine of rock, known as the Brig o' Trams, projecting into the sea between two deep narrow gulleys. Great care is required when visiting this site.
☎ 01667 460232
www.historic-scotland.gov.uk

Castle Varrich
155 E3

0.5 mile (1km) from the village of Tongue. Ruin located above Kyle of Tongue on a promontory. Steep path to castle accessible from the gate beside the Royal Bank of Scotland. A 14th century MacKay stronghold. Beautiful views along Kyle of Tongue.

Cawdor Castle
148 D5

5 miles (8km) south west of Nairn on the B9090 off the A96. Cawdor Castle is the name romantically associated by Shakespeare with Macbeth. The medieval tower and drawbridge are still intact and generations of art lovers and scholars are responsible for the eclectic collection of paintings, books and porcelain to be found in the castle. There are beautiful gardens, five nature trails, a nine-hole golf course and putting green, gift, book and wool shop with a wide range of Scottish knitwear and children's clothes.
☎ 01667 404615
www.cawdorcastle.com

Chapel of Sand
150 A5

In Laide, north of Gairloch. Said to have been constructed by St Columba in the 6th century. Parts of the intricately carved windows of the chapel are still intact and a large remnant of an arch can be seen.

Childhood Memories Toy Museum
141 E3

50 yards (50m) from Strathspey Steam Railway in Boat of Garten. Housed temporarily in the village hall, the collection contains over 2500 toys, dolls, teddy bears and a working train set. Children's quizzes. Attractions for all ages. Beautiful location.
☎ 01479 831609
www.boatofgarten.com

Chisholms Highland Dress
142 B2

47 – 51 Castle Street, Inverness. Display of kilt-making and of Scottish Highland dress. There are also models in Highland dress and uniforms from 1745 to the present day. Tartans, swords and other weapons on show.
☎ 01463 234599

Choraidh Croft Farm Park
154 D3

On the western shore of Loch Eriboll on the A838 between Durness (7 miles/11km), and Tongue (22 miles/35.5km). Britain's most northerly farm park with over 40 different breeds of friendly animals, a pets' corner and museum showing crofting life over the last 150 years. Good location for artists, photographers and bird and animal enthusiasts of all ages.
☎ 01971 511235

Claggan Crafts
132 C5

Morvern, 4 miles (6.5km) from Lochaline on the A884. Knitwear workshop producing an extensive range of made-to-measure garments using varied designs with themes taken from wildlife, animals and sport. Pet markings can be matched from photograph and knitted on a sweater. High quality, locally produced crafts – glass, ceramics, leatherwork plus cards and prints featuring local views.
☎ 01967 421240
www.picturesinstitch.plus.com

Clan Cameron Museum
134 A1

Achnacarry, Spean Bridge. 5 miles (8km) from the Commando Memorial on the B8005. Signposted. The history of the Cameron Clan, its involvement in the Jacobite Risings and the subsequent resurgence of the clan. Visitors can also learn about the story of Achnacarry and its wildlife. There are sections on the Queen's Own Cameron Highlanders and the Commandos who trained at Achnacarry during World War II. The building is on the site of a croft burned by Cumberland's soldiers in 1746.
☎ 01397 712090
www.clan-cameron.org

Clan Macpherson Museum
140 C5

Clan House, Main Street, Newtonmore. 15 miles (24km) south of Aviemore on the A86. Museum depicting the history of the Clan Macpherson with portraits, photographs and other Macpherson memorabilia.
☎ 01540 673332

Clansman Centre
139 F4

Canalside, Fort Augustus. On the A82, 38 miles (61km) west of Inverness at the southern end of Loch Ness. See how the 17th century Highland clans lived, ate and survived inside a reconstructed turf house. Hear a live presentation by an authentically dressed clansman, including clothing and weapons demonstration. Craft shop and scottish armoury.
☎ 01320 366444
www.scottish-swords.com

Clava Cairns
143 D4

Near Culloden, off the B9006, 6 miles (10km) east of Inverness. Two chambered cairns and a ring cairn in a row, each surrounded by a circle of stones. Of late Neolithic or early Bronze Age date. An extensive and well-preserved site in a beautiful setting.
☎ 01667 460232
www.historic-scotland.gov.uk

Clog & Craft Shop
139 G3

Invermoriston, Loch Ness, 25 miles (40km) south of Inverness on the A82. Leather goods manufacturer and clog-maker. Watch production of leather goods and clogs. Gifts and crafts.
☎ 01320 351318

Clootie Well
143 C3

Munlochy, south of Fortrose, Black Isle. Wishing well dedicated to St Boniface (or Curidan). Although no trace of it can now be found there is said to have been a chapel on this site. The trees and fence around the well are draped with thousands of rags. To have your wish granted you must spill a small amount of water three times on the ground, tie a rag on a nearby tree, make the sign of the cross and then drink from the well. Tradition states that anyone removing a rag will succumb to the misfortunes of the original owner.

Clynelish Distillery
153 D4

Brora, 58 miles (93km) north of Inverness on the A9. The original Clynelish Distillery was built in 1819 by the Marquis of Stafford, later to become Duke of Sutherland. The superb quality of Clynelish whisky was so much in demand that only private customers at home and abroad could be supplied. Trade orders were refused. The distillery was extended in 1896 by the Leith Whisky blenders, Ainslie and Co. In 1967 the new Clynelish Distillery was built alongside the original building with three times the production capacity. Clynelish is available as a 14-year old single malt and is the heart of Johnnie Walker's Gold Label blend.
☎ 01408 623000
www.highlandescape.com

Cnoc Freiceadain Long Cairns
156 C2

6 miles (9.5km) west south-west of Thurso. There were originally several round cairns here which, at a later date, were combined to form these two unexcavated Neolithic long-horned burial cairns, set at right-angles to each other. Forecourt horns are still visible under the grass.
☎ 01667 460232
www.historic-scotland.gov.uk

Cobb Memorial
140 A2

Between Invermoriston and Drumnadrochit by the A82. A cairn commemorates John Cobb, the racing driver, who lost his life near here in 1952 when attempting to beat the water speed record, with his jet speedboat, on Loch Ness.

Commando Memorial
134 B1

Off the A82, 11 miles (17.5km) north east of Fort William. An impressive sculpture by Scott Sutherland, erected in 1952 to commemorate the commandos of World War II who trained in this area. The three gigantic bronze figures stand proud in battledress, woollen caps and climbing boots looking out across the Great Glen. Fine views of Ben Nevis and Lochaber.

Confectionary Factory Visitor Centre
133 G3

Old Ferry Road, North Ballachulish, on the A82, 13 miles (20km) south of Fort William. Displays of products and an explanation of the history of Islay tablet, its origins on Islay and reason for the use of goats' milk. Also speciality Scottish food shop. Scenic views of Ballachulish bridge.
☎ 01855 821277

Corrieshalloch Gorge
147 E2

Braemore, 12 miles (19.5km) south east of Ullapool, on the A835. Here is one of the finest examples of a box canyon in Britain, forming a spectacular 200ft (61m) deep, mile-long gorge. A viewing platform stretched across the gorge looks up towards the Falls of Measach.
☎ 01445 781200
www.nts.org.uk

♣ Corrimony Cairn
139 F1
In Glen Urquhart, 8.5 miles (13.5km) west of Drumnadrochit. A chambered burial cairn surrounded by a kerb of stone slabs, outside of which is a circle of standing stones.
☎ 01667 460232 www.historic-scotland.gov.uk

✹ Cotton Mill
152 B5
In Spinningdale, between Dornoch and Bonar Bridge. The ruins of an 18th century cotton mill destroyed by fire in 1808.

▦ Courthouse Museum
143 D2
Church Street, Cromarty, 25 miles (40km) north of Inverness on the A832. The courthouse, which dates from 1773, has been converted into an award-winning museum interpreting the history of the well-preserved town of Cromarty. Displays include a reconstructed trial in the 18th century courtroom, prison cells, animated figures and costumes. A personal tape tour of the town is included in the admission price.
☎ 01381 600418 www.cromarty-courthouse.org.uk

✹ Craggan Fishery and Golf Course
141 F2
Craggan, 1 mile (2km) south of Grantown-on-Spey on the A95. An 18 hole par 3 golf course suitable for individuals and families of all levels. Fly fishing and bait fishing for adults and children. Daily flying displays and archery at the falconry centre.
☎ 01479 873283 www.cragganforleisure.co.uk

▦ Craggan Mill Restaurant, Crafts and Art Gallery
141 F2
1 mile (1.5km) south of Grantown-on-Spey on the A95. Old converted water mill displays local crafts and paintings, wooden sculptures, dried flowers and wrought iron work in art gallery. Restaurant.
☎ 01479 872288

✹ Craig Highland Farm
138 A1
Situated between Plockton and Achmore on shore road. Rare breeds farm and animal sanctuary situated in bay on shore of Loch Carron. Visitors can feed the llamas, ponies, donkeys, goats and poultry and observe the owls, pigs and rabbits. Low tide gives access to Scottish Wildlife Trust island via Coral Beach heronry.
☎ 01599 544205

✝ Croick Church
151 G5
At Croick 9 miles (14.5km) west of Ardgay. Made famous in 1845, during the Highland clearances, when many of the tenants of nearby Glencalvie were evicted to make way for sheep. They took refuge in the churchyard and even now names scratched on the east window bear witness to their distress.

✹ Culbin Sands RSPB Nature Reserve
149 E3
Nine miles of coastline between Nairn and Findhorn Bay. The reserve has sandy beaches, saltmarsh, mudflats and shingle ridges. Thousands of ducks and waders winter here and in the summer you can see butterflies, dragonflies and wild flowers.
☎ 01463 715000 www.rspb.org.uk

✹ Culloden Visitor Centre
143 D4
Culloden Moor on the B9006 5 miles (8km) east of Inverness. Site of the battle on 16 April 1746, when the forces of Bonnie Prince Charlie were defeated by the Hanoverian army, so ending the Forty-Five Jacobite uprising. Turf and stone dykes which played a crucial part in the battle have been reconstructed on their original site. Visitor centre with Jacobite exhibition, displays, audio-visual programme and bookshop.
☎ 01463 790607 www.nts.org.uk

⚱ Dalwhinnie Distillery Visitor Centre
135 F1
Dalwhinnie, off the A9, 50 miles (80km) north of Perth. The highest distillery in Scotland at 1073ft (326m) above sea level, opened in 1898. Tour guides explain the secrets of distilling. The exhibition features the history and geography of the area, and the classic malts.
☎ 01540 672219

▦ Dandelion Designs & Images Gallery
144 B4
The Captain's House, Stein. On the B886, Waternish Road, between Edinbane and Dunvegan. A craft workshop and gallery. A local artist demonstrates craft work and painting techniques. Situated in a fine listed building on the shore of Loch Bay with spectacular views.
☎ 01470 592218 www.dandelion-designs.co.uk

▦ Dingwall Museum
143 B2
Town House, High Street, Dingwall. 11 miles (18km) north of Inverness via the A9 and A835. The award-winning museum contains a reconstructed smiddy and kitchen; military room and artefacts relating to the history of the ancient burgh. Special attractions including giant jigsaws for children. Changing exhibitions and activities such as spinning and blanket stamping.
☎ 01349 865366

✹ Divach Falls
139 G2
A82 from Inverness through Drumnadrochit, turning right at Lewiston onto Balmacaan road (Falls signposted). Car park at top. A 100ft (30.5m) fall above the village of Drumnadrochit. The falls are overlooked by Divach Lodge where J. M. Barrie once stayed.

❖ Dochfour Gardens
143 B5
Dochgarroch, on the A82, 5 miles (8km) south west of Inverness. Fifteen acres (6ha) of Victorian terraced garden at the north end of the Great Glen with panoramic views over Loch Dochfour. Magnificent specimen trees, naturalised daffodils, rhododendrons, water garden and extensive yew topiary. Pick your own raspberries and strawberries.
☎ 01463 861218

✹ Dolphins and Seals of the Moray Firth
143 C4
Tourist Information Centre off the A9, just north of the Kessock Bridge. The Moray Firth contains a resident population of over 140 Bottlenose Dolphins and there are also large populations of Common and Grey Seals. This exhibition includes information about the dolphins, a video display, children's activities and a reference corner and interpretive staff. Visitors may watch the dolphins and hear them communicate and echo-locate their food through an underwater hydrophone system.
☎ 01463 731866

✝ Dornoch Cathedral
152 C5
Dornoch, on the A9, 40 miles (64km) north of Inverness. A small well-maintained cathedral founded in 1224 by Gilbert, Archdeacon of Moray and Bishop of Caithness. Partially destroyed by fire in 1570 and restored 1835–37, and again in 1924. The fine 13th century stonework is still visible. There are 27 magnificent stained glass windows.
☎ 01862 810357

✹ Dornoch Lochans
148 C1
Davochfin Farm, 1 mile (2km) west of Dornoch on Cuthill Road. A trout fishery with four well-stocked ponds. Also pitch and putt, croquet and boule and golf driving range. All equipment can be provided.
☎ 01862 810600 www.dornochlochans.co.uk

✹ Dounreay Visitor Centre
156 B2
Dounreay, on the A836, 9 miles (14.5km) west of Thurso. The Dounreay Visitor Centre tells the story of the remarkable work carried out at this nucelar power station in the past, the present and looking into the future, which can be easily understood and enjoyed by the whole family. Visitors can also hear how UKAEA Dounreay is developing world-class expertise in decommissioning, waste management and environmental reclamation of the site.
☎ 01847 802572

✹ Drum Farm Centre
140 A2
The Village Green, Drumnadrochit, 12 miles (19km) south of Inverness on the A82. Family-run livestock farm. Lots of play activities including straw barn, indoor sandpit, play tractors and classroom. Feed and stroke the animals. Tractor trailer rides.
☎ 01456 450788 www.drumfarm.co.uk

✹ Dulsie Bridge
149 E5
Off the A939 from Ferness, take the B9007 south, turn right onto an unclassified road to Dulsie. An old stone bridge dating from 1764 spans the spectacular Findhorn Gorge at this well-known beauty spot.

♣ Dun Beag Broch
136 C1
1 mile (2km) west of Bracadale, Isle of Skye. A fine example of a Hebridean broch, apparently occupied until the 18th century. Visitors can see the remains of the stairway, a side cell and the gallery built into the 13ft (4m) thick walls.
☎ 01667 460232 www.historic-scotland.gov.uk

♣ Dun Canna
150 D5
Ardmair, north of Ullapool. The site of a Viking Fort. Also a flat pebble beach with good swimming.

♣ Dun Domaigil Broch
155 D4
10 miles (16km) south of Hope. A well-preserved broch standing to a height of 22ft (6.5m) above the entrance passage.
☎ 01667 460232 www.historic-scotland.gov.uk

▦ Dunbeath Heritage Centre
153 G2
Old School, Dunbeath. Housed in the birthplace of author Neil M. Gunn. Historical detail has been extensively portrayed with a tableau of beautifully sculptured and dressed life size figures depicting Dunbeath inhabitants from the present back to its early settlers. The tableau is surrounded by displays, models and stained glass. Ancestral research, heritage trail, fishing and a bookshop.
☎ 01593 731233

✹ Duncansby Head
157 F1
The north east point of mainland Scotland, 18 miles (29km) north of Wick. The lighthouse on Duncansby Head commands a fine view of Orkney, the Pentland Skerries and the headlands of the east coast. A little to the south are the three Duncansby Stacks, huge stone needles in the sea. The sandstone cliffs are severed by great deep gashes (geos) running into the land. One of these is bridged by a natural arch.

✹ Dunnet Head
157 D1
B855, 12 miles (19km) north east of Thurso. This bold promontory of sandstone rising to 417ft (127m) is the northernmost point of the Scottish mainland. There are magnificent views across the Pentland Firth to Orkney and a great part of the north coast to Ben Loyal and Ben Hope. The windows of the lighthouse are sometimes broken by stones hurled up by the winter seas.

▦ Dunrobin Castle & Garden
152 D4
Off the A9, 1 mile (2km) north of Golspie. Set in a great park with magnificent formal garden overlooking the sea. Dunrobin Castle was originally a square keep, built circa 1275 by Robert, Earl of Sutherland, after whom it was named Dun Robin. For centuries this has been the seat of the Earls and Dukes of Sutherland. The present outward appearance results from extensive changes made 1845 – 50. Fine paintings, furniture and a steam-powered fire engine. Falconry displays and museum.
☎ 01408 633177

Dunvegan Castle · 144 B5

On the A850, 1 mile (2km) north of Dunvegan village, Isle of Skye. Historic stronghold of the Clan Macleod, set on the sea loch of Dunvegan, the home of the chiefs of Macleod for 800 years. Possessions on view include books, pictures, arms and treasured relics. Trace the history of the family and clan from the days of their Norse ancestry through 30 generations to the present day. Boat trips from the castle jetty to the seal colony. Extensive gardens and grounds. Audio-visual room. Clan exhibition with items belonging to Bonnie Prince Charlie.
☎ 01470 521206 www.dunvegancastle.com

Eas Coul Aulin Falls · 151 E2

At the head of Loch Glencoul, 3 miles (4.5km) west of the A894 near Unapool. The tallest waterfall in Britain, dropping 658ft (200m). Seals and the occasional elusive otter may be seen on the loch.

Eathie Burn · 143 D3

Rosemarkie, north of Fortrose, Black Isle. Fossils may be found on this attractive foreshore.

Edinbane Pottery · 144 C4

Edinbane, just off the A850. 14 miles (22.5km) from Portree, 8 miles (13km) from Dunvegan, 48 miles (77km) from Skye bridge. Workshop and gallery, specialising in both wood-fired and saltglaze handmade functional pottery. Work in progress may be seen.
☎ 01470 582234

Eilean Donan Castle · 138 A2

Dornie, on the A87, 8 miles (13km) east of Kyle of Lochalsh. On an islet (now connected by a causeway) in Loch Duich, this picturesque and inhabited castle dates back to 1214. It passed into the hands of the Mackenzies of Kintail who became the Earls of Seaforth. In 1719 it was garrisoned by Spanish Jacobite troops and was blown up by an English man o' war. Now completely restored. Visitors can explore every part of the castle from the Banqueting Hall to the bedrooms. Includes a recreated kitchen with sights, sounds and smells.
☎ 01599 555202 www.eileandonancastle.com

Embo Beach Anchor · 152 D5

Embo, north of Dornoch. The anchor probably came from the Prussian barque Vesta which was wrecked in 1876. It came ashore 300 yards (275m) north of the village and Embo fishermen rescued all 11 crew.

Fairy Glen RSPB Nature Reserve · 143 D3

Rosemarkie, Black Isle, 16 miles (26km) from Inverness. One mile of attractive woodland glen with a stream and two waterfalls, on the edge of a coastal village. Lots of woodland plants to see, and breeding dippers and grey wagtails. The glen has many tales and legends connected with it and is reputed to be the home of a black witch.
☎ 01463 715000 www.rspb.org.uk

Falls of Foyers · 139 G2

Foyers, on the eastern shore of Loch Ness. Car park in village, then walk. These falls, which are particularly spectacular in spate, are surrounded by woodland trails. The falls were visited and written about by Robert Burns.

Falls of Glomach · 138 C2

18 miles (28km) east of Kyle of Lochalsh, north east off the A87. At 370ft (112m), this is one of the highest waterfalls in Britain, set in a steep narrow cleft in remote countryside. The falls are well worth the 5 mile (8km) walk from the car park at Dorusduain.
www.nts.org.uk

Falls of Shin · 152 A5

Lairg, off the A836, 5 miles (8km) north of Bonar Bridge. Waterfalls in a beautiful wooded section of the Achany Glen. Popular for watching salmon leaping as they migrate upstream on their annual journey to the spawning grounds in the headwaters of the River Shin. The salmon can be seen from April to November. The visitor centre is a popular stop.
☎ 01549 402231 www.fallsofshin.com

Faraid Head & Balnakeil Bay · 154 C1

North of Durness, the Balnakeil area is of outstanding nature conservation interest for its outcrops of Durness limestone and the associated plant communities. Faraid Head, behind the beautiful Balnakeil beach, is a narrow headland with dunes, coastal grasslands and steep cliffs. During the summer months a ranger service is operated from the Tourist Information Centre where advice on guided walks and areas of wildlife interest can be obtained.

Farigaig · 140 A2

By Inverfarigaig on south side of Loch Ness, 18 miles (29km) south west of Inverness. Farigaig Forest offers excellent views over Loch Ness and across Inverfarigaig to Dum Dearduil, the site of a vitrified Iron Age fort dating from around 500 BC. The forest comprises large specimen conifers, introduced from America during the last century, and a mixture of native trees including birch, rowan, alder, ash, willow, hazel, elm and oak.
☎ 01320 366322 www.forestry.gov.uk

Ferrycroft Countryside Centre · 152 A4

A Tourist Information Centre in Lairg where visitors can learn about Sutherland. The audio-visual displays show the many changes to Sutherland's landscape from the Ice Age to the present day. Themes include forest cover, inhabitants, hydro-electric schemes, wildlife, conservation and archaeology. There are indoor puzzles and a play area for children. Visitors can also book accommodation, buy maps and books, exchange currency and obtain angling permits. Archaeological trail and forest walks.
☎ 01549 402160

Flow Country · 157 E4

At Golticlay, just north of Rumster Forest on the Lybster to Achavanich road. A view of the open peatlands of central Caithness. To the west, beyond Loch Rangag and Loch Ruard, these ancient peatlands have remained unchanged for thousands of years. Blàr nam Faoileag National Nature Reserve is visible and is part of the largest single expanse of actively growing blanket bog remaining in Britain. These peatlands, with their extraordinary surface patterns of pools and ridges, collectively form what is commonly known as the Flow Country.

Forsinard RSPB Nature Reserve · 156 A4

RSPB Visitor Centre, Forsinard Station, Forsinard. On the A897, 26 miles (41.5km) inland from Helmsdale. A nature reserve forming 20,751 acres (8398ha) of rolling peatland in the heart of the world-famous Flow Country. The unique blanket bogs contain thousands of bog pools, with insect-eating plants, dragonflies and many uncommon birds. Guided walks (May – Aug) and self-guided trail.
☎ 01641 571225 www.rspb.org.uk

Fort George · 143 D3

Visitor Centre, off the A96, by Ardersier, 11 miles (17.5km) east of Inverness. A vast site of one of the most outstanding artillery fortifications in Europe. It was planned in 1747 as a base for George II's army and was completed in 1769. Since then it has served as a barracks. It is virtually unaltered and presents a complete view of the defensive system. There is a reconstruction of barrack rooms in different periods and a display of muskets and pikes. Includes the Queen's Own Highlanders Regimental Museum.
☎ 01667 462777 www.historic-scotland.gov.uk

Fortrose Cathedral · 143 D3

In Fortrose, 8 miles (13km) south south-west of Cromarty. The surviving fragments consist of the 13th century vaulted undercroft of the chapter house and the south aisle of the nave, a 14th century vaulted structure, both finely worked, with two canopied monuments and other memorials.
☎ 01667 460232 www.historic-scotland.gov.uk

Fyrish Monument · 143 C2

Above village of Evanton on Fyrish Hill, off the A9. Curious monument erected in 1782 by Sir Hector Munro who rose from the ranks and distinguished himself at the relief of Seringapatam. The monument is a replica of the gates of the Indian city of Negapatam, the scene of one of Munro's military victories. It was built to provide work at a time of poverty and unemployment in the Evanton area. There are stunning views over the Cromarty Firth.

Gaelic Whiskies - Whisky Exhibition · 137 G3

An Oifig, Eilean Iarmain, Sleat, Isle of Skye. On the A851, 8 miles (13km) south of Broadford. Pràban na Linne (meaning 'the little whisky centre by the Sound of Sleat') is the only whisky company with its headquarters in the Hebrides. An exhibition about whisky is located in historic buildings, once the Isle Ornsay harbour shop.
☎ 01471 833266

Gairloch Heritage Museum · 146 A2

Achtercairn, in Gairloch, on the A832 70 miles (112km) north west of Inverness. A heritage centre displaying all aspects of life in a typical west Highland parish from the Stone Age to the present day, including archaeology, fishing, agriculture and domestic arts. Reconstructed crofthouse room, schoolroom, dairy and shop. The local lighthouse and preserved fishing boats are outside. Archive and library.
☎ 01445 712287 www.gairlochheritagemuseum.org.uk

Gairloch Marine Life Centre & Sail Gairloch · 146 A2

At Gairloch harbour on the A832. Porpoise, dolphin and whale surveys have been conducted for the Sea Watch Foundation for over ten years. At the centre, visitors can see photo displays, video and computer presentation, maps and charts along with survey records. The whole of marine life is covered, from jelly fish through to birds, seals and whales. Sail Gairloch Cruises take place daily subject to weather conditions and demand.
☎ 01445 712636 www.porpoise-gairloch.co.uk

Garvamore Bridge · 140 A5

6 miles (9.5km) west of Laggan Bridge, 17 miles (27km) south west of Newtonmore. This two-arched bridge at the south side of the Corrieyairick Pass was built by General Wade in 1735.

Glass Creations · 156 D2

Thurso Glass Studio, Riverside Road, Thurso. On the banks of the river Thurso with uninterrupted views of salmon, seals and otters. The studio uses the lampworking method to create glass items and sculptures. Demonstrations in glass blowing on request. Small orders completed for visitors on holiday.
☎ 01847 894017 www.glasscreations.ukf.net

✷ Glen Affric `139 E2`
From the A831 at Cannich take the unclassified road south to Loch Affric. Known as one of the most beautiful glens in Scotland, Glen Affric is a mix of high mountains, lochs, rivers and part of the ancient Caledonian Pine forest. Main features include Dog Falls in the lower Glen, Loch Affric and the wilder West Affric owned by the National Trust for Scotland. The glen is also an excellent place for all types of walking. See also Beauly Firth and Glens Trust.

✷ Glen Nevis Visitor Centre (Ionad Nibheis) `134 A2`
1.25 miles (2km) up Glen Nevis, located 2 miles (3km) east of Fort William. Information on the history, geology, flora and fauna of Ben Nevis and Glen Nevis. Ranger guided walks during June, July and August.
☎ 01397 705922

Glen Ord Distillery Visitor Centre `143 B3`
Just off the A832 on the outskirts of Muir of Ord, 15 miles (24km) west of Inverness. The sole survivor of nine distilleries which once operated around Glen Ord. Licensed in 1838. The tour and exhibition show the history of the Black Isle and the main processes of distilling. Complimentary tasting.
☎ 01463 872004   www.glenord.com

✷ Glencoe `134 A4`
Visitor Centre, Glencoe, Ballachulish. On the A82, 17 miles (27km) south of Fort William. Dramatic and historic glen, scene of the 1692 massacre of part of the MacDonald clan by soldiers of King William. Its name translates as Valley of Weeping. Its steep sided mountains offer superb walking and climbing. Red deer, wildcat, golden eagle and rare arctic plants can be seen among the breathtaking peaks and spectacular waterfalls. Ranger service. Video programme on massacre. Display on history of mountaineering.
☎ 01855 811307   www.nts.org.uk

Glencoe & North Lorn Folk Museum `134 A4`
Off the A82 in Glencoe village. A local museum in four heather-thatched buildings and two outbuildings. Many exhibits reflect Highland rural life, history, geology and wildlife.
☎ 01855 811664

Glencoe Ski Centre `134 B4`
Kingshouse, Glencoe. On the A82, 30 miles (48km) south of Fort William, 12 miles (19km) from station at Bridge of Orchy. Scotland's original ski centre, Glencoe is renowned for its exhilarating skiing and friendly atmosphere. For skiers and boarders of all standards, Glencoe provides on-site facilities including ski and snowboard school and hire departments. A diversity of terrain for snowboarders includes jumps, drop-ins and wide open runs. The chairlift and restaurant are open in summer.
☎ 01855 851226   www.ski-glencoe.co.uk

Glenelg Brochs `138 A3`
About 8 miles (13km) south east of Kyle of Lochalsh. Two Iron Age broch towers standing over 30ft (9m) high, with well-preserved structural features.
www.historic-scotland.gov.uk

✷ Glenelg Candles Arts & Crafts Centre `138 A3`
In Glenelg, 2 miles (3km) from car ferry to Skye and 7 miles (11km) from Shiel Bridge on the A87. A candle workshop where visitors can see demonstrations of handmade Highland landscape candles, or browse among paintings by local artists, books and gifts.
☎ 01599 522313   www.glenelgcandles.co.uk

Glenfinnan Monument `133 F1`
Information Centre, Glenfinnan, on the A830, 18.5 miles (30km) west of Fort William. Set amid superb Highland scenery at the head of Loch Shiel, the monument was erected in 1815 in tribute to the clansmen who died for the Jacobite cause. It is on the site where Bonnie Prince Charlie raised his standard in 1745. Displays and audio-visual programme in information centre.
☎ 01397 722250   www.nts.org.uk

Glenfinnan Station Museum `133 F1`
Station Cottage at Glenfinnan station. Restored station containing a museum illustrating the history of the West Highland railway line through objects and photographs. Steam train runs from the station to Fort William and Mallaig during the summer. Woodland walk and viewpoint.
☎ 01397 722295

✷ Glenfinnan Viaduct `133 F1`
At Glenfinnan, near Loch Shiel. Spectacular 21 arched railway viaduct built in 1901 and one of the first large constructions made of concrete.

Glenmorangie Distillery Visitor Centre `148 C1`
On the A9, 0.5 mile (1km) north of Tain. Describes 150 years of the distillery's history. Personal and informative tours, and free sample.
☎ 01862 892477   www.glenmorangie.com

✷ Glenmore Visitor Centre `141 E3`
7 miles (11km) along Ski Road from Aviemore. The Glenmore Forest Park is situated in the foothills of the Cairngorm National Nature Reserve. Caravan and camping site, visitor centre, car parks and picnic areas. Waymarked walks, off-road cycle routes, lochside activities, bird watching. Ranger services. Guided walks and tours.
☎ 01479 861220   www.forestry.gov.uk

✷ Gramayre Studio `138 A1`
An Cuilionn, Achmore, Stromeferry. 10 miles (16km) north of Kyle of Lochalsh, just off the A890. Working craft studio and sales area, featuring hand printed linocuts and colourful papier-mâché items finished in unusual papers. Also hand crafted cards, notelets, gift tags and unique gift packaging.
☎ 01599 544264

Grantown Museum & Heritage Trust `141 F2`
Burnfield House, Burnfield Avenue, Grantown-on-Spey. Located at Burnfield House, a refurbished school originally built in 1865. The permanent exhibition tells the story of Sir James Grant's Town – a fine example of a planned town – bringing the history of Grantown-on-Spey to life through audio-visual and traditional displays.
☎ 01479 872478

✝ Grey Cairns of Camster `157 E4`
Off the A9, on the Watten Road, 5 miles (8km) north of Lybster. Two Neolithic chambered burial cairns – one long with two chambers and projecting 'horns'; one round with a single chamber.
☎ 01667 460232   www.historic-scotland.gov.uk

Groam House Museum `143 D3`
High Street in Rosemarkie on the A832, 15 miles (24km) north east of Inverness. Award-winning Pictish museum. The centre-piece in a stunning display of locally-found stones is the magnificent 8th century Rosemarkie cross-slab. Part of the nationally important collection of original work by George Bain, the artist responsible for the revival of Celtic art, is also exhibited. Temporary exhibitions of local history or Pictish interest.
☎ 01381 620961

✷ Halistra Pottery `144 B4`
Halistra, Waternish, Isle of Skye. Situated on the Waternish peninsula, one of the craft centres of Skye, this is a purpose built gallery and open plan workshop allowing visitors to see the pottery being made. Wonderful views across Loch Dunvegan to the outer isles.
☎ 01470 592347

Handa Island Ferry Trips `154 A4`
Handa Island, 6 miles (10km) north of Scourie, is internationally famous for its sea bird colonies including the largest breeding colony of guillemots in Britain. The island is also renowned for its magnificent Torridonian Sandstone cliffs, which rise to a height of 400ft (122m) along the dramatic northern edge of the island. From this viewpoint you may also see much of the area's marine wildlife such as dolphins, porpoises, seals and the occasional whale. A footpath circles the island. No dogs allowed.
☎ 01971 502340

✷ Hartmount Woodturning & Cabinet Making Studio `143 D2`
Tigh an Fhraoich, Hartmount, off minor road to Scotsburn, 3 miles (5km) south of Tain. Family business (member of the Guild of Master Craftsman) with over 35 years experience. Custom-built woodworking shop and display area. Work produced to client's requirements. Courses throughout the year, one-to-one tuition.
☎ 01862 842511

Highland & Rare Breeds Croft `139 F4`
Fort Augustus. Footpath walk around enclosed fields containing red deer, highland cattle, various breeds of sheep, goats, pigs, hens and pheasants, ducks and shetland ponies.
☎ 01320 366433

Highland & Rare Breeds Farm `151 E3`
On the A835, 15 miles (24km) north of Ullapool. The Scottish Farm Animal Centre has over 36 breeds of animals, ancient and modern, including Highland cows, Hebridean ewes and Muscovy ducks. Set in 15 acres (6ha) of farmland, river and mountain scenery. A croft has been adapted for conservation. A working organic farm has an exhibition of farm tools, farming demonstrations, guided tours and information sheets.
☎ 01854 666204

Highland Folk Museum, Kingussie `140 C4`
Duke Street, Kingussie, 12 miles (19km) south west of Aviemore off the A9. An open air museum, partly housed in an 18th century shooting lodge. Features a Black House from Lewis, a clack mill and exhibits of farming equipment. Indoors, a fine display of barn, dairy, stable and an exhibition on Highland tinkers. Special features on costume, musical instruments and Highland furniture. See also the other site of the museum at Newtonmore.
☎ 01540 661307   www.highlandfolk.com

Highland Folk Museum, Newtonmore `140 C5`
Aultlarie, in Newtonmore off the A9, 15 miles (24km) south west of Aviemore; 65 miles (104km) north of Perth. A fascinating glimpse into 300 years of social history in the Highlands – an 18th century farming township with turf houses authentically furnished with box beds and cruisie lamps; an early 20th century school complete with many of its original fittings; a clockmakers workshop; curling hut and pond; and working croft. See also the other site of the museum at Kingussie.
☎ 01540 661307   www.highlandfolk.com

Highland Museum of Childhood `143 A3`
The Old Station, Strathpeffer, on the A834, 5 miles (8km) west of Dingwall. Located in part of the old station, the museum tells the story of childhood in the Highlands over the last century. A fascinating collection of over 270 dolls from all over the world and an extensive display of toys and games including Victorian board games.
☎ 01997 421031   www.hmoc.freeserve.co.uk

✷ Highland Stoneware `150 C2`
Lochinver, Assynt, Sutherland. Highland Stoneware was formed in 1974, and has built an international reputation for quality and innovation. Visitors can watch the craftspeople at work to see the full range of making and decorating skills used in creating their unusual and distinctive pottery.
☎ 01571 844376   www.highlandstoneware.com

Highlands & Skye

Highland Wildlife Park **140 D4**
Kincraig, Kingussie, on the B9152, 7 miles (11km) south of Aviemore. Visitors can discover Scottish wildlife, from native species to those creatures long extinct, and explore themed habitats on foot. Cars can be driven around the main reserve (those without a car will be driven by staff). Brightwater Burn is an otter habitat with walkways and pools. Themed special events at weekends. Managed by the Royal Zoological Society of Scotland.
☎ 01540 651270

Highland Wineries **143 B4**
Moniack Castle, off the A862, 7 miles (11km) west of Inverness. A family business in a 16th-century castle producing country wines, liqueurs, meat and game preserves, all made by hand. Tour, tastings, video and talk by tour guide.
☎ 01463 831283

Hill o' Many Stanes **157 E5**
At Mid Clyth, 4 miles (6.5km) north east of Lybster. More than 22 rows of low slabs arranged in a slightly fan-shaped pattern, which may have formed a prehistoric astronomical observatory.
☎ 01667 460232   www.historic-scotland.gov.uk

Hilton of Cadboll Chapel **149 D2**
At Hilton of Cadboll, 12 miles (19km) north east of Invergordon. The foundation remains of a small rectangular chapel.
☎ 01667 460232   www.historic-scotland.gov.uk

Hugh Miller's Cottage **143 D2**
Off the A832 in Church Street, Cromarty, 22 miles (35km) north east of Inverness. Birthplace of Hugh Miller (1802 – 56), famous stonemason, geologist, writer and church reformer. Furnished thatched cottage, built circa 1698, with restored cottage garden. Many of Miller's belongings, including fine fossil collection. Video about his life.
☎ 01381 600245   www.nts.org.uk

Hunters of Brora **153 E4**
Brora, Sutherland. The most northerly vertical woollen mill in Europe, producing real Shetland wool and cloth. The company is 100 years old, located in a new, purpose built mill. The cloth is sold to local estates, Saville Row and New York. Home furnishings, carpets, rugs, wool, tweed, gifts and clothing in Hunters yarns and fabrics.
☎ 01408 623500

Hydroponicum, Garden of the Future **150 C4**
Achiltibuie. A pioneering indoor garden created for the 21st century, overlooking the beautiful Summer Isles. Guided tours take visitors around modern growing houses, each with different climatic zones. Here lush, sub-tropical fruit trees, exotic flowers, scented plants, vegetables and herbs all grow without the use of soil or pesticides.
☎ 01854 622202   www.thehydroponicum.com

Iceberg Glassblowing Studio **143 B5**
Victoria Buildings, in Drumnadrochit on the A82. A glass-blowing studio manufacturing both solid and hollow glassware, mostly small delicate pieces including vases, Christmas decorations, animals, and modern jewellery. Visitors can see the manufacturing process.
☎ 01456 450601

Insh Marshes RSPB Nature Reserve **140 D4**
Ivy Cottage, Insh, Kingussie. The most important area of floodplain wetland in Britain with nearly 1000 pairs of wading birds breeding on the marshes. This is an important wintering ground for wildfowl, including whooper swans from Iceland. Varied wetland plants. Otters. Flower rich meadows, butterflies and other insects.
☎ 01540 661518   www.rspb.org.uk

International Otter Survival Fund **137 F2**
On the A87 near Broadford on the Isle of Skye. Guided walks by prior arrangement around the island, with a description of the history, ecology and conservation of the otter.
☎ 01471 822487   www.otter.org

Inverewe Garden **146 A1**

Poolewe, on the A832, 6 miles (10km) north east of Gairloch. A world-famous garden created from a once-barren peninsula on the shore of Loch Ewe by Victorian gardener Osgood Mackenzie. Exotic plants from many countries flourish here in the mild climate created by the North Atlantic Drift. Spectacular lochside setting among pinewoods, with superb views.
☎ 01445 781200   www.nts.org.uk

Inverlochy Castle **134 A2**
2 miles (3km) north east of Fort William. A fine well-preserved 13th century castle of the Comyn family in the form of a square with round towers at the corners. The largest tower was the donjon or keep.
☎ 0131 668 8800   www.historic-scotland.gov.uk

Inverness Museum & Art Gallery **142 B2**
Castle Wynd, Inverness. Displays of natural and human history of Inverness and the Highlands. Features exhibition of Highland and Inverness silver, weapons and musical instruments. Temporary exhibitions and events.
☎ 01463 237114

Isle of Skye Brewing Company **144 C3**
Adjacent to the pier at Uig (on the A856). A brewery which produces several cask-conditioned real ales, most of which have won awards, and its own cold-filtered bottled beers. Visitors can tour the brewery (brewing permitting – please telephone ahead). As well as its own range of beers the company sells a wide range of other Scottish bottled beers, wines and brewery souvenirs.
☎ 01470 542477   www.skyebrewery.co.uk

J. F. Lindsay Targemaker **143 C4**
Balquhidder, Main Street, North Kessock. 4 miles (6.5km) north of Inverness off the A9, take first junction left after Kessock bridge. Small workshop making high quality hand-crafted reproductions of original Jacobite targes (shields). The targemaker is happy to answer questions. Photos may be taken holding targe and sword. Targes, swords and other items for sale.
☎ 01463 731577   www.targemaker.co.uk

Jack Drake's Inschriach Alpine Nursery **141 D4**
On the B970, 4 miles (6.5km) south of Aviemore. Show garden and alpine plant nursery growing a wide range of alpines, heathers, dwarf shrubs and dwarf rhododendrons.
☎ 01540 651287   www.kincraig.com/drakesalpines

Jacobite Cruises **143 C4**
Tomnahurich Bridge, Glenurquhart Road,1 mile (1.5km) west of Inverness town centre on the A82. Round trips, one-way journeys to and from Urquhart Castle, and combined coach and cruise tours, follow the Caledonian Canal onto Loch Ness. Enjoy dramatic scenery along the way. See also Caledonian Canal and Urquhart Castle.
☎ 01463 233999   www.jacobitecruises.co.uk

Jacobite Steam Train **134 A2**
Fort William railway station. This round trip crosses the famous Glenfinnan viaduct (stopping at the village of Glenfinnan), passes through the country's most westerly mainland railway station at Arisaig and the silver beaches of Morar before reaching Mallaig. Great views en route of the Isles of Rum, Eigg, Muck and Canna, and the southern tip of Skye.
☎ 01463 239026   www.westcoastrailway.co.uk

James Pringle Weavers **143 C4**
Holm Mills, Dores Road. On the B862, 1.5 miles (2.5km) south west of Inverness. Tartan is woven in an original mill dating back to 1798. Weave your own piece of tartan. Also cashmere, lambswool, tweeds, whisky and golf equipment.
☎ 01463 223311

John o' Groats **157 F1**
John o' Groats claims to be the most northerly point of mainland Scotland, but in fact Dunnet Head, to the west, is. Named after Jan de Groot, a Dutch ferryman who settled there in the 16th century.

Kerrachar Gardens **151 D1**
Kerrachar, Kylesku, Sutherland. On the south shore of Loch a` Chairn Bhain. Situated in an extremely remote and beautiful location, Kerrachar is only accessible by a 30 minute boat trip from Kylesku. The gardens contain a wide range of shrubs and perennials, including many unusual species, some of which are for sale. New areas are still under development.
☎ 01571 833288   www.kerrachar.co.uk

Kildonan Church **153 E2**
10 miles (16km) north of Helmsdale on the A897 Strath of Kildonan road. Walk up track from Kildonan Farm. The present church, completed in 1896, contains the old pulpit with the foot marking of Alexander Sage, minister from 1787 – 1824, a man of 'great bodily weight'. His son, the Rev Donald Sage wrote Memorabilia Domestica, an interesting account of Highland life in the 18th and 19th centuries.

Kilmorack Gallery **143 A4**
Old Kilmorack Church, 2 miles (3km) west of Beauly along the Cannich road. Exhibition and sale of work by the Highland's leading artists. The gallery is housed in a spectacular 18th century church which remains largely unchanged since it was re-cast in 1835.
☎ 01463 783230   www.kilmorackgallery.co.uk

Kilravock Castle **148 D5**
Croy, 6 miles (10km) west of Nairn on the B9101. The extensive grounds and garden of this 15th century castle are noted for the large variety of beautiful trees, some centuries old. There are sports facilities and a tree garden, nature trails and river host an abundance of wildlife.
☎ 01667 493258   www.kilravockcastle.com

Kilt Rock **145 E3**
Off the A855, 17 miles (27km) north of Portree, Skye. Can be seen from the road. Care should be taken not to go too near the edge of the cliff. The top rock is composed of columnar basalt, the lower portion of horizontal beds, giving the impression of the pleats in the kilt. There is a waterfall nearby.

Kinloch Forest & Letir Fura Walk **137 F3**
4 miles (6km) south of Skalamus at Sleat, Isle of Skye. Letir Fura is a ruined township located in Kinloch Forest, a fine example of native woodland. The 4 mile (6km) walk overlooks the Sound of Sleat providing excellent views and good opportunities to see local wildlife.
www.forestry.gov.uk

Kintail & Morvich **138 C3**
16 miles (26km) east of Kyle of Lochalsh, north off the A87. A west Highland estate which includes the Falls of Glomach and the Five Sisters of Kintail, four of which are over 3000ft (914.5m). The site of the Battle of Glen Shiel, which took place in 1719, is within this area, 5 miles (8km) from Morvich. The best access to the mountains is from the Countryside Centre at Morvich.
☎ 01599 511231   www.nts.org.uk

✳ Kirkaig Falls — 150 D3
Inverkirkaig, south of Lochinver. Popular beauty spot and walk.

✳ Knockan Studio & Craft Centre — 151 E3
On the A835, 14 miles (22.5km) north of Ullapool. A jewellery/lapidary workshop where Scottish gemstones are cut and set. Workshop viewing area. Selection of Scottish crafts, knitwear, pottery, glass. Also at Ullapool.
☎ 01854 666261 — www.knockanstudio.com

⚓ Knocknagael Boar Stone — 143 C4
In Highland Council Offices, Glenurquhart Road, Inverness. On ground floor of council chambers. A rough slab incised with the Pictish symbols of a mirror-case and a wild boar. Can be viewed at any time through window.
☎ 01667 460232 — www.historic-scotland.gov.uk

🐾 Kylerhea Otter Haven — 137 G3
Kylerhea on the Isle of Skye is a superb place for otters – and from the hide you may be lucky enough to see them. Specially constructed paths are designed to protect the habitat and the wildlife, and visitors should keep to the designated paths and leave the shoreline undisturbed. Success in seeing an otter will be mostly down to your own skills in field craft, an element of luck, and patience. As well as otters, there are falcons, waders, sea birds and seals in the area.
www.forestry.gov.uk

❀ Lael Forest Garden — 147 D1
6 miles (9.5km) south of Ullapool on the A835 to Inverness. Extending to 17 acres (7ha), the garden was set aside in 1933 for interesting and ornamental trees of native and foreign origin. The oldest specimen trees were planted around 1870 and there are now some 150 different trees and shrubs.

🏛 Laidhay Croft Museum — 153 G1
Laidhay, on the A9, 1 mile (2km) north of Dunbeath. An early 18th century croft complex with stable, dwelling house and byre under one rush thatched roof. Separate cruck barn with winnowing doors. Completely furnished in period style. Crofting hand tools, machinery and harness on view.
☎ 01593 731244

✳ Landmark Forest Heritage Park — 141 E2
Carrbridge, on the B9153 (old A9), 7 miles (11km) north of Aviemore. Scotland's most exciting heritage park with wild watercoaster ride, nature trail, treetop trail, Clydesdale horse, steam-powered sawmill demonstrations, forestry skill area, viewing tower, maze, adventure play area and microworld exhibition.
☎ 0800 731 3446 — www.landmark-centre.co.uk

🏛 Last House Museum — 157 F1
John o' Groats, Caithness. A local history museum featuring photographs and a collection of artefacts. Also photographs of shipwrecks in the Pentland Firth, Scapa Flow and views of Stroma. All postcards purchased are stamped with the Last House in Scotland and John o' Groats' postmarks.
☎ 01955 611250

🏛 Laurence Broderick Sculpture Exhibition — 137 G3
Gallery An Talla Dearg, Eilean Iarmain, Isle Ornsay, Isle of Skye. On the A851 between Broadford and Armadale, 8 miles (13km) from Broadford. A gallery displaying the work of the sculptor, especially carvings of otters. Work in various stones, including Skye marble, and in bronze. Sculptor usually available to discuss his work and to do demonstrations.
☎ 01767 650444 — www.laurencebroderick.co.uk

🍂 Ledmore & Migdale Wood — 148 B1
Spinningdale, between Dornoch and Bonar Bridge on the A949. One of the largest oakwoods and colony of juniper bushes in the north of Scotland. Also Scots pine, birch, hazel, willow, and ash trees. An area of great archaeological interest – to date 28 different features have been recorded, including several chambered cairns dating from over four thousand years ago. There are also waymarked trails.

⚓ Leisure Marine — 138 A1
32 Harbour Street, Plockton, 6 miles (9.5km) north of Kyle of Lochalsh. Calum's Seal Trips at Plockton, made famous by the television programme Hamish Macbeth. Views of seals guaranteed, or money back. Spectacular scenery. Boat hire and private charter.
☎ 01599 544306

🏛 Lime Tree Studio Gallery — 134 A2
The Old Manse, Achintore Road, Fort William. Houses a continually changing exhibition of landscape paintings, mainly of north west Scotland. Extensive workshop programme and stained glass exhibition. Accommodation also available.
☎ 01397 701806 — www.limetreestudio.co.uk

🏛 Little Gallery — 136 C1
7 Portnalong, Isle of Skye, 3 miles (5km) west of Talisker distillery on the B8009. Overlooking Loch Harport, the gallery displays etchings, prints and watercolours depicting the Cuillin, Skye landscapes and the native flora and fauna.
☎ 01478 640254 — www.mtn.co.uk/skye-artist

✳ Loch Eriboll — 154 D3
Situated between Tongue and Durness in the north of Sutherland. Reputedly the deepest sea loch or inlet in Britain. Both the loch itself and its shores are steeped in history. Despite the inhospitable landscape of today, archaeological remains indicate that people have lived here for at least the last 4000 years.

🐦 Loch Garten Osprey Centre — 141 E3
Off the B970, 8 miles (13km) north east of Aviemore. A public viewing facility overlooking the tree-top nest of ospreys. Direct viewing with telescopes and binoculars; CCTV transmits pictures of the nest to the centre.
☎ 01479 831694 — www.rspb.org.uk

🏃 Loch Insh Watersports — 140 D4
Kincraig, 7 miles (11km) south of Aviemore. Watersports include sailing, windsurfing, canoeing, salmon/trout fishing and rowing. Dry ski slope skiing, mountain biking, archery. Hire and instruction. The 2 mile (3km) interpretation/fun trail and stocked fishing lochan were especially designed with wheelchair users in mind. Children's adventure area.
☎ 01540 651272 — www.lochinsh.com

✳ Loch Morar — 133 D1
South east of Mallaig. Said to be the deepest freshwater loch in Britain and the home of Morag, a monster with a strong resemblance to the Loch Ness Monster.

⚓ Loch Nam Uamh Cairn (The Prince's Cairn) — 132 C1
Off the A830, south of Arisaig. The loch is famous for its association with Bonnie Prince Charlie. The memorial cairn on the shore marks the spot from where Prince Charles Edward Stuart sailed for France on 20 September 1746, after having wandered round the Highlands as a fugitive with a price of £30,000 on his head.

✳ Loch Ness — 143 B5
This striking 24 mile (38.5km) long loch in the Great Glen forms part of the Caledonian Canal which links Inverness with Fort William. Up to 700ft (213m) deep, the loch contains the largest volume of freshwater of any lake in the British Isles. Famous worldwide for its mysterious inhabitant, the Loch Ness Monster, it is also ideal for cruising and sailing.

🏛 Loch Ness 2000 — 143 B5
In Drumnadrochit on the A82, 15 miles (24km) south of Inverness. A fully automated multi-room presentation takes visitors through themed areas describing Loch Ness from the pre-history of Scotland, exploring the cultural roots of the story in Highland folklore; and into the present controversy and all the phases of investigation and exploration. Includes the world's largest inflatable and one of the world's smallest submersibles. Also Loch Ness boat trips aboard the famous Deepscan, and themed shops.
☎ 01456 450573 — www.loch-ness-scotland.com

✳ Loch Ness Clayworks — 140 A2
Bunloit, Drumnadrochit. Situated in a beautiful area with stunning views, this is a small and prolific pottery producing a wide range of colourful artistic and domestic pieces including mugs, bowls, plates, jugs, vases, oil lamps, night lights and more. Items can be purchased.
☎ 01456 450402

✳ Loch Ness, Original Visitor Centre — 140 A2
Drumnadrochit. The story of Loch Ness, the monster, and other mysteries of the area is presented in a wide-screen cinema. Various gift shops.
☎ 01456 450342 — www.lochness-centre.com

⚓ Loch Shiel Cruises — 133 E1
On the A830, 15 miles (24km) north west of Fort William. Pleasure cruises from Glenfinnan and Acharacle on Loch Shiel, one of Scotland's most beautiful and historic lochs. A wide variety of rare wildlife, best seen from the water.
☎ 01687 470322 — www.highlandcruises.co.uk

✳ Loch-an-Eilein Pottery — 141 D4
Rothiemurchus, 3 miles (5km) south west of Aviemore on the Loch-an-Eilein road. Small rural craft pottery making terracotta domestic wares, glazed in blues and greens. The pottery is situated on the Rothiemurchus estate near Aviemore. Hands-on make your own pot activity on Thursdays.
☎ 01479 810837

✳ Lochindorb — 141 E1
Unclassified road off A939, 10 miles (16km) north west of Grantown-on-Spey. On an island in this lonely loch stand the ruins of a 13th century castle, once a seat of the Comyns. It was occupied in person by Edward I in 1303 and greatly strengthened. In 1336 Edward III raised the siege in which the Countess of Atholl was beleaguered by the Regent Moray's troops. In 1371 the castle became the stronghold of the Wolf of Badenoch, the vicious Earl of Buchan who terrorised the area. The castle was dismantled in 1456.

⟳ Logie Farm Riding Centre — 149 E5
Logie Farm, Glenferness, on the A939, 10 miles (16km) from Nairn. A riding centre with quality horses and ponies. Traffic-free riding, stunning scenery, an extensive cross-country course, show jumping and dressage areas, outdoor arena and first class instruction. Riding holidays for adults or unaccompanied children.
☎ 01309 651226

🏛 Luib Croft Museum — 137 E2
Luib on the Isle of Skye. On the Broadford to Sligachan road, 36 miles (57.5km) from Dunvegan in the heart of the Cuillins. Depicts living conditions in the early 20th century. Exhibition of maps from 1750 – 2000 and information about a recently discovered Viking Farm.
☎ 01471 822427

🎭 Lyth Arts Centre — 157 E2
Lyth, 4 miles (6.5km) off the A99 between Wick and John o' Groats. Regular performances by touring drama, music and dance companies, presenting the work of professional British and international artists. Up to ten new exhibitions of contemporary fine art shown simultaneously each season, ranging from local landscapes to the work of established British and foreign artists.
☎ 01955 641270

✳ Made in Scotland — 143 E4
Station Road, Beauly, 12 miles (19km) north west of Inverness on the A862. One of Scotland's largest craft centres, housing the cream of Scottish designer and handmade products.
☎ 01463 782821

🏛 **Mallaig Heritage Centre** `137 F5`

Station Road in Mallaig centre between railway station and Marine Hotel, off the A830. Exhibits and displays all aspects of the history of Mallaig and West Lochaber – social history, crofting, fishing, railway archaeology, maritime history, and the Knoydart clearances. Children's quizzes.

☎ 01687 462085   www.mallaigheritage.org.uk

✳ **Mallaig Marine World** `137 F5`

The Harbour, Mallaig. An imaginatively laid out aquarium and exhibition featuring local marine species. A fishing display features the Mallaig fishing fleet and a video illustrates boats at work.

☎ 01687 462292

🏛 **Mary-Ann's Cottage** `157 E1`

At Dunnet, 10 miles (16km) east of Thurso. A cottage built in 1850 by John Young. The croft was successively worked by three generations of the family, ending with Mary-Ann and James Calder. All the furniture, fittings and artefacts are original, the way of life and working practices changing little over the generations.

☎ 01487 892303

🏛 **Maryck Memories of Childhood** `151 E1`

Unapool, on the A874, 0.5 mile south of Kylesku bridge, midway between Ullapool and Durness. The exhibition includes dolls, doll's houses, teddy bears and toys from 1880 to the present day. The craft shop has a range of items for sale, most made in Scotland and some handmade locally. Toys and dressing up opportunities for the under 8s (parental supervision required).

☎ 01971 502341

✳ **Meadow Well** `156 D2`

Located in Thurso this was once a major source of the local water supply and where the local fishwives gathered to sell fresh fish.

🚤 **Moray Firth Dolphin Cruises** `142 B1`

Shore Street Quay, Shore Street, Inverness. The Moray Firth dolphins are the largest resident population in Britain. Moray Firth Dolphin Cruises operate the M.V. Miss Serenity, which will carry 90 passengers in comfort. The company participates in the International Dolphin Watch programme. A good opportunity to see common and grey seals, porpoise, minke whales, terns, gannets, razor bills, kittiwakes and ospreys.

☎ 01463 717900   www.netmedia.co.uk/users/dolphins

🏛 **Nairn Museum** `149 D4`

On the A96, 15 miles (24km) from east of Inverness. A local history museum with five rooms of displays and a changing exhibition each month. Local and family history research room and children's area.

☎ 01667 456791

⚑ **Neil M. Gunn Memorial Viewpoint** `143 B2`

Heights of Brae, Strathpeffer. Memorial viewpoint for the author Neil M. Gunn, who lived nearby.

✳ **Neptune's Staircase** `134 A2`

Off the A830 at Banavie, 3 miles (4.5km) north west of Fort William. A picturesque series of eight locks, built between 1805 and 1822, which raises Telford's Caledonian Canal 64ft (19.5 m) in less than 0.5 mile (1km). There are stunning views of Ben Nevis.

✳ **Nevis Range** `134 A2`

Torlundy, on the A82, 7 miles (11km) north of Fort William. Britain's only mountain gondolas take passengers to 2150ft (655m) on Aonach Mor beside Ben Nevis. Spectacular views of the Highlands and islands. Mountain restaurant, bar and shop at 2150ft (655m). Walks. Britain's largest downhill mountain bike track with gondola access. Scotland's highest winter ski and snowboard area, ski school and ski hire (Dec – May).

☎ 01397 705825   www.nevis-range.co.uk

🦅 **Nigg Bay Bird Reserve** `143 D1`

Cromarty Firth, north of Invergordon. Bird reserve. The best access is along the shore from Barbaraville.

✳ **North Shore Pottery** `157 E5`

Mill of Forse, Latheron, south east Caithness. Studio and showroom located in a restored oatmeal mill. Visitors can see the potter at work, creating hand thrown pots, salt-glazed and reflecting the local landscape.

☎ 01593 741777

✳ **Northern Lights Candles Workshop** `143 B4`

Lentran, 5 miles (8km) west of Inverness on the A862 towards Beauly. Located in a converted crofters cowshed made from railway sleepers. Family business where a large variety of candles are handmade using simple tools, moulds and methods. Visitors can watch candles being made.

☎ 01463 831332

✳ **Northern Natural History** `153 E4`

Greenhill, on the A9, 1.5 miles (2.5km) north of Brora. Taxidermy workshop with work for sale.

☎ 01408 621500   www.nnh.co.uk/taxidermy

🏛 **Northlands Viking Centre** `157 F2`

Auckengill, Keiss, on the A99, 10 miles (16km) north of Wick. A display explaining the heritage of Caithness including the pre-Viking kingdom of the Catti and the Norse settlers. Features models of the Viking settlement at Freswick, a Viking longship and currency.

☎ 01955 607771

✳ **Old Man of Stoer** `150 C1`

2 mile (3km) walk from Stoer Lighthouse, north of Lochinver. This is the most westerly point of Sutherland and on a clear day it is possible to see the Hebridean Island of Lewis.

🏛 **Orbost Gallery** `144 B5`

4 miles (6.5km) south of Dunvegan off the A863. Paintings and prints of the landscape of Skye and adjacent highlands. Also caligraphy, wood engravings and a selection of antique prints. Picture framing service available and artist's materials on sale.

☎ 01470 521207

✳ **Orcadian Stone Company** `152 D5`

Main Street, Golspie, 60 miles (96.5km) north of Inverness on the A9. Exhibition covering 1600 square ft (488m) on two floors. The ground floor includes highland rocks, minerals and fossils, a geological model of Assynt, a diorama of Glencoul and interpretive panels. The upper floor contains worldwide minerals, chosen for beauty and scientific interest. Gift shop specialises in mineral specimens, stone giftware, semi-precious stone jewellery, geological books and maps.

☎ 01408 633483

✳ **Ord of Caithness** `153 F3`

At the hairpin bends on the A9, north of Helmsdale. From here there are spectacular views of the Caithness coastline. In the early morning or late evening, herds of red deer can often be seen.

✳ **Ord Summit** `152 A4`

West of Lairg village, Sutherland. Dotted with burial mounds, hut circles, a burnt mound (a type of ancient barbecue) and topped by two chambered cairns dating back 5000 years. The view from the summit of the Ord is stunning.

✳ **Parallel Roads** `134 C1`

Glen Roy, unclassified road off the A86, 18 miles (29km) north east of Fort William. Stretching for miles in a horseshoe curve around Glen Roy these parallel roads are gravel terraces about 30ft (9m) wide. They mark the three progressively lower levels of an ice age loch which slowly drained as the glacier damming it melted.

✳ **Plodda Falls** `139 F2`

From Drumnadrochit take the A831, turning left before Cannich onto the unclassified road to Tomich. Waterfalls 100ft (30.5m) high in the spectacular surroundings of well-established broadleaf and pine forest, south of the village of Tomich. They are particularly impressive when in spate. There are viewing platforms above and below the falls.

⚑ **Port-na-Con Souterrain** `154 D2`

0.5 miles (1km) north of Port na Con pier, near Durness. Marked by two cairns at the east side of the road, this is a well preserved souterrain (Iron Age store room). Take extreme care and enter at your own risk.

🏛 **Queen's Own Highlanders Regimental Museum** `143 D3`

At Fort George, 14 miles (22.5km) east of Inverness. A regimental museum with collections of medals, uniforms and other items showing the history of the Queen's Own Highlanders, Seaforth Highlanders, The Queen's Own Cameron Highlanders, and Lovat Scouts.

☎ 01463 224380

✳ **Quirang** `145 D3`

Off unclassified Staffin to Uig road, 19 miles (30.5km) north of Portree, Isle of Skye. An extraordinary mass of towers and pinnacles into which cattle were driven in times of trouble. A rough track (not suitable for the elderly or infirm) zigzags up to the Needle, an imposing obelisk 120ft (36.5m) high. Beyond the Needle, in a large amphitheatre, stands the Table, a huge grass-covered rock mass where it is said that Shinty used to be played. Impressive views.

🧍 **Raasay Outdoor Centre** `137 E1`

Raasay House, on Raasay, an island off Skye. A variety of activities are on offer at the centre, complemented by the island's abundance of wildlife, forestry, scenic mountains and landscapes. Qualified instruction in windsurfing, sailing, kayaking, rock climbing, abseiling, mountain biking, expeditions, forest trails, archery and orienteering. The centre, set in a Georgian Mansion is surrounded by four acres (1.6ha) of woodland and lawns.

☎ 01478 660266   www.raasayoutdoorcentre.co.uk

🌿 **Ravens Rock Forest Walk** `152 A5`

At Linsidemore on the A837. A delightful and under-frequented walk alongside the deep gorge of the Allt Mor Burn, through old mixed woods of mature conifers and beech trees. The paths are easy and there is plenty to keep children interested. The partially suspended path leads you upward to magnificent views over the burn towards Strathoykel.

✳ **Red Kite Viewing** `143 C4`

On the Black Isle at the north end of Kessock Bridge, Inverness, off the A9 northbound. The red kite is one of the most beautiful birds of prey in Europe. Using a closed-circuit television camera system, live pictures are beamed back to a monitor in the North Kessock Tourist Information Centre where RSPB staff are on hand to assist. From the comfort of the Tourist Information Centre, and safe in the knowledge that these rare birds are not being disturbed, you may have the chance to see close-up pictures of wild red kites nesting in the Highlands.

☎ 01463 731505   www.rspb.org.uk

⚑ **Red Smiddy** `146 A1`

Poolewe, north east of Gairloch on the A832. Poolewe was an important centre for early ironworking and the remains of Scotland's earliest blast furnace – the red Smiddy – lies close to the village on the banks of the River Ewe.

✱ Reelig Glen `143 B4`

At Moniack, 8 miles from Inverness. 1 mile (0.5km) south of the A862 Inverness to Beauly road. Woodland walk with viewpoint and picnic place. A feature is the number of specimen trees on the walk, with some of the tallest trees in Britain. Leaflet available from Forest Enterprise, Smithton.
☎ 01463 791575   www.forestry.gov.uk

❈ Revack Estate `141 F2`

Revack Lodge, on the B970, 1 mile (2km) south of Grantown-on-Spey. Ten miles of woodland walks and trails, adventure playground, walled garden, ornamental lakes, exotic orchid houses, stocked fishing and a garden centre in a 350 acre (141ha) sporting and farming estate.
☎ 01479 872234

✱ Rhue Beach `150 C5`

West of Ullapool. A good family beach, with safe swimming and also the possibility of catching a glimpse of seals and various sea birds.

🏛 Riverside Gallery `142 B2`

11 Bank Street, in Inverness town centre by the River Ness. Original paintings and prints by local artists. Scottish landscapes, sporting, natural history and still life are all featured.
☎ 01463 224781

✱ Rogie Falls `147 G4`

2 miles (3km) west of Strathpeffer. The word Rogie comes from the Norse language and means splashing foaming river. From the suspension bridge which spans the falls, leaping salmon may be viewed.

✱ Rossal Interpretive Trail `155 F4`

1 mile (1.5km) from the car park at Syre, on the B873 Altnaharra to Bettyhill road, Sutherland. A pre-clearance village of great historic interest. Several displays and explanations.

✱ Rothiemurchus Estate `141 D4`

Rothiemurchus, on the B970, 1.5 miles (2.5km) from Aviemore. Guided walks, Landrover safari tours with countryside rangers. A range of tours for groups to see Highland cattle, deer and the fishery, Loch an Eilein. Various photographic viewpoints. Loch and river fishing, clay pigeon shooting and off-road driving can be booked at Rothiemurchus visitor centre. Fresh and smoked trout, venison and quality foods are available from the farm shop. Quality Scottish knitwear and craftwork from the Old School shop. Card shop. Visitor centre at Loch an Eilein.
☎ 01479 812345   www.rothiemurchus.net

✱ Ruthven Barracks `140 C4`

On the B970, 0.5 mile (2km) south of Kingussie. The ruins of an infantry barracks erected in 1719 with two ranges of quarters and a stable block. Captured and burned by Bonnie Prince Charlie's army in 1746.
☎ 01667 460232   www.historic-scotland.gov.uk

✝ St Andrew's Cathedral, Inverness `142 B3`

Ardross Street, on the west bank of the River Ness, below Ness Bridge, ten minute walk from railway and bus stations. The cathedral church of the Diocese of Moray, Ross and Caithness, the first new cathedral to be completed in Britain since the Reformation. Built 1866 – 69 in the Gothic style to the design of Alexander Ross. Features twin towers with a ring of ten bells, octagonal chapter house, monolithic pillars of polished Peterhead granite, stained glass, sculpture, carved reredos, angel font after Thorvaldsen (Copenhagen), founder's memorial, icons presented by the Tsar of Russia. In beautiful riverside setting.
☎ 01463 233535

✝ St Duthus's Chapel `148 C1`

Tain. Built in the 11th or 12th century and now in ruins. Robert the Bruce's wife and daughter were captured here in 1306. James IV made an annual pilgrimage to this chapel.

🏛 St Fergus Art Gallery `157 F4`

Wick, Caithness. The gallery is situated in an attractive 19th century building that also houses the town's library and county archives. Exhibitions change regularly and include a touring exhibition and work by artists in the Highlands. All mediums are catered for, from sculpture, painting and ceramics to jewellery and handmade paper.
☎ 01955 603489

✝ St Mary's Chapel `156 C2`

Off the A836, 6 miles (9.5km) west of Thurso. A simple dry-stone chapel, probably 12th century.
☎ 01667 460232   www.historic-scotland.gov.uk

✱ Sandwood Bay `154 B2`

4 miles (6.5km) walk north from Kinlochbervie, north west Sutherland. A relatively undisturbed bay with great views. The beach is said to be haunted by a bearded mariner and is also witness to Britain's most recent recorded sighting of a mermaid.

✱ Scottish Kiltmaker Visitor Centre `142 B2`

Hector Russell Kiltmaker, 4 – 9 Huntly Street, Inverness. Scotland's only visitor attraction devoted to the kilt. You can learn all about its history and development, its tradition and culture, as well as how it is worn today. Audio-visual, costume and tartan displays create a colourful, authentic and memorable experience. You can also see kilts being made in the world's largest kiltmaking workshop.
☎ 01463 222781

⋎ Sea Eagle Viewing `145 D5`

Portree, Isle of Skye. Located in the Aros Experience. Displays and camera footage of sea eagle and grey heron nest sites. RSPB staff are present between May and September.
☎ 01478 613649   www.rspb.org.uk

⛵ Seafood Cruise `137 G2`

8 Forestry Houses, Achmore, by Kyle. Scenic boat tours offering marvellous views of the local scenery and wildlife, and a delicious meal of freshly caught fish and seafood, prepared by the seafood restaurant based in the railway building at Kyle of Lochalsh. A unique and enjoyable experience.
☎ 01599 577230

⛵ Seal Island Cruises `134 A2`

Town Pier in Fort William, next to the Crannog Restaurant, just off Fort William bypass on the shore of Loch Linnhe. A variety of boat trips. See a working salmon farm and a colony of grey and common seals on Seal Island (90 minutes), learn the history of Fort William on a cruise around the bay (50 minutes) or indulge in an evening buffet cruise with a full meal provided (90 minutes).
☎ 01374 705589   www.crannog.net

✱ Shieldaig Island `146 A4`

Situated in Loch Torridon, off Shieldaig village. This 32 acre (13ha) island is almost entirely covered in Scots pine, which once formed vast forests covering much of the Scottish Highlands.
☎ 01445 791368   www.nts.org.uk

✱ Shilasdair `144 B4`

Carnach, Waternish, Isle of Skye. 22 miles (35km) north west of Portree on the A850, then the B886. Fleece from the owner's flock of fine woolled sheep is dyed in the traditional Hebridean manner with natural dyes augmented by indigo, logwood and cochineal. A unique range of yarns are available in kits and finished garments. Dye garden, spinning workshop and dyehouse open to visitors.
☎ 01470 592297   www.shilasdair-yarns.co.uk

🏰 Sinclair & Girnigoe Castle `157 F3`

Noss Head, near Wick. Built by Earl William Sinclair in the 1470s. The older part of the castle, Girnigoe, dates from between 1476 and 1486. The new wing, locally known as Castle Sinclair, was built in 1607. The castle was largely destroyed during a siege in 1690.

♟ Sir Hector MacDonald Monument `143 B3`

Overlooking the town of Dingwall from the Mitchell Hill Cemetery. This monument was erected in memory of General Sir Hector MacDonald (1853 – 1903) who became an outstanding soldier, starting his career in the Gordon Highlanders. Known as Fighting Mac, he was born in the nearby Parish of Ferintosh.

🏰 Skelbo Castle `152 C5`

Located north of Dornoch at Skelbo. This site was probably chosen by invading Norsemen for the protection of the ships, beached on the shores of Loch Fleet, in the 9th century. The ruins can be seen from the roadside.

🏛 Skye Museum of Island Life `144 C2`

Kilmuir, on the A855, 5 miles (8km) north of Uig. An interesting museum of rural life housed within a group of thatched cottages. It depicts the lifestyle of the crofting community of the island a century or so ago and displays a wide range of agricultural tools and implements. One house is furnished with period furniture.
☎ 01470 552206

⋎ Skye Serpentarium `137 F2`

The Old Mill, Harrapool, Broadford. On the A87, 8 miles (13km) north west of Kyleakin. A unique award-winning reptile exhibition and breeding centre in a converted water mill. Visitors can watch a world of snakes, lizards, frogs and tortoises in bright natural surroundings. Also a refuge for neglected and illegally imported reptiles. Frequent informative snake handling sessions. Baby snakes for sale.
☎ 01471 822209   www.skyeserpentarium.org.uk

✱ Skyeskyns `144 B4`

Waternish, on the B886, 4.5 miles (7km) from the A850, 19 miles (30km) north of Portree. Showroom visitors are offered guided tours of the tanning workshop, the only one of its kind in Scotland. They can see the traditional tools of the trade in use – the beam, paddles, drum, buffing wheel, combs and iron. Demonstrations of rare tanning skills and hand-finishing of finest lambswool rugs. Wide range of leather goods.
☎ 01470 592237   www.skyeskyns.co.uk

✱ Smithy Heritage Centre `146 B5`

On the A896, 1 mile (2km) east of Lochcarron. A restored smithy with information on the history of the building, the business and the blacksmith who worked in it. Walk through a plantation of native trees. Speakers, demonstrations and crafts at advertised times.
☎ 01520 722246

✱ Smoo Caves `154 D2`

In Durness, Sutherland. This impressive limestone cave has formed at the head of a narrow coastal inlet. An easy and safe access path has been made from the road above leading into the cave. With its entrance at least 100ft (30m) wide this is arguably one of the largest cave entrances in Britain. A wooden pathway extends into the cave and allows viewing of the second inner chamber where the Allt Smoo falls from an opening in the roof above. In the outer cave there is an ancient midden which would indicate that Stone Age man once lived here.

⚲ Smoo Innercave Tours `154 D2`

11 Druimbhlar, Durness. A 15-minute boat trip to and walking tour of Smoo Innercave, featuring the cave and its natural history, archaeology and geology.
☎ 01971 511704

✱ Spean Bridge Woollen Mill `134 B1`

On the bridge at Spean Bridge next to Spean Bridge railway station. A picturesque weaving mill in a former farm steading. Angus McLeod, resident weaver, demonstrates his craft, weaving tartan and tweed on Hattersley pedal looms. Clan Tartan Centre, whisky tasting, Scottish knitwear, crafts and gifts.
☎ 01397 712260

✱ Spey Valley Smokehouse   `141 F2`
Achnagonalin, on the outskirts of Grantown-on-Spey on the B970. With a history of salmon smoking since 1888, the Spey Valley Smokehouse offers visitors the opportunity to experience the traditional smoking process in the most modern facilities. Gourmet salmon products available for purchase.
☎ 01479 873078

✱ Speyside Heather Centre   `141 E2`
Skye of Curr, Dulnain Bridge. Off the A95, 9 miles (14.5km) from Aviemore, 6 miles (9.5km) from Grantown-on-Spey. An exhibition, craft shop, garden centre and show garden, with heather as a speciality. Includes the famous Clootie Dumpling Restaurant and a gallery and antiques shop.
☎ 01479 851359   www.heathercentre.com

✱ Speyside Horn & Country Crafts   `141 D4`
Rowan Tree Restaurant, Loch Alvie, on the B9152, 2 miles (3km) south of Aviemore. Visitors can hear about and see the wide variety of horns used today and see a demonstration in which craftsmen show techniques developed by the Scottish tinkers (advisable to book demonstration in advance).
☎ 01479 811503   www.speyside-horn.co.uk

✱ Split Stone   `156 A2`
1 mile (1.5km) east of Melvich in the north of Sutherland. Local history says that an old woman was returning from a shopping trip and was chased by the devil. She ran round and round the stone and the devil in his temper split it. The woman escaped.

⛴ Statesman Cruises   `151 E1`
Kylesku, on the A894 between Ullapool and Cape Wrath. Cruises along a sheltered sea loch to Britain's highest waterfall, seeing seals and cubs during season. Commentary explains sights seen during the cruise.
☎ 01971 502345

✱ Storehouse of Foulis   `143 C2`
Foulis Ferry, Evanton. 16 miles (26km) north of Inverness on the A9, 1 mile (1.5km) north of Cromarty Bridge. Discover the secret of the Munro clan and explore the stories of seven centuries of land and people brought to life in the rogue's gallery. Son et lumière shows. Also information on the behaviour of seals, which visitors might see from the shore.
☎ 01349 830000   www.storehouseoffoulis.co.uk

✱ Storr   `145 D4`
Two miles (3km) from the A855, 8 miles (12.5km) north of Portree, Isle of Skye. A series of pinnacles and crags rising to 2360ft (719m). No access, but can be seen from the road. The Old Man of Storr, at the east end of the mountain, is a black obelisk, (160ft/49m) high, first climbed in 1955. Visitors can see Storr from the main road; due to erosion it is now closed to walkers.

🏛 Strathnaver Museum   `155 G2`
Clachan, Bettyhill, 12 miles (19km) east of Tongue. A local museum housed in the former parish church of Farr. Shows the story of the Strathnaver Clearances and the Clan Mackay. Collection of local artefacts, including prehistoric and Pictish items.
☎ 01641 521418

✱ Strathspey Steam Railway   `141 E3`
Aviemore Station, Dalfaber Road, Aviemore. 35 miles (56km) south of Inverness. A steam railway, re-opened in 1978, and running between Aviemore and Boat of Garten (5 miles/8km).
☎ 01479 810725   www.strathspeyrailway.co.uk

✱ Struie Viewpoint   `148 B1`
South of Dornoch Firth on the B9176. Overlooking the picturesque Dornoch Firth. The Sutherland mountains are marked on an indicator board.

✱ Studio Jewellery Workshop & Gallery   `147 D4`
At the railway station in Achnasheen. Craft centre incorporating jewellery/silversmithing workshop. Viewing windows allow visitors to watch work going on, but demonstrations are not given. Silver and gold jewellery and small silverware are on sale, together with other craft items. Rare breed sheep and ducks.
☎ 01445 720227

⛴ Summer Queen Cruises   `150 D5`
1 Royal Park, Ullapool, 55 miles (88km) north west of Inverness on the A835. Boat trips to the Summer Isles, an attractive group of islands, the largest of which is Tanera Mhor. Pleasure cruises give views of seals, birdlife and extraordinary rock formations. A four-hour cruise takes in all the Summer Isles and lands on Tanera Mhor where visitors can purchase the unique Summer Isles stamp. Also a two-hour cruise around the Isle of Martin.
☎ 01854 612472   www.summerqueen.co.uk

✱ Tain Through Time   `148 C1`
Tower Street, Tain, 1 mile (2km) off the A9. Comprises St Duthus's Chapel and Collegiate Church, which was an important medieval pilgrimage site; the Pilgrimage visitor centre with an audio-visual interpretation of the history of Tain; and Tain and District Museum offering an insight into the local history.
☎ 01862 894089   www.tainmuseum.demon.co.uk

🍾 Talisker Distillery Visitor Centre   `136 C1`
Carbost, Isle of Skye. On the B8009, just off the A863 where it joins the A87 at Sligachan. The only distillery on Skye. An exhibition tells the history of the distillery and its place in the community.
☎ 01478 614308

✱ Tarbat Discovery Centre   `149 E1`
Portmahomack. Housed in a beautifully restored 18th century church, records show that this site had a church on it as early as the 13th century. Recent archaeology has revealed the remains of a wealthy 8th century Pictish monastic community, the finds from which are displayed in the treasury. A recreated archaeological pit explains how the valuable artefacts were uncovered. St Coleman's Gallery describes how the local community has developed over the ages.
☎ 01862 871351   www.tarbat-discovery.co.uk

✱ Three Follies at Auckengill   `157 E2`
Auckengill, on the A9 Wick to John o' Groats road, 6 miles (9.5km) south of John o' Groats. The first folly on the left was a boats lantern; the second held a barometer, a log book and weather information; the third is known as Mervin's tower, built for a small boy who spent all his time with the workmen. The motto means hasten slowly.

🏛 Thurso Heritage Museum   `156 D2`
Town Hall, High Street, Thurso. A varied collection which includes historical Pictish stones, fossils, relics of the flagstone industry, local military memorabilia, and reconstructions of granny's kitchen and living room. Historical perspective of local figures in the community, and photographic history of the area.
☎ 01847 892692

✱ Timespan Heritage Centre & Art Gallery   `153 F3`
Dunrobin Street, Helmsdale, 70 miles (112.5km) north of Inverness, on the A9 to John o' Groats. Award-winning Timespan features the dramatic story of the Highlands, including Picts and Vikings, murder at Helmsdale Castle, the last burning of a witch, the Highland Clearances, the Kildonan Goldrush, and the North Sea oilfields. Scenes from the past are re-created with life-size sets and sound effects. Audio-visual presentation. Herb garden, beside Telford's bridge over the River Helmsdale. Art gallery with changing programme of exhibitions by leading contemporary artists.
☎ 01431 821327   www.timespan.org.uk

🍾 Tomatin Distillery   `140 C2`
Tomatin, just off the A9, 15 miles (24km) south of Inverness, buses from Inverness or Aviemore. One of Scotland's largest malt whisky distilleries and over one hundred years old.
☎ 01808 511444

✱ Torridon Visitor Centre   `146 B4`
Off the A896, 9 miles (14.5km) south west of Kinlochewe. Around 16,000 acres (6475ha) of some of Scotland's finest mountain scenery whose peaks rise over 3000ft (914m). Of major interest to geologists, Liathach and Beinn Alligin are of red sandstone, some 750 million years old. The visitor centre at the junction of the A896 and Diabaig road has an audio-visual presentation on the local wildlife. Deer museum (unmanned) and deer park open all year. Ranger led walks in season.
☎ 01445 791221   www.nts.org.uk

✱ Touchstone Maze   `143 A3`
Strathpeffer, west of Dingwall. A large-scale labyrinth pathway amongst standing stones and turf walls. The maze has been built to incorporate alignments with sun and moon positions.

🏛 Toy Museum   `144 B5`
Holmisdale House, Glendale, Isle of Skye. 7 miles (11km) west of Dunvegan. Award-winning toy museum, with a unique display of toys, games and dolls from Bisque to Barbie, Victorian to Star Wars. Includes Meccano's largest model, the Giant Blocksetting Crane. Also on display are early examples of Pinball.
☎ 01470 511240   www.toy-museum.co.uk

✱ Treasures of the Earth   `133 G2`
Corpach, 4 miles (6.5km) from Fort William, on the A830. This is a large collection of gemstones and crystals, displayed in recreated caverns and mines, just as they were found beneath the earth. Nuggets of gold and silver, aquamarines, red garnets, rubies, opals and diamonds are amongst many other gemstones and crystals on display, some weighing hundreds of kilos.
☎ 01397 772283

🏛 Trotternish Art Gallery   `144 D2`
Kilmaluag, Duntulm, Isle of Skye. 25 miles (40km) north of Portree on the A855. Working landscape gallery set in a beautiful part of Skye with magnificent and spectacular pinnacles and cliffs. Wide selection of originals, and mounted photographic work. All artwork exclusive to gallery.
☎ 01470 552302

🐦 Udale Bay RSPB Nature Reserve   `143 D2`
0.5 mile (1km) west of Jemimaville, Black Isle. Part of the vast spread of sand and mud deposits of Nigg and Udale Bays National Nature Reserve. Udale Bay is a mecca for birdwatchers. Herons, greylag geese, widgeon, teal, mallard, goldeneye and shelduck can all be found here in good numbers. A new hide has full disabled access and can comfortably accommodate ten people. Colourful display panels tell visitors about the varied birdlife.
☎ 01463 715000   www.rspb.org.uk

🏛 Uig Pottery   `144 D3`
Uig, Isle of Skye. A pottery making unique and functional pieces.
☎ 01470 542421   www.uigpottery.co.uk

✷ Ullapool Museum & Visitor Centre `150 D5`

7 – 8 West Argyle Street, Ullapool. Housed in an A listed historic building, a former Telford Parliamentary Church. The award-winning museum interprets the natural and human history of the Lochbroom and Coigach area. This includes the establishment of Ullapool by the British Fisheries Society in 1788 and the voyage of the Hector in 1773, the first emigrant ship to sail direct from Scotland to Nova Scotia. The museum displays objects, photographs, community tapestries and quilts, and uses audio-visual and computer technology. Maps and records are available for study. There is also a tape tour of the town.
☎ 01854 612987

✎ Urquhart Bay Wood `143 B5`

On the north shore of Loch Ness, 1 mile (1.6km) east of Drumnadrochit. Under restoration by the Woodland Trust. The wood lies between the Rivers Enrick and Coiltie and is one of the best surviving examples of ancient wet woodland in Europe. It is a habitat full of birds, mammals, fish and insects. Waymarked walks.
☎ 01764 662554   www.woodland-trust.org.uk

🏛 Urquhart Castle `140 A2`

On the A82 beside Loch Ness, 2 miles (3km) south east of Drumnadrochit. The ruins of one of the largest castles in Scotland, which fell into decay after 1689 and was blown up in 1692 to prevent it being occupied by Jacobites. Most of the existing remains date from the 16th century and include a tower. Built on the site of a vitrified fort. See also Jacobite Cruises.
☎ 01456 450551   www.historic-scotland.gov.uk

✷ Victoria Falls `146 A2`

Off the A832, 12 miles (19km) north west of Kinlochewe, near Slattadale. Waterfall named after Queen Victoria who visited Loch Maree and the surrounding area in 1877.

✷ Waltzing Waters `140 C5`

On the main street in the village of Newtonmore. Indoor water, light and music spectacular in theatrical setting.
☎ 01540 673752

⚜ Wardlaw Mausoleum `143 B4`

Kirkhill, 7 miles (11km) west of Inverness on the A862, signposted from Inchmoke. This grade A listed burial mausoleum was built in 1634 onto the east gable of the 13th century church. The mausoleum was altered in 1722 at which time a most exceptional bartran tower was added and the interior was recast to allow the incorporation of a very elaborate memorial to Thomas Fraser, the 12th Baron Lovat.
☎ 01463 831324

✷ Water Sampling Pavilion, Strathpeffer `143 A3`

Strathpeffer, west of Dingwall. An opportunity for visitors to sample the sulphur waters, which made Strathpeffer Spa renowned as a destination for Victorians.

✷ Waterlines `157 E5`

Lybster, Caithness. The visitor centre explains the natural heritage of the east Caithness coast and the history of Lybster harbour, once the third most important herring port in Scotland. Live CCTV on bird cliffs, also wooden boatbuilding display. Shower and laundry facilities for yachts.
☎ 01593 721520

✷ Well of Seven Heads `139 F4`

Off the A82 on the west shore of Loch Oich. A curious monument inscribed in English, Gaelic, French and Latin and surmounted by seven men's heads. It stands above a spring and recalls the grim story of the execution of seven brothers for the murder of the two sons of a 17th century chief of Keppoch.

✷ West Affric `139 F1`

22 miles (35.5km) east of Kyle of Lochalsh, off the A87. Stretching over 9000 acres (3642ha), this important wild and rugged landscape adjoins the NTS property at Kintail. West Affric is magnificent and challenging walking country, and includes one of the most popular east-west Highland paths. This was once the old drove road taking cattle across Scotland from the Isle of Skye to market at Dingwall.
☎ 01599 511231   www.nts.org.uk

✷ West Highland Dairy `138 A1`

Achmore, Stromeferry, Kyle. 0.3 mile (0.5km) from Achmore village. Small commercial dairy producing sheep and goat's milk cheese, an award-winning blue cheese, dairy ice cream and Cranachan, a traditional Scottish dessert. A small flock of milking sheep enable the dairy to run short courses on all aspects of dairying.
☎ 01599 577203

✷ West Highland Heavy Horses `137 F4`

Armadale Castle, Sleat, Isle of Skye. Based at Armadale Castle Gardens. Various tours in horse-drawn, traditionally built, all-weather dray: up to Armadale Castle or along the stunning coastline. Private evening bookings and training available. All visitor facilities available at Armadale Castle Gardens.
☎ 01478 660233   www.gael.net/heavyhorse

🏛 West Highland Museum `134 A2`

Cameron Square, Fort William. The museum was founded in 1922 and its collections cover all aspects of Highland life. The museum is world renowned for its Jacobite memorabilia including a secret portrait of Bonnie Prince Charlie.
☎ 01397 702169

✷ Whaligoe Steps `157 F4`

At Ulbster. Three hundred flagstone steps descend the steep cliffs to a small quay below, built in the 18th century during the herring boom. Care should be taken in wet or windy conditions – the steps are not suitable for the young or infirm.

⛨ Witch's Stone `148 D1`

In the Littletown area of Dornoch. An upright slab bearing the date 1722, marking the place where the last witch in Scotland was burned.

⛨ Wolfstone `153 E3`

Situated in a lay-by, 6 miles (9.5km) south of Helmsdale at Loth. The stone marks the spot where, in 1700, the last wolf in Scotland was killed.

✷ Working Sheepdogs `140 D4`

Leault Farm, Kincraig, Kingussie. 6 miles (10km) south of Aviemore on B9152. Displays of up to eight border collies and their skilful handlers. Traditional hand-shearing displays – visitors can participate. Also ducks, puppies and orphan lambs. Visitors can learn about the working day of a Highland shepherd.
☎ 01540 651310

✷ World of Wood `137 F2`

Old Corry Industrial Estate, Broadford, Isle of Skye. The story of a tree from a seed to the various articles created from wood. The planting, harvesting and sawmilling stages, as well as many wood craft trades are displayed. General woodworking tools are on display and some are available for use by young or old – the foot powered pole lathe can be operated by even the very young. A variety of items of wood craft are on sale.
☎ 01471 822831

Outer Islands

The Outer Islands are for those looking for a totally different holiday experience.

Although geographically separate, the Western Isles, Shetland and Orkney all share a remote scenic splendour. They also share a strong sense of history. Settlers arrived on the islands in Neolithic times and many of the archaeological remains from that era are renowned world-wide. For centuries Orkney and Shetland were also Viking strongholds and this heritage and ancestry is reflected in the people as well as their legends, myths and traditions. In the Western Isles the old Gaelic way of life lives on in crafts, language and music.

Loch Seaforth

Harris

Western Isles

The Western Isles, a 130 mile (209km) long chain of islands lying to the north west of Scotland, offer a unique experience. The combination of land, sea and loch has produced landscapes which have been designated areas of outstanding scenic value.

Map pages in this region

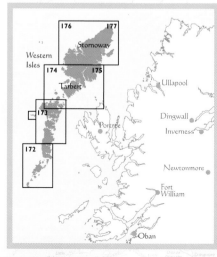

Western Isles Tourist Board

26 Cromwell Street, Stornoway, Isle of Lewis, HS1 2DD
☎ 01851 703088

www.witb.co.uk

Shetland

A cluster of over 100 islands set between Scotland and Scandinavia, Shetland shares something of the character of both countries, while guarding a rich local identity. Magnificent seascapes and fine seabird colonies are among the many features of these untamed islands.

Shetland Race weekend

Orkney

Orkney is made up of 70 islands, rich in historical and archaeological remains. Here you will find villages, burial chambers and standing stones built before the Great Pyramids of Egypt.

Old Man of Hoy, Orkney

Map pages in this region

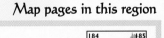

Shetland Islands Tourism

Market Cross, Lerwick,
Shetland, ZE1 0LU
☎ 01595 693434

www.visitshetland.com

Orkney Tourist Board

6 Broad Street, Kirkwall,
Orkney, KW15 1NX
☎ 01856 872856

www.visitorkney.com

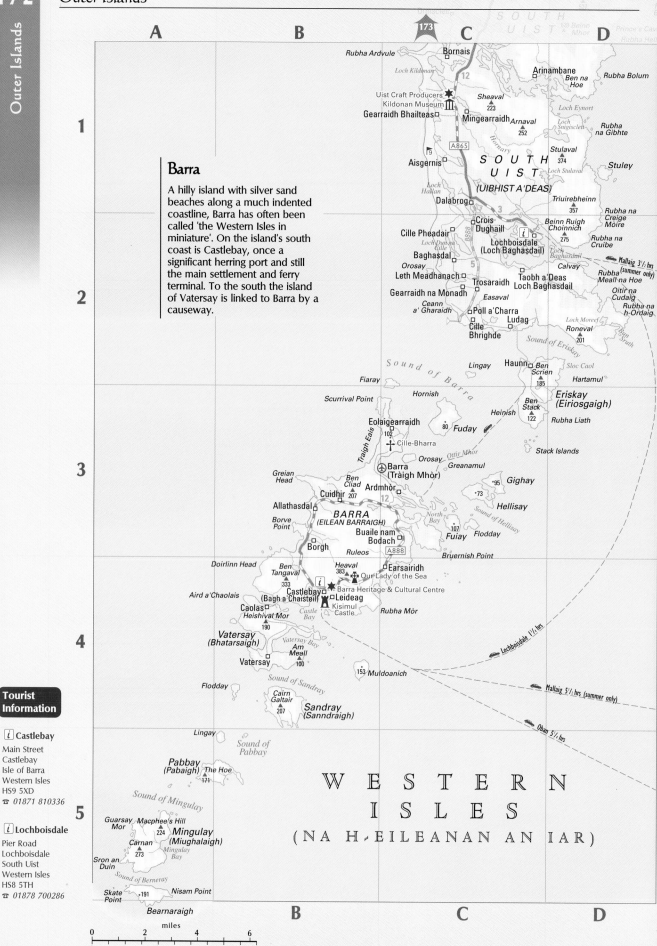

Barra

A hilly island with silver sand beaches along a much indented coastline, Barra has often been called 'the Western Isles in miniature'. On the island's south coast is Castlebay, once a significant herring port and still the main settlement and ferry terminal. To the south the island of Vatersay is linked to Barra by a causeway.

Tourist Information

i Castlebay
Main Street
Castlebay
Isle of Barra
Western Isles
HS9 5XD
☎ 01871 810336

i Lochboisdale
Pier Road
Lochboisdale
South Uist
Western Isles
HS8 5TH
☎ 01878 700286

SOUTH UIST (UIBHIST A'DEAS)

BARRA (EILEAN BARRAIGH)

Eriskay (Eiriosgaigh)

Vatersay (Bhatarsaigh)

Sandray (Sanndraigh)

Pabbay (Pabaigh)

Mingulay (Miughalaigh)

WESTERN ISLES (NA H-EILEANAN AN IAR)

miles
0 2 4 6
kilometres
0 2 4 6 8 10

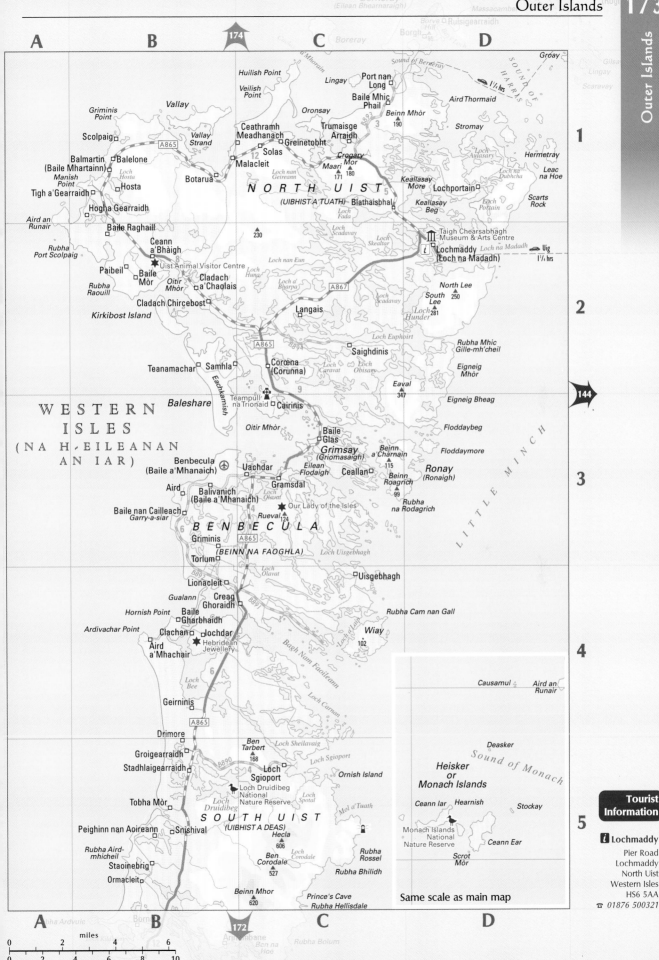

A B 174 C D

Killegray

Berneray
(Eilean Bhearnaraigh)

Massacamb

Stranndaí
(Rogh

Gilsay
Lingay
Scaravay

Sound of Berneray
Borve
Hill
Ruisigearraidh
Borgh

Groay
Groay

SOUND OF HARRAS

Huilish Point
Veilish
Point

Lingay
Port nan
Long
Baile Mhic
Phail

Aird Thormaid

Scaravay

1

Vallay

Griminis
Point

Oronsay
Trumaisge
Arraidh

Beinn Mhòr
190

Stromay

Hermetray

Scolpaig
Ceathramh
Meadhanach
Greinetobht

Loch
Aulasary

Leac
na Hoe

Balmartin
(Baile Mhartainn)
Balelone
A865
Valley
Strand
Solas
Malacleit

Crogary
Mòr
Maari
171 180

Keallasay
Mòre
Lochportain

Loch na
Dubhcha

Manish
Point
Hosta
Loch
Hosta
Botarua

NORTH UIST
(UIBHIST A'TUATH)

Blathaisbhal

Keallasay
Beg

Loch
Portain
Scarts
Rock

Tigh a'Gearraidh
Hogha Gearraidh

Loch
Fada

Aird an
Runair

Baile Raghaill

Loch
Scadavay
Loch
Skealtar
Taigh Chearsabhagh
Museum & Arts Centre

2

Rubha
Port Scolpaig

Ceann
a'Bhàigh
Uist Animal Visitor Centre

Loch
Huna
Loch nan Eun

i Lochmaddy
(Loch na Madadh)
Loch na Madadh
Uig
1¾ hrs

Paibeil
Baile
Mòr
Cladach
a'Chaolais
Loch a'
Bharpa

North Lee
250

Rubha
Raouill
Cladach Chircebost

A867
Loch
Scadavay
South
Lee
281

Rubha Mhic
Gille-mh'cheil

Kirkibost Island
Langais
Loch
Hunder

Teanamachar
Samhla
Corcena
(Corùnna)
Loch
Caravat
Loch
Obisary
Saighdinis

Eigneig
Mhòr

WESTERN
ISLES

Eachkamish

A865
9
Eaval
347

Eigneig Bheag

144

(NA H-EILEANAN
AN IAR)

Baleshare
Teampull
na Trionaid
Oitir Mhòr
Cairinis

Floddaybeg

LITTLE MINCH

Baile
Glas

Floddaymore

Benbecula
(Baile a'Mhanaich)
Uachdar
Grimsay
(Griomasaigh)
Eilean
Flodaigh
Ceallan
Beinn
a'Charnain
115

Ronay
(Ronaigh)

3

Aird
Balivanich
(Baile a'Mhanaich)
Gramsdal
Loch
Olavat
Beinn
Roagrich
99
Rubha
na Rodagrich

Baile nan Cailleach
Garry-a-siar
Rueval
124
Our Lady of the Isles

BENBECULA

Griminis
A865

Torlum
(BEINN NA FAOGHLA)
Loch Uisgebhagh

Uisgebhagh

Lionacleit

Gualann
Creag
Ghoraidh
B891
Rubha Cam nan Gall

Hornish Point
Baile
Gharbhaidh

Ardivachar Point
Clachan
Iochdar
Hebridean
Jewellery

Wiay
102

4

Aird
a'Mhachair

Bagh Nam Faoileann

Loch a'Laib

Causamul
Aird an
Runair

Loch
Bee

6

Loch Carnan

Geirinis

Deasker
Sound of Monach

Drimore
A865

Ben
Tarbert
168
Loch Sheilavaig
Loch Sgioport

Ornish Island

Heisker
or
Monach Islands

Groigearraidh
B890
4
Loch
Sgioport
Loch
Spotal

Ceann Iar
Hearnish
Stockay

Stadhlaigearraidh
Loch Druidibeg
National
Nature Reserve
Mol a'Tuath

Ceann Ear

Tobha Mòr
Loch
Druidibeg

Monach Islands
National
Nature Reserve

5

Peighinn nan Aoireann
Snishival

SOUTH UIST
(UIBHIST A DEAS)
Hecla
606
Rubha
Rossel

Scrot
Mòr

Rubha Aird-
mhicheil
Loch
Corodale

Staoinebrig
Ben
Corodale
527
Rubha Bhilidh

Same scale as main map

Ormacleit
Beinn Mhor
620
Prince's Cave
Rubha Hellisdale

A B 172 C D

Rubha Ardvule
Bornal
Rubha
na Hoè
Rubha Bolum
Sheaval

Tourist
Information

i Lochmaddy
Pier Road
Lochmaddy
North Uist
Western Isles
HS6 5AA
☎ 01876 500321

miles
0 2 4 6
0 2 4 6 8 10
kilometres

OUTER HEBRIDES

Liongam
Aird Bheag
Kearstay
Gob na h-Airde Moire
Aird Mhòr
Loch Thealasbhaidh
Loch Bodavat
Loch Benisval
Morsgail For
Sgeir Moil Duinn
Sron Romul 308
Loch Resort
Ulladale
Beinn a'Bhoth 308
Scarp
Mas a'Chnoic-chuairtich 386
Mullach na Reidheachd 295
Rapaire 453
Sgianait 425
Loch Voshimid
Stulaval 579
Huisinis
Loch a'Ghlinne Mòr
Husival Mòr 489
Tirga Mòr 679
Ullaval 659
NOR HARR
Hushinish Point
Hushinish Bay
Arda Beaga
Leosaval
Forest of Harris
Oreval 662
(CEANN A TUATH NA
Horsanish
Gobhaig
Abhainnsuidhe
Cleiseval 511
Uisgnaval Mòr 729
Mul dh
Rubha Bhuic
12
Taransay Glorigs
Soay Beg
Soay Sound
Miabhag
Bun Abhain Eadarra
West Loch Tarbert
Soay Mor
Aird Asaig
Ben Raah 267
Taransay
Beinn Dhubh 506
Taobh S
Aird Vanish
Paible
Losgaintir
Ceann Reamhar 467
Rubha Sgeirigin
Sound of Taransay
South Harris
Corran Seilebost
287
Rubha Romagi
Seilebost
Forest
Toe Head
Rubha Mas a'Chnuic
Buirgh
23
Clett Nisabost
East Stocklett 175
339 Chaipaval 365
Sgarasta Mhòr
Bulabhall 354
Heileasbhal Mòr 384
An Coileach 386
Aird Mhige
Liceasto
Leac a'Li
Shillay
Bleaval 398
SOUTH HARRIS
Clu
Traigh na Cleavag
Maodal 251
Loch Langavat
(CEANN A DEAS NA HEARADH)
Seallam! Exhibition & Genealogy Centre
Northton (Taobh Tuath)
Bràigh nam Bàgh
Aird Leimhe
Manais
Beinn a'Chàrnain 196
Fleoideabhagh
Ard Manish
Baile-na-Cille
Pabbay
Carminish Islands
Mas Garbh
Aird Mhighe
Cuidhtinis
Quinish
Loch Steiseval
Roneval 459
Boirseam
Rubha Quidnish
Ensay
Leverburgh (An T-òb)
A859
Ceann a'Bhàigh
Killegray
Cairminis
Strondeval
211
Lingarabay Island
Strannda
Rodel (Roghadal)
St Clement's Church
Berneray (Eilean Bhearnaraigh)
Rubha Vallarip
Massacamber
Renish Point
Borve Hill
Ruisigearraidh
Borgh
85
Bàgh Loch
Boreray
Gròay
Gilsay
Huilish Point
Lingay
Lingay
Port nan Long
Aird Thormaid
Scaravay
Veilish Point
Baile Mhic Phail
Stromay
Oronsay
Beinn Mhòr 190
Hermetray
Ceathramh Meadhanach
Trumaisge Arraidh
3
Greinetobht
12 Solas
Crogary Mòr 180
Keallasay More
Lochportain
Leac na Hoe
Malacleit
Maari 171
NORTH UIST
(UIBHIST A'TUATH)
Blathaisbhal
Keallasay Beg
Scarts Rock

miles
0   2   4   6
0 2 4 6 8 10
kilometres

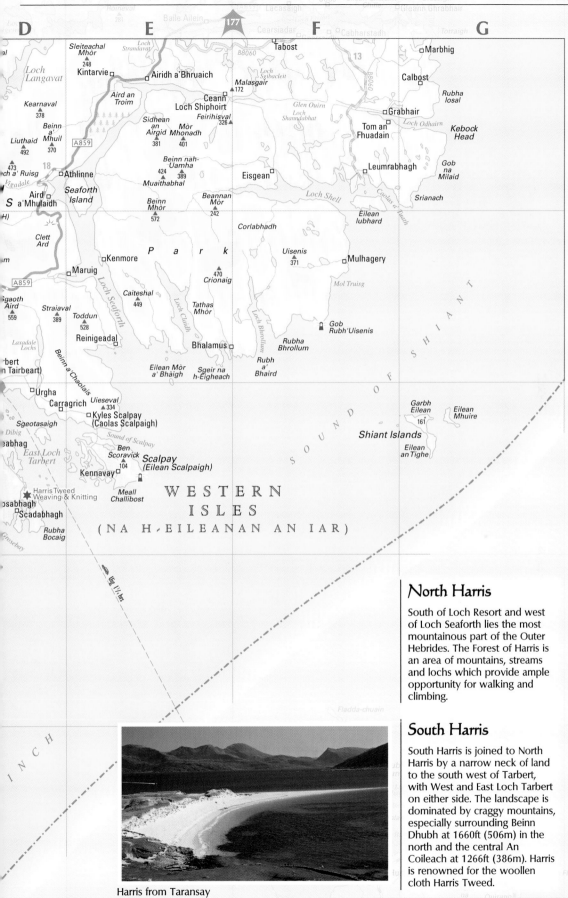

D   E   177   F   G

Loch Airich
nt A-Acla

Loch
Ceps Eilean Chaluim Orasaigh

Gleann Ghrabhair

Tabhaigh
Mhòr

207

Roineval

Baile Ailein

Lacasaigh

Cearsiadar

Cabharstadh

Torraigh

B8060

Loch Airigh
nt A-Acla

Sleiteachal
Mhòr
248

Kintarvie

Loch
Langavat

Loch
Strandavat

Airidh a'Bhruaich

B8060

13

Tabost

Marbhig

Kearnaval
378

Aird an
Troim

Beinn
a'
Mhuil
370

Liuthaid
492

A859

ch a' Ruisg
473

18

Sidhean
an
Airgid
381

Mòr
Mhonadh
401

Malasgair
172

Ceann
Loch Shiphoirt

Feirihisval
326

Loch
Sgibacleit

Calbost

Rubha
Iosal

Vigadale

Athlinne

Beinn nah-
Uamha
424

Grabhair

389

Muaithabhal

Beannan
Mòr
242

Tom an
Fhuadain

Loch
Shanndabhat

Glen Ouirn

Loch Odhairn

Kebock
Head

Seaforth
Island

Beinn
Mhòr
572

Eisgean

Leumrabhagh

Gob
na
Milaid

Aird
a'Mhulaidh

Loch Shell

Caolas a'Ruith

Srianach

Clett
Ard

P a r k

Corlabhadh

Eilean
Iubhard

gaoth
Aird
559

A859

Kenmore

Maruig

Caiteshal
449

Crionaig
470

Uisenis
371

Mulhagery

Straiaval
389

Toddun
528

Tathas
Mhòr

Mol Truisg

Reinigeadal

Bhalamus

Rubha
Bhrollum

Gob
Rubh'Uisenis

S O U N D

O F

S H I A N T

Laxadale
Lochs

Beinn a'Chaolais

Eilean Mòr
a' Bhàigh

Sgeir na
h-Eigheach

Rubh
a'
Bhaird

bert
n Tairbeart)

Urgha

Carragrich

Uieseval
334

Kyles Scalpay
(Caolas Scalpaigh)

Garbh
Eilean
161

Eilean
Mhuire

Sgeotasaigh

Dibig

Sound of Scalpay

Shiant Islands

Eilean
an Tighe

East Loch
Tarbert

eabhag

Ben
Scoravick
104

Scalpay
(Eilean Scalpaigh)

Kennavay

Harris Tweed
Weaving & Knitting

Meall
Challibost

W E S T E R N
I S L E S

osabhagh

Scadabhagh

(N A H - E I L E A N A N A N I A R)

Rubha
Bocaig

Grosebay

I N C H

Uig 1½ hrs

Fladda-chuain

North Harris

South of Loch Resort and west
of Loch Seaforth lies the most
mountainous part of the Outer
Hebrides. The Forest of Harris is
an area of mountains, streams
and lochs which provide ample
opportunity for walking and
climbing.

1

2

3

4

South Harris

South Harris is joined to North
Harris by a narrow neck of land
to the south west of Tarbert,
with West and East Loch Tarbert
on either side. The landscape is
dominated by craggy mountains,
especially surrounding Beinn
Dhubh at 1660ft (506m) in the
north and the central An
Coileach at 1266ft (386m). Harris
is renowned for the woollen
cloth Harris Tweed.

5

Harris from Taransay

Kilvaxter

Kingsburgh

Flodigarry

Tourist
Information

i **Tarbert**

Pier Road
Tarbert
Isle of Harris
Western Isles
HS3 3DG
☎ 01859 502011

D   E   F   G

Vaternish
Point

Monkstadt

Linicro

Uig

Balgown

Sùidh'
a' Mhinn

Quiraing

The
Needle

Digg

Staffin Island

Stenscholl

Staffin

Rubha Garbhaig

Kilt Rock

Brògaig

Bhaltos

Brida
Buidhe

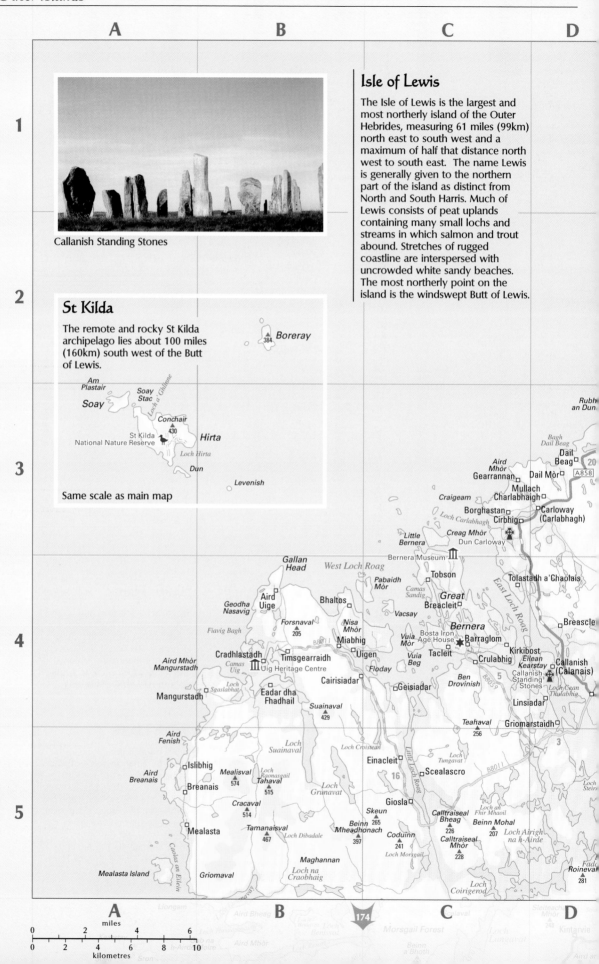

Callanish Standing Stones

Isle of Lewis

The Isle of Lewis is the largest and most northerly island of the Outer Hebrides, measuring 61 miles (99km) north east to south west and a maximum of half that distance north west to south east. The name Lewis is generally given to the northern part of the island as distinct from North and South Harris. Much of Lewis consists of peat uplands containing many small lochs and streams in which salmon and trout abound. Stretches of rugged coastline are interspersed with uncrowded white sandy beaches. The most northerly point on the island is the windswept Butt of Lewis.

St Kilda

The remote and rocky St Kilda archipelago lies about 100 miles (160km) south west of the Butt of Lewis.

Am Plastair
Soay Stac
Soay
Loch a' Ghlinne
Boreray
384
Conchair
430
St Kilda
National Nature Reserve
Hirta
Loch Hirta
Dun
Levenish

Same scale as main map

Aird Mhòr
Gearrannan
Dail Mòr
Dail Beag
A858
20
Bagh Dail Beag
Rubh an Dun
Craigeam
Mullach Charlabhaigh
Borghastan
Loch Carlabhagh
Cirbhig
Carloway (Carlabhagh)
Little Bernera
Creag Mhòr
Dun Carloway
Bernera Museum
Tobson
Tolastadh a'Chaolais
Gallan Head
West Loch Roag
Pabaidh Mòr
Camas Sandig
Great Breacleit
East Loch Roag
Breasclet
Aird Uige
Bhaltos
Geodha Nasavig
Forsnaval
205
Nisa Mhòr
Vacsay
Bernera
Bosta Iron Age House
Barraglom
Kirkibost
Fiavig Bagh
B8011
Miabhig
Vuia Mòr
Tacleit
Crulabhig
Eilean Kearstay
Callanish (Calanais)
Aird Mhòr Mangurstadh
Cradhlastadh
Camas Uig
Timsgearraidh
Uig Heritage Centre
Uigen
Vuia Beg
Floday
Ben Drovinish
B8059
Callanish Standing Stones
5
Loch Cean Thulabhig
Mangurstadh
Loch Sgaslabhat
Eadar dha Fhadhail
Cairisiadar
Geisiadar
Linsiadar
Suainaval
429
Teahaval
256
Griomarstaidh
Aird Fenish
Loch Suainaval
Loch Croistean
Little Loch Roag
Loch Tungavat
B8011
3
Islibhig
Mealisval
574
Loch Raonasgail
Tahaval
515
Loch Grunavat
Einacleit
Scealascro
16
Loch Steir
Aird Breanais
Breanais
Cracaval
514
Giosla
Skeun
265
Calltraiseal Bheag
226
Beinn Mohal
207
Loch an Fhir Mhaoil
Loch Airigh na h-Airde
Mealasta
Tamanaisval
467
Loch Dibadale
Beinn Mheadhonach
397
Coduinn
241
Calltraiseal Mhòr
228
Loch Morsgail
Fada Roineval
281
Mealasta Island
Griomaval
Maghannan
Loch na Craobhaig
Loch Coirigerod

miles
0   2   4   6
0 2 4 6 8 10
kilometres

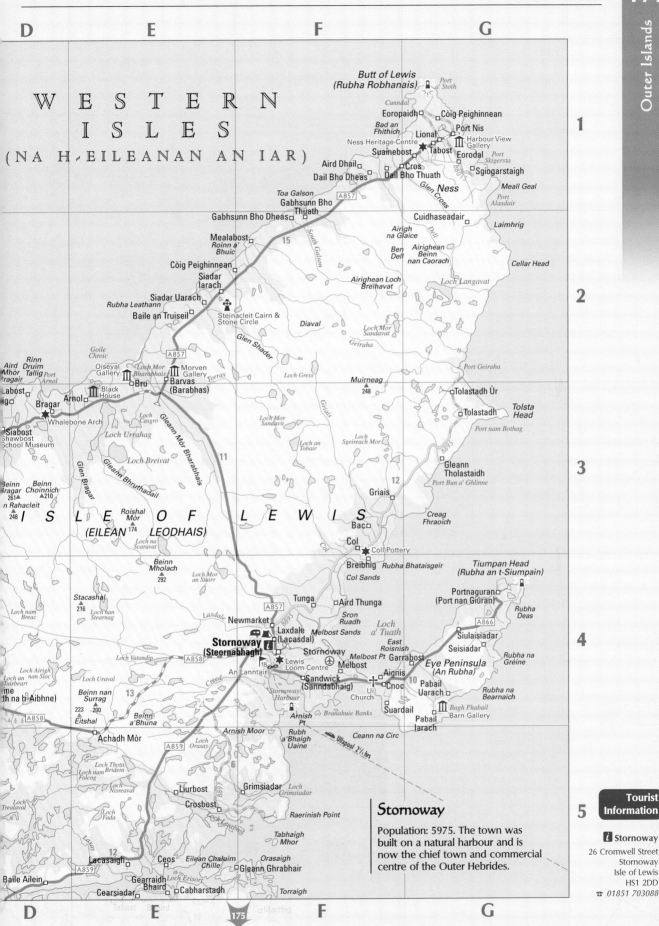

D E F G

W E S T E R N
I S L E S
(NA H'EILEANAN AN IAR)

Butt of Lewis
(Rubha Robhanais)
Port a' Stoth

1

Cunndal
Europaidh
Còig Peighinnean
Bad an
Fhithich
Port Nis
Lional
Harbour View
Gallery
Ness Heritage-Centre
Suainebost Tabost
Eorodal
Aird Dhail
Dail Bho Thuath Sgiogarstaigh
Dail Bho Dheas Cros
Port Skigersta
Glen Cross Ness
Meall Geal
Port Alasdair

Toa Galson
Gabhsunn Bho
Thuath
A857
Cuidhaseadair
Laimhrig
Gabhsunn Bho Dheas
Mealabost
Roinn a'
Bhuic
15
South Galson
Airigh
na Glaice
Ben
Dell
Airighean
Beinn
nan Caorach
Cellar Head

2

Còig Peighinnean
Siadar
Iarach
Siadar Uarach
Rubha Leathann
Baile an Truiseil
Steinacleit Cairn &
Stone Circle
Diaval
Airighean Loch
Breihavat
Loch Mor
Sandavat
Geiraha
Loch Langavat
Port Geiraha

Glen Shader
Loch Gress
Muirneag
248
Tolastadh Ùr
Tolsta
Head

Goile
Chroic
A857
Torray
Griais
Loch Mor
Sanduvit
Loch an
Tobair
Tolastadh
Port nam Bothag

Rinn
Aird
Mhòr
Druim
Tallig
Port
Arnol
Oiseval
Gallery
Loch Mor
Bharabhais
Morven
Gallery
Bru Barvas
(Barabhas)

Labost
Arnol
Black
House
Whalebone Arch
Loch
Casgro
Loch Urrahag
Loch Sgeireach Mor
Gleann Tholastaidh
Port Bun a' Ghlinne

3

Bragar
Siabost
Shawbost
School Museum
Loch Breivat
11
Griais
Creag
Fhraoich

Beinn
Bragar
261
Beinn
Choinnich
210
n Rahacleit
248
Gleann Bhruthadail
Glen Bragar
Gleann Mòr Bharabhais
Roishal
Mòr
174
Loch na
Scaravat

I S L E   O F   L E W I S
(EILEAN   LEODHAIS)
12
Griais
Baç
Col
Coll Pottery

Beinn
Mholach
292
Loch Mor
an Stairr
Breibhig
Col Sands
Rubha Bhataisgeir
Tiumpan Head
(Rubha an t-Siumpain)

Stacashal
216
Loch nan
Stearnag
Laxdale
Tunga
Aird Thunga
A857
Sron
Ruadh
Melbost Sands
Loch
a' Tuath
Portnaguran
(Port nan Giùran)
Rubha
Deas

Loch nam
Breac
Newmarket
B895
Laxdale
(Lacasdal)
Stornoway
Melbost Pt
East
Roisnish
Garrabost
A866
Siulaisiadar
Seisiadar
Rubha na
Gréine

4

Loch Airigh
nan Sloc
Loch an
Tairbeart
h na h-Aibhne)
A858
Beinn nan
Surrag
13
Loch Vatandip
A858
Stornoway
(Steornabhagh)
Lewis
Loom Centre
18
An Lanntair
Aignis
Melbost
Cnoc
Ui
Church
Eye Peninsula
(An Rubha)
Pabail
Uarach
Rubha na
Bearnaich

me
223
200
Beinn
a'Bhuna
Eitshal
Creed
Sandwick
(Sanndabhaig)
10
Suardail
Pabail
Iarach
Bagh Phabail
Barn Gallery

Achadh Mòr
A859
Loch
Orasay
6
Arnish Moor
Rubh
a'Bhaigh
Uaine
Ullapool 2¼ hrs
Ceann na Circ
Stornoway
Harbour
Arnish
Pt
Brànahuie Banks

Loch Thota
Loch nam
Falcag
Loch
Nisreaval
B897
Liurbost
Grimsiadar
Loch
Grimsiadar

5

Loch
Trealaval
Crosbost
Raerinish Point
Stornoway

Population: 5975. The town was
built on a natural harbour and is
now the chief town and commercial
centre of the Outer Hebrides.

Loch
Fada
Tabhaigh
Mhor

Loxay
12
Lacasaigh
A859
Ceos
Eilean Chaluim
Chille
Orasaigh
Gleann Ghrabhair
Baile Ailein
Cearsiadar
Gearraidh
Bhaird
Cabharstadh
Loch Erisort
Torraigh

D E F G

**Tourist
Information**

i **Stornoway**
26 Cromwell Street
Stornoway
Isle of Lewis
HS1 2DD
☎ 01851 703088

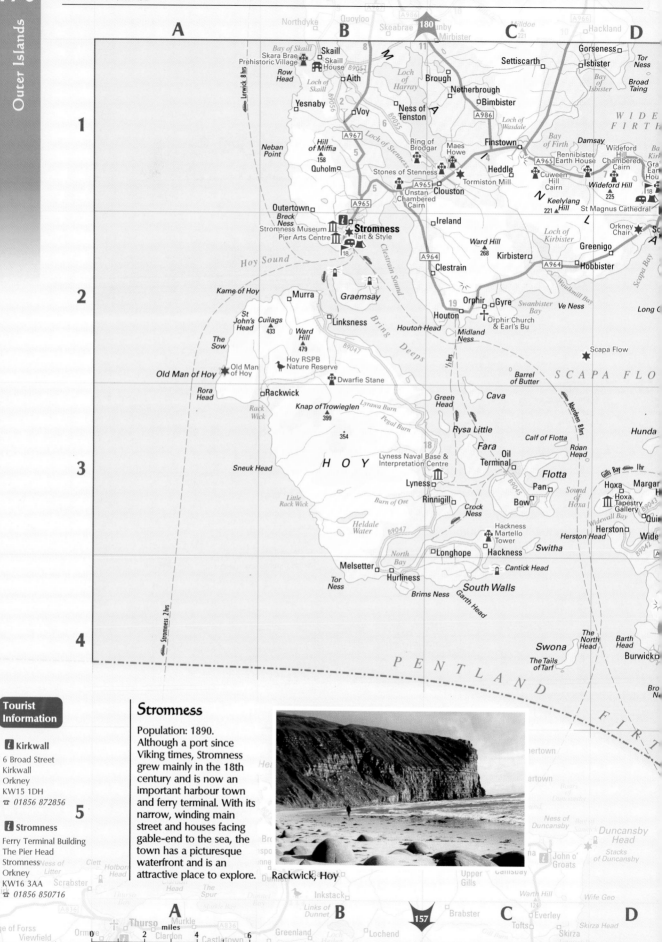

Rackwick, Hoy

Tourist Information

ℹ️ **Kirkwall**

6 Broad Street
Kirkwall
Orkney
KW15 1DH
☎ 01856 872856

ℹ️ **Stromness**

Ferry Terminal Building
The Pier Head
Stromness
Orkney
KW16 3AA
☎ 01856 850716

Stromness

Population: 1890.
Although a port since Viking times, Stromness grew mainly in the 18th century and is now an important harbour town and ferry terminal. With its narrow, winding main street and houses facing gable-end to the sea, the town has a picturesque waterfront and is an attractive place to explore.

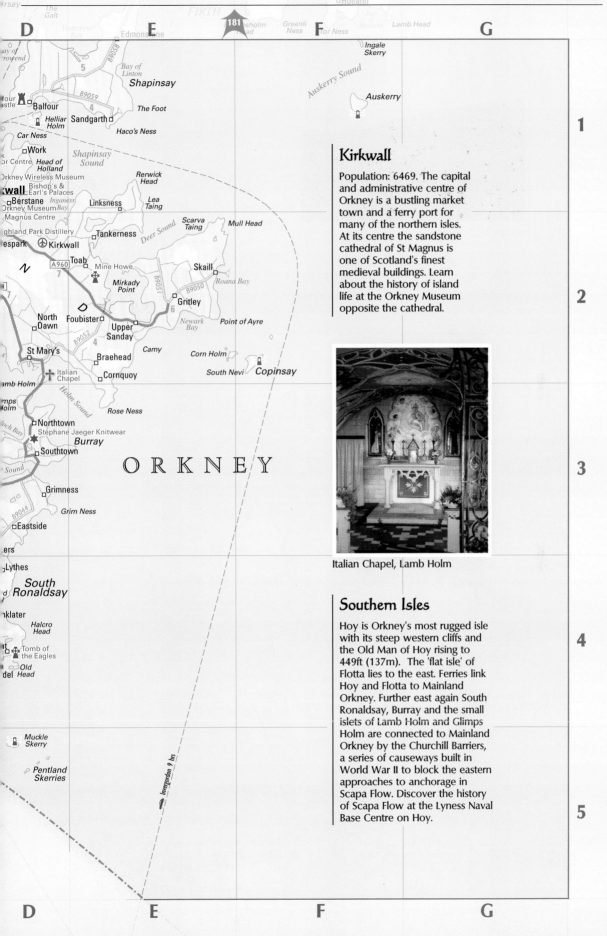

Kirkwall

Population: 6469. The capital and administrative centre of Orkney is a bustling market town and a ferry port for many of the northern isles. At its centre the sandstone cathedral of St Magnus is one of Scotland's finest medieval buildings. Learn about the history of island life at the Orkney Museum opposite the cathedral.

Italian Chapel, Lamb Holm

Southern Isles

Hoy is Orkney's most rugged isle with its steep western cliffs and the Old Man of Hoy rising to 449ft (137m). The 'flat isle' of Flotta lies to the east. Ferries link Hoy and Flotta to Mainland Orkney. Further east again South Ronaldsay, Burray and the small islets of Lamb Holm and Glimps Holm are connected to Mainland Orkney by the Churchill Barriers, a series of causeways built in World War II to block the eastern approaches to anchorage in Scapa Flow. Discover the history of Scapa Flow at the Lyness Naval Base Centre on Hoy.

Faraclett Head, Rousay

ORKNEY

The Bore

Mull Head

Papa Westra

Papa Sound

Bow Head

Aikerness

Papa Westray

Knap of Howar

Holland

Holm of Pa

Westray

Holm of Papay Chambered Cair

Noup Head

Rackwick

St. Mary's Medieval Church

Backaskaill

Ouse Ness

Head of Moclett

Gentlemens' Cave

Noltland Castle

Pierowall

Westray Heritage Centre

Broughton

Braehead

Spo Ness

Monivey

Bis Geos

Westray

4

B9067

Skelwick

8

B9066

Inga Ness

Midbea

Bay of Tuquoy

Stanger Head

Langskaill

Cross Kirk Medieval Parish Church & Norse Settlement

Berst Ness

Twiness

Rapness

Skea Skerries

WESTRAY FIRTH

Point of Huro

1½ hrs (summer only)

Rapness Sound

Faray

Sacquoy Head

Saviskaill Head

Rusk Holm

Fers Ness

Bring Head

Saviskaill Bay

Faraclett Head

Eday

Rousay

Wasbister

B9064

Kili Holm

Sou

Costa Head

Muckle Water

Sourin

Mae Ness

Skea

Midhowe Broch & Cairn

Taversoe Tuick Chambered Cairn

St Magnus Church

Egilsay

Geo Lu

Brough Head

Brough of Birsay

Eynhallow

Westness

Blotchnie Fiold

250

9

Fall of War

A966

Abune-the-Hill

Costa

Knowe of Yarso Chambered Cairn

Brinian

Rousay Sound

Earl's Palace

Birsay

Eynhallow Church

Blackhammer Cairn

Muckle Green Holm

Birsay Bay

Loch of Swannay

Broch of Gurness

Eynhallow Sound

Cubbie Roo's Castle

Marwick Head

Loch of Boardhouse

Evie

Aiker Ness

Wyre

Marwick

Kirbuster

Redland

Wood Wick

Gairsay Sound

Sweyn Holm

Ness

Outshore Point

A967

Twatt

Burn of B9057

Tingwall

Shapinsay

Isbister

Loch of Hundland

Hillside

Gairsay

The Galt

Northdyke

B9056

9

Quoyloo

A967

Beaquoy

10

Click Mill

Milldoe 221

A966

10

Hackland

Veantrow Bay

Edmons

Skeabrae

A986

Dounby

Mirbister

Gorseness

Bay of Furrowend

B9058

Bay o Linte

Bay of Skaill

Skaill

8

11

Settiscarth

Isbister

Tor Ness

Balfour Castle

Balfour

Skara Brae Prehistoric Village

Skaill House

Brough

Broad Taing

Bay of Isbister

5

4

Row Head

B9057

Loch of Skaill

Netherbrough

Helliar Holm

Sandgarth

B9059

Aith

Loch of Harray

Bimbister

Haco's N

Yesnaby

A967

Voy

Ness of Tenston

A986

Loch of Wasdale

WIDE FIRTH

Bay of Kirkwall

Work

Car Ness

Shapinsay Sound

Ren

Neban Point

Hill of Miffia 158

Quholm

5

Ring of Brodgar

Maes Howe

Finstown

Bay of Firth

Damsay

Rennibister Earth House

Wideford Hill Chambered Cairn

Grain Earth House

Ortak Visitor Centre

Head of Holland

Orkney Wireless Museum

5

A967

Stones of Stenness

Loch of Stenness

Tormiston Mill

Heddle

A965

Cuween Hill Cairn

Wideford Hill 225

18

Kirkwall

Bishop's & Earl's Palaces

Orkney Museum

Berstane

Inganess Bay

Linksness

Outertown

A965

Unstan Chambered Cairn

Clouston

Keelylang Hill 221

St Magnus Cathedral

Orkney Chair

178

Greenigo

Orkney Museum

Scapa

St Magnus Centre

Highland Park Distillery

Rer

Breck Ness

Stromness Museum

Pier Arts Centre

Stromness

Tall & Style

miles

Ward Hill 268

Kirbister

Loch of Kirbister

Tradespark

Hobbister

Kirkwall

Toab

Mine Howe

A961

A964

Clestrain

Ireland

Outertown

0   2   4   6
miles

0   2   4   6   8   10
kilometres

Tourist Information

i **Kirkwall**

6 Broad Street
Kirkwall
Orkney
KW15 1DH
☎ 01856 872856

D E F G

1

North Ronaldsay
Point of Sinsoss
Tor Ness
North Ronaldsay
Hollandstoun
Linklet Bay
Bride's Ness
South Bay
Strom Ness

2

North Ronaldsay Firth

3 hrs (summer only)
Holms of Ire
THE NORTH SOUND
Whitemill Point
Tofts Ness
Scar
Burness
Otters Wick
Sandquoy
North Loch
Scuthvie Bay
North Bay
B9068
B9069
Bay of Lopness
Start Point
4
7
Newark
Broughtown
Sanday
Roadside
Cata Sand
Sanday
Overbister
Red Head
Grey Head
Calf of Eday
B9070
Kettletoft
Sty Wick
Bay of Newark
ick House
Calfsound
4
Backaskail Bay
Quoy Ness
Quoyness Chambered Tomb
Els Ness
Tres Ness

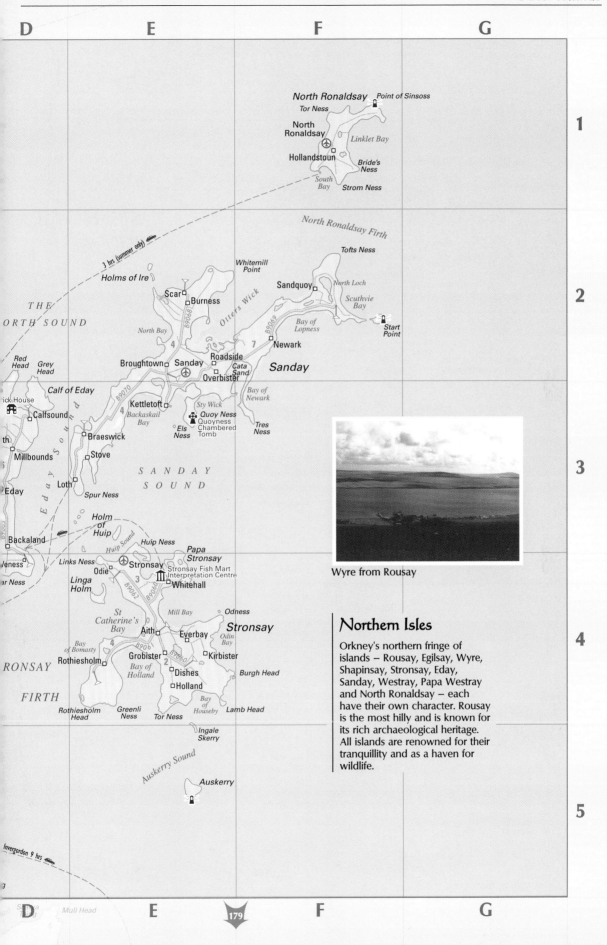
Wyre from Rousay

Braeswick
Millbounds
Stove
SANDAY SOUND
3
Eday
Loth
Spur Ness

Holm of Huip
Backaland
Huip Sound
Huip Ness
Papa Stronsay
Links Ness
Odie
Stronsay
Stronsay Fish Mart Interpretation Centre
Whitehall
eness
ar Ness
Linga Holm
B9062
B9060

St Catherine's Bay
Mill Bay
Odness
Aith
Everbay
Stronsay
Odin Bay
4
RONSAY FIRTH
Bay of Bomasty
Rothiesholm
4
B9061
Grobister
2
B9060
Kirbister
Bay of Holland
Dishes
Holland
Burgh Head
Rothiesholm Head
Greenli Ness
Tor Ness
Bay of Houseby
Lamb Head

Ingale Skerry

Auskerry Sound
Auskerry

Northern Isles

Orkney's northern fringe of islands – Rousay, Egilsay, Wyre, Shapinsay, Stronsay, Eday, Sanday, Westray, Papa Westray and North Ronaldsay – each have their own character. Rousay is the most hilly and is known for its rich archaeological heritage. All islands are renowned for their tranquillity and as a haven for wildlife.

5

Invergordon 9 hrs

D E F G

Mull Head
Skaill

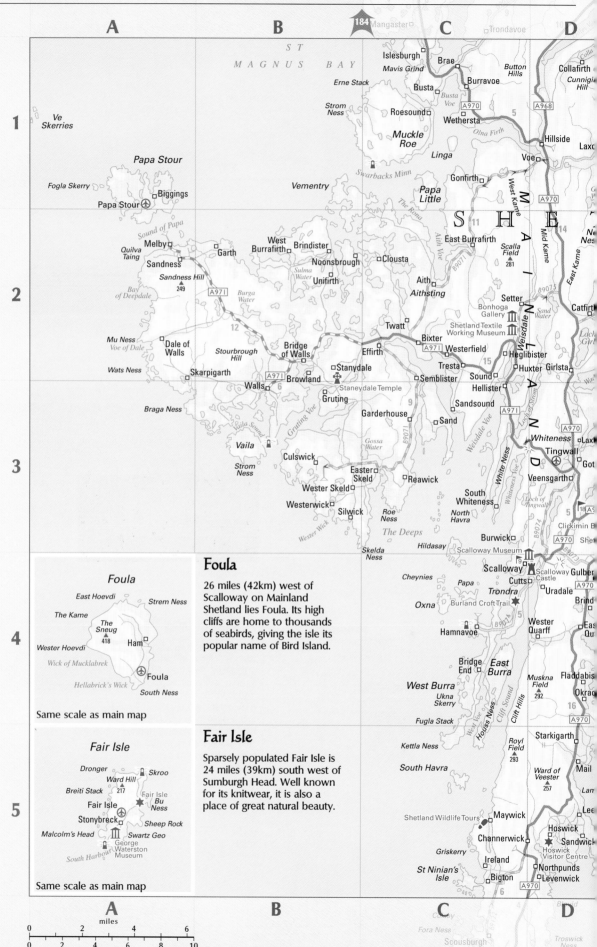

St MAGNUS BAY

Ve Skerries

Papa Stour

Fogla Skerry

Biggings

Papa Stour

Sound of Papa

Melby

Quilva Taing

Garth

Sandness

Sandness Hill 249

Bay of Deepdale

Burga Water

Mu Ness

Voe of Dale

Dale of Walls

Stourbrough Hill

Wats Ness

Skarpigarth

Braga Ness

West Burrafirth

Brindister

Noonsbrough

Vementry

Sulma Water

Unifirth

Bridge of Walls

Browland

Walls

Stanydale

Staneydale Temple

Gruting

Vaila

Culswick

Strom Ness

Vaila Sound

Gruting Voe

Wester Skeld

Easter Skeld

Reawick

Westerwick

Silwick

Wester Wick

Roe Ness

Gossa Water

The Deeps

Skelda Ness

Islesburgh

Brae

Mavis Grind

Busta

Burravoe

Button Hills

Collafirth

Cunnigi Hill

Erne Stack

Strom Ness

Busta Voe

A970

Roesound

Wethersta

A968

Muckle Roe

Linga

Olna Firth

Hillside

Laxe

Swarbacks Minn

Voe

The Rona

Gonfirth

West Kame

A970

Vementry

Papa Little

SHE

11

East Burrafirth

Scalla Field 281

Mid Kame

N Ne

East Kame

Clousta

Aith

Aithsting

B9071

Setter

Catfirt

Bonhoga Gallery

Shetland Textile Working Museum

Sand Water

Loch Girl

Twatt

Bixter

A971

Westerfield

Heglibister

Huxter

Girlsta

Effirth

Tresta

Sound

15

Semblister

Hellister

Stanydale

Whiteness

Laxe

Sandsound

A971

Tingwall

Sand

Garderhouse

Weisdale Voe

Veensgarth

Got

Whiteness Voe

South Whiteness

North Havra

Loch of Tingwall

5

18 A9

Burwick

Clickimin B

B9074

A970

She

Hildasay

Scalloway Museum

184 Mangaster

Mangaster

Trondavoe

Collaf

Sullom

Graven

Foula

26 miles (42km) west of Scalloway on Mainland Shetland lies Foula. Its high cliffs are home to thousands of seabirds, giving the isle its popular name of Bird Island.

Cheynies

Papa

Oxna

Burland Croft Trail

Scalloway Castle

Scalloway

Cutts

Gulber

Uradale

A970

Trondra

Brind

Hamnavoe

B9074

Wester Quarff

Eas Qu

Bridge End

East Burra

Muskna Field 292

Fladdabis

Okra

West Burra

Ukna Skerry

16

A970

Fugla Stack

Houss Ness

Cliff Sound

Cliff Hills

Fair Isle

Sparsely populated Fair Isle is 24 miles (39km) south west of Sumburgh Head. Well known for its knitwear, it is also a place of great natural beauty.

Kettla Ness

Royl Field 293

Starkigarth

South Havra

Ward of Veester 257

Mail

Larr

Lee

Shetland Wildlife Tours

Maywick

Hoswick

Sandwick

Channerwick

Hoswick Visitor Centre

Griskerry

Ireland

St Ninian's Isle

Bigton

A970

Northpunds

Levenwick

6

Fora Ness

Scousburgh

Skelberry

Troswick Ness

Foula (inset)

East Hoevdi

The Kame

Strem Ness

The Sneug 418

Wester Hoevdi

Ham

Wick of Mucklabrek

Foula

Hellabrick's Wick

South Ness

Same scale as main map

Fair Isle (inset)

Dronger

Skroo

Ward Hill 217

Breiti Stack

Fair Isle

Bu Ness

Stonybreck

Sheep Rock

Malcolm's Head

Swartz Geo

George Waterston Museum

South Harbour

Same scale as main map

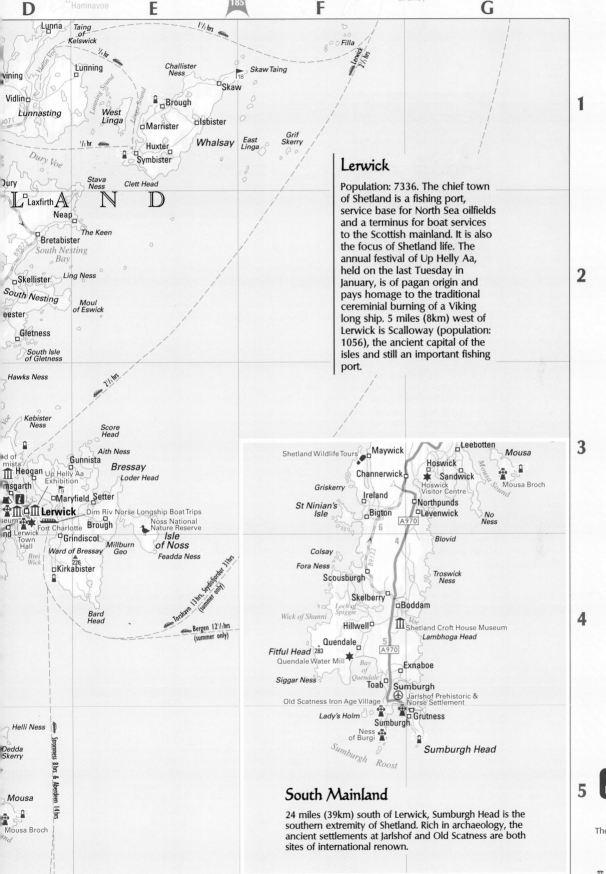

185

D   E   F   G

Linga
Holm

Out Skerries   Bruray
Housay   Out Skerries
Grunay

Hamnavoe

Lunna Ness
Lunna Voe

Lunna
Taing of Kelswick
1¼ hrs
Filla

Valla Voe
vining
Lunning   ¼ hr
Challister Ness
18   Skaw Taing

Lerwick 2½ hrs

Vidlin
Brough   Skaw
Lunnasting   West Linga
Marrister   Isbister
Huxter   Whalsay

1

Dury Voe
½ hr   Symbister
East Linga
Grif Skerry

Stava Ness
Clett Head

Dury
Laxfirth   N   D
Neap   The Keen
Bretabister
South Nesting Bay

Skellister   Ling Ness
South Nesting
eester   Moul of Eswick
Gletness
South Isle of Gletness

2

Lerwick

Population: 7336. The chief town of Shetland is a fishing port, service base for North Sea oilfields and a terminus for boat services to the Scottish mainland. It is also the focus of Shetland life. The annual festival of Up Helly Aa, held on the last Tuesday in January, is of pagan origin and pays homage to the traditional cereminial burning of a Viking long ship. 5 miles (8km) west of Lerwick is Scalloway (population: 1056), the ancient capital of the isles and still an important fishing port.

Hawks Ness
2½ hrs
Kebister Ness
Score Head
Aith Ness
d of mista   Gunnista   Bressay
Heogan   Up Helly Aa Exhibition   Loder Head
nsgarth
Maryfield   Setter
Lerwick   Dim Riv Norse Longship Boat Trips
seum   Fort Charlotte   Brough
nd   Lerwick Town Hall   Grindiscol   Noss National Nature Reserve
Brei Wick   Ward of Bressay   Millburn Geo   Isle of Noss
226   Feadda Ness
Kirkabister

Torsham 13hrs, Seydisfjordur 31hrs (summer only)
Bergen 12½ hrs (summer only)

Bard Head

3

Leebotten
Shetland Wildlife Tours   Maywick   Mousa
Hoswick
Channerwick   Sandwick
Griskerry   Mousa Broch
Ireland   Hoswick Visitor Centre   Mousa Sound
St Ninian's Isle   Bigton   Northpunds
Levenwick   No Ness
A970

Colsay   Blovid
Fora Ness   6   4
Scousburgh   Troswick Ness
Skelberry
Loch of Spiggie   Boddam
Wick of Shunni   Hillwell   Voe
Shetland Croft House Museum
A970   Lambhoga Head
Quendale   5
Fitful Head   283
Quendale Water Mill   Exnaboe
Bay of Quendale
Siggar Ness   Toab   Sumburgh
Old Scatness Iron Age Village   Jarlshof Prehistoric & Norse Settlement
Lady's Holm   Sumburgh   Grutness
Ness of Burgi   Sumburgh Head
Sumburgh Roost

4

South Mainland

24 miles (39km) south of Lerwick, Sumburgh Head is the southern extremity of Shetland. Rich in archaeology, the ancient settlements at Jarlshof and Old Scatness are both sites of international renown.

Stromness 8 hrs & Aberdeen 14 hrs

Helli Ness
Dedda Skerry
Mousa
Mousa Broch

5

Tourist Information

Lerwick
The Market Cross
Lerwick
Shetland
ZE1 0LU
☎ 01595 693434

D   E   F   G

	A	B	C	D

Shetland puffins

Unst

S H E T L A

North Shetland

Yell, Unst and Fetlar are all linked to each other and to Mainland Shetland by ferry. Green and fertile Fetlar is known as 'The Garden of Shetland', it is a sparsely inhabited island of pastoral farmland. Yell is an island of wild moor where coastal walks give the opportunity to spot whales, seals, otters and dolphins. Unst is the most northerly isle; its indented coastline offers both towering cliffs and beautiful beaches.

Geo

Ramna Stacks

Gruney

Garmus Taing   Point of Fethaland

Uyea   Whale Geo

Hellir

Y

E

L

L

South Wick   Isbister

A970

Hevdadale Head   North Roe   S

North Roe   Burra Voe   O

Muckle Holm   U

The Castle   N

Roer Water   9   D

The Faither   Head of Broug

Muckle Ossa   Housetter

Ronas Hill   Neap of Skea   Ness of Sour

450   Collafirth   Colla Firth

The Clifts   A970   Quey Firth   Brother Isle

Head of Stanshi   Hamnavoe   Heylor   Voe   Ollaberry   Lamba

Esha Ness   Ure   Braehoulland   Eela Water   5   Uynarey

Tangwick Haa Museum   10   Burnside   A970   Urafirth   Gluss Isle   Little Roe

B9078   Tangwick   B9079   Brough   Toft

Stenness   Hillswick   Gluss   Bardister

Brae Wick   4   Sullom Voe Oil Terminal   Mossba

Baa Taing   Burraland   Firt

Isle of Nibon   Uro Firth   A970   Sullom   A9

ST MAGNUS BAY   8   Graven

Sullom Voe   9

Mangaster   Orka Voe   Trondavoe   10   Dales Voe

Islesburgh   Brae

Mavis Grind   Button Hills

ST   Collafirth

MAGNUS BAY   Busta   Burravoe   Cunnigill Hill

Erne Stack

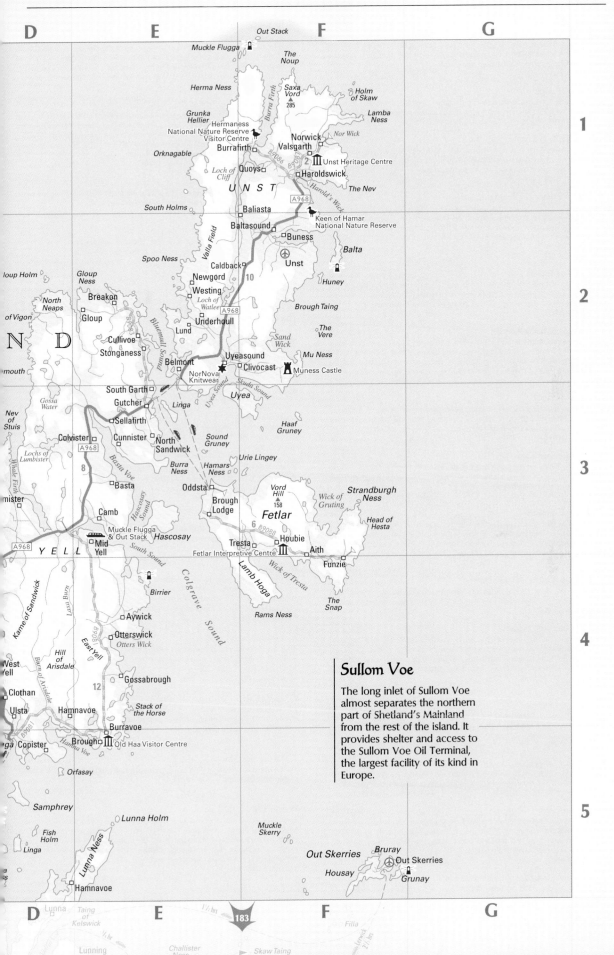

Sullom Voe

The long inlet of Sullom Voe almost separates the northern part of Shetland's Mainland from the rest of the island. It provides shelter and access to the Sullom Voe Oil Terminal, the largest facility of its kind in Europe.

An Lanntair 177 F4

Town Hall, South Beach, Stornoway, Isle of Lewis. On the seafront in Stornoway adjacent to ferry and bus station. The main public arts facility in the Western Isles since 1985. A forum for local, national and international arts, promoting a diverse year-round programme of exhibitions and events.
☎ 01851 703307   www.lanntair.com

Balfour Castle 179 D1

Shapinsay Island, Orkney. Guided tours by member of family around this Victorian castle with original furnishings and 3 acre (1.2ha) walled garden.
☎ 01856 711282

Barn Gallery, The 177 G4

Eagleton, Lower Bayble (Pabail Iarach), Isle of Lewis. 6 miles (10km) from Stornoway on the Eye Peninsula. A small gallery displaying the original work of four artists, in watercolour, oil, pastel, acrylic and liquid wax.
☎ 01851 870704

Barra Heritage & Cultural Centre 172 B4

Dualchas, 0.3 mile (0.5km) west of Castlebay pier. Local history exhibition in Gaelic and English in a high tech environment. Art exhibitions. Local artefacts and old photographs. The centre also runs the Dubharaidlt Thatched Cottage Museum. This is a restored house in a magnificent secluded location 3 miles (5km) north west of Castlebay. No cars.
☎ 01871 810413

Bernera Museum 176 C4

Bernera, Isle of Lewis. On the B8059, 2 miles (3km) from Bernera Bridge. The museum displays information on genealogy, archaeology and historical sites. Also archives, old photographs and a lobster fishing exhibition in summer.
☎ 01851 612331

Bishop's & Earl's Palaces 179 D1

Watergate, Kirkwall. The Bishop's Palace is a 12th century hall house, later much altered with a round tower built by Bishop Reid between 1541 and 1548. A later addition was made by the notorious Patrick Stewart, Earl of Orkney, who built the adjacent Earl's Palace between 1600 and 1607 in a splendid Renaissance style.
☎ 01856 875461   www.historic-scotland.gov.uk

Black House 177 E3

At Arnol, on the A858. 15 miles (24km) north west of Stornoway. A traditional Hebridean thatched and chimneyless house dating from the 1870s with byre, attached barn and stackyard. Furnished with a peat fire in the hearth.
☎ 01851 710395   www.historic-scotland.gov.uk

Blackhammer Cairn 180 C4

North of the B9064 on the south coast of the island of Rousay, Orkney. A long Neolithic cairn bounded by a retaining wall with a megalithic burial chamber divided into seven compartments.
☎ 01856 751360   www.historic-scotland.gov.uk

Bød of Gremista 183 D3

Gremista, 1.5 miles (2.5km) north of Lerwick town centre. A restored 18th century fishing booth, the birthplace of local shipowner and politician Arthur Anderson. Displays tell the story of Anderson's life and service to Shetland, and of the fisheries 200 years ago. Also recreated room interiors of the kitchen and bedroom.
☎ 01595 694386

Bonhoga Gallery 182 C2

Weisdale, 12 miles (19km) west of Lerwick. Displays local, national and international art and craft exhibitions. Plus the Shetland Textile Working Museum.
☎ 01595 830400

Bosta Iron Age House 176 C4

Great Bernera, at the end of the B8059, north west Lewis. The adjacent archaeological site was excavated in 1996 to reveal a complex of several Iron Age houses. A full-scale replica of one house has been built nearby, using authentic construction methods, and gives a fascinating insight into the way of life of the inhabitants 1500 years ago.
☎ 01851 612331

Broch of Gurness 180 B4

Evie, off the A966 at Aikerness, about 14 miles (22.5km) north west of Kirkwall. An Iron Age broch over 10ft (3m) high, surrounded by stone huts, deep ditches and ramparts.
☎ 01856 751414   www.historic-scotland.gov.uk

Brough of Birsay 180 A4

On the island of Birsay, at the north end of mainland Orkney. 20 miles (32km) north west of Kirkwall. The remains of a Romanesque church and a Norse settlement.
☎ 01856 841815   www.historic-scotland.gov.uk

Burland Croft Trail 182 C4

Burland, Trondra, Shetland. 3 miles (5km) from Scalloway. Follow the waymarked route through this working croft. See the croft animals such as sheep, Shetland cattle, Tamworth pigs, and Shetland ducks and geese which have been re-introduced as a result of detailed research.
☎ 01595 880430

Callanish (Calanais) Standing Stones 176 D4

At Calanais, off the A858, 12 miles (19km) west of Stornoway, Isle of Lewis. A unique cruciform setting of megaliths second in importance only to Stonehenge. Erected about 3000 BC. An avenue of 19 monoliths leads north from a circle of 13 stones, with rows of more stones fanning out to the south, east and west. Inside the circle is a small chambered tomb.
☎ 01851 621422   www.historic-scotland.gov.uk

Carrick House 181 D3

Eday, Orkney. Historic private house dating from the 17th century, built by John Stewart, Earl of Carrick. The house was the scene of the capture of Pirate Gow in 1725. It was renovated into a larger house in the mid 19th century. Built of local sandstone, harled and crow-stepped in the traditional Orkney style. The guided tours take in the house, garden and other parts of the island. Spectacular views.
☎ 01857 622260

Cille-Bharra 172 C3

At Eolaigearraidh (Eoligarry), at the north end of Isle of Barra. The ruined church of St Barr, who gave his name to the island, and the restored chapel of St Mary formed part of the medieval monastery. Among the preserved gravestones there was a unique stone carved with a Celtic cross on one side and Norse runes on the other. A replica of this stone now stands in Cille-Bharra.
☎ 01871 810336 (Castlebay Tourist Office)

Click Mill 180 B4

At Dounby, on mainland Orkney. The last surviving and working horizontal water mill in Orkney, a type well represented in Shetland and Lewis.
☎ 01856 841815   www.historic-scotland.gov.uk

Clickimin Broch 183 D3

About 1 mile (2km) south west of Lerwick, Shetland. A good example of a broch tower with associated secondary buildings of Iron Age date.
☎ 01466 793191   www.historic-scotland.gov.uk

Coll Pottery 177 F3

In township of Col on the B895, 6 miles (9.5km) north east of Stornoway. A working pottery making a wide range of items, from the unique marbled ware of the Hebridean range and the traditional figurines of the Highlands and Islands, to the collectible range of MacKatts of Glen Kitloch.
☎ 01851 820219

Cross Kirk Medieval Parish Church & Norse Settlement 180 C2

At Bay of Tuquoy on the south coast of the island of Westray, Orkney. A roofless 12th century Romanesque church. Remains of a Norse settlement to the west.
☎ 01856 841815   www.historic-scotland.gov.uk

Cubbie Roo's Castle 180 C4

On the island of Wyre, Orkney. Probably the earliest stone castle authenticated in Scotland. Built circa 1145 by Norseman Kolbein Hruga, it consists of a small rectangular tower enclosed in a circular ditch. Nearby are the ruins of St Mary's Chapel, late 12th century in the Romanesque style.
☎ 0131 668 8800   www.historic-scotland.gov.uk

Cuween Hill Cairn 178 C1

On the A965, 0.5 mile (1km) south of Finstown, Orkney. A low mound covering a Neolithic chambered tomb with four cells. When discovered, it contained the bones of men, dogs and oxen.
☎ 01856 841815   www.historic-scotland.gov.uk

Dim Riv Norse Longship Boat Trips 183 D3

Lerwick, Shetland. Harbour tours on a working replica of a Norse longship.
☎ 01595 693097

Dun Carloway 176 C3

On the A858, 1.5 miles (2.5km) south of Carloway and 16 miles (25.5km) west north-west of Stornoway, Isle of Lewis. This 2000 year old round defensive tower is one of the best preserved Iron Age brochs in Scotland. One wall rises over 70ft (21m). There is also an interpretation centre.
☎ 0131 668 8800   www.historic-scotland.gov.uk

Dwarfie Stane 178 B2

Towards the north end of the island of Hoy, Orkney. A huge block of sandstone in which a Neolithic burial chamber has been cut. No other known example in the British Isles.
☎ 01856 841815   www.historic-scotland.gov.uk

Earl's Palace 180 A4

In Birsay at the north end of mainland Orkney, 11 miles (17.5km) north of Stromness. The gaunt remains of the courtyard palace built in the 16th century by Robert Stewart, Earl of Orkney.
☎ 01856 721205   www.historic-scotland.gov.uk

Eynhallow Church 180 B4

On the island of Eynhallow, Orkney. The ruins of a 12th century church and a group of domestic buildings.
☎ 01856 841815   www.historic-scotland.gov.uk

Fair Isle 182 A5

Between Orkney and Shetland. One of Britain's most isolated inhabited islands. Most famous for the intricately patterned knitwear which bears its name, a traditional craft which continues today. Fair Isle is important for birdlife, and offers many opportunities for ornithological study. The island also has much of archaeological interest, and traditional crofting is still in evidence.
☎ 01463 232034   www.nts.org.uk

Fetlar Interpretive Centre 185 F3

Beach of Houbie, on the island of Fetlar, 4 miles (6.5km) from the car ferry. Museum and visitor information centre with interactive display on Fetlar's history, folklore, flora, fauna and geology. Extensive archive of photographs, audio recordings and historic local film. Award-winning exhibition on the history of antiseptic surgery.
☎ 01957 733206   www.zetnet.co.uk/sigs/centre

Fort Charlotte — 183 D3
In the centre of Lerwick in Shetland. A pentagonal artillery fort, with bastions projecting from each corner and towering walls. Built in 1665 to protect the Sound of Bressay from the Dutch, but taken by them and burned in 1673. Rebuilt in 1781.
☎ 01466 793191   www.historic-scotland.gov.uk

George Waterston Museum — 182 A5
Auld Schule, Fair Isle, Shetland. Maps the social history of the island with displays of agriculture, fishing, shipwrecks, textiles, natural history and archaeology.
☎ 01595 760244

Grain Earth House — 178 D1
At Hatston, about 1 mile (2km) north west of Kirkwall, Orkney. A well-built Iron Age earth house with an underground chamber supported on stone pillars.
☎ 0131 668 8800   www.historic-scotland.gov.uk

Hackness Martello Tower — 178 C3
At Hackness, at the south east end of the island of Hoy, Orkney. An impressive tower (one of a pair) built between 1813 and 1815 to provide defence against the French and American privateers for the British convoys assembling in the sound of Longhope. Renovated in 1866 and used again in World War I.
☎ 01856 841815   www.historic-scotland.gov.uk

Harbour View Gallery — 177 G1
Near Butt of Lewis, 28 miles (45km) north of Stornoway on the A857. Artist's studio gallery in a scenic location at the northern tip of the Isle of Lewis. Contemporary, original watercolours by island based artist Anthony J. Barber. Also prints and cards.
☎ 01851 810735   www.abarber.co.uk

Harris Tweed Weaving & Knitting — 175 D3
4 Plockropool, on Golden Road, 5 miles (8km) south of Tarbert. Visitors can see Harris tweed being woven. Also demonstrations of warping, bobbin winding and wool plying.
☎ 01859 511217

Hebridean Jewellery — 173 B4
Located at Iochdar at the north end of South Uist near Benbecula. Celtic jewellery shop and workshop. Visitors can see five jewellers working with silver, gold and gemstones. Commissions undertaken.
☎ 01870 610288

Hermaness National Nature Reserve Visitor Centre — 185 F1
Shorestation, Burrafirth, Unst, Shetland. On the B9086, 3 miles (5km) north west of Haroldswick. An interpretive display for the neighbouring Hermaness National Nature Reserve. Simulates the sights and sounds of the sea bird cliffs. Useful for those unable to visit the reserve.
☎ 01957 711278

Highland Park Distillery — 179 D2
Holm Road, 1 mile (2km) outside Kirkwall, Orkney. A 200 year old distillery and the most northerly whisky distillery in the world. Visitors can tour the distillery and traditional floor maltings (still in use). Most days there is also a kiln burning.
☎ 01856 874619   www.highlandpark.co.uk

Holm of Papay Chambered Cairn — 180 D1
On the island of Holm of Papa, Papa Westray, Orkney. A massive tomb with a long narrow chamber divided into three, with 14 beehive cells opening into the walls.
☎ 01856 841815   www.historic-scotland.gov.uk

Hoswick Visitor Centre — 182 D5
Hoswick, Sandwick, 14 miles (22.5km) south of Lerwick. Previously a weaving shed and now an exhibition of old weaving looms and radios. The history of the area is illustrated with photographs of mining, crofting, fishing and knitting.
☎ 01950 431215

Hoxa Tapestry Gallery — 178 D3
Neviholm, Hoxa, Orkney. On Mainland 3 miles (5km) from St Margaret's Hope and 18 miles (29km) south of Kirkwall. The gallery shows the work of Leila Thomson who weaves in the High Gobelin technique. Her theme is the life and the landscape of Orkney. Visitors can watch her weaving, view her work and take tuition courses.
☎ 01856 831395   www.hoxatapestrygallery.co.uk

Hoy RSPB Nature Reserve — 178 B2
Ley House, Hoy, Orkney. RSPB site close to the Old Man of Hoy sea stack. Visitors will see and hear a wide range of birds, including skylarks, sea birds, peregrines and golden plovers. The site contains the highest hill in Orkney, natural field landscapes, lochans and a population of mountain hares. Also Rackwick Crofting Museum, the remains of a Bronze Age settlement and Berriedale, the remnants of Britain's most northerly woodlands.
☎ 01856 791298   www.rspb.org.uk

Italian Chapel — 179 D2
Lamb Holm, Orkney. On Mainland at St Mary's, 7 miles (11km) south of Kirkwall. Two Nissen huts transformed into a chapel by Italian prisoners of war during the construction of the Churchill Barriers in World War II. A beautiful interior is the result of their ingenuity and craftmanship. Painting of Madonna and Child by Domenico Chioccetti.
☎ 01856 781268

Jarlshof Prehistoric & Norse Settlement — 183 G5
On the A970 at Sumburgh Head, 22 miles (35km) south of Lerwick. An extraordinarily important site with a complex of ancient settlements within 3 acres (1.2ha). The oldest is a Bronze Age village of oval stone huts. Above this there is an Iron Age broch and wheelhouses, and even higher still an entire Viking settlement. On the crest of the mount is a house built around 1600. The displays explain Iron Age life and the history of the site.
☎ 01950 460112   www.historic-scotland.gov.uk

Keen of Hamar National Nature Reserve — 185 F2
Keen of Hamar, on the A968, 1 mile (1.5km) east of Baltasound. An important botanical site with unique habitat and landscape. A number of specialist plants grow on the serpentine soil.

Kildonan Museum — 172 C1
8 miles (13km) north of Lochboisdale on the A865 to Lochmaddy, South Uist. Recently renovated, the museum displays information on local history. Craft shop. Occasional music performances in the evening, see local notices for details.
☎ 01878 710343

Kisimul Castle — 172 B4
On a tiny island in the bay of Castlebay, Isle of Barra. For many generations, Kisimul was the stronghold of the Macneils of Barra, widely noted for their lawlessness and piracy. The castle is at least 550 years old. Restoration was commenced in 1938 by Robert Lister Macneil of Barra and completed in 1972.
☎ 01871 810313   www.historic-scotland.gov.uk

Knap of Howar — 180 C1
On the west side of the island of Papa Westray, Orkney. Probably the oldest standing stone houses in north west Europe. Two Neolithic dwellings, approximately rectangular with stone cupboards and stalls.
☎ 01856 841815   www.historic-scotland.gov.uk

Knowe of Yarso Chambered Cairn — 180 C4
On the island of Rousay, Orkney. A Neolithic oval cairn with concentric walls enclosing a chambered tomb divided into three compartments.
☎ 01856 841815   www.historic-scotland.gov.uk

Lerwick Town Hall — 183 D3
In Lerwick town centre on a commanding site on the ridge in the older part of the town known as Hillhead. The chief attraction is the series of stained glass windows representing leading personalities in the early history of the islands, from Norwegian inhabitation in the 9th century to the pledging of the islands to Scotland in 1469.
☎ 01595 744502   www.scapaflow.co.uk/sfvc.htm

Lewis Loom Centre — 177 F4
3 Bayhead, Stornoway, Isle of Lewis. An enjoyable introduction to the history of Harris tweed. Information on sheep breeds and plant dyes, and demonstrations of hand spinning, looms and all aspects of producing finished cloth. Craft shop selling mostly local produce, tweeds and knitwear.
☎ 01851 704500   www.lewisloomcenter.co.uk

Lyness Naval Base & Interpretation Centre — 178 C3
Lyness, Hoy, Orkney. Exhibition of photographs and artefacts cover the period when Scapa Flow was a key anchorage for the British Royal Navy in both World Wars. Housed in a converted pump house at the former Lyness naval base. There is a Naval Cemetery nearby.
☎ 01856 791300   www.scapaflow.co.uk/sfvc.htm

Maes Howe — 178 C1
Stenness, off the A965, 9 miles (14.5km) west of Kirkwall, Orkney. The finest megalithic (Neolithic) tomb in the British Isles, consisting of a large mound covering a stone-built chamber with cells in the walls. Runic inscriptions were carved in the walls by Vikings and Norse crusaders. Admission, shop and tearoom are at the nearby 19th century Tormiston Mill.
☎ 01856 761606   www.historic-scotland.gov.uk

Midhowe Broch & Cairn — 180 B3
On the west coast of the island of Rousay, Orkney. An Iron Age broch and walled enclosure situated on a promontory cut off by a deep rock ditch. Adjacent is Midhowe Stalled Cairn, a huge and impressive Neolithic chambered tomb in an oval mound with 25 stalls. Now protected by a modern building.
☎ 01856 841815   www.historic-scotland.gov.uk

Mine Howe — 179 E2
Veltitigar Farmhouse, Tankerness, Orkney. Unique to Europe, this mysterious Iron Age archaeological site was re-discovered in 1999 and further excavated in 2000 by television's Time Team. 26ft (8m) underground, down deep steps, there is a small chamber with two side chambers. Related to the site there is a broch, round howe and long howe.
☎ 01856 861234

Morven Gallery — 177 E2
Upper Barvas, 12 miles (19km) west of Stornoway, Isle of Lewis. Fine art by local painters and sculptors. Ceramics, tapestry, carvings and designer knitwear. Talks, slide shows and conference facility. Workshops and children's activities.
☎ 01851 840216

Mousa Broch — 183 D5
On the island of Mousa, Shetland. The finest surviving Iron Age broch tower, standing over 40ft (12m) high. The stairs can be climbed to the parapet.
☎ 01466 793191   www.historic-scotland.gov.uk

Muckle Flugga & Out Stack — 185 E3
Depart from the pier, Mid Yell, Yell. All-day guided tour by motor boat to the seal islands of Yell Sound, the sensational cliffs of the west coast of Unst, around Muckle Flugga lighthouse and Out Stack at the northern tip of Shetland and on to the Scottish National Heritage Centre at Hermaness National Nature Reserve at Burrafirth.
☎ 01950 422493   shetland.wildlife.tours@zetnet.co.uk

Muness Castle — 185 F2
At the south east corner of the island of Unst, Shetland. A late 16th century tower house with fine detail and circular towers at diagonally opposite corners. The most northerly castle in the British Isles.
☎ 01466 793191   www.historic-scotland.gov.uk

✱ **Ness Heritage Centre** `177 G1`

Towards the Butt of Lewis, 28 miles (45km) from Stornoway on the A857. A unique insight into the social and cultural heritage of the Western Isles. Over 500 artefacts and 7000 photographs illustrate the lifestyle of a people carving out an existence on the very edge of Europe. Genealogical information spanning 250 years is an invaluable resource to visitors tracing their family histories and the adjoining tele-centre offers technological support and DTP services.
☎ 01851 810377

♟ **Ness of Burgi** `183 F5`

At the south eastern point of Scatness, Shetland, about 1 mile (2km) south west of Jarlshof. A defensive stone blockhouse, probably from the Iron Age, with some features resembling a broch.
☎ 01466 793191   www.historic-scotland.gov.uk

🏰 **Noltland Castle** `180 C2`

On the island of Westray, Orkney. A fine ruined Z-plan tower built between 1560 and 1573, but never completed. Remarkable for the large number of gun loops and the impressive winding staircase.
☎ 01856 841815   www.historic-scotland.gov.uk

✱ **Nor/Nova Knitwear** `185 E2`

Muness, Uyeasound, Unst, Shetland. Hand spinning, knitting and all things to do with wool. Lace knitting for shawls and stoles. Shetland sheep.
☎ 01957 755373

🐦 **Noss National Nature Reserve** `183 E3`

Noss Island, Shetland. On an island off the east coast of Bressay by Lerwick. A unique three-hour tour of some of Europe's finest scenery and wildlife habitats. Visitors can see up to 100,000 sea birds and dozens of seals at close range. Spectacular caves, sea statues and rock arches. Entertaining commentary on geology, local history and folklore of Bressay and Noss islands. Puffins visible before second week in August.
☎ 01950 422483

🏛 **Oiseval Gallery** `177 E2`

James Smith Photography, Brue, Isle of Lewis. An exclusive collection of photographic landscapes and seascapes of the Outer Hebrides, including images of St Kilda.
☎ 01851 840240   www.oiseval.co.uk

🏛 **Old Haa Visitor Centre** `185 E5`

Burravoe, Yell, Shetland. The oldest building on Yell, with exhibitions on local flora and fauna, arts and crafts, and local themes of historic interest. Photographs, video and sound recordings of local musicians plus story telling. Genealogical information by arrangement. Craft shop and art gallery.
☎ 01957 722339

✱ **Old Man of Hoy** `178 A2`

North west coast of Isle of Hoy, Orkney. A 450ft (137m) high isolated stack (pillar) standing off the magnificent cliffs of north west Hoy. The Old Man of Hoy can also be seen from the Scrabster to Stromness ferry. A challenge to experienced climbers.

♟ **Old Scatness Iron Age Village** `183 F5`

A970 Virkie, Sumburgh, Shetland. Iron Age Broch and village with excavations in progress. Village stands up to head height. Replicas of some buildings. During excavations (July – August) living history and displays. Further facilities are under development.
☎ 01595 694688   www.shetland-heritage.co.uk/amenitytrust/

✱ **Orkney Chair** `178 D2`

St Ola, Kirkwall, Orkney. In Orphir Road (A964), 1.5 miles (2.5km) from town centre. See craftspeople at work making traditional Orkney chairs.
☎ 01856 873521   www.orkney-chairs.co.uk

🏛 **Orkney Museum** `179 D1`

Tankerness House, Broad Street, Kirkwall. Opposite St Magnus Cathedral. The museum describes island life through 6000 years, with additional special exhibitions. It is housed in a merchant-laird's mansion, with courtyard and gardens, dating from 1574.
☎ 01856 873191

🏛 **Orkney Wireless Museum** `179 D1`

Kiln Corner, Junction Road, Kirkwall, Orkney. A museum explaining Orkney's wartime history which involved an intense communications network of radio and telephones to protect the home fleet in Scapa Flow. Details of a secret radar station. Also displays of domestic receivers, valves, rare equipment, gramophones, transistors. Special display of Italian POW crafts.
☎ 01856 871400

✝ **Orphir Church & the Earl's Bu** `178 C2`

By the A964, 8 miles (13km) west south-west of Kirkwall, Orkney. Earl's Bu are the foundation remains of what may have been a Viking palace. Nearby are the remains of Scotland's only 12th century circular medieval church.
☎ 01856 841815   www.historic-scotland.gov.uk

✱ **Ortak Visitor Centre** `178 D1`

Hatston Industrial Estate, Kirkwall, Orkney. A permanent exhibition with a video presentation describing how modern jewellery is made and telling the story of Ortak. In July and August visitors can watch a silversmith at work.
☎ 01856 872224

✱ **Our Lady of the Isles** `173 C3`

North of South Uist, Western Isles. On Reuval Hill - the Hill of Miracles - is the statue of the Madonna and Child, erected in 1957 by the Catholic community with contributions from all over the world. The work of Hew Lorimer, it is 30ft (9m) high.

✝ **Our Lady of the Sea** `172 B4`

Heaval, on the Isle of Barra, Western Isles. Heaval is the highest point in Barra at 1257ft (383m), and on the slopes of the hill is erected an attractive statue of the Madonna and Child, symbol of the islanders' faith.

🏛 **Pier Arts Centre** `178 B2`

Victoria Street, Stromness, Orkney. Former merchant's house (circa 1800), coal store and fishermen's sheds which have been converted into a gallery. Permanent collection of 20th century paintings and sculpture as well as changing exhibitions.
☎ 01856 850209   www.pierartscentre.com

✱ **Quendale Water Mill** `183 F4`

Quendale, Dunrossness, Shetland. 4 miles (6.5km) from Sumburgh Airport. A restored 19th century over-shot water mill with displays of old croft implements, photographs and family history. Souvenirs and local crafts in reception area.
☎ 01950 460969   www.quendalemill.shetland.co.uk

♟ **Quoyness Chambered Tomb** `181 E3`

On the east side of Els Ness on the south coast of the island of Sanday, Orkney. A megalithic tomb with triple retaining walls containing a passage with a main chamber and six secondary cells. Neolithic.
☎ 01856 841815   www.historic-scotland.gov.uk

♟ **Rennibister Earth House** `178 C1`

On the A965 about 4.5 miles (7km) west north-west of Kirkwall, Orkney. A good example of an Orkney earth house, consisting of a passage and underground chamber with supporting roof pillars.
☎ 01856 841815   www.historic-scotland.gov.uk

♟ **Ring of Brodgar** `178 B1`

Between Loch of Harray and Loch of Stenness, 5 miles (8km) north east of Stromness, Orkney. A magnificent circle of upright stones with an enclosing ditch spanned by causeways. Neolithic.
☎ 01856 841815   www.historic-scotland.gov.uk

✝ **St Clement's Church** `174 C4`

At Rodel, at the south end of the Isle of Harris. A fine 16th century church built by Alexander MacLeod of Dunvegan and Harris. Contains his richly-carved tomb.
☎ 0131 668 8800   www.historic-scotland.gov.uk

🐦 **St Kilda National Nature Reserve** `176 A3`

60 miles (96.5km) west of the Isle of Harris. Evacuated in 1930, these remote islands are now a World Heritage Site, their sea bird colonies and rich in archaeological remains. Each year NTS work parties carry out conservation work. For details of access contact NTS Regional Office on telephone number below.
☎ 01631 570000   www.nts.org.uk

✝ **St Magnus Cathedral** `178 D1`

Broad Street, Kirkwall, Orkney. Founded by Jarl Rognvald and dedicated to his uncle, St Magnus. The remains of both men are in the massive east choir piers. The original building dates from 1137–1200, but sporadic additional work went on until the late 14th century. It contains some of the finest examples of Norman architecture in Scotland, with small additions in transitional styles and some early Gothic work.
☎ 01856 874894

✱ **St Magnus Centre** `179 D2`

Kirkwall, Orkney. A source of information on St Magnus and his cathedral. A 17 minute video, Saga of Saint Magnus, tells the story of St Magnus in six languages. Study library. Spectacular views of the east end of St Magnus Cathedral.
☎ 01856 878326

✝ **St Magnus Church** `180 C3`

On the Isle of Egilsay, Orkney. The complete, but roofless, ruin of a 12th century church with a remarkable round tower of the Irish type. Dramatically sited.
☎ 01856 841815   www.historic-scotland.gov.uk

✝ **St Mary's Medieval Church** `180 C2`

At Pierowall on the island of Westray, Orkney. The ruins of a medieval church with some finely lettered tombstones.
☎ 01856 841815   www.historic-scotland.gov.uk

🏰 **Scalloway Castle** `182 D4`

In Scalloway, 6 miles (9.5km) west of Lerwick, Shetland. A fine castellated mansion built in 1600 in medieval style by Patrick Stewart, Earl of Orkney. Fell into disuse in 1615.
☎ 01466 793191   www.historic-scotland.gov.uk

🏛 **Scalloway Museum** `182 C4`

Main Street, Scalloway, 7 miles (11km) west of Lerwick. Artefacts and photographs cover the history of Scalloway over the past 100 years. A major section is devoted to Scalloway's unique role in World War II, when it was a secret base for Norwegian freedom fighters, as 16 Norwegian fishing boats ran a shuttle service to Norway carrying in weapons, ammunition and radio sets, returning with refugees. Realising the importance of this operation, the US Government donated three submarine chasers which operated between 1942 and 1945.
☎ 01595 880783

✱ **Scapa Flow** `178 C2`

Sea area, enclosed by the mainland of Orkney and the islands of Burray, South Ronaldsay, Flotta and Hoy. Major naval anchorage in both wars and the scene of the scuttling of the German High Seas Fleet in 1919. Today a centre of marine activity as Flotta is a pipeline landfall and tanker terminal for North Sea Oil.

✱ **Seallam! Exhibition & Genealogy Centre** `174 B4`

Seallam! Visitor Centre, Northton, Isle of Harris. 17 miles (27km) south of Tarbert on the A859. A major exhibition on the Hebrides and a genealogical resource.
☎ 01859 520258   www.seallam.com

🏛 **Shawbost (Siabost) School Museum** `177 D3`
Shawbost (Siabost), 19 miles (31km) north west of Stornoway, Isle of Lewis. Created under the Highland Village Competition of 1970, the museum illustrates the old way of life in Lewis.
☎ 01851 710212

🏛 **Shetland Croft House Museum** `183 F4`
South Voe, Boddam. On an unclassified road, east of the A970, 25 miles (40km) south of Lerwick. A 19th century drystone and thatched croft, consisting of inter-connected house, barn, byre, kiln and stable with watermill nearby. Furnished throughout with period implements, fixtures and furniture.
☎ 01950 460557

🏛 **Shetland Museum** `183 D3`
Lower Hillhead, Lerwick. A museum covering all aspects of Shetland's history and prehistory. Archaeology from Neolithic to medieval times including early Christian sculpture, Viking grave finds, medieval domestic and fishing items. Maritime displays cover fisheries, merchant marine and shipwrecks. Models, fishing gear, maritime trades. Agriculture and domestic life collection, including basketwork, peat cutting, 19th century social history. Costume display and textiles.
☎ 01595 695057   shetland.museum@zetnet.co.uk

🏛 **Shetland Textile Working Museum** `182 C2`
Weisdale Mill, Weisdale. 7 miles (11km) west of Lerwick, take the A971 and turn right on the B9075 for 0.6 mile (1km). A unique collection of Shetland textiles illustrating the history of spinning, knitting and weaving in the islands from their earliest development to the present day. Workshops in spinning and knitting arranged and visitors have the opportunity to see demonstrations of local craft skills.
☎ 01595 830419

🐾 **Shetland Wildlife Tours** `182 C5`
Longhill, Maywick. Half-day to seven-day wildlife tours throughout the Shetland Islands with expert naturalist guides.
☎ 01950 422493

🏠 **Skaill House** `178 B1`
Breckness Estate, Sandwick. Beside Skara Brae, 5 miles (8km) north of Stromness. The most complete 17th century mansion house in Orkney. Built for Bishop George Graham in the 1620s, it has been inhabited by successive lairds, who have added to the house over the centuries. On show – Captain Cook's dinner service from his ship the Resolution, and gunroom with sporting and military memorabilia.
☎ 01856 841501   www.skaillhouse.com

⚑ **Skara Brae Prehistoric Village** `178 B1`
On the B9056, 19 miles (30km) north west of Kirkwall. The best preserved group of Stone Age houses in Western Europe. Ten one-roomed houses from a former fishing village are joined by covered passages and contain stone furniture, hearths and drains. They give a remarkable picture of life in Neolithic times. There is a full scale replica of a complete house.
☎ 01856 841815   www.historic-scotland.gov.uk

⚑ **Staneydale Temple** `182 B2`
3.5 miles (5.5km) east north-east of Walls, Shetland. A Neolithic hall, heel-shaped externally and containing a large oval chamber. Surrounded by the ruins of houses, walls and cairns of the same period.
☎ 01466 793191   www.historic-scotland.gov.uk

⚑ **Steinacleit Cairn & Stone Circle** `177 E2`
At the south end of Loch an Duin, Shader, 12 miles (19km) north of Stornoway, Isle of Lewis. The remains of an enigmatic building of early prehistoric date.
☎ 0131 668 8800   www.historic-scotland.gov.uk

★ **Stephane Jaeger Knitwear** `179 D3`
Littlequoy, Burray, Orkney. Near Echnaloch, off the A961, 12 miles (19km) south of Kirkwall. A knitwear workshop in a traditional Orkney building. Garments are made from wool spun and knitted from the undyed natural fibres of the workshop's own sheep and cashmere goats. Hand-spinning demonstrations on request. Also collector's pieces incorporating coloured pure cashmere, merino and silk yarns.
☎ 01856 731228   www.visitorkney.com/stephjaeger

⚑ **Stones of Stenness** `178 C1`
Between Loch of Harray and Loch of Stenness, about 5 miles (8km) north east of Stromness, Orkney. The remains of a stone circle surrounded by traces of a circular earthwork.
☎ 01856 841815   www.historic-scotland.gov.uk

🏛 **Stromness Museum** `178 B2`
52 Alfred Street, Stromness, Orkney. A museum of Orkney maritime history and natural history – birds, eggs, fossils, butterfiles and moths, fishing, whaling, Hudson's Bay Company, the German fleet in Scapa Flow. Changing exhibitions.
☎ 01856 850025

🏛 **Stronsay Fish Mart Interpretation Centre** `181 E4`
At ferry pier, Stronsay, Orkney. A visual collection of herring fishing and farming memorabilia from Victorian times.
☎ 01857 616360

🏛 **Taigh Chearsabhagh Museum & Arts Centre** `173 D2`
Lochmaddy, North Uist, Western Isles. Local museum and art gallery with over 2000 archive photos of North Uist from the 1950s and 1960s.
☎ 01876 500293   www.taigh-chearesabhagh.org

★ **Tait & Style** `178 B2`
Old Academy, Back Road, Stromness. A showroom where visitors can see a collection of pure wool fashion and furnishing accessories hand-crafted from a specially developed felting technique.
☎ 01856 851186

🏛 **Tangwick Haa Museum** `184 B5`
Eshaness, Shetland. About 40 miles (64km) north of Lerwick via the A970 and the B9078. Museum in a restored 17th century house built by the Cheyne family. Shows various aspects of life (agriculture, fishing, spinning and knitting) in Northmavine through the ages, using photographs and artefacts. Exhibition changes annually.
☎ 01806 503389

⚑ **Taversoe Tuick Chambered Cairn** `180 C4`
On the island of Rousay, Orkney. A Neolithic chambered mound with two burial chambers, one above the other.
☎ 01856 841815   www.historic-scotland.gov.uk

⚑ **Teampull na Trionaid** `173 C3`
Cairinis (Carinish), close to the A865, North Uist. Ruined remains of an important ecclesiastical site, founded by Beatrice, daughter of Somerled, Lord of the Isles, in about 1203 on the foundations of an earlier place of worship. A major centre of learning in medieval times.

⚑ **Tomb of the Eagles** `179 D4`
Liddle, on South Ronaldsay, 20 miles (32km) south of Kirkwall. Tour starts at museum and proceeds to 5000-year-old tomb. Also a Bronze Age house. Wildlife to see en route.
☎ 01856 831339

★ **Tormiston Mill** `178 C1`
On the A965 about 9 miles (14.5km) west of Kirkwall, Orkney. An excellent late example of a Scottish water mill, probably built in the 1880s. The water wheel and most of the machinery have been retained. Now forms a reception centre for visitors to Maes Howe.
☎ 01856 761606   www.historic-scotland.gov.uk

✝ **Ui Church** `177 F4`
At Aiginis, off the A866, 2 miles (3km) east of Stornoway, Isle of Lewis. Ruined church (pronounced eye) containing some finely carved ancient tombs of the Macleods of Lewis.

🏛 **Uig Heritage Centre** `176 B4`
Crowlista (Cradhlastadh), Uig, 33 miles (53km) west of Stornoway on B8011. The centre contains an exhibition of local artefacts from the early to mid 20th century. Also photographs, croft histories, a turn of the century replica thatched house interior and displays of shoemaker's tools, blacksmith, fishing, weaving and agricultural implements.
☎ 01851 672456

★ **Uist Animal Vistor Centre** `173 B2`
Kyles Road, Bayhead (Ceann A' Bháigh), North Uist. 13 miles (21km) from ferry terminal at Loch Maddy on west coast of Uist. An all weather attraction for the family. Hebridean sheep (and fleeces, wool, knitwear), Soay sheep from St Kilda, rare Eriskay ponies, Scottish wildcats and birds of prey. Games area, bouncy castle.
☎ 01876 510233

★ **Uist Craft Producers** `172 C1`
Kildonan Museum, Kildonan, 8 miles (12.5km) north of Lochboisdale, South Uist. Craft workshops on view and crafts for sale – spinning, knitting, weaving. Photographic display of local history.
☎ 01878 700483

🏛 **Unst Heritage Centre** `185 F1`
Haroldswick, Unst, Shetland. Local history and family trees of Unst.
☎ 01957 711528

⚑ **Unstan Chambered Cairn** `178 B1`
About 3.5 miles (5.5km) north east of Stromness, Orkney. A mound covering a Neolithic stone burial chamber, divided by slabs into five compartments.
☎ 01856 841815   www.historic-scotland.gov.uk

🏛 **Up Helly Aa Exhibition** `183 D3`
St Sunniva Street, Lerwick, Shetland. An exhibition of artefacts, photographs, costumes and a replica galley from the annual fire festival of Up Helly Aa. Audio-visual show.

🏛 **Westray Heritage Centre** `180 C2`
7 miles (11km) from ferry terminal, minibus to Pierowall village during summer. A display on the natural heritage of Westray. Many children's hands-on activities. Large collection of black and white photos. Information on local cemeteries. Local memories of wartime, schooldays, Noup Head lighthouse, sports, kirks and sea transport.

★ **Whalebone Arch** `177 D3`
Bragar, on the western side of the Isle of Lewis. This arch is made from the huge jawbone of a blue whale that came ashore in 1920.

⚑ **Wideford Hill Chambered Cairn** `178 D1`
On the west slope of Wideford Hill, 2 miles (3km) west of Kirkwall, Orkney. A fine Neolithic chambered cairn with three concentric walls and a burial chamber with three large cells.
☎ 01856 841815   www.historic-scotland.gov.u

Battlefields

Battlefield sites are part of Scotland's national heritage. Some sites, such as Bannockburn and Culloden have visitor centres. Others may be marked by information panels or monuments which stand testament to thousands of lives lost several centuries ago.

Airds Moss 1680 `23 D4`
Site of skirmish between Royalists and Covenanters.

Alford 1645 `120 A2`
The site of the battle where the Royalist Marquis of Montrose defeated the Covenant army two months after his victory at Auldearn.

Ancrum Moor 1545 `18 D2`
The site of the battle in which the Scots repelled English raiders after a dispute following the death of James V over the betrothal of the infant Mary, Queen of Scots to Henry VIII's son, Edward. The decisive victory helped to unify Scotland.

Auldearn 1645 `149 E4`
The site of the Marquis of Montrose's tactical defeat of the Covenanters in the Civil War.

Bannockburn 1314 `70 D1`
Where the Scots under Robert the Bruce defeated the English under Edward II, gaining independence and national identity. The battle is commemorated at Bannockburn Heritage Centre.

Barra Hill 1308 `120 C1`
Battle where Robert the Bruce decisively defeated John Comyn on Christmas Eve.

Bothwell Bridge 1679 `56 C4`
The battle in which the Covenanters were heavily defeated by Scottish loyalists led by the Duke of Monmouth and Claverhouse.

Carbisdale 1650 `152 A5`
The scene of Montrose's defeat by the Earl of Sutherland. The main battle was fought on a craggy hill, Creag a' Choineachan.

Corrichie 1562 `116 A1`
The site where the Earl of Huntly was defeated by followers of Mary, Queen of Scots, led by Moray.

Culloden 1746 `143 D4`
Where the Jacobean cause led by Prince Charles Edward Stuart was finally defeated by the Duke of Cumberland on 16th April 1746. About 200 Jacobites were lost on the field, but around 2000 more were killed in the subsequent pursuit. Culloden was the last battle fought on British soil.

Dunbar 1296 `43 F2`
Site of the defeat of John Balliol by Edward I.

Dunbar 1650 `43 F2`
Battle where Cromwell defeated Charles, Prince of Wales, and his Scottish army under David Leslie, hampering the Royalists' campaign in the north.

Falkirk 1746 `71 D3`
The battle site where a Jacobite army of Highlanders defeated the Hanoverian army, led by Henry Hawley.

Glen Trool 1307 `9 F1`
Bruce's Stone marks the site of the rout of the English by Robert the Bruce's men in 1307.

Glencoe Massacre 1692 `134 A4`
The site where the MacDonald clan of Glencoe were killed on the orders of Sir James Dalrymple when they were six days late in signing their peace with William of Orange.

Glenshiel 1719 `138 B3`
Where the Jacobites, backed by Spain, were defeated by George I's army.

Harlaw 1411 `120 C1`
The site where Donald, Lord of the Isles, tried to claim the Earldom of Ross and was defeated by the Earl of Mar.

Haughs of Cromdale 1690 `141 G2`
The site where government forces defeated the Jacobites in 1690.

Inverlochy 1429, 1431 and 1645 `134 A2`
Inverlochy Castle was built in the 13th century and was the scene of battles in 1429, 1431 and 1645. In the last and most important battle the Covenanters, led by Argyll, were defeated by Montrose. This led to Charles I breaking off negotiations with Parliament and ultimately to his defeat.

Invernahavon 1370 or 1386 `140 B5`
A battle of uncertain date between Clan Cameron and the rival Clan Mackintosh, supported by Davidsons and Macphersons. The Mackintoshes and their followers suffered heavy losses, although the battle ended with the Camerons in flight.

Keppoch 1688 `134 B2`
The site of Scotland's last real clan battle, caused by a territorial dispute between the MacDonalds and the Mackintoshes.

Killiecrankie 1689 `101 F3`
The site of the battle where Government troops were defeated by the Jacobites in 1689.

Kilsyth 1645 `56 C2`
Battle site, now covered by Townhead Reservoir, where Montrose defeated the Covenanters, killing some 6000 of the enemy with the loss of only ten men.

Langside 1568 `56 A3`
The site where Mary, Queen of Scots' forces were defeated by Moray after her escape from Loch Leven.

Loudoun Hill 1307 `23 E3`
Battle site where Robert the Bruce defeated Earl of Pembroke.

Mauchline 1648 `22 C4`
On this battle site there was a skirmish between Covenanters and English troops, the outcome of which is uncertain.

Methven 1306 `96 A3`
Site where Robert the Bruce was defeated by the Earl of Pembroke.

Nechtanesmere 685 `98 C1`
Where Egfrith of Northumbria was killed by the Picts, ending Anglian incursions into this area.

Philiphaugh 1645 `18 B2`
On this site, after defeating the English, Scottish leader Sir David Leslie took prisoners to Newark Castle and murdered them in cold blood.

Pinkie 1547 `42 C2`
(Also known as the Battle of Inveresk or Musselburgh.) The Duke of Somerset, regent to Edward VI, sought to impose a betrothal treaty between English and Scottish monarchs, leading to battle in 1547. Although the English were victorious, they failed in their objective as Mary, Queen of Scots was sent to France to marry the Dauphin.

Prestonpans 1745 `42 D2`
The site of a battle where the English Government forces defeated the Jacobites as part of the 1745 Jacobite uprising.

Redeswire Fray 1575 `19 E4`
Site of the last significant Borders skirmish between the English and the Scots, marked by a stone.

Rullion Green 1666 `42 B3`
Battle site where 1000 Covenanters were defeated by superior Crown forces under General Dalziel.

Sherriffmuir 1715 `81 F5`
Where the Jacobite army under the Earl of Mar fought the army of George I, led by the Duke of Argyll.

Stirling Bridge 1297 `70 D1`
Where Scots under William Wallace routed the English under Warenne.

Strath Oykel 1369 or 1406 `151 G4`
A bloody battle of uncertain date between Clan Mackay and rival Clan Macleod, which ended with heavy losses for the Macleods. The conflict gave the name of Tuiteam Tarvach, meaning plentiful fall or great slaughter, to the vicinity.

Strathpeffer 1411 `143 A3`
Site of affray between Munros and Macdonalds and commemorated by the Eagle Stone.

Tibbermore 1644 `96 A3`
Site of first battle between the Royalist Marquis of Montrose and the Covenanters, in which Montrose was victorious, gaining control of Perth.

Turiff 1639 `124 C3`
Site of the first skirmish in the Civil War, known as 'Trot of Turriff', where Royalist Gordons defeated the Covenanters.

S ir Hugh T. Munro originally published *Tables of Heights over 3000 Feet* in the 1891 edition of the Scottish Mountaineering Club Journal. His name has given rise to these 284 Scottish mountain peaks higher than 914m. At the list's conception it was considered an arduous lifetime challenge to climb them all. There are now over 2000 'Munroists' who have completed the feat.

Munros

Munro name	Height (m)	Page & grid reference
Ben Nevis	1344	134 A2
Ben Macdui	1309	114 A2
Braeriach	1296	114 A1
Cairn Toul	1293	114 A2
Sgor an Lochain Uaine	1258	114 A2
Cairn Gorm	1245	114 B1
Aonach Beag	1234	134 A2
Carn Mòr Dearg	1223	134 A2
Aonach Mòr	1221	134 A2
Ben Lawers	1214	94 D1
North Top	1196	114 B1
Carn Eighe	1183	138 D2
Beinn Mheadhoin	1182	114 B1
Mam Sodhail	1180	138 D2
Stob Choire Claurigh	1177	134 B2
Ben More	1174	80 B3
Leabaidh an Daimh Bhuidhe	1171	114 C1
Stob Binnein	1165	80 B3
Beinn Bhrotain	1157	114 A2
Cac Carn Beag	1155	114 D3
Derry Cairngorm	1155	114 B2
Sgurr nan Ceathreamhnan	1151	138 C2
Bidean nam Bian	1150	134 A4
Sgurr na Lapaich	1150	139 D1
Ben Alder	1148	135 D2
Geal Charn	1132	135 D2
Ben Lui	1130	79 G4
Creag Meagaidh	1130	134 D1
An Riabhachan	1129	138 D1
Binnein Mòr	1128	134 B3
Ben Cruachan	1126	79 E3
Carn nan Gabhar	1121	101 F2
A' Chràlaig	1120	138 C3
An Stuc	1118	94 D1
Meall Garbh	1118	94 D1
Sgor Gaoith	1118	141 E5
Stob Coire Easain	1116	134 C2
Stob Coire an Laoigh	1115	134 B2
Aonach Beag	1114	135 D2
Monadh Mòr	1113	141 E5
Tom a' Chòinich	1111	139 D2
Carn a' Coire Bhoidheach	1110	114 D3
Sgurr Mòr	1110	147 E2
Sgurr nan Conbhairean	1110	138 D3
Meall a' Bhùiridh	1108	134 B4
Stob a' Choire Mheadhoin	1106	134 C2
Beinn Ghlas	1103	94 D1
Mullach Fraoch-choire	1102	138 C3
Beinn Eibhinn	1100	135 D2
Creise	1100	134 B4
Sgurr a' Mhaim	1099	134 A3
Sgurr Chòinnich Mòr	1095	134 B2
Sgurr nan Clach Geala	1093	147 D2
Bynack More	1090	141 F4
Beinn a' Chlachair	1088	135 D2
Stob Ghabhar	1087	134 B5
Beinn Dearg	1084	147 E1
Schiehallion	1083	100 D4
Sgurr a' Choire Ghlais	1083	147 E5
Beinn a' Chaorainn	1082	114 B1
Beinn a' Chreachain	1081	94 A1
Ben Starav	1078	134 A5
Beinn Dòrain	1076	80 A2
Beinn Heasgarnich	1076	94 B2
Stob Coire Sgreamhach	1072	134 A4
Bràigh Coire Chruinn-bhalgain	1070	101 F2
An Socach	1069	138 C1
Meall Corranaich	1069	94 D1
Glas Maol	1068	102 A2
Sgurr Fhuaran	1068	138 B3
Cairn of Claise	1064	114 C4
Bidein a' Ghlas Thuill	1062	146 C1
Sgurr Fiona	1059	146 C1
Na Gruagaichean	1055	134 B3
Spidean a' Choire Leith	1054	146 B4
Toll Creagach	1054	139 D2
Sgurr a' Chaorachain	1053	146 C5
Stob Poite Coire Ardair	1053	134 D1
Beinn a' Chaorainn	1052	134 C1
Glas Tulaichean	1051	101 G2
Geal Charn	1049	135 E1
Sgurr Fhuar-thuill	1049	147 E5
Carn an t-Sagairt Mòr	1047	114 D3
Chno Dearg	1047	134 C2
Creag Mhòr	1047	94 A2
Glas Leathad Mòr	1046	143 A2
Beinn Iutharn Mhòr	1045	101 G2
Cruach Ardrain	1045	80 B3
Stob Coir' an Albannaich	1044	134 A5
Meall nan Tarmachan	1043	94 C2
Càrn Mairg	1041	100 C4
Sgurr na Cìche	1040	138 B5
Beinn Achaladair	1039	94 A1
Meall Ghaordie	1039	80 C2
Sgurr a' Bhealaich Dheirg	1038	138 C3
Carn a' Mhaim	1037	114 A2
Gleouraich	1035	138 C4
Carn Dearg	1034	135 E2
Am Bodach	1032	134 A3
Beinn Fhada	1032	138 C3
Carn an Righ	1029	101 G2
Ben Oss	1028	79 G4
Càrn Gorm	1028	100 C4
Sgurr a' Mhaoraich	1027	138 B4
Sgurr na Ciste Duibhe	1027	138 B3
Ben Challum	1025	80 A2
Sgorr Dhearg	1024	133 G4
Mullach an Rathain	1023	146 B4
Stob Dearg	1022	134 B4
Aonach air Chrith	1021	138 C4
Ladhar Bheinn	1020	138 A4
Beinn Bheòil	1019	135 E2
Carn an Tuirc	1019	114 C3
Mullach Clach a' Bhlàir	1019	141 D5
Mullach Coire Mhic Fhearchair	1019	146 C2
Garbh Chioch Mhòr	1013	138 B5
Cairn Bannoch	1012	114 D3
Beinn Ime	1011	75 E4
Beinn Udlamain	1010	100 B2
Ruadh-stac Mòr	1010	146 B3
Saddle, The	1010	138 B3
Sgurr an Doire Leathain	1010	138 C4
Beinn Dearg	1008	101 E2
Sgurr Eilde Mòr	1008	134 B3
Maoile Lunndaidh	1007	146 D5
An Sgarsoch	1006	114 A3
Carn Liath	1006	139 G5
Beinn Fhionnlaidh	1005	138 D2
Devil's Point, The	1004	114 A2
Sgurr an Lochain	1004	138 C3
Aonach Meadhoin	1003	138 C3
Sgurr Mòr	1003	138 B5
Beinn an Dòthaidh	1002	80 A1
Sàil Chaorainn	1002	138 D3
Sgurr na Carnach	1002	138 B3
Meall Greigh	1001	95 D1
Sgorr Dhonuill	1001	133 G4
Sgurr Breac	1000	147 D2
A' Chailleach	999	146 D2
Sgurr Choinnich	999	146 C5
Stob Bàn	999	134 A3
Ben More Assynt	998	151 F2
Broad Cairn	998	114 D3
Stob Diamh	998	79 E3
Glas Bheinn Mhòr	997	134 A5
Spidean Mialach	996	138 C4
An Caisteal	995	80 A4
Carn an Fhidhleir	994	101 F1
Sgor na h-Ulaidh	994	134 A4
Sgurr Alasdair	993	137 D2
Sgurr na Ruaidhe	993	147 E5
Spidean Coire nan Clach	993	146 B4
Carn nan Gobhar (Lapaichs)	992	139 D1
Carn nan Gobhar (Strathfarrar)	992	147 E5
Sgairneach Mhòr	991	100 B2
Beinn Eunaich	989	79 F3
Sgurr Ban	989	146 C2
Conival	987	151 F2
Creag Leacach	987	102 A2
Druim Shionnach	987	138 C4
Gulvain	987	133 G1
Lurg Mhòr	986	146 C5
Inaccessible Pinnacle	986	136 D2
Ben Vorlich	985	94 D4
Sgurr Mhòr	985	146 A3
An Gearanach	982	134 A3
Ciste Dhubh	982	138 C3
Mullach na Dheiragain	982	138 C2
Creag Mhòr	981	95 D1
Maol Chinn-dearg	981	138 C4
Stob Coire a' Chairn	981	134 A3
Beinn a' Chochuill	980	79 F3
Cona' Mheall	980	147 E1
Slioch	980	146 C3
Beinn Dubhchraig	977	80 A3
Meall nan Ceapraichean	977	147 E1
Stob Bàn	977	134 B2
Stob Coire Sgriodain	976	134 C2
A' Mharconaich	975	135 F2
Carn a' Gheoidh	975	114 C4
Carn Liath	975	101 F3
Stuc a' Chroin	975	80 D4
Beinn Sgritheall	974	138 A3
Ben Lomond	974	80 A5
Sgurr a' Ghreadaidh	973	136 D2
Meall Garbh	968	100 C4
A' Mhaighdean	967	146 C2
Sgorr nam Fiannaidh	967	134 A4
Ben More	966	77 G4
Sgurr na Banachdich	965	136 D2
Sgurr nan Gillean	965	137 D2
Carn a' Chlamain	963	101 F2
Sgurr Thuilm	963	133 F1
Meall nan Con	961	152 A1
Beinn nan Aighenan	960	79 F2
Meall Glas	960	80 B2
Sgorr Ruadh	960	146 B4
Stuchd an Lochain	960	94 B1
Beinn Fhionnlaidh	959	79 E2
Saileag	959	138 C3
Bruach na Frithe	958	137 D2
Stob Dubh	958	134 A4
Tolmount	958	102 B1
Carn Ghluasaid	957	138 D3
Tom Buidhe	957	102 B2
Sgurr na Coireachan	956	133 F1
Stob na Broige	956	134 A4
Sgòr Gaibhre	955	134 D3
Am Faochagach	954	147 F2
Beinn Liath Mhòr Fannaich	954	147 E2
Beinn Mhanach	954	94 A1
Meall Dearg	953	134 A4
Sgurr nan Coireachan	953	138 B5
Meall Chuaich	951	135 G1
Meall Gorm	949	147 E3
Beinn Bhuidhe	948	75 E3
Sgurr Mhic Choinnich	948	137 D2
Creag a' Mhaim	947	138 C4
Driesh	947	102 B2
Beinn Tulaichean	946	80 B4
Carn Bhac	946	114 B3
Meall Buidhe	946	138 A5
Bidein a' Choire Sheasgaich	945	146 C5
Carn Dearg	945	140 B4
Sgurr na Sgine	945	138 B3
An Socach	944	114 B3
Sgurr Dubh Mòr	944	137 D2
Ben Vorlich	943	75 E3
Stob a' Choire Odhair	943	134 B5
Carn Dearg	941	134 D3
Carn na Caim	941	135 F1
Beinn a' Chroin	940	80 A4
Binnein Beag	940	134 B3
Luinne Bheinn	939	138 A4
Mount Keen	939	115 F3
Mullach nan Coirean	939	134 A3
Beinn na Lap	937	134 C3
Beinn Sgulaird	937	79 E2
A' Bhuidheanach Bheag	936	100 C2
Beinn Tarsuinn	936	146 C2
Am Basteir	935	137 D2
Sròn a' Choire Ghairbh	935	139 E5
Meall a' Chrasgaidh	934	147 D2
Beinn Chabhair	933	80 A4
Cairnwell, The	933	102 A2
Fionn Bheinn	933	146 D3
Maol Chean-dearg	933	146 B4
Meall Buidhe	932	100 A4
Beinn Bhreac	931	114 B2
Ben Chonzie	931	95 E2
A' Chailleach	930	140 B4
Bla Bheinn	928	137 E2
Eididh nan Clach Geala	928	147 E1
Mayar	928	102 B2
Meall nan Eun	928	79 F2
Moruisg	928	146 D4
Ben Hope	927	155 D3
Seana Bhraigh	927	147 E1
Beinn Narnain	926	75 E4
Geal Charn	926	140 A5
Meall a' Choire Leith	926	94 D1
Beinn Liath Mhòr	925	146 B4
Stob Coire Raineach	925	134 A4
Creag Pitridh	924	135 D1
Sgurr nan Eag	924	137 D3
An Coileachan	923	147 E3
Sgurr nan Each	923	147 D3
Tom na Gruagaich	922	146 A3
Sgaith Chuil	921	80 B2
An Socach	920	138 C2
Carn Sgulain	920	140 B4
Gairich	919	138 C5
A' Ghlas-bheinn	918	138 C2
Creag nan Damh	918	138 B3
Ruadh Stac Mòr	918	146 C2
Sgurr a' Mhadaidh	918	137 D2
Beinn a' Chleibh	917	79 G4
Carn Aosda	917	114 C4
Geal-chàrn	917	135 E2
Meall na Teanga	917	139 E5
Ben Vane	916	75 E4
Beinn Teallach	915	134 C1
Sgurr nan Ceannaichean	915	146 C5
Beinn a' Chlaidheimh	914	146 C2

Index to place names & places of interest

The following is a comprehensive listing of all named places and places of tourist interest which appear in this atlas. The places of tourist interest are in purple type and they are also listed and described in the separate Places of Interest section for each region. National Nature Reserves (N.N.R.) are also indexed in purple although they are not included in the regional Places of Interest sections. The letters and numbers around the page edges form the referencing system used in this atlas. The place name is followed by a page number and a grid reference specific for that page. The place can be found by searching that grid square. Where more than one place has the same name, each can be distinguished by the abbreviated administrative area name shown after the place name, for example Acharn *Arg. & B.* can be found on page 79 in grid square F3.

Administrative area abbreviations

Aber.	Aberdeenshire	Edin.	Edinburgh	N.Lan.	North Lanarkshire	Shet.	Shetland
Arg. & B.	Argyll & Bute	Falk.	Falkirk	Ork.	Orkney	Stir.	Stirling
D. & G.	Dumfries & Galloway	Glas.	Glasgow	P. & K.	Perth & Kinross	W.Dun.	West Dunbartonshire
E.Ayr.	East Ayrshire	High.	Highland	Renf.	Renfrewshire	W.Isles	Western Isles
E.Dun.	East Dunbartonshire	Inclyde	Inverclyde	S.Ayr.	South Ayrshire		(Na h-Eileanan an Iar)
E.Loth.	East Lothian	Midloth.	Midlothian	S.Lan.	South Lanarkshire	W.Loth.	West Lothian
E.Renf.	East Renfrewshire	N.Ayr.	North Ayrshire	Sc.Bord.	Scottish Borders		

Airport information

Aberdeen Airport
International & Scheduled flights
Farburn Terrace, Dyce, Aberdeen, AB21 7DU
☏ *01224 722331*
www.baa.co.uk/main/airports/aberdeen

Barra Airport
Scheduled flights
Eoligarry, Castlebay, Isle of Barra, HS9 5YD
☏ *01871 890212*

Benbecula Aerodrome
Scheduled flights
Benbecula, Western Isles, HS 5LA
☏ *01870 602310*

Campbeltown (Machrihanish) Airport
Scheduled flights
Campbeltown, Argyll, PA28 6NU
☏ *01586 553797*

Dundee Airport
Scheduled flights
Riverside Drive, Dundee, DD2 1UH
☏ *01382 643242*

Edinburgh Airport
International & Scheduled flights
Edinburgh, EH12 9DN
☏ *0131 333 1000*
www.baa.co.uk/main/airports/edinburgh

Glasgow Airport
International & Scheduled flights
Abbotsinch, Paisley, PA3 2PF
☏ *0141 887 1111*
www.baa.co.uk/main/airports/glasgow

Glasgow Prestwick International Airport
International & Scheduled flights
Prestwick, KA9 2PL
☏ *01292 479822*
www.gpia.co.uk

Inverness Airport
Scheduled flights
Inverness, IV2 4BD
☏ *01463 232471*
www.justplanecrazy.co.uk

Islay Airport
Scheduled flights
Glenegedale, Port Ellen, Isle of Islay, PA42 7AS
☏ *01496 302361*

Kirkwall Airport
International & Scheduled flights
Kirkwall, Orkney, KW15 1TH
☏ *01856 872421*

Stornoway Airport
Scheduled flights
Melbost, Stornoway, Isle of Lewis, HS2 OBN
☏ *01851 702256*

Sumburgh Airport
Scheduled flights
Sumburgh, Shetland, ZE3 9JP
☏ *01950 460654*

Tiree Airport
Scheduled flights
Tiree, TA77 6UW
☏ *01879 220456*

Wick Airport
Scheduled flights
Wick, Caithness, KW1 4QS
☏ *01955 602215*

Edinburgh Airport

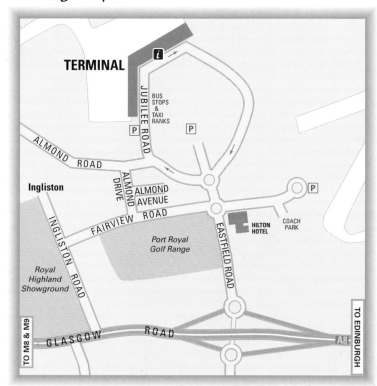

Glasgow Airport